ALSO BY CHRISTOPHER ISHERWOOD

THE ANIMALS

THE ANIMALS

Love Letters Between

CHRISTOPHER ISHERWOOD

and DON BACHARDY

Edited and with an introduction by

KATHERINE BUCKNELL

FARRAR, STRAUS AND GIROUX   NEW YORK

Farrar, Straus and Giroux
18 West 18th Street, New York 10011

Copyright © 2013 by Don Bachardy
Introduction and notes copyright © 2013 by Katherine Bucknell
All rights reserved
Printed in the United States of America
Originally published in 2013 by Chatto & Windus, Great Britain
Published in the United States by Farrar, Straus and Giroux
First American edition, 2014

Grateful acknowledgment is made for permission to reprint the
following material:
"A Critical Guide to the Galleries: La Cienega" by Henry J. Seldis and William
Wilson copyright © 1970. *Los Angeles Times*. Reprinted with permission.
Material by Lincoln Kirstein copyright © 2013 by the New York Public Library
(Astor, Lenox and Tilden Foundations).

Library of Congress Cataloging-in-Publication Data
Isherwood, Christopher, 1904–1986.
    The Animals : Love Letters Between Christopher Isherwood and
Don Bachardy / edited and with an introduction by Katherine Bucknell.
        pages cm
    Includes index.
    ISBN 978-0-374-10517-4 (hardback) — ISBN 978-0-374-71211-2 (ebook)
    1. Isherwood, Christopher, 1904–1986—Correspondence.   2. Bachardy,
Don, 1934—Correspondence.   3. Love-letters.   I. Bachardy, Don, 1934–
II. Bucknell, Katherine, editor of compilation.   III. Title.

PR6017.S5 Z48 2014
823'.912—dc22
[B]

                                                            2013041939

Farrar, Straus and Giroux books may be purchased for educational, business,
or promotional use. For information on bulk purchases, please contact the
Macmillan Corporate and Premium Sales Department at 1-800-221-7945,
extension 5442, or write to specialmarkets@macmillan.com.

www.fsgbooks.com
www.twitter.com/fsgbooks • www.facebook.com/fsgbooks

1 3 5 7 9 10 8 6 4 2

Let's put our faith in the Animals. They have survived the humans
and will survive.

Inscribed by C.I. in a copy of Down There on a Visit *that he gave D.B.,*
February 14, 1963

Contents

Introduction

From February 14, 1953 until January 4, 1986 the conversation between Christopher Isherwood and Don Bachardy never stopped. When they were apart, they continued by letter, telegram, and telephone a dialogue of intimacy, depth, and urgent, tender concern. They first exchanged letters in February 1956 when Isherwood took the twenty-one-year-old Bachardy on a tour of Europe. On their way home via England, where the winter was harsh, Isherwood went alone to Cheshire to visit his mother and brother for a few days while Bachardy stayed behind in their London hotel because Isherwood wished to spare him the primitive accommodation and the cold at his mother's manor house, Wyberslegh Hall. This very first pair of letters shows how, in absence, they both reassessed their three-year-old relationship, valuing it the more for being separated. This first pair of letters also mentions the animal identities which expressed the instinctive, unbreakable bond that had already formed between them. "I miss rides through London on old Dobbin," wrote Bachardy:

> ... (especially in the snow yesterday) and think a lot about him, sleeping in a strange stable, eating cold oats out of an ill-fitting feedbag and having no cat fur to keep him warm. And don't let them put any frozen bits in his mouth. And tell him an anxious Tabby is at the mercy of the RSPCA and counting the days till his return.[1]

In their most private interactions, Isherwood was a stubborn grey workhorse, Dobbin; Bachardy was a skittish, unpredictable white kitten usually called Kitty. Over the years, these "pet" personalities were to be elaborated upon and decorated by each of them with stories and events from literature and life, evolving as a camp that allowed Isherwood and Bachardy to masquerade and to play about the serious matters of

1. Bachardy letter, Feb. 1, 1956, p. 6.

love and commitment and thereby to reveal themselves more fully to one another. They generally spoke of the Animals in the third person, distancing themselves from the sentimentality in which their Animal identities allowed them to indulge. Although these grew more complex over time, one of the most important characteristics of the Animals remained their simplicity, their innocence of ulterior motive. The Animals embodied the instinctive life—the submission to creaturely needs and to a humble, unforeseeable destiny.

The Animals are homosexuals and never would or could deny this. The Animals are thirty years apart in age, but nevertheless must be together. The Animals have busy social lives, many shared and separate friends, and even outside love affairs, yet some of their most contented waking hours are spent nestled together in the dark, watching films and munching junk food. The Animals have intensely cerebral artistic lives and enormous ambition, but their subverbal bond makes intellectual and professional activities seem merely worldly and unimportant. The Animals fight, sometimes savagely, run away from one another, suffer blinding pangs of loneliness, and yet always return to their basket, their silent world of warmth and comfort. They never accuse or absolve; they don't experience guilt or regret; they live in the present rather than the past or the future. Foolish or wise, their behavior is characteristic, ritualistic, unavoidable; they don't consider why they do what they do. They will always be together, and The Others—in general straight people, but also sometimes any outsiders—enter their world for brief spells only and, however welcome or involved they may seem there, are always turned out again in the end.

When Isherwood died in 1986, his full set of tiny, white-jacketed Beatrix Potter story books still stood on his library book shelves. These had been among his favorite nursery reading, and the animal world portrayed in them—in both narrative and watercolors—offers a miniature comic universe in which character brings about both action and consequences, including suffering, but in which humor and compassion prevail over moral judgement.

In 1925, when he was twenty-one and working in London as secretary to the string quartet of Belgian violinist André Mangeot, Isherwood composed some poems to accompany sketches of animals, some dressed in human clothes, which were drawn by eleven-year-old Sylvain Mangeot, the beloved younger son of the household. The poems and pictures were published much later as *People One Ought to Know* (1982). They are clumsy compared to Beatrix Potter, but they offer an equally broad range of characters, delineated with resourceful and eccentric detail.

With his friend Gore Vidal, Isherwood shared another camp, borrowed from *The Wind in the Willows*; they called one another Mole (Isherwood) and Toad (Vidal), pointing up the fussy, self-important rivalry in their relationship, but also the natural dignity and heroism, the shared wish to be the best they could be, to show off for the world and one another, and to make one another's lives more interesting than they might otherwise have been. Mole and Toad are courteous, noble, and gentlemanly as well as petty and striving. Of course, Isherwood and Vidal were also laughing at the smallness and unimportance of any two creatures anywhere anytime—apart from to one another.

The ability to create a world, a safe and separate milieu, was a great gift of Isherwood's. As a homosexual, he spent decades half-hidden below the surface of ordinary social activity. For many, such a buried life might have been lonely, painful, angry, colored by bitterness, guilt, even self-loathing. But Isherwood knew how to spread hay around his stable, put up bright wallpaper, and attract a good-looking and entertaining crowd. He drew Bachardy into his semi-secret realm, and they made their lives into the finest private party in town. On New Year's Eve, 1960, Isherwood wrote in his diary:

> Very good relations with Don, all this time. Yesterday evening—I forgot to record—we did something we haven't done in ages; danced together to records on the record player. A Beatrix Potter scene—the Animals' Ball.[2]

The second set of letters Isherwood and Bachardy exchanged were about a year and half after the first, in June 1957, when Bachardy's spring semester at Chouinard Art Institute ended; he marked the start of his summer vacation by travelling alone to New York to stay with Lincoln Kirstein. In June 1958, Bachardy made a similar trip, travelling first to New Orleans to stay with his close friend, Marguerite Lamkin, a dialogue coach on the original production of Tennessee Williams's *Cat on a Hot Tin Roof.* Isherwood remained behind, working, at the house they were then renting in Santa Monica. He enormously enjoyed the dramatic,

2. *The Sixties, Diaries Volume Two: 1960–1969 (D. 2)*, p. 38.

closely observed report Bachardy sent him of the attempted suicide of Marguerite's father. Throughout the Isherwood–Bachardy letters, figures and events familiar from Isherwood's diaries are discussed by both correspondents with even greater candor than in the diaries; many others are mentioned here for the first time. Bachardy, the sexy, turbulent boy, proves to be a thoughtful, articulate, and highly analytical writer with as broad and penetrating an interest in human character as his mentor, and with a startlingly robust voice.

Generally, it was Bachardy who left home for a few days or weeks to stay with friends, to travel, to work, or to combine all these things. He wanted to lead an independent life and to explore the world and his talent on his own terms. Isherwood was determined not only to let him, but also to encourage him because, in fact, Bachardy found it psychologically daunting to leave home alone at all. It took all his nerve and self-discipline to pull away from his sheltered life with Isherwood and from their productive day-to-day regime. The energy he invested in departing left him, in younger years, so emptied that he typically arrived at his destination wondering why he had come. But as the letters intermittently make clear, the relationship with Isherwood survived and succeeded partly because of these separations.

In 1960, Bachardy got his first big assignment as a professional portrait artist when Tony Richardson asked him to draw the cast of *A Taste of Honey* for exhibition in the Broadway theater lobby, and this led to several other East Coast jobs—drawing posters for Tennessee Williams's *Period of Adjustment* and Julie Harris's *Little Moon of Alban*. By 1961, Bachardy was ready for a much bigger step, and he moved to London to study at the Slade School of Fine Art. He intended to remain for six months, supported mostly by funding from a Californian acquaintance wealthy enough to act as a patron of the arts. The Animals found the parting excruciating, and at first Bachardy found it so difficult to be alone that he was unable to work and felt, for a time, both disappointed and overwhelmed by the Slade. Yet he craved the challenge of solitude, and writing to Isherwood strengthened him. They reported their activities to one another in minute detail, keeping their daily concerns very much in one another's thoughts and never allowing their intimacy to dwindle. Bachardy soon involved himself with Isherwood's circle of London friends, and he grew close to the painter Keith Vaughan, with whom he was studying at the Slade, to the socialite doctor Patrick

Woodcock, and to Cecil Beaton. Before long he was painting five hours a day, and he went often to the theater and movies, sharp reviews of which cram his letters to Isherwood throughout the decades.

Isherwood tried to lose himself in work. He completed the draft of his new novel, *Down There on a Visit,* and worked with Charles Laughton preparing a Plato monologue for Laughton to perform as a one-man stage show. At the same time, he chased down some extra funds inherited from his mother and, with Bachardy's help, pursued London scriptwriting jobs so that he could afford to join Bachardy from April to October 1961. When his final draft of "Paul," the last section of *Down There on a Visit,* was complete, Isherwood posted it ahead, and Bachardy, who had read an earlier draft in September 1960, wrote back praising it highly. Bachardy also drafted a passionate critique, which he never mailed, warning Isherwood to cut what they referred to as the hashish section, based on their visit to Paul Bowles in Tangier in October 1955, and later published separately as the short story, "A Visit to Anselm Oaks."

They had discussed the cut before, and Isherwood was relying on Bachardy and on Isherwood's school friend Edward Upward for guidance. In his letter of March 11, 1961, Isherwood says, "You and Edward will have to decide about this." Since their years together at Repton and Cambridge, Upward had read all Isherwood's work before publication, and he would continue to do so, but Bachardy's opinion now mattered most. In his draft letter, which perhaps reflects telephone and face-to-face conversations about the book, Bachardy argues that experimenting with drugs should not be presented alongside the narrator's religious journey as if it were equally serious or important. The hashish episode seemed to Bachardy more in the nature of a "cheap thrill,"[3] a merely chemical adventure that involves no inward transformation or spiritual or philosophical work on the narrator's part and which is not a path to anything more. He worried that Isherwood's candor would invite sceptics to dismiss his religious beliefs as if they, too, were a brief experiment or even a moment of irresponsibility, like being drunk at a party. He was at pains to foresee and forestall critical attacks from outsiders, and his tone is at once protective, adult, and proprietary, even as he prepares with humility and maximum efficiency to pass the typescript quickly to Upward for his opinion.

3. Bachardy draft, Mar. 26, 1961, p. 73.

The private view on October 2, 1961, for Bachardy's debut show at the Redfern Gallery, heavily attended by celebrities and press, was a moment of triumph and fulfilment for both Isherwood and Bachardy. By the time Isherwood returned to Santa Monica, Bachardy was launched on a new phase of professional activity. He was inundated with portrait commissions in London, and he began to plan a second show for January 1962 at the Sagittarius Gallery in New York. But when the Animals met in New York, Bachardy's success came between them. There were more portrait commissions, many social opportunities, and a hectic pace affording little privacy. On his return to Santa Monica, it was Isherwood's turn to draft a letter that he did not send: "Won't write a Kitty and Dobbin letter. That's sentimental. Though it's a beautiful poetic sentimentality. But I think we can still talk to each other by our own names—I mean, even when we're not mad." The magical intimacy seemed to be shattered, the pet names dropped as if they were masks for a show that was over. The Animals had become two ordinary, separate people again: "I realize I am deeply selfish. You admit that you are . . . My selfishness is that I want you to stay with me. Your selfishness is that you ask yourself couldn't you do better; considering you are young."[4]

Bachardy came home in late February, 1962, and they returned to established modes, but the emotional tension was to get much worse over the following year and a half. Bachardy struggled to capitalize on his achievements as a portraitist and fashion illustrator and to progress with his painting, and he explored an independent sexual and romantic life that profoundly changed his relationship with Isherwood. In principle, each encouraged the other to have outside sexual affairs, but such was the intensity of the attention that they had, until now, focused on one another that neither was really prepared for the seismic emotional shifts that would come about when this attention was directed, even in part, elsewhere. The Animal essence of their relationship relied on close and constant physical interaction, on uncontested physical possession, and, especially on Isherwood's side, on being together from twilight to dawn. In fact, Isherwood found it very hard to spend nights alone. Early in 1963, Bachardy became absorbed in a love affair with Bill Bopp, and Isherwood repaid him by spending the night in their own bed at

4. Isherwood draft, Jan. 27, 1962, p. 115.

Adelaide Drive with Paul Wonner, a close friend who, they both knew, had just the qualities that might offer a genuine threat to Bachardy's place in Isherwood's affections, in particular the animal sensuality Isherwood so adored in Bachardy. Wishing to allow one another freedom, both found it difficult to be entirely honest about outside sexual activities and the emotions they prompted; in fact, Isherwood thought too much honesty was destructive. But he believed their Animal personae had a mythic power that could keep the relationship alive: "I often feel that the Animals are far more than just a nursery joke or a cuteness. They *exist*. They are like Jung's myths. They express a kind of freedom and truth which we otherwise wouldn't have."[5]

Nevertheless, in April 1963, the Animals parted. Isherwood went north to San Francisco, where he lived in a borrowed house and gave some lectures. Bachardy turned into "the blackest of black cats,"[6] so tense that he was almost unable to function and the more miserable for being alone with himself and the things about himself that he did not like. Isherwood returned for Bachardy's birthday in May, but the meeting was a disaster. On Bachardy's birthday card, he wrote, "I dreamed Dobbin died . . ."[7]

But they did not give up. By June, they were living together again, and by the end of September, Bachardy felt less distressed and was able to work a little. On Christmas Eve, Isherwood wrote from India, where he had travelled with his guru Swami Prabhavananda to celebrate the one-hundredth anniversary of the birth of Vivekananda and to observe the final vows of two Hollywood monastics, John Yale and Kenneth Critchfield, "[T]his is not my life and could never become my life," a realization about monasticism that was to form the basis of his last novel, *A Meeting by the River*. His life was with Bachardy: "I want to talk Cat-Horse again."[8] On his return journey, they had a happy rendezvous in New York, where Bachardy was arranging an autumn exhibition at the Banfer Gallery. By the time Isherwood arrived alone in Santa Monica, they had agreed that Bachardy would design the cover for *A Single Man*, Isherwood's masterpiece inspired by the fear of losing him.

In June 1964, Bachardy travelled abroad with a new lover and another

5. Isherwood letter, Mar. 11, 1963, p. 126.
6. Bachardy letter, Apr. 16, 1963, p. 129.
7. Isherwood greeting card, May 18, 1963, p. 137.
8. Isherwood letter, Dec. 24, 1963, p. 139.

friend to Egypt, Greece, and Austria. Isherwood recorded in his diary on May 26, "This is Don's 'birthday present' for his thirtieth birthday. He wanted to do it 'with my blessing.'"[9] A sea change had come about. And the word "blessing" is a key to the new dynamic in their relationship, which had been recast as, fundamentally, father-son or guru-disciple. A lover who betrays is harder to forgive than a prodigal son who wanders and returns. The prodigal son receives unconditional love and is always welcomed home, whatever the emotional cost; Bachardy was now free to wander and philander as he liked. His reports of his travels with his two age-mates are like those of a student backpacker—eyefuls of monuments and scenery, differing cultural attitudes to money and how it should be dished out, confidential grumbles about strange food and the lack of privacy and independence.

He was in New York again for the opening of his show at the Banfer Gallery in October while Isherwood assembled *Exhumations* and worked on a film script of *The Sailor from Gibraltar* for Tony Richardson. The exhibition led, as always, to new interest in Bachardy's work, and at the start of 1965, he settled in New York for what proved to be six months, drawing the dancers of the New York City Ballet and the actors of the American Shakespeare Festival on a commission from Lincoln Kirstein. Isherwood began teaching a writing seminar at UCLA and got to work on *A Meeting by the River*, but after visiting Bachardy briefly in late January and early February, he was lonely for him and wrote often with tempting gossip such as what was afoot on the set of Gavin Lambert's film, *Inside Daisy Clover*. "Old Dub thinks and thinks of his dear Kitty and is happy to do whatever Kitty says, because he now belongs to Kitty entirely and will just try to be useful in the few ways old horses can."[10] Meanwhile, Bachardy brooded, somewhat in the way that Isherwood had done in the late 1940s and early 1950s before he met Bachardy, on how he was meant to spend his life:

> Kitty is continually rejecting possible bowls of cream and yet he doesn't know quite what he wants instead—except that he does long to devote all of his fur to *something*. To painting, to Ramakrishna, to old Dub, maybe even to all three. He realizes he has never made up his mind really. He has always been testing and tasting, dipping his paw in here, his tail in

9. *D.* 2, p. 339.
10. Isherwood letter, Mar. 10, 1965, p. 181.

there, trying a tunnel as far as the point where his whiskers touched the sides. But then sometimes Kitty feels that perhaps this is the nature of life, at least of his life, a succession of glimpses, some satisfying, some not. Perhaps, he thinks, the state of waiting, of expectation, of near desperation sometimes, is a quite rewarding, maybe even profound state to be in, if he can just manage to accept it and go along with it.[11]

Nevertheless, he was drawing portraits, painting in oils as well as in acrylics, and socializing with writers, painters, composers, actors, dancers, and musicians, and he sent Isherwood insightful and acerbic assessments of New York cultural life.

In mid-February 1966, Bachardy again established himself in New York, this time for a little over two months. His drawings of the New York City Ballet were to be reproduced for sale at performances, and while he oversaw the engraving and printing, he did portraits several times a week. In September and October the same year, he remained in Santa Monica while Isherwood travelled to Austria to draft a television script about the song "Silent Night." Isherwood's travelogue home has the easy brilliance of an old hand returning to a familiar German-speaking world and taking in with pleasure some previously unknown sights.

He returned by way of England, and reported from there his excitement as he began to burrow into family papers for the book that he was eventually to call *Kathleen and Frank*. He also sent Bachardy news of their ever-growing circle of English friends. One was to figure significantly in their lives:

Last night I saw Patrick Procktor (who sends you much love) and went with him and Bob Regester and the director named Anthony Page (not sure you'll remember him—quite bold, youngish, rather nice) to that Chinese restaurant in Limehouse—"New Friends"—and then on a tour of pubs.[12]

Within a year and a half, Isherwood's new friend Anthony Page was to become a new and very particular friend of Bachardy, and Bachardy's 1968 letters reveal that his relationship with Page was to come closer than any other to separating Bachardy from Isherwood altogether.

11. Bachardy letter, Mar. 3, 1965, p. 182.
12. Isherwood letter, Oct. 16, 1966, p. 230.

Meanwhile, in May 1967, Isherwood returned to London for about a month to promote *A Meeting by the River*. While he was there, he worked towards arranging another London exhibition for Bachardy and sent him catalogues from shows that he saw of Francis Bacon and Patrick Procktor. He spent time with some of his oldest friends, and again visited his brother at Wyberslegh to consult family papers.

Bachardy's letters from Santa Monica during these two trips fizz with maturing enthusiasm about his work and with his characteristically tough observations about the friends and acquaintances he and Isherwood shared at home. Harsh though he could be towards false pride, bad manners, or lack of consideration for sensitive feelings, he nearly always extended benevolence to the shy, the underdog, and those without self-confidence. He was a great one for spotting a light hidden under a bushel. His reports to Isherwood humorously exaggerate his own demanding and haughty demeanor towards their friends, and thus obliquely reveal how he longed for Isherwood to spoil him with the loyalty and understanding that Bachardy was never able to find elsewhere. They also show how grateful he was. He gave dutiful accounts of the income flowing from the stage musical *Cabaret* (based on Isherwood's novel *Goodbye to Berlin* and playing to packed houses on Broadway since November 1966) and of the resulting taxes. All the while, he worked steadily in his studio towards a Los Angeles exhibition in November 1967.

Bachardy spent a month in New York from late August to September 1967, then in April 1968 he flew to London for what he thought would be a two-and-a-half-week trip. But, almost certainly as a result of Isherwood's introduction, he became romantically involved with Anthony Page. One postponement of his return led to another. Such was his absorption with this new relationship that Bachardy didn't even get in touch with other London friends, for a time not even with his favorite, Marguerite Lamkin. He forgot to tell Isherwood about the death of Iris Tree, one of Isherwood's closest and most long-standing women friends, and he didn't attend her memorial service. By the end of April, he was obliged to warn Isherwood not to telephone him at Bob Regester and Neil Hartley's, where he was supposedly staying: "Don't call me here except in an emergency. I feel very uncomfortable around Bob & Neil and so spend most of my time away."[13] For the time being, he didn't say where.

13. Bachardy letter, Apr. 30, 1968, p. 283.

Page had hired Bachardy to draw portraits for a John Osborne play that he was directing at the Royal Court, *Time Present*, and, in his letters to Isherwood, Bachardy makes much of the genuine difficulties of the personalities involved, in particular Osborne himself and the notoriously challenging Jill Bennett, then becoming Osborne's fourth wife. He soon revealed to Isherwood that he was staying with Page, but he presented it as an uncomfortable, makeshift arrangement, acceptable only while he reluctantly completed the portraits. And he said Page was caught up in a complicated affair with another man on the premises:

Old Cat misses his Angel Horse so very much and thinks of him so much and pines for his warm basket with the huge Hide cushion which comforts him so. But Kitty is being terribly fussed by these Show Biz people who keep plucking at his fur and spinning him around . . . I am staying with Anthony Page (68 Ladbroke Grove, W. 11). I was so ill at ease at Bob and Neil's that I asked him if he would put me up for a few days. The place is very primitive (but still preferable to Bob's) and though much more inconvenient than Cadogan Square, I at least can get a ride into town in the morning when Anthony goes to rehearsal. He has been having [. . . an] affair of many months with a guy named Norman who lives in the flat above with a lover [. . .].

Cadogan Square is a few blocks from the Royal Court; Page's flat in Notting Hill is probably twenty minutes away by car and longer by tube. The letter tells no lies, but it is a careful delivery of truths that avoids articulating the real excitement of his involvement with Page. "I am very fond of Anthony and he is fun to be with," Bachardy writes, but he goes on to imply that Page hardly notices him and that Isherwood would be equally involved in the friendship if Isherwood, too, were in London:

. . . much of the time he is so wrapped up in the play and rehearsals that he can't really concentrate on anything else. He still talks of the possibility of your writing this thriller for him though I hear nothing that makes me think it might really happen. It could very easily happen if you were here. He is a terribly out-of-sight-out-of-mind person.[14]

14. Bachardy letter, May 2, 1968, pp. 287–288.

On May 8, Bachardy mentions again the possibility that Isherwood might write the screenplay for the French thriller Page was thinking of adapting, *The Praying Mantises*, and although he dismisses the novel as contrived and reiterates that Page is too busy with his stage play to focus seriously on it, he nevertheless gives Isherwood the name of the American publisher and tentatively offers himself as a collaborator: "... a kitten might lend a paw if asked. That way the Animals could put their heads together out of the basket as well as in. But you might hate it and think it unworkable. Anyway, we'll see."[15] On May 15, he sends a long explanation of why he will not be home for his birthday—delays in printing the theater program in which his drawings were being included—and a critique of Page's movie-directing skills in *Inadmissible Evidence*. On May 18, he assures Isherwood his return is imminent, but then on May 29, he writes to say he has begun a set of drawings for a new Osborne play, *The Hotel in Amsterdam*. He finally returned to Los Angeles on June 10, two-and-a-half weeks having become two-and-a-half months. Through all this time, Isherwood never wrote a letter to Bachardy, because he constantly expected him to return, and because he wanted Bachardy to feel the pressure to do so, rather than be allowed to relax into a routine of back-and-forth exchanges. Bachardy's letters are full of reassuring assertions that he longs impatiently to be with Isherwood, and he encloses with them pictures of helpless, damp-eyed kittens clipped from glossy magazines. A cruel truth, though, about the Animal personae is that they could be deployed falsely, and thereby maintain a sentimental fiction of harmony when there was none.

Like any set of conventions, the Kitty and Dobbin life achieved a reality all its own, and Bachardy drew on this resource adeptly now and at other times when he was inwardly preoccupied with an emotional trajectory that had nothing to do with Isherwood. Despite the betrayal this implies, it allowed Bachardy to maintain a balance among a variety of conflicting needs in his own life. He created private space in which to have the kind of sexual and romantic experiences Isherwood had had before the two of them met, and which Isherwood knew Bachardy envied and desired; meanwhile, he continued to make the necessary ritual observances to their household gods. It was not unlike the way in which Isherwood kept up his meditation and prayers through periods

15. Bachardy letter, May 8, 1968, p. 290.

of spiritual dryness in the hope that feelings of belief and refuge in Ramakrishna would return. Isherwood's diaries make clear that he knew at least a little about many of Bachardy's affairs, sometimes because Bachardy told him and sometimes because he recognized the signs. Although he occasionally rebelled against too much intimacy with outsiders, he certainly preferred an open relationship to losing Bachardy altogether. He himself had love affairs, too, or at least plenty of sex with boys and men he found attractive. Sometimes he even had sex with people he didn't find all that attractive. In one letter, he entertained Bachardy with details of a date with a "skinny Maths professor":

> He really is quite bright and has a nice little house all to himself on 15th St., and a little money apparently, which is a drag because he wants to "return my hospitality." He is very closet, or rather, not even that; just restrained and somehow reserved for something, like a folded napkin. He played the piano to me afterwards, Brahms, quite fairly nicely but not well. I imagine he would be good to draw; his face is rather endearing when playing, like a fish rising to the surface. The enormous advantage of mathematics is that it can't be explained so one is excused from all that.[16]

Bachardy's offer of himself as a collaborator for Isherwood is another inspired combination of self-interest and shared interest. He tells Isherwood repeatedly that Page is obsessed with his directing work, and it seems clear that Bachardy wanted to enter Page's world more completely, to be not just an artistic observer recording it, but also a creator participating in it. It's unlikely this was simply in order to get Page's attention; hanging around with Page, Osborne, Jill Bennett, and the other actors in *Time Present* might make anyone ambitious to join in. Bachardy had been a constant movie-goer since childhood; he was a natural critic; and he had begun haunting the theaters and tried writing a play about his family in 1956, the very first time he was alone in London. A few years later, he and Isherwood had worked together on a stage adaptation of *The World in the Evening*; they titled it *The Monsters*, completing a draft in 1959 which they showed to Dodie Beesley and Cecil Beaton. Bachardy possesses just the sort of obsessive temperament suited to the intensely communal and temporary interaction of staging a play, and it suited Isherwood's needs

16. Isherwood letter, Oct. 19, 1968, pp. 329–330.

to be used as a ticket to involvement in this way. Isherwood had already conceded that he was there to serve Bachardy, and he meant it. A new dynamic for the Animals would certainly contribute to keeping their bond alive and strong.

When Auden realized in 1929 that Isherwood was not in love with him and never would be, he had proposed that they write a play together. They went on to write four, and they continued to be intimately involved with one another for more than a decade, partly because of this, while other boyfriends came and went. Collaboration formed a central theme of their lifelong friendship, and Auden later wrote that collaboration was more satisfying to him than any erotic bond: "In my own case, collaboration has brought me greater erotic joy—as distinct from sexual pleasure— than any sexual relation I have had."[17] By the end of the 1930s, when they finished their last play together, they had stopped having the occasional schoolboyish sex that each wrote and spoke about. Their relationship was now primarily intellectual. The Bachardy-Isherwood bond had begun very differently, as a real love affair, and it retained that aura permanently; still, in times when erotic energies were flowing elsewhere, securing the bond by other means, however manipulative, was politic and smart.

Isherwood and Bachardy spent the summer of 1968 together, and Bachardy's suggestion that "the Animals could put their heads together out of the basket as well as in" took quick and unforeseen shape: they adapted Isherwood's novel *A Meeting by the River* into a stage script, a project Isherwood originally initiated with the writer and director Jim Bridges. In October, Bachardy returned to London and to Page, carrying a copy of the script.

In his first letter home, Bachardy diplomatically reports his impression that Page "rather dreaded my visit." Page was absorbed in a feud with Tony Richardson over Richardson's upcoming production of *Hamlet* starring Nicol Williamson. It was Page's brainchild, which he had planned to direct himself, but Richardson had hijacked the project and was doing it without Page. Instantly seeing how to achieve traction in this heated London scene after several months of absence, Bachardy placed a call to Richardson, "just to go on record right away as not being part of this stew. The fact that I left Anthony's number is bound to intrigue

17. Unpublished 1964 Berlin diary, quoted in Edward Mendelson, *Later Auden* (2000), pp. 471–472.

Tony and ensure our meeting."[18] Bachardy also contacted other London friends almost as soon as he had arrived. The return of his interest in a wider social circle coincides with a renewal of authentic warmth and concern in his correspondence with Isherwood and suggests that the affair with Page was now both less intense and less secret.

Bachardy had tea with David Hockney and Peter Schlesinger, and he wrote to Isherwood about the double portrait of himself and Isherwood that Hockney had begun in Los Angeles early that year:

> After the preparation provided by you and Anthony, I was not at all horrified by the likeness of me, which really does seem quite a likeness now. I think he's been working on it since either of you saw it. In fact, the figure of me is in grave danger of being *over*worked. Otherwise I very much like the painting.[19]

Isherwood had made himself available for sittings in California during the spring while Bachardy was absent in London. Eventually, Hockney moved the canvas to London to finish it, by which time Bachardy had gone home for the summer. So Hockney had painted Bachardy mostly from photographs. The wobble in the Isherwood-Bachardy relationship was evident enough to Hockney, who later recalled his impression that Bachardy "nearly stayed" with Page.[20] In the painting, Isherwood turns towards Bachardy attentively, and Bachardy looks out at the viewer, half his face veiled by shadow, his expression charged but unrevealing. In fact, his expression appears frozen in a state of sparkling and unreal excitement, almost as if he were conscious of being a gorgeous object, a magnet for attention. Isherwood's slightly more relaxed posture conveys natural human feeling, and his head, even though we cannot see his whole facial expression, implies a capacity for private commitment and understanding because it is turned to his beloved with a gaze that dismisses all others. The painting is looked on by many as a seminal public image of a successful gay relationship, and part of its interest and power derives from the way in which it reflects the threats to that relationship even though it does not record them. (Perhaps the painting also played a role in preserving the relationship by institutionalizing it.)

18. Bachardy letter, Oct. 9, 1968, p. 302.
19. Bachardy letter, Oct. 11, 1968, p. 309.
20. In conversation, May 24, 2012.

In his letters, Bachardy played down any domestic harmony with Page. He wrote that Page was going without him to Dublin to see a play, mentioned that he was up to work in the morning long before Page was out of bed, reported that Page was often surrounded by other people so it was difficult to talk to him, and described Page talking on the phone while he himself hung around waiting. But the Animals were so close and knew each other so well that even from 6,000 miles away, Isherwood sensed how potent the connection with Page was, and he was anxious in ways that he only half articulated:

> Angel Love, I had such a terrifically vivid dream of you this morning, at exactly seven. You were absolutely *there*, but at the same time I knew you weren't, you were sort of sliding away from me. It was terribly painful and you didn't really want to go, but then I woke up . . ."[21]

In fact, Bachardy needed Isherwood's support as he struggled with the romance and considered what to do with the script of their play. After a week, Isherwood was urging him to show the script to Tony Richardson and to Page just for their opinion, and the next day he wrote, "I am now *certain* that it is good, not only intrinsically but even as it stands, and I don't care, I feel just as I usually do about my books, *somebody* will like it and it will be performed somehow."[22] Bachardy was too proud and too clever a strategist, both personally and professionally, to offer the play to Page or anyone else unless they were likely to pay it serious and empathetic attention, but he guarded his treasure so closely that he began to kill off his own enthusiasm, and he felt increasingly reluctant to put himself forward as a playwright: "I've lost confidence in showing *[A] M[eeting] by [the] R[iver]* to anyone with my name on it."[23] When their agent Robin French read the play back in Los Angeles, he pronounced it "perfect," and so Isherwood tried to buoy up Bachardy without pressuring him, letting go of the idea of showing it to their London stage friends: "I do think we are going to have to take some sort of plunge, at least as soon as you get back here . . . But, I repeat, if you decide not to show it or admit to anyone that you have a copy with you, that's entirely up to you."[24]

21. Isherwood letter, Oct. 15, 1968, p. 311.
22. Isherwood letter, Oct. 15, 1968, p. 310.
23. Bachardy letter, Oct. 12, 1968, p. 313.
24. Isherwood letter, Oct. 16, 1968, p. 314.

Finally, on October 15, Bachardy told Richardson about the play: "Though he was interested and thought it a good idea and was impressed by all the work you've been doing lately, he did *not* ask to read the play. Should I ask him to read it? Let me know what you think."[25] It was not just that Bachardy needed Isherwood's support in this and all other decisions, but that he sometimes seemed to doubt he even existed when Isherwood was not there. He visited Richardson, and his next letter to Isherwood included two paragraphs explaining that Richardson's real reason for wanting to see him was to further his feud with Page:

> I think I am considerably a more desirable guest in Tony's house now that Tony knows I am staying at Anthony's. . . . Tony has not dared to ask me anything about my relations with Anthony, but that too I'm sure makes me a more eligible guest—Tony hopes that Anthony will get jealous. Anthony, in fact (and it is to be said in his favor), makes no objection whatsoever to my seeing Tony. Quite the contrary, he too is eager for news of the other side.

Much though he wanted to be noticed in his own right and for his own talents, Bachardy found it hard to believe it when he was, and he relished this complex web of intertwining loves and hates in which multiple passions and identities generated unpredictable energies. Richardson surely did enjoy exploring the effects of his triumph over Page in the way Bachardy describes, but it seems likely he was also fond of Bachardy. Bachardy tells Isherwood with genuine surprise in the same letter, "He was very friendly and amazingly relaxed and communicative."[26]

In this and similar episodes, Bachardy describes himself as if he were primarily a medium through whom others interacted. When Leslie Caron invites him to supper, "She recognized the telephone number I left yesterday as Anthony's and invited him to dinner, too. I suspect he may be a large reason for her cordiality to me. Her dear little calculating French mind could hardly fail to take into account a smart young director about town." When he hosts Marguerite Lamkin at lunch, "One thing helped: John Schlesinger turned up there and came over very friendly and I introduced them. Marguerite said later in very respectful tones, 'He's so talented,' so I gather she was impressed." Tony Richardson

25. Bachardy letter, Oct. 16, 1968, p. 321.
26. Bachardy letter, Oct. 16, 1968, pp. 321–323.

invites him to dinner, but "most certainly because Tony guessed I was having dinner with Anthony. He would so love to have been able to spirit me away as well as Nicol Williamson."[27] What's remarkable here is not so much Bachardy's concern for the status of his boyfriend, or the snobbery and cruelty common among their circle of friends, but rather the frankness with which he exposes them. Most people would attribute such thoughts to others and pretend they themselves did not have them. Minimizing his own importance, Bachardy gets right underneath everyone else's skin. He sees their most hidden thoughts, the thoughts they hide even from themselves, or which hover just below consciousness. This ruthlessly penetrating style of observation conforms to his sense of how he worked as a portrait painter, too; in later years, he was to describe himself as impersonating his sitters.[28] For the span of a sitting, he watches so closely that he gains access to an internal chemistry and "becomes" his sitter.

His biggest act of impersonation was, of course, his impersonation of Isherwood himself, in voice, manner, and taste, steadily perfected over the decades. To some, he now seems to be a reincarnation of Isherwood, though, in fact, he is also very different. Following Isherwood's example, Bachardy kept diaries for many years, but only when he was living with someone else—that is, with Isherwood and, after Isherwood's death, with his subsequent longterm boyfriend Tim Hilton. He asserts that he was of little interest to himself when he was alone.[29] To Isherwood, he was always of interest, and he was obviously confident that he fully existed in Isherwood's eyes, just as Hockney observed in his double portrait. There was no one Isherwood wanted to talk to in the way that he wanted to talk to Bachardy, and no matter how much time they had together, Isherwood never stopped wanting to hear what Bachardy had to say. Moreover, Isherwood wanted to make an example of their life together and of their determination to be happy, partly because a sense of greater purpose gave relief from the narrow inner experience of sorrow and longing. Imagining their relationship from the outside gave it a reality and steadiness Isherwood could not always feel. When Bachardy was away in London with Anthony Page, Isherwood wrote with a characteristic mixture of seriousness and camp:

27. Bachardy letter, Oct. 18, 1968, pp. 331–332.
28. In conversation, Oct. 2006.
29. In conversation, Oct. 2011.

Thinks of his Darling all the time, the constant dialogue with him goes on, what he would say to this or that, how he would react. Breakfast seems not worth fixing and even the few steps to the deck are a drag, but Dobbin has great style and appears because, after all, we belong to Our People and seeing that life goes on in the Casa helps them so much in the miserable existences they lead in their squalid huts.[30]

As Bachardy's second London visit with Page stretched on, his letters became more open about the friendship. Isherwood went to see Page's film, *Inadmissible Evidence,* in Los Angeles, and he thought much more highly of it than Bachardy. He even asked Bachardy to pass on his praise to Page, thereby delicately attempting to participate in their friendship. Perhaps this made Bachardy feel the status quo was approved. Bachardy's assignment to draw posters for Page's revival of Osborne's *Look Back in Anger* fell through, but he was busy with numerous other commissions. He revealed to Isherwood that he and Page were getting on better and even conceded that Page was highly intelligent and multitalented:

> His danger is that he is really too bright. He is capable of doing so many things quite well but none of them really well enough unless he concentrates. Did I tell you he can draw surprisingly well and also plays the piano and once considered a concert pianist's career? And in spite of all his success in the theater I don't think he's quite given up thoughts of these other careers which take on added attraction when things go wrong in the theater . . . I think he does really enjoy directing while he's doing it, and what is so impressive in watching him do it is his ability to concentrate. Every ounce of his nervous energy is poured into attending to what's going on onstage and the actors feel it and respond to it and therefore often enjoy working for him more than anybody else.[31]

But other letters continue to lament Page's disorganization, his habitual lateness, usually because of his work, and when Bachardy himself was working, "a childish, mischievous desire to rile me if he can. I think my patience irks him a lot. . . ."[32]

All the while, the Animals kept up a steady traffic of gossip about

30. Isherwood letter, Oct. 17, 1968, p. 319.
31. Bachardy letter, Oct. 20, 1968, p. 337.
32. Bachardy letter, Oct. 23, 1968, p. 349.

their many friends in Los Angeles and London, the day-to-day ones and the famous ones like Paul Bowles, Tennessee Williams, Gore Vidal, and John Gielgud. By the end of October, Isherwood finally got going for real on *Kathleen and Frank*. Then, just as Bachardy prepared to return home, Page indeed tested his patience as well as Isherwood's by asking Bachardy to draw a new poster for *Hotel in Amsterdam*. Paul Scofield was leaving the play, to be replaced by Kenneth Haigh. Isherwood cried out in dismay when Bachardy phoned to tell him. But Page had also, on October 27, begun reading the script for *A Meeting by the River*. Halfway through, he took the script to the Royal Court, where he asked an assistant, playwright and director Nicholas Wright, to read it. Bachardy received this as an insult:

> I was *furious* and lost my temper in a way I have never done with him before. As you can imagine, he was very surprised. We had quite an argument. This is another reason why I didn't want to leave yesterday, in a cloud of ill feeling.
>
> Apparently the assistant adored it though, and even called after midnight on Monday to enthuse about it, but I was still so cross I wouldn't speak to him. I'm sure a production at the Court could and would be arranged if we wanted it. But as far as I'm concerned we don't—anyway not without the very best cast and director. Anthony has not yet said anything about wanting to direct it himself but I'll bet he's seriously considering it.[33]

Bachardy at last returned to Santa Monica in time to vote in the presidential election on November 5. Isherwood evidently loved him the more for the absences and obstacles Bachardy created in their lives. Cast in the role of the steady and dependable Dobbin, he acted more and more in keeping with his Animal character as he grew older, even though in youth he had been as mercurial and restless as his young lover. Perhaps it was the memory of his younger self that he loved in Bachardy; certainly this allowed him to understand and to sympathize with Bachardy's temperamental behavior and continual changes of heart. He signed off his letters to Bachardy with childlike sketches of himself as a clunky old horse, a horse sometimes shedding tears and always

33. Bachardy letter, Oct. 30, 1968, p. 356.

lonely for his kitten. Bachardy loved the sketches because he knew how Isherwood struggled to make them, hampered as he was by arthritis in both his thumbs and, increasingly, with Dupuytren's contracture, which began as a lump in his left palm and gradually contracted the little finger of his left hand into a rigid, curled claw. Drawing came easily to Bachardy, and it moved him that Isherwood would clumsily attempt it when he could far more easily express his adoration in words.

In April 1969, Bachardy again went to London to stay with Page and to do portraits of the Earl and Countess of Harewood, scandal-ridden members of the royal family and the British musical world. Harewood was a first cousin of the Queen, in line to the throne, and a patron of opera, on which he wrote with expertise; the countess was an Australian violinist who bore his child out of wedlock while he divorced his first wife to marry her. The commission had been arranged by the ballet critic Richard Buckle, who had designed the wildly popular exhibition of Cecil Beaton photographs at the National Portrait Gallery the previous year, and who was proving to be a very useful friend to Bachardy. In London, Bachardy also finalized his own arrangement with the National Portrait Gallery, to sell the gallery his 1967 drawing of Auden, and he delivered the portrait in person. Isherwood again set to on a regime of work and socializing to fill the time. His stage adaptation of George Bernard Shaw's story "The Adventures of the Black Girl in Her Search for God" had opened at the Mark Taper Forum, where it was playing to mixed reviews and big audiences, so he was a little occupied with publicity, and he pressed on with *Kathleen and Frank*. He kept Bachardy updated on old and new friendships, in particular "the two little boys," Jim Gates and Peter Schneider, who charmed and intrigued him: "they were just sort of magically involved with each other and I saw a great deal of the relationship I had with Edward Upward at Cambridge in it."[34] He always begged Bachardy not to forget him, and he continued to supply all the latest news from the Hollywood Vedanta Center where, since 1939, he had been a member of the congregation and a disciple of its leader, the Indian Ramakrishna monk, Swami Prabhavananda.

When Bachardy arrived this time at Page's flat in London, he was greeted by Page's new assistant, the young, not-yet-famous Stephen Frears, a rival in so far as he was in command of Page's telephone.

34. Isherwood letter, Apr. 19, 1969, p. 367.

Bachardy had to wait a long time to contact Richard Buckle and arrange his first sitting with the Harewoods, which took place at Harewood House near Leeds. He was later to work again with them in London. As Bachardy now engaged with the highest echelons of the "poshocracy" that Isherwood had eschewed since his adolescent friendship with the rebellious, downwardly mobile Upward, Isherwood found it in himself to be entirely interested in Kitty's progress there, and increasingly expressed in his letters unnuanced animosity for anyone who made Bachardy's life at all difficult or who snubbed him in any way. In fact, much like siblings who squabble privately at home but unite against outsiders, Bachardy and Isherwood brooked no criticism, apart from their own of one another.

The success of *Cabaret* had led to plans for a film. Bachardy had actually delayed his London trip waiting for developments because the project promised a new opportunity for collaboration. Then, not long after he finally left Los Angeles on April 17, 1969, Isherwood wrote to say that he had sold the film rights for "about 6 or 7 thousand a year for six years."[35] Yet another Anthony, Anthony Harvey, was mooted to direct it, and Isherwood and Bachardy were offered $25,000 for a treatment and $60,000 for the screenplay itself. Isherwood told Bachardy that he was beginning right away to prepare for the job by attending a screening at MGM of *I Am a Camera*, the film version of the first, nonmusical stage adaptation of *Goodbye to Berlin*. But the deal was not yet final. Since Bachardy's work with the Harewoods was going well and further London portrait commissions were coming in, Isherwood did not press him to return home. Instead, on his own, Isherwood spoke to Harvey on the telephone, met with him, made notes from their conversation, and began to think about problems in the story that would need solving and about which he and Harvey didn't agree.

Bachardy's reports of his friendship with Page sound far more relaxed than during his two previous visits. Then, about a week into his trip, Bachardy suddenly wrote to tell Isherwood that he had moved out of Page's flat that very morning and moved in with Buckle in Covent Garden. "I've felt very uncomfortable with Anthony for several days and I knew there would be a row if I stayed on." Page was so occupied with work that Bachardy found it impossible to communicate with him. He

35. Isherwood letter, Apr. 23, 1969, p. 375.

was planning a new production of Middleton's *Women Beware Women*, which he had directed successfully for the Royal Shakespeare Company in 1962, but the new production fell apart, and that evidently triggered the rise in tension:

> The fact is, I think we are chemically an unsafe mixture and, being as we were in very confined quarters, there was bound to be an explosion if I didn't get out. I'm very sorry in a way, but glad at least to have found this out without too much unpleasantness.[36]

Isherwood, by contrast, had proved by now that he was an entirely safe mixture with Bachardy. As he observed several times in his diaries, nothing was as important to him as their relationship, neither his work nor his religion. Or more exactly, with regard to the latter, he understood his love for Bachardy as a way of expressing his devotion to Ramakrishna. Simply by sitting still and waiting, he maintained his position in Bachardy's affections, and his professional achievements and the fresh opportunities they brought—for example, the *Cabaret* job—worked like a lodestone, helping to pull Bachardy home:

> A kitten's drooping whiskers suddenly stiffened this morning at the sound of that Old Naggin neighing, and his tired little heart started beating so quickly. Kitty is delighted by the news. It probably would never have happened if Kitty hadn't come to England. How Kitty looks forward to working side by side with his Dear . . . I sent a telegram this afternoon after confirming a reservation on Pan Am Fl. 121 arriving Tuesday May 6 at 5:35 p.m.[37]

Meanwhile, Bachardy saw Page again, and he told Isherwood the meeting was a success. "[T]he big mistake," he wrote, "was in staying at Ladbroke Grove,"[38] implying that he and Page could have a romance but could not make a home together. On May 1, he wrote to say that he had spent the night with Page, and soon after that he went off with him for a weekend in Devon. But he returned to Santa Monica as promised to work with Isherwood on *Cabaret*, and then to travel with him to Tahiti

36. Bachardy letter, Apr. 25, 1969, p. 388.
37. Bachardy letter, Apr. 30, 1969, p. 398.
38. Bachardy letter, Apr. 30, 1969, p. 398.

and Australia, where they visited the set of *Ned Kelly* and discussed with Tony Richardson yet another script on which they might collaborate, based on Robert Graves's *I, Claudius* and *Claudius the God*. From Sydney, Bachardy phoned Page and arranged to visit him again in London from August 18.

Isherwood and Bachardy now had three projects in the offing: their own play *A Meeting by the River*, the film of *Cabaret*, and a proposed Claudius film. Bachardy's first business on arriving in London in August 1969 was to push forward their original collaboration, *A Meeting by the River*, in the hope of a London production directed either by Anthony Page or Jim Bridges. Various producers lined up to back them. Bachardy's letters are full of directors and actors who might or might not participate. Many were close friends, all of them juggling other commitments or hopes, and the timing and sensitivities of each proposed involvement is fantastically complex. Mischief is suspected of those who back away, and those who are not wanted seem keenest to take part. Bachardy expresses strong and shifting opinions about who can be trusted, who is any good, who is a friend. In the midst of all this, he mentions in a postscript to Isherwood that the newest of their three projects doesn't actually interest him. With little work invested, it was to go nowhere, even though with its intrigues, spying, and manipulation it offers obvious comparisons with his own situation and style of behavior: "*I, Claudius* is such a bore. . . . What drudgery it is to get through it."[39]

The negotiations over *A Meeting by the River* dragged on until Bachardy finally went home to Los Angeles to get on with his painting career. The following winter, January 1970, he and Isherwood returned to London together to continue trying to get their play staged, and they made some significant changes to the script in response to requests from directors and producers. In March 1970, Bachardy again went home to Los Angeles for a show of his work at the Irving Blum Gallery. The affair with Page had evidently died away, and the Animals now temporarily switched roles, with Isherwood fighting their corner in the London theater world while Bachardy set himself to a work routine at home and did the domestic chores. Jim Gates had moved into their house at Adelaide Drive as a housesitter, and was still living there; Bachardy got on with him contentedly enough. He had some Los Angeles commissions to do

---

39. Bachardy letter, Aug. 21, 1969, p. 409.

as a result of his show there, which was well reviewed, and he took up their social life where Isherwood had left off, including regular dates with Evelyn Hooker, Jo Masselink, Chris Wood, and Elsa Lanchester, and frequent visits to the bedside of Gerald Heard, who had suffered so many slight strokes that he and everyone else had lost count. The project Bachardy most enjoyed during this period was watching George Cukor films with Gavin Lambert, who was preparing to write his book about Cukor. The letters are confidential and unguarded, and Bachardy reports on his amorous adventures as if they were now a source of shared pride.

In London, Isherwood continued to work on *Kathleen and Frank*. He wrote home about his trip to Paris and the South of France with Hockney and Schlesinger, during which they stayed with Tony Richardson. He also reported on the opening of Hockney's retrospective at the Whitechapel, a smash hit, and further visits to aging friends like the writer Dodie Smith and her husband Alec Beesley. Mostly he felt he was wasting his time without Bachardy:

> The things I don't regret about this trip are that we did all that truly valuable work on the script, that I got a lot more material for my book from Richard and that I made the trip in France with David & Peter (but that would have been more fun with you along).[40]

He did not feel the least discouraged, however, by directors and actors turning their play down:

> I am now more than ever convinced that the play is *good* and so I feel strangely exhilarated, as I often do when I'm convinced that The Others are wrong. Also I feel that all these minus votes are preparing for some big plus in the near future.[41]

Indeed, there never was a London production. *A Meeting by the River* was staged successfully in Los Angeles, and then went to Broadway, where it was an instant and complete failure. Their *Cabaret* film script wasn't used at all. Such things no longer mattered much to Isherwood, and his attitude sheltered Bachardy, who might otherwise have been more

---

40. Isherwood letter, Apr. 6, 1970, p. 432.
41. Isherwood letter, Apr. 7, 1970, p. 434.

vulnerable to disappointment. Isherwood felt most alive in a posture of opposition to The Others. Succeeding and thereby becoming part of their world offered only a kind of deadening banality. His relationship with Bachardy was the center of his life, and their close companionship strengthened Isherwood in his stance against conformity with established social groups.

The challenges that Bachardy never ceased to offer not only held Isherwood's attention, but were a tonic to his love. His last message in this book was written in 1970 to accompany a now forgotten birthday gift that Isherwood hoped might please Bachardy, "a silly way of saying how much Dub loves Kitty and wishes him all the things that can't be given...."[42] He lived only to please Bachardy, and he tried all the harder precisely because Bachardy did not make it easy. Bachardy was like the heroine of a courtly romance or a princess in a fairy tale, for whose love the greatest challenges were laid down. Isherwood was not only the steed, but also the knight riding off on the required quest. In 1969 on Bachardy's birthday, Isherwood wrote an Animal tale, a kind of Beatrix Potter story about himself as a Don Quixote figure who stumbles off with the highest intention, his ideal love for his Dulcinea embodied in a creaturely, sweaty, and inept effort at fulfilment:

There was an old Dobbin who wanted to give Kitty something of a certain shape and color which he had lost part of, so he went to a place in Sta. Monica and they said better go to a place where they sell men's clothes, and they said have you tried the hotel but the hotel didn't know. So old Dob went to Pacific Palisades where the lady said no unfortunately but I hear there's a place on Ventura Boulevard at Coldwater Canyon where they have *nothing else.* So Dub trotted over the hill and how hot it was and the flies got under his hat and stung him but he found out where it was and they said sorry but our Mr. So-and-So has taken them all to the Pan Pacific where there's a Home Show—so Drabbledug trotted back over the hill dragging his tail through Laurel Canyon through all the dust and he got into the Pan Pacific and they laughed at him and tried to run him out but he neighed and reared and at last he found Mr. So-and-So who was kind but said I've sold them all. But Mr. So-and-So told him to go to Gorham, just off San Vicente, and there, in a pet shop of all places, he

42. Isherwood note, May 18, 1970, p. 439.

found some—and this isn't really what he was thinking of but he hopes
Kitty will like it—anyhow it's truly a token of Love on Kitty's birthday.[43]

The gift Isherwood had in mind was not even the gift that he finally
found or gave, and Bachardy has again long since forgotten what it was,
but the love it betokened was unchanging. It seems fitting that such an
Animal token was found in a pet shop.

The last letters in this book were written in 1970, roughly halfway
through the Animals' life together. After that, they were apart only for
brief spells, and they relied on the telephone. In their thirty-three years
together, Isherwood never entirely got the measure of Bachardy, who
never ceased to fascinate and intrigue him. Although Bachardy looked up
to Isherwood, admired, emulated, and needed him, he always kept him
in the role of supplicant, subjecting him to ceaseless tests. Isherwood
was more experienced, more self-confident, older, and much sooner to
die, and they both knew that Bachardy's exercise of power was, in these
respects, only a kind of game, a private, specialized camp in which they
both willingly engaged. Neither of them was able to achieve control over
the unexpected turns of mood and conviction to which Bachardy was
utterly subject, the blossomings of sweetness, the outbreaks of storm.
And this, thrillingly, dramatically, shaped their Animal destiny.

43. Isherwood note, May 18, 1969, p. 404.

Textual Note and Acknowledgements

This volume contains all the letters between Christopher Isherwood and Don Bachardy that are known to survive. The text is based on a typescript made by Don Bachardy in the early 1990s. He arranged the letters chronologically, and added missing dates by consulting Isherwood's day-to-day diaries as well as his own diaries and recollections. Where letters crossed in the post, he sometimes overruled strict chronology in favor of the clearest narrative trajectory. I have preserved his sequence in all but a few cases where he and I were able to establish a correction or improvement together.

Bachardy made a very small number of revisions to the text of his own letters; in general, I have not retained these, but instead have restored what he first wrote. A few of his changes have been preserved for clarity, and a very small number of similar changes have been made in Isherwood's letters. Changes in Isherwood's letters are marked with square brackets. I have retained many abbreviations and typographical and handwritten anomalies to preserve the character of the correspondence, and I have included nearly all of the sketches and annotations with which many of the letters are embellished, as well as some of the cuttings enclosed in or glued (by Bachardy) to the letters.

Style and spelling are American. Where Isherwood and Bachardy don't habitually adopt the same spellings, I have allowed Isherwood's to prevail.

Headings to the letters reflect what Isherwood or Bachardy wrote or typed at the top of the page, and square brackets mark dates and locations supplied by Bachardy, mostly from envelopes and postmarks. Both Isherwood and Bachardy meticulously wrote return addresses on the outside of their correspondence. Bachardy saved Isherwood's letters inside their envelopes; Isherwood discarded envelopes. Isherwood often used air letters when writing abroad, a single sheet that folds to form its own envelope and with a designated space for postal addresses; Bachardy used air letters, too, as he grew older. I offer a brief description of each item, in square brackets at bottom left, whether autograph or typed, stationery where notable, enclosures, and some other details.

The letters form a private and informal conversation, and many readers will need guidance to recognize the friends mentioned and to follow references and jokes. I have relied solely on traditional footnotes, in order to avoid having any editorial voice intervene on the page between the two main speakers. The letters are grouped so that each new section represents a new period of separation, however brief, between Isherwood and Bachardy. In general, the first footnote in each section tells where each of them was and why they were apart. Much additional information is available in Isherwood's diaries, and I hope that readers of the diaries will skim my notes here without feeling burdened by material with which they are already familiar. At the same time, I hope it will be possible for readers new to Isherwood to start with this volume of letters if they so choose. Dates in square brackets in notes are not confirmed.

I could not have begun or finished my part in preparing this book without Don Bachardy's continuing readiness to answer questions. He is a tenacious worker and utterly unafraid to speak candidly about the past. Many other people have also helped me with great resourcefulness and patience, including: Francis Bator; Kate Bland; Zennor Compton; Julia Connolly; Paul Cox, Associate Curator (Reference Collection), National Portrait Gallery; Thomas J. Devine; Mareika Doleschal, Collections Librarian, Shakespeare Centre Library and Archive, Stratford-upon-Avon; Jason Epstein; Robert Gore, Visual Arts Librarian, UCLA Arts Library; Phyllis Green; Mandy Greenfield; David Hannah; Selina Hastings; Tim Hilton; Dr. Anthony Hippisley; David Hockney; Sue Hodson, Curator of Literary Manuscripts, the Huntington Library, San Marino, California; Nicholas Jenkins; the staff at the London Library, including Alice Dowhyj and especially Gosia Lawik; Mary Marshall; Richard Marston; Edward Mendelson; Nicky Nevin; John Julius Norwich; Susannah Otter; Anthony Page; Christopher Phipps and Ben Murphy who both worked on the index; Darryl Pinckney; Sarah Punnett; Ned Rorem; Robert Silvers; Christopher Simon Sykes; Ann Totterdell; Robert Winckworth, Archives Assistant, UCL Records Office; Gloria Vanderbilt and Katie Arnold-Ratliff; Hugo Vickers; Natalie Wall; Ruth Warburton; Edmund White; Luke Ingram and Kristina Moore at the Wylie Agency.

Also at the Wylie Agency I would like to thank Sarah Chalfant for her unfailing engagement with whatever questions books and life present. Our publishers, Clara Farmer and Jonathan Galassi, have been warmly committed to all things Isherwood, and Rowena Skelton-Wallace always sees how to improve, but never criticizes.

To their mild surprise and evident amusement, my family are still on the Isherwood journey, and I am so grateful for their company.

The letters are deposited at the Huntington Library, San Marino, California.

Letters

Wednesday [February 1, 1956]   High Lane, Cheshire[1]

Dearest Donny,

I wonder so much what you are doing, and I hope so much that you're having fun and interesting adventures. Wednesday! And when you get this it will be Thursday—and then there will only be Friday, Saturday, Sunday . . . But I mustn't get rattled. I keep looking out anxiously at the snow which fell last night and wondering if more will fall and block the roads. But I'll get through somehow—like in that Courbet at the National Gallery.[2] This house is as damp as a sponge, and *cold*—you can see your breath even when standing by the fire—and the sheets are damp like graveclothes and the books on the shelves smell of corpses. And in the kitchen and scullery there are very old smells of dried fat in skillets and old old black rags that are quite frighteningly filthy in a 19th century way, like something out of *Oliver Twist*.

I don't say all this just in complaint. A lot of it is hilariously funny, or very touching, and I'm glad I came alone because it's really easier to take. I spend a lot of time scrubbing things. If *only* the pipes don't freeze!

My mother[3] is absolutely marvellous—sharp as a needle, sees well, hears perfectly, remembers everything, talks all day long. Poor Richard[4] is turning rapidly in[to] a prematurely aged freak—his face around the nose is dark purple (bad circulation, I guess) and he has lost several of his teeth in front and he walks with a stoop and keeps his head down. But he is so kind and gentle and anxious to help. He fills my bed with

1. Isherwood and Bachardy were winding up Bachardy's first trip to North Africa and Europe with two months in England, January 7 to March 11, 1956. On January 30, Isherwood travelled alone to Wyberslegh, his childhood home, to spend a week with his mother and his brother. He posted this letter to the Cavendish Hotel, Jermyn Street, London, where Bachardy was staying in the room they had shared.
2. *The Diligence in the Snow* (1860).
3. Kathleen Bradshaw Isherwood (1868–1960).
4. Isherwood's brother, Richard Graham Bradshaw Isherwood (1911–1979).

hot water bottles, leaving marks on the sheets because his poor hands are chronically covered with coal dust. He is forever building fires or making tea which is pure liquid brass. They have two white cats. The female has a black smudge over one eye and she is fat with kittens, fathered by the other cat, her son. She is one of the best-looking cats I have ever seen, and she doesn't give a shit about any of us.

If I didn't hate the cold so, I'd admit that this place is marvellously beautiful. Cobden Edge, the first ridge of moorland behind the house, is all white and there is a strange orange light on the snow; the bare trees are so black against it. Cheerful stamping men in mufflers bring milk and newspapers—from which I see that Emlyn Williams and Charlie Chaplin were both at Korda's funeral. Maybe Molly will fix for you to meet him—and/or *Lady* Olivier, who was there too?![5]

Unless I send a telegram to the contrary, I will arrive at Euston Station Monday afternoon at 1:55. No need to meet me if you have something else to do. I just tell you so you'll know approximately when I'll be at the hotel—about 2:30. Leave word for me there if you're not coming to the station. (But I hope you do!)

Imagine—this is the first letter I ever wrote you! I think about you all the time, and about times I might have been kinder and more understanding, and I make many resolutions for the future—some of which I hope I'll keep.

In any case,

all my love,

Chris.

[*Autograph letter on printed letterhead of Wyberslegh Hall, High Lane, Stockport, Cheshire*]

5. Hungarian-born British director and film producer Alexander Korda (1893–1956) died January 23; he was cremated privately, but there was a star-studded memorial service at St. Martin in the Fields in London on January 31. Welsh playwright, screenwriter, and actor Emlyn Williams (1905–1987) and his wife, Mary (Molly) Carus-Wilson (d. 1970), an actress under her maiden name, Molly O'Shann, were close friends of Isherwood and Bachardy. Charlie Chaplin had also been a friend, but he refused to see Isherwood after Isherwood allegedly peed on the Chaplins' sofa while drunk at a party in 1950 or 1951. Isherwood hoped Molly Williams might be able to introduce Bachardy to Chaplin and also to actress Vivien Leigh (1913–1967), second wife of Laurence Olivier. Olivier had been knighted in 1947, making her Lady Olivier, a title little known to Americans. Isherwood and Bachardy met and became friends with Leigh only in 1960.

February 1, 1956 [London]

Dear Chris,

It is freezing here. It snowed most of yesterday, and even began to lay on the iron steps outside the window. But today it is all gone, and though clear & sunny, it is much colder. I am still in bed (it's past 12) because it's the only warm place. I have been reading, and working on my play! I am amazed—I worked three and a half hours yesterday morning and three hours this morning, and now I have eight pages of solid notes and, I think, a very good outline for the first two acts! I've managed to think up a surprisingly well-constructed plot (although there is not much of a story) and already I know roughly what the third act will consist of. I feel quite silly, especially in the afternoon and early morning, when I think of writing this play, but nevertheless it is going well and it is fun. It's a very heavy drama—I hope this isn't a mistake—and not very original, but with a few surprises. As of yet, you have not appeared. It may very well be a thing of the past by next Monday—I really haven't written more than just a few snatches of dialogue yet.[1]

John (I don't even know his last name yet—Cuthbert's friend[2]) called yesterday morning and took me to *Fresh Airs* last night. I thought it was dull and trivial, and very poorly organized and produced. Too much really amazingly trashy sentiment. I thought a revue was essentially based on gags and laughs, but right in the middle of supposedly funny skits were very serious, straight-faced sentimental numbers with nothing but the corniest lyrics. There were endless sets and costumes, all ugly, and the most amateurish dancing and pantomiming I've seen out of high school. Here and there were a few amusing gags, all very proper except for a terribly shocking skit about a Paris pissoir and some "asides" from Max Adrian (who got in drag, too), but the funniest thing was a political skit making fun of America doing her all to make Germany happy.[3]

John and I got along well—he's really very nice and has a lot of the same difficulties that I've got, so there's quite a bit for us to talk about. I took him to dinner at the Comedy and we had drinks at the hotel before

1. The play, about Bachardy's parents, was soon abandoned.
2. Cuthbert Worsley (1907–1977), leftist English writer, theater critic, and schoolmaster, lived with a much younger companion, John Luscombe.
3. The Laurier Lister revue at the Comedy Theatre starred Lister's longterm companion, Irish comic actor Max Adrian (1903–1973), with Rose Hill, and Moyra Fraser. It won an Ivor Novello Award.

dinner. He even invited me to spend a few days with him and Cuthbert, but I firmly refused—for various reasons. I think he is interested in me, but I most definitely don't reciprocate any kind of similar interest. No one else has called and I haven't made any calls myself.

Yesterday I saw *The Constant Husband* with Rex Harrison and Margaret Leighton (it was very boring) and *A Life at Stake* with Angela Lansbury and Keith Andes, a quickie thriller made on location in L.A. with a weak, silly story but still interesting. She was good. You don't have to bother with either film, though.[4] The day before I saw *White Cargo*, which was mild fun, and *Moulin Rouge*, which was still beautiful but unbelievably trashy and pompous and self-consciously chic, and in places really foul. Huston gives himself away in this.[5] I saw *The Boyfriend* in the evening. It's not nearly as good as in New York and seemed very "joke's over" this time after one act. But I had a seat in the front row and flirted unmercifully with the chorus boys all through it.[6]

But I miss rides through London on old Dobbin (especially in the snow yesterday) and think a lot about him, sleeping in a strange stable, eating cold oats out of an ill-fitting feed bag and having no cat fur to keep him warm. And don't let them put any frozen bits in his mouth. And tell him an anxious Tabby is at the mercy of the RSPCA and counting the days till his return.

Love, Ak

P. S. Don't forget about the movies.[7]

[*Autograph letter*]

. . .

4. Isherwood had known British film star Angela Lansbury (b. 1925) since World War II, when she was brought to Hollywood for safety during the Blitz. British actors Rex Harrison (1908–1990) and Margaret Leighton (1922–1978) became friends later, and both are mentioned below.

5. John Huston (1906–1987), American director, screenwriter, and actor, directed the original 1952 film. Isherwood had been friendly with him since about 1950.

6. Sandy Wilson's musical had been running in London since 1953; Isherwood and Bachardy had seen the New York production (which opened in September 1954) at the start of their long trip abroad, in mid-October 1955, when they flew from Los Angeles to New York and spent ten days there before travelling to Tangier by ship.

7. Bachardy was reminding Isherwood to film his mother and brother and Wyberslegh.

Sunday June 16 [1957]   [Santa Monica]

Dearest Don,

This is just a quick note to tell you that you are sadly missed here and much thought about.[1] I do hope you are having a wonderful time, in spite of Marguerite being away.[2] Will she be back before you leave?

Would you like me to do something about the work table you wanted for your room? Will Reid[3] is back and has fixed the front door. If you will tell me exactly what it is that you want, I can get the work started. It occurs to me that perhaps we could work out a more compact way of storing the stuff you have in those two chests of drawers upstairs—maybe buy another filing cabinet? As I understood you, you were thinking of getting a door and putting it on legs to make your work table, so that it would go over the chests of drawers. But maybe we could put the chests of drawers in the downstair bedroom—in front of the window?

When you see John Goodwin be sure to find out all about Japan, and what we should see there. Maybe get a couple of his capsules.[4]

Am going on the beach in an hour or so, where I shall meet Ted,[5] also

1. Isherwood was writing from 434 Sycamore Road, Santa Monica, where he and Bachardy lived from 1956 to 1959. Bachardy was taking a holiday in New York, June 13 to June 30, 1957, between semesters at the Chouinard Art Institute where he first enrolled in July 1956.
2. Marguerite Lamkin (b. *circa* 1930), American socialite and dialogue coach, then lived in New York but was visiting her family at home in Monroe, Louisiana.
3. William Wallace Reid, Jr. (1917–1990), the carpenter, was the son of silent-film star Wallace Reid (1892–1930).
4. John Goodwin (1912–1994), American poet and novelist, wealthy and well-travelled, later published *A View from Fuji* (1963), a novella based on his time in Japan. Isherwood and Bachardy visited there on October 8, 1957 at the start of a four-month trip to the Far East, Calcutta, London, and New York. Goodwin began taking mescaline in the mid-1950s; Isherwood had tried it twice in London in 1956.
5. Ted Bachardy (1930–2007), Don Bachardy's brother.

Scott[6] and his new friend. Tonight I'm dining with Evelyn.[7] Yesterday I went up to Vedanta Place for the Father's Day lunch. Swami asked after you and greatly regretted your absence and invited you to Trabuco on the 4th,[8] about which I was vague, knowing how you hope to go to the Cottens'.[9] (No invite yet.) Actually, yesterday would have been a kind of preview of Indian embarrassment for you. We were the only guests of honor and you would have had to sit with me between the two swamis under a sort of canopy, wearing flower garlands! Afterwards there was a religious play in the temple, quite good. When it was over, I congratulated the director—a complete stranger to me—who replied: "I just tried to make it into the maddest camp I knew how." That's what Vedanta is coming to!

Last night I had supper with Jerry Lawrence,[10] and his various young actor friends—including Jack Larson.[11] Jerry made like he had hardly lived through our separation! I don't dig this. If it is just an act, and it must be—*why?* He sent warmest greetings to you. Larson was very intense, puzzled, boyish, searching, etc. I talked too much, but escaped with an un-upset stomach even after eating fruit salad and drinking a little brandy! Jerry is finishing another play for Broadway this fall.[12]

Have also seen Hayden and Rod.[13] They think Jim[14] is getting very crazy. Jo and Ben[15] are away for the weekend. The weather is gorgeous,

6. Scott Schubach, a wealthy doctor.

7. Evelyn Hooker (1907–1996), American psychologist and psychotherapist.

8. Swami Prabhavananda (1893–1976), Hindu monk of the Ramakrishna Order, founder of the Vedanta Society of Southern California, which had a temple at Vedanta Place, Hollywood, and a monastery in Trabuco Canyon southeast of Los Angeles. He was Isherwood's guru from 1939 onward. Father's Day was celebrated annually by the congregation in honor of their gurus—the swamis, monks, and nuns at Vedanta Place. American Independence Day on the Fourth of July was celebrated annually by the monks at Trabuco.

9. Joseph Cotten (1905–1994), American actor, and his first wife Lenore Kipp (d. 1960), friends of both Isherwood and Bachardy.

10. Jerome Lawrence (1915–2004), American playwright.

11. Jack Larson (b. *circa* 1933), American actor, playwright, librettist, best known for playing Jimmy Olsen in the original 1950s T.V. series, "The Adventures of Superman."

12. Probably *The Gang's All Here* (1959), with his partner Robert Lee (see below, p. 167).

13. Hayden Lewis and Rod Owens, companions since the mid-1940s when Isherwood first met them; they ran a ceramics business, making dinnerware and ashtrays.

14. Jim Charlton (1919–1998), American architect, trained by Frank Lloyd Wright; a close friend since 1948 and an intermittent romantic interest of Isherwood.

15. Jo (*circa* 1900–1988) and Ben (1919–2000) Masselink, American sportswear and swimsuit designer and American novelist and T.V. writer. They never married, though she used his name when they lived together. Her professional name was Lathwood, from a brief early marriage.

but it misses Kitty. Tell Kitty to remember that old Dobbin will be lovingly waiting when K. is tired of his travels.

Love as always, Chris.

Thursday, June 20. After we talked on the phone this morning, the mail arrived and there was my letter—the one I wrote you—returned from the Gladstone! So I'm sending it back to you.[16] Have a wonderful time. I do miss you *terribly*. I called your mother [17] and told her I'd heard from you and all was well. All other news when we meet. All my love, C.

[*Typed letter, signed, with autograph addition*]

Monday June 25 [1957, New York]

Dearest Chris—

I can't tell you how much I miss you, how often I think about you, and how even much, much more I love you after having been away from you *so long*. So many times I've thought and thought about you, especially how tiny you are and how much tinier you must be all alone in that big house, & I've wanted to come right home as fast as I could because nothing means anything without you—you're all I care about and I don't care where I am or who I'm with as long as you are there. It seems so silly sometimes that I should be here in N.Y. without you, but then I feel it's a kind of sentence & endurance test that I must go through with and complete. Although it may not sound like it, this trip has been an enormous success. I think I've learned much more about myself, & become more self-confident and secure—I know what I like and whom I like and there is so much that is exciting that I can look forward to knowing, and yet it all doesn't matter because I'm really happy just thinking about you and looking forward to being home again.

There is so much to tell about what's happened to me and whom I've seen that I will save it all till I see you—I've written it all down in my

16. Isherwood added this note across the top of the June 16 letter, which he had previously posted to Bachardy at the Gladstone Hotel in New York. On arriving in New York, Bachardy decided to stay at the East 19th Street townhouse of poet and ballet impresario Lincoln Kirstein (1907–1996) instead of at the Gladstone.
17. Glade De Land Bachardy (1906–1990).

big book[1] so I won't forget any of it. I did see *Hotel Paradiso* and loved it and laughed so hard—I went backstage to see Angela afterwards and she was so sweet and looked wonderful.[2] I've just gotten back from a weekend with John Goodwin at Fire Island—he wants you to write him and he will then write back all addresses, including one for peyotl buds in Texas which are even *nicer* than mescaline, which he doesn't have any of at present. Everyone sends much love. Truman is in Bridgehampton[3] and, although very cordial, very unable to see me. Tennessee and Frank[4] have been angels, and Lincoln and Jen, too.[5] I can't tell you how relieved I felt when I found out Marguerite was in Monroe, although I shall never forgive her, quite. It has all been so exciting—

Your friend is being brutally HAD at this moment by an ENORMOUS pussy-cat!

that was Lincoln[6]—he is back from the country & we are all having dinner downstairs tonight, in a few minutes in fact, so I must tell horsey once more how much I love him and long to be home with him.

His most adoring Kitty

P.S. Your letter came and I think we should wait until I'm home to put up my work table. I hope you didn't neglect to tell Jack Larson you had a terrible, fierce, very possessive tiger cat who was due back *any* minute, with great sharp talons and an enormous appetite for intense, puzzled, boyish, searching actors.

[*Autograph letter*]

• • •

1. Bachardy's diary. He began to keep one in 1953, at Isherwood's suggestion, but became a steady recorder only in the mid-1960s. He made one of his longest entries so far on this first solo trip to New York.
2. Angela Lansbury's Broadway debut, also starring Bert Lahr, in Peter Glenville's adaptation of Georges Feydeau and Maurice Desvallières' 1894 farce *L'Hôtel du libre échange*.
3. Truman Capote (1924–1984), American novelist, had a house there.
4. Tennessee Williams (1911–1983), American playwright, and Frank Merlo (1921–1963), his Italian-American companion.
5. Jenson Yow, artist and curator, a friend of Lincoln Kirstein, had a room in his house.
6. Italics passage and drawing in Kirstein's hand.

Dearest Chris—

I don't know what you'll make of all this, or if you will have heard by the time you get this. It's written in terrific haste as you will understand because I've hardly had a moment. I just wanted to get it all down in any way I could—reading back through it I can hardly believe that it's all true, but it is.

I'm flying to N.Y. Saturday morning at 8:30 and arriving 4:15. No news from Lincoln yet. I'll call him as soon as I arrive.

I miss my angel horse terribly and think of him all the time and look forward every minute to seeing him again and telling him all the tales of my travels. Take good care of my horse. His Kitty loves him so much.

June 17[2]

We spent the day—Marguerite, Henry Guerriero,[3] Tom Wright[4] and I—at Tom's cabin in the country on the edge of a swamp. We had lunch and played canasta till after five. When Marguerite and I got back to the house it was almost six. We had agreed to meet Henry at eight for dinner and since we were both tired we separated and went to our rooms to nap before dressing. I paused at the garage which is directly under my room and stared into the window at the three miniature dogs who were locked inside and squealing to get out—fat Mayno, a miniature white poodle named Camille and a small pug. I then unlocked my door and once inside I closed it behind me and found myself completely in the dark.

1. Bachardy was staying with Marguerite Lamkin and her family; he arrived June 16 from Los Angeles.
2. Bachardy enclosed this separate, dated narrative in his note.
3. American painter and sculptor (b. 1929), from Monroe, settled in Los Angeles.
4. American writer (b. *circa* 1927), also from Louisiana and settled for long periods in Los Angeles.

I didn't know where the light switch was so I started upstairs, feeling my way. Just before I reached the top I thought I could hear Marguerite calling from far away. It was Marguerite. She was nearer. She was in my room. I could hear her moaning like a wounded dog. I was still in the dark, fumbling for the door knob at the top of the stairs, unable to find it and on the verge of panic. I called to Marguerite and finally she opened the door from the inside and I stumbled in.

"Don, something *terrible* has happened." She was wide-eyed and trembling, on the verge of hysteria. "My father's shot himself." Her hands darted about, clutched at me, squeezed each other, pulled at her hair. "What'll we do?" she cried. "There's blood *all over*!"

Before she dashed frantically back to the other part of the house where her father's room was I found out from her that her father had shot himself in the temple but was still alive. He was with her mother and the doctor had been sent for. "You mustn't come," she said. "It's too awful."

She was gone. I could hear nothing. Suddenly she was back, more frantic than ever. "We must pray," she cried, "That's the only thing that can save him." She grabbed my hand and kneeled by my bed, pulling me down beside her. She clasped her hands to her mouth and hunched her shoulders. "Pray, Don!" she implored. She was a terrified little girl. I sat beside her on the floor dumbfounded and helpless, while she prayed.

She was gone again. I looked out of my window onto the front lawn, the doctor arrived, then Mr. Lamkin's sister Marguerite, then Susie and Cookie in a taxi.[5] I heard a deep, horrible wail, then Susie exclaiming, "Lawdy! Lawdy!" The ambulance arrived and two men, one middle-aged, the other young, both dressed in street clothes, brought a stretcher across the lawn and in through the front door. After a few minutes and much shuffling they reappeared on the lawn carrying the stretcher on which Mr. Lamkin was lying, his face up and his eyes open, a white bandage around his head with strips of white tape down one side of his face. A blanket covered everything else but his bare shoulders. In a moment they were gone and Marguerite was with me again. "Did you see?" she asked. "No," I lied. She had changed out of her matador pants and blouse and was hooking up a short dark blue dress. I got a jacket and we went downstairs. Mrs. Lamkin stood very straight at the foot of

5. The Lamkins' longtime housekeeper and her helper; they had previously left for the day.

the stairs, her face taut and grim, her mouth set in forced composure. "Calm yourself, Marguerite." Her voice was low but firm and level. I searched her eyes for tears. There were none. Her eyes did not meet mine but concentrated on Marguerite. "I'll follow you in my car and meet you at the hospital. Drive carefully, Marguerite."

In the car Marguerite calmed down considerably and began going over the events of the past half hour. "Isn't this the most awful thing that could possibly happen? I can't believe it, Don. I'm in a daze. That this should happen during your visit. You're always with me when something awful happens to me." She giggled. Serious again. "Daddy'll never live through this. You should have seen the room—blood everywhere! Susie's cleaning it up now. She'll never get it out of the carpet. Susie was hysterical when we told her what had happened. We had to shake her to keep her from screaming. I don't know how Mother can be so calm. It must have happened just a few minutes before we got home. When I came in the door I heard Mother calling, 'Marguerite! Marguerite! Come quick!' She said she'd come home just a few minutes before I did and found blood all over the bed. She thought Daddy had had a hemorrhage. He was in the bathroom leaning over the sink. 'You're hemorrhaging,' she told him. He said 'I shot myself, and it wasn't an accident.' Imagine, Don, how despondent he must have been. He's been despondent for a long time. His health is bad. He almost died last year. It's his heart. He's often told me he didn't want to live. If only I'd been home maybe it wouldn't have happened. He got the gun out of *my* closet. It's been there for a long time, I've seen it! If only I hadn't gone out today."

Mrs. Lamkin arrived at the hospital a moment before us though she had left the house after we had. The three of us went inside and were sent to a room on the third floor which was empty when we arrived. We each of us took up posts in three corners of the room and stood silently like three grim sentries, each staring at the empty bed in the middle of the room. After a few minutes the door opened and the same two men in civilian clothes entered carrying the same stretcher with Mr. Lamkin on it, looking exactly the same as he had on being taken from the house: eyes open staring motionlessly up, his head in the same bandage which was now half saturated with blood on one side. I could see now that he was wearing an undershirt, the whole front of which was stained with blood. The stretcher was set down on the floor at our feet and a third man came in and together the three men lifted the pale over-sized body of Mr. Lamkin onto the bed and covered him, shoes and all, with a sheet up to his neck. The three men left the room. Mrs. Lamkin went to the bed and took Mr. Lamkin's hand and held it tightly. Again the three of us stood silently, staring down at the bed occupied now by the motionless Mr. Lamkin.

A year or more before, the doctor who came finally was telling us, Mr. Lamkin suffered from blood clots in his arteries and so since then he'd been given medication to thin his blood. Now his blood no longer clotted and it was too dangerous to operate (to take the bullet out) before more medication with the opposite results could be given and have time to take effect—4 hours at least. During these 4 hours X-rays would be taken, tetanus and other shots given, blood transfusions made.

We had nothing to do but wait. Mrs. Lamkin asked only for a Coke. A few relatives, called in to help by Mrs. Lamkin during some split-second lull in the proceedings, had arrived. One of them, Marguerite's 75-yr.-old Uncle Tom, after he'd established who I was and where I'd come from, began telling me how Mr. Lamkin always has the little dogs up in his room when he gets home from the office and that's how the "accident" must have happened. He was cleaning his gun and one of the little dogs jumped up and jarred his hand and the gun went off.

Marguerite was now firing nervous questions at her mother. "Did you call Hillyer Speed yet?[6] Does Veda know?" (Veda is Mrs. Lamkin's sister.) Mrs. Lamkin, still cool and in control, said she'd decided *not* to call Veda tonight because she was at the country club playing cards with a lot of women who would all come running down to the hospital with Veda and spread the news all over town in no time. Mrs. Lamkin asked Marguerite and me to go back to the house and drive Susie and Cookie back home.

On the way back to the house Marguerite told me they'd agreed to say that her father was taking his gun out of the top drawer of a bureau and somehow or other it had gone off. "Ridiculous," she said, but somehow in a few days everyone would believe it, "Even me," she said. "Why even Mother, when I found her in the bathroom with Daddy leaning over the sink bleeding, already she was saying to Daddy 'You know it was an accident. What else could it be?' And Daddy had just told her it was no accident. I just can't get over how calm Mother is. You know, she put on lipstick before she went to the hospital. Imagine!"

6. Marguerite's brother, Hillyer Speed Lamkin (b. 1928), American novelist and playwright.

Marguerite, with a quick glance in the rearview mirror, raked her hand through her hair. "I must look awful." She dashed upstairs as soon as we got back to the house to check on Susie's progress in cleaning up the blood. From downstairs I heard her say: "Susie, I'll put the pistol away before there's another accident. Susie! It's *covered* with blood!" She indulged herself with a gasp of horror.

While I was waiting at the foot of the stairs I heard Cookie, Susie's enormous, 15-year-old colored helper (one-month pregnant illegitimately), humming in the kitchen. She came into the dining room carrying a sponge and pail, met me at the stairs and, stopping her humming suddenly, walked slowly back up to Mr. Lamkin's room.

Marguerite, back downstairs, was at a loss for something to do. "Let's have a drink," she said, "but don't tell anybody we've been drinking. Aunt Marguerite can't stand drinking. I can hear her now. 'We were all at the hospital with poor Bano (Mr. Lamkin) and there they were—drinking!' She'd never forget it either."

While we were sipping our Bloody Marys in the sun parlor and staring through the open windows at the heavy darkness outside, Marguerite was mulling over the disaster again. "I'm still so dazed I don't know what's happening to me. He was conscious, Don. He even knew the doctor when he came into the room. They talked together. I heard the doctor ask him what caliber the bullet was and Daddy said '34.' There was blood all over the bed. Poor Mother. I should go back to the hospital." Susie limped into the room, exhausted by her work. She began pulling the curtains across the windows. "Sit down, Susie," Marguerite said. "Uh-uh," Susie grunted, "I don't want to sit down." "You have to rest, Susie, you're tired." "I'm going into the kitchen to sit down and read the paper," she said as she left the room. "You know she found a piece of his skull on the floor," Marguerite whispered when Susie was gone, "Isn't that awful!"

We drove Susie and Cookie home and then went on to the hospital. We learned that when they took Mr. Lamkin down to have his X-rays they took the pillow out from under his head and he started to bleed internally. He was in a coma now. Mrs. Lamkin had called Speed in New York and told him to come but didn't tell him what had happened to his father, only that he was in hospital. Marguerite decided to stay with Mrs. Lamkin who already had a cot in the room and I was to be driven back to the house by Uncle Tom. Stepping into the elevator we met Veda and four lady companions from the country club coming out. Veda was wide-eyed and tragic and the four ladies bobbed their heads and looked intent. "What's happened to Bano?" Veda said, "Hillyer Speed called me from New York. Where *is* Bano?" She and the four ladies rushed past us down the hall before we could speak.

Uncle Tom drove me back and I spent the night alone in the house.

June 19

Speed is here now. He arrived late yesterday afternoon but I've hardly seen him or Marguerite as they've been sitting up in the hospital room with Mrs. Lamkin, who refuses to leave. Mr. Lamkin is in a semicoma. His very critical condition has not changed since Tuesday.

The newspaper reports, though bitchy, give no explanation of the shooting. Only Mrs. Lamkin, Marguerite, Susie and I know the truth, & so it is very top secret. Tom and Mrs. Wright are like beasts driven wild by curiosity.

[*Autograph letter, pencil*]

Saturday June 21st   The Stables, Sycapaw Road[1]

Dearest Don,

Your letter, with the truly horrendous diary excerpt, just arrived. I enjoyed it so much that I quite forgot to feel sorry for anybody. Honestly, this is literature! The *things* you put in! Like Marguerite saying, "She'll never get it out of the carpet!" and the phoney explanation about the little dog jumping up, and Marguerite saying, "I must look awful."

Paul Millard[2] called me and gave me the news yesterday. As a matter of fact, he unintentionally scared the shit out of me by the way he did it, beginning, "Marguerite asked me to call you and tell you myself. Mr. Lamkin shot himself. And Don was there—" And for a moment, I felt sick to my stomach, absolutely sure Paul was going on to tell me that this poor crazy man had gone berserk and shot *you*, too! So that, when I realized that he was the only casualty, I felt nothing but utter relief! I didn't tell him this!

1. Isherwood posted this from Sycamore Road to Kirstein's house in New York where Bachardy was again staying.
2. American actor turned real-estate investor.

Until I know definitely what the "line" is, I'll play safe by saying nothing whatsoever about this to anyone here. Jo and Ben (who send their love) keep asking are you having a good time. I think I faintly roused their suspicions by being a little unconvincing, but [I] hope it will be true after you get to New York. My love to everyone there. I do hope this hasn't spoiled your trip. At least, it won't have been uneventful!

Nothing so earthshaking has happened here—only a few small surprises and gossip items so far, which will be better kept and served on ice when you return. I wish you would definitely let me know one thing: suppose Jo and Ben propose one of those coming-home suppers, *not* including meeting you at the airport, which I shall do alone—do you want to accept? You will understand why I ask this: maybe you would rather first decide how much you mean to tell them!

Old Dobbin doesn't sleep so well, missing that tiny cat. He longs so to hear the patter of paws on the floor again and hopes by that time it will be cleaner for kitty to walk on—Dorothy is bringing some new soap Monday.

All my love and constant thoughts and longings to be together again—

Chris

I'll write Marguerite a brief line of sympathy in a day or two, if Mr. L. dies. Paul seemed to think it was certain he would.

[*Typed letter, signed*]

June 26 [1958, New York]

Dearest Angel—

I miss you so much. I think of you all the time and long so to be back in my basket, close to Dobbin. It seems like ages since I left my horse—so much has happened, and yet so little, too. I hate not being busy. I want to work my head off when I get home, even if it never leads to anything or makes me world-famous. I just want to work. That and being with Dobbin are all that matter to Kitty, and being with Dobbin matters more than anything.

New York is nice, much cooler than last year. I wish I knew though exactly why I came. I'm enjoying myself and yet I'd so much rather be home with you. It's all kind of "as if," my being here. I keep saying to myself it's all so exciting, a lone cat in the big city, no holds barred, sky's the limit. And yet if I stopped pushing I don't think I'd get up in the morning at all. It's such an effort just to call people. There seems little point or pleasure in seeing most people, and yet I like it when it happens and enjoy being with them. Lincoln has been just wonderful, nicer than ever before, and Jen so sweet, too. I can't tell you how relieved in a way I was to find out Julie and Manning were out of town (in Ireland or England or somewhere making this ghastly Irish film!)¹ but I was sorry to miss John Goodwin who stays out on Fire Island most of the time now. He was a little put out that I hadn't written to say I was coming. I've seen Tennessee and Frank and am having dinner with them again tonight. They are well and are leaving for Portugal this weekend. News about the plays I've seen and other people I will keep.

Lincoln has gotten me by some devious means (though I still have to pay) a seat on a fast nonstop tourist plane which arrives in L.A. on Monday morning at, forgive me, 6:30 a.m. or thereabouts. I shall telegraph you the flight no., and exact time when I know for sure, but please, *don't* break your neck to get out to the airport on time. I could always have breakfast at the Flight Deck there and meet you back at the ticket counter around 8, though it would be nice to have breakfast with you.

I'm going to the country tomorrow afternoon to stay the weekend with Lincoln and see, God give me courage, *Hamlet* and *Midsummer Night's Dream*. Hardly my two "favorite" Shakespeares.² It is suddenly so dark I think it's going to rain so I must rush out and mail this before I get soaked. Just know that Kitty is counting the minutes till he's reunited with his most sacred treasure-horse. All my love, Don.

[*Autograph letter*]

. . .

1. Julie Harris (b. 1925), American actress, and her second husband Manning Gurian, a stage manager and producer. She was starring in *Sally's Irish Rogue*, released in the U.S. as *The Poacher's Daughter* (1958).
2. At the American Shakespeare Festival Theater in Stratford, Connecticut. Kirstein's country house was in nearby Westport, and he had founded the festival with two others in 1955.

Sunday [October 2, 1960]   [Santa Monica]

It was wonderful hearing Kitty's voice on the phone this morning.[1]
And yet old slow-reacting Dobbin couldn't manage to tell him everything
he was feeling—how proud he is of Kitty and how he loves him and how
grateful to him he is, every day. How wonderful he has made Dobbin's
life, having Kitty to love and think about and hope for and be so proud
of. It's almost too wonderful that Kitty should have all this talent, and
Dobbin is so glad of that, but more for Kitty's sake than for Dobbin's,
because Dobbin would have loved him anyway. And yet Dobbin is so
glad. . . . And he will try. Dobbin misses Kitty so much—but not that he
wants to cut Kitty's trip short by a single second, as long as Kitty has any
reason to stay on.

In great haste, because Dobbin has to canter out and listen to that
wicked old Elsa mooing.[2]

Love always,

D.

[*Typed letter, initialled*]

•   •   •

1. Bachardy had flown to New York on September 30, 1960 to supervise the framing and
exhibition of his drawings of the cast of Tony Richardson's New York stage production of
A Taste of Honey. He was staying with Julie Harris and Manning Gurian.
2. Elsa Lanchester (1902–1986), British actress, was appearing that night in *Elsa Lanchester—
Herself* at Royce Hall, UCLA.

[October 14, 1960 Santa Monica[1]]

Dearest Lovehorse—

I had the inspiration to suggest to Cheryl Crawford when she called that I could use the understudies as models so all is well and I am leaving as planned at 8:30.[2]

I will call you as soon as I know what is what and let you know my fate. Please think of Kitty and wish for his success. Kitty loves his dear horse so much, more than anything in the world, and he will miss him terribly. All Kitty's love,

[*Autograph letter, pencil*]

1. On October 14, 1960, Bachardy joined Tennessee Williams in Wilmington, Delaware, to design posters for Williams's *Period of Adjustment* opening there. The trip was uncertain until the last moment because he had returned home only on October 6 from working on *A Taste of Honey* in New York, and he then fell ill with tonsillitis. This hasty farewell note was left at home–145 Adelaide Drive, Santa Monica, where he and Isherwood had settled in September 1959. Isherwood was away at the University of California at Santa Barbara (UCSB) from October 13 to October 15, delivering one of his series of lectures, "A Writer and His World," and also teaching. His UCSB appointment as a visiting professor at large and a visiting professor of English lasted from July 1 to December 31, 1960.
2. Cheryl Crawford (1902–1986), American stage producer, was putting on four Williams plays, of which *Period of Adjustment* was the last. She and Williams evidently feared that Bachardy would arrive too late for the lead actors, tired by rehearsals and performances, to pose for his posters, which had to be printed before the play opened.

[October 26, 1960, Philadelphia[1]]

Dearest Treasure Dub—

How very very much he is missed by his Kitty. He is so loved and thought about by Kitty, every day, all the time. Kitty longs so to lay his head against that long mane and feel that knobbly foreleg around him again. Kitty is desperate for his horse and his basket and every day away from them is more difficult for him, but Kitty must not give up. He must be tougher than anyone ever dreamed. He really is a lot tougher than even Kitty thought, and this whole thing is a question of stamina. Everything is going *marvellously* well, but it just takes so *long!* One thing leads to another. James Daly has just commissioned him to draw his whole family (he is the star of Tennessee's play and is part of a family of six!)[2]

I'm leaving Philadelphia tonight after the show (I'm here for the cast drawings of *Period of Adjustment*) and have been staying at a much dumpier hotel than the one above[3], called the Sylvania. Last night there was a drunken party on the other side of my door that began at six a.m. Julie and Manning are here (Philadelphia) too, for the first opening of *Little Moon* this Friday night. The address is the Forrest Theater, Walnut Street, Philadelphia, if you want to send a telegram. They have both been angels, so terribly nice to horsey's Kitty. Both my poster designs have been accepted and production has started on the one for *Period* and production is pending on the *Little Moon* poster until the Philadelphia notices Saturday morning. I think it has a good chance to succeed—I saw a run through the other day—the play is the most awful claptrap; bogus sentimentality about imaginary religion, but Julie is better than I've ever seen her. I cried through practically the whole play. I'm coming to Phil. again for the opening. I love my darling so much, and miss him so. All his Kitty's love, K.

---

1. Bachardy followed *Period of Adjustment* from Wilmington to Philadelphia, where he was also designing posters for Julie Harris's new play, *Little Moon of Alban* by James Costigan.
2. American stage and T.V. actor James Daly (1918–1978) had three daughters and a son with his wife, actress Hope Newell (1921–2009), before they divorced in 1965. Two of the children also went into acting, Tyne Daly (b. 1946) and Tim Daly (b. 1956).
3. That is, than the hotel named on the stationery he was using.

Kitty will try to get back to the Stable early next week—a telegram will be sent. K.

[*Autograph letter, pencil, on letterhead of St. James Hotel, Walnut at Thirteenth Street, Philadelphia*]

NEW YORK, N.Y.
NOVEMBER 2, 1960

CHRISTOPHER ISHERWOOD

145 ADELAIDE DR. SANTA MONICA CALIF.

ARRIVING FRIDAY AFTERNOON WILL TAKE BUS PLEASE PREPARE BASKET LOVE=K

[*Western Union Telegram*]

· · ·

[January 23, 1961, Santa Monica[1]]

Dobbin dear:

Please remember to call Doris (tell her I loved her etc. & explain about not coming backstage)[2] and Peter Shaw (Wm. Morris—CR 47451 or home GL 62553)[3] and please remember Kitty, and remember that Kitty loves his horse, more than anything in the world. K.

[Autograph note]

Monday night [January 23, 1961, New York[1]]

My darling Horse—

He can't know how much his Kitty misses him. He has thought of him all day and felt so lonely and unhappy. So terribly alone. He never guessed what it would be like to really leave his dobbin and not know that he would see him again in a week or two weeks. Kitty feels really lost without his only dear and the whole idea of going to England now seems pointless and silly, irresponsible and empty. To trade his Dobbin

1. On January 23, 1961, Bachardy flew to New York on his way to London, where he planned to study painting at the Slade School of Fine Art. He left this note behind at Adelaide Drive.
2. Doris Dowling (1923–2004), American actress; Isherwood and Bachardy saw her in Pirandello's *Six Characters in Search of an Author* at UCLA the night of Bachardy's departure, then rushed away so Bachardy could pack and finish other chores before catching his late-night flight.
3. Peter Shaw (1918–2003), British actor and producer; he was a studio executive at MGM and also an agent and, later, an executive at the William Morris Agency. His wife was Angela Lansbury. Lansbury was in the cast of the New York production of *A Taste of Honey*, so Bachardy had recently drawn her with the four other cast members, and he had asked Isherwood to phone Shaw about some detail of the exhibition in the theater lobby.

1. Bachardy was staying again with Julie Harris.

even for an absolute guarantee of success, let alone a half-baked attempt at it, seems wildly ridiculous and Kitty feels sorry and foolish and so alone. He can't possibly accept now the idea of six months without his darling, or anything near that. Kitty must believe that his horse will be with him again very soon, no matter what. Kitty can't think of a life without his horse very near.

Julie and Manning are very well and good to Kitty—really very sweet. Peter[2] is impossible—I think even Julie is beginning to think so. She is doing "He Who Gets Slapped" for television now with Richard Basehart and does "The Heiress" soon after with Farley Granger for T.V. also.

Kitty went to see *Bye Bye Birdie* tonight—really only because as he was walking by the theater the doorman offered him a ticket for free. Someone hadn't shown up and the show had only been on fifteen minutes. The only real thing to recommend the whole contraption is a really young set of chorus boys, two or three quite cute and saucy ones. But oh! N.Y. musicals—the idea of going to one of them to be cheered up, of all things, is pathetic. So boring and heavy and conventional. And so hideously decorated, except for the boys.

It's only about 12° here but it doesn't seem cold—only very dry and exhilarating. Dobbin could have a good trot and enjoy snorting his hot breath in great fumes. Kitty misses his cart so[,] and so hates dragging his tail through the slush.

More depression almost than Kitty could bear was produced by reading Wyatt's play on the plane.[3] Perhaps the most unbelievably bad and nauseating and really insane play he's ever read. Seriously, Wyatt *must* be insane, or else *so* sloppy and trashy, and gabby! I can't say one kind word for the whole *endless* mess. The only thing to do is pretend I didn't have a chance to read it.

I am worried about the Stravinskys being offended that I didn't call to say goodbye.[4] It was bad of me but please explain and say I left so suddenly that I didn't have a chance to talk to *anyone*. I will write them a nice note, but please make it all right with them anyway.

---

2. Peter Gurian, their young son.
3. Wyatt Cooper (1927–1978), American actor, screenwriter, editor, and later, fourth husband of Gloria Vanderbilt. His play was called *how do you like your blue-eyed boy / MISTER DEATH*.
4. Russian composer Igor Stravinsky (1882–1971) and his second wife, Vera (1888–1982), a Russian painter, close friends of Isherwood since 1949. They lived in West Hollywood.

Dearest Dub, please seriously plan to come and be with Kitty as soon as possible. Nothing matters as much to Kitty as being with his angel—even if Kitty has to come back to Calif. to do it. Please think of Kitty and take scrupulous care of himself.

All Kitty's love K.

Tuesday morning [January 24]

Loveliest—

I talked to the McKinnons' broker this morning and he doesn't think he can put the deal through by Thurs. evening so I may have to stay in N.Y. a few days longer. I will know for sure tomorrow because I am having lunch with him.[5] I am having dinner tonight with Wystan and Chester—Wystan was very affectionate on the phone and had heard your lectures were a great success.[6] Lunch with Marcia[7] today. It was snowing again this morning when I woke up. Oh if only my horse were with me—everything would be all right. Kitty thinks of him all the time and needs him so and loves him so very much. K.

[*Autograph letter on printed letterhead "Julie Harris"*]

January 26 [1961]   [Santa Monica]

My darling Kitty,

I'm writing this only a few hours after talking to you in New York, because I want there to be a word from Dobbin waiting for K. when he arrives in London.[1] Talking on the phone really is frustrating in a way,

---

5. Bachardy's London studies were paid for by Russell and Edna McKinnon, wealthy Californians. She was ten or fifteen years older than her husband, and the money may have been hers; he was personally attracted to Bachardy. The broker was selling assets to advance cash.
6. W.H. Auden (1907–1973), English poet, one of Isherwood's closest friends, with whom he had written four plays and a travel book, and Auden's companion Chester Kallman (1921–1975), American poet, with whom Auden collaborated on opera libretti. The lectures were the series of eight, "A Writer and His World," that Isherwood had given during the previous autumn at UCSB.
7. Marcia King; she taught fashion illustration at Chouinard, where Bachardy became friendly with her. She was about five or ten years older than he, and they often drew together.

1. Sent c/o English poet Stephen Spender (1909–1995) and his wife, concert pianist Natasha Litvin Spender (1919–2010), 15 Loudoun Road, St. John's Wood, London, where Bachardy planned to stay.

and yet it's at least the live mew and neigh; and I think the Animals should phone each other from time to time while Kitty is in England, just to reassure them. Of course, I know just how terrible Kitty must be feeling, because Dobbin feels awful too. But I do believe it will get a lot easier for Kitty when he has settled down to work and the London life. But he must never forget Dobbin and Dobbin's love; he must know that they're always there and waiting for him when needed. And by all means let's see if some kind of job can't be organized for D. in England in a little while.

At the same time, sweetheart, let's not forget that your instinct told you to be on your own for a while. I know that now seems, as you say, pointless and empty; but no instinct is quite pointless. It has to be treated with respect. And it is just because Dobbin loves Kitty *for keeps* and wants to stay with him for the rest of his life, that he is determined not to have Kitty depending on him in the wrong way, because that always leads to resentment deep down later. Dobbin always has before him the horror of his mother and Richard; and however utterly different that case may have been[,] it still wouldn't have arisen if my mother could have set R. free when he was still young. Not that anyone could compare Kitty with poor R. But you have to understand that situation to understand Dobbin's qualms.

As a matter of fact, I really am most optimistic about the possible effects of this Slade School venture, on your work and on you and, therefore, on me. But let's see and play it by ear; and let's be quite relaxed about the possibility that you *may* decide to leave at any moment. No undue heroics. Kitty may be brave but not *too* brave.

Sentimental Dobbin likes to wear Kitty's old pair of sneakers. He feels he's near K. then. He has moved into the back room, and the basket is being preserved until Kitty's return and all the blankets and even the pad cleaned!

Tonight, the Stravinskys. Tomorrow, probably Gavin[2] and Tom [Wright]—at Tom's invitation. Saturday—ugh—possibly the Andrews dinner party for Alan (*Wisdom of Insecurity*) Watts.[3] Saturday lunch, at

2. Gavin Lambert (1924–2005), British novelist, screenwriter, and biographer.

3. Oliver Andrews (d. 1978), Californian sculptor, and American actress Betty Harford (b. 1927), then his wife, were close friends with British mystic, Beat guru, and author Alan Watts (1915–1973), known as a Zen Buddhist. Bachardy read *The Wisdom of Insecurity* (1951) in the spring of 1960 and told Isherwood he would never be quite the same again afterwards.

the Swamitage, for Amiya's birthday.⁴ And so forth. But at least Dobbin isn't wasting the Animals' money on riotous living.

I keep right on with the novel⁵ and still hope to finish it in March or maybe earlier—it's so hard to tell.

Frank Wiley, with a friend, just stopped by to deliver the manuscript of his Sta. Barbara campus queer novel.⁶ I haven't been able to face Wyatt's death-house dialogue yet. But I must, very soon.

Dobbin will work hard and drive carefully and think of Kitty all the time, and keep radioing his love across the waves.

All his love, as always—D.

Kitty's letter on notepaper stamped "Julie Harris" might produce a fascinating scandal in a divorce court. "Miss Harris challenged to name Dark Horse—signed herself 'Kitty'!"

[*Typed letter, initialled*]

Sunday January 29 [1961]   [Santa Monica]

My dearest sweet love,

[I]t's now five minutes to five, our time, and I feel like someone outside the gas chamber, because I know you are taking off at eight New York time and won't be getting my message. This morning I got such a strong urge to call you and wish you bon voyage and just hear your voice again; but I thought I would catch you easily at one-thirty, our time, and I called Julie's and you'd gone to the airport and then I went through the most torturing thing of trying to page you, and they were idiots beyond all description and finally got me a Mr. Mackardie, on another flight altogether! And then it got to be late and I was almost glad, because I didn't want to fuss you at the last moment with the phone, and make you miss a good seat.

4. Amiya (1902–1986), née Ella Sully in England, had been housekeeper to Swami Prabhavananda and his Hollywood hostess Carrie Mead Wyckoff (Sister Lalita) in the early 1930s, and then became a Vedanta nun. In 1952, she returned to England to marry George Montagu, 9th Earl of Sandwich (1874–1962), whom she met when he visited the Hollywood Vedanta Society.
5. *Down There on a Visit* (1962).
6. Frank Wiley (not his real name) had been in Isherwood's seminar at UCSB; he later served in the navy.

I've already written twice to England, so you'll have something when you arrive. The second letter was just enclosures: some kind of vouchers referring to the McKinnon money, which you may or may not need, and a letter from Julie's producer about the drawing you did of Julie, which you may or may not want to give her. You should get them before you get this.[1]

A few more questions:

Quite by accident I noticed a book on your shelf, *From Ibsen's Workshop*, taken out of the Los Angeles Public Library Dec. 6. Should I return this?

Do you want the copies of *Film Facts* sent on to you?[2]

Do you think I ought to call McKinnon? No, I guess not. I mean, it is somehow insulting if I thank him in any way, however indirectly. If he is doing me any kind of a favor it's unintentional!

Day before yesterday, I had supper with Tom Wright and Gavin was there and he said he'd been offered a movie job in England, for late March or April, doing a script of Graham Greene's *England Made Me*. The producer is John Sutro. Gavin had turned it down. So I said, I'll try for it, and I called Ivan Moffat,[3] who offered to write Sutro at once and ask him if he is interested in having me. It's a very *long* shot—but I just want you to know that I have already started trying to get over there and be with Kitty. Don't say anything about it to anyone, of course.

Sarada,[4] whom I talked to at Amiya's birthday party at Vedanta Place, said how much she liked you. The party was awful. Amiya so *loud*, and ZaSu Pitts was there, and the women were fawning on her as a big star,[5] which embarrassed her to death—she seemed nice—and embarrassed Swami too. But he did everything to make the party go.

Today I have been working all day on my novel; and now I'll work and work and work.

1. All sent c/o the Spenders. The vouchers, from the brokers Fahnestock & Co., 65 Broadway, New York, were for the sale on January 25 of 100 shares of Oklahoma Natural Gas, generating $3,308.86 net of taxes and commission, and 24 further shares generating $786.69 net, sums which Bachardy could collect from any of their offices. The January 25 letter from Julie Harris's producer, Mildred Freed Alberg, lamented the mixed reviews and early closing of *Little Moon of Alban* on Broadway and asked Bachardy to help locate "your beautiful sketch of Julie" so that it could be framed.
2. Bachardy had a subscription.
3. Ivan Moffat, British-American screenwriter (1918–2002), then living in Los Angeles. He was the son of Isherwood's close friend Iris Tree.
4. American nun of the Ramakrishna Order (d. 2009).
5. ZaSu Pitts (1894–1963), a major silent-movie star, was later known as a comedienne in talkies, and also on Broadway and on T.V.

I'll write to Kitty nearly every day for a while until he settles down, because I know it helps to get letters; but Kitty isn't to answer if he's too busy. Dobbin will understand.

Sweetheart, in all the years we've been together, I've never felt closer to you than I do now. Please know that I'm constantly thinking of you and be certain of my love, always and always. D.

[*Autograph letter*]

5:30 Monday [January 31, 1961, London]

My darling—His letter was waiting for Kitty when he arrived this morning and Kitty was so glad—his dear, sweet Horse had been thinking of him. A wonderful letter that helped Kitty so much—Kitty was very frightened and wide-eyed and ruffled and then there was Dobbin's love and assurance to calm him. And Kitty had been thinking so much of his Horse and wanting him and needing and loving him so much. During the flight here he wrote two wild incoherent letters to his round darling which are almost indecipherable now—and very repetitious—over and over again how much he loves his dear and how close he feels to him and how much he wants him. Kitty was bad—he sat up drinking in N.Y. with Marcia until it was so late that when Kitty got to the airport the plane was already sealed and they had to roll up the stairs and open the plane to let bad Kitty on—he knew how cross his old Dobbin would be and he was ashamed. But he so hated going so much farther away from his darling. Stephen and Natasha seemed very distracted and embarrassed this morning—maybe because K. was so befuddled. Stephen fixed some fatty, uncooked bacon for him and fried an egg (in the leftover grease) that was warm on the bottom and cold on the top. The smell of the gas stove brought England back to K. with such terrible clarity. Natasha has been practising all day for a concert tomorrow—with such grim determination it sounds as though she were playing with her jaw. K. went to bed right after breakfast and slept for six hours and now feels somewhat recovered. But oh the sadness of this house—this clammy, jammed, sad little room of Matthew's[1] with a

---

1. Matthew Spender (b. 1945), son of Stephen and Natasha; later, he became a sculptor and author.

bed of such weak lumpiness Dub would have a bad back for a week. And do you remember the bathroom? In the middle of his toilette K. nearly cried with depression and discomfort. But all this is good because it will make K. get out and find himself a place to live right away—which will relieve Stephen and Natasha, too. Tonight I am having dinner with Stephen and, if he can arrange it, the man in charge of establishing me at the Slade—a Mr. Jenkins[2]—at Stephen's club. I want to start to school tomorrow if I can, the next day at the latest. Coldstream[3] is having a nervous breakdown according to Stephen and so definitely out of the picture. Natasha has just come in and brought me some delicious tea and been very nice. I realize she is beside herself with anxiety about this concert. My dearest, I think of you constantly and love you with all my heart. K.

[*Autograph letter*]

Tuesday January 31 [1961]   [Santa Monica]

My dearest love,

[Y]our cable arrived this morning to say you enrolled at the Slade and are flat hunting.[1] I long for your first letter; but, as I said before, *never* drive yourself to write to me, because you'll have ten million things to do, I know. Dobbin will write a lot, especially at first, because he has more time for it. I hope his first letter was awaiting Kitty at Stephen's? Since then, I have sent two more—one of them just with enclosures. I have two more legal receipts of what money you got from McKinnon. Will send them later, if needed. It's probably better you have them, because I just might forget where I put them, later on, when they were needed.

Grey weather, and cold. Dobbin sleeps in the back room, in pajamas, under piles of blankets. He is very well though so sad, and aches all over

2. I.E. Tregarthen Jenkin (1920–2004), secretary and tutor at the Slade, once an aspiring painter and, in 1938–1939, a part-time Slade drawing student.
3. William Coldstream (1908–1987), English painter, Slade Professor of Fine Art and Head of the Slade School.

1. The cable is lost.

from going to the gym. There are wonderful machines to make him less round. And he'll cycle too.

The little picture of Vera's got framed and I picked it up and have hung it on the wall facing the front door, just between the steps up to the dining area and the door of the living-room closet. It looks good and somehow makes the whole living room quite a bit less bare.[2]

Wyatt Cooper came by yesterday and I was quite tactful but begged him to cut out the Jesus conversion in his play and make all kinds of changes. Then I went out to supper with Claire and Rod Steiger. It was really quite a bore, but I didn't care; I ate and drank. Claire is going very soon to England to be in the Sartre play at the Royal Court.[3] I still have no more news about the possible job on the Graham Greene film; but I'm sure Ivan wrote to Sutro, as he promised. If that falls through, I'll keep trying. We'll manage something. The date I have in April, to speak at the Pasadena synagogue, can easily be cancelled;[4] but I'm pretty well committed to the three reading dates in March—12th, 19th, 26th— because they are bringing out a brochure and making a lot of special publicity and it would be awfully bad for business to break them.[5] Not that I wouldn't, instantly, if one mew of despair was uttered by Kitty.

If I work like mad all through February, I *could* finish the revision of "Paul" by the end of it.[6] But it's quite an if. I do think what I've done is a huge improvement.

Gielgud[7] also cabled me today to know if our address is still the same as the one he has—it is—because Alec Guinness[8] is coming over and he wants us to meet. I'll write John, but I expect you will be seeing him very soon yourself. My much love to him and Pat Woodcock[9] and all who should have it.

2. Oil on canvas, by Vera Stravinsky, purchased at a recent show.
3. English actress Claire Bloom (b. 1931) was the second wife, from 1959 to 1969, of American actor Rod Steiger (1925–2002). She was about to appear in Sartre's *Altona* directed by John Berry.
4. April 2, "A Writer's Approach to Life."
5. "The Voices of the Novel," three Sunday-evening readings at UCLA: "The Forefathers: Dickens, Conrad, Brontë, Joyce, and Others," "Our Group and Its Older Brothers: Joyce, Hemingway, and Others," "The Young Novelists: Williams, Capote, Kerouac, Mailer, Bradbury, and Others."
6. The fourth and last section of *Down There on a Visit*.
7. John Gielgud (1904–2000), British actor and director.
8. British actor (1914–2000).
9. Patrick Woodcock (1920–2002), British doctor; his patients included many theater stars like Gielgud.

I still haven't bought a doorbell but I will. Dorothy[10] is supposed to tell me about a gardener when she comes on Friday this week. The front bedroom is closed, all the blankets cleaned, and the pad; it looks very grand and historical, like Chapultepec or somewhere.[11]

We had quite a quake the other day, it seems, but no one felt anything and I carefully examined all the cracks and could find no enlargements.

Another letter from Jo and Ben on some remote island, weeping over the wonderfulness of fishing and swimming.[12]

Half past six here. And over there my dear sweet beloved sadly missed angel-cat will be in the deepest of his sleep amidst his fur! How Dobbin's heart signals to him, long-love-waves which just barely stir his whiskers! Take care of yourself, darling Kitty. D.

[*Typed letter, initialled*]

Casa de los Animales[1] Friday Feb. 3rd [1961]

My darling love,

[J]ust got the first letter from Kitty in England—heartrending—and it made me remember the squalor so vividly. I do hope that by now Kitty has found some relatively clean basket? I know he will let me know as soon as he does, but meanwhile I must send this to Stephen's. Oh, I can't bear to dwell on all that pain—rushing to the airport—which explains why I couldn't get through to you on the phone before the plane started—too dreadful. But Dobbin would treasure the letters Kitty wrote him, however drunkenly, if Kitty will let him see them? Please!!

A tearing wind today with very bright hot sunshine. Dorothy was here, complaining of arthritis, very bad in her face. She asked to be remembered. Dobbin aches all over from going to the gym, plus the

---

10. Dorothy Miller (d. 1979), cook and cleaner to Isherwood and Bachardy.
11. The castle in Mexico City used by Emperor Maximilian I as his official residence and abandoned after his 1867 execution. Isherwood and Bachardy saw it in December 1954 with Jo and Ben Masselink.
12. In the Caribbean, where they went annually after visiting Ben's father, who lived in Florida.

1. The Animals' House, i.e., 145 Adelaide Drive, Santa Monica.

wind whistling through his old joints—but he likes the gym because it's small and cheerful and clean and not full of muscle men. Jeffrey Hunter goes there, and is very friendly.[2] In fact everyone is, but not in a bad way Kitty would disapprove of.

Sweetheart, couldn't you call me long-distance on our anniversary, the fourteenth of this month? I guess you can reverse the charges; but even if not it is worth it. If you were to call me very late that day—eleven or twelve midnight—it would be early in the morning of the same day here. If you wanted to call at ten, Dobbin wouldn't mind; that would be six a.m. And so on. *Do* call and speak to Dobbin and reassure him.

I'm now in correspondence with Wystan and Chester. They plan to be in England anyhow at the end of June, beginning of July. It is a choice between then and the beginning of April in New York for us to confer on the musical of *Goodbye to Berlin*. The deal seems almost definitely on. *I* favor England in June–July, because I hope to be there anyway and because you will be there so we can discuss the whole thing together. Which reminds me—as soon as you know—can you give me some idea when your Slade summer term is over, etc.?

I have heard nothing yet about the possible Graham Greene movie job. But I will keep trying all sorts of things. Mrs. Degener of Curtis Brown seems to think that Lewenstein *might* be induced to pay my fare to England for this conference—and of course if I arrived months earlier that would be no skin off their noses; it'd cost them the same.[3] Then again, I'm becoming curious to know if my mother didn't leave me some money—aside from the share of the furniture, etc. If there *is* money in the bank, even Amiya agrees that I should spend it, because she says Richard would never accept it anyway—I mean, he would never accept my share.[4] So that might be a way of getting over, independently of everybody. I will write to the lawyer about it . . . Meanwhile, if you get any opportunity to poke Tony Richardson[5] into

---

2. Jeffrey Hunter (1926–1969), American actor. The gym was Lyle Fox's, in Pacific Palisades.

3. Auden, Kallman, and Isherwood first worked on a musical of *Goodbye to Berlin* in the spring of 1959 for American producer Frank Taylor; now London impresario Oscar Lewenstein was interested. Cindy Degener was head of the dramatic department at Curtis Brown, Isherwood's and Auden's first literary agency.

4. Kathleen Isherwood died June 15, 1960; Isherwood had passed his share in physical property to his brother Richard.

5. British stage and film director (1928–1991).

coming up with a job, please do so. I *know* I could get some job once I was over there.

Angel, I'm sure all this will gradually work out for us. And I know that things will begin to look quite a bit less dreary for Kitty if he finds the work at the Slade satisfactory and if nice people are nice to him. BUT NOT TO FORGET DOBBIN! ABSOLUTELY FORBIDDEN!!!!!!

I enclose some more legal papers about the McKinnon money. Either they are duplicates or the whole thing is even more complicated than I imagined. However, you had better have them all with you . . . Also, this from *Look* which is rather sweet, though what the white horse is really doing there I can't imagine and don't altogether like the idea of.[6]

Monroe Wheeler[7] is in town. I shall have supper with him tomorrow night; Sunday morning he flies back east. He wrote a nice note to both of us, inviting us to supper. He was thrilled to hear about your going to London.

On Sunday, I guess the delayed luncheon given by Marguerite and Gavin for Bill Inge[8] will take place. Will let you know all about that. Claire and Rod Steiger have invited me *again*, to what is I imagine a larger affair, an informal buffet supper.

Amiya is eager to get your new address before she leaves, which will be on Thursday 9th. I'm having her and Prema[9] to supper on Monday next; I rather dread it.

No news yet how Elsa's show went in New York. I remembered to send her a telegram. Charles should be back soon.[10]

I keep right on with my novel. It *could* be ready the end of this month, but I doubt it and I know I mustn't rush too frantically. It is really coming along. And I am so thankful for this occupation, because without it I think being alone in this house would be quite unbearable. Not that I don't adore the house. It is the best of them all. But every corner is

6. Enclosure lost.

7. (1899–1988), director of exhibitions and publications at the Museum of Modern Art in New York.

8. William Inge (1913–1973), American playwright.

9. Prema Chaitanya (1913–2000), American monk of the Ramakrishna Order. He was born John Yale and, like all Ramakrishna monks, was renamed when he made his first vows of renunciation. Later, after his final vows in 1964, he was called Swami Vidyatmananda; see below, p. 138.

10. Lanchester opened *Elsa Lanchester—Herself* on February 4 in New York before taking it on tour. Charles Laughton (1899–1962), British actor, was her husband.

full of memories of Kitty; and sometimes Dobbin just wails "Kitty . . . Kitty . . . Kitty . . ." to himself. At least, there won't be much to remind Kitty of Dobbin—especially not at the Slade School. I never even set foot in it. How *tiresome* of Coldstream to have a nervous breakdown! *Why?*

Dobbin must stop now, so he can get this to the post office before it closes and find out how many stamps are needed.

He loves Kitty with all his heart; and when the Animals are together again, he will treasure Kitty even more than ever before. D.

[*Typed letter, initialled*]

Tuesday February 7th [1961]   [Santa Monica]

Sweetest love,

I haven't written for three days. Hoping to hear the address you moved to, if you already have moved. But I fear these blizzards in the East may be holding up the mails from England, unless they send them over Greenland.

I do hope, by now, that my darling has settled down a little and started to enjoy his work, and that people are being nice to him? Like, for example, Gielgud and Pat Woodcock—not to mention Mary Ure[1] and Tony [Richardson]—are you seeing them? Amiya has been urging me to give your address; but she can easily call Stephen and get it anyway, and she certainly won't be in London for quite a while, though she returns to England on Friday.

On Sunday, Marguerite and Gavin finally gave their lunch. It was as they say a success, although I was raging with guilt because I missed a whole day of work. The belle of the ball was—Dennis Hopper![2] Bill Inge and Monroe [Wheeler] and Gavin were just drooling over him. He's quite a nice boy but not attractive and so mannered. He wore a black blouse, tight thin black pants and a New York pallor, and looked exactly like Hamlet. Charlie Brackett[3] raved about your work, talent, charm, until one would have thought he'd discovered you. In fact, it is now becoming fashionable to talk about you

---

1. British actress (1933–1975).
2. American actor (1936–2010).
3. American screenwriter and producer (1892–1969).

at parties in a knowing, I-always-said-he'd-go-far way; several people were doing it. Agnes Moorehead sent her love; she is going off to Sicily to play a bandit moll or something.[4] Peter Glenville[5] was a handsome bore in tennis-anyone white shorts. Minnelli's new wife seemed quite mad, and Minnelli was [looking after] her.[6] Larry Harvey was his sunbeam self. Gavin tells me —I'd already left—that he announced he was secretly married to a young British actor, square and hideous, in a scraggy red beard, who is playing in *Mutiny on the Bounty*—"and John Ireland's my mistress," Larry added, "I don't know how much longer I can keep it out of the gossip columns, I'm sure."[7] As for Marguerite, she was busy dancing The Madison. Everybody knows about the break with Rory,[8] who returns today; and everybody sides with Marguerite, who has been badly treated, it's said. Marguerite has been accusing Rory right and left of boyfucking ... Believe it or not, just as I wrote that, Marguerite called me! She asked about you and had I heard any more, which I haven't, since I last spoke to her. Rory is still in New York, not coming back till the weekend. M. didn't say anything about any of that. Some say that no mail is coming out of New York, and Idylwyld still closed by this ghastly blizzard. Thank God you made it over there before all this started. Glenway, to whom Monroe talked long-distance, has been shut up in their farm for days and days.[9] What a nightmare country!

I plod on with my novel. It goes very slowly and yet it does go and I know I mustn't rush; but it certainly won't be finished till after the end of February. The weather here is fine but quite cool. I was even chilly cycling into Sta. Monica yesterday. I do quite a bit of that, now. And I've stopped feeling stiff from the gym.

In my last letter, I suggested your calling me from London on the

4. Agnes Moorehead (1900–1974), American actress; the film was *Jessica* (1962), in which she had a supporting role.
5. British actor and director (1913–1996).
6. Denise Minnelli, third wife from 1960 to 1971 of American director Vincente Minnelli (1903–1986).
7. Laurence Harvey (1928–1973), Lithuanian-born South African actor, played the Christopher Isherwood character in the film version of *I Am a Camera* (1955). John Ireland (1914–1992) was a Canadian-born American actor. Harvey married three times, but reportedly also had male lovers.
8. Rory Harrity, American actor, was Marguerite Lamkin's second husband from 1959 to 1963. The Madison, a line dance that became a craze in 1960, is still familiar from the musical and film *Hairspray*.
9. Glenway Wescott (1901–1987), American writer, was Monroe Wheeler's longterm companion. They lived in Manhattan and shared a house on Wescott's brother's farm in New Jersey.

14th—sometime between 10 p.m. and midnight, your time. I must have been crazy, because I believed that this would be 6–8 a.m., California time! Actually, of course, you could call early in the morning of the 14th and reach me around midnight of the 13th—or you could call in the evening of the 14th, at 7 p.m. or 8 p.m., and reach me during the morning of the 14th. If you can plan ahead, let me know. If not, I'll try to stay home all or most of the day anyway. That is, unless you think the whole thing is unpractical.

All my love to my own sweet dear Kitty. These first two weeks have gone by like lead. I hope they weren't so long for Kitty.

Will write again soon—D.

[*Typed letter, initialled*]

February 6, 1961 [London]

My dearest love:

To start with the good news: Sybil and Richard Burton have let me have their house in Hampstead to live in, since Richard is committed to *Camelot* until next December and that means they will be in New York till then.[1] The house is very comfortable and snug, just built a few years ago and so fitted with all the modern conveniences that we would take for granted. Richard offered it to me when I went backstage after *Camelot* to see him. I thought at the time it would be so much better to find my own place and be absolutely on my own in some stylish little flat in the center of London—Hampstead seemed *so far out!* Three days of hunting for some such stylish little flat, dealing with housing agents and lodging bureaus and tedious landladies, cured me of any such notion. I was so desperate I called Sybil in N.Y. and was fully prepared to beg for the house—but she was terribly sweet and said but of course I could stay there and told me she had called me at Julie's the day before, not knowing I had gone, to confirm Richard's offer. Anyway, I am in the house now, sitting up in their double bed in fact, thinking, as always, of

---

1. Welsh actress Sybil Williams (b. 1929) was the first wife of Welsh actor Richard Burton (1925–1984); their London house was 11 Squire's Mount. The musical *Camelot* had been running on Broadway since December 1960, and Bachardy had seen it when he stopped in New York on his way to London.

my darling Dobbin and how terribly I miss him—but more of that later. Richard's brother Ivor (Jenkins) and his wife Gwen (whom we met when they were in Los Angeles about a year and a half ago) have a house of their own directly across the street and have been very kind and helpful to Kitty and are so eager to please. The house I'm in is legally theirs because Richard is supposed to be strictly a resident of Switzerland, so they know their way around it and explain everything to dense Kitty. And it is not so far away from town after all—it takes me less than half an hour to get to the Slade on the underground and I don't even have to change trains. And aside from the joys of having a really motel-modern and clean bathroom, a civilized kitchen and central heating (almost unknown here), it is a relief to be away from the Spenders. There was something very wrong with my being there. The truth is, I have never liked either of them really and going there was asking for trouble. They made me feel very ill at ease, as though they were frightened of being made to assume any responsibility for me. Stephen took trouble to take me out to dinner one night and then took me to the Slade to introduce me, but he made it all seem perfunctory and made me feel I was putting him out. Natasha just disappeared to bang away at the piano all day and the second evening I was there Stephen asked me if I could be out because they were having a dinner party and had as many people as could be sat around the table. All this is of course understandable, and yet I couldn't help feeling uncomfortable and in the way. And of course it was altogether a bad time for me and I probably read all kinds of meaning into their behavior because I was so upset.

The person who has been an angel is Patrick Woodcock. I called him in desperation and he immediately understood how I was feeling and was so kind and warm and helpful. He has taken charge of entertaining me and has already managed, aside from everything else, not only to get me into Covent Garden but for a very glamorous opening—Britten's opera of *A Midsummer Night's Dream*. He got me a seat in the second row, dead center! Of course the opera was a bore (except for John Piper's sets) but it was fun to see Covent Garden at its best. Paul Anstee[2] and Patrick went together and we all had dinner afterwards. I talked to John Gielgud on the phone only—he has gone to N. Y. now to direct Hugh Wheeler's

2. Interior decorator and longtime companion to John Gielgud until the early 1960s.

play[3] & will be gone at least six weeks. Keith Vaughan[4] turns out to be one of Patrick's dearest friends and we all had drinks on Sunday. Keith is very shy and we haven't yet really made contact but I am hoping.

Oh, my dearest darling, I've tried to keep this letter fairly bright but I really am so awfully sad and I miss you so very much and need you so. I really don't know now whatever possessed me to come to this place. The only thing I seem to have done really is to create more problems rather than solve any. Everything that I thought was wrong with my life in California, all the problems I felt trapped by there, I have brought with me to London, and I have left the dearest treasure I had behind me, unguarded. I certainly never knew before how much I need you, my love, good or bad as it may be. I do need you and feel lost without you and long to hide myself in your mane and sleep warm against your flanks. I honestly don't know what I'm doing here, and the thought of painting, of wanting to paint, is farthest from my mind. The Slade is really no different from any other school I've been to, sloppy, dirty, disorganized—bored teachers and bored students and bored models. Mind you I've spent less than a day and a half there and yet I feel I know it—I can smell the same old smells and sense the same situation that always makes me retreat into my fur and hide there, silently disapproving and scared at the same time, paralyzed with apathy. I honestly feel at this moment that I don't want to paint and have nothing to say and no business pretending I have. It is so humiliating to feel this way and to have to admit it, but I do feel utterly helpless and meaningless, sad and lost, neurotic and silly, and *guilty* for having spent all this money and built up all this production—for what? To feel more insecure than ever before and for no reason at all except what's inside of me—everything would be all right but for that. I just feel so embarrassed and scared, and for no real reason, I know.

Later

I've just been to Loudoun Road and two dear letters from my sweetheart were waiting for me. My dearest, I want you so much—and

---

3. *Big Fish, Little Fish*, the first play by English writer Hugh Wheeler (1912–1925) who later became known for his collaborations with Stephen Sondheim; he also wrote mystery thrillers under the name Patrick Quentin.
4. English painter and diarist (1912–1977).

I want to please you and make you proud of me, and now I want to tear up all the sick complaining and depressing stuff I've been indulging in, but you said in your letter you wanted to read everything, and I've been writing *for hours*—if I had time for my journal I could get all that stuff out of my system. Anyway, it's probably just that it's been a bad day today—I feel low but I know myself well enough not to think that today has any relation to tomorrow as far as my moods go. I will probably feel splendid tomorrow and feel all kinds of zest for "the challenge." Please don't fear that Kitty will crumble. He believes that his Dobbin will always be there and that belief is so precious to Kitty. It really keeps him going when all else fails. Nothing will ever take Dobbin's place and nothing will ever be so bad that Kitty will feel he can't rely on his horse. I can't help needing you my darling, but I will try to be better and stronger. But don't be surprised if I suddenly fly back to the basket. I certainly want to, terribly, but writing this letter has helped somewhat. I can at least face the thought of tomorrow.

I so wish I could have written my love a happy letter—it hasn't all been bad, and Patrick is very steadying and sympathetic and I do feel he will be very reliable. I must just give this thing a fair try—but my head is most certainly out of the clouds and now that I know that I'm prepared to come back to the basket a failure, I feel I can stand to stay here a little longer, just in case Kitty's courage reappears. But know my dearest that I am always thinking of you and loving you and wanting you.

I haven't called anyone besides Patrick—I haven't really wanted to see anyone and anyway I very psychosomatically lost my London address book so it will be difficult if I do feel up to calling anyone.

February 7, 1961

Better this morning, in spite of a sore throat—never have I known such psychosomatic behavior! But at least I do have a doctor here if it doesn't go away instantly. I have decided to ignore it and go to the theater tonight.

The Slade really is a bore, I'm afraid, and now I've got to invent some other nucleus of activity—perhaps even that most dreaded of dread, painting on my own. I hope Keith will give me some encouragement and guidance, but I do feel so awfully silly about telling him my woes. I know so well what any sensible intelligent person would say, what I say to myself in fact, "Do you or don't you? Shit or get off the pot." And honestly I can't lean on him too heavily. He has his life and already gives up two days of his week to the Slade which I think he himself quite disapproves of, anyway. But I will see, my love. You know me so well and know that a week from now I may have almost forgotten the blues and fears of today. I do think it was a GHASTLY mistake coming here, but I must be here for some reason or other, and perhaps I will find it out. It may be that the grass is nowhere greener than in Dobbin's meadow. And to really know that is worth a trip to England. Foolish Kitty should have known that long before now.

The Sutro deal sounds good but God knows where Kitty may be by the end of March—the 26th—an eternity away. But I promise to send up HOH's (Horse, Oh Horse) if and when necessary.

Of course I will call you on the 14th—I've almost called you so many times already—and my number at the house in Hampstead N.W. 3 (11 Squire's Mount) is SWIss cottage 3718. The telephone people are supposed to come to fix it today—I can get calls on it but can't call out (a good thing, too, I'm thinking) but I will call you on the 14th, if not before.

Please keep sending those love-waves and Kitty will try very hard to concentrate—he's so receptive now anyway, and a stir of the whiskers by Dobbin's love-waves is worth endless hi-fi broadcasts from anywhere else. And don't worry about Kitty—he gets very rattled but if the house really catches on fire Kitty will run out as fast as he can to keep from singeing his limp but still white fur.

I love my darling very very much. K.

P.S. The horse Kitty loves has always been an old grey mare, so sweet and dear, and *never* one of those greedy and faithless white stallions. And besides, grey is more becoming to Kitty's white fur. Two white animals would never do.
XXXXXXXX K.

[Autograph letter, ink and pencil]

February 10, Friday. [1961]   Casa de los Animales

Own sweetest one,

[Y]our letter, dated February 7, just arrived. Oh, how happy I was to hear from my darling, even in sadness! I never supposed it would be easy for Kitty—certainly not at first—but I am glad he has the nice Burton house and I am so glad about Pat Woodcock. I feel such gratitude to him, because he has helped Kitty; he shall be rewarded somehow, by some great horse-gesture, one day before long. What could Dobbin do that he would like?

Yet, on the other hand, I don't want to mix in too much in any of this—because it can never be insisted on too often that what's done for Kitty is done for Kitty, not for Dobbin. That's why I don't want to meet or speak to the McKinnons, anyhow not yet.

Today, also, a very short letter arrived from Stephen, obviously full of guilt, about what a rush he has been in and how he hopes to meet you often during the lunch hours! "He seems quite well and elated and very keen to get working." That's so like my Kitty, even when he's weeping so bitterly inside, he sparkles. But he mustn't be too heroic. Tell Pat *everything*. And be quite utterly frank with Keith Vaughan; I *know* he's a good person, I feel it instinctively; and as soon as you make a move, he'll respond.

Stephen writes, "Mr. Jenkin of the Slade received him with enthusiasm and told me that they thought very highly of the drawings and were very pleased to have him." But, honey love, as I have told you 10,000,000,000,000 times, there is no law ordained by me or anyone else that says you *have* to be a painter, or anything. Sure, Dobbin loves to feel proud of his Kitty, but, whatever Kitty does or doesn't do, Dobbin will always feel proud of him because he knows what it means to be Kitty and what an achievement that is. Let any of them try it who think they can! Ha!

I *know* one thing: win, lose or draw, six months from now you will tell me, "The trip to London was" (whatever it was) "BUT IT WAS WORTH IT." Never mind about the Slade or painting or any of that; I mean worth it in the only way that counts. It will contribute to Kitty's funds of experience-know-how-understanding. I am *sure*. But Dobbin does not want Kitty to come to the conclusion simply that Dobbin reigns supreme; that's depressing as well as untrue. Dobbin would just like to be loved more than anyone else. He is in constant touch with Kitty through love-waves. Some places are very painful; like driving back from Hollywood at night along that bit of Sta. Monica Boulevard between Sepulveda and Veteran—the thought comes stabbingly, "Why are you going home, Dobbin? There's nobody there." But Dobbin is brave. He goes home. He hasn't been drinking much or roaring around, and he won't. The novel is a great support; always something to be gotten on with. And he likes to exercise at the gym. It is sad in his little bed, though. And this morning he found himself pouring two glasses of Tiger's Milk![1]

Hope this will reach you before you phone on Tuesday. I'll tell you the news then, such as it is. This letter is more about feelings. But it will make Dobbin happy to hear his Kitty's mew. He does so look forward to that.

With all my love to my darling,

D. XXXXXXXX

[*Typed letter, initialled, autograph additions*]

Sunday, February 12 [1961, London]

(If this reaches you before: I will call you between 7–8 p.m. London time, about midday for you, on the 14th—just letting you know.)

My only love,

I have just collected your letter of February 7 from Loudoun Road—it cheers Kitty so to know that his dear horse is thinking of him and to have even a slip of paper with the smell of the stable about it brings the pink back to Kitty's nose.

I do hope old Dub was not disturbed by silly Kitty's more than somewhat hysterical last letter. Kitty feels much better now, though he still misses his horsey so terribly and thinks of him all the time and hopes he is not as lonely as poor Kitty gets sometimes, though as I say, things are better, though I don't know exactly why or believe that things will necessarily *stay* better.

I hope your February 7 letter was the last to Loudoun Road. I think I have decided to dispense altogether with the Spenders, at least for the time being. I realize they have become my London villains and I am going to make use of them as such—so important to have villains to attach one's

1. Powdered protein mixture added to milk.

sulks to. I went this evening like a thief in the night to collect my mail—only Natasha's old deaf mother was in the house. She is ridiculously deaf. After yelling into her portable microphone an elaborate explanation of who I was and what I wanted, I still had to write it all down for her on the back of an envelope. And wouldn't you know, she's so blind she could hardly read what I'd written. Anyway, Kitty scampered away with his letter in his mouth, so happy to have news of his Dobbin that his paws hardly touched the pavement all the way to the tube station.

I went to the Royal Court Theatre last Thursday evening to see Tony and Mary. I had no way of calling them first so I had to catch them at the tail end of a rehearsal.[1] They were of course very surprised, and surprisingly cordial—Mary gave me a hug—and after watching a bit of the rehearsal they broke for the day and Mary took me for drinks at the pub next to the theater with the actor who plays De Flores—Robert Shaw, an arty, scruffy inhabitant of Boresville, but quite nice—and then to see the house she's just bought very nearby. An enormous, rather battered Regency house with five floors counting the basement, obviously bought with an eye to accommodating John, who is in Wales for three weeks.[2] The house will be really nice when fixed up and may even entice John. Jocelyn Rickards is a confiding patient of Patrick's and according to her Mary has "nothing to offer" John, more than implying that she has. But all judgement, or some of it anyway, will be suspended until I meet her. I'm longing to.[3]

Tony of course had to rush off right after the rehearsal for a conference with David Merrick,[4] who never seems to be far away. I did see Tony for a few seconds before he had to rush off again to a dinner party, and because he was in a hurry he pretended offense at not being called the moment I'd arrived—he was intrigued though to know why I was in

1. For Thomas Middleton and William Rowley's The Changeling (1622), which Richardson was directing. Mary Ure was playing Beatrice, opposite Jeremy Brett as Alsemero.

2. Ure was then married to British playwright John Osborne (1929–1994), but she was having an affair with Robert Shaw (1927–1978) and gave birth to Shaw's child later that year, on August 31, 1961. After the child was born, she divorced Osborne and, in 1963, married Shaw, with whom she had three further children.

3. Jocelyn Rickards (1924–2005), Australian-born artist and costume designer, was then having an affair with Osborne; they lived together from early 1960 to the autumn of 1961, while he was married to Ure.

4. American producer (1911–2000); he took Tony Richardson's 1956 Royal Court production of John Osborne's Look Back in Anger to Broadway in 1957.

London, probing all the while for some telling little clue to my having left old Dub *forever*. He was like a dog smelling a bone—his appetite was up and he was all wild-eyed and nervous from the rush and the scent of disaster. He said he would call this weekend but hasn't and it is already 7:45 Sunday evening—but I didn't think he would call and I've planned to write all kinds of letters this evening that are weighing heavily—I haven't written one word to my mother or Ted or Julie or the Burtons, but Dub comes first *ALWAYS!*

I saw *Saturday Night and Sunday Morning* yesterday. I don't like it much. I was quite bored, though Albert Finney *is* good. But it is an actor's picture and that is always boring in the end. All depends on the character and Finney's performance and halfway through you realize you are watching just an actor feeling confident in front of a camera and though he is quite sweet it is not enough. You feel the picture has not been directed at all, unless by Albert Finney.[5]

As for the Slade, I went to a life drawing class every day this past week and got thoroughly bored drawing two thoroughly bored Negroes, both with beards and exactly like American Negroes except for the lack of southern accents, which is curiously disconcerting—I find I keep listening for it. The school is, after all I'm afraid, like most schools, and nobody there is going to hold my hand or paint my pictures for me. I had drinks with Keith Vaughan and Ramsay McClure[6] today— Ramsay has lent me his easel which is terribly sweet—and Keith spoke somewhat frankly about my position at school. Since I am a special student, to whom the privileges of using the school and its facilities have been given but nothing else, none of the instructors is going to pay very much attention to me. It is assumed that I know what I'm about and don't need or want instruction—which was probably Cecil's setup when he studied there.[7] And I must say, I asked for just such a setup and so I can't very well squawk, not loudly at any rate. Keith spoke to a painter friend of his named Prunella Something who lives in Chelsea and has just had quite a successful showing of her work here. She said

5. Czech-born British filmmaker Karel Reisz (1926–2002) directed British actor Albert Finney (b. 1936), and Tony Richardson produced the film. Bachardy and Isherwood got to know Finney later that year, in June, when Richardson was directing him in Osborne's *Luther*.
6. British painter (1924–1981), Vaughan's longterm companion since the late 1940s.
7. Cecil Beaton (1904–1980), British photographer, theater and film designer, author. He attended the Slade intermittently as a part-time student from 1953 to 1956.

when told of my situation that I should certainly have gone to study in Chelsea at some school there.[8] It begins to occur to me as I write that perhaps this woman may be a key to something for me. You always said I needed a woman in order to make any kind of contact and I think you're right (except for one very ͙s͙p͙e͙c͙i͙a͙l͙ exception) and so I think I will follow up this Prunella—she is a friend of both Keith's and Patrick's and is described by them as a "sensitive" painter, "but still good." But one thing I have learned from being here—I must do it myself. I must want to do it enough to get over the awful fear and dread of beginning. I always knew this, I think, but was never really up against it like I am now—there is really nothing else *to do*. So, I have hired a model for next Saturday (a marvellous, fat, lisping woman who looks like an old Bette Davis and behaves like a young Clara Bow—she has been modelling at school) and I shall begin working in one of the bare rooms in the house, which is only partially furnished—three of the rooms are bare or nearly bare, and all have a northern light, ideal to the point of being spooky for a studio, especially the dining room downstairs which has a bare floor. The model fees are astoundingly low here—six shillings an hour, about 90¢ I guess—as compared to anywhere from $3.50 to $5.00 in Los Angeles. In the meantime, I am having my first portrait sitter tomorrow. A novelist named Hester Chapman—you probably know of her—who is a good friend of Patrick's and Rosamond's and should be fun to draw.[9] Patrick took me to dinner at her house and we got along very well. Patrick also had me to dinner with Mai Zetterling and her husband.[10] They are nice and she is a prospective victim of mine.

Dearest love, a tiresome request—could you please send me, if you can find them, the addresses and phone numbers of the following: Amiya (the country and London), Forster,[11] Tutin,[12] Emlyn and Molly [Williams], Henry (Green) Yorke and Dig (she was born to be drawn),[13]

8. Prunella Clough (1919–1999) lectured at the Chelsea School of Art, where she had once been a student; she had a retrospective at the Whitechapel Gallery, September–October 1960.
9. Hester Chapman (1895–1976), also a biographer, was a longtime friend of English novelist Rosamond Lehmann (1901–1990).
10. Mai Zetterling (1925–1994), Swedish actress, and David Hughes (1911–2005), English novelist, who was her husband from 1958 to 1979.
11. E.M. Forster (Morgan) (1879–1970), English novelist.
12. Dorothy Tutin (1931–2001), English actress; she played Sally Bowles in the London stage production of *I Am a Camera*.
13. Henry Yorke (1905–1973), English novelist, wrote under the name Henry Green; his wife Adelaide was known as Dig.

Cecil most importantly, the Tynans,[14] Francis Bacon[15] just in case I feel very bold, William Plomer,[16] even John Lehmann[17] (Beatrix[18] too if you have it—she would be almost too good to draw). And would you ask Gavin again for the name of the hotel at which Lenya[19] is staying and for Diane Cilento's[20] phone number. All the rest—Rosamond, Gielgud, Paul Anstee, etc. I can get from Patrick. God knows if I shall ever call any or all of them, but I just might. I might as well in fact, what can I lose? That is rather my attitude in general now—what can I lose that I haven't already lost, or at least left behind. If I thought for one split second that I might lose my dear colt I would be in Santa Monica tomorrow with boots and a lasso. And you know what they did in *The Misfits?*[21] Only Dobbin would be trotted right back to the stable. Oh, Kitty worries so about his darling and wants so much to be near him again. I didn't get a chance to talk to Tony about our plot but I will when I see him next. Dobbin would even, I think, feel quite at home in this house. There is wall-to-wall carpeting so he could even take off his horseshoes indoors and pad about like he likes to. Kitty longs so to hear again his old dear shuffling about and neighing and snorting. All Kitty's love always, K.

[*Autograph letter with enclosure*[22]]

February 16, Thursday [1961]   C. de los A.

My darling dearest love,

Just got your sweet long letter and a dear picture of Kitty with it. I would like to write reams to you but am in such a rush today because

---

14. Ken Tynan (1927–1980), English theater critic, and his first wife, American actress and writer Elaine Dundy (1921–2008).
15. Irish-born painter (1909–1992).
16. British poet and novelist (1903–1973).
17. English author and publisher (1907–1988).
18. Beatrix Lehmann (1903–1970), English actress, youngest sister of John and Rosamond.
19. Lotte Lenya (1900–1981), Austrian actress and singer, known for her roles in Brecht-Weill musicals.
20. Australian actress (b. 1933).
21. Rounded up wild mustangs and sold them to be slaughtered for dog food. Isherwood and Bachardy had seen the 1961 film on January 10 in a projection room at Paramount Studios.
22. A color illustration, cut from a magazine, of a long-haired white cat on which Bachardy wrote, "To remind my dear Dobbin of his loving Kitty—with all Kitty's thoughts and love. K."

Charles is coming to weep and work on the Plato.¹ Mostly weep. Oh dear—next to my darling's return, nobody's arrival will make me happier than Terry's² next week because then Charles will be out of my hair. I cannot believe in the sincerity of such noisy public love. Imagine if the Animals made such a spectacle of themselves! But they are too well-bred and their feelings are too deep.

It was so wonderful hearing his dearest Kitty's voice on the phone. And, you know, it's too ridiculous to be stingy about such an important thing; why don't we talk to each other at least once a week? Why not call me a week from yesterday; next Wednesday the 22nd? I'll wait home all morning, so you can call any time between, say, three in the afternoon and eight in the evening, London time. It is such a joy hearing my Kitty's voice.

Great news! John Sutro just cabled to Ivan, "We are most interested in Isherwood." So now I am writing Sutro myself today; but it must surely mean that he's prepared to make an offer. And of course I'll agree to anything halfway reasonable, because it's a good job. More of this when I hear from him.

Here are the addresses: *The Countess of Sandwich* The Cottage, Hinchingbrooke, Huntingdon. (Huntingdon 52) London number: Trafalgar 1726. Don't know London address. *E.M. Forster* King's College, Cambridge. (Cambridge 4411). *Dorothy Tutin* (I only have her parents' address: 11a Tregunter Road, S.W. 10 Fremantle 9597) but her barge is tied up off Cheyne Walk, Chelsea.³ *Emlyn Williams* 15 Pelham Crescent, London S.W. 3 (Kensington 2045) *Henry Yorke* 16 Trevor Place, S.W. 3 (Kensington 4781). *Tynans* I only have a phone number: Enwright 95675. You could get him of course through whichever newspaper he's writing for now. *Bacon,* can't find him. Rupert Doone and Robert Medley would know.⁴ My address for them is 5 The Grange, S.W. 19 (Wimbledon 7128). *William Plomer* Rossida, Stonefields, Rustington, Sussex. *John Lehmann* (haven't got Beatrix) 31 Egerton Crescent, S.W. 3. (Kensington 0568). *He'd* know where Bacon was, I think. Please see him—otherwise he'll sulk.

---

1. Isherwood and Charles Laughton were writing a play for Laughton about Socrates.
2. Terry Jenkins (1936–2009), British model and aspiring actor with whom Laughton was having an affair.
3. Tutin lived on a houseboat on the Thames.
4. Rupert Doone (1903–1966), English dancer, choreographer, and theatrical producer, founder of the Group Theatre, which staged Auden and Isherwood's plays in the 1930s; and his longterm companion, Robert Medley (1905–1994), English painter, theater designer, and teacher.

And you can bitch Stephen to him if you're in the mood. He'll adore that. Gavin sends his love and says *Lotte Lenya* was staying at the Grosvenor House, Park Lane; she said she'd be moving but is sure to have left an address. *Diane Cilento's* number is Park 9965. And (if you dare!) *Vivien Leigh's* private number is Sloane 1955. Be sure to visit the *Mrs. Stone* and *Lolita* sets soon.[5] Patrick would like that, wouldn't he?

I can never be grateful enough to him for all he has done for my darling. And even if he may have introduced Kitty to some *numbers* which Dobbin doesn't wish to know about, well, Dobbin is only happy if Kitty finds consolation—ONLY NOT TOO MUCH!! Dobbin seems to catch hints in Kitty's letters of concern about possible *riders* Dobbin may be finding? Kitty is not to worry. If anyone tries to get a firm seat on the saddle, Dobbin rears and they go flying off again. Dobbin only longs for the day when he'll be with Kitty. These lectures, as I told you, run till March 26. I have told the Pasadena people I can't do April 16. They pleaded and pleaded and finally I said, Well, April 2.[6] So I *could* leave the 4th, if all goes well. That's really not so long, is it? We'll soon be through February. The chief reason for not coming earlier is that I really do want to finish "Paul" first and show it to Gerald, so I get any shit or bitchery about his portrait out the way at once.[7]

Am taking care of the picture of Julie today.[8] Will write again very soon and hope to hear from my so much missed darling.

D.

LONGING TO HEAR ABOUT AMSTERDAM [9]

[*Typed letter, initialled*]

---

5. Vivien Leigh was starring in *The Roman Spring of Mrs. Stone* (1961), Gavin Lambert's screenplay of Tennessee Williams's novel. Lotte Lenya also had a role. Stanley Kubrick (1928–1999), also a friend, was directing *Lolita* (1962), and yet another friend, Shelley Winters (see below, p. 118), was playing Lolita's mother.
6. To speak at the synagogue, as mentioned above, p. 31.
7. Henry FitzGerald Heard (Gerald) (1889–1971), Irish writer, broadcaster, philosopher, religious teacher, was the model for Augustus Parr in *Down There on a Visit*.
8. Isherwood was sending Bachardy's drawing of Julie Harris to her producer, Mildred Freed Alberg, in New York.
9. Patrick Woodcock had planned a weekend in Amsterdam, but Bachardy decided not to go.

Friday [February] 17th [1961]   [Santa Monica]

Dearest sweet love,

Today was the Ramakrishna birthday puja,[1] and I got back here early and have been fussing with bills, checks, etc. Now I think I'll write a little to my darling, because I miss him so and writing makes me feel better, and there were things I forgot to say when I wrote the day before yesterday.

Enclosed is another letter about the McKinnon money, and the brochure of my forthcoming UCLA lectures. Isn't it AWFUL? I really feel so sorry for that poor colored boy who drew the picture.[2] He will never hear the last of it, especially as one of Dr. Kaplan's assistants, who is in charge of the brochure, is a queen and an utter bitch. [. . .][3] Meanwhile, I haven't yet thought much about the lecture I'm giving at Riverside on Monday,[4] much less these UCLA readings. And I'm really getting a little bit rattled about "Paul," because it goes so slowly and there are so many interruptions. For example, now Laughton is all excited about his reading tour and I have to hear all his ideas. And we have been working on the bit of Plato (the Wings passage from the *Phaedrus*) which he's going to include, and I must say, it sounds very good indeed, now, and Charles is wildly enthusiastic about our collaboration. The only *good* thing is that he keeps saying that now I must be paid for my extra work in connection with the tour. We shall see . . .

Did I tell you I saw Inge's film, directed by Kazan,[5] *Splendor [in] the Grass?* It's really an awful lot made out of nothing, but some of the shots are absolutely beautiful, and Natalie Wood is really quite good. As for Warren Beatty, Gavin tells me he isn't nearly as sexy in real life as on

1. Vigil marking the birth of Ramakrishna (1836–1886), the Hindu holy man whose life and teachings sparked the modern renaissance of Vedanta. The ceremony of worship runs from the evening into the small hours of the morning.
2. A black artist called Bill Brown.
3. Abbot Kaplan (1912–1980), an economics professor and university administrator, ran UCLA Extension, the continuing education program for which he hired Isherwood to lecture.
4. University of California at Riverside, where he lectured on February 20 and was entertained at the home of philosophy professor Philip Wheelwright.
5. Elia Kazan (1909–2003), Turkish-born Greek-American stage and film director, also an actor and producer, and a proponent of Method acting. Isherwood and Bachardy first met him in 1955, when Kazan directed Tennessee Williams's *Cat on a Hot Tin Roof.*

screen. Maybe you will have met him by now, if you go on the *Roman Spring* set. And do find out if he is really having this affair with Vivien Leigh, or is that all just publicity?[6]

The puja this evening was a *shambles!* Because Swami got the bright idea, why have them all lining up and taking ages bowing down to the shrine, so he came out himself and tried serving instant relics to each of us where he or she sat. But it got all confused, and some people were getting seconds and others couldn't get near him! According to sour old Prema, there was one woman dead drunk, who just sat in bliss and kept getting touched and touched and touched by the relic tray! They all asked after you. Thank goodness, Swami Ritajananda is *not* going to Paris, but will stay right here. Prema is agitating to get Vandanananda kicked upstairs, that is, made head of one of the other centers![7]

And did I tell you Rory [Harrity] came to see me—yes, I must have, because it was the day before you called. Since then I have heard nothing from or about either of them, but I am having supper with Gavin on Sunday and no doubt there'll be some gossip floating around by then. Also, nothing from—Hope,[8] Glenn,[9] the Stravinskys, Jennifer and David[10]—in fact, nothing, period. Old Dobbin is abandoned, but he doesn't care about that. He only wants his Kitty, and until that can happen, he will just dully work and work like an old carthorse. All will be better after Tuesday, because at present Charles insists on treating me as a companion in love-suffering, and he absolutely does not understand how Dobbins suffer and anyhow wouldn't be interested. So roll on, Terry. Terry is going with him on the reading tour and it will last eight weeks,[11] so he won't even notice I'm gone for quite a long while.

6. American actor Warren Beatty (b. 1937) played the love interest in both *Splendor in the Grass* (1961) and *The Roman Spring of Mrs. Stone*; his affair with co-star Natalie Wood (1938–1981) is well known, but the one with Vivien Leigh is affirmed only by insider gossip.
7. Ritajananda, an Indian monk of the Ramakrishna Order, was Prabhavananda's chief assistant at the Hollywood Vedanta Society from 1958 to 1961, when he did in fact leave to run the Vedanta Center at Gretz, near Paris. Swami Vandanananda, a fellow monk, remained in Hollywood and eventually became chief assistant. Later, Vandanananda returned to India and rose to be General Secretary of the whole order.
8. Hope Lange (1931–2003), American actress.
9. Glenn Ford (1916–2006), Canadian-born actor, then having a love affair with Lange.
10. American actress Jennifer Jones (1919–2009) and her second husband, producer David Selznick (1902–1965).
11. Laughton was giving dramatic readings throughout the U.S. from Shakespeare, the Bible, and other classic literature.

Dearest treasure, there is no cure for being catless—let no one tell you there is. It is just dull hell, getting steadily duller and more hellish. But I shall simply apply myself and work and the time will pass. But Kitty is not to be sad—Dobbin will be sad for both of us—and he is to enjoy himself, and not pine for Dobbin, but to be very very happy to see Dobbin when he comes!

D. XXXXXXXXXXXX
Hope you call Wednesday!

[*Typed letter, initialled, autograph additions*]

Thursday, February 23 [1961]   [Santa Monica]

My dearest love,

[I]t is such a good idea, our talking to each other on the phone. I don't care *how* much it costs. There's something about hearing your voice; I know then *that you're really there.* And yet, there are things I can't say on the phone which I can say in letters. So here's another of them.

But I'm actually writing to tell you a bit of bad sad news: Ted has flipped again—you were so right when you said that his wanting to come to England with me was crazy. He went voluntarily into the same place, Edgemont Hospital on Hollywood Blvd., 4841. It was Bart who told me this on the phone, this morning. So then I called the hospital, and Ted has been transferred from the nonviolent to the violent ward and can't be talked to, at least not today. I only pray he won't pull another of his escapes. Bart says his stealing still goes on, all the time; and altogether thinks the outlook black, because this attack follows so soon on the other one . . .[1] Oh dear, I wish I liked Bart better. He really has behaved very well in some of these crises, and yet there is always a sour note. (It should be said in Bart's defence that he just had a bad accident

---

1. Ted Bachardy was a manic-depressive schizophrenic. His attacks began in 1945, when he was fifteen years old: periods of manic, self-destructive behavior followed by nervous breakdowns and long stays in mental hospitals. Usually, the attacks were at least a year apart. His most recent attack had been almost exactly a year earlier, in February 1960, during which he ran away from the sanatorium. He sometimes shoplifted and had been arrested for this. Ted's friend, Bart Lord, was an amateur actor and a show-business fan; they had been lovers and lived together during the 1950s.

on the freeway—ran out of gas and was bumped into by a car behind, and got a whiplash and is staying away from work.) I'll call Vince[2] later on and see if there's anything I can do. But of course it's so awkward visiting the hospital, lest I run into your father[3] . . . Ted seems to be in a friendly mood toward both of us. He asked Bart to get in touch with me; and he told him how sweet you had been to him and Vince lately.

No news about the Graham Greene film yet. Charles expects Terry's arrival in the small hours of tomorrow morning. I have nothing to expect except giving supper to Olga Fabian tomorrow night.[4] Brother! Then on Sunday, I must entertain Brian Bedford, who is here in *Five Finger Exercise*;[5] so I shall take him to Jerry Lawrence's to see the flower of California Youth—Jimmy Bridges,[6] Jack Larson and Dean Campbell![7] Next week, I'm going up to Santa Barbara to collect the tape of my lectures and see the Warshaws[8] and Douwe.[9]

We have had a real *Wuthering Heights* windstorm. I was quite afraid it would smash the workroom windows right out; that end of the house seemed to be taking the full blast. But old Dobbin managed to go to sleep amidst all the commotion.

Here's a mad little picture Krishna took of me, God knows when, and pressed into my hand last night, when I was up at Vedanta Place.[10]

Oh, sweetheart, it is good to know that you aren't forgetting old Dobbin, but, even with the phone calls and letters and stiff upper

---

2. Vince Davis, another boyfriend, with whom Ted lived for about four years after splitting from Bart Lord.
3. Jess Bachardy (1905–1977), a mechanic for Lockheed Aviation, refused to meet Isherwood until 1968.
4. Olga Fabian (1885–1983), Viennese actress, played Fräulein Schneider in the original Broadway production of *I Am a Camera* (1951).
5. Bedford (b. 1935), British stage actor and, later, director, had first appeared in this Peter Shaffer play in London in 1958, then in New York in 1959. Gielgud directed it.
6. James Bridges (1936–1993), American actor, screenwriter, and director, lived with Jack Larson from the 1950s onward.
7. American musical comedy actor, singer, dancer, and singing coach.
8. Howard Warshaw (1920–1977), American artist, taught at UCSB; his wife, Frances, previously married to Mel Ferrer, was wealthy. Isherwood stayed often with them while he was a visiting professor.
9. Douwe Stuurman (1910–1991), American classicist, was a professor in the English department at UCSB.
10. Swami Krishnananda, an American monk of the Ramakrishna Order, obsessively tape recorded and photographed Swami Prabhavananda's lectures and classes; this photograph of Isherwood has been lost.

muzzles and noses, it still is rather *hell*—just the *non*-Kitty quality of the view from this window, or anything. Does it take separations like this to make two people realize how lucky it was they met? And what does it take to keep them remembering it, when they're together again? It seems to Dobbin, now, that he will *never* forget, even for a moment . . . Well—let's see.

Will send off the Kitty-clothes and things in a day or two.

All Dobbin's love and daily thoughts—

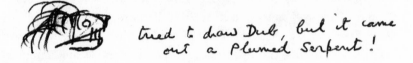

tried to draw Dub, but it came out a Plumed Serpent!

Will expect your call Wednesday morning, March 1st.

[*Typed letter, autograph additions*]

Thursday evening, February 23 [1961]   [Santa Monica]

A whole month since my Kitty left, today! I wrote him this morning but I hadn't realized this—God it seems ever so much longer than that—so I will send him some more words of love. It is all very well, the way Dobbin calls Kitty a treasure. But now and then Dobbin is specially hit by the word and realizes that a treasure is something absolutely irreplaceable, and something you may quite easily lose unless you take the greatest care of it. And then he feels really desperate!

Dearest love, all around us I see people who simply do not know that they have someone's love, and they just throw it away again, out of vanity, mostly; they think it's just nothing and lots more where that came from. We won't make that mistake, will we?

Old Dobbin is sitting at home, all alone, and no wind tonight. He has eaten frozen beef hash and string beans and pineapple sherbert. He has decided not to drink for quite a while. And he eats lots of celery because someone said Kinsey[1] said it makes you potent—but don't misunderstand Dobbin, he needs the energy for other things, like

---

1. That is, Alfred Kinsey (1894–1956), the American sex researcher.

finishing his novel. That *will* be a rush, and I still don't know if I can or not. Shall know in a couple of weeks. The new part about the Salton Sea is quite amusing, I think. There is a scene at the volcanic mud-pots. I have gone there on a picnic with two women from the seminar, and Gerald arrives to bring the news of the scandal with Paul.[2] And then there is a bit I rather like: "I glanced questioningly at Augustus, but he seemed lost in contemplation of one of the Mud Pots. At length he murmured, ['Y]es—' softly and thoughtfully, as though agreeing with some remark it had just spat out."

Here are two things I forgot in my letter this morning. Stanley Kubrick's home number is Primrose 5043 and his number at the studio is Elstree 1600. Cuthbert Worsley and John Luscombe: 126A Harley Street, London W. 1.

Bart and Vince both called tonight. Very pessimistic. The doctor wants Ted to have shock treatment again and your father so far refuses because he feels Ted would never forgive him. And, on top of that, the doctor feels it is a very bad sign that this relapse has come so soon after the last one. He fears it'll get worse. However, it may all be alarmism; we have to wait until some better men have been consulted.

Friday evening, Feb. 24. Olga Fabian just left. Jesus, what a bore evening! She quoted to me all the poems she used to read aloud in colleges, in absolutely incomprehensible English. Waiting for her bus made me so late that I missed seeing Terry, who is over with Charles in the other house. They've gone to bed.

This morning I got a huge slab of work done, so feel good. This afternoon I went to [Flax]. The man there remembered you and said you would want the combined brush and pen.[3] So I hope that's right? I bought two. I have located a parcel-wrapping place in Pacific Palisades (which is much better for mailing because of the parking) and I hope to take all your things there bright and early and get them mailed off.

No word about Ted today. I'll get some news over the weekend.

Goodnight, my darling own Kitty,

D.

2. Paul was modelled on Denham (Denny) Fouts (*circa* 1914–1948), the widely admired Florida-born bisexual courtesan who died a drug addict in Rome.
3. Flax Art Supplies in Westwood; Bachardy used a Japanese bamboo pen with a brush at one end and a whittled bamboo point at the other end to be dipped in ink for drawing.

Sat. morning Feb. 25.

Just sent the clothes off, *air freight*, because I couldn't bear to think of my Kitty waiting a month for them. They *should* take 4–5 days.

[*Typed letter, initialled, autograph additions*]

February 27 [1961, London]

My own darling horse—

Two letters today from my dearest, one in the morning which Kitty read at breakfast before going off to school, and the other was waiting for Kitty when he came home this evening so tired out and rained on but instantly revived by his Dub's dear words. And Kitty's heart was nearly broken when he found that sweet picture of his old darling, all colored and so happy—just like Kitty remembers him. It is sitting up next to Kitty's bed right now and Horsey's eyes are watching Kitty very closely.[1] My dearest love, I think of you all the time and miss you more every day, and I realize now how terribly much I love you, so much that it worries Kitty sick to think of his Dub all alone, so far away. You are the only thing in my life I really care about and the idea of being without you, really without you, of not being able to look forward to being with you again *soon*, closer than ever, makes Kitty frantic. I will never forget how awful it's been these last endless weeks without you, with this scary grim feeling behind everything I do that my life is meaningless without you and it's only the constant thought of you, the natural assumption that you are near me and thinking of me, that makes being here possible. How angry it makes me when I think it has taken this drastic ghastly separation to make me aware of really how very, very much I love you, my dearest. And I can't bear the prospect of another month without you. I am so lonely for you now, sitting up in bed in this big dark house, I want to cry. I'm so sleepy I can hardly hold my pen, but writing to you helps Kitty to feel a little bit closer to his darling Dub.

These are all the notices of *The Changeling*. As you will see, they are all good for the production and Tony is enormously pleased.[2] By the time

1. Enclosure lost.
2. The play opened February 21. The enclosures are lost.

you get this letter I will have talked to you on the phone so I will save all news. I did get a wild letter from Ted the day after I talked to you last week. It is so soon for this to happen again—I think it does look very bad indeed. I've not heard a word from my mother, though.

Please let me know the moment you hear something definite about the Sutro-Graham Greene film. And do try to avoid any delays in coming here if you possibly can. I've told everyone you're coming at the beginning of April, including John Lehmann—I had a drink with him and Alexis[3] tonight. Seeing Morgan on Wednesday—but all is empty without my horse love. Kitty adores the little self-portrait of Dub and knows how difficult for Old Dub to hold a pen with his hoof.

All Kitty's love to his dearest. K.

I love the Mud Pot scene with Augustus—so true and typical of Gerald, too.

[*Autograph letter*]

Saturday March 4th. [1961]   145.

My dearest love,

Your dear letter was waiting when I got back from Santa Barbara yesterday. It made Dobbin cry, both with sadness and joy. Joy that Kitty loves him so, but sadness to think of him in the "big dark house." Oh, honey, I would like to rush over to you when I hear that; and yet you know that I must stay and get these things settled and done. Quite aside from everything else, it means an extra thousand dollars for the Animals, which they badly need. But, *no matter whether the Sutro film works out or I get travel money from Lewenstein*, I will definitely prepare to come over the first week in April. Once I am with my Kitten, all will be well and things will work out this way or that way.

No sign of Jo and Ben yet. I expect them any day.

Vernon Old called. He has gotten married again, to a girl from San Francisco and says they are very happy. He sent you his love. I am to

3. Alexis Rassine (1919–1992), Lithuanian-born South African dancer, of Russian parentage; he had a flat in Lehmann's house.

see them before I leave. She is studying to be a teacher, at L.A. State, in English literature. So she would probably have been in my class if I had gone back there![1]

It was nice, going to Sta. Barbara again. I had such a strong reassurance of the friendship of the Warshaws. They both sent you their love. Now I feel that this is a relationship which will continue.

Last night to see Brian Bedford in *Five Finger Exercise*. It really is crap and Culver is simply atrocious. And the new boy who plays the German is worse than the other one.[2] But I must say Brian was really quite good! He will be back in London about the same time I shall be going there, with his American friend;[3] and is anxious we shall all get together.

I am still working desperately at the novel. Now I almost begin to dare to say I shall get through it. I am within sight of the final episode in Europe. But I have a feeling there may be a drastic revision of the hashish part. An awful lot of it is irrelevant or merely campy. The story is now much more definitely about Paul—and so far it is just as long!

Dearest sweetheart, I want to whizz this off to you tonight. I am sick to my stomach when I think of you being so unhappy. I do pray that it isn't like that all the time?

Laughton is now in a tizzy, because, after rehearsing with Terry for several days for this test,[4] he is beginning to doubt if Terry really could ever be an actor! I tell him to go ahead at all costs and risk the test. He can't back down now. If he does, Terry's confidence in him will be shattered. Oh dear—!

Sweet darling—we'll be talking on Wednesday. Till then, all my love. And *never* doubt Dobbin's faithful devotion. It couldn't ever ever change.

As always,

D.

[*Typed letter, initialled*]

---

1. Vernon Old (not his real name), Isherwood's first American boyfriend, was a painter and tutored Bachardy in the late 1950s. He had been married once before and had a son. Isherwood taught at Los Angeles State College from September 22, 1959 to June 1960.
2. British actor Roland Culver (1900–1984) played Stanley Harrington; other members of the cast were Jessica Tandy, Juliet Mills, and American actor Robert Dowdell (b. 1932) as the German tutor, replacing British actor Michael Bryant (b. 1928) who played the role in London and on Broadway.
3. Probably Jack Allen, an actor and restaurateur; see below p. 235.
4. That is, screen test, arranged by Laughton.

Sunday
March 5 [1961]
London

My only darling,

Kitty has been very clever, he thinks. Instead of talking to Tony directly, I spoke to his friend George[1] about your being sent for. George is very understanding about separations and in general is much in favor of holding relationships together. Also he likes doing favors and arranging things and whispering into Tony's ear, which he's promised to do, not necessarily letting on that I asked him to do so. I spoke to him on Friday and have not heard anything from him yet about it, but it just might work. The important thing is to get my treasure here—then Tony can be as unreliable as he wants. Even if this other film doesn't materialize we can live here as cheaply as in California anyway. In fact, Kitty will keep his horse—there is still more than a thousand pounds in cat money in the bank here. That will certainly last the Animals till summer at least.

Had dinner last night with Keith Vaughan at Patrick's. We talked about my attitude to painting practically the whole evening. I was very frank about my opinions and problems and though nothing was really accomplished it was good talking to Keith and hearing what he had to say, which was quite sound. Still, the problems are all mine and I'm still grappling with them every day. I'm bound to arrive at some conclusions sooner or later. Right now I'm still at the mercy of good and bad days, sometimes feeling I can do it and sometimes not having the faintest idea of what it is I want to do. But I like working at the Slade now and feel quite relaxed there.

I saw a marvellous production of *Romeo and Juliet* at the Old Vic last week—the first time I've ever really gotten right through a performance of Shakespeare without being bored. It's terribly well directed and acted and marvellous to look at. The production was directed and designed by an Italian named Zeffirelli.[2] Patrick took me backstage afterwards to meet the actors and Zeffirelli was there with Fellini (the film director) and so I met them both briefly. Zeffirelli is queer and quite attractive with blue

1. George Goetschius (1923–2006), American sociologist; he had a live-in relationship with Tony Richardson from 1954 to 1959.
2. Franco Zeffirelli (b. 1923) cut the text of *Romeo and Juliet* for his first-ever stage production and made the fight scenes long and realistic. His stars were Judi Dench (b. 1934) and John Stride (b. 1936).

eyes and silvering temples. Fellini looked like an enormous Wop business man, fat with curly black greasy hair, etc., but probably quite nice.

Also saw at Covent Garden a ballet about Ondine with Margot Fonteyn as Ondine and music by Hans Henze and choreographed by Freddy Ashton. I loved the whole thing—Fonteyn is really wonderful and all the business with the water sprites is perfect camp.³ Ashton was there and remembered me and asked me to call him which I will do— he was very friendly and asked after you and was very pleased when I said you would be coming here soon.

Cecil should be back here from New York before long. I saw Emlyn Williams in a production of three one-act plays and went backstage afterwards to see him.⁴ Molly was there too, having just come back from a month in Barbados and looking very tan and at least fifteen years older than when last seen. They were both very friendly and said they would call me. They haven't yet, but I am out a lot of the time so I may call them. Saw the Tynans at the opening of *The Changeling*. They also said they would call but I've not heard from them yet.

Kitty still pines for his dearest Dub, more and more every day, and longs only for the day when a van pulls up in front of Kitty's house with old Horsey, all blinkered and blanketed, standing up in the rear. How Kitty will spin and dance and lavish his darling with pink kisses and scratchy licks.

All Kitty's love, always, XXXXXXXXX

K.

[*Autograph letter*]

Saturday March 11th, 1961 [Santa Monica]

My dearest darling,

I *must* get a word off to you tonight but it will only be very short, because I'm so behindhand with everything. I have been working like

---

3. Frederick Ashton (1904–1988), Peruvian-born British dancer and choreographer, created the 1958 ballet about the water nymph Ondine especially for Fonteyn (1919–1991), longtime Prima Ballerina of the Royal Ballet, and commissioned German composer Hans Werner Henze (1926–2012) to write the score.
4. *Lunch Hour* by John Mortimer, *The Form* by N.F. Simpson, and *A Slight Ache* by Harold Pinter at the Arts Theatre.

a demon to get "Paul" finished, and I really believe I'll do it by next Tuesday! But tomorrow there will be my first lecture at UCLA and *nothing* is prepared. And yesterday night I got so hopped up on coffee and Dexamyl[1] that I couldn't sleep, and got up at six and started working again. So I must sleep tonight!

I'm still doubtful about the hashish scene. I cut it and cut it but it doesn't seem to me to belong. Maybe it is far too late to introduce all these characters, and yet in a way they're needed. You and Edward[2] will have to decide about this. There really is no hurry. I just want to have the main bulk of the book finished and out of my hair.

Charles and Terry are now going to do a simple interview-test for Billy Wilder.[3] Next week. Charles has been pestering me so much with the material for his reading tour. I won't let him in this house, because he sits and sits. I go over there.

Jo and Ben are back and send you their warmest love. I have only seen them once so far because you can imagine all the luaus and stuff people are throwing for them.[4]

I talked quite a long while to Ted. He is out and quite rational. But *still* he said something about coming over to London!

Another very cooperative letter from Sutro. It does look as if the deal might really go through.

But I will come over anyway to my own love. He must not be left any longer or he will begin not to miss Old Dub so much, and then Dub would arrive and be an anticlimax.

The legs came off the couch in my study. Not the legs which you put on, but the board to which they were nailed. This board was merely glued on; so Mr. Callahan[5] is nailing it on right now.

Sweet darling love, I love you so very very much, and you are all my life to me and my reason for doing anything and not just relapsing into gloom. Richard writes such strange half-mad letters from Wyberslegh,

1. Dextroamphetamine, an upper, combined with a barbiturate, amobarbitol, to offset its effect.
2. Edward Upward (1903–2009), English novelist and schoolmaster; Isherwood's closest friend from schooldays at Repton and university at Cambridge. Isherwood showed Upward work in progress throughout his life.
3. Austro-Hungarian-born American film director, producer, screenwriter (1906–2002).
4. They had been on their annual, several-months-long trip to Florida and the Caribbean, and were being welcomed home with parties, including at least one Hawaiian-style feast.
5. A handyman.

full of hate against the local people. Resentment is certainly the hereditary disease of our family and it is only thanks to Kitty that old Dub is able to keep it in the background. Oh, he does adore his darling Kitty so!

Looking forward to Wednesday's call from his dear.

With always always love,

D.

Less than a month, now!

[*Typed letter, initialled, autograph additions*]

March 13, 1961 [London]

My dearest darling,

His kitten thinks and thinks about his horse every day and pines so for him and plans and plans for the arrival of his treasure. Kitty has already bought lots of hay and strewn it about the house so old Dobbin will feel at home right away. Kitty's even made a nest of hay which he sleeps in every night so he'll be sure to smell right for his old dear.

As you say in your letter of the 4th, the important thing is that you get here, as soon as possible—then we'll go from there. Something is bound to turn up, even if Sutro or Tony don't produce. Tony has gone off to Manchester to start the filming of *A Taste of Honey* without a word about Dub's shipment, but Kitty is seeing his friend George for dinner this week and will do more prodding with his paw, the claws ever so slightly unsheathed for added emphasis. Tony is such a queen! We mustn't forget that and so not rely too heavily on him.

Katkin is painting and painting away, five hours every day, with little results so far but he is still determined that something will come of all this. I have the most unsubstantiated superstitious feeling that I will only start to do anything interesting once I have painted out this mass of conventional ideas and timid, boring prejudices and fears I have about what a painting is *supposed* to be. Again, it is all a matter of belief in myself. And I think I can only be forced to that by this tedious process of eliminating bit by bit all the obstructive nonsense that is sitting dully between me and what I would like to do and would enjoy doing. I can really only do this myself, and though it helps to have someone to encourage me and make suggestions, the real battle is with myself. I have tried to explain to Keith my problems and to a certain extent I think he understands, though it doesn't really matter if he does or not as long as I do.

Keith is a funny, astringent little thing—full of sourness and disapproval and yet at heart I think he is probably quite sweet and affectionate in a cool sort of way. He is suffering from disenchantment and disappointment and feels somehow he has been taken advantage of and used badly and rather than let that happen again he strikes first. He is quite frank and tough in his criticisms and inclined to sound a little snide though I don't think he means to. His ass has just gotten terribly tight with stored resentment against what he thinks is the cheap success and undeserved praise that has been lavished on people he disapproves of, Cecil Beaton for one. Keith's mouth got very small and tight as he mentioned in passing that my position at the Slade was like that of other "special" people who had studied there (his tone implied superficial, pretentious people who sashay about disregarding protocol and giving themselves airs) like Cecil or Peggy Ashcroft's daughter or Coldstream's maiden aunt, etc.[1] He doesn't quite know he's doing it, but he's really attacking anyone who thinks of himself as special or outside of official channels, anyone who has the gall to dare to push and demand special treatment—because he himself always put up with ordinary circumstances and made his way on his own. He suspects me of being frivolous and unsturdy, pampered and self-pampering—and yet I still think he likes me. At least he thinks I'm quite ridiculous and helpless, and sympathetic in spite of being absurd. And so in the end he's quite well disposed towards me and helps me and takes an interest, all of which I'm glad of. The only thing is he's only at the Slade two days a week and even on those days he is only around for a few minutes. Nevertheless, I've never worked so hard at painting and one way or another I will come up with something.

I am keeping up the portrait drawing, too—I drew Rosamond on Saturday and did three really quite good drawings. She really liked them I think and wants to buy them and suggested that I draw her daughter-in-law.[2] Hester Chapman is wild about the drawings I did of her and is

1. The daughter of English actress Peggy Ashcroft (1907–1991) was Eliza Hutchinson (b. 1941). Coldstream's aunt is unidentified, and is perhaps only a figure of speech.
2. Mary Makins (Mollie) (b. 1935), second wife from 1959 to 1984 of Hugo Philipps (1928–1999); in 1989 she married John Julius Norwich.

going to try to get one of them put onto the book jacket of her new book. She also has relatives and such she wants me to draw.

Elaine Tynan just called a few minutes ago and suggested we have dinner tonight—at 10:30 though, because she's working on a play. I was just going to complain to my Horse about the wicked Tynans because it's been weeks since I called them. Molly and Emlyn are still in Kitty's small black ledger, second only to Miss Ure who is unequalled in her abuse and negligence of the poor lonely Kitten—not one finger of hers has been lifted to stroke Kitty or even acknowledge his forlorn presence. Hell has no fury (or memory) like that of an unpetted pussy.

I did have tea yesterday with Pat Trevor-Roper[3] who was very nice though suffering more than I'd remembered from the great English malady—snide disapproval, of almost everyone we talked about. Freddy Ashton was awfully sweet to me and we got along terribly well and laughed a lot—he is really amusing and so sympathetic. He sends his love to you. Cecil is back from N.Y. but off to Paris. He should be back by now though—I will call him tomorrow. Patrick had me to dinner on Friday with Pamela Brown,[4] who I liked a lot, and a colored dancer named Christine Something who was from Santa Monica.

I see so many plays that I will soon run out. Last week I saw Tutin in *The Devils* by John Whiting, based on *The Devils of Loudun*.[5] She plays a depraved, sex-craving hunchback nun and is surprisingly good, though I thought the play artificially sensational and very predictable in its would-be profound meaning and approach to religion. It is surprising though how she has developed her technique—the once thin scratchy voice is very rich and versatile now. But oh dear how dull to dwell on naughty nuns. (GOOD LINE)

So glad that my dear is in sight of the end of the book. I hope it is still going well. I long to read it. Love to Jo & Ben, the Warshaws, too, but not Brian Bedford. He better not be trying any five finger exercises on my hooved darling. All my love, K.

[*Autograph letter*]

3. Patrick Trevor-Roper (1916–2004), British ophthalmologist.
4. English star of stage and screen (1917–1975).
5. Whiting (1917–1963) adapted Aldous Huxley's 1952 historical novel for the Royal Shakespeare Company.

The Basket. Saturday March 18 [1961]

My darling,

After talking to you this morning, I decided to get the typescript of "Paul" off to you right away; so I rushed it to the post office before it closed and you should have it before this letter, if not at the same time.

Since I talked to you, my curiosity overcame me, because there had been no call from Gerald about it, so I called Michael.[1] He was very grand and said that Gerald and he had decided not to discuss it until they'd both read it. (I'd never said Michael *might* read it, as it happens.) Of course, said Michael, we're rather full up next week, but maybe we could discuss it on Wednesday. Well, I got boiling mad, but didn't show it, and said merely that I had to have the manuscript back at once, so would he please finish it tonight. Gerald has read it already. What all this bodes, I don't know; but I have a nasty feeling that it won't be pleasant. Oh well, fuck. I don't really care. I cared much more that Gavin liked it; indeed said it was much the best thing I'd ever written. But what I really want to know is what you'll think of this revision; have any of the values of the original been lost, in your opinion. And then what Edward will think. His address is: 154 Turney Road, Dulwich, London S.E. 21. His telephone number is, or was, Brixton 1817. Of course I would like to hear from him—I know I shall from you—*before* I see him; that is, I hope he'll write me about the story. There should be plenty of time for that.

Charles was over here all this afternoon. Terry apparently *looked* very good in the test—which, as I think I told you, was just an interview; no acting. But his accent was terrible. So now it's thought that he should try to improve it. So he will stick around with Charles, go on tour with him in April, etc. Charles is coming to England in July to make a picture for Disney, and he says he will speak to Disney about my working on the script which needs polishing.[2] The only point of doing this would be that Disney is a far more reliable payer than either Sutro or Tony. Well, we shall see. All I know is, I must get to my Kitty and be with him again at all costs. Dobbin

1. Jay Michael Barrie (1912–2001), friend and secretary to Gerald Heard from the late 1940s; once a singer, he had lived until 1955 as a monk at Trabuco, the monastery sixty miles south of Los Angeles that Heard founded in 1942 and gave to the Vedanta Society in 1949.
2. That is, American producer, director, animator Walt Disney (1901–1966); the project did not go forward.

will have so much to tell Kitty about his love, when he sees him. How he has realized what a priceless treasure he has. And the risks one takes with love are *hair-raising*. And yet, in a way, it seems as if one has to keep taking them. Because I'm sure you will agree that it was good that Kitty went to England the way he did—even though it made both the poor Animals suffer so.

Am going down now to have supper with Jo and Ben, and to be shown all their latest slides of their winter fishings and swimmings etc. Well, I'm glad Kitty will be spared that one! Tomorrow, Evelyn Hooker is giving me supper early at the Miramar—which I shall never really like again because it was from there that they took Kitty away in a basket, mewing so, that grim morning—and then we are going to my recital or whatever you call it at UCLA. I'll read *Sherlock Holmes, Moby Dick,* Virginia Woolf, Joyce, Conrad, Wells and Ray Bradbury.

It's a cold but beautiful night, with the very new moon shining over the ocean and the last light just going. My Kitty is sound asleep, I hope, in his fur. A breath of love will make his whiskers stir at this moment, but it won't wake him. Maybe he'll smile in his sleep, and begin to dream of fat little birds and juicy mice.

All my love, darling sweet adored treasure, D.

Just spoke to your mother on the phone. Ted is out of hospital, but she feels he isn't properly cured yet. She wrote you, but got her letter back because it was insufficiently stamped. I explained to her about postage to England and the advantage of using these air letters.

[*Typed letter, initialled*]

Tuesday March 21 [1961, London]

My darling Horse,

Here is a picture of his Kitty, already watching the skies for the great iron bird that is going to deliver his old dear Dub to him.[1] How Kitty's whiskers and fur tingle with excitement and expectation. Kitty's Easter vacation starts tomorrow and lasts for a whole month, so Kitty will be able to devote every moment to making his dear snug and comfortable.

1. Bachardy enclosed a black-and-white photograph cut from a newspaper of a long-haired white cat looking up.

I talked to Cecil yesterday and he was so sweet and has invited me to the country at Easter time, for five days. I was quite dreading the holiday which would seem endless in London with everything firmly shut down, but now I'm really looking forward to it.

I went to Brighton on Sunday with Patrick and had lunch and spent the afternoon with Richard Addinsell,[2] who has a flat there. He is very nice, and cozy to be with in the nicest English way. And the weather was beautiful—the first time Kitty had been at the sea since he went away from the stable and his only love. Kitty thinks of nothing but his Dobbin's arrival and counts the seconds. All Kitty's love.

P.S. George says Tony has agreed to send for you any time, but wants to be coaxed and pleaded with, which is rather difficult since he is in Manchester. I will call him tomorrow. The idea is that you will come here to work on the book of the musical.[3] But under no circumstances should you change your reservations of the sixth because Tony is so unreliable and now very much involved with this film. Once here, you can probably arrange to be given the cost of the ticket to England. Or perhaps Sutro will pay your fare here and Tony the fare back. In any case, just come. That is all Kitty cares about.

All love and Kitty kisses, K.

[*Autograph letter with enclosure*]

Wednesday morning
March 22 [1961, London]

My only love,

His dear letter and his precious story have just arrived, both smelling so deliciously of HORSE that Kitty's nostrils are in a state of nervous excitement. He has rubbed himself all over, the furriest parts and all, with Dub's scent.

I can't wait to start "Paul" but I will restrain myself until I have enough time to read it right through in one sitting and then write

2. British composer (1904–1977), especially of film music.
3. That is, the Berlin musical. Richardson and Oscar Lewenstein, partners on many productions, were evidently both interested at this point.

immediately. Then I will call Edward and arrange to take it out to him. I think I can read it tomorrow morning. Today I must have lunch with Tony's friend George and try to negotiate further to finance my darling's mailing. Tonight I am seeing a stage designer Loudon Sainthill and his friend for dinner. The friend is either one of the head people or even *the* head person at the Redfern and I am taking the old display of drawings along to show them.[1] Today will be the last day of school. Friday I must definitely begin work here at the house, or I'm afraid I never shall. Of course I dread it. I met just outside of the Slade the other evening by purest chance Amiya. She was out shopping with her chauffeur. It was so odd running into her like that—I felt as though I were recognizing someone in a dream. I'm having dinner tomorrow evening with Morgan at the Reform Club. John Lehmann and I have both been very nice to each other. Freddy Ashton let me draw him yesterday—I am not pleased with the drawings but he sweetly said he would sit again. I can't remember if I told you in yesterday's letter that Cecil has invited me to the country for five days at Easter.

To bring in the saddle bag when my dear gets transported: a large bottle of Dexamyl, a can of ordinary black pepper & Kitty's blue denim jacket.

All my love XXXXXXX K.

I long so to have my own dear near again. I love you so much more than anything in the world. Please be very careful of Kitty's old Dobbin.

I will call on Sat. I do hope the "recitals" are going well.

[*Autograph letter*]

Sunday [26 March 1961, London]

My own darling—

"Paul" is absolutely sensational. I didn't give you any idea at all yesterday how really marvellous I think it is. You have lost none of the original values—far from it. There is so much now that is so much better than before, and you know how much I loved it when I first read

---

1. Loudon Sainthill (1918–1969), Australian-born painter and theater designer, and Harry Tatlock Miller (1913–1989), Australian-born writer, critic, and curator, who was a director at the Redfern Gallery in Cork Street.

it. So much, in fact, that I was a little afraid of reading it again, afraid it would be changed or not as good as I'd remembered. But none of it. I was even more excited by it than before. I *laughed* so much, and cried, too, and was so moved by Paul. His character seemed even clearer and more lifelike to me this reading. And Augustus is a triumph. *So* much better than before—absolutely adorable and silly and yet not superficial or bogus but really *about* something. Gerald should be so marvellous. And the episode at Eureka is infinitely improved. And the *pachuco* affair so convincing and right now.[1] Kitty is so proud of his darling, so proud and pleased and happy. How Kitty cried to think his own treasure had worked so hard and created with his heavy hooves and horse mind such a marvellous story.

Kitty has taken several notes about minor things he wants to discuss with his dear when he has him here, little questions and thoughts that Kitty had while reading "Paul." In fact, Kitty longed to read it right through again but knew that Dub wanted Edward to have it as soon as possible, so Kitty took it off this afternoon and delivered it personally—a good thing, too, because Edward said they were all going off to the Isle of Whyt (Wyte, Wight?) on Wednesday.[2] I do hope he will read it right away and write to Dub before he goes off.

My dearest sweetheart, I'm really so excited about this book—I can't tell you enough or give you any idea really how impressed and thrilled Kitty is. Kitty looks forward to telling his Horse more when the Animals are reunited and Kitty can purr endless endearments into his darling's soft ears.

Waiting impatiently for his only treasure,

his loving and devoted

K. XXXXXXXXX

[*Autograph letter*]

1. The episode with the teenage Mexican-American gang members; *pachucos* were a particular, self-identified social group, with their own slang and style of dress.
2. The Upwards had a family home in Sandown, Isle of Wight, and spent all their holidays there.

Wednesday March 29th. [1961]   [Santa Monica]

Dearest sweet treasure,

Just got your dear letter with praise of "Paul." I am so happy you like him. Somehow he is specially yours. This whole book is for you. It will be dedicated to you of course. But it will also be sort of privately dedicated in a way only Kitty and Dobbin will understand, because this is Dobbin's way of laying the best he knows how to do at Kitty's paws. It is a little tiny token of all the love and gratefulness he feels. *Merci, Kitty, d'avoir existé!*[1]

I am sending a carbon copy of this letter to one address and this one to the other, so you will hear from me as soon as possible, even if you are down in the country with Cecil. (But, horrors, I have just realized I don't have his country address! Will get it if I can.)

I now have my passport and my ticket. My plane is BOAC flight 592, arriving North London Airport at 5:50 p.m. (London time) on Friday afternoon, April 7th.

I have the pepper and 100 Dexamyls. I thought I knew what the denim jacket looked like, but now I'm almost sure that the one you mean is the very light sky-blue jacket. If this is wrong, send me a cable. Otherwise, that's the one I shall bring.

If you want to call me at the very last moment, I shall be having supper that night with Jo and Ben and can certainly be reached there between seven and eight on the evening of April 6th. Gladstone 47221.

That's all for now, because Dobbin must simply fly to see the income-tax man.

All my love and kisses and longing thoughts of the Animals' sweet meeting.

D.

Stupid gaga old Dobbin sent the other copy of this letter off with only 7 cents stamps on it. Now he doesn't know if it'll be returned here, or sent on to London for cat money. So it seems best to send *this* copy to London, too. I have now found the name of Cecil's village from our 1957 pocket diary, so will send a cable there for Easter.

No word from Sutro yet. But what the hell. I feel sure something good

1. Thank you, Kitty, for being!

will come up, sooner or later. Even if it doesn't, we'll manage. *All* that matters is to feel the beat of that little pink coral heart under the fur.

These photos just arrived from Santa Barbara.[2]

[*Typed letter, initialled, with autograph additions and enclosures*]

Sunday [March 26, 1961, London]

My own darling,

I've finished reading "Paul." I have various reservations beyond page 130. As I said to you yesterday on the phone, everything up to that point is marvellous—better than I'd remembered, and by this time my memories of it had taken on such proportions I was more than a little apprehensive about reading it again. But really, I loved it even more, and was terribly moved by it. Augustus Parr is so much more effective now, and I adored Paul, and I laughed so much. The *pachuco* affair and

2. Six black-and-white snapshots of Isherwood in his UCSB office, one with colleagues and two with an unidentified student.

the episode at Eureka are so much more convincing and amusing and completely under your control.

My reservations about the last part may well be due to a breaking of the spell. Because I couldn't finish last night, I came to the end part this morning without the full warm-up from the first 130 pages. I want so much to reread the whole thing, but I know you want Edward to have it as soon as possible so I will wait until after he's read it. Then I can see if it's only my mood of this morning. I hope, too, that by then you will be right here so I can tell you exactly what, if anything, still bothers me.

Kitty finds it very difficult to put his claw right on the trouble. The whole Anselm Oakes episode seems now in some way invented and out of place, compared to the reality and seriousness of the California part. I am bothered terribly by Paul's motives for taking you to such a tacky successor to Augustus Parr. [It] seems queeny of him in the wrong way, and the whole idea of Hell and his exploration of Evil seem glaringly like "ideas," compared with the feeling I got from the earlier parts that it was all happening and that the ideas, though certainly there and important, were so much a part of the events. The intent behind the events, the idea or whatever it is I mean, seems to take over in the last part and becomes much more apparent, and therefore out of style, as well as being not as convincing in relation to the first part.

A great deal of my reaction is due largely to my vision of what your critics will be able to misread into the last part. You have been so frank and open and uncautious that I'm afraid "the Others" will dismiss *everything* as hocus-pocus and claim that your attitude to Augustus Parr's teachings is no more serious than your attitude to hashish dreams, and they will accuse you of dabbling irresponsibly in "the unusual" for its own sake. I know one can't let fears of what "the Others" will think interfere with one's work, but I am scared that you have made it too easy to find fault with your actions in the Paris scenes.

Your firm self-criticism, of which I am liable to complain, is perfect in the earlier parts of "Paul," an ideal buffer between you, the worldly, successful writer, and the exotic thing you are doing. Your relentlessly dim view of yourself, which nevertheless permits you to go on with Augustus's teaching, is terrific, and makes your experiences all the more impressive. Perversely enough, I felt a slight lack of this self-critical analysis of your behavior in the Paris scenes. Would the cynical "I" of California have permitted himself any such participation in an obviously "evil," bogus situation created by someone like Anselm? I fear devastating parallels between Anselm and Augustus will be seen by your detractors. And your victimization by Anselm creates an impression of vulnerable susceptibility which is completely lacking in your character in the first part of the story.

I know you are not *really* victimized, you don't really take Anselm seriously at any point, but the fact that you are *there*, unable to control or defend yourself should an humiliating raid take place, is certainly inconsistent with the "I" of California. I think further explanations of your "mood," your attitude to the events of the Paris evening are necessary, and, I hesitate to suggest it, a little more about Paul's mood and attitude, to Anselm in particular. Any suggestion of naughtiness or gullibility, on either of your parts, should be avoided. There should be no self-indulgence for the sake of what could be called a cheap thrill.

The description of your experiences under the hashish is certainly not the description of a cheap thrill, but I'm afraid it may nevertheless be called one by people who think in prejudiced generalities, and most everybody does when it comes to drugs. And the lack of a serious, scientific approach to drugs in Paris will reflect unfavorably on your very serious and careful approach to God in California. You and Paul will be called hysterics out for *any* thrill, and I know this is not only not your intent but, in your frankness, open-mindedness and unpretentiousness, you have left yourself too much open to the misconstruing and deliberate misunderstanding of others. The "I" of the story should in some way recognize and resist the possible humiliation or embarrassment of being caught in Anselm's den, not by the police necessarily but by some malevolent associate of Augustus, who might read a newspaper report of an arrest.[1]

I think it is the old stand I'm taking again, about your having too little respect for the "I" of the book. Your tone with him is still too critical, too unrelenting. In the first part of "Paul" you are there long before

---

1. The letter breaks off here, and a new attempt begins, below, revising the preceding three paragraphs.

anyone else to judge yourself and then, all of a sudden, all caution seems thrown to the wind and you are allowing yourself to be taken in by an old fake. But isn't it a luxury to allow oneself to be any kind of victim? Would the "I" who is struggling in California have allowed this indulgence? I don't know really. Somewhere I feel you are consciously dismissing all respectable, sensible behavior and saying it's not as easy as all that, and Paul's refusal to be classified or behave in any logical sense is marvellous, but somehow his preoccupation with "evil" doesn't convince me, and I can't think he wouldn't have called Anselm a little fool as well, except the absence of surface "seriousness" in Anselm, as in the Existentialists, would probably interest Paul. I am all confused now and *must* read it again, when my darling is very near I hope, breathing warmly into Kitty's fur.

The reunion with Waldemar in Berlin is so good, but I felt a little uneasy about finding Ronny and Ruthie sitting up in the bar. I will stop picking. I have not elaborated at all on what is so terrific about the book. And *never*, for one minute, am I the least bit alarmed about my few misgivings. I feel it is just a matter of Dub's turning a tiny screw with his deft hoof, and instantly bringing everything into perfect focus. I do think it is a question of hanging onto Paul—I want to know what *he's* doing while you are under the drug. And if he has really gone beyond you in a sense with his drugs, would he bother to show you Hell? Wouldn't he disdain showing you? I wonder that he would take the chance of your perhaps not getting the intended reaction and just going headlong into a delicious orgy. Paul is just a little bit too openly serious about his final experiences. In the California scenes he never allows himself to show this seriousness, at least to you, but I feel it is *always* there.

I am going to call Edward now and arrange to take the manuscript to him today, if he can be reached. All my love to my adored and constantly anticipated Horsey from his tiny K.

[*Draft letter, not mailed, original now lost*]

Saturday, April 1 [1961]   Reddish House,
                                                  Broadchalke, Salisbury[1]

My own darling Horse—

His little telegram came this morning to make Kitty very happy. And
Cecil was pleased, too, and sends his love to you. He is going to New
York on Thursday but will only stay a week and so will be back here soon
after my dear is installed in his new stable.

We all arrived here about five on Thursday afternoon after a
nightmare two hours on the train, which was so jammed with holiday
weekenders that Cecil and I couldn't even sit together. "We all" includes
a set designer named Alan Tagg, whom Cecil has also invited with what
I begin to suspect is his unerring flair for bringing the wrong people
together—you remember Froska Monster, I know.[2] Tagg is a sandy-
haired, soft-spoken man of about thirty-five who looks like Jean Marais,
but his would-be handsome face is prematurely lined with deep, sour
furrows. He is a precious, rarified queen with a fake-shy manner which
doesn't nearly conceal an intense, mean, jealous little nature. He has
worked with Cecil on various shows and does plays here on his own as
well—Billy Liar is the only one I've seen and that seemed quite good,
though it's difficult to tell from one set.[3]

Cecil apparently likes him—he must like him to have him around
so much—but Tagg still takes great pains to speak Cecil's language and
be very much "in" with him, which may be for my benefit. I think he is
probably somewhat jealous of me. I wouldn't be surprised if Cecil, in his
curious and surprising tactlessness, didn't tell him I was quite a good
artist, or something else to alarm him—set designers so seldom can

1. Cecil Beaton's country house in Wiltshire.
2. Euphrasis (Frosca) Munster, a Russian émigré who lived in Paris in the 1920s; though
married at the time, she had been the last lover and also a subject of bisexual English painter
Christopher Wood, an opium addict, who threw himself under a train in 1930. Isherwood and
Bachardy had met her on a previous visit to Beaton's country house and had shared a train
compartment with her on their return to London. She spoke French all the way, excluding
Bachardy and intensely irritating Isherwood.
3. Tagg (1928–2002) worked with the English Stage Company at the Royal Court, where he
made his name with the set for Look Back in Anger (1956). Jean Marais (1913–1998) was the
beautiful French actor who was Cocteau's lover and starred in his Beauty and the Beast (1946)
and Orphée (1949). Bachardy spent most of one night that weekend in Tagg's bed with him,
and later a night or two at Tagg's London flat. Neither Beaton nor Isherwood knew.

draw and usually feel bothered because of it. But whatever his attitude to me may be, we would never in a million years like each other and any hint of similarity between us would only make each watch the other more closely. This in itself is quite enough to make me feel trapped for the weekend, and more than a little bored.

The effort to be nice to Tagg is very tiring, and the strain of it makes it very difficult for me to relax with Cecil, who anyway is *not* the easiest person in the world to feel at ease with. For one thing, I'm always aware of his trigger-sensitivity, which can be released by the slightest tainted breath. And yet he expects frank and firm opinions, and for one to take a stand—but it had better be the right stand. In the past two days I've really seen Cecil more clearly than ever before and, though I'm interested, I can't help being bored at the same time, and depressed.

In a funny kind of way, Cecil's not a gentleman. He is much too self-centered to be really concerned with people beyond the outward forms of politeness, and these keep slipping, particularly under close observation, and I see enormous selfishness and more than a little vulgarity in him. His sensitivity, if exposed to anything unrefined or unpretty, is exaggerated to the point of hysteria. To spend a night or two, for instance, in an ordinary hotel room, becomes exquisite torture for him.

Yet, though the room I am staying in here has all the appearances of style and comfort, I am exquisitely uncomfortable in it. Because it is more or less his dressing room, the closet is nearly full to capacity and there is no room to hang my clothes or drawers to put my socks and underwear into. I share his bathroom, but the door from it to his bedroom won't close because the carpet's too thick and so I can never make a sound without his hearing it if he's in his room. After Cecil has taken his bath I must wait at least half an hour for the water to be lukewarm. This morning while he bathed he had records of lessons in Italian playing over the loudspeaker system so loudly that I could hardly read my newspaper. All of this he apologizes for profusely, but in a self-excusing tone which gives little satisfaction to anyone else.

And any kind of communication with Cecil in this weekend's setup is nearly impossible. Either this queen, Tagg, is primly present, or else Cecil's poor old mother, who is greatly aged since we were here together, is wandering about. When I arrived I was terribly shocked to see her. She floated stiffly into the hall like a great pale blowfish, with small, watery, unseeing eyes and wisps of white hair like fins at the sides of her head. She didn't remember me and indeed forgets me in the course of a sleep.

Obstinately deaf and repetitiously talkative, she takes great delight in teasing Cecil, which she does by asking him the same question two or three times in the course of a few minutes, or by nagging him for drink and then changing her mind. Last night she asked for more wine, which Cecil is terribly stingy with—he seldom provides more than a glassful at dinner. When Cecil ignored her, she asked Tagg for more and he, queeny-solicitous, gave her some of his unfinished glass. As Cecil was removing the dessert plates she asked again for some wine. Cecil lost his temper and snapped: "Will you wait *one minute*?! I'm exhausted doing all the butling myself and you'll just have to wait. Now will you be quiet?" His tone was very sharp and she was clearly offended, having heard every word without the slightest difficulty. When Cecil finally went down to the cellar and brought up another bottle of wine, she immediately got up to go to her room, turning her back on Cecil and very sweetly saying goodnight only to Tagg and me.

I can't blame Cecil for getting irritated, but still it is very embarrassing when he does. He also makes funny remarks about his mother while she is in the room and says she only enjoys making him fag for her.

[*Unfinished draft letter, original now lost*]

·   ·   ·

Kitty loves his dear more than anything in the world.

[*Autograph note*]

Monday October 16th [1961]   Casa de los Animales

Dearest own treasured love,

I must get a few lines off to you tonight although they will be hasty and not say all I want to. Oh, when I unpacked the suitcase this afternoon and found the Kitty had slipped a note of love in amongst the suits, tears ran down Old Dobbin's muzzle. He sent Kitty a cable last night to tell him that all Dobbin's love was in London with Kitty.

The flight was all right, except that we waited another hour and a half, much of it actually on the runway with the engines going. The pilot frankly said that he had hoped to leave and then just found he couldn't; it had thickened up again. For a while I, and the other passengers, really thought we were going to be sent back home to wait till tomorrow. But then off we shot and of course after the first thousand feet it was bright sunshine all the way. Jo and Ben met me at the airport, and I really don't feel exhausted and I believe I will sleep normally. If not, I have Jocelyn's pills. (Am not used to this tyepwriter!)

The Casa looks beautiful beyond all belief, specially polished up by Dorothy. We met this morning, over at the Laughtons',[1] and kissed. (I

1. Bachardy concealed this note in Isherwood's suitcase as Isherwood packed to leave London for Los Angeles on October 15. Isherwood had arrived April 6, 1961, and stayed with Bachardy at the Burtons' house in Hampstead. In England, he continued work on *Down There on a Visit*, which was accepted for publication by Methuen, and he worked with Auden and Kallman on the Berlin musical. He also visited his brother twice at Wyberslegh and reviewed his mother's estate arrangements with the family lawyer in London to obtain the money left to him in her will.

discovered from Jo and Ben that she was anyhow planning on kissing *me!*) Jo also says that she was so delighted because you wrote her and put "love." She is really an angel, and looks a little slimmer, I think.

Terrific heatwave here. It was a hundred and five *on the beach* yesterday. Today isn't so bad. But anyhow this house is always cool and I am sleeping in the workroom again. The sun is setting right into the ocean already. Oh, how beautiful it would all be, if Kitty were here!

Do you want me to call the McKinnons? If so, to say what, and at what number?

A tiresome thing—I came away without the notes and beginning of the new Ramakrishna chapter.[2] They should be all together and on the top shelf but one, of the right-hand bookcase in the dining room. Nothing much to mail—just a few pages. You could put them into one of the envelopes. Now that I think of it, I am ashamed of the sloppy way I left all that stuff. The truth was, I was feeling so utterly wretched at parting from my dear. But I am so proud of him too and want him so much to take every opportunity he gets in London and not come back prematurely. I have never *known* what real pride was until I saw my Kitty that night at the Redfern in his triumph.[3]

I called your mother this morning but no answer. I will try again tomorrow and I will call Ted and Vince this evening. I have already made quite a lot of contacts and dates, as I want to keep busy. For example: tonight, Gerald and Michael, tomorrow, Jo and Ben, Wednesday, Swami, Thursday, Jerry Lawrence, Friday, Paul Millard, Saturday, Laughtons, Sunday, Ivan Moffat, Monday, Carter and Dick![4] Chris Wood[5] is in New York. Gavin and Tom Wright I saw today, just before their departure on a tour by car to Oak Creek, Canyon de Chelly, etc. etc. So I gave them a lot of dope and lent them a map.[6] They begged me to come with them,

1. Dorothy Miller also cleaned for Charles Laughton and Elsa Lanchester, who owned 147 Adelaide Drive next door to Isherwood and Bachardy.
2. For the biography Isherwood was writing, *Ramakrishna and His Disciples* (1965).
3. Bachardy's first-ever gallery show opened at the Redfern, October 2, 1961, with a glamorous, well-attended party.
4. Carter Lodge (d. 1995), American business manager and former lover of English playwright John van Druten, and Dick Foote, American actor and singer, Lodge's subsequent longterm companion.
5. English man of means (d. 1976); he lived with Gerald Heard in London in the 1930s, emigrated with Heard to Los Angeles in 1937, and remained a member of Heard's circle after the breakup of their domestic relationship.
6. Isherwood had made several similar tours, once with Bachardy, see below, pp. 174 and 191. Dope is American slang for information.

and in a way it would have been fun, but I have to stay on deck here. They sent you their best love.

I called Paul Millard because I thought it was tactful, from your point of view. He was bubbling with enthusiasm. He said: "I really look forward completely to seeing you," whatever that meant. He tells me Dorothy Parker[7] is in town. Also that [a friend of] the Brackett[s] is being held on a charge of rape. He used to go into the apartments of middle-aged women, always in the Norma Place area, and threaten them, with a sheet over his head and just a hole in it to look through. It seems that Charlie thought this hugely funny, when it was found out. However, I'll believe all this when I hear more details!

The Heinz 57 Varieties people sent me a whole case of goodies—canned soups, sauces, etc.—with a note congratulating me on my 57th birthday!

The Pearson's Liquor Store has been turned into a sort of Tudor mansion, almost too grand to enter; and you should see the poor old San Vicente market. It's as bad now as the Westward Ho.[8] All my love, and let me hear from you soon—I was going to say; but can you imagine the stupidity of that half-witted old Dobbin—he typed it all on part of the letter that was going to be on the outside, so it is a complete fuckup and I must put it into an envelope!

Never mind, I'll write some more while I'm at it. Did you see the two terrible notices poor Alan Sillitoe got?[9] I don't know if I should write him. Maybe better just you call him and make my apologies. However, I very much liked The Fox in the Attic, the Richard Hughes book I took with me on the plane.

I'm starting back at the gym tomorrow, and today I ate Tiger's Milk[10] and lots of carrots and everything healthy.

Be *sure* to let me know about any reviews![11]

---

7. Leftist American poet, short-story writer, journalist, critic (1893–1967).

8. Both had been turned into "super" markets.

9. Sillitoe (1928–2010), British poet, novelist, and playwright, had become well known with his first novel *Saturday Night and Sunday Morning* (1958) and a short-story collection *The Loneliness of the Long Distance Runner* (1959), both made into films. *Key to the Door* (1961), his third novel, was badly received.

10. It also came in bar form, but Isherwood probably meant that he drank it as previously.

11. For the Redfern show. The opening was covered by *The Evening Standard* in Donald Purgavie's "In London Last Night," Oct. 3, p. 18, and reviews appeared in *The Times*, Oct. 6, p. 20. and *The Arts Review*, Oct. 7–21, p. 16.

Oh, that money of my mother's has arrived already and been deposited in our account—$14, 038.50!!! So the Animals will not starve. The money from Methuen's hasn't arrived, however, at the Chase Manhattan. I hope the English didn't grab it.[12]

Mountains of second-class mail—including all kinds of books and appeals for charities, and your film magazine sent regularly. Now I have to attend to the problem of the trees. I don't think we should cut down the live ones, do you?

All my love, sweetest angel and goodnight.

Drub.

[*Typed letter, signed*]

October 19, Thursday. [1961]   La Casa.

Nothing yet from my Kitty, which doesn't surprise me, knowing how busy he is, but I think I'll send off another signal from the western stable. So far, I've sent a cable, and a letter, and a bottle of Sebb[1] which should have arrived, as it went airmail, unless it was seized by the customs or exploded at 40,000 feet.

Am still in the process of tidying up. I got the mountains of second-class mail read through and destroyed and the trash people removed it all yesterday. This morning a rather sultry fire inspector, masked by thick dark glasses, called and informed me that we have to clear the whole slope, including the city land, right down to the road. However, I don't think this will really cost much extra, because Mr. Gardner is going to do it; and anyhow it is ridiculous to stick around arguing with the city over a few bucks when there is this quite alarming fire hazard right below the house, and it's the house that would burn, not the city.[2]

I started the gym again on Tuesday and am going again today. Very stiff but already responding to the old reins, and filling myself up with

12. His advance for *Down There on a Visit*, which he hoped was not subject to U.K. taxes.

1. Dandruff shampoo.
2. Mr. Gardner, who had recently painted the house, was to cut down dead trees and clear brush on the slope below 145 Adelaide.

Tiger's Milk and stuff to get that Dobbin to prance. I still have this funny sticky feeling in my jaws. No trouble about sleeping, except that Dobbin never really relaxes when not in the basket.

Dorothy came this morning. She was saying how Elsa (whom I'm seeing, with Charles, next Saturday) is always rushing around. "Even Mr. Bachardy, who's such a little flashlight, can't compare with her!"

This evening, I'm going to see the Rod Steiger Hemingway show, with Jerry Lawrence. Big thrill!

Saw Swami last night. He sent you his love. They all seem to be going along as usual up there, except that Tito[3] has developed really quite crazy persecution delusions, though very friendly with me personally. Tito came to Prema and complained that one of the boys was being mean to him and willing him to leave, so Prema said deadpan, "That's nothing—I happen to know that he's secretly in love with you," and apparently this satisfied Tito for the moment.

Am seeing Gerald this afternoon. He and Michael are taking off before long for the Virgin Islands, to talk to a man who is studying porpoises and has discovered that the porpoises are very much amused at being studied.

I'm going to write Richard and Sybil Burton. Maybe you should too. Did I leave you their address? It's 201 Via Appia Antica, Rome.

Have talked to Glade. Ted now has a job in an art store, the one on Beverly Drive in Beverly Hills! I haven't talked to him yet. Phoned a couple of times but couldn't catch him. I have terrifying visions of him arriving with little gifts for you of monster easels and ten-foot canvasses!

I'm dying to hear how the show has been going and what commissions, and all of your prospects and plans. I know how busy Kitty is and understand, but even a postcard with a few facts would bring some comfort to the old horse.

Quite nice weather here, though no longer hot. Grey foggy mornings. Haven't had time for the beach yet.

As always, Kitty's faithful and devoted old

Rubdub.

[*Typed letter, signed*]

3. Tito Renaldo, Mexican actor, intermittently a monk at the Vedanta Society.

Thursday, October 19 [1961, London]

My own dear Drub—

His lovely long sweet letter arrived this morning to comfort poor
sad Kitty, alone in the *cold* stable with only the smell of the old horse
to fill his empty hours, and make him cry with loneliness for his old
dear. All the little and big things Dub left behind him make Kitty all
the sadder, and just the sight of his tattered blanket makes pussy's heart
sink. Kitty's only consolation is his work, which he has thrown himself
into with all his strength, going out at 9 a.m. and not getting back till
nearly 8 in the evening, too tired to eat. I've not only been doing two
commissions a day but lots of fashion drawings as well. I reckon I've
made $450 in the last three days alone. The only reason I'm home this
morning is that Mrs. Gratsos[1] called while the cat was sat down in front
of a small dish of porridge (there was nothing else he could find to eat
because there was no one to shop for him and the stable cupboards were
almost bare) to say that she was satisfied with the drawings I'd already
done and no point in doing more. I'm drawing Dig this afternoon, and
every day for a week is booked with commissions.

Your bookings sound as formidable, and just the thought of all those
names makes the forlorn cat long so for his old cushion and the things
he used to know, all of them soaked with, and reeking of, Horse.

It has turned very cold here since that sinister fog on Sunday that
took Kitty's old darling away from him, and Kitty has had to brush up
his coat to its full winter glory, especially since he couldn't make the
central heating work and had finally to ask old Mr. Cowan to make it
go for him, which he did and now the house is gradually warming up,
with all kinds of gurgling sounds in the walls which echo through the
deserted stalls. (Kitty has just noticed a great dog watching him from
a car parked outside the house—maybe he's waiting for Kitty to step
outside so he can chase him and pounce on him.)

It would be nice if you could call the McKinnons, though I don't know
their number. The address of the house is 1106 Sutton Way, but they
might be staying at the Beverly Comstock on Wilshire Blvd. according to
their last letter, while workmen are in their house. If you do talk to them,

1. Wife of Constantine "Costa" Gratsos, Greek ship owner who managed Aristotle Onassis's
companies and was his closest friend and confidant.

give them my love and tell them about the show and its success and that I am busy doing commissions. Stanley Hall[2] has just arranged for me to draw Godfrey Winn,[3] whom I talked to this morning and he says he will have the drawing published in a magazine, very large.

Gavin and Tom's trip reminds Kitty of his first view of the big world, when he was tiny and pink and furless, tucked into a leather pouch slung over Dobbin's neck with Dobbin's mane to keep him warm and protect him from the harsh glare.

I will call the Sillitoes and make your apologies, though he would probably appreciate a short note from you, as would Hester, whom I talked to this morning also making apologies for you.[4] She instantly offered me dinner next week—which is terribly sweet of her but oh what it means for poor Kitty who will have to hide all his fur and strap down his ears and pretend [he] isn't an Animal.

About the trees—I don't know—wouldn't it be cheaper to have them all taken out now? It really depends on our balcony plans. Anyway, whatever seems best to you. Love to Jo & Ben, Gerald & Michael, etc., Dorothy too, and of course, as always, all Pussy's love to his only treasure.

[*Autograph letter*]

Darling Dub—I've searched the bookshelves, and indeed the house, and no sign of *any* Ramakrishna material—only lecture notes in an envelope and a day-to-day book from Valbonne[1] of any possible urgency. If you want these I will send them air mail immediately, otherwise bring them with me or send them surface when I leave.

XXXXXX K.

[*Autograph note, probably enclosed in Bachardy's letter above*]

2. English wig maker and makeup artist (1917–1994).
3. English actor, newspaper columnist, and novelist (1906–1971).
4. Sillitoe and his wife, American poet Ruth Fainlight (b. 1931), had evidently invited Isherwood for supper before he left London. So had Hester Chapman.

1. Isherwood's record of their visit to the South of France, where he and Bachardy stayed September 6–16 at a farmhouse, La Baumette, that John Osborne had rented and was sharing with Tony Richardson and other friends at Valbonne, near Nice.

Monday October 23 [1961]   La Casa.

My sweet love's first letter arrived today. Oh, how happy it made old Dub, although he is sad to think of poor Kitty's sadness and shivering[,] unshopped-for[,] in the fog. If only I could bring the Casa with all its comforts, including weather, right over the ocean and put it up on the Heath,[1] so Kitty would have his proper basket!

On Thursday I saw *A Short Happy Life*, Rod Steiger's Hemingway circus. It is the worst thing *ever*. Not that Rod is so terrible as all that; it's the utter confusion of the script.[2] A guy, who's evidently the character out of "Snows of Kilimanjaro" but also Hemingway, is dying, and he has visions from the past. He sees his old friends, who are also somehow characters from his books, playing scenes out of Hemingway. The actor (Dullea from Don's *Hoodlum Priest*[3]) who is Hemingway as a young man is also the bullfighter from *The Sun Also Rises*. They mime a bullfight on the stage, in which the bullfighter gets killed, and it is *exactly* like people trying to shoo a bat out of the room with sheets! After it was all over, I unwillingly went to Rod's dressing room and found him quite unperturbed. He is too vain to be depressed, even though it is folding without a New York run. A woman came in and said, "At last, a *man* on the stage—a real gutsy *man!*" Rod bowed and said, "Thank You, Ma'am."

Laughton *very* impressed by your Auden drawing; and there was a lot more about your being like Sharaku. He feels he is marvellous in *Advise and Consent*. They've nearly finished it now and then he *may* direct the Lawrence-Lee *Diamond Orchid*, about Evita Peron.[4]

[The case of that poor friend of Charlie Brackett] is much more serious than I had realized. The last rape he attempted, he hurt a woman very badly with a brick, and she *may* die. He is quite nuts, apparently. His great aggression seems to be against [his own mother]!

---

1. That is, Hampstead Heath, a short walk from the Burtons' house.
2. By Hemingway's friend, American writer A.E. Hotchner (b. 1920).
3. American actor Keir Dullea (b. 1930) appeared with Don Murray (b. 1929) in *The Hoodlum Priest* (1961), which Murray also co-wrote.
4. Bachardy's drawing of Auden was reproduced on the cover of the catalogue for his Redfern show. In July 1960, Laughton had loaned Bachardy a book of Sharaku's portraits of Kabuki actors, advising Bachardy to study the eighteenth-century Japanese printmaker because he felt Bachardy's talent was similar. Laughton's supporting role in Otto Preminger's *Advise and Consent* (1962) proved to be his last. He did not direct Jerry Lawrence and Robert Lee's *Diamond Orchid*; it opened on Broadway only in 1965, directed by José Quintero (see below, p. 167).

Colin Wilson[5] is coming by this evening and then I'm going to have supper with Carter and Dick. Chris Wood is coming back from New York, and I'll see him Thursday with Gerald. And Friday supper with Jo and Ben and Anne Baxter and her husband.[6] I saw Ivan Moffat and Kate[7] last night. They seemed radiantly happy and sent you their love—I mean, Ivan did. He was very affectionate, and actually kissed me on arrival, which he never has before! Altogether, old Dub's stock seems to have risen in his absence. Quite a lot of people seemed really pleased he was back. Everywhere there are enquiries about Kitty and his show. Kitty's propaganda really did its work. I don't think you would have any difficulty in arranging one here, if you wanted.

What has happened about reviews? Have you sold any more pictures? How are you getting along with the Redfern people?

Yes, I would like the envelope containing the transcriptions of my Santa Barbara lectures—if that's what they are, and not just notes. The notebook can be thrown away. But could you airmail the lectures? Stupid old Dub must have mislaid the Ramakrishna notes. He will just have to begin again.

Oh, Dub does miss Kitty so dreadfully! It is so sad without him, and everything seems so empty. But Dub must be busy too. He is correcting the American proofs, right now. Loves his dear so and longs to see those whiskers come sidling around the doorway and the dear white paws coming down the steps from the plane.

All Drub's love

D.

[*Typed letter, initialled*]

5. English novelist and critic (b. 1931).
6. Anne Baxter (1923–1985), American actress, and her second husband Randolph (Ranny) Galt, an outdoorsman and adventurer.
7. Katharine (Kate) Smith (1933–2000), English aristocrat, Moffat's second wife from 1961 to 1972.

Thursday October 26 [1961] [Santa Monica]

My dearest love,

Another little bulletin. I imagine you prefer getting a lot of short ones to a few long ones?

I have just been talking to Russell McKinnon on the phone. He tells me he has written you, and he wants me to tell you that money will be available whenever you need it; he says he is shy of talking to you too much about this for fear you will be annoyed, because you are so fine and sensitive. (He never saw Kitty grab a plump sparrow in his quick little fine sensitive claws.) He wants you to stay in Europe and visit France and Italy and see all the pictures. What did I think? I said I thought it was marvellous that he had given you all these opportunities.

In a curious way, I felt embarrassed and even rather a heel, and yet that's nonsense. *Of course* I want you to do and have everything you need and go everywhere and see everything; and *of course* I want you to come back home. And of course there is a certain opposition there. But it is really nonsense to feel guilty about it, because I know that you're acting freely and doing what seems best. And if I get too impartial about it, that's merely a kind of camp noble. The only thing that really matters is that you know I am *right here* when needed. *Always.*

Have written to Hester Chapman. But, horrors, no address for Sillitoe. Could you send it in your next?

Incidentally, Russell M. said that Edna is definitely dying. The cancer hasn't been arrested. If he doesn't mention this it's probably better to pretend not to know it. Maybe better anyway.

Do you remember an English girl who was up at the Vedanta center, Joan Ray—called Doya—I think you talked to her one time quite a bit? She left the center and became very alcoholic, and then cured herself and got a job. And then a few days ago she killed herself with pills. They had the funeral today.

All the trees have been cut down, below the Casa. It seemed best. The couple of live ones looked awkward alone, and now we are all clear. When the slope below the footpath was cleared, it was found to be littered with empty pint bottles thrown by drunks from cars!

Have seen Ted and Vince, who were quite sweet and friendly though a bit embarrassed somehow. We talked only about You and Films. We're meeting up with Glade next week to go see *Breakfast at Tiffany's.*

I found to my astonishment that Jo had read *The Heart in Exile* while we were away, and thought it marvellous! I feel she somehow got a new angle on us Unfortunates.[1] There is a new John Rechy story about hustling in the July–August *Evergreen*, very touching.[2] He is really a very romantic writer.

I finished and sent off the proofs of the American edition of my novel the day before yesterday. So that's that. I kind of wish I could placate Tony Bower somehow, as he is just bitchy enough to make a fuss. And yet, really, the character of Ronny is very harmless now, even quite sympathetic.[3]

Did I tell you I signed on for the next term at Los Angeles State College[?] This is still provisional. And if, for example, you had a show in New York, I could take time off for it.

Your *Film Facts* keep coming and there's a nice fat stack of them. Tonight I'm having supper with Chris Wood, Gerald and Michael. Tomorrow with Jo and Ben and Anne Baxter and husband.

All Dobbin's fondest love and thoughts. He misses Kitty so terribly, but Kitty is to stay in England as long as the cream lasts!

XXXXXXXXXX Drub.

Grey weather today and colder. Have had the heater on for the first time.

[*Typed letter, signed*]

Monday October 30 [1961, London]

My dear old darling Dub,

Your fourth letter arrived this morning to cheer the Pussy and make him think all the more about his much loved Horse. Kitty loves Dub's little bulletins coming regularly to reassure him—so much better than a few long ones. Kitty has been very busy and hasn't been able to write as often as he would like, but he knows his dear wants him to finish up here as soon as possible so he can get back to his own special cushion under his darling, between those four knobbly legs like great bedposts.

My show closed on Friday with another ugly little scene about

1. *The Heart in Exile* (1953) by Rodney Garland (a pseudonym, possibly for Adam de Hegedus) is a novel about gay life in London after World War II.
2. "A Quarter Ahead," *Evergreen Review*, Vol. 5, No. 19.
3. Tony Bower (1911–1972), American editor and, later, art dealer, was the model for Ronny.

frames, 16 of which I'm now expected to pay for, each about 50 shillings. There is no point in arguing any further since they are determined to see themselves as the generous benefactors of an ungrateful snip. Rex[1] actually came out with, "I don't remember hearing one word of thanks from you, not one word," in a very throaty voice. But I have been promised a statement in black and white this week. Eric helped me with the sixteen frames and drove me up to Hampstead with them. He's been terribly sweet to me. I've told him definitely that I will stay at Squire's Mount as long as I'm here. I thought it best and the least trouble really. It would have been uncomfortable with him and a little messy. I realized there were some strings attached to his offer, in the nicest way certainly, but still there. He has commissioned me to do a drawing of Bob Jackson at my usual fee.[2] I've done one session with Bob, four drawings, all quite good likenesses and one very good as a drawing, but even Eric is dissatisfied with something that isn't *his* view of Bob, regardless of the quality of the drawing. So I will have to have another go at it with Bob. I am doing at least two sittings every day almost. I don't even have time to get to the gym. When I am not doing a commission I arrange for someone like Julian Jebb[3] or Walter Baxter[4] to sit for me. The drawings of Julian are my best in a long time. He is marvellous to draw and very sweet. He took me afterwards to the Natl. Film Theatre to see one of the festival films—*Une aussi longue absence* with Valli. It was absolute hell, thanks mostly to Marguerite Duras.[5] The next time I see that woman's name in any film credits I shall leave the theater immediately. Julian and I had dinner at the Nag's Head because Kitty asked to be taken to the place where his own had been watered and fed. Most or a lot of the evening after that was spent with Julian on the phone to Elaine, who has just had another big blow-up with Ken and taken again to drinking in a big way—she'd been drunk for

1. Rex de Charembac Nan Kivell (1899–1977), director of the Redfern since 1931, originally from New Zealand.
2. Eric Falk (1905–1984), English barrister, was Isherwood's schoolmate at Repton. Bob Jackson was his longterm companion.
3. British journalist, filmmaker, BBC producer (1934–1984).
4. British novelist (1915–1994), a friend of E.M. Forster.
5. *Such a Long Absence* (released in the U.S. as *The Long Absence*) was written by Marguerite Duras with Gérard Jarlot, directed by Henri Colpi, and starred Alida Valli and Georges Wilson. It was co-winner of the Palme d'Or at the Cannes Film Festival in May 1961 and of the Prix Louis Delluc.

two days. I'd never known she had had a drinking problem. Apparently that's why she hasn't been drinking all of this year—not a liver ailment as she'd led us to believe that day with Truman. Ken is in Vienna with some woman now. It was his departure and a few scenes of hysteria before which have set her off. Diane Cilento is going to do her play, and Tony I'm told really does want to direct it.[6] I've not heard a peep from Tony. There is definitely frost there but I don't really care very much. Al and Christopher, too, have been turned against me I think—neither has called and I think they might have, considering our efforts with Christopher.[7] But if I really wanted to see them I would call myself. I think best to let the whole thing with Tony be forgotten for now. He'll get over it. And anyway he's not indispensable, to either of us.[8] Jocelyn has been very sweet and I think is really fond of me. Not seen much of Patrick so far but will go there after dinner tonight. I thought I might try to see the Thorndike play first. Not a raging success but apparently she really cuts loose, which is what I want to see.[9]

Did some drawings of Kathie Parrish, one very good indeed. I think they may buy it.[10] They took me to lunch afterwards with Jack Lemmon[11] at the Vendôme. He says he will sit for me day after tomorrow.

Cecil did indeed talk to Count Rasponi of the Sagittarius Gallery in N.Y.[12] I got a letter from him a few days after Cecil left London. He says it is possible, if he likes my work etc. that I could have a show there the first two weeks of January 1962. I've sent him lots of photographs of my things and am waiting to hear from him. If he does come across with a definite offer it would be quite a good plan. I would stay here till early in December and then go to N.Y., where we could meet and have one of our nice N.Y. Christmases. Wouldn't that be nice? I will write to you as soon as I hear from him.

---

6. Cilento appeared in Elaine Dundy Tynan's play *My Place* in 1962, but the director was John Dexter.

7. Al Kaplan, wealthy American doctor, and his companion Christopher Lawrence.

8. It was indeed forgotten; Bachardy no longer recalls the cause of the frost.

9. British actress Sybil Thorndike (1882–1976) was starring as the sixteenth-century Spanish nun in Hugh Ross Williamson's play *Teresa of Avila*.

10. Kathleen Parrish (1918–2011), American script reader and editor, was the wife of American actor, film editor, director, and author Robert Parrish (1916–1995).

11. American actor (1925–2001).

12. Lanfranco Rasponi (d. 1983) was a publicity agent for Italian opera singers and New York restaurants and a society party fixer. He ran the gallery on the side to showcase young artists.

No further acknowledgements of my show in the papers here. But odd commissions still keep coming up. For instance I'm drawing Richard Buckle[13] this afternoon. He saw the drawings of Julian and was very impressed I think. Also Morgan wants me to draw May.[14] And this photographer John Hedgecoe who took those pictures of me for *The Queen* (I've drawn both him and his wife) has suggested arranging for me to draw Henry Moore—a friend of his (he's doing a book of photographs of Moore and of his work—and taking pictures of us while I'm doing the drawings. Good if it comes off.[15] John Osborne and Tutin still being evasive but I've not had time really to pin them down. If the N.Y. show is set I will really get to work and polish off as many more celebs as possible. If the N.Y. deal fizzles out I will try to be back at the Casa by Thanksgiving—Jo wrote a sweet letter suggesting it. Please tell them how busy I am and give them my love.

The Stravinskys and Bob[16] have been here two weeks and not a word from them. I don't know where they are and have called Stephen several times to reach them but can't get onto him. It's probably some bitchery of Stephen's that I've not been called.

Have just been on to Stephen and then to Bob at the Savoy. They are leaving today but their plane has been delayed so I am going by there at 2:30. I have just decided to make it up with Stephen I think—for no real reason, except that I don't really feel cross with him anymore.

I've done some nice drawings of Dig and am going to lunch there on Sunday to draw them both. Another expense account dinner at L'Ecu de France with Bill Bridger[17] and Terry. I'm drawing Terry on commission Wednesday morning. I've done drawings of Nick Eden[18] and Stanley Hall has arranged for me to draw Godfrey Winn this Thursday, on

13. British ballet critic, exhibition designer, and, later, biographer (1916–2001).

14. May Buckingham, wife of Forster's policeman lover, Bob Buckingham. She was a nurse.

15. John Hedgecoe (1932–2010), then staff photographer for *Queen* magazine, photographed sculptor Henry Moore at work for many years, resulting in exhibitions and three books. Hedgecoe's first wife, from 1960 to 1995, was Julia Mardon; she was a friend of Moore's daughter Mary and introduced Hedgecoe to the Moore family. Bachardy did not draw Moore and never met him.

16. Robert (Bob) Craft (b. 1923), American musician, conductor, critic, author; he was Stravinsky's closest colleague and a member of his household.

17. Bridger worked at the modelling agency which employed Jenkins. He had hosted Isherwood, Bachardy, and Jenkins at the same restaurant on July 11.

18. Nicholas Eden, 2nd Earl of Avon (1930–1985), served in the Queen's Royal Rifles and was later an ADC to the Queen, and a Tory politician.

commission—I think I told you already. Michael Franklin is coming to be drawn here Saturday afternoon and wants me to do Terry (Rattigan) if I'm in N.Y. at Christmas time.[19] Julian Jebb has commissioned me to draw John Gathorne Hardy[20] on Friday and I'm coping with five Attenboroughs on Sunday week.[21] Lord Amherst[22] is tomorrow morning's subject. I've done more drawings of Gladys Cooper—she wants to put one up outside the theater, for free of course, the old sly bird of time, but I will do it.[23] She has been nice to me and any publicity is good. Gerald Hamilton did bring Maurice Richardson to my show with great complicated arrangements. No word in his column yet but Gerald assures me there will be (small good now that the show is over).[24] I'm having dinner with Gerald on Thursday, Hester next week. Whatever you wrote to her it really hit the mark. She was *terribly* pleased and called just to say so. The Sillitoes (not seen or called yet by me): [. . .] Pembridge Crescent, W. 11.

Must fly now to see the Stravinskys. I will give them your love.

Terry was very anxious to have news of Charles, whom I don't think he's heard from for a long time. Is there a cooling in the old cauldron?

Sad about Doya—I do indeed remember her. And astonishing about [that poor friend of Charlie Brackett].

I wonder how your evening with Anne Baxter was. How I long for some good old seasoned movie stars.

Really must go now. All my love to my own, only, old, adored darling, who must know how much he is missed and loved by his small furry friend. XXXXXXXXXXXXXXXXXXXXXX Kitty

[*Autograph letter*]

19. Michael Franklin was the longterm companion of British playwright Terence Rattigan (1911–1977).
20. British biographer, social historian, novelist (b. 1933).
21. Richard Attenborough (b. 1923), British actor, film director, producer; his wife, British actress Sheila Sim (b. 1922); their three children, Michael (b. 1950), later a theater director, Jane (1955–2004), later an arts administrator, Charlotte (b. 1959), later an actress.
22. Jeffrey John Archer Amherst, 5th Earl Amherst (1896–1993), was a partner in the Redfern Gallery.
23. Cooper (1888–1971), British actress, was then appearing in Peter Mayne's *The Bird of Time* at the Savoy Theatre.
24. Gerald Hamilton (1890–1970), Anglo-Irishman of various pursuits and a shady reputation, was the original for Mr. Norris in Isherwood's *Mr. Norris Changes Trains*. Maurice Richardson (1907–1978), a regular reviewer for *The Observer*, ran the "Londoner's Diary" in the *New Statesman*.

Saturday [November] 4 [1961]   [Santa Monica]

My own dearest love,

[N]othing from you for nearly two weeks now. Of course I know so well how difficult it is to get around to writing anything when you are so busy and also living up in Hampstead and having to drag home exhausted and go out again in the morning. But I worry just the same. Santa Monica seems so far from my Kitty. And then, I have promised Swami to go down to Trabuco tomorrow Sunday and I won't be back here till Tuesday night, the 7th. So, as soon as you get this, if you haven't already sent a letter, will you send a cable? Just a word to know that Kitty is safe and hasn't forgotten. Please don't be cross with anxious old Dubbin for asking this. He is so sad and he worries so.

Meanwhile, you will have heard or very soon be hearing from the McKinnons, who have impulsively decided to come to Europe and buy things. He called me and told me this a few days ago. And he said he was sending you a cable.

Gavin and Tom Wright are back from their trip, and I have seen Gavin's house which is really very nice indeed and not at all in a hole. In fact it is as high or higher than ours and you can see it from our windows. It is right below the big house which dominates the Canyon on the top of Amalfi. Gavin is busy working on his novel; hopes it will be ready by Xmas.

Colin Wilson spent a day here and I took him to see Huxley[1] and also Laughton and Gavin. And Henry Miller[2] appeared and came along too. I thought he was an absolute sweetie pie, but he has bad marks from Jo because he allegedly got drunk at Peter and Alice's,[3] used obscene language AND—made eyes at Ben! At Jo and Ben's I also met Anne Baxter again, with her great hunk of a husband, Ranny Galt. Rather a tasteless hunk though anxious to be pleasant. They raved about Australia and only succeeded in making the people sound the vilest ever.[4]

Howard Warshaw stopped by to see me and was hugely impressed by your Auden drawing on the catalogue. Everybody I meet seems to have

1. Aldous Huxley (1894–1963), English novelist, intellectual, and utopian.
2. American novelist (1891–1980).
3. Peter Gowland (1916–2010), American photographer and camera maker, and his wife Alice, who directed his photo shoots.
4. They had been living on a cattle station in the Outback.

absorbed the news of your show and of course I blow the trumpet as loud as it'll blow.

Gore here for a short visit, assured me we shall visit Jackie and Jack and you shall draw them. He loves the Kennedys as much as ever and stays frequently at the White House. The word going around now is NO WAR, but the bomb-shelter racket flourishes.[5] Gore says he is terrified of fascism in this country, a few years from now.

The Picasso exhibition is very good here and also they showed a Picasso film, made by Clouzot. It would have fascinated you because it showed different stages of a painting and how he keeps abstracting and elaborating.[6]

I went to a strange wake-like party at the Bracketts'. Xan[7] all in black. Nothing was said about [Charlie's friend] until I got alone with Charlie, after seeing a truly disastrous T.V. film of *The Power and the Glory* with Olivier and Julie; at their all-time worst. Then Charlie suddenly declared that the whole business had been much exaggerated, the woman [his friend] hit wasn't going to die, and [the friend] himself could be completely cured, it was only one lobe of the brain which was affected. Whether Charlie really believed all of this or was just trying to reassure himself, I don't know.

Sweetheart, please send a tiny word to your adoring D.

[*Typed letter, initialled*]

Monday November 6. [1961, London]

My dearest, only Dub—

He has been so much thought about, this past week especially. Kitty is so afraid sometimes that when he's near his darling he doesn't really

---

5. Gore Vidal (1925–2012), American writer, shared a stepfather with Jacqueline Bouvier Kennedy (1929–1994), wife of President John (Jack) F. Kennedy (1917–1963). The Berlin crisis, which had worried Isherwood throughout the summer in London, reignited when East German police stopped an American diplomat at Checkpoint Charlie, demanding to see his passport although his Occupation Forces license plates entitled him to travel freely throughout Berlin. On October 27 and 28, U.S. and Soviet tanks faced off a few hundred yards from the wall, until Kennedy and Khrushchev agreed to back down.
6. The exhibition at UCLA, two hundred fifty works loaned by Californians, opened on Picasso's eightieth birthday. The film was *Le Mystère Picasso* (1955), *The Mystery of Picasso*, a documentary by Henri-Georges Clouzot.
7. Alexandra (Xan) Larmore, Charlie Brackett's daughter; she was married to his assistant, James Larmore.

let him know how very very much his Pussy loves him, and treasures him more than anything in the world. There is nothing else in the whole world as near and dear to Kitty as his old Horse, and Kitty does miss him so much. And in his small, cluttered, crazy cat head Dobbin is the one thing about which Kitty never doubts his feelings, though he worries that maybe he hasn't made them clear enough to his sweetheart-Horse. And it's more than loneliness and missing his Drub that make Kitty want his old dear so much.

Kitty was given a great surprise on Friday when he got a telegram from the McKinnons saying they would be at the Dorchester today! Perhaps you know about this? Anyway, I've called the hotel and they neither have a reservation for them nor any room for them tonight. The Mayfair where they stayed before also has no reservation for them. What to do? I don't even know if they have my phone number. They will just have to write to me. It will be difficult to see them too because I have Heather Sears[1] to draw this afternoon, Jack Lemmon again tomorrow afternoon after lunch with Gerald Hamilton and Robin Maugham[2] (who wants to commission me according to Gerald), the Albee plays[3] with Patrick tonight and dinner with Norman Frank[4] and Chita Rivera[5] afterwards, and dinner with Hester tomorrow night. And yet I hate to say to them they have to wait their turn. I will at least see them and have a drink maybe, that is if I find out where they are. I might see them Wednesday night instead of having a suspicious sounding dinner with Bill Bridger at his flat in order "to show him my drawings of Terry" in the hope of a sale. I think he wants a little of Kitty's fur for his 25 guineas, as well. The drawings of Terry are fair, one especially is a nice drawing but the ones that are most like him are too unflattering. He is one of the most difficult and dullest of subjects, but he was sweet and we got along all right.

Lunch yesterday with the Yorkes—they really are adorable people

---

1. British actress (1935–1994).
2. English barrister, soldier, author (1916–1981), a nephew of Somerset Maugham.
3. *The American Dream* and *The Death of Bessie Smith.*
4. American advertising executive and, later, T.V. producer and director (1925–2007).
5. American musical star (b. 1933); she had opened in the London production of *Bye Bye Birdie* in June. Bachardy saw only the New York production on January 23, 1961, when the show had already transferred twice and she had been replaced by Gretchen Wyler, but he and Isherwood had seen Rivera in the original *West Side Story.*

but oh so sad. Henry was quite muddled with drink by the end of the afternoon and though he let me do four drawings I would hardly say that he sat for me. His head wagged like Mr. Huggins's of Mesa Rd. when he was stalking his prey,[6] but without any intent in Henry's head—just a listless wag. And Dig sat behind me and watched, sweetly trying to keep Henry still but only managing to make it worse for both of us. She is so heartbreaking, trying to keep everything, including Henry himself, in one piece. I did four more drawings of her after lunch—some of my very best I think—and I'm going to give her one. The drawings of Henry were done so quickly I don't know if they are any good at all.

A letter from Count Rasponi of the Sagittarius Gallery on Thursday to say—"Haven't you anything else besides portraits? We cannot have a show of only portraits. I cannot tell you how expensive it is to run a gallery in New York, and I cannot base a show on the question mark of how many portrait commissions we can get" and so on. I wrote back a rather marvellous letter I think, which I will show you, but I think you'll agree with me it looks quite definitely no deal. Just as well. Thanksgiving with my darling in California is a much more attractive idea.

I'm having dinner with Joe Ackerley on Friday. Queenie was put to sleep today week. Nancy told me this morning—Joe of course has been very upset.[7] He spent the weekend with Raymond Mortimer.[8]

Sold two drawings on the spot to Godfrey Winn (40 guineas) when I went to draw him Thursday. Though the drawings weren't bad and he was quite nice and polite, I think he liked Kitty more than his drawings. Michael Franklin (Rattigan's friend) came on Saturday and was a quite cozy subdued little mouse and sat well and was very good to draw.

Saw the Stravinskys last Monday for about an hour—they were all friendly but not the least bit feeling there was any need for explanations or excuses or apologies for neither having called me nor having gone to my show. They were all in their fussed grand state, a little dazed from lunch and drink, not completely conscious, smiling but not recognizing. It was as though I were seeing them in a huge room filled with people.

6. Mr. Huggins was a big, malevolent, long-furred old cat, yellowish dark-grey stripes with yellow basilisk eyes; Bachardy thought of him as a ruthless, slow-moving hunter.
7. J.R. (Joseph, Joe) Ackerley (1896–1967), English author and editor, had an intensely intimate relationship, described in My Dog Tulip (1956), with his Alsatian, Queenie. Nancy West was Ackerley's sister.
8. English literary and art critic (1895–1980).

They were also in a state because of the indefinite delay of their plane. I would almost bet that when we meet again in California they will quite have forgotten we met in London. They hadn't even really registered that I'd been living here since January. I must stop now.

All my love to my dearest Drub from his loving fur. More news when I hear from the Sagittarius. Till then all Kitty's most loving thoughts.

Nick Reid very sweetly gave us all these prints for free.[1] They are certainly better than I'd expected. He says we can have extra prints of any of them at cost. A short note of thanks and praise if you have a moment I know would be appreciated. [. . .] Philbeach Gardens, S.W. 5.

[*Autograph letter with enclosures*]

Tuesday November 7 [1961]   La Casa

Dearest Own,

Got back from Trabuco to find the big package of lecture notes with your dear letter. Now I understand why there was a gap in communication. Your package went off on Oct. 31st and wasn't delivered here till yesterday. The customs apparently suspected it of something, because there was a stamp on the envelope saying "supposed liable to United States customs duties" and then another stamp "passed free, United States Customs, Los Angeles." I can't see that they opened it, but maybe they did. How embarrassing if they read your letter, except that I really don't think the Animals' language is intelligible to humans!

You will have read in the papers about our fire. It is still making a

---

1. Bachardy enclosed the photographs and this note about Reid, a young British photographer who photographed him and afterwards came to the Burton house in Hampstead to photograph Isherwood. Bachardy drew Reid and swapped him one drawing for some of the photographs, which are now at the Huntington Library in San Marino.

dull red volcano on the far skyline, somewhere behind Pacific Palisades as I write this. It must have been very bad yesterday, while we were up at Trabuco; all three swamis[1] and me. Now there seems absolutely no danger; but houses were burned just the other side of Sunset on Saltair, and quite near the Uplifters'—causing Peter and Alice Gowland to begin to pack—and I have just been talking to Jerry Lawrence, who is a bit worried because of a movement of fire toward the sea near Castellamare, the Joe Cotten country. There is ash all round the Casa, and I'm glad we had the brush cut, bare as it now looks.[2]

Dobbin hopes Kitty wasn't cross because he wrote that letter all worried. He knows how hard Kitty has to work, and is *so* proud of him, but still the silly old thing gets disturbed. *Of course* he will join Kitty in New York for Christmas if the show goes through—and surely it will? Should we write Julie and Manning, or what's best?

I am most displeased with the Stravinskys, and I hope they apologized humbly, after slighting the Animals' hospitality.

Will write to Sillitoes, although that novel really is unpraisable; and to Nick Reid, although there are very few of the pictures I like even a little. None do Kitty justice, and you cannot catch Dobbin like that. He always has to pose for his candid pictures; otherwise all you see is a horse's skull.

Have just had supper with the Masselinks, who send you their love and keep saying how awful if they go away without seeing you again. They still hope you will be there for Thanksgiving. But Dobbin hopes more that you will get the show. Although you almost *might* afford the little extra luxury and come back to take a look at the basket? I still love the old Casa, but I know this—I will live anywhere rather than be separated from Kitty for long periods, because Dub gets so sad he has no delight in anything.

Both fires have disappeared from the skyline now. So I will take off

1. Prabhavananda, Ritajananda, and Vandanananda.
2. The fire—L.A.'s biggest ever—started November 6 in Sherman Oaks and spread west to Bel Air and Brentwood. It took 2,500 fire fighters twelve hours to control it, and it smouldered in some neighborhoods for several days; 3,500 people had to leave their homes. A day later, another fire started in Santa Ynez Canyon, five miles to the west. Pacific Palisades is about three miles north of Adelaide Drive along the coast, spreading inland to the east. The Uplifters' was a Prohibition-era drinking club and ranch retreat in heavily wooded Rustic Canyon just beyond the eastern end of Pacific Palisades (the property is now Rustic Canyon Park). Joseph Cotten lived closer to the coast, in Castellamare, in a house high above the ocean.

for Hollywood—it's nearly ten in the evening—and attend the Kali puja,[3] which will go on till 4:00 a.m.! At least I can make japam[4] for the Animals. And it will please Swami. He has been very sweet. He asked after you and sent love. Swami Ritajananda leaves on Friday to take over the French center outside Paris.

Since you wrote, Terry called Charles long-distance and so presumably got his news. He is all excited again about Plato, which is a bore, but we have a good gimmick for the whole thing. I'll tell you about it. But not now.

All dearest love to Dobbin's dear. Dobbin thinks of him always and loves him so.

D.

[Typed letter, initialled]

Friday. November 10. [1961, London]

Darling Angel Drub—

Kitty has been so worried about the stable and his basket, and the thought of his old dear being threatened by flames makes Kitty frantic. He knows how wild-eyed and panicky his horse can get. Whom can I trust to have the good sense to put a sack over his head and lead him to safety? Kitty doesn't like to think of him bolting into the street with all those terrible fire engines screaming by. Please write to calm poor anxious pussy.

Saw the McKinnons on Wednesday night. They both seem very much the same. The evening went quite well I think, partly because they asked two other women, one a painter who stayed to have dinner with us at Claridge's, and partly because there was lots to drink. Russell was really quite surprised at the number of martinis Kitty had downed without a ripple in his fur. Edna drank quite a bit, too, and talked more than ever before. She was really very sweet and really fond of me, too, I think. The moment she was out of earshot Russell was filling my head with the horrors of her state. She

3. The late-autumn vigil celebrating the four-armed Hindu goddess Kali, Divine Mother and Destroyer, consort of Shiva. She was Ramakrishna's Chosen Ideal, and for a number of years he worshipped her image exclusively.
4. That is, repeat one of the names for God, probably his own mantra. Isherwood counted repetitions on a Vedanta rosary of 108 beads, one hundred repetitions towards his own (and in this case Bachardy's) spiritual progress and eight repetitions for mankind, before reversing the rosary at the 109th bead, which hangs down with a tassel on it and represents the guru.

went to bed after dinner and Russell and I went to see the paintings of this woman, one of which he bought out of politeness. In the taxi on our way back Russell stuffed fifteen pounds into my hand ("for the cab fare") and held my leg very paternally. He said he's making arrangements with the Hanover Bank to transfer some more money into my account here, which should take a month he thought. I didn't tell him I was planning to go. What should I do? Will I have to be here to acknowledge the money or shall I just let it happen, if it's going to? I thought anyway I would leave what's left of the money in my account at the bank, here. Russell said I should take a trip to the Continent or even to the States for a while. I felt they were a little surprised and maybe slightly upset that I wasn't in school again and was instead carrying on with these commissions. I think they regard my show as an interference with their plans for me. They're right in a way. They left early Thursday morning for Switzerland and may be back here in a few days' time if they don't like what they see there.

No word yet from the Sagittarius. I do feel it's most certainly off, though. Nothing has or will happen with the Hirsch and Adler gallery[1] that the Redfern said was interested. Just talk I think. So I am just finishing up my commissions here which are now thinning out and I think I will be more or less free to go in two weeks' time.

Please let me know what you think I should do about the extra McKinnon money ("a Christmas present" as Russell calls it—he apologized profusely for not bringing me anything from California, till I wanted to hide under the table).

Gerald Hamilton arranged for us to be taken to lunch by Robin Maugham, who wants me to draw someone named Winifred on Sunday week. Willie was too sick (now in Switzerland anyway) even to be seen by me according to Alan.[2] John Osborne wrote a card filled with guilt, love, busyness and a refusal to be drawn.

All Kitty's dearest love to his sweetheart Horse, about whom he thinks and worries so.

[Autograph letter]

---

1. Probably the Hirschl and Adler Gallery, founded in 1952 by Norman Hirschl and Abraham Adler, in New York.
2. William Somerset Maugham (1874–1965), English playwright and novelist, and Alan Searle (1905–1985) his secretary, companion, and heir, also English.

Friday November 10 [1961]   [Santa Monica]

Another letter from my sweet Kitty, dated Tuesday 7th, so it came quick. Two letters from me hadn't arrived when you wrote it; the one written on the 5th and the one on the 7th. In one of them I told you about the coming of the McKinnons. By this time I guess you will have contacted them. How typical of them not to make reservations or arrangements! I gave them your phone number, though.

It is disappointing about the Sagittarius Gallery. I had felt perfectly sure that the whole thing was set. But something else will come up. And all I can think about is that I will see my Darling soon. Then we can decide if we want to go to New York and seek our fortune there. Gore, who was here, offers an invitation to spend Xmas with him, Howard[1] and the Paul Newmans;[2] and he insists that the White House has its welcome mat out. Maybe you can draw Jackie. Gore promises to promote this. He has a new play opening early in January.[3]

A slight jolt from Mr. Sidebotham, the lawyer managing my mother's estate. He writes to say that the tax people have found some extra charges and that he may have to ask me to return some of the fourteen thousand dollars he sent me! I wrote back very coldly, saying the money was practically spent and he must be more specific, and I must have a proper govt. tax bill "for my legal adviser." I don't know why, but I suspect some fraud. I have never trusted that man. But I'm not too worried, because, at the worst, there is always the other half of the money which comes from London, not Stockport and which should be arriving before long. And then we haven't touched a cent of the Simon and Schuster advance.[4] And there are various projects on foot which I'll tell you about later. Incidentally, I hope you will confer with somebody about your British tax before you leave?

My stay at Trabuco was very peaceful, and Swami was marvellous. I often think that I am really the richest horse in the world, having these two marvellous blessings in my life. I envy *no one*.

The fire burned on all through Wednesday; yesterday it was all over, though of course it can spring up again from embers, if there is another

1. Howard (Tinker) Austen (1928–2003), American companion to Vidal from 1950.
2. American actor (1925–2008) and his actress wife, Joanne Woodward (b. 1927).
3. An adaptation of Friedrich Dürrenmatt's *Romulus the Great*, about Romulus Augustulus, last emperor of the Western Roman Empire; it ran from January to March 1962 on Broadway.
4. For the U.S. publication of *Down There on a Visit*.

wind. Now it is beautiful not too hot weather. From our windows, you could see the bombers dumping borate on the hills to put the fire out. One of them was nearly licked up by a huge flame which swept up at it as it dove. The Casa looks huge and bare, with all the trees cut down; rather like the great palace at Lhasa. The Laughtons are paying to have the trunks sawn up into small pieces for firewood on condition they get half of it, which is a fair deal, and we shall have as much as we need for the winter, I think. Charles is now hot on the trail of Plato again and I think we are going to produce something really interesting. Otherwise I just get on with my Ramakrishna chore,[5] and go to the gym. Yesterday I had a long conversation there with Jeff Hunter about *The King of Kings.* Haven't seen it yet. He was much hurt because *Time* had described him as a flabby New York chorus boy.[6] Actually, his figure is quite good but he is plump, and very very SMALL. When you get home, I want to discuss with you what I can do to adapt the hashish scene out of my novel so it can be published as a separate piece in some magazine.[7]

Perhaps neither of the Animals tells the other enough how much he loves him. But it is very difficult, during all the day-to-day moods and fuss, and the constant preoccupation with cream and hay. The Animals must just have faith and remember the times when they're apart from each other, because then it immediately becomes absolutely obvious that there is no treasure but that furry love. The daily life is like weather, sometimes it's good, sometimes cloudy, but the sun is always there, in back of it. What Kitty must particularly remember is how very proud Dobbin is of him; that's another thing Dobbin doesn't say often enough. Kitty is going to be a very great artist and a very great cat. That night at the Redfern, Dobbin knew what real triumph is. (But fuck those miserly queens.)

With *all* love and longing to see his dear treasure,

D. XXXXXXXXXXXXXXXX

[*Typed letter, initialled, with autograph additions*]

5. That is, the biography.
6. American actor Jeffrey Hunter (1926–1969) played Christ in Nicholas Ray's 1961 epic life story *King of Kings,* narrated by Orson Welles. The *Time Magazine* reviewer called Hunter "a fan-mag cover boy with a flabby face, a cute little lopsided smile, baby-blue eyes and barely enough histrionic ability to play a Hollywood marine . . . the pallid, simpering, chorus-boy Christ of the religious-supply shoppes." (Friday October 27, 1961).
7. Isherwood did cut the hashish scene from the novel, and eventually he published it as a short story, "A Visit to Anselm Oakes," in *Exhumations* (1966).

Monday November 13 [1961]   [Santa Monica]

Only sweet Angel Kitten,
    Just got yours of November 10th. I hope you are getting mine? If you
have, you'll know that our fires are safely out—though today there are two
more, in Altadena and in Sunland—miles away but there's a tremendous
golden brown smudge all the way out over the ocean, greatly improving
the sunset! Am just back from lunch with Nehru[1] and soon off to dinner
with Evelyn Hooker—and people still say California is provincial! Nehru
was really quite sweet, and it was a small lunch, only fourteen of us in his
suite at the Ambassador, so we could all talk to him. "We" was Brando,[2]
Irving Stone,[3] Will Durant,[4] Danny Kaye,[5] Nehru's sister[6] and some other
Indians and wives. Nehru was like a prim but sympathetic schoolmistress
(out of The Corn is Green[7]). You feel that all the other world leaders are
more or less backward boys in her class. Brando made quite an ass out of
himself, trying to talk real philosophical, but I liked him as I always do.
Stone's wife[8] is enough to ruin his career, and as for Mrs. Durant,[9] she
actually asked Nehru, "Mr. Prime Minister, do you still enjoy doing your
job?" To which Nehru replied, "Well, one must say—er—enjoy is—er—
perhaps hardly the word one would have chosen." It seems absolutely
incredible, and at the same time reassuring, that a person like him could
be one of the most influential men in the world.
    I think you are right not to take any more of the McKinnons' money

---

1. Jawaharlal Nehru (1889–1964), Prime Minister of India from 1947 to 1964.
2. Marlon Brando (1924–2004), American actor.
3. American historical novelist (1903–1989).
4. American historian and philosopher (1885–1981).
5. American singer, comedian, actor (1913–1987).
6. Nehru's sister, Vijaya Lakshmi Nehru Pandit (1900–1990), politician and diplomat, was then leader of India's delegation to the U.N. But in his diary for this period, Isherwood records that Nehru's daughter was present at the lunch, and contemporary photographs at the Nehru Memorial Museum and Library in New Delhi show Indira Gandhi (1917–1984), who became Prime Minister of India in 1966, with her father on the California trip. See The Sixties, Diaries Volume Two: 1960–1969 (D.2), November 14, 1961, p. 135.
7. By their friend Emlyn Williams, based on his own life, and in which he starred on stage. Isherwood preferred Sybil Thorndike as the schoolteacher Miss Moffat in the stage version and dismissed Bette Davis in the film.
8. Jean Stone (191[1]–2004), his editor.
9. Ariel Durant (1898–1981) co-authored the last four volumes of her husband's eleven-volume The Story of Civilization; they won a Pulitzer Prize for volume ten.

as long as you aren't going to play their game and go to school. Sooner or later, you will have to tell them, with the utmost sweetness, that you can accept no strings to anything they give you. At the same time, don't penalize yourself. Take enough to cover all your expenses. I think you should tell them you are coming back to the States for a while. They did, after all, suggest that. And, you know, sweetheart, I do think you should try to get a show in New York soon, don't you? Should we go there and promote it together, at Xmas? Couldn't Tony Bower help? (Simon and Schuster have just succeeded in losing my corrected proofs, and also write that they're putting different lettering on the jacket and will send a proof of that.)

But maybe you feel differently? Maybe you want to paint for a while and forget the portrait racket? We must discuss all of that. What I really feel about the McKinnons, I guess, is that you should now be very very clear that they cannot under any circumstances direct your career or your life. If they want to help you without making any conditions, that's wonderful. I know it will be difficult to say this to them, but the sooner you do it the easier and the less chance of recriminations later.

Tell me when you want to get your car fixed up ready for you.

Did you ever give Heywood Hill those books I left behind in the house to be mailed on to me? They don't seem to have arrived yet. One of them was the rather valuable early edition of my Baudelaire translation, another that old guide to the Peak District which I used to use as a boy.[10]

How Dobbin longs to see his dearest Kitty again! But Kitty must take his time and do everything he needs to do first. Old Dub has so many chores the days pass quickly enough, but the nights are sad.

All the Horse's dearest love to his own Mr. K.

D. XXXXXXXXXXXXX

[Typed letter, initialled, with autograph additions]

10. G. Heywood Hill Ltd. is the bookseller at 10 Curzon Street in London. Isherwood's translation of Charles Baudelaire's *Intimate Journals* with an introduction by T.S. Eliot was published in a limited edition by the Blackamore Press in London and Random House in New York in 1930. *The Peak District of Derbyshire and Neighbouring Counties* by M.J.B. Baddeley, eighth edition (London, 1903), had been given to Isherwood by his grandmother, Emily Machell Smith, in April 1918, and he retrieved it from Wyberslegh during his visit there in July 1961.

Thursday. November 16. [1961, London]

Darling Angel Drub—

Your letter of the 10th arrived yesterday morning. There is still no word from the N.Y. swine—I don't know whether to wire him or just assume the whole thing is off. In any case I don't think I can be back by Thanksgiving. Though most of the commissions are done, there is still enough work to keep me busy through next Wednesday. Richard Buckle this afternoon (he has turned out to be very nice indeed, full of praise for and interest in my work, suggesting various people for commissions and being very sweet in general—to my complete surprise), a friend (Mrs. Davall) of Heather Sears tomorrow morning, and Tutin (barring a likely fit of exhaustion) tomorrow evening in Stratford.[1] Simon Fleet's friend Martin Newell[2] on Saturday and Lady Hulse,[3] a friend of the McKinnons, on Sunday. This is a duty job to please the McKinnons. Also on Sunday Edmund Tracey, a music critic for *The Sunday Times*[4] and a friend of Eric, who arranged the commission.

Lunch with Angus and Tony[5] at the Jardin on Monday and a chance to draw them afterwards I hope, to Brighton on Tuesday for a final session with Rattigan's friend Michael Franklin,[6] and Mrs. Sutton (the last of the Redfern customers to be dealt with, excepting the Duchess of Leeds who wrote a terribly sweet letter saying she couldn't come to London from Jersey because her husband had just had his *other* leg off) on Wednesday.[7] In between times I hope to get at Chita Rivera whom I've met several times with Patrick and like enormously, though she'll be the devil of a sitter I'll bet.

1. Where Tutin was appearing as Desdemona to Gielgud's Othello in Zeffirelli's disastrous production for the Royal Shakespeare Company. Mrs. Davall is unidentified.
2. Newell was an aspiring painter. Fleet (1913–1966), whose real name was Harry Carnes, was a socialite antiques expert who entertained continuously at his Chelsea house, the Gothic Box. He was a close friend of Richard Buckle and of Cecil Beaton.
3. Probably Lucy Elizabeth Smitheyt Spain, fourth wife of Sir Hamilton Westrow Hulse, 9th Baronet (1909–1996), a barrister.
4. Tracey (1927–2007) was in fact music critic for *The Times Educational Supplement* and occasionally for *The Observer*.
5. Angus Wilson (1913–1991), British novelist and literary critic, and his companion and secretary, Anthony Garrett (b. 1929), formerly a probation officer.
6. They lived there together in a house Franklin was decorating.
7. John Francis Godolphin Osborne (Jack), 11th Duke of Leeds (1901–1963), and his third wife, Caroline Fleur Vatcher (1931–2005), last-ever Duchess of Leeds, born and buried in Jersey. She was an artist under the name Caroline Leeds and had two subsequent husbands. Mrs. Sutton is unidentified.

Gladys Cooper sent me a typed letter with a signature you wouldn't believe possible, the 50 megaton variety beside which Crawford's would look like a modest Hiroshima mushroom.[8] The purpose of the letter was to say, "Could I have your lovely drawing of me," the old sly bird. I'm going to let her have it, partly because she's been very sweet and partly because she wants the worst drawing of the lot. "The most beautiful play in London" closes on Saturday and she goes immediately to N.Y. to do A Passage to India, with Eric Portman and without Tony Richardson.[9]

Saw Joe Ackerley and Nancy on Monday night. She cooked an elaborate supper for me and both of them were so affectionate and kind to Pussy. They walked me back to the tube station even and Joe paid my fare back to Hampstead. The flat was delightfully calm and quiet without that wretched smelly dog but Joe still minds terribly about her and misses her, says the flat seems so empty without her. According to Joe's description they came to get her like they came for Blanche in the last scene of Streetcar, with a hypodermic syringe to calm her and all—this way Joe's last sight of her was in his flat while she was still alive. Terribly tragic and yet silly, almost more tragic because it's silly. Nancy is obviously delighted and herself again, mistress unchallenged.

I took to Bill Bridger the drawing of Terry last night (he gave me a check on the spot) and then he took me to supper at a nearby dump on the Earls Court Road. I was more than willing to sing for my supper but I couldn't think of the words, any words. He is the dullest little man. But he was delighted to make, with great hush and airs of indiscretion, the announcement that he and Terry "had been together" for two and a half years. I mustered as much inoffensive surprise as I could.

I'm giving Dig a framed drawing (she had the irritating good taste to pick one of the best, but I will have it photographed to show my horse) and little by little I am managing to use up most of the frames I've

8. Bachardy was familiar with the signatures of film stars such as Joan Crawford (1905–1977) because he had collected them at premieres throughout his adolescence. He drew Joan Crawford only later, on February 9, 1974, and she added a message and autograph so large that he was unable to exhibit the portrait.

9. Cooper played Mrs. Moore and Portman played Mr. Fielding in the 1962 Broadway production of Santha Rama Rau's adaptation. Tony Richardson was mooted to direct it, but instead the producers settled on Donald McWhinnie.

been stuck with. Lunch at Jocelyn's on Monday, just the two of us. We really get on well together, even all by ourselves. She was full of lots of interesting history about Loudon and Harry.

Nick Eden has also taken a drawing I did of him, and Georgia Brown[10] finally bought one of herself for her mother.

Saw *The American Dream* and liked the production but really don't think much at all of Albee. Hated everything about *Death of Bessie Smith*.

Suddenly I must fly! It's after twelve and I'm expected at Buckle's at one.

Dearest magic horse, don't stop thinking of pussy because he loves his horse so and keeps him so close to his heart always, and that small hard cat head is always occupied by the horse, which doesn't leave very much room for anything else. Kitty misses his dear so very very much and will fly to the stable as soon as he can get everything settled here.

All Kitty's Love.

[*Autograph letter*]

Friday. November 17. [1961, London]

Dearest only Horse—

Your letter of the 13th arrived this morning. Loved your description of lunch with Nehru—old Dub leads such a glamorous life, and when you think that most horses his age would be standing out in a quiet meadow sleepily munching grass, or on their way to the glue factory. But not Kitty's slippery mare.

I've thought too of maybe going to N.Y. anyway, regardless of this ass at the Sagittarius not coming across. But if I do I should certainly go on my way back to California, which would mean writing Julie, sending my drawings from the show to N.Y. rather than to California and all kinds of things. Do you think it's worth it to save my fare? I do feel I would like to try painting again but also dread being depressed by it in California and feeling I haven't anything else to turn to. And will you mind leaving Santa Monica again so soon, and being in N.Y. when your book comes out?

---

10. English singer and actress (1933–1992), then known for her roles in *The Threepenny Opera* at the Royal Court and *Oliver!* in the West End.

Please write as soon as you can and tell me your feelings. You are right, I think, about what I should do regarding the McKinnons. I hope I will be able to see them here again before I go, to make things clear. I didn't know I was to give the books you mentioned to Heywood Hill but I will certainly do it right away, and send my *Sally Bowles* and *Conspirators* along, too. They are all still here in the house. Had a drink with Phil Burton last evening—he's coming over to see my drawings today. His play was a disaster and he's very sad.[1] All Pussy's furriest love to his beloved colt.

🐾 X ⅄ X ⅄ ⅃⅄ X ⅄ X ⅄ X ⅄ X ⅄ X X X

[Autograph letter]

Saturday. November 25. [1961, London]

Dearest Stallion—

You will have gotten my telegram when you read this. I had a letter yesterday morning from the Sagittarius saying I could have a show there from January 2 to 13th, if I wanted it. Of course when they put it that way, "if you want it," I wasn't sure that I did. First of all it's a terrible time of year for a show, just after Christmas when no one is in a buying mood or even a looking mood. Then I will have to pay for all the frames and invitations, etc., myself, and all this expense combined with the very lukewarm interest on the part of Rasponi and Co. made me think it might be best to turn it down. But then I talked to Cecil last night (Truman is here now and we all went to the world premiere of *The Innocents*[1]) and he encouraged me to do it—said in spite of everything he thought it would do me good. He also said Rasponi was reliable, a gentleman and a good business man, all of which impressed me, particularly coming from Cecil. So I have decided to do it.

I am writing the Sagittarius today to say I will be coming soon, also

1. Philip Burton (1904–1995), Welsh schoolmaster, playwright, director, BBC drama producer, was teacher and mentor to Richard Burton, who became his legal ward and took his name by deed poll. The play may have been *Twelfth Night*, which he directed that year with the Shakespeare Festival Players at the Library of Congress in Washington, D.C.

1. Truman Capote and William Archibald wrote the screenplay, based on Henry James's *The Turn of the Screw*.

writing Julie and Manning to ask if we can stay with them, and if so how soon. I will wait for their answer and then, if it's all right with them, I will make plans to fly to N.Y. as soon as possible, having made all arrangements (getting the house here in order and sending on drawings and excess baggage to N.Y. and California) in the meantime. If Julie and Manning can't put us up I will write to Lincoln and ask if he can. As soon as I hear either way I will let you know and you can come to N.Y. in your own time. I want to be there as soon as possible to start preparations for the show and do all the things I didn't do with the Redfern show. So don't do anything until you hear from me but plan to be in N.Y. at least by Christmas—it's been a long time since the Animals have had a white Christmas. Kitty is quite excited at the thought of it and so longing to be with his old dear treasure again—he's thought so much of him this last week and missed him more than ever. What a remarkable, irreplaceable, unmatchable, and adorable darling Kitty's old horse is.

I will write as soon as I hear from Julie, and if I can get reservations, leave soon after, so that I may be in N.Y. by the time you get my letter. So it's probably best if you don't write again to London—don't want any horse missiles left lying around for bad, unanimal eyes to make use of. Rest assured that Kitty will make a place for his Horse and send for him the moment it's warm and nice.

All of pussy's best love to his dearest angel.

XXXXXXXXXXXXXXXXXXXX K.

PUSSY-FOOTNOTE:

The evening last night was quite fun, except for the film which really is not much good, worse even than I'd thought. I felt a coolness in the reception of it—the usual chanting of "great—great" had a hollow sound to it. Truman was very nervous and edgy. Jimmy Woolfe[2] gave an elaborate dinner in a private room at the Mirabelle afterwards, for nineteen people and a white pussy who got his dish put right on the table. Truman, Cecil, Deborah and Peter[3] (all of whom send love to you),

2. James Woolfe (1919–1966), British film producer; a backer of The Innocents. He had produced I Am a Camera (1955) with his brother John Woolfe (see below, p. 247).

3. Deborah Kerr (1921–2007), Scottish-born actress who starred as the governess in The Innocents, and her second husband since 1960, German-born American novelist and screenwriter, Peter Viertel (1920–2007), also married once before.

Jack Clayton,[4] the Irwin Shaws,[5] the Parrishes, the Bryan Forbeses,[6] the Attenboroughs, Ricky Huston,[7] Harry Kurnitz,[8] Martita Hunt[9] (at last I've met her) were all at dinner. Out of the twenty the cat's pencil had done its work with nine, the most distinguished nine, too. I'm going to call Martita Hunt and hope to make it an even ten. Truman is being interviewed for Ken Tynan's show tomorrow,[10] then a big party at Richard Buckle's afterwards.

[*Autograph letter with autograph enclosure*]

Monday November 27 [1961]   [Santa Monica]

Sweetest treasure,

Your cable arrived this morning, and I am THRILLED to hear that you have got a show after all. I do think it was essential to get one right away, and even if you had come back here we would have had to go to New York and try to get one. Of course I am sad that I won't see you for another two and a half weeks or so; I was so looking forward to welcoming my darling toward the end of this week. But the time will pass.

There is so much to discuss with you. Particularly the Socrates project, which we have now reopened and I think really invented a quite fascinating and original way of doing. Sort of Pirandelloish, but different. However, more of that when we meet.

Great weepy scenes with Glenn Ford, who has been told by Hopey that he's not to go around with her any more. Having said this, Hope does go around with him but then gets drunk and tells him she doesn't want to! Glenn is so appallingly *loyal* and moons over her, and is really moved to genuine tears of self-pity. It is very tiresome having to advise

4. (1936–1992), British director of *The Innocents*. He and Woolfe had previously had a big success with *Room at the Top* (1959).
5. American novelist, playwright, screenwriter (1913–1984) and his wife, the former Marian Edwards, an actress and chorus girl from Los Angeles. Shaw was a longtime friend of Viertel.
6. English actor, director, producer, screenwriter, novelist (b. 1926), and his second wife, English actress Nanette Newman (b. 1934).
7. Enrica (Ricki) Soma, Italian-American ballerina (1930–1969), fourth wife of John Huston.
8. American playwright, novelist, and screenwriter (1908–1968).
9. Argentine-born British actress of stage and screen (1900–1969).
10. "Tempo," a U.S. arts show aired on ABC T.V. on Sunday afternoons.

him, especially as I privately believe there is no hope for him (pun unintended!). She is just bored pissless by him now.

Jo is in a fuss because her daughter is visiting her with the husband whom neither she nor Ben likes. And oh, there is something so strange there—Jo has never told Peter and Alice even or any of their other friends that she *has* a daughter, and now she is afraid it'll be discovered![1] I don't really understand this at all. Surely it can't be that she thinks it dates her?! And, according to Jo, Ben minds so terribly. WHY?

I'm going into town now to see Carter Lodge, to get advice about an offer I've had to have a screenplay of *Prater Violet* done. Something whispers to me not to agree but wait and see how the new novel does first. I do so wish I could talk it all over with you. You always have some kind of angle on these things.

Sweet love, I am bursting with joy and pride about your New York show, and I long for the day we meet again. Oh God I do get so terribly lonely. And even if I were to live in the midst of a mob, everything would still be empty and stupid and solitary without the brush of a kitten's whisker and the touch of his furry paw.

Will write again as soon as I get your letter. I do hope Julie can put us up. If she refuses, what should we do?

Always, Dub

[*Typed letter, signed*]

Thursday, December 6. [1961, London]

Dearest Treasure-Drub—

Just a tiny minute to write my darling a little note to tell him how terribly rushed and fussed Kitty has been these past days. I had so much work to do at the last minute this past week that I couldn't even get packed and organize the shipping to California of all the stuff I've accumulated at the house. I literally had to cancel my Sunday morning flight on Saturday night. But I have turned this delay to my advantage

---

1. Before settling in Santa Monica, Jo had a son and daughter with a North Dakotan, Ferdinand Hinchberger, whom she did not marry. She was married only once, briefly, to another man, Jack Lathwood. The daughter, Betty, married Fran Arizu, a Mexican.

and am having the catalogue for the N.Y. show printed here (much cheaper that way), which will cut down the number of things I will have to do in N.Y. when I finally get there. I called the gallery in N.Y. and prepared them for a late arrival next week. They said they would warn their framer to stand by for an emergency job. Otherwise they did not sound alarmed. A man at Methuen's is taking charge of the printing of the catalogue here and it is possible I will have the work finished by Tuesday next and if so I will send my clothes on by mail and take the catalogues with me on the plane. All this is of course subject to delay. The drawing of Igor stretched out on the sofa is being used for the cover. I think it might look very nice if all goes well.

Eric has been very helpful and has produced an accountant to advise me on my tax situation, which doesn't seem as serious as I thought. I am drawing the Duchess of Leeds tomorrow morning and going to the Redfern in the afternoon to try to get as much money out of them as I can. I sent off by surface the Jenkins's bag stuffed with clothes and three other parcels of drawings, paints and more clothes this morning.[1] They will arrive in California sometime in February I'm told. I will pay all of the cost of shipping etc. here before I go.

I sent Julie a cable saying I was delayed and will send the Dub and her another cable each as soon as I know when I will get to N.Y. I missed the McKinnons on their way back through London. They are in N.Y. now and maybe I will see them when I get there. Richard Buckle has been very kind and helpful to the pussy and given him advice and help with his problems. But nobody is quite like Kitty's old Bay when it comes to guidance and encouragement. Kitty needs his dear very much and misses him so and longs for him and so looks forward to his White Horse Christmas. All the cat's love to his dear. Horse's only Sainta Claws.

[Autograph letter on letterhead of Savoy Hotel, London[2]]

1. The Jenkins's bag was a spare given to Bachardy by Richard Burton's brother and sister-in-law, Ivor and Gwen Jenkins, when they were Bachardy's landlords in 1961.
2. Bachardy was not staying there.

NEW YORK NY[1]
DECEMBER 11, 1961

ISHERWOOD
145 ADELAIDE DR SANTA MONICA CALIF

STRAY KITTEN FOUND IN NY MEWING FOR A HORSE IF YOU KNOW
THIS CAT COME AT ONCE = NYSPCA =

[*Western Union Telegram*]

. . .

1. Bachardy flew to New York overnight December 9–10 and spent the weekend with Paul
Millard at a friend's apartment, without telling Isherwood or the Gurians where he was. He
had been having an affair with Millard in California, before he left for the Slade, and after
nearly a year without meeting, they ended it that weekend.

Friday morning.   [26 January 1962]

Sweetest love,
    Just a hoof-scribble to say we are nearly in Chicago,[1] well on time.
A director of a hospital who dined opposite me, wearing a huge wedding
ring, informed me that "Richard Burton's voice is full of sex"!
    Love my darling.
    Thinking so much of Kitty—
    Dub.

Something I forgot to tell you—of the books I left behind, the *Julius
Caesar* is the copy with pages missing, so it's useless. They gave me
another in its place. *The House of Mirth* belongs to the Gurians. The
others I just don't want.

[*Autograph letter*]

[January 27, 1962]

    Won't write a Kitty and Dobbin letter. That's sentimental. Though
it's a beautiful poetic sentimentality. But I think we can still talk to each
other by our own names—I mean, even when we're not mad.

---

1. Isherwood was en route from New York to Los Angeles by train. He had flown to New
York on December 12, 1961, where he met Bachardy at the Gurians'. They saw many friends,
visited Gore Vidal at his country house in Barrytown, attended the opening of Vidal's play
Romulus in Philadelphia and New York, and prepared for Bachardy's opening on January 2,
1962, including framing the pictures and sending out catalogues. Bachardy did many portraits
throughout this period; Isherwood met several times with his editor and others at Simon
and Schuster about his new novel, *Down There on a Visit*, and picked up the first copies. When
Isherwood set off for Los Angeles on January 25, Bachardy remained at the Gurians'.

I realize I am deeply selfish. You admit that you are. But that doesn't stop me loving you. And perhaps we would get along better on the basis of being admittedly selfish. I said a true thing when I said I didn't like being "good" any more than you didn't like being "bad."

You are so much the reason for my life—my writing, the house, my teaching. You say, that's just accident. Anyone could have been the reason. No. You know that's not true.

My selfishness is that I want you to stay with me. Your selfishness is that you ask yourself, couldn't you do better; considering you are young. So my selfishness is really much more sinister than yours.

Am writing this halfway through my first scotch of the evening, in the vista dome, going through the desert beyond Needles. But I'll copy it out if I mean it tomorrow . . .[1]

[Draft letter on train ticket envelope, now lost]

Tuesday, January 30. [1962]   [Santa Monica]

My own Love,

Just a brief note of assorted news and stuff.

The crates came all right and they weren't crates but quite manageable packages wrapped in burlap which I was able to pick up from Gavin's by myself and stash away in a corner of the back room. Only five dollars to pay for the trucking fee; so I guess the total charge was $25.00—plus of course what you paid in London.

Which reminds me, I can't find any record of having paid that travel agency, so shall send the money for my ticket to France.[1]

Ask Bob Craft about this show of pictures, etc., of Stravinsky. He mentioned it to me, but I forgot to tell you, I think. You ought to get in on it. I expect Wystan would lend his.[2]

1. Isherwood copied this letter into his diary, and it is printed in D.2, pp. 157–158, but he did not mail it to Bachardy. Needles is the California town at the borders with Nevada and Arizona.

1. When they stayed with Tony Richardson at La Baumette, near Valbonne, in September 1961.
2. "Stravinsky and the Dance," at the Wildenstein Gallery in 1962 in honor of Stravinsky's eightieth birthday on June 18, including photos, snapshots, paintings, drawings, keepsakes, and memorabilia. Auden owned one of Bachardy's drawings of Stravinsky.

Be sure to contact Jen and get that poem of Wystan's from him.[3]

This has been the third marvellous gold day with temperature in the high eighties. The sun still sets right in the middle of the bay. I have been to the gym twice already and plan an intensive course. Also, yesterday, on the beach and into the ocean. It was icy. Ted is coming down tomorrow. I have talked to him on the phone but not yet to Glade. Tonight I am going to see the Houseman production of *Measure for Measure* at UCLA with Ivan and Kate Moffat. Gavin says it's good. If it is and you come back in time, I'll gladly go again. But I doubt if you will come in time as it only runs until February 7. I am also going to *Throne of Blood*,[4] and of course I'll see that again with you, if you haven't seen it in New York. Don't know how long that's running.

Gavin fears that Tom Wright is falling in love with Michael Hall![5] Mike Steen,[6] met on the beach, thought Tennessee would arrive tomorrow. But you probably know about this. On Friday I'm going to L.A. State to get my parking pass, find out which classrooms I have and sign that old loyalty oath for the millionth time.[7] Still, as long as one keeps being asked, "Do you still love me?" I suppose one can't complain.

I found Dorothy well but shaken by flu. Everybody has had it here. The plants looked yellowish but are being given revival treatment in the garden. Nothing was damaged or stolen. All your back issues of *Film Facts* have arrived.

Gerald and Michael had flu so badly that they cancelled their trip to see the dolphins.[8]

---

3. "The Platonic Blow," beginning, "It was a Spring day, a day for a lay," rumored to have been written by Auden in 1948; it circulated in typescript until it was first published in 1965 (see below, p. 211), and evidently Jenson Yow had a copy.

4. Akira Kurosawa's 1957 adaptation of *Macbeth*, set in medieval Japan, was released in November 1961 in the U.S.

5. American actor and, later, antique dealer (b. 1927).

6. American stuntman, actor, author (1928–1983), born Malcolm H. Steen; he was from Louisiana, where he was friendly with Tom Wright and Speed Lamkin.

7. He was to start teaching there again in February, two literature courses and a creative writing course. Beginning in 1949, at the dawn of the McCarthy era, the State of California required university employees to affirm their loyalty to the state constitution and to forswear beliefs or membership in groups advocating overthrow of the U.S. government—for instance, communist beliefs or groups.

8. In the Virgin Islands, see above, p. 82.

Last night I had dinner with the lovestruck Jerry Lawrence.[9] You'll probably see him before this letter.

I wrote from Chicago to you, Julie and Jack Kelly,[10] thanking them.

Sweetheart, I miss my dear. Tell that busy frisky cat not to forget his old faithful Dubrin, and come back before long to the Casa—but preferably *not* to arrive on a Tuesday or a Thursday, or it may not be possible to meet him with his velvet cart and prepare all the proper comforts for a travelworn tabby.

Como siempre, El Dub.

[*Typed letter, signed*]

Monday February 5. 1962 [New York]

Dearest only Drub—

Poor Kitty misses his old darling so much and suffers so in the big, cold, grey city, without the warmth of Horse's round body and the reassuring smell of hay. Lonely cat couldn't even bear to be fed his breakfast cream in the Animals' place, and now every morning he casts about, alone and unbrushed, drifting into any nameless place with only the smallest hope of some stray kindness. At best Kitty is shoved into a corner with a dirty saucer of skim milk.

Dub's dear letter did come to comfort Pussy, though the days since then have been long and hard. But Kitty struggles on, working bravely every day, and making some progress.

Yesterday he did some drawings of Frank and one of Tennessee, only one, but at least it's the best so far. Also, Tennessee took the cat into the country in a black limousine to see his crazy sister, Rose, at a place called Stony Lodge where, after a gruesome dinner, the cat was even made to draw crazy Rose.[1]

9. Lawrence regularly fell in love; this time, it may have been with Larry Paxton. See below, p. 119.
10. J. Terry Kelly (d. 1989), antique dealer and party designer who decorated John F. Kennedy's inaugural dinner in 1961. His companion, dancer and librettist Erik Johns (1927–2001), was a devotee at the New York Vedanta Society. Kelly gave an all-male party in New York the night before Isherwood left.

1. Rose Isabel Williams (1909–1996), a schizophrenic, was given insulin shock treatment and a lobotomy in her early thirties and spent the rest of her life in institutions. Stony Lodge Hospital is in Ossining, New York, overlooking the Hudson.

The cat's tail brush also dealt with Marianne Moore[2] on Friday, and she was so kind to him, and stroked him and showed him little pictures and toy mice and her old watercolors. Though she didn't have one of her own, Kitty felt she really liked cats. One of the drawings, in her usual three-cornered hat which Wystan objects to, is even quite good.

Wystan and Chester have been very sweet. Wystan has commissioned me to draw Elizabeth Mayer,[3] which I'm doing on Thursday. They had me to dinner one night. Irving Drutman and Michael De Lisio[4] have also been kind to a kitten.

Julie and Manning, Marian and Jay[5] and particularly Bill Inge, all praise "The Dub's Story" very much.[6] Tennessee was upset because he hadn't got his copy yet, so Kitty gave him his own because he thought his old Horse would have wished it.

Did more, older, drawings of Anita Loos,[7] which she liked even more than the first ones, also some flying claw impressions of Shelley,[8] who was as impossible a sitter as I had expected. Terry Rattigan took the cat, in his best night-black bow, to the opening of A Passage to India[9] and then to dinner with Margaret Leighton at 21—they were both surprised that such a tiny pussy could make more than mewing sounds. Margaret quite drunkenly said she thought all my drawings of her were awful, though this was only after I told her frankly, because she told me to be frank, that a brand new emerald-studded brooch she'd just bought looked rather like a piece of costume jewelry (those were her own words to me!)—but all was well in the end. She is mad to marry Terry and wildly

2. American poet (1887–1972).
3. German émigré translator and editor (1884–1970); she hosted Auden in her Manhattan and Long Island homes and became his close friend.
4. Drutman, an editor and a songwriter, had advised Cocteau on his 1946 film Beauty and the Beast. De Lisio was his longterm companion.
5. American actress Marian Winters (1924–1979), who won a Tony Award for Best Supporting Actress playing Natalia Landauer in the original stage production of I Am a Camera, and her husband, Jay Smolin, a lawyer.
6. That is, Down There on a Visit.
7. American playwright, screenwriter, novelist (1888–1981), creator of the art of silent-film captions and author of Gentlemen Prefer Blondes (1925); she had been a close friend of Isherwood since 1939.
8. Shelley Winters (1922–2006), American actress; she played Natalia Landauer in the film of I Am a Camera. (She had the same surname as her stage predecessor Marian Winters only by coincidence.)
9. On January 31.

possessive about him and feared that she might have to compete with a ball of fur—imagine! But Kitty was gracious and made his pussition perfectly clear to her—as though a Rat could *ever* follow a Horse.[10]

A Passage to India is inept as a play, and yet it has a great deal of atmosphere occasionally, and Gladys Cooper is terribly good, so is the Indian.[11] But [Eric] Portman is awful and Anne Meacham completely wrong.[12] Still it is worth seeing, particularly the first act. It gets progressively worse and of course the scene at the caves is bad, vague and silly at the same time.

This afternoon the cat's eye is on the Davidova,[13] tomorrow Leueen Goodyear[14] and Virgil Thomson,[15] who is a commission from Igor. I saw them all only once at a big cocktail party given for them by Arnold Weissberger.[16] Igor was terribly sweet, hugged and kissed me (Weissberger nearly fainted) and so was Vera. Bob [Craft] strangely cool. David Selznick and Ethel Merman[17] were there (she wished Igor a happy birthday and he said, "It's not my birthday," and there was a deadly hush). Also Jerry Lawrence who is supposed to take Larry[18] and me to *Who'll Save the Plowboy*[19] on Thursday.

Lotte Lenya is written in to be drawn on Wednesday and (if she doesn't beg off again) that will be the last of the things I really wanted to do here. The cat is planning to be with his horse for their anniversary, which is a Wednesday, if nothing comes up to make him stay (can't think what could).

Vogue magazine called to say my drawing of Emlyn will be in the

10. Leighton was then appearing in *The Night of the Iguana*, which Bachardy and Isherwood had seen with Williams in preview, December 27, 1961, the night before it opened, and for which Leighton won a Tony Award. She had also won a Tony for Rattigan's *Separate Tables* in 1956 and had appeared in other Rattigan plays. She had recently divorced her first husband, Laurence Harvey.
11. Zia Mohyeddin (b. 1933), Pakistani actor trained at the Royal Academy of Dramatic Arts, who had made his 1960 London debut in the same role, Dr. Aziz.
12. Mary Anne Meacham (1925–2006), American actress, noted for her roles in Tennessee Williams's plays and, later, in the soap opera "Another World"; she played Adela Quested.
13. A Russian friend of Vera Stravinsky and especially of George Balanchine; she reportedly attended every performance of the New York City Ballet and even rehearsals.
14. English actress Leueen MacGrath (1914–1992), then married to Stephen Goodyear. Her five husbands also included, from 1949 to 1957, George S. Kauffman, with whom she co-wrote the book for *Silk Stockings* (1955) and other Broadway musicals.
15. American composer, music critic, author (1896–1989).
16. Show-business and arts lawyer (1907–1981); Stravinsky was a client.
17. American musical comedy star (1908–1984).
18. Larry Paxton (d. 1963), a young Los Angeles friend then working in an art gallery in New York.
19. By Frank Gilroy (b. 1925).

February 15 issue (I'll believe it when I see it)[20] and the Oleg Cassini job is still on,[21] though his fall collection will not be ready till April—I could, if I still want to, do the drawings anytime in the late spring or early summer. I've told the advertising agency that I'm going to California very soon and gave them my address and phone there.

Betsy von Furstenburg and husband[22] bought one of the drawings of her, and Tennessee paid me for the Leighton (she's getting it whether she likes it or not) and Terry [Rattigan] gave me $150 for the drawings of Michael [Franklin]. John Knowles wants to buy a drawing I did of him (he wrote that college book[23] and his *Morning in Antibes* is just coming out) and I drew Marian Smolin, and Joanne [Woodward] & Paul [Newman] again.

That's all news for now. The next word you have may be a telegram to say the cat is rushing back to his dear stable-izer on the next jet plane, his tail a booster jet stream. All love to his only Love. Tabby

[Autograph letter]

La Casa. Wednesday February 7. [1962]

Dearest Love,

Your dear letter arrived this morning, so full of news, and how sweet a Kitty to find time to write it with his tiny tired paw. It would be lovely if he was here for the Animals' Day,[1] especially as they missed being together last year. If he were to arrive late on Tuesday, Dobbin *could* meet him. I think he could get to the airport, direct from State College, by about eight-thirty in the evening. On Wednesday, of course, he would be free any time.

Went back to work at L.A. State yesterday. Mobs of people, and my

20. It appeared in U.S. *Vogue* with Williams's story "They Loved Each Other," p. 90.
21. Drawings of the Paris-born American fashion designer (1913–2006) and of actress Merle Oberon in one of his gowns, for ads in *Vogue* and *Harper's Bazaar*.
22. Elizabeth von Fürstenburg-Hedringen, German baroness and, as Betsy von Furstenberg, Broadway actress (b. 1931), and her French-born first husband, Guy Vincent Chastenet de la Maisonneuve, a mining engineer known as Guy Vince.
23. *A Separate Peace*, based on his high-school years at Phillips Exeter Academy, from which Knowles (1926–2001) graduated in 1945 before attending Yale.

1. That is, their anniversary, February 14.

classes jammed. It will be all right, I guess. But now I have three classes in a row on Tuesdays, and that *is* tiring. Dubbin is also going religiously to the gym—five times last week!—and laying off bread and butter and suchlike; but I fear it'll be a long while before he loses his roundness.

A letter from the Masselinks, on some particularly exotic spot in the Hawaiian Islands, and a letter from Jim [Charlton], *still* in Kyoto. He has had clap but continues to love the Japanese. Says nothing about returning. And then a very sweet note from Anita, who has read and liked the first episode of my novel. She writes, "Don's jacket is very moving and I feel that by the time I finish the book it will be almost unbearably so; a record of how cruel life is and at the same time how seductive, as your works always reveal so poignantly." I don't really quite understand what this sentence means, but it is obviously high praise for both of us! I was astonished that she signs herself "your devoted." I think you must have a great deal to do with all this enthusiasm. It's something new. She writes of your drawings of her that they are "so full of character that they give me a fresh impression of myself."

I shall see about getting your car put into running order. Have got the license plates. Talked to Parker today about renewing the insurance. He is finding out about all this.[2]

It's grey here now and has been foggy and sad. Today is raining and there is a wind getting up, so let's hope it blows some fine weather along.

Read the first forty thousand words of Gavin's novel.[3] It is almost frantically readable. Maybe a bit too nervous and smart-alecky. I long to hear your opinion. The *Measure for Measure* production was just awful. Terribly acted, and the most tasteless Gay Nineties Viennese decor and costumes. Was also much disappointed in *Throne of Blood*. But I think that'll still be on when you come back.

Elsa [Lanchester] and Michael Hall (now her constant companion) were down at their house and called me over, and then Charles got on the line. He is in bed in hospital in New York, and he asked if you were in town and if you could come and visit him. I was vague, vague. On being pressed for your phone, I gave him a number which I now realize was almost certainly wrong. So that's that. If you *do* want to see him, however—Flurrance Nightcat—he's at the Hospital for Special Surgery,

---

2. Charles Parker, their tax accountant, also managed their paperwork.
3. *Inside Daisy Clover* (1963).

535 East 70th St. Poor old thing, he has cracked his collarbone. Terry [Jenkins] is in attendance. [Charles] is very cold whenever Elsa suggests coming, according to her.

All my love to my Darling, and awaiting his telegram, Dub.

Love to Julie and Manning.

[*Typed letter, signed, with autograph addition*]

. . .

Tuesday 10th [July 1962]   [Santa Monica]

After hearing his sweet kitten purring down the phone,[1] Dob went trotting out to do errands, including mailing the drawings for Kitty. Got home to find the enclosed card for Kitty from Grimes. So you'd better contact the woman she mentions and say the prints have gone off already to the other address?[2]

Also, Mrs. Strauss called in a flap, because she'd been expecting Kitty to come and draw her and, pray, where was he? So I soothed her as best I could, said he had left in mad haste to capture a very unexpected huge mouse, and that no doubt in the excitement of the chase he had forgotten and would be very contrite and sad when he remembered, and especially if he was suffering from indigestion from gobbling the mouse up too quick.

A card for you from Ned Rorem[4] announces his arrival in L.A. next Friday. It is signed "affection, Ned." Hm.

Dob thinks so much of his kitten and will be sad till his return. Len Kaufman is calling by for Doris's easel this afternoon.[5]

Tell Lincoln I send my love. But it's really all for that furry treasure. Drub

[*Typed letter, signed*]

1. Bachardy flew to New York just after midnight on July 9–10, 1962, to draw Oleg Cassini. He stayed with Lincoln Kirstein.
2. Bachardy drew American musical comedy star Tammy Grimes (b. 1934) on June 3, and Grimes was trying to get the drawings published in a magazine. The enclosure is lost, but evidently Isherwood posted photostats of the drawings to a Miss Thwaites at an address previously supplied to Bachardy. Bachardy had also drawn Grimes twice in New York, December 28 and 29, 1961, when she was still appearing in *The Unsinkable Molly Brown* for which she won a Tony Award; it closed in February 1962.
3. The size of the mouse was exaggerated by Isherwood to placate Mrs. Strauss, but Cassini was at the height of his fame, dressing Jacqueline Kennedy in the White House.
4. American composer and writer (b. 1923).
5. Doris Dowling had taken up painting as an amateur and loaned her easel to Bachardy who did not have his own. Len Kaufman was her third husband.

July 13 [1962]   [Santa Monica]

Dearest love,

[T]his is to enclose three things you may like to have. I opened
Stephen's letter because I thought it might be something I could cope
with, and Miss Thwaites's letter for the same reason. The photostats have
been returned, but they have been clumsily handled and show small
tears at the sides. I don't think they are to be trusted with drawings. As
for the King letter, maybe you will want to see her while in New York.[1]

I saw Al Spar yesterday and he is going to set us up as a sort of
corporation or firm or whatever. It is perfectly legal and it saves a lot on
taxes. Only thing is, we have to have a name! Any suggestions? I do hate
those very invented-sounding names like Carviv or Monox. How would
Casa do? But maybe it's too usual.[2]

Lovely weather here. Am working very hard. A gloom-filled visit to
poor Charles yesterday.[3] The plumbing and electricity have been okayed
by the inspectors, so we can hope for more action next week. The man
came in to measure for the mirrors; an estimate will be phoned in later
today.[4]

I keep wondering what Wondercat is doing. Shan't be happy till he's
home again. All an old horse's love to his darling,

Drubbin

[*Typed letter, signed*]

·   ·   ·

1. The enclosed letters, from Stephen Spender, Miss Thwaites, and Bachardy's friend, Marcia
King, then still living in New York, have not been traced.
2. Spar was a lawyer and accountant; he merged Isherwood's and Bachardy's finances as
Bee-Eye Enterprises—for Bachardy-Isherwood. He was recommended by Carter Lodge in
particular because Lodge was working on a deal to make a potentially lucrative musical of *I
Am a Camera*.
3. Laughton had been released from the hospital in New York and had returned to Los
Angeles; although inclined to deny it, he was dying of cancer.
4. Isherwood and Bachardy were making improvements to 145 Adelaide Drive, including
lining one wall of the dining room with mirrors and turning the garage into a studio for
Bachardy.

Monday morning. [March 11, 1963]   [Santa Monica]

You have just left,[1] and oh dear I feel so miserable, at the complexity of everything and the difficulty I have in talking to you. I mean, I really understand so much much more than I can express in conversation. There's your painting problem. Almost nothing I can do about that. I often feel you don't even want my sympathy, but just for me to get the hell out and leave you alone. That's perfectly all right, but it's among the many things we don't seem to be able to say to each other without hurt feelings on my side, irritation on yours. (The irony of it is that you can help *me*, with my writing problems, very considerably; so the situation is one-sided.) Then there's Bill.[2] If only we could talk about that! But I guess it's impossible, because you feel that I am trying to own the relationship or sponsor it, or whatever you say, just by talking about it. But all I really want you to know is that I do see why it has to be, and I am glad about it—much more than that, I really do accept it as part of our life together. But even if I say *that* much, it sounds sort of possessive, as though I were trying to make it into a mere colony of the Kitty-Dobbin empire. Anyhow, I won't pretend that I adore being alone, those evenings. But that's my business. It has always been a weakness of mine, and one which I should get over. It's childishness, really. Something to do with the dark. Because during the daytime I couldn't be happier by myself.

---

1. Bachardy set off for Phoenix, Arizona, by car that morning and returned the evening of March 15. A show of his work was planned to open at the Phoenix Museum of Art on April 16, and he had made a previous trip in January to draw portraits of two prominent local residents, Frank Lloyd Wright's widow Olgivanna Wright (1898–1985) and Clare Boothe Luce (1903–1987), editor, playwright, Republican congresswoman, ambassador, and wife of *Time-Life* magnate, Henry R. Luce. By the beginning of April, Bachardy was to cancel the show because it had become political and burdensome. In Phoenix, he stayed with Edward ("Bud") Jacobson, a lawyer involved with civic affairs.
2. Bill Bopp (b. 1932), with whom Bachardy was having a relatively serious affair. Bopp was an administrator at the Burroughs Corporation, the data-processing company, and lived in an apartment in Hollywood.

Well, anyhow—that is connected with these involvements I create. And there I have to admit, you are right, I am motivated, at least to some extent, by a queeny competitive bitchiness. I see now that the thing with Paul was really inexcusable.[3] I simply cannot fathom how I can have been so thick-skinned. But, there again, if only we could talk! Like the evening before last, I had actually just stayed the night at the house where I'd been drinking, purely and simply because they didn't want me to drive back drunk.[4] But I couldn't tell you that, because telling you would have suggested that you minded; and that's the kind of minding we never talk of. We only either kid each other about it, or get angry. Oh—I am so saddened and depressed when I get a glimpse, as I do so clearly this morning, of the poker game we play so much of the time, watching each other's faces and listening to each other's voices for clues. And then you say, for example, Dobbin's in a strange mood, and then things start to get tense. And, because I know this, I start playacting to get them untense again, and that makes everything worse. And you are much the same. Although, somehow or other, you always seem franker than I am. Is that because you can afford to be? Am I scared of you? Yes, in a way. But I really almost wish I could be *more* scared. How can I explain that? It's hard. But, to try to get at what I mean, I was so happy the other day when you said that about Dobbin having been a jailer and now being a convict.[5] I sort of wish that were true all of the time. Masochism? Oh, Mary—what do I care what it's called? I only know that it isn't a *wrong* thing for me to feel. Our relationship is really so very very strange. No wonder it gives us trouble. I mean, I often feel that the Animals are far more than just a nursery joke or a cuteness. They *exist*. They are like Jung's myths. They express a kind of freedom and truth which we otherwise wouldn't have . . . I have written all this and maybe, having read this far, you will say, what an egomaniac. I have quite other problems, you will say, which have nothing to do with him. Yes, I know that. And again, if I say I would like to talk about them, you may reply

3. Paul Wonner (1920–2008), American painter, spent the night with Isherwood at 145 Adelaide Drive on February 28; it was "inexcusable" because they slept in Isherwood and Bachardy's own bed. Bachardy was out of town for the March 1 opening of a show of his drawings in Stanford. Before and after his trip, Bachardy himself spent numerous evenings and nights away from Adelaide Drive with Bill Bopp.
4. Isherwood stayed with Haven Lucas, Alan Harlan, and a friend of theirs called Henry, on March 9.
5. On March 5, "Dub used to be my jailer, now he's Kitty's convict." D.2, March 6, 1963, p. 269.

that I am merely trying to get possession of them. (I mean, basically, the feeling you have mentioned of fear—what is going to happen to you.) Oh sweetheart, I probably ought not to send you this letter at all. Perhaps you feel nothing but sick of my interference. (I don't forget how you said how you had those feelings of sheer hatred while you were up at Stanford.[6] But then again, I am going to send the letter, because the one thing I do want you to know is that I *care*. I really do ache with misery when the wires are crossed. But then, I realize, it is sheer egotism to talk about caring. Oh shit . . . I feel I have somehow gotten something said, but I don't quite know what. I love you. C.

In case I forgot to tell you, I suppose I shall have to go to *The Hollow Crown* with Cecil, on Thursday night.[7]

[*Typed letter, initialled*]

• • •

6. Bachardy had driven to Stanford on February 26 for the opening of his show and returned March 2.
7. Dorothy Tutin was touring with the Royal Shakespeare Company in this "Royal Revue" about the kings and queens of England; Isherwood and Beaton saw it on March 14.

April 13 [1963]   2424 Jones St. San Francisco 11¹

Own sweetcat,

Well, the drive took only seven hours and thirty-five minutes, door to door. I did everything correctly, despite the fact that they don't mark the turnoff properly from the Sacramento road. On the speedometer it was 403 miles. The Volkswagen kept comfortably at seventy-five whenever required. It was a beautiful day but last night it started to rain and it has been drizzling on and off today. This house is overwhelmingly *moderne*, and there are many gigantic abstracts, probably by Frank²— awful anyway. I have a lot of fun riding up and down in the elevator. This street goes straight down to Fisherman's Wharf, with Alcatraz in the background. Quite a good view from the roof.

Yesterday I saw Stanley Miron,³ who is much involved with a true-unto-death boy of twenty who won't leave him alone, also there's Zeigelita,⁴ also Bob in England still faithful.⁵ Yes, poor Stanley is indeed quite a bore. Today I have been quite alone, just wandering around the streets and looking at the Chinese and the shops, which is fun for a while. I have resolved this time to learn the geography of this city properly. It will all have to be done on foot, because there is absolutely nowhere to park.

1. Isherwood drove to San Francisco on April 12 and settled in a house borrowed from a painter, Mason Wells. He and Bachardy had agreed to spend some time apart, and Isherwood wanted Bachardy to remain at Adelaide Drive. An English-professor friend, Mark Schorer, arranged for Isherwood to lecture at Berkeley during May, and Isherwood wanted to be alone to work on his new novel.
2. Frank Hamilton (b. 1923), American painter, was the younger companion of Mason Wells.
3. An attractive Jewish doctor who lived and practised in San Francisco. Isherwood and Bachardy first met him in London. Stanley Miron is not his real name.
4. John Zeigel (b. 1934), American scholar of ancient and modern literature, newly an assistant professor of English and humanities at California Institute of Technology; a former love interest of Isherwood.
5. James Robert (Bob) Regester (193[2]–1987), American theatrical producer and advertising executive, later the longterm companion of Neil Hartley (see below, p. 157).

I don't know if you recall, but Mason Wells sent me a couple of tickets for some theater or other. I find I have lost them. They may just possibly be between the pages of the Forst's catalogue of hams and sausages which I left behind, in that metal tray where I keep letters to be answered, on my desk. Would you look, like a sweet love, and send them to me if they're there?

I enclose some blue stamps for Arlene.[6]

Miss my sweet kitty and hope so that his work will go well. Will be thinking of him always and hoping he hasn't forgotten his tiresome but devoted old horse, Dub-dub

[*Typed letter, signed*]

Tuesday, April 16, 1963 [Santa Monica]

Dear Stallion:

Very little of any interest to report. Old Cat is just coming out of a *deep* sulk, one that any horse would thank his stars for having missed. I suppose it's partly the usual feline reaction to being left so terribly alone, also the failure so far of any attempts to paint—not that there have been many. A petit point rendering of that blond dancer you met and a half-hearted fling at stilling that restless, tiresome head of Gia Scala's[1] have just about managed to put me off completely. On Sunday I couldn't even *draw* Dick Hopper[2]—a fairly frequent companion, incidentally, which will give you a vivid idea of the zest of Kitty's social life A.D. (After Dubbin).

Did see *The Trial* and didn't like it, though it is marvellously photographed and done with great energy. I admit that it was shown to the blackest of black cats, on the eve when his power was at the zenith, and Hell hath no Furry like a black cat bored. And he was bored. It seemed to me a quite simple, ordinary "idea" all tarted up and arted up

6. Arlene Drummond, their temporary cleaning lady while Dorothy Miller took several months off for her high blood pressure. Blue Chip Stamps, a loyalty scheme, were dispensed with purchases of groceries, gas, and other necessities, pasted into books by consumers, and then traded for housewares, kitchen and garden equipment, home beauty gadgets, and tools.

1. English-born actress (1934–1972), of Italian and Irish background.
2. Richard Hopper, American dress designer. He was a classmate of Bachardy at Chouinard in the 1950s and later worked with Edith Head, who won numerous Academy Awards for her costumes.

in the hope that mystification might pass for significance. Some of it is amusing, and much of it amusingly done, but oh the tedium of the absurd. Perkins is the only actor who has more than a glorified guest appearance—and do *you* want to see a movie with Perkins in every scene of every reel? Also, something which particularly irritates me, a very bad soundtrack, as is usual with Welles. Lots of inept dubbing and wagging mouths with no sound coming out. The whole movie sounds as though it were made in a vault.[3]

Went to life class last night and tonight I am dining at Rudi Gernreich's[4] and then after supper drawing Peggy Claxton[5] in some of his clothes. I don't have very high hopes of any great success. I've never liked drawing her but I could hardly hex her to Rudi since she was his idea and she works a lot for him. Tomorrow I will sit in on Oliver's class at UCLA[6] and Thursday night Cecil has invited me to see *Mondo cane*.[7] Friday night I'm to eat and draw with Wonner and Brown.[8]

I've sorted out of this mail most obviously unimportant stuff, though none of what's left looks important.[9] I'm sorry the Wells house is disappointing. I know what you mean about those Hamilton paintings—the school of controlled madness. The later ones are even better, what I call planes and stains.

Now that the cat-funk is over (I hope) Kitty may be able to think himself into some sort of positive state. A little thinking might not do him very much harm anyway, as long as he can avoid getting caught up in that old meaningless activity which is his usual cure for thinking. He's going to try.

3. Orson Welles's 1962 adaptation of Kafka's novel *The Trial* (1925), which Welles directed and in which he acted with American actor Anthony Perkins (1932–1992). Jeanne Moreau and Romy Schneider were among the other actors.

4. Viennese-born costume and fashion designer (1922–1985).

5. Peggy Moffitt (b. 1939), American model and actress, married to photographer Bill Claxton.

6. Oliver Andrews taught art at UCLA.

7. *Dog World*, a 1962 Italian documentary film written and directed by Gualtiero Jacopetti, Paolo Cavara, and Franco Prosperi, released in April 1963 in the U.S. It uses mostly real archival footage to present bizarre, depraved, and shocking cultural practices around the world.

8. That is, Paul Wonner and his long-established companion Bill Brown (1919–2012), also an American painter who used various names professionally: W.T. Brown, W. Theo Brown, W. Theophilus Brown, and Theophilus Brown. (Brown was white, and should not be confused with the black artist, Bill Brown, mentioned on pp. 50 and 178.)

9. The enclosures were not saved.

But he misses his old Drub, in spite of himself, and can't help loving him, in all but the worst of moods. XXXXXXXX K.

[Typed letter, initialled, with autograph additions]

Friday April 19 [1963] 2424 Jones. S.F. 11

Own sweetest Fur,

Got the dear letter yesterday. I do hope Black Puss will scat for a while and let you work. Why don't you go and see Swami one day, for a little while? I don't mean tell him anything or ask any advice. But sometimes just being with him has done something for me. Or one uses him to do something for oneself.

I am trying very hard to fill in all the time left empty by these bastards who have done nothing at all to organize lectures for me. I work on my novel and the Ramakrishna book every day, and I am doing the exercises prescribed by the Royal Canadian Air Force booklet. They are very good and don't require any props. And I have finished *Eternal Fire*,[1] which I adore; and am reading *Salt*, by Herbert Gold, which I rather hate, and him too. He is so dreary and Jew-sour. Tomorrow there is a party to celebrate the coming-out of this novel of his. Tonight dinner with Cecil and this rather nice Englishwoman who married a columnist here, the tough manly type who writes about sports with a beerbelly.[2] Yes, I like them. Don't like Bill & Paul's friends Donald Houghton and Byron Meyer very much, or any of the *rico* queers I have met[3]—oh how nastily they smell of their money and their beautiful houses; theirs really is quite stunning, an octagon, built more than a hundred years ago. This Wells house isn't so bad, it's just well-carpeted and dead, with huge bored-to-death plants. It is only bearable to be alone in; then you can wander around naked and fart at the paintings, and mutter. Frank may be pretty far gone, but he has to stand aside and award the laurel wreath to Mason himself. How could a great grown man spend hours and days and years doing those ver-

1. By Calder Willingham.
2. Mary McCabe, second wife of Charles McCabe (1915–1983), columnist for the *San Francisco Chronicle*.
3. That is, rich queers. Houghton and Meyer were trustees of the San Francisco Ballet Association and belonged to the Society for Encouragement of Contemporary Art. Meyer was in real estate and property management.

tical daubs? It is sad, really, except that I do not find the rich so very sad.

Houghton and Meyer took me to the San Francisco Ballet and there I espied Tony Duquette and Beegle. They had designed a thing called *Fantasma*.[4] Nothing in the world really but a remake of *Giselle*. The huntsman who gets taken over by the spook maiden and then killed by the spook attendants. I think the huntsman, a boy named Robert Gladstein,[5] was the worst dancer I have ever seen; he didn't have the most beautiful legs I have ever seen, but they were stunning. Nobody else worth mentioning. Tony had fashioned nipperkin-tipperkin costumes, in which the "dancers" whirled, with flying scarves and ribbons; it was like a fight in a bargain basement.

My first two lectures (out of a total of three, so far!) are next Tuesday.[6] I already went over there and had a talk with the students, who were exceptionally bright and exceptionally homely. Not *one*![7] Oh, I may possibly whizz over to the University of Nevada, at Reno, I think, sometime next week, and give a talk there. I am wild to pick up some more money, just on principle; besides, it costs a bit, living here, even with planned meal-cadging. I don't eat here except breakfast; there is a local kind of fishcake which is acceptable. The colored lady comes in and calls me Mr. Issuewood.

Lots of rainstorms, and also bright sunshine. The bay is magnificently beautiful. I lie on the roof when I can and sun. Also I walk all over the area and am learning its geography at last. Kitty would have clapped his paws and laughed from the bottom of his furry heart to see Drub hopelessly stuck on a vertical bit of Jones Street, high up Russian Hill, and trying to cling to passing houses with his hooves. But it is wonderful for the legs.

Thinks of his dear so very much and sends thoughts of love and prays that [K]itty will find a way out of his sad self.

Old Drubrubbin

[Typed letter, signed]

---

4. Tony Duquette (1914–1999), Los Angeles artist and designer of sets and costumes, domestic interiors, and jewellery, and his wife, painter Elizabeth Johnstone, known as Beegle. In 1955, Bachardy had briefly worked as Duquette's assistant. The ballet programme, on April 18, also included *Original Sin* and *Variations de Ballet*.
5. (194[3]–1992), later a principal dancer, ballet master, and assistant director of the San Francisco Ballet and then ballet master of the Dallas Ballet; he was also a choreographer.
6. Isherwood delivered "The Autobiography of My Books—I" on April 23 at Berkeley and, later the same day, "Influences," at the San Francisco Public Library. His two subsequent Berkeley lectures were "The Autobiography of My Books—II" on April 30 and "III" on May 8.
7. That is, not one was good-looking.

Tuesday, April 30, 1963 [Santa Monica]

Dear Horse:

This is all the mail of any importance to date.[1] I've weeded out all the obvious advertisements and stuff of that kind, and paid all the bills. I'm sorry to be so long in getting this to you. I hope there is nothing that has been seriously delayed.

I've not written before because I haven't had anything to tell you. I am going through an awful time. The screws are on. I can't remember a more difficult time. I can't paint, I can't read, I can't relax—or rather I *don't* do any of these things. I can't even seem to think in any kind of reasonable, constructive manner. Something is terribly wrong and not only do I not know what to do about it, I don't even know what it is that is wrong, or why. Fits of doubt and gloom keep descending. I try to fight them off but I seem to have fewer and fewer weapons.

And yet, in spite of all this, there is somewhere the vague feeling that there is a point—if I can only find it. This experience must produce some result. I only hope it will be reassuring in some way. So far, not yet. I need you, terribly sometimes. It shocks me how much. I don't want to need you. I want to be able to rely on myself. I have so many years of bad habits, selfishness and weakness to overcome. I sometimes feel it's almost hopeless to try to change, but then I don't know what else to do. I don't have any other choice which is acceptable to me. It seems I must change.

I don't like depressing you with all my woes. That's why I've not written. I don't want you to worry about me. I must do this alone. I must get through by myself. And I try hard to love you instead of just needing you.

Your overwrought
Pussy

[*Typed letter, signed*]

---

1. Enclosures not preserved.

May 1 [1963]   2424 Jones St. San Francisco 11

My darling Kitty,

Just got your letter. Naturally, I feel upset about your being upset. But not exactly anxious. I mean, I know that no one can be the person you are without going through some terrible times. But you have never been weak and, even if you can't see it in yourself, it is obvious to me that you are getting stronger and stronger. You will come through this bad time— oh yes, and go into others, no doubt. But first you will come through this one, and everything will be better, and in a new way. I am sure of that.

How I wish I could help you! If there is anything I can do to help, you must always tell me. You must tell me even if it's something which you think might hurt my feelings. Because I mustn't be weak or selfish either. And, as you often pointed out, a form my selfishness can take is wanting everything in the garden to be lovely, or seemingly lovely, so I needn't get upset about it. Tell me honestly, would it help if I stayed away longer? I have to stay here until the 15th, and I've been assuming that I will drive back down on the 15th, 16th or 17th, to be there for your birthday.[1] But if you feel you would be better without me right now, I shall understand, believe me, and I could stay on in this house a while longer and maybe later stay a week or two with friends. Please be absolutely frank about this.

I think about you all the time and love you very very much, and I pray for you too. I try not to be possessive about you, and I do think I am improving, a bit at least. I have never in my life gone so *far* in a relationship with anyone before. In a way, I feel as if we *couldn't* be separated any more. I don't mean, physically, of course.

Cecil Beaton called this morning and said you had spent a delightful evening together, so I knew that kitten with his truly aristocratic courage and style had smiled, despite the pain under his fur. And I'm sure every hair of it was perfectly coiffured and in place.

Perhaps it's just because *I* find discussion helpful that I keep suggesting you should talk to people—but, have you considered Gavin? Evidently he has just been through a bad time himself. But maybe you don't want to do that. And of course he may be away, in New York.

I am going ahead with lectures, talking to classes, advising students. No geniuses or beauties have appeared yet. I keep on with my work,

1. On May 18.

exercise, sunbathe on the roof, give interviews. James Baldwin[2] is coming up next week to lecture and I may meet him. Am not mad about Mason and Frank's friends, but do like Cecil's friend Mary McCabe. As for Kin,[3] I'm not quite *quite* sure. I hope Cecil doesn't notice I feel this. Probably he wouldn't care, anyway.

Enclosed is a letter for you you sent on by mistake. Two checks to be deposited.[4] Has the house been fumigated yet? If it's a bore, never mind. No hurry.

I am not absolutely sure you have the phone number here. It's Prospect 52424. Just in case. For obvious reasons, I don't want to make long-distance calls from this end.

Kitty must always remember how Dobbin misses him and loves him. But Dobbin doesn't want to come back until Kitty feels he won't interfere with solving Kitty's problems. And Kitty must believe that Dobbin does not want to use his love as a sort of blackmail or to make Kitty feel guilty. It's just something Kitty can have whenever he wants it. Always.

Drub

[*Typed letter, signed*]

Friday 10th [May 1963]   [San Francisco]

Have just heard from Frank Hamilton that he is returning on the 15th, that is next Wednesday. So I shall get out of here on Tuesday and go to stay with Ben Underhill[1] until Friday, and then, when you arrive, we can get a motel room while you're here.

Ben Underhill's address is [. . .] Julius Street, San Francisco 11 and his phone is GA 16739. So please let me know c/o him when you are coming.

Did anyone tell you about Larry Paxton's death? He died last Tuesday, in a diabetic coma. The story is that some Christian Science woman

2. American writer (1924–1987).
3. Kin Hoitsma (b. 1934), a romantic interest of Beaton's; he fenced for the U.S. in the 1956 Olympics and afterwards taught humanities, philosophy, and religious studies at a community college in the San Francisco Bay area.
4. Enclosures not preserved.

1. Not his real name; a schoolteacher.

persuaded him to give up taking insulin. The funeral was today. They asked me to speak. Oh, it was ghastly—the absurd dolled-up corpse lying in the open casket, and the raddled half-drunk ex-show-biz mother not quite knowing what went on, and the teenage half-brother, a great big football boy clinging on to my arm and stroking my hand all through the service (it was obviously sheer nerves; he just didn't realize what he was doing!) and Larry's great friend, a Greek, who flew here from New York—at the end of it all, he suddenly let out a great roar of frustration and despair, and banged against the casket with his fists.

My back is a bit better, I think, but still tiresome.

We have had rain but wonderful sunshine in between, and the bay looks absolutely marvellous. It's so beautiful to watch the ships.

My lectures are all given, now, so I hope to get back to the novel.

Sweet love, I think and think and think about you, and I ache inside with sadness that you are unhappy. I long and pray for you to find your way out of this. There is nobody else in the whole world who matters to me in the way you do, and I can't even help you, except by staying away. Oh God, there seems to be so much sadness, everywhere you look. We ought all to be so gentle with each other. But I won't be gloomy, I promise, when you come up here. I feel, more and more, an absolute fear of giving way to gloom; that would be the last straw. Although the funeral this morning was so awful, it was a kind of relief because it took my mind right off of me and my problems, all the time it was going on.

I read the sonnet by John Donne which begins, "Death, be not proud—"

Oh, when I see my Kitty again I *must* find some way of making him happy, even if it's only for his birthday. I long to see him frolic and play and chase his tail. I do love him so.

D.

[Typed letter, initialled]

·   ·   ·

[May 18, 1963]   [Santa Monica]

I dreamed of Kitty.

I dreamed Dobbin died and someone said, "Was he very beautiful?"
and Kitty said "No."

[Printed Hallmark card, signed, with autograph note enclosed in an envelope marked "For dearest Fluffcat
on his birthday"]

·   ·   ·

Christmas Eve. [1963] Belur Math [West Bengal, India][1]

Dobbin is thinking so much about his Kitty on their first separated Xmas. Not that this could possibly be less like Xmas, here. I am to read the Sermon on the Mount out aloud in the temple this evening, but that's just camp. The weather is perfect, not too hot, and the new guesthouse where I'm staying is a whole lot more comfortable than the one you and I stayed in. Swami Nikhilananda of New York is here with four Western devotees, who are like characters of E.M. Forster's—one of them is an Italian countess dressed as a Hindu nun, another, a wealthy American inventor. I don't know whose character I am. I feel absolutely not here. No alcohol, not even any more Librium,[2] has left me with a vast appetite. Swami is marvellous; he is absolutely himself, and yet he fits in perfectly and blesses the faithful, in droves. I take the dust of every swami's feet, and all manner of people take the dust of mine and I'm not even embarrassed. It is all a charade. And yet India is teeming all around us and Calcutta is as filthy as ever, and that matters—it is horrific—and yet not altogether depressing, because much is being done about it. Prema says he will stay here and join in the work. Arup[3] is literally sick with horror and will leave as soon as he can. I think of nothing but January 7, when I fly to Rome—followed by New York a couple of days later. Meanwhile I shall faithfully yak about Vivekananda as contracted—to the Parliament of Religions, the Women's College, the

1. Isherwood was at the Ramakrishna monastery near Calcutta for the centenary of the birth of Vivekananda and for the sannyas, the second and final vows of renunciation, of two Hollywood monks, Arup and Prema. He flew to Tokyo on December 18 with Swamis Prabhavananda and Krishnananda, then on to Calcutta on December 21. He posted this letter to Bachardy c/o Lincoln Kirstein in New York.
2. Gavin Lambert had suggested that Isherwood take Librium, beginning a few days before the journey, to cope with travel dread.
3. Arup Chaitanya, American disciple of Swami Prabhavananda, born Kenneth Critchfield and later, after his sannyas vows, called Swami Anamananda.

Vivekananda High School, etc. etc.[4] In a daze, I observe how beautiful and curious and comic the life is here. I sit watching the boats on the Ganges. I read Willa Cather.[5] But this is not my life and could never become my life. The only realities here for me are Swami, Prema, Arup and Krishna—whom I have become much more intimate with since our day together in Tokyo, where he bought Jap cameras, giggling like a schoolboy.[6] I know this letter isn't making sense; because this place isn't making sense—though it will probably make a good story in retrospect. I am not at all miserable or sick—only bored and lonely. I long to see you, my darling treasured Kitty. Away from you, I can't talk, I don't feel this is my language or my world. I want to talk Cat-Horse again.

Don't forget old dazed dumb doddering Dobbin. Will send a cable in due course.

All my love, sweetheart,

from that

D.

[Autograph letter]

· · ·

4. Swami Vivekananda (1863–1902), born Narendranath Datta and later also known as Swamiji, was Ramakrishna's chief disciple. He led the other followers after Ramakrishna's death, founded and administered the Math and Mission, and travelled twice to Europe and America, where he lectured and initiated disciples who started the first Western Vedanta centers. Devotees gathered from all over the world to mark his centenary, and Isherwood and many others addressed numerous large and lengthy meetings over a period of several weeks.
5. *The Song of the Lark.*
6. On December 20, during a layover on their journey to India, Krishna bought a new camera and tape recorder to continue his documentation of Swami Prabhavananda's activities.

Sunday [January 26, 1964]   [Santa Monica][1]

Dearest Love,

Just to let you know I arrived safely, to find the house more or less in one piece. There was an earthquake, described by Dorothy as, "It sounded like the Chinese were coming," and as a result the floor of the front bathroom is just a bit more cracked. Nothing else. A windstorm blasted those traily plants in boxes which used to hang on the deck, and broke a limb from the tree, but nothing serious. The garden is growing up all right. Some more rain got into your studio but no damage; I moved a stack of drawings out of reach, in case there is more. Today is cold and grey.

Yesterday I had sort of flu and stayed in bed and slept hours and hours. Today I'm better. Friday, Gavin and I went to see Burton and Liz, who were at bay in the Beverly-Wilshire, en route for Toronto and *Hamlet*. They were very sweet, when we finally got to them through a cordon of newsmen, photog[rapher]s and cops, and we had supper together and Richard seemed quite terrific and not really fat at all. "The Beach of Falesá" seems very much on, and I (and you, if you are free) will go to Boston in March and see *Hamlet* and make the final arrangements.[2]

Mountains of Xmas cards for both of us. There was one from Jimmy Daugherty[3] (looking for it today I can't find it) so maybe you should call him. Also a little juju candy man from the Smolins. Also there are

1. Posted to Bachardy at the Hotel Chelsea in New York, where Bachardy had moved from Kirstein's apartment. On his return from India and Rome, Isherwood had joined Bachardy in New York, arriving January 10, 1964, and leaving for Los Angeles by himself on January 23.
2. Burton and American star Elizabeth Taylor (1932–2011), who began their romance in 1962 on the set of *Cleopatra*, did not marry until March 1964 after securing divorces from Sybil Burton and Eddie Fisher. Gielgud was directing Burton in *Hamlet*, which opened in Toronto in January and then in Boston prior to a sold-out Broadway run from April to August 1964. Burton owned the rights to Robert Louis Stevenson's "The Beach of Falesá" and first asked Isherwood in 1960 to write a screenplay of it, but the project faded away.
3. A young black craftsman, gay, who painted and glued decorative designs for the Duquettes.

some brushes and pencils for you, left, I presume, by Jim Cole; he said he would do this. But no note and no money.[4] I called Frank Wiley who says he has heard nothing from Jim so far.

The house is very clean and calm, after India. I have been walking around in white socks and there isn't one speck of dirt on them. Dorothy is coming tomorrow, but more as a social call. So far I have just spoken to her on the phone.

Am driving up Wednesday to see the Wonner-Brown show.[5]

Jo and Ben write that they will be home in about a week.[6] I wrote back asking them to have supper with us/me the evening they return.

Dobbin misses his dear love and hopes he will be able to come back soon. The time in New York with his Kitten was a very happy one for him. That camera-mad Roddy McDowall[7] has sent a really rather sweet picture of the Animals, in front of a window, waiting to be fed.

Love from a wheezy but ever-faithful old Horse,

Drub

A Mr. A.M. Sheridan Smith writes from Methuen: "As Mr. White[8] will be going away shortly he asked me to write to you about the jacket for *A Single Man*. I wonder if you have any ideas on the matter? Don Bachardy's design for *Down There On a Visit* was particularly successful, I think."

I replied, saying that you were going to design the jacket and that you already had a good idea for it, and would they please write and say what the deadline is. If you care to write him (not necessary, I think) the new address is: Methuen and Co. Ltd. 11 Fetter Lane. London E.C. 4.

Why is it that one remembers so much to say after one has signed a letter?

I have an idea for the jacket of *A Single Man* (I mean, one of them, as I suppose you'd do two different ones). A wrecked automobile turned over in a ditch. It's horribly corny—but I keep thinking of it. What do you say?

4. Cole, an attractive blond friend who had served in the military, sat for Bachardy and bought one of the portraits, paying partly in art supplies.
5. At Esther Bear's gallery in Santa Barbara.
6. They were travelling in Asia, including to Japan, Hong Kong, Macau, Thailand, and Cambodia.
7. British actor and photographer (1928–1998).
8. Isherwood's editor, J. Alan White, chairman of Isherwood's British publisher, Methuen & Co.

Further adventures of Dorothy. Our cesspool backed up and filled both toilets and the kitchen sink with stinking water. Am just a bit skeptical about this. All seems well now—and how could it have backed up all that far?

Two or three youths attempted to rob a house on Mabery Road. The police chased them. They ran up our steps to the gate. One of them yelled, "It's locked!" so they turned around and ran down again, into the arms of the cops. This, the most improbable story of the year, is also told by Dorothy, who claims she watched the whole thing from the balcony! Well—maybe I misunderstood her . . .

Your car isn't here. I presume your father still has it. Tried calling Ted, but so far no answer. Maybe I don't have the right number.

[*Typed letter, signed, with typed additions*]

January 26. 1964 [New York]

Dear Beloved Roan—

Here are notices of *After the Fall*. The only time almost that I have agreed with Walter Kerr.[1] In spite of the mixed reception I'm told it is impossible to get seats before March.

Little has happened since you left. I did get to draw James Baldwin. He sat as still and as long as he could, which was neither very still nor very long, but I do like him. There is something silly and adorable about him and his face is marvellous to draw. One of the drawings is not bad—at least it's very like him. I'm supposed to go again next Sunday, though something may well prevent the sitting. He is certainly trying to do too many things at one time. The hour and a half I spent in the apartment was full of incident; odd characters roaming about, constant telephone calls, sudden conferences with apparent strangers, delivery boys wandering in and out, wild hoots of forced laughter—but all vaguely controlled from inside by Baldwin, around whom everything

---

1. Isherwood and Bachardy saw a preview on January 17 of *After the Fall*, Arthur Miller's play based on his marriage to Marilyn Monroe. Opening night was January 23. Walter Kerr (1913–1996), in the New York *Herald Tribune*, described the play as ". . . a confessional which Arthur Miller enters as a penitent and from which he emerges as a priest . . . neither an especially attractive nor especially persuasive performance," Jan. 24, pp. 1 and 11.

was circling. Among other things he is having a play produced by the Actors Studio, though he does not have any great love for them or the Strasbergs. Mrs. Strasberg was one of the people who telephoned while I was there and after being told Mr. Baldwin was hopelessly busy and unable to come to the phone, said she only wanted to ask two little questions. Baldwin's answer to this report was: "That means a good forty-five minutes."[2]

I also drew Gower Champion very successfully (Mrs. Champion said she'd like to buy one for him)[3] and Philip Johnson,[4] unsuccessfully. Hannah Arendt[5] was a very serious-grand Jewish bitch of the Upper West Side (if she's the most intelligent woman Wystan has ever met we must introduce him to Thelma Schnee[6]).

Kitty is very lonely and misses his only Animal friend and dreads another long week in the cruel dirty old city. He plans to move into Marguerite's on Wednesday and fly back to the basket Sunday or Monday evening. With loving devotion,

His Fur

[*Autograph letter on letterhead of Hotel Chelsea at Seventh Avenue and West Twenty-third Street, New York*]

• • •

2. Baldwin had written *Blues for Mr. Charlie* at the suggestion of Elia Kazan, who was to direct it, but Kazan left the Actors Studio, and Baldwin continued the project amid public tension with Lee and Paula Strasberg, the Method Acting gurus who took over the Actors Studio.
3. Gower Champion (1919–1980), American actor, dancer, and director and choreographer of Broadway and Hollywood musicals, and his first wife, actress and choreographer Marjorie (Marge) Celeste Belcher (b. 1919), who was his dancing partner.
4. American architect (1906–2005), a close friend of Lincoln Kirstein; see below, p. 190.
5. German-born philosopher and political theorist (1906–1975).
6. American psychologist and parapsychologist (1918–1997); she was also an actress and wrote film and T.V. scripts.

June 5 [1964]   [Santa Monica]

Dearest Love,

Nothing from you yet, which doesn't surprise me. But I feel I should send you a word. Unless I hear from you tomorrow, I'll mail it c/o American Express in Athens and hope you'll get it sometime.[1]

The same dull weather continues. Dorothy says it is explained by the underground tests: "They've shaken the veins of the earth." She has just shampooed the rug. It looks as brown as ever, but is cleaner, I guess. Now we hear from England that Vanessa has left *The Seagull* and won't be in *St. Joan* because of illness. Siobhán McKenna will take her place.[2] Tony should be out here by the end of next week, say around the 12th. According to Robin French,[3] everybody is expecting me to come back to work on the script,[4] soon after that. Meanwhile I am starting on the commentaries to the various pieces in my *Exhumations* book.

Went to see Gerald two days ago. He still seems sad and shaky. Jack Jones was there, wearing an incredible white cowboy outfit with light golden shit-colored cowboy boots. (I knew at once who he was supposed to be—the handsome young cowboy who lay dying in the

1. Bachardy flew to London on May 25, then on to Egypt where he joined two friends, travelled to Greece with them, and afterwards continued alone to Austria. The trip marked his thirtieth birthday.
2. English actress Vanessa Redgrave (b. 1937) was then married to Tony Richardson, who was directing the English Stage Company in both plays. *The Seagull* closed May 30, and Irish actress Siobhán McKenna (1923–1986) opened in Bertolt Brecht's *St. Joan of the Stockyards* on June 11. McKenna had starred in several productions of George Bernard Shaw's *St. Joan* and in 1956 had made the cover of *Life Magazine* costumed as Joan of Arc.
3. Hollywood agent (b. 1936); he ran Chartwell Artists with his father, Hugh French, and they became Isherwood's film agents in 1963.
4. Of *The Loved One*, which Isherwood adapted for Richardson from Evelyn Waugh's novel. He had finished writing the screenplay on May 22, and was waiting to do rewrites.

"Streets of Laredo" song!)⁵ They sent their love. Jack is doing nothing but photography at present. Also, last night, I had supper with Chris Wood. He has a new dachshund puppy named Beau, quite sweet and not so stinky. Chris says he (not the puppy) only weighs 127 lbs.!

I'm afraid Ted is still off. He calls me quite a bit. A couple of days ago he announced that he has found a new agent, a Mr. Samuels, of the Cora-Lee (?) Agency.⁶ Apparently this man accosted him while he was collecting unemployment insurance, and they had an interview at his office and the agent was encouraging. However, Ted still has enough sanity to be taking temporary help-out jobs and looking around for a steady one. He keeps urging me to spend an evening with him.

Both Prema and Arup are somewhat in the doghouse with Swami (who sends his love to you). Prema because he intrigued behind Swami's back to get taken on at the French center by Ritajananda. Arup because he has been getting very grand about what he calls his status as a swami. He said to one of the girls who had asked him to carry something, "How dare you ask a swami to do that!" So Swami told him that being a swami only means you must be the servant of servants and humbler than the dust. And you must be truthful in all things—unlike Prema.

Chris Wood gave me a pair of Japanese binoculars which reveal all the secrets of the Canyon. You'll be horrified to discover how well everybody must be able to see us!

The letter from Max Granick turned out to be a bill for $64—four frames at $15 each, delivered to the Banfer Gallery. Shall I pay it? Also there is a bill from Standard Oil. Do you want that taken care of?⁷

June 6. Nothing from you yet, so I'll conclude and send this off. This morning, an advance copy of *A Single Man* arrived. I don't think they have got the jacket quite right in front, but your drawing looks very strong and absolutely first-rate and is properly credited to you. The idiots put the

---

5. Jack Jones, American painter, was a disciple and friend of Gerald Heard. He was about the same age as Bachardy. "The Streets of Laredo" includes the line "I see by your outfit that you are a cowboy," though it's addressed by the dying cowboy who is already wrapped in white linen to the cowboy who passes by.
6. Possibly the Coralie Agency.
7. Max Granick was a New York picture framer, for the Metropolitan Museum of Art and smaller galleries, and also a noted collector of African and tribal art. Bachardy had a show of drawings opening in New York on October 27 at the Banfer Gallery, run by Tom Ferdinand and Richard Bennet. The bill from Standard Oil was for gas for his car.

"About the Author" note smack facing the last page of the story, although I told them not to. An abject letter of apology from Schwed[8] about this.

Three days ago, Ben had to go up to Monterey for a couple of days to get some material for a new television series. So I saw Jo alone and she confided to me that Ben still absolutely refuses to see Betty's children; he cannot bear to think of Jo as a grandmother, indeed probably a great-grandmother in the near future. "But after all," she added, "I am very lucky. It isn't as if he ran around after girls or drank." Dobbin's eyes, under his great lashes, were lowered to the floor.[9]

I have just heard that Tony Richardson won't be returning until the 15th, so shall take a tiny trip, early Monday till late Wednesday, to Big Sur. Am driving with Bart Johnson[10] for lack of someone more thrilling. I just feel I want to get away from this greyness, and going to San Francisco would be too elaborate.

Will you give Lee my regards and ask him, should I invest another five thousand in the same stocks, through his friend; or put the money in a savings account?[11]

That guy whom we met, who was going to caretake for Jack Larson, is said to have reduced the house to a pigsty and to be stepping out with Ralph, Mirandi's husband[12]—this from Gavin.

Hope that dearest kitten is having a wonderful romp amidst the pyramids. His old battered brumbie thinks of him so, and gets so sad in the basket he turns and lies right across it in his sleep, searching for that lost puss. He longs to see his dear fur again.

Love, Dubbin

[*Typed letter, signed*]

---

8. Peter Schwed (1911–2003), Isherwood's editor at Simon and Schuster.
9. As Jo was to discover during the next few years, Ben Masselink had a drinking problem and at least one young girlfriend.
10. Not his real name. A schoolteacher and aspiring writer.
11. Lee Garlington, a tall, good-looking blond known for his decade-long affair with actor Rock Hudson, was one of Bachardy's travelling companions and also a current sexual interest. He had struggled as an actor and turned to stockbroking.
12. Ralph Levy (1920–2001), American T.V. and movie director and producer, married to Miranda Speranza Masocco, a friend of the Stravinskys.

June 5, 1964 [Cairo]

Dearest Horse—

I've been in Egypt now nearly a week. This trip is certainly one of the strangest experiences of my life. I hardly know from day to day what I think of it all. There have been some marvellous high points and some terrible low. Of course I have more than once decided the whole set-up was a ridiculous mistake and to pull out immediately was the only sensible solution. Then, something magic has happened and it all seems the most amusing, wonderful adventure. Anyway, nothing like this trip has ever happened to me before and I guess that in itself is something.

It is not surprising to me that the basic experience I am having is that of travelling with two almost complete strangers, of being with them practically every moment. This afternoon is really the first time I have managed to be alone for a couple of hours. I could write postcards and do all kinds of things in their presence I never thought I could do, but I could not sit down with them in the same room and write to you. So I am now downstairs at a writing desk in one of the big lounge rooms of the Semiramis Hotel in Cairo. It's a very attractive hotel, old-fashioned & heavy, and right on the Nile. At first we had a room with balcony on the Nile but since we've come back from Luxor we have a room on the other side which is almost as nice. At least it's air-conditioned which is really a necessity here, this time of year anyway, if any sleep is going to be had. The first night we spent in a quite fun but really terrible dump called the Ismalia House, with cockroaches, lumpy beds, sinister-looking cutthroat-type Arab servants and no air-conditioning. We all slept for about an hour the whole night. Lee had diarrhea and stomach cramps to make matters worse, and had to keep getting out of bed and going down the hall to the toilet. That has been more or less cured now, though he still has threats of it from time to time. Both he and Henry were suffering from the strain and exhaustion of travelling for more than a month by the time I arrived, and no wonder. If that month was anything like this last week in Egypt there is no good reason why they aren't both in hospital.

Henry[1] is very feminine, pale and passive, shy and hesitant, and very like an old maid. He is really quite sweet and I sincerely like him. He sees the fun in almost everything, including himself, and will laugh and joke

1. Bachardy and Garlington's companion is not identified.

in the most trying circumstances. At heart he trembles with fear of the foreigners, whatever color, and deeply suspects them, but still he fights on bravely, trying hard to see the romance in what he's doing in spite of the harsh realities in the foreground. His great fault is stinginess and all of his suspicions of the others express themselves in his always-present certainty that he is being cheated, taken advantage of, robbed, or, failing any of those, at least being followed by some unsavory character with an insidious design. But all of this he freely confesses and even tells terribly funny stories about what has happened to him. His description of being taken to a steam bath establishment in some squalid town somewhere in the middle of India made me laugh till the tears came—and I'm sure it was all true. He is really very sympathetic—for him this trip in a way is a last fling. He is 36, though he looks much younger, and really is an old maid, still living with his parents and an older sister who sings popular songs in night clubs and has been a great influence on him obviously. He has accompanied her in her act on the piano occasionally—he plays popular music in a flowery, old-fashioned manner which exactly suits his personality. We get along very well indeed, which teaches me my first impressions of people are not necessarily accurate.

Lee is scoutmaster on the trip, partly by choice and very real qualifications for the job and partly because Henry from the beginning forced him into the role by being helpless about money and reservations and tickets. It is usually Lee who deals with hotel managers and pays bills and arranges tours, and he is very admirable in his efficiency. He has one of those information books for tourists for every place he's been and he really uses the information. He knows all about combined hotel & railway tickets with reductions, what meals should cost, what the proper rate of exchange is, and all that an experienced tourist should know. He and Henry are agreed in their determination not to pay one half cent more than anything should cost, and they are indefatigable in their efforts to Jew everyone down to their basic price. I have often been shocked by their behavior and so embarrassed I've wanted to crawl on the floor with humiliation. But nevertheless they have caught many a crooked Arab with his pants down and it amazes me what a little persistence will do—I have seen the smoothest Arabs with many years of experience in dealing with tourists suddenly, without batting an eyelash or suffering the least embarrassment, turn around and offer us the same service for half the price they were asking just a moment before. The Arabs anyway are very shady and dishonest about money, though very friendly and often charming in other ways. And in a way I think they admire someone who can bargain intelligently. I've certainly learned a lot about spending money unnecessarily and the laziness and embarrassment that goes with it and how very much this laziness and embarrassment are used by people, particularly the Arabs, in getting an outlandish price.

We are doing all the tourist attractions, which is really just about all we could do in the time, but it is often great fun if I can make myself relax towards the otherwise terrible effort and strain of travel. I see this trip as a lesson in patience and have already made some improvement, but I know the greatest tests are by no means behind me. I am of course surprised to find out what a selfish, mean little bitch I can be, if I allow myself the extravagance, as I have too often in the past. And yet I also have to watch out for the bitchery of being too agreeable and easy going. There are moments when the only decent thing to do is to object and to speak up, though in the case of tipping I feel it would be letting the team down if after fierce haggling and pinching of piastres I suddenly step forward and magnanimously spread around the dough—and even worse if I tip surreptitiously.

This last week seems like many and already London is far away in my mind. The major feeling I got, perhaps to be expected in so short a visit, was that I could not ever really think of living there—not even in the best of circumstances. Patrick was very sweet, though busy, and I didn't get to spend all that much time with him. He and I did go to a cocktail party in Noël Coward's room at the Savoy and had dinner with Noël alone afterwards which was very nice and amusing. I liked Noël far better than I ever had before.[2] Joan Sutherland[3] was at the cocktail party and looked gloriously ridiculous. Also went to Cecil's house for lunch and also to Ivan & Kate's for lunch—they've got an awfully nice big spacious house with a garden as well as one of those drooling objects in the nursery. Ivan is fat and somehow broken—you may be seeing him very soon. Jocelyn & her new husband Leonard Roseman[4] were both very sweet and I think

---

2. English playwright, composer, director, actor, singer (1899–1975); Isherwood first met him in 1947, but Bachardy recalls this as the first and only time he himself met Coward, so he may have meant that he liked him privately more than as a performer.
3. Australian soprano (1926–2010).
4. Leonard Rosoman (1913–2012), British painter, her first of two husbands. The marriage quickly failed, though legally it lasted from 1963 to 1970.

quite happy—I had a very snug dinner with them. They especially, I mean Jocelyn, sent loads of love to you. Everyone in fact, including Harry Miller. I actually collected more than $100 from the Redfern and also about $300 left in the bank account, so I should not find myself pressed for money. It makes pinching pennies, though, all the funnier.

We will probably go to Alexandria tomorrow for two days and then to Athens. We've not decided how to see the islands yet⁵—whether to take a tourist boat for several days or try to do it independently as we've done so far. In any case, I won't be in any one place for more than a day or two for the next two weeks. I would love to hear from you but I don't know where would be the best place to reach me. I would guess Athens with a note to forward to Rome after June 15 with a note to forward to Vienna after June 18. But then, I don't even feel I can guarantee absolutely that I won't suddenly decide to give the whole trip up and whiz back to the basket. It is impossible for me to see around the nearest corner. But even if I do decide to throw up the trip, I still feel that just this last week has been worth it. I think that in my slow-reacting way I've had a quite strange and marvellous time already.

This letter doesn't seem to have told you anything really—but I will resist the usual impulse to rumple it up and start all over just because I know I may not get the chance to write again for days.

Please remember poor Kitty and know that he is thinking so much about his dear Dub. There were lots of Victorias in Luxor and so many sweet, knobbed, skinny dobbins that Kitty stroked longingly as he whispered soft endearments into their dusty velvet ears.

All my love

Your bedraggled but always adoring,

K.

[Autograph letter]

5. That is, the Greek islands.

June 10. [1964, Greece]

(We will be back in Athens on the 13th and will stay there at least through the 15th, then a tour of the islands and possibly Istanbul. I will write when I know.)

Dearest Rub Dub.

I am on a ferry boat now between Iteas and Aigiou.[1] We spent the night in Delphi which was the end of the first day of a tour of the Peloponnesus. We left Cairo on Saturday, the day after I wrote to you, and flew to Athens, having decided against going to Alexandria. We were three nights in Athens, which was a welcome change from Cairo, cooler, more convenient and comfortable in a European way, and the Greeks are not quite as tricky to deal with as the Arabs, though they are still *far* from being trustworthy.

We have rented a car and driver for this tour very cheaply through an American friend of Lee's who has lived in Greece several years, speaks the language and enjoys organizing our time here. His name is Peter [. . .] and he has come along with us on this tour. He is a road company version of Donald Richie[2] or a non-Jewish Chester Kallman, if you can believe that such a thing exists. Peter is tall with thin blond hair and a haggard face, much older looking than his age, which Lee claims is only 31 or 32. He is in the process of getting his doctorate in medieval Greek history, which he is quite intelligent about, and is full of stories both historical and personal. The personal stories are less interesting, a lot of them about a brute of a Greek soldier-lover who swore everlasting devotion to Peter but was finally betrayed by Peter's insatiable appetite for, from what I can make out, anything in trousers. His frantic sex talk is neither attractive nor original and he is continually referring to us all as his sisters, or those Hollywood actresses, or just plain girls. Of course this often wears thin on all of us but we feel a tour alone with Peter in a private car is still very much preferable to an American Express bus tour which is actually more expensive as well.

1. Crossing the Gulf of Corinth between the mainland and the Peloponnesus.
2. American writer (b. 1924), expert in and exponent of Japanese movies; Bachardy thought him facile and a little too pleased with himself.

The drive yesterday from Athens to Delphi was spectacular. I had never expected such dramatic landscape in Greece—tall mountains, jagged cliffs, red earth, cliff-hanging villages—not unlike the Sorrento-Amalfi country. And the setting of the Delphic temple ruins more than makes up for my boredom with just plain ruins. This is also true of the Acropolis which is high enough to give a marvellous view of Athens & the surrounding sea and country, in case you get tired of admiring the world's most beautiful and architecturally perfect building. The Greeks themselves are friendly, quite short, more varied and attractive than I'd expected (at least when young) and the food is good in spite of being often greasy and heavy.

I have already survived an eye infection and am just getting over what in Cairo is called Pharoah's revenge, both results of being in Egypt. My adaptability and resilience surprise even me. I am quite good-humored and self-controlled most of the time, in spite of very trying circumstances. This trip has now lost the uncertain quality I wrote about from Cairo and has become a pure exercise in self-discipline. I have resigned myself to the rigors and discomfort, mental more than physical, of this holiday junket and I find that by expecting the worst I am sometimes rewarded with second-best worst, which is bearable but not my idea of "fun." Still I do feel this experience has its moral object—if only to teach me in future to follow my self-protective instincts. In the meantime, a monk-like acceptance of the will of God is the mental attitude I am striving for. And I think a great deal of my dear old Horse. Yesterday I bought some blankets for him and a fur rug for his stable. How glad this frazzled old puss will be to see his kind, patient, understanding Dobbin again. But not before he has served all of his time on this pleasure road.

All my love. C. XXX

[*Autograph letter*]

June 16. [1964, Austria]

Darling Rub Dub—

Suddenly the cat is alone in Vienna, of all places. And how depressing it is—grey, civilized, sensible and overwhelmingly *middle class*, very safe and dull. It makes me feel I know and dread the whole of Europe. I long for the sick heat of Cairo, the filth and the disorganization, anything rather than this dead safety. At least in Cairo one is aware that at any moment one could fall down dead in the gutter whereas in Wien (what a repulsive and appropriate sound the name produces) one would be hygienically carried away by some nondescript public servants in serious grey uniforms.

In other words, I'm feeling quite sad. The trip has failed, we've all parted and gone our separate ways, and I am in a dazed state, not knowing why on earth I am in Wien but at the same time feeling a detached amusement at the meaningless[ness] of my being here. The only reason I can produce for myself is that having spent so much money to get over here it seems criminal not to see as much as possible, since it doesn't cost any more as far as transportation goes. But this attitude can't last and I think I will probably be back in Santa Monica before very much longer. In fact, very soon.

I've just had an elaborate and quite expensive meal in an elegant restaurant, recommended to me by Wystan, whom I am seeing tomorrow. It is the first time I have spent money on myself in any considerable way since this trip started, what with all the determined economy at the start. But I suddenly caught sight of myself in an unflatteringly lit shop window and realized how much weight I'd lost—so I ate lots of bread and butter, rich sauces and a peach melba in a would-be outdoor street-café arrangement, with heavy sheets of glass between me and the passersby to kill the illusion. I felt very exquisite and apart, and the food really was good.

I arrived early this afternoon and so made use of the time and saw what I'd really come here for—the Klimts and the Schieles. The Klimts, the oils anyway, are a disappointment. They are, many of them anyway, much greyer in color than they seemed in reproductions, grey like old Wien is grey. There are marvellous ones, too—the Judith with the head of Holofernes is as good as I'd hoped. The watercolors and drawings are what I'd expected, too. The Schiele oils are actually better than any I'd seen—there is one really magic one. I have lots of inspiration now which I hope I can hang on to.[1]

I will take a morning train to Kirchstetten—Wystan said he'd meet me at the station—and will spend the night there.

1. The Klimts and Schieles that Bachardy saw are in the Leopold Museum and the Österreichische Galerie Belvedere.

June 18.

Back in old Wien after a very pleasant day with Wystan. To my amazement the house is quite cozy and comfortable, even almost neat. It must be due to the elderly couple who look after the place. The house is undistinguished-looking but Wystan & Chester have put in a proper kitchen and there is an adequate bathroom. And there are trees all around, a wood at the back of the house, or rather the front—it doesn't make much difference I guess, there really doesn't seem to be a proper entrance. The garden has lots of fruit trees, especially nice black cherries which I stuffed myself with, and vegetable gardens and strawberries and currants and raspberries, lots of roses and country flowers. I really can imagine a life there, but thank God it's not mine!

Wystan cooked single-handed two very good meals (admittedly I was very hungry) and drove me to Krems on the Danube—very quaint and picturesque and absolutely grimsville. I would die of sadness if made to stay in this country. Even the architecture fills me with gloom. We saw an exhibition in Krems of 11th–13th-century Christian art and no wonder they're all so humorless—what a beastly religion it is, made far worse in this climate, and such ugly, painful objects were produced by it. Oh for the pagan worship of a sun god.

Wystan let me read part of his Dag Hammarskjöld book. Wystan's foreword is very good but I could hardly read the parts by H.— apparently no humor whatsoever, and so tortured and self-obsessed, and intellectual to the point of meaninglessness a lot of the time, as far as I could tell, and terribly repetitious.[2]

Wystan seems in very good shape, somewhat thinner, too. Of course he sends his love to you.

I haven't even told you yet that I met Chester in Athens quite by accident. He was there for only a few days. He was sitting at a table in the main square and called to me as I passed by on my way to the American Express. He looked ghastly beyond belief that first morning but pulled himself together later on. We saw a lot of each other for a couple of days. He is in the midst of an affair with a 25-year-old Greek soldier, a palace guard in fact who gets to wear one of those tutus and show lots

2. *Markings* (1964) was the diary of the Swedish civil servant and diplomat (1905–1961), who served as the second Secretary General of the U.N.; it was found in his house in Manhattan after his death in a plane crash in Northern Rhodesia, en route to the Congo. Auden translated it from Swedish with Leif Sjöberg, as well as writing the foreword.

of well-shaped, white-stockinged leg, with those silly black pompons on his shoes. Chester could talk of nothing else but their love—boring incident after boring incident, over and over. I began to think he'd gone quite mad. The boy sounds like a rotter, though quite beautiful in a dull way, judging from the endless photographs Chester showed me.

I am debating whether or not to go to Copenhagen for a day to see some paintings or just come straight back to California. One thing for sure, I want to beat it out of Wien as soon as possible. I may even be back before this letter gets to you.

It is foolish to call this trip a failure. It's much more than that really. At least I've found out a lot of things about myself I didn't know—that's something, I guess. I will try to "learn" from this experience. I will tell you the details of the story when I get home—too much to go into on paper, and anyway I'm still figuring out what happened myself. Miss my dear old warm Brumby.

His forlorn old Pussy.

[*Autograph letter*]

. . .

Oct. 19 [1964]   [Santa Monica][1]

Mailed the negative prints (air mail) and the album (surface mail) to you c/o Banfer Gallery today.[2] Hope they arrive all right.

Have just taken Truman on the Greystone lot.[3] Now to see *Topkapi* with Chris W. My writing shakes because it's on my knee, not because of drink!

All my love & thoughts & devotion always— D.

[*Autograph postcard*]

[Friday, October 23, 1964]   [Santa Monica]

Dear precious fluffcat

These arrived & I opened them, thinking I would pay and save Kitty trouble. But I see where you have to sign that you got the pictures undamaged, so I can't.[1]

Hope the other things—photos & album—arrived all right?

[An ex-monastery boy][2] came by to see me. I don't think he'll go back. He and his friend have started threesomes—already! Phil Anderson, and *his* friend, had supper with me.[3] Phil has a job looking after the Charles

---

1. Posted in Hollywood to Bachardy at the Chelsea Hotel in New York, where he was preparing for the opening of his show at the Banfer Gallery.
2. Probably photostat negatives and an album of prints, both of Bachardy's celebrity work, to further promote him to the gallery.
3. Greystone was the Beverly Hills mansion where Tony Richardson was shooting scenes for *The Loved One.*

1. Probably invoices, now lost, for works shipped east for the Banfer Gallery Show.
2. An American monk who later left the Ramakrishna Order.
3. A big, dark, good-looking American medical student met on the beach; his friend, Bob Rosen, was an assistant director and production manager on T.V. serials.

Lederers' retarded son.[4] Tonight, supper with the Richardsons. The party for Cecil's show is on Monday.[5] I shall try to phone you during your opening, at the Banfer, but I don't know the time. *The Sailor from Gibraltar* goes better.[6] I have all the necessary house papers.[7] Am seeing Evelyn Hooker soon—I think she's about to crack up. Hope Kitty is being as pure as Dub's being faithful—

D.

[Autograph letter]

November 4. [1964]   The Casa

Came back after a long day to find this darling letter from my love,[1] and how happy it made Dubbin, who misses his sweet dear so and has no one but his furry angel. How he loves him!

The bad Fox, whose smell offended Kitty's delicate nostrils and made him sneeze, has been put safely in a box; and old Mrs. Luce's latest attempt to rule the United States has failed.[2] Tony had a victory party to which he invited several Fags for Goldwater, who sulked, and Neil was very cross and said things very loud about "our *real* friends."[3] Vanessa arrives next Monday, and Budd is looking tragic.[4] I am working over at their house now and have a wonderful secretary, a Jewish girl

---

4. Charles Lederer (1910–1976), American screenwriter and director, had been a friend since the 1940s when he and Isherwood both had studio writing jobs, possibly at MGM.
5. Beaton was having a show of drawings locally at the Rex Evans Gallery.
6. Richardson had hired Isherwood to make a screenplay from *Le Marin de Gibraltar*, the novel by Marguerite Duras.
7. Isherwood picked up the house grant deed and title insurance from Santa Monica Bank on October 23, probably in connection with the arrangements for merging their finances and property.

1. The letter, evidently sent from Hotel Chelsea where Bachardy was still staying, has been lost.
2. Barry Goldwater (1909–1998), the Republican senator from Arizona, was defeated by Lyndon Johnson (1908–1973) in the presidential election on November 3. Clare Boothe Luce was an outspoken supporter of Goldwater.
3. That is, "*real* friends" who would have supported Johnson, not Goldwater. Neil Hartley (1916–1994), American stage and film producer, helped bring Tony Richardson's plays to the U.S., and he was producing *The Loved One* for him, their first of many movies together.
4. Budd Cherry, Richardson's creative assistant on *The Loved One*, and just then enjoying an affair with him.

who is really bright.[5] But I have to bash out a batch of pages by the weekend.

Which reminds me that the yachting trip which Tony planned is definitely off—so I will be home for Kitty's Sunday call.

I wrote John Goodwin suggesting we should go to Santa Fe for Xmas.[6] He said yes—but he wants to know soon, because otherwise he will plan to go down to Mexico. What do you think?

All Dobbin's faithful love—

loves his fur-heart,

D.

A letter from Jo & Ben sounds as if they are secretly hating Europe.

Have you talked to Stephen Spender about Natasha? It seems she is very sick. Cancer?[7] He wants to spend a night here late in November, between lectures.

Dr. Dubbin has ordered D. off drink till Kitty returns.

[Autograph letter]

Nov. 15, [1964] just after talking to you—   [Santa Monica]

Dearest sweet love—

(No, I have not gone sick, these things[1] were printed up for me and sent, unasked for, as a thank-you gift by a German woman in the Valley who had written asking me some question about Berlin in the thirties, which I couldn't answer!)

A big hunt—I still can't find your checkbook—only the record of some checks written early in 1964. So I'm sending $500 from my New York account. As it's the same branch, they should be able to cash it or transfer it to your account without any delay.

I do understand very well why you must not come back until you

5. Carole Gister.
6. Goodwin had a house there.
7. She underwent two operations for breast cancer in 1964 followed by radiotherapy.

1. That is, the notepaper Isherwood was writing on.

have done this work.[2] I long to be with you again, but I'm not really unhappy, because I think about you all the time, and you are with me. You are the only reason for so much of what I do—but what a good reason! The best possible!

Take the greatest care of my darling furry treasure.

Dwrubbe.

[*Autograph letter on 4¼″ × 5½″ printed notepaper headed "Christopher Isherwood"*]

. . .

2. Lincoln Kirstein had asked Bachardy to draw portraits of thirty dancers in the New York City Ballet.

Sunday night [January 10, 1965, New York]

My dearest Only Drub—

I'm sorry for being so down on the telephone this morning. I've had a terrible day, due largely to drinking too much last night—the first time in a long while and oh how silly and wrong it is to drink—and I've been depressed all day as a result. And even though I realized it was mostly the effect of the drink I still couldn't get over it. I do hope my dear pony is keeping his muzzle out of that old liquor trough. It is so bad for him, too, and Kitty worries so about his falling down and not being able to get up again. Kitty is determined not to slip now—as though his little life weren't difficult enough already—and he would feel so reassured to know his darling wasn't getting all liquored up, too.

This apartment is weighing on me terribly.[1] I dread the thought of having to fit it out with towels and sheets, pots and pans, etc. I never realized what it meant to move into a completely unfurnished place. I deeply regret having gotten involved but I don't know what else to do now except to go ahead with it. I hope it may not seem so bad once I get into it. It really is quite a pretty apartment though now it seems so *un-me*. And I hate having to occupy my mind with it instead of throwing myself instantly into my work.

And then seeing today all this marvellous furniture Lincoln was loaning to me. I wanted to cry. Three dirty, badly worn wicker chairs with rusted iron legs, a beat-up wicker table, a long, narrow, useless bench, a Japanese chest, an old wooden box and that was it. I loaded them into the car, though. What else could I do? My only alternative would be to buy stuff and I'm going to have to spend enough money as it is. Rouben[2] has given me an old cheap little bed which I guess will

1. Bachardy had been borrowing Budd Cherry's apartment on East 68th Street, but was planning to move to 418 West 20th Street, Apt. 1, which he had rented for two hundred dollars a week. He intended to stay in New York for at least two months and perhaps as many as five.
2. Rouben Ter-Arutunian (1920–1992), Soviet-émigré set and costume designer for ballet, opera, and film. He designed the set for *The Loved One* and was then working for the New York City Ballet.

have to do for Kitty's basket for the present. I think I ought to move into this place right away or else I never will have the nerve. The telephone is supposed to be hooked up on Tuesday.

The whole idea of being here seems utter madness now and I miss my darling Horse so terribly. I think about him and worry so about him and long just to stroke his muzzle and feed him a nice sweet carrot. It seems so wrong and unnecessary for the Animals to be apart. Nobody understands about them really, and whatever they think or say or do, they will never be able really to keep the Animals apart. None of them could ever guess how the Animals love and understand each other. I love my Horse now more than ever and I know in my heart that nobody, nothing, could ever take his place. Dub is the one dear treasure in Kitty's world and He means more to Kitty than anything else. And nothing could ever really come between the Animals now. All my love to my darling from his cat.

[*Autograph letter*]

Monday [January 11, 1965, New York]

My dearest Old Drub—

I have been thinking about you so much today, and missing you terribly, and wishing I could just see you and be with you and talk to you, all at once and right away. I often get so lonely for you but today a great wave of wanting you hit me.

Please take so much care of yourself and always know and remember that I love you in my deepest of hearts. Everything about you, every last detail of you that I know, I love.

Your adoring
Fur.

[*Autograph letter*]

Tuesday [January 12, 1965, New York]

Darling Cat Horse—

Kitty started to work yesterday drawing the actors of the Shakespeare company.[1] Six actors in one day, two drawings of each. It was a great relief to be working again and though the cat's paw was very shakey during the first few drawings, by the end of the afternoon he was fairly much back in form. Luckily the leading actors (Ruby Dee of *Carmen Jones* and *Raisin in the Sun*,[2] and a fluffy-haired, piss-actory, would-be boy who plays Romeo[3]) were scheduled to be drawn in the afternoon and by that time the cat's paw had thawed out sufficiently so that he could hold the pencil properly. All the actors were very pleased with the drawings (not necessarily any indication that they're good) and both Romeo and Ruby Dee even showed signs of wanting to buy their drawings. Ruby Dee is playing Katherine in *Taming of the Shrew*.

Lincoln hasn't seen the drawings yet. But even when he has I probably won't know what he really thinks of them. When I first showed him the drawings I did of Alicia Markova[4] he said they were too fussy, too labored, too heavy. This afternoon I saw him for a few minutes to discuss the Shakespeare company program and he told me the drawings should all be like those I did of Markova which are really the best of the drawings I did in the last few months, because they're much stronger and have much more form than the others. Kitty kept his pink tongue rolled up tight—it would only make Lincoln angry to be told he was contradicting himself. And I don't think he will ever be able to know sufficiently what he thinks to be consistent. Anyway, he says he will pay me $2,500 for all the drawings (about 30 actors, a director & a producer) so I guess the only thing to do is just to get on with the work as best as I can.

The telephone has been installed in the apartment now (Chelsea 23409) and I got sheets and towels. I will probably not move in until Friday. Rouben has given me a very basic type bed which I can sleep on

1. Kirstein had now also commissioned Bachardy to draw actors from the American Shakespeare Festival, with which he had been involved since helping to found it.
2. African-American actress Ruby Dee (b. 1924) appeared in the Broadway play (March 1959– June 1960) and the film (1961) of *A Raisin in the Sun*, but she was not in the 1943 musical or the 1954 film of *Carmen Jones*. Dorothy Dandridge (1922–1965) starred in the film.
3. Terrence Scammell (b. 1958), Canadian actor.
4. British prima ballerina, choreographer, and teacher (1910–2004), retired from the stage since 1963; Kirstein arranged the sitting.

until I can get a better one. The Salvation Army has quite good ones, surprisingly enough, for very little money. I went there this morning and bought a simple chest of drawers for $22. It is dark and battered now but after Kitty has clawed off the old peeling finish and rubbed it down with his pads it might do for the basket room of the Casa—it's about the same height and also slim.

The Cat is going to see Collin tonight in her play, called *The Family Way*, which is opening tomorrow night.[5] I still haven't heard a good word about it. I talked to Anita and Marguerite this morning, both of whom send you their love and hope to see you the end of the month. Kitty will certainly have a double bed sometime next week and so he would have a place to tuck up his dear Brumby if the book can be finished in time.[6] Marguerite's first words (in bated breath) when I told her I had this apartment were: "Is Chris upset?" I assured her there was absolutely no disaster to celebrate and that Kitty was more devoted to his dear than ever before. Anita, when told where the apartment is, said I should, like a lady doctor friend of hers who practices in bad districts, always carry a bottle of ammonia with me—with an easily uncorkable cork—it *blinds*, but only temporarily.

Later

It is intermission. Collin's play is sincerely shocking—one of the most unintentionally dirty plays I've ever seen and Collin's part one of the most unsympathetic ever presented. And it is all so predictable. Collin is good, I guess, if such a thing is possible in such a part. The more convincing she is the more horrible she seems. And a dear little moppet, two of them in fact, to add to the charm of the evening. If my Dubbin were here Kitty would have to put on his blinkers and tuck his ears under his hat or else he'd rear for sure.

Dearest angel pony, please take care of that dear old carcass that Kitty cherishes and never forget that Kitty loves him more than anything in the world. Dubbin's and Kitty's lives are inseparable now.

All of a cat's love,

Fur

---

5. Collin Wilcox (1937–2009), American stage, film, and T.V. actress, also known as Collin Horne and sometimes credited as Wilcox-Horne or Wilcox-Paxton. *The Family Way*, by Ben Starr, closed after five performances.
6. That is, *Exhumations: Stories, Articles, Verses*.

Later
Collin's play (and I told her) is even worse than I thought. It's really foul and intentionally dirty. Till Sunday, your angry cat.

[*Autograph letter*]

January 18 [1965]   [Santa Monica]

Dobbin is so full of love for his Kitten that he has to send him a hoof-written note. How Dub grieves to think of that shivering cat out in the winter snow! Soon he must come to the big city and find him. Drubbin has very sharp ears and will hear that beloved mew and track it down.

Tom Wright, his saucy though slightly cockeyed dancer friend Flavio Aguilar,[1] Carter Lodge, Peter Gowland and Michael Sean[2] *all* arrived nearly simultaneously, yesterday afternoon. Peter had come to put up the Bernhardt poster,[3] which he did with Michael's help. Michael goes around a lot with the Gowlands, it seems, and talks of going to Europe with them. Jo says he is a freeloader. I went into the water with her yesterday. It was icy, but hot on the beach. Carter adores Mexico. He and Dick have built their house—on the coast, near Puerto Vallarta (spelling?)—and we are invited; they will stay *forever* and become Mex citizens. Tom Wright will not stay forever. He wants out—and Flavio wants in the New York City Ballet—he danced with Melissa Hayden[4] in Mexico City, in *Combat*. Just one variation.

I enclose some mail for you.[5] At first I was going to pay the bills; then I thought maybe this only confuses your accounts? Let me know what I should do.

1. Born in Mexico, where he danced for the national ballet company; Wright gives him this false name when he tells about their relationship in *Growing Up with Legends: A Literary Memoir* (1998).
2. Aspiring actor (b. 1938) and a protégé of Bill Inge; his real name, by which he was later known, is Allan Carter.
3. An 1898 Alphonse Mucha poster of his drawing of Bernhardt costumed as Medea, Isherwood's favorite Mucha poster. Bachardy bought it from Anthony Holland, an actor and amateur collector who needed money. They positioned it just inside the door at Adelaide Drive to avoid light damage.
4. Canadian ballerina (1923–2006), longtime star of the New York City Ballet.
5. Enclosures not preserved.

Do love my darling so much and look forward to seeing him soon. The Casa is going to be a bower of greenery when Kitty comes padding home.

XXXXXXX
Rubbin
(Old Faithful)

[Autograph letter]

• • •

February 12 [1965, New York]

My Darling Dubbin—

Kitty is so lonely and sad without his Dear, now.[1] He dreamt about him all of last night and I think probably cried out for him several times but there was no one to hear him. Kitty misses him so, and The Casa and the sea and Kitty's dear little work place with his things. More than I hate N.Y. I hate this propaganda spread around by people who live here about its being the only city *really*, the only place one can live and work and "be stimulated." It is all nothing but desperate self-hypnosis. Marguerite is the only person I know who complains bitterly about living here and that's one of the reasons why I like seeing her. She has badly injured her foot by simply turning her ankle as she was crossing a street. Two little bones are broken and the tendons torn (much worse than broken bones because they take longer to heal) and so she is confined to her bed, with occasional hops around her apartment, for three weeks anyway. She is very upset by the whole situation, almost more upset than I've ever known her to be. She displayed yesterday a very morbid, decadent-Southern masochism about being sick and threatened by doctors and hospitals, which was only occasionally counteracted by the driving, career-girl Marguerite who is irritated and impatient when confronted by any kind of incapacity. Career-girl Marguerite insisted on forcing an ignorant new colored maid to cook and serve an elaborate sit-down lunch to the two of us, which required masochistic invalid Marguerite to hop painfully from bed to table and then from table to kitchen in order to find the proper serving spoons for the helpless maid.

---

1. Isherwood had flown to New York January 25 and stayed there with Bachardy until February 6.

She hurt her foot on the way to Sharman Douglas's[2] apartment where she and Sharman were giving a god-awful, crash-jam Bore party for Kate Moffat who is in town for several days (Ivan is in Los Angeles so probably you have heard from him). Marguerite was forced to make a detour to an emergency hospital but nevertheless showed up at the height of the party with cane and bandaged foot, being supported by various solicitous males, her wild hairdo in even wilder disarray, and beside herself with groans of pain and nervous chatter. She was the spectacle of the party though all of the women complained bitterly and openly of her shameless tactics. Kate carefully kept her back to Marguerite the whole time I was there.

I fled as early as I could to participate in an even greater fiasco which at least was much more amusing in a morbid sort of way—the first N.Y. performance of *Diamond Orchid*, the night before it opened.[3] I had asked Jerry if I could see it and he said, rather than getting me a seat which I would gladly have paid for, "Meet me outside and I'll get you in somehow. There'll be some space somewhere—you can watch it with me—we may have to roam around a bit—" all in order I suppose to get out of paying for my seat. Anyway, I did get a seat in the back row of the main floor which wasn't all that bad because it's a small theater, and I had the honor of sitting next to Gilbert Miller,[4] the illustrious, doddering ass who produced it. The play, as you know, is incredibly poor, old-fashioned and carefully protected from all threat of intrusion by the interesting nature of its subject matter. Jennifer West, who I personally do not find sympathetic as an actress, is not wholly without talent, but certainly very badly cast in this.[5] The production is, surprisingly enough, very cleverly and effectively designed[6] and Quintero has done the best he could with the play. I met Quintero in the lobby and he was very effusive and "so glad I had come" and "we must meet afterwards" but then slunk away cowardly after the performance before I could bring up the delicate subject of the money he owes me.[7]

2. Douglas was a New York socialite (1928–1996) known for her friendship with Princess Margaret.
3. *Diamond Orchid*, by Jerry Lawrence and his longtime collaborator and companion, American playwright and lyricist Robert (Bob) Lee (1918–1994), opened February 10 and closed February 13 after five performances.
4. Broadway impresario (1884–1969).
5. West, American actress (b. 1939), starred as the Evita Perón character, Paulita.
6. By David Hays, a five-time Tony Award winner for set design.
7. José Quintero (1924–1999), Panamanian-born theater director, commissioned Bachardy to draw his portrait, and he had not yet paid for it.

The behavior of Jerry and Bob Lee on the eve of their opening would take pages to describe and I do not want to dwell that long in negativism. Bob Lee, I *know*, is insane and I believe totally removed from what I would call reality. He is Jerry's familiar, his Frankenstein monster, his alter-evil, and I think he has gone so far that even Jerry has trouble controlling him now. Together, they give the pursuit of success new, deeper meaninglessness. I did have one glimpse of unfeigned emotion. Jerry insisted (after I told him truthfully I thought it was his best play—he misunderstood and thought I was exaggerating) that I go backstage to see Jennifer West. I did, and got the big treatment with a kiss which surprised us both. And then, Jerry saw it—the original Hirschfeld drawing of Jennifer West as "Paulita," hanging on the wall of her dressing room.[8] "Where did you get it?" he cried in disbelief. José Quintero had bought it from Hirschfeld and given it to Jennifer that night, before the performance (you of course remember Jerry's collection of Hirschfelds) and scooped Jerry. (Relations between them before this apparently had not been at all good.) From where I stood I could see Jerry's face as he stared at the Hirschfeld, a more genuine look of true desire than I have ever before seen on it, mixed with a hopeless doggy despair and an underlying mean resentment. Pure Tableau.

You will not get this before we talk on Sunday so I will tell you then about your book which I have been reading with pleasure, even the things I've read before, though I am doubtful about the Ford Madox Ford article. Not having read *Parade's End*, your description of the plot, in all seriousness, made it sound unintentionally quite hilarious. And, horror of horrors, you even refer to Valentine Wannop as a "whole, sane individual." I realize Old Dub was still a racy colt when he wrote that, but even so his muzzle might still deserve the tiniest flick of the crop. Though of course you explain in the introduction that no changes have been made.[9] Cat must fly out to begin his grim chores. All his thoughts and his dearest love are with his only love, his treasured Brumbie. XXXX K.

[*Autograph letter*]

---

8. Al Hirschfeld, American caricaturist (1903–2003), was known for his black-and-white line drawings of theater stars in character; they often appeared alongside reviews.
9. "*Parade's End* by Ford Madox Ford" was one of seven essay-reviews Isherwood wrote for an American magazine, *Tomorrow*, between October 1950 and July 1951. For *Exhumations*, as Bachardy makes clear, he made no changes, not even to the line to which Bachardy objected.

Casa, Monday. [February 15, 1965]

My dearest Love,

[T]hat sweet catletter arrived this morning, as hoped for. Yesterday on the phone Dobbin wanted to say something about the anniversary[1] but somehow couldn't; too many people have been too glib on such occasions. I'm sure Jerry Lawrence excels at such speeches. Still and all . . . The encounter of Kitty and Dobbin was and is such a miracle that I can think of it almost objectively. The chances against were about the same as those of a flying saucer from another galaxy finding the earth. And where would Dobbin have been if they hadn't met—and if Kitty hadn't loudly mewed to be taken indoors? I seriously doubt if that old horseheart would have found the strength to go on pounding or if the hoof would ever have been raised to thump out any more of its stabletalk on the typewriter. So what? No, what's really important is, will Kitty, looking back, not regret the firing of that Valentine's arrow? That, no one can say yet. All that is certain is Dub's love, as long as that old tail can whisk. Kitty must never doubt that. Kitty must always know, with absolute certainty, that Dub loves him and is there, waiting.

Dub is waiting, absolutely at Kitty's disposition. That is all he knows. So he can't really ever say things like, leave New York. Kitty must decide. If anything good is coming of the New York stay, then Dub can honestly say that he is resigned to Kitty's remaining on there. Nor must he lure Kitty home with reminders of the softness of the basket cushions and the warmth of the sunshine. (Right now, it isn't very.)

How awful that sentence is in the Ford Madox Ford review! I hadn't reread it. I agree that the plot of the whole book is crazy—but my making it seem so was not unintentional. I guess I will leave the review in, however, because it does make a few good points.

I started the new novel[2] yesterday, as promised. It is almost certainly a false start, but that's nothing against it. I will try to add a page to it every day.

Of the manuscripts submitted by students at UCLA,[3] three (out of eight) appear to be thunderingly queer.

1. February 14, Valentine's Day.
2. *A Meeting by the River.*
3. Where Isherwood had started teaching on February 9.

Was disappointed by Bill Brown's show yesterday.[4] The Masselinks bought a great big landscape which is quite pretty, however. All the usual people were there. Jack Larson expressed violent dislike of Henry Kraft[5] (behind his back) and Budd Cherry took shines to John Zeigel. Jack Larson is very happy because he has at last finished his opera.[6] Virgil Thomson is here but only briefly; he has quarrelled with the people at UCLA and won't be a professor there, after all.[7] Both Jack and Jim [Bridges] were quietly pleased at the failure of *Diamond Orchid*, but they insist that Bob Lee is the fiend and that Jerry does not realize this!

Give my love to poor Marguerite.

Maybe Kate will have joined Ivan by tomorrow, when I'm to see him.

All my love, darling, and don't forget how I am missing you, and thinking of you, all the time. You are my whole life. There isn't any part of it you don't enter into, now; and all my hopes are about you.

XXXXXXXXXXX

D.

[Typed letter]

Wednesday Night [17 February 1965, New York]

My darling Horse,

His dear letter arrived today and cheered Old Cat so much. Kitty has been very low these last days. This place has seemed so grim and awful since that Dub galloped away and left Kitty so forlorn, with only his unattended fur to protect him. Kitty spends most of his time just padding about sniffing the corners where the Drub stood and feeling so lonely for the warmth of those smooth old flanks.

Drub is the most important thing in Kitty's life and without the constant thought of Him, Kitty couldn't [go] on, wouldn't want to. But Dub is by Kitty's side always, that dear muzzle bending over him with

4. At the Felix Landau Gallery on La Cienega Boulevard in Los Angeles.

5. Not his real name; an aspiring photographer and a one-time love interest of Bachardy.

6. A libretto for *Lord Byron*, which Larson wrote for Virgil Thomson to set.

7. The quarrel was probably about how much he would be paid, and it was soon resolved; see below, pp. 171 and 191.

those great dark wet eyes looking soulfully down at him. And Kitty concentrates very hard on his Dear and then he doesn't feel so lost.

There must be *some* point to being here though, and I must find it.

The very *awfulness* of being here makes me think there must be some point to it all. I suspect that Kitty might be paying the terrible price for all his complaining amidst the cushions of his beloved basket. Anyway, Kitty is going to be as brave as he can and try hard to last till Easter.

He still rarely goes out in the evenings, except to drawing class. During the day he has been doing nudes of Bob Christian[1] and Dick Gain[2] (some of his best) and almost no portraits since finishing with the actors, which is a relief. The painting bug is nipping at Kitty but he so dreads the effort and cost of setting up a studio here. Tomorrow night I draw Mimi Paul[3] again at the theater, in makeup, and Friday I have invited Anita to lunch and a movie. I've not seen her since our Russian Tea Room lunch.[4]

Tonight I had dinner with Virgil alone in his apartment. He was extremely sweet and comforting and I think he is fond of Old Kitty and made Kitty especially fond of him by speaking very highly of Kitty's Thoroughbred.

I didn't press him for an opinion of Jack's libretto and so he didn't give one, but he did speak affectionately of Jack and Jim. He is going to UCLA again in March.

Last night I had dinner with Lincoln & Fidelma,[5] and Margaret French,[6] with whom I was stuck for the evening. We went to the ballet and I took her home afterwards on the subway. She is very shy but there is something very good about her. We actually got along quite well—Kitty at least tried to sparkle, remembering his Old Stablemaster's lessons.

One positive accomplishment of these last awful weeks—Kitty has

1. Robert Christian (1939–1983), American actor, especially on T.V. soap operas "Search for Tomorrow," "Another World," and, later, "All My Children."
2. Richard Gain, American ballet dancer, in *Camelot* (1960) on Broadway, for Jerome Robbins in "Ballets: USA," and in Martha Graham's company.
3. Principal dancer for the New York City Ballet.
4. On January 29, with Isherwood.
5. Kirstein's wife since 1941, Fidelma, née Cadmus.
6. Margaret Hoening French (d. 1998), American painter, married since 1937 to Jared French (1905–1988), also a painter; in the late 1930s, they had formed the PaJaMa photographic collective with the painter Paul Cadmus, Fidelma Kirstein's brother and Jared French's one-time lover. Jared French lived mostly in Italy from 1961.

broken his record of regularity with his beads and is now determined to set new records.[7]

Marguerite is rallying, rather sooner than was expected. I have dates to draw Joe LeSueur,[8] a silly, would-be-grand ass, I'm afraid, and Frank O'Hara,[9] much nicer, at the weekend. Part of Kitty's not unfamiliar "keeping busy" campaign. A still Cat is an ill Cat.

But everything boils down to Kitty's undying devotion to his only Treasure—the great encounter of his life, without whom nothing has meaning. Distance can't separate the Animals, not for long anyway, and time only makes Kitty cherish His Dear more than ever.

All Kitty's loving thoughts, always,

P.S. The notices of *Diamond Orchid*, in case you are interested and haven't already seen them.[10] Also, a recent, ever-so-slightly-posed, portrait for Dubbin's desk.

[*Autograph letter with enclosures*]

February 23 [1965, New York].

Dearest beloved Drub—

The enclosed is a recent portrait of Kitty in a very characteristic pose: gazing heavenward with paws crossed in virtuous modesty.[1] The field of red, aside from setting off Kitty's white purrity, is symbolic of the Animals' Valentine's Day anniversary.

7. That is, making japam; Bachardy had been initiated by Prabhavananda in 1962.
8. Aspiring playwright, screenwriter, and critic (192[4]–2001), originally from California.
9. American poet and art critic (1926–1966); LeSueur had been his companion since 1955.
10. The play reviews are lost.

1. Full-color magazine illustration, 8¼" × 8½–8¾", cut with uneven bottom edge from longer page, head and paws of white kitten with blue eyes on vivid red ground, inscribed "For Drub from his loving Fur."

Kitty so wishes his darling Drubbin were here to escort him uptown to see the Bette Davis movies—there is a festival of them now, including *Jezebel* (which Kitty saw yesterday afternoon and loved, as always, until they sent the dobbins off to the lepers island in the end and made Kitty cry) and *The Sisters* (which starts today—Kitty can hardly wait to see the San Francisco earthquake!), *Dangerous* (which Kitty has never seen) and *The Letter*. A real feast for Kitty, but like most of his meals nowadays, a lonely feast.

Kitty hardly has any appetite anymore and has to force himself to eat. He so often forgets to be hungry when he doesn't see that Old Dub standing there with his muzzle buried in the feedbag. Sometimes just the smell of oats or the sight of a carrot will remind Kitty to nourish himself.

Virgil called yesterday and said he wanted to buy one of my drawings of him—the best one in fact. He agreed to $150. Last week he said to please let him know if ever I needed money and I think this is probably a development of that idea but is nevertheless very sweet and thoughtful. He did say though that he would have to take down some pictures in order to hang one the size of mine.

I had a drink with Rouben last night. He leaves today for Rio, where Hale Matthews[2] is already and where Tony and Neil are likely to be before long. Carole[3] told me too that Tony and Neil will probably be in Los Angeles in about two weeks to supervise some looping by Morse.[4] Of course the nature of all these plans is extremely fluid.

The ballet season is in Texas now for three weeks so Kitty has to scare up models and concentrate on classes. Bob Christian posed for me last week but he goes out of New York to some place in the suburbs this week for a small part in a production of *A Streetcar Named Desire* with Nina Foch[5] playing Blanche. I thought I might travel into the sticks just to see it—I've never seen it on stage and I can't imagine how she can manage it. There might just be some fun to be had. Maybe I will ask Tennessee

2. Broadway producer; Bachardy drew him around this time. He recalls that Matthews was wealthy and plump, and that one morning he woke up in bed with him, though he cannot remember why.
3. Carole Gister, the secretary working for Richardson and Isherwood.
4. Robert (Bobby) Morse (b. 1931), American actor and Broadway musical star known for his much later role as Bertram Cooper in the T.V. series "Mad Men," had trouble with his British accent in *The Loved One*, so Richardson audio-taped Morse reading aloud from a script, then looped his dialogue back into the film in post-production.
5. American stage, screen and T.V. actress (1924–2008).

if he wants to go with me. Joe LeSueur, not the most believable teller of stories, told me there was a great scene at the ballet the other evening when Tennessee commented loudly at the opening of *Swan Lake* that the dummy swans looked like birds in a shooting gallery and was told by some cruel man nearby to shut up because he was old and finished. Tennessee got up and left, according to the story.

Kitty has thought often lately of the Animals' dear trip to Monument Valley and the thought occurred to him that the Animals might celebrate their 12th Anniversary with a second honeymoon there at Easter— the same time of year as before.[6] It is just a thought that Drub might consider. The important thing is that the Animals will be together— wherever that is doesn't matter. *All* of a cat's love and devotion to his darling, sacred Horse, always. K.

[*Autograph letter with inscribed enclosure*]

La Casa, Wednesday. [February 24, 1965]

Kitty's dear letter just arrived and made Dobbin very happy. Again and again he kissed the portrait of Kitty with his wet muzzle. It is *exactly* how Kitty looks when at his prayers or watching a plump juicy bird on a tree.

Oh dear, how slowly the time passes! Five long days, and then all of March to drag through. But now I find that we get our week's holiday before, not after Easter. So if we are to leave town I would be free to leave on April 9th, or even the afternoon of the 8th. My next class would be on April 20th. I think it would be lovely to go to Monument Valley, and now the road is much better, Gavin says. But if we are to go we should book a room at the lodge, as it will be around holiday time.

Am so happy that Kitty has Bette Davis to comfort him. I would love to see *The Letter* again. There hasn't been much in movies out here. *La Notte* is being shown on Western, and something at the Toho. Too far to go alone to.

6. Two and a half months after their relationship began in 1953, Isherwood and Bachardy drove through Arizona and New Mexico to Monument Valley in Utah, then home through Nevada. The trip was during Bachardy's so-called Easter vacation from college, but in fact took place during early May. See below, p. 191.

Out of the blue, Caskey[1] called, said he was selling his Palm Springs house and all his belongings and leaving America, first to Australia, then maybe later to Europe. Could he see me? I said yes on the impulse, then regretted it; but when we met—we had lunch together at Ted's—it was strangely remote. He has a belly and looks battered and much older; all that I expected. But his real oldness seemed to be inside. He seemed quite without interest in me or in anybody much, kept grumbling peevishly about the horrors of this country and how much everybody drank, and said that people bored him so that he had to drink. Everything was somebody else's fault. But he wasn't a bit drunk and he only drank one scotch. He was like the kind of sulky cantankerous middle-aged Irishman you meet in a bar. What made him so curiously unyouthful was that he seemed to have lost all his bitchiness. . . . I really don't know why he wanted to see me. We parted quite casually. His only reference to you was polite praise of the drawing on the back of A Single Man. But he didn't seem to care about anything, really. I suspect that he has turned into his father.

Had supper with Jerry Lawrence and David Smith.[2] Jerry is really upset about the reception of Orchid, I think. He kept saying that it was the fault of their casting; she[3] just wasn't up to it on the opening night. But he claimed that she had been marvellous when you saw it. Great enthusiasm for you and for your beauty. When David arrived it was embarrassing, rather, because he and I had so much to talk about— David has got a job working with juvenile delinquents and he was really very interesting. Jerry was bored. He sat beside David, pawing him from time to time, and then started to fall asleep. So I left early.

I do hope you go to the Foch-Christians Streetcar production; though it would be even funnier with Bob playing Stanley! I long to hear your account!

I don't suppose this will thrill you greatly, but it might be fun: Gavin says they want you to draw the principals in his film.[4] The drawings would probably be used in the promotion. Pakula[5] agrees to this idea. It could be done anytime in April or even as late as May.

---

1. William (Bill) Caskey (1921–1981), American photographer; Isherwood's boyfriend from 1945, when they met, until 1951.
2. A student of Isherwood's at L.A. State in 1962, and afterwards an admiring friend.
3. That is, Jennifer West.
4. Inside Daisy Clover, based on his 1963 novel.
5. Alan Pakula (1928–1998), American director, screenwriter, and producer, was producing the film.

I do sincerely like Jack Larson's libretto. I think it will really work. In fact, I now think it is almost the ideal way to do a Byron opera. The great difficulty about Byron is his death because it's symbolically so great and noble but actually he just got a fever, as he might have done equally well while fucking in Italy. So the death scene is bound to be somewhat false, at least in an opera. This way, you avoid it altogether. . . . I would love to hear what Virgil really thinks of the libretto.

I have quite a lot of manuscripts to read, about fourteen, and I have already coped with four. Am now in the middle of the first of two volumes of an immense weepy queer tragedy, about some character who is so sad because he can never find *real* love. It reminds me of Stevens's cry of desperation, "We've got enough problems *with* windows!" and this reminds me of The Greatest Tory Ever Sold, which is said to be the Egg of Eggs. . . .[6] But, to get back to UCLA, I am really very dissatisfied with myself and this class which I imprudently said I'd hold. Of course it ought to have been a small group, but that was impossible, because who is to choose the members of such a group, and how? What has happened is that a mob of sensation seekers, anthropologists, psychologists, women, philosopers, teenagers, beats and German Jews collects every Tuesday at three and I am supposed to cope with them for two hours. The first week we had about fifty, the next seventy, the next ninety plus. It is just awful, and dull, because they all want to talk, and they bore me and each other and then blame me for not moderating the discussion. Yesterday we bogged down in the most futile argument about what Jung really means by a myth. I was so discouraged that I talked to them quite brutally and said that if we couldn't manage to get along better I would close the class. . . . The trouble is simply, as always, that I am not an intellectual. I can get by with double-talk on the platform but I am quickly bored and always want to change the subject and tell jokes. Unfortunately, my public lecture[7] was taken by quite a few people as a serious statement about something—so I got off on the wrong foot. . . . Alas, this is just one more instance of how much Dub needs that Cat. Kitty can always advise him about these things

6. When George Stevens (1904–1975) was directing *The Greatest Story Ever Told*, an historical adviser told him that despite Leonardo da Vinci's portrayal of the Last Supper in his fresco, there were no windows in the room where the meal actually took place. The film was released at Easter, at the same time as seasonal candy eggs, with a huge promotional campaign targeting Christians in particular, but Isherwood had heard that ticket sales were poor.
7. "Writing as a Way of Life" at Macgowan Hall Playhouse on February 10.

and warn him when he is neighing up the wrong tree, and making an old donkey out of himself instead of a horse with sense

Am plugging on with the novel. Not a ray of light, yet, but then I hardly expect any for a while. I have to bore myself to the point of desperation before the inner voice will speak.

Dear sweet beloved Kitty[,] I love you so and give thanks only that you exist. Even in absence you are so near to me and support me through so much. When I found you I found the great jewel which all but the very few would envy with tears, except that they can't even remotely imagine what it would mean to find it. Never forget old Dub, and pray for him as Dub does for Kitty, piously crossing his hoofs.

All my love to my much-missed darling, eternally,

Drub

The packet of nuts was mailed to Kitty yesterday.

[*Typed letter, signed*]

Wednesday [March 3, 1965]   [Santa Monica]

Beloved Catkin,

Dobbin is so lonely. He keeps trotting up the ramp to [the] mailbox, restless and uneasy, but there is no mail at all today, so no word from his Love. It is beautiful weather but cold, and the old casa feels that it will never be warm again till Kitty comes. Without him, southern California is a joke in bad taste.

Gavin just phoned from the pier where they are shooting *Clover* to say that it is going to be amusing today and wouldn't I come. But I must take Kate Moffat to see Gloomy Robards in *Hughie*,[1] and then go on to Vedanta Place.

Yesterday, Lee Prosser and his wife Mary[2] arrived by car from Missouri and moved into the Tumble Inn. They are both very young and fat and

1. After a six-week Broadway run, Jason Robards Jr. (1922–2000) toured in José Quintero's production of Eugene O'Neill's two-character play, opening in Los Angeles at the Huntington Hartford Theater.
2. Prosser (1944–2011), later an author and a student of shamanism, witchcraft, and Wicca, was a Vedanta devotee; Mary was his first of three wives.

she looks at you with slitty eyes squidged together by the fatness of her cheeks. She seemed so stupid that it was probably slyness. Imagine, little Prosser (he is half Dobbin's size and weighs 165!) has stuck himself with this lump at the age of twenty. But then, why not?

Connie Wald[3] just called to ask if we (she cannot get through her head that you are still in New York) would come to supper tonight to meet a perfectly brilliant young French doctor and the Levants.[4] She then sang a short psalm about your brilliance.

Dobbin has a sore boil on his tongue.

The class at UCLA went better yesterday but it is a drag. Never have I felt less marvellous.

Ended up paying approximately $10,600.00 in federal and state income tax! But still didn't have to dip into our savings accounts. Maltin[5] only charged $150 which I think was reasonable, under the circumstances. He is sending your tax papers to you in a few days.

Bill Inge is getting very thick with the Catholics and may join the Church. This is confidential, he says.

I called [Paul] Wonner and [Bill] Brown and went there on Monday night. They also invited Gavin and Nigger Brown,[6] I guess to cover up any possible intimacy. The evening went politely, with cautious questions about you and New York by Bill. Nigger Brown has given up his job to be an artist. It is sad because I feel sure he can't, but I suppose it is good to try.

A cunt just called and asked me to edit her little film about animals. When I refused, she got nasty and said she had been a Vedantist for fifteen years.

I have read *Daisy Clover* and don't like it much. It doesn't seem to be about anything and there is far too much about that dreary character, The Dealer.[7] But I suppose the strong cast will carry it. . . . However, I do quite like the beginning of Bill Inge's novel.[8] It's sort of Willa Cather with lots of sex, and surprisingly queer.

The ass who interviewed me the other day called. Told him in future

3. Hollywood hostess, widow of screenwriter and producer Jerry Wald, for whom Isherwood worked in the 1950s.
4. Oscar Levant (1906–1972), American composer, pianist, actor, talk-show host, and his wife, June.
5. Arnold Maltin (not his real name), Isherwood and Bachardy's accountant.
6. The younger black artist also called Bill Brown.
7. Isherwood was reading Lambert's screenplay of his novel; Daisy's mother deals Tarot cards.>
8. *Good Luck Miss Wyckoff* (1970).

to send stamped addressed envelopes when he writes me. Dobbin is cross today because his tongue is sore.

Very sad because his Kitty is away. Love from his poor old D.

[*Typed letter, initialled*]

March 10 [1965]   [Santa Monica]

My darling,

Nothing from his Kitty yet but will write and send a little gossip from Hedda Horse.[1] Chiefly from the movie world. On Monday, I went on the pier to watch them filming the first scenes from *Daisy Clover*. It was a glorious day and the black limousines of the wicked producer looked wonderfully sinister against the Japanese blue ocean with cumulus clouds behind over the hills. And Christopher Plummer all in black, attended by Roddy, also in black, was truly evil in the manner of Peter Shaw or Vincent Price as he crossed to greet Natalie, who is supposed to be living in a shack on the pier.[2] I can't say Natalie looked fifteen but she looked like actresses who play fifteen are supposed to look, which is of course much better for film purposes; and Betty Harford was just not to be believed, in elbow gloves and a hat.[3] I'm afraid only that she may seem too much bigger than life, like an actress out of the Moscow Art Theater. But Gavin says she is wonderful in the rushes. And Ruth Gordon[4] was on hand (I didn't see her in costume and makeup) as The Dealer. She is very amusing and amazingly spry. She told how Bobby Morse was so bad in the stage production of *The Matchmaker* that they were going to throw him out, but Equity wouldn't allow it, and then on

1. Cf. Hollywood gossip columnist Hedda Hopper (1885–1966).
2. Natalie Wood played the defiant teenage tomboy who wins a movie contract with Hollywood producer Raymond Swan, played by Canadian actor Christopher Plummer (b. 1929). Roddy McDowall was Swan's assistant. The pair arrives at the shack on the Santa Monica pier in two enormous limousines, wearing black overcoats and black chesterfield hats in the ocean sunlight. American actor Vincent Price (1911–1993) often played villains, and possibly Isherwood saw Peter Shaw do the same in his early career as an actor, though Isherwood may have had in mind the professional persona of the real-life Shaw, super agent and studio executive.
3. As Daisy's older sister, Gloria Clover Gostlett.
4. American Broadway star, playwright, screenwriter (1896–1985).

the opening night he was marvellous and saved his career.[5] Well, they had all better be good, because the director is about as inspiring as a tree stump. Mulligan is so square that he seems unable to walk properly.[6]

On Sunday evening Tony and Neil had arrived from Rio and I saw them Monday night. They brought so much scuttlebutt that I can only skim it. Here are some items: Rouben is having a terrific affair with Hale Matthews (you probably know this—if it's true). Right after having the baby,[7] Vanessa had to go to a hospital to have a lump removed from her neck. The surgeon said it was the remains of gills, and that some humans have these vestiges of the period when we were fish. (With my famous tact, I said, oh so she's a mermaid!) Terry Southern is divorcing his wife and marrying this girl of his.[8] John Calley is marrying Julie Andrews;[9] [they say] he muff-dives her every night. They are still planning to do *Forbidden Dreams* and then *Gibraltar* this summer. Jean Genet walked out on Tony owing him a lot of money. Genet thinks Moreau is a lousy actress.[10] Tony feels (for the first time in his life, he says) that he has made a good film: *The Loved One.* (I saw it Tuesday morning, and it is certainly improved by cutting; but I doubt if you will like [it] any better.) Tony seems to be avoiding Budd, and indeed a whole lot of other people, and it is a big bore, pretending one doesn't know he's in town, especially as the word has gone out all over California that he's here.

Jo and Ben say that Anne Baxter and her husband are on the skids.

Peter Viertel called, very friendly. He and Deborah are in town for

5. In the original 1955 Broadway production Gordon played Dolly Gallagher Levi, and Morse played Vandergelder's apprentice, Barnaby Tucker.
6. Robert Mulligan (1925–2008), American movie and T.V. director.
7. Joely Kim Richardson, a second daughter, was born January 9 in London.
8. American novelist, essayist, and screenwriter Terry Southern (1924–1995), who rewrote Isherwood's script for *The Loved One*, was having an affair with Canadian-born dancer and actress Gail Gerber; she had a non-speaking role in the film. In fact, Southern remained married to his second wife, Carol Kauffman, until 1972.
9. American movie producer and studio executive John Calley (1930–2011) was co-producer of *The Loved One.* He did not marry his then girlfriend, English Broadway and Hollywood musical star Julie Andrews (b. 1935).
10. French writer Jean Genet (1910–1986) offered his original screenplay *Les Rêves interdits, ou L'Autre versant du rêve (Forbidden Dreams, or the Other Side of the Dream)* to Richardson's producer Oscar Lewenstein, and Richardson hired Genet to make necessary rewrites for the film. Genet asked to be paid in advance, and then, after a week working with Richardson in London, disappeared. French actress Jeanne Moreau (b. 1928), in fact a friend of Genet's, was Richardson's choice for the lead, and they went ahead with the film, released as *Mademoiselle* (1965). Richardson hired Marguerite Duras to complete the rewrites. Moreau also starred in Richardson's *The Sailor from Gibraltar,* for which Isherwood had already completed the script.

some time; she is doing a film comedy with Sinatra and Martin.[11] Am to see them next week.

A medium sent a message to Laura which he claimed he received from Aldous. Aldous warns Laura to give up using drugs and says he has made a terrible mistake and that he knows now that he has set back his whole spiritual development by having used them and gotten others to use them, and that he is in some sort of a hell! Laura is sceptical but disturbed about this.[12]

Does Kitty ever play the tapes Dobbin made for him?[13]

Old Dub thinks and thinks of his dear Kitty and is happy to do whatever Kitty says, because now he belongs to Kitty entirely and will just try to be useful in the few ways that old horses can. He only wants to be near his furry darling and keep him warm or carry him to places and wait for him.

X X X X X X X X X X X X X X XXXXXXXX D.

Just a word of love to my sweet Kitty to slip into this letter, although I was listening to that dear mew only a short while ago. Today, he seemed very close, and yet so cruelly far.

Bill Inge was in *again*! He had to bring me some revised sheets of the manuscript of his novel—which I haven't even opened yet! Must read some in the car after *The Threepenny Opera*[14] and before going to Jack & Jim's for *Les Abysses*.[15] Bill Inge said, "Don has become an *artist*—it's very exciting." What you were before is better not asked—like our chest which Tony Duquette wanted to paint black to hide its nature![16]

---

11. *Marriage on the Rocks* (1965), starring Frank Sinatra, Deborah Kerr, and Dean Martin.
12. Huxley began experimenting with mescaline, LSD, and psilocybin in the early 1950s and wrote about drugs in *The Doors of Perception* (1954), *Heaven and Hell* (1956), and *Island* (1962). Laura Archera (1911–2007), his Italian second wife, a concert violinist in youth and later a psychotherapist, used LSD therapy on some of her patients and injected Huxley on his deathbed at his request.
13. Of Isherwood reading poems aloud.
14. The 1962 German film version, starring Kurt Jurgens, Hildegarde Neff, and Gert Fröbe, dubbed in English, was playing at local movie theaters.
15. *The Depths*, Nikos Papatakis's 1963 French film based on the real-life murders by the Papin sisters of their landowning employers, was released in the U.S. in November 1964. Jack Larson and Jim Bridges were probably taking Isherwood to see it at a studio screening room.
16. Duquette advised them on interior decoration in the 1950s. Isherwood and Bachardy acquired the chest when they bought 434 Sycamore Road with its furniture in 1956. They never painted it black, but they did eventually get rid of it because it was so cumbersome and heavy.

I am working a lot on my novel again. It seems very exciting but all wrong. Probably a novel without dialogue is an impossible bore. I long to finish the first draft so you can read it when you return.

Have just watered the deck plants and driven off a female trespasser. Now for the boredom of Brecht. Do you remember that shatteringly ugly performance of the *Opera* we half-saw on Hollywood Boulevard?[17]

All my love, sweet Angel—

Drub.

[*Typed letter, initialled, with autograph note enclosed*]

The Anti-Casa.
Wednesday [March 3, 1965, New York]

My Darling Drub—

There is not much to tell my Dear. Kitty's life in N.Y. seems to be getting more and more uneventful, and yet I can't help feeling it is all part of an important phase in a kitten's small life, a terrible, frightening, mysterious turning point which must occur but which nevertheless makes Kitty tremble. One thing is for certain: never before has Kitty asked himself so often what *is* his tiny life all about. He asks himself over and over, "What does he want?" "If not this, then what?" Kitty is continually rejecting possible bowls of cream and yet he doesn't know quite what he wants instead—except that he does long to devote all of his fur to *something*. To painting, to Ramakrishna, to Old Dub, maybe even to all three. He realizes he has never made up his mind really. He has always been testing and tasting, dipping his paw in here, his tail in there, trying a tunnel as far as the point where his whiskers touched the sides. But then sometimes Kitty feels that perhaps this is the nature of life, at least of his life, a succession of glimpses, some satisfying, some not. Perhaps, he thinks, the state of waiting, of expectation, of near desperation sometimes, is a quite rewarding, maybe even profound state to be in, if he can just manage to accept it and go along with it.

All these thoughts and so many more occupy Kitty unceasingly and somehow or other Kitty will make up his mind and devise a plan of action, if only because he must. But that dear Dubbin is always in his

17. Starring Lotte Lenya, on November 13, 1960.

thoughts, near him, supporting him, and being loved by him with all of a cat's heart and soul.

This cat-soul searching may sound very silly if Kitty allows himself to reread this letter, so he will mail it off right away, just to get some kind of word to his Horse to make him know how much Kitty thinks of him.

I do hope Gavin has my drawing of José Quintero. If not, it is in my studio, framed and all, and would you be sure to see that Gavin gets it, because I am writing Quintero again to ask for my money. Also, I got a bill from the telephone co. in Pacific Palisades charging a monthly service rate of $10.35, from 2/19–3/18 (Feb. 19–March 18, I presume) which seems an awful lot to pay for a telephone on vacation rates. Perhaps, if there is no mistake, it ought to be turned off altogether. Would you please call them about it? I will wait to send a check until I talk to you on Sunday.

The drawings of Frank O'Hara on Sunday afternoon came out quite well. He was a good sitter, and I think he is a sweet man. At least he spoke well against Lauren Betty Bacall Bogart Robards, which endeared him to me.[1] Joe LeSueur, too, is nice—cozy, chatty, gossipy, indiscreet about his affairs, and altogether surprisingly (to me) feminine. I had not imagined him at all like that. I went with Frank O'Hara to have a drink with Joe Sunday evening. Joe's current love was there, a 21-year-old, gangling, grinning, bespectacled, joke Perkins-type boy named Joe Brainard.[2] He's a would-be shy, somewhat calculating tease, but quite friendly in spite of all. His pop art work, mostly object collages (Jack & Jim have two small inferior ones) is not bad if you go along with it. I will, for a few steps anyway. Went to Lincoln's for dinner afterwards with Richard Buckle (not at his charming best) and a dwarf Jewish sculptress from England who is unexpectedly nice.[3] Lincoln is still manic and oh! so difficult and boring to be with.[4] I think a lot of Buckle's edginess was due to having been subjected to Lincoln all weekend long in the country.

Kitty is off by his cat-self this afternoon to see *The Letter*, to soothe

1. American star Lauren Bacall (b. 1924) was originally called Betty Joan Perske; she was Mrs. Humphrey Bogart from 1945 until Bogart's death in 1957 and then Mrs. Jason Robards from 1961 to 1969. Bachardy had been trying to get her to sit for a portrait.
2. American artist and writer (1942–1994), born in Arkansas. He reminded Bachardy of actor Anthony Perkins: tall, dark, handsome, self-conscious, and preppy.
3. Astrid Zydower (1930–2005), born in Germany, near Posen, now Poland. Her parents died at Auschwitz after sending her with two older siblings to England for safety in 1939. She was 4′ 10″ tall. Buckle admired her Shakespeare busts and introduced her to Kirstein, who bought one for his Shakespeare festival. She and Kirstein became close friends.
4. Kirstein was bipolar.

his tortured soul. How he wishes he had his Nag to ride him there. Kitty could hide his puss in Drub's mane when they get out the gun (Kitty is always so shocked by any violence).

All of a kitten's love to own, darling Horse.

[Autograph letter with glued-on addition]

Tuesday [March 9, 1965, New York]

My Precious Pony—

Kitty thinks so much about his darling Treasure and misses him terribly and sometimes he just doesn't know what to do without his Old Drub. And yet, in spite of the pain Kitty suffers because he's separated from Horse, he always feels that Dubbin is with him in his heart, and he knows he can talk to Him when he's in trouble and Old Drub will answer with love, and comfort Kitty. Dubbin's love strengthens Kitty, and keeps him going, and Kitty returns that love twofold. If nothing else has been accomplished by this exile in N.Y., at least it has revealed to Kitty for always the incredible value of his priceless Pearl, his own Pony, who was right there grazing in Kitty's backyard all the time. Kitty can never love him enough but that is not going to keep him from trying.

Lincoln is very impressed by your letter about turning the poems into a stage piece.[1] He can't understand why you won't come here to live (and incidentally be on hand to be made use of). "It'll take six months at least to get the show done," he says, inferring that you will have to be here at least for that length of time. It doesn't occur to him that he might go to California for six months. At heart, he is terribly spoiled and self-

1. *Rhymes of a PFC* (1964), which Kirstein was expanding for *Rhymes and More Rhymes of a PFC* (1966). Kirstein had been sending Isherwood poems for comment, and a copy of Kirstein's "Bobby" that survives among Isherwood's papers at the Huntington Library in San Marino, California, suggests that Kirstein tried assigning characters to speak the verses of the poem he had already published in the 1964 volume. Kirstein evidently destroyed Isherwood's letter, with others. No post-1962 correspondence from Isherwood survives in the Jerome Robbins Dance Division at the New York Public Library. (PFC: private first class.)

indulgent. What he really wants is another jester for his already crowded court. He has more people now than he can ever afford to pay attention to separately for more than twenty minutes at a time. He has quarreled Forever with Richard Buckle but quite fails to understand why. Buckle, never the most patient and understanding of creatures at his best, I'm sure, has reacted to middle age by becoming more impatient than ever, and Lincoln, in his senseless, blundering, drunken mismanagement, kept throwing Buckle off his "schedule." They actually quarreled because Lincoln disrupted Buckle's schedule. Buckle had arrived at the house to discuss business and found the place full of unexpected people (Andrew Wyeth's 19-year-old son[2] and Hylie Selassie's (sp?) grandson)[3] and flew into a rage. Anway, Buckle leaves on Friday.

Lincoln says that I will have a check for $2,000 tomorrow—the remainder of my fee for doing the drawings of the actors. I am glad my return to California does not depend on the fact of that check's being placed in Kitty's paw tomorrow. Though Lincoln is so unpredictable. I might well be given a check for $2,500. I must say I don't feel bad about receiving such extravagant payment for my efforts when Lincoln tells me he is going off to Japan next week, for a rest, and taking with him both Danny and Freddy Maddox,[4] just for company. If Lincoln is going to throw his money around, I see No reason why Kitty should be criticized for taking off his little hat (very respectfully) and catching a coin or two.

Kitty is drawing regularly, and painting, too. The painting is not right yet, but, wonder of wonders, fun to do, even working with oils. I can't understand it and tremble to think this attitude won't last.

Frank O'Hara & Joe LeSueur have arranged for me to draw Larry Rivers,[5] maybe sometime next week. I can't imagine what I'm going to do with him but I'm curious enough to take the dare.

2. James (Jamie) Wyeth (b. July 6, 1946), younger son of American painter Andrew Wyeth (1917–2009) and already an accomplished artist in his own right. Kirstein was a family friend and agreed to pose for his portrait, which Jamie completed early in 1966.
3. Haile Selassie (1892–1975), Emperor of Ethiopia from 1930 to 1974, had six grandsons born between 1947 and 1960. Kirstein's guest was probably the eldest, Prince Paul, Duke of Harrar (b. 1947); the next, Crown Prince Mikael (b. 1950), would then have been only fifteen.
4. Artist and teacher Dan Maloney had been an intimate friend since 1949 when Kirstein first became infatuated with him; he sometimes lived in Kirstein's house and later married. Fred Maddox, an architect, whom Kirstein met in about 1963, also sometimes lived at East 19th Street, and later became Kirstein's companion in old age.
5. American proto-pop artist, jazz musician, and filmmaker (1923–2002); he had two wives, many girlfriends, five children, and an intense friendship with O'Hara, evidently sexual for a time.

They showed Kitty *Metropolis* last night and he clapped his paws with joy (only momentarily forgetting his grief).[6] Buñuel's *Diary of A Chambermaid* with Jeanne Moreau opens tomorrow but Kitty will try hard to wait to see it with his D.

Endless Cat kisses and bottomless baskets of love for his adored Nag. K.

[Autograph letter]

Wednesday [March 17, 1965]   [Santa Monica]

Dearest Love,

Old Dub felt so hideously depressed last night. A cold wretched day, and a tiresome unrewarding class, and his rough old tongue was sore where it scraped against his bridgework and the root canal which was supposed to have been cleaned out has started another abscess and his cold still bothers him and his bang on the head still hurts[1] and he was too tired to work and there was nothing he wanted to read and no films on the telly and Jim [Charlton] and Bill Caskey asked him to supper but he didn't feel like it, so he stayed home and got sadder and sadder, after eating a horrid T.V. chop suey, and was so terribly lonesome for Kitty. All will be well, he thought, if I can just hear him mew once, so he called N.Y., forgetting about the answering service which answered and took his name, but Kitty didn't call back, so now Dub is worried a bit, though of course Kitty may have been out or even out of town. . . . Tonight, horror, a lecture by Howard Warshaw at UCLA to which Fran has forced me to go,[2] am taking Bill [Brown] and Paul [Wonner]. Tomorrow, worse horror, the dinner at USC at which we are to talk about Huxley. . . .[3] Well, never mind. As long as Kitty comes back soon. Only wants to be with Kitty.

6. Bachardy went to the film alone; he describes himself in the third person for Isherwood's amusement.

1. Isherwood got drunk at the Masselinks' with Julie Harris and James Murdock on March 13, fell, and hit his head on the bathtub.
2. Titled "Vision Made Visible."
3. Isherwood, Laura Huxley, American film director George Cukor (1899–1983), and Robert Hutchins (1899–1977), former Dean of Yale Law School, former President of the University of Chicago, founder of the Center for the Study of Democratic Institutions in Santa Barbara, and chair of the editors of the *Encyclopaedia Britannica*, reminisced about Huxley on stage, following a memorial dinner for four hundred Friends of the University of California Libraries.

Silver lining department: Simon and Schuster enthusiastic about *Exhumations*, though they may want to take out as many as half a dozen pieces, according to Curtis Brown.

Loves Kitty so.

Rub

[*Typed letter, signed*]

Wednesday. [March 24, 1965, New York]

Most Adored Drubbin—

Kitty is spending most of today indoors. His whiskers haven't been trimmed and his fur is all dishevelled and he is sitting in an untidy heap in that uncomfortable junk chair, first forcing himself to swallow a few bits of lonely breakfast, then trying to interest himself in the events of the non-cat world via the newspaper, and finally seeking consolation in Vivekananda.

Yesterday was a very busy day—class in the morning, then getting back all the drawings of the Shakespeare co., then to the framers, then to draw a ridiculously, girlishly pretty young hairdresser friend of Anthony's named Gerard Bollei,[1] then to an evening class and then to see a late showing of *The Firefly* at the theater where they showed the Animals that Doris Day–Rock Hudson movie[2] (Kitty's great eyes teared momentarily when he saw the seats they had been together in, but then Jeanette MacDonald managed to cheer Kitty for a bit—she really is one of the best unconscious comediennes—and also there were lots of Dobbins in the movie, including a big fat white one that Allan Jones rode and in one scene he even has to give Jones a great lippy kiss—they paid them very well in those days[3]).

Monday night Anthony, whom I hadn't seen for weeks because John Goodwin had been here (I discovered that from Robbie Campbell[4] who goes to my gym now), took me to see a British play called *All in Good Time* which, in spite of Donald Wolfit, was very well acted but terribly

1. Bollei ran the in-house salon at the Plaza Hotel and later founded his own larger salon nearby on 57th Street. Anthony Russo, the longtime companion of John Goodwin, was also a hairdresser. Bachardy found him to be a unique personality and once went to bed with him.
2. *Send Me No Flowers* (1964), on February 2.
3. Jones and MacDonald played spies in the 1937 musical set during the Napoleonic Wars; Jones, a trick rider, rode his own horse, Smokey.
4. A young, pretty black lover of American Broadway producer Arnold Saint-Subber (1918–1994).

sentimental and, in its artful smallness, very artificial and pretentious. It's all about a pair of newly marrieds who don't screw for the first six weeks of marriage because of family tensions and rivalries. Not my most favorite subject and I'm sure you can get the smell of it.[5]

Anthony was very sweet as usual but told me nothing about John, I suppose because I didn't ask. There's nothing I really want to know about him. We had dinner afterwards with Anthony's fellow hairdresser Gerard and his not-so-pretty but much more attractive young friend named Jerry, who works at Edward Albee's producing company office. They chattered away like magpies and were really very silly but not hard to be with. They both treat Anthony and me like middle-aged gentlemen. They had been to see the musical adaptation of Arthur Laurents's *Time of the Cuckoo* which has had a cool reception here, thought to be dull. The boys had quite liked it but that's no recommendation.[6]

One funny term I'd not heard before: when Gerard was asked by the very wised-up waitress at the French restaurant where we ate "What do you do?", he answered after a gulp and a pause, "I'm a coiffurist."

Before the theater on Monday I saw *All About Eve* again. It finally seems quite dated and strangely naive in spite of many still very good qualities. Bette Davis is good but Anne Baxter seems very clumsy and heavy-handed now and there is an awful lot of strained "bright" dialogue.

Sunday night I had a drink with a pair of Budd Cherry's friends who called me on Budd's suggestion. Luckily I was smart enough to refuse a dinner invitation because they are very ordinary, would-be-grand-but-can't-be-anything-but-boring rich queens of an uncertain, uninteresting age. Their method of entertaining guests gave me the feeling that every once in a while, in the midst of their richly decorated townhouse boredom, they suddenly get what they think is an urge to benefit humanity but which is really just a lonely wish to show off their finery to someone, anyone, and so they fling open the great paneled doors and let any scatter-brained silly rush in. I realize I am developing the most violent prejudice against the rich, but I can hardly bear to be with any of them now.

Afterwards I went with Joe LeSueur to a concert which included the N.Y. premiere of one of Ned's pieces—something for two singers with

5. By Bill Naughton, who also wrote *Alfie*, directed by Donald McWhinnie; Wolfit (1902–1968) played the father of the bride.
6. *Do I Hear a Waltz?*, adapted from the 1952 play with music by Richard Rodgers and lyrics by Stephen Sondheim.

words by Frank O'Hara. It seemed really quite nice but meant nothing to me, except the boy who sang was big and cute. As for the music, it was little more than an obstacle to understanding the words.[7]

I had a drink with Joe, Ned & Frank after the concert and that was pleasant. Their world is quite a tight circle made up of people who reinforce each other's standards and beliefs. Frank O'Hara is their leader and Virgil is their honorary father. There is quite an elaborate court, complete with hangers on, which is the foundation of this group, and though I quite like most of the people I've met within the confines, there is a slight provincial quality underlying, a smug New York superiority which, though it doesn't condemn heretics, does manage to create an air of patronage and pained sympathy toward "the others." At least I like and feel more at home with these people than I do with what they refer to as "the uptowners."

I have had a fuss with Rouben because I heard from John Gielgud's friend Martin[8] that Rouben had been gossiping to them about me. Martin was quite innocent in letting me know that Rouben had been talking, thinking that I wouldn't mind, that I would even be flattered to think I was being discussed at all. Apparently Rouben had gone on about how unhappy I was in N.Y., just because I had had dinner with him one evening when I was feeling particularly low and Kitty let slip a little moan or two, mostly about how he missed his Rub-Dub. Rouben anyway had talked like a bone-stupid ass about the horrors of living with one person for several years and losing one's precious individuality which had already made me realize he was not material for a cat-friend. Kitty doesn't stand still for any maligning of his Old Horse, even of the most indirect kind.

Coincidentally, Lincoln has apparently broken forever with Rouben, who has Lincoln to thank for his first break. Lincoln was originally cross because Rouben dared to criticize Lincoln for allowing John Braden (and therefore not Rouben) to design a ballet for him, especially since the ballet was an awful flop and John Braden's work lousy. Then, Lincoln found out that Rouben had betrayed John Braden, who had worked with

7. *The Quarrel Sonata*, later retitled *Four Dialogues for Two Voices and Two Pianos*; Ned Rorem asked O'Hara to write him some verses in 1953 so he could compose something for Robert Gold and Arthur Fizdale, the piano duo, with tenor and mezzo soprano. It was first performed in Rome in 1955. The New York tenor was John Moriarty (b. 1930), later a conductor and vocal coach.
8. Martin Hensler, a Hungarian; he met Gielgud in 1960 and was his companion for the rest of Gielgud's life.

him, by telling a Broadway producer that John was incompetent. John had given Rouben's name as reference.[9]

Lincoln has also quarreled forever with Philip Johnson,[10] and Lincoln is also leaving today for Montgomery, Alabama, to observe the demonstrations as poet-historian,[11] which gives you a rough idea of his state of mind. The landlady is coming in to see Kitty in a few moments so Kitty will speak of his imminent departure for Nagland and subsequent arrival of Freddy Maddox in the apartment. Will tell the outcome on Sunday. Every ounce of a Kitten's honeyed devotion to his Horse who means more to Kitty than anything in the world.

[Autograph letter]

Wednesday [March 24, 1965]   [Santa Monica]

My own Sweetpaws,

Dobbin is late today writing to his dear, which will probably mean this won't arrive till Furday. Have been struggling with the second draft of the novel. It's still all wrong but much more interesting to write, this way; a completely new form (for me) and one which seems to fit the material much better. But the question remains: is it interesting at all? Kitty will have to decide.

Anyhow, as Igor sweetly said the other day, "As long as I am working

9. Braden continued as an assistant designer of costumes and sets at the New York City Ballet. He was a relatively longtime sex partner of Kirstein, and Kirstein was perhaps in love with him, but Braden had a domestic partner, and on his side the relationship with Kirstein was more of a professional obligation. Braden also had a brief but intense affair with Bachardy, who did two drawings of him.

10. This important friendship survived the quarrel. Like Kirstein, Johnson was a Harvard graduate, a millionaire in his own right since youth, bipolar, gay, and obsessed by Modernism. He founded the Department of Architecture and Design at the Museum of Modern Art, and designed with Richard Foster the New York State Theater at Lincoln Center, completed in 1964, commissioned and partly funded by Kirstein as a home for the New York City Ballet.

11. Martin Luther King marched from Selma, Alabama, March 21, arriving at the steps of the capitol in Montgomery on March 25 with thousands of non-violent demonstrators as part of the struggle for voting rights in Alabama. Two previous marches had been beset by fatal violence, attracting national publicity; this third march was federally sanctioned and protected by the Alabama National Guard and the FBI. President Johnson supported the marchers; he submitted voting rights legislation to Congress on March 17, and the Voting Rights Act of 1965 was signed on August 6.

I am very content," and that's how I feel. Dobbin is recovering from his ailments again, it seems. And he has been rigid in his refusal of all firewater and fermented oats. Not even a sip till Kitty returns.

Happening to look at an old diary, I see that we actually left for Monument Valley early in May, a whole month later than we plan to, this time.[1] I must try to find out from the Auto Club how it will be now. Maybe still snow. Should we rent a car? I know Kitty hates to ride far in the Volkswagen. And should I reserve a room at the Lodge? I see that it only took us three nights to get there, and that was the long way around, by Gallup. The nearer way, it could certainly be reached on the third day.

Got a strange note from Julie, apologizing for not having called back before leaving. "The last few days were long and hard and I felt so melancholy on top of that and I didn't want to spread my misery on you over the telephone. I feel so close to you and feel that if only I could talk to you it would help me so much but now we're 3,000 miles apart again." I hardly know what to write to her. I'm afraid of saying too much. Can it be that she is *really* dissatisfied with Manning?

The irony of it is, I am trying to write a blurb about her for Roddy McDowall's book of photographs. I think I already told you about this, and how Gavin was conned into writing something for my picture in it? Haven't read this, but Roddy assures me it's "beautiful"![2]

Tonight I'm going with Gavin to a dress rehearsal of Virgil's *Four Saints in Three Acts*.[3] I feel this is expected, and it is so much less depressing than going to a regular sit-down concert. Jack and Jim will be there of course and that nice photographer from England, Michael Cooper. I have given him your phone number in New York because I feel pretty sure you will like him, and he knows so many of our friends.[4]

The weather is still poor, either too cold or too windy or both. But Dobbin is happy thinking that he will see his dear soon, longing for that silver mew and the touch of that treasured paw and the beat of that

1. The trip was May 4–10, 1953, when Bachardy had a so-called Easter break from college. In fact, Easter Sunday had fallen on April 5 in 1953; in 1965, it was to fall later, April 18.
2. *Double Exposure: A Gallery of the Celebrated with Commentary by the Equally Celebrated* (1966), pp. 28–29, 106–107.
3. Thomson was conducting his 1934 opera on Gertrude Stein's libretto at Schoenberg Hall, UCLA.
4. Cooper (1941–1973) worked for *Vogue*. He became close to Robert Fraser and the Rolling Stones and later did cover photography for *Their Satanic Majesties Request* (1967) as well as for the Beatles' *Sgt. Pepper's Lonely Hearts Club Band* (1967).

huge heart within that tiny envelope of fur. (Which reminds me, I will try to remember to pick up a bead bag from the bookshop when I go to Vedanta Place.)

Love from a devoted old horse who is waiting day and night with his saddle on, ready for his Kitten's commands,

Rub

[Typed letter, signed]

• • •

Tuesday [25 May 1965, New York]

Most-treasured Plug—

His dear missile arrived this morning to cheer and encourage poor Kitty, who was feeling very depressed and cross and upset.[1] Yesterday was a bad day—a series of minor irritations and then dinner with Ned Rorem and his new friend. I say "new" only to distinguish him from the previous friends of Ned. He is really the dreariest of old-fashioned sulkers, with the most artificial scowl and would-be serious deep grumble. The only justification I could find for the scowl was the hideousness of his droopy smile, which, accidentally appearing from time to time, betrayed a very usual kind of timid insecurity and grovelling weakness. He is not even young, and his skin has that terrible N.Y. yellow-greyness of the sick and sour. Even though one is forced to make do here, I really think Ned is scraping the bottom of the barrel unnecessarily soon. And, to make matters worse, this guy turns out to be an "artist," for want of a crueller word.[2] A big slick commercial-type still life of his hangs over Ned's fireplace and in the self-consciousness of my arrival, I falsely, grossly praised it. By falsely and grossly I mean that I said "I like it" with that awful hollow enthusiasm of the embarrassed liar. My retribution was soon to follow. After dinner they invited themselves to my apartment and then asked to see some of my work, which I showed them. To my amazement, Ned's friend had the effrontery to dare to deliver a crit., telling me what he thought my work "needed," and in the most unbelievably cliché art-school jargon. Ned, himself, who has no idea who Klimt was, *also* dared to criticize one of the drawings and to tell me which *one* of them was really "successful." I

1. Bachardy visited home in Santa Monica, April 3–May 20. Isherwood's first letter to him on his return to New York was posted May 23 to the apartment on West 20th Street and is lost, although the envelope survives.
2. Joe Adamiak, a graphic artist; he designed the layout for *The Paris Diary of Ned Rorem* (1966) and took the cover photo.

was speechless with anger and nearly at one point threw them out of the apartment, but then Kitty regained his composure, his true grandness returned, and he realized it could not possibly matter *what* this pair might think or might not think about his work.

Their rudeness (of which they seemed blissfully unaware, making it all the more damaging for them) was only valuable as farce. Being rude is the current N.Y. mode of behavior, and the kind of rudeness that's really "in" lacks even the somewhat saving grace of premeditation. Anyway, Drub would have been proud of Kitty's self-control. Though Kitty might just allow himself, when next he encounters Ned, to suggest to him that he play some of his music so that Kitty, being as ignorant of music as Ned is of art (not having even heard of Klimt after a two-month exhibition at the Guggenheim has only just ended![3]), might make a few helpful criticisms.

Virgil was in his usual good form and my reaction to Paul Bowles after the many years since I've seen him was still the same.[4] I don't like him. I get a bad smell off him. There is something about him which is false, right down to the roots of his passive, long-suffering negativism. His face has become set in a superior-wry grimace of ironical despair, but I suspect the despair only exists to feed his cold, ruthless appetite [for it]. But he was reasonably charming in his cool, charmless way, and asked after you, and said as though he'd never really expected anything more, that you'd not in all these years written to him, but then caught himself up quickly and said that, for that matter, neither had he written to you.

Wednesday [26 May]

Kitty is feeling better today, though for no good reason. In fact, I had dinner with Lincoln last night and he told me the pavilion, which is being built especially to display my drawings, is *not* being built, for a variety of sound and unsound reasons which might well have been gone into months ago. I can't help feeling a great relief, though Lincoln says he wants to put the drawings up somewhere else, in the theater I think he said, but I believe I can get out of that or maybe only have a

3. "Gustav Klimt and Egon Schiele," February 5–April 25.
4. Bachardy had an extreme, paranoid reaction to Bowles (1910–1999), the American composer and writer, when he and Isherwood took hashish with Bowles in Tangier in 1955. He had seen Bowles only a few times afterwards, perhaps most recently at the opening of Tennessee Williams's *Sweet Bird of Youth* in Philadelphia in 1959.

few put up. So there seems no real reason now for me to stay on here, except to get rid of this apartment and make up my mind about what to do with the stuff I've accumulated. This apartment of Brian Bedford and Stanley Papich's[5] that Jack & Jim said was available turns out to be in a dreary state of confused ownership with priority phantom tenants ready to move in and out at a moment's undelivered notice. So the Cat may be back, bag and baggage, quite suddenly one day, before Dubbin can clear the stable of all the pretenders to the basket.

Lincoln is at least fairly sane now and therefore filled with overwhelming resentment. He is also quite thin.

Thursday [27 May]

Joe LeSueur arrived. I took him to dinner at the Spanish restaurant in the Chelsea. We had a nice, chatty evening. I like him, and he tells *all* that is going on without malice, or at most very little and very understandable malice.

Talked to Lincoln this morning. He still wants to keep on this apartment and Freddy Maddox is ready to move in the moment I get out. Not having to dispose of all of the furniture and equipment I've accumulated is really a relief. And even if the Bedford-Papich place were available, it already has a bed, chairs, sheets, towels, etc., so I would have to pay to have all my stuff sent out to Santa Monica, which would be a bore and hardly worth it. Lincoln repeated his plan to put up "some" of my drawings at Stratford, so I will have to stick around long enough to see to the framing, though I doubt if it will be considered necessary for me to be present at the installation.

Lincoln gave me two tickets for the Gala Preview of *Don Quixote* (with Balanchine dancing Quixote) tonight.[6] I've invited Joe LeSueur to go with me because I couldn't think of anyone else worthy, besides Virgil who is already going.

Purrverse Kitty, having written yesterday's summation of Paul Bowles, called him last night to ask him to let me draw him. He didn't even know that I draw but said reluctantly he would sit on Saturday afternoon.

---

5. Papich, an American dancer, was a replacement in *West Side Story* on Broadway in 1957 and had other small roles.
6. The Russian choreographer (1904–1983) and co-founder with Kirstein of the New York City Ballet and the American School of Ballet created the ballet for his nineteen-year-old muse Suzanne Farrell whom he cast as Dulcinea; he was sixty-one when he opened in the title role.

After all, Chat Maître (the artist) is above personal judgements and His piercing objective eyes see only the Truth.

Joe just called to say he can't go tonight—he's giving a cocktail party and says he would feel too rushed, and would be embarrassed to leave his guests, so I don't know who to ask now.

Kitty is going to draw a singer-commedienne-dyke named Kaye Ballard this afternoon.[7] I met her at Brian & Stanley's on Sunday. She is really quite nice, rather Martha Raye-ish to look at, and is especially likable because she went on at length about the glories of Kitty's art.

Poor feverish Puss (he is sitting up this minute without a stitch on, not even his collar, it is so hot and steamy since yesterday) misses his Old dear Dubbin so, and loves him more than ever. Kitty is quite often moved to tears by the sweetness of his devotion to his Old Plug. Kitty will get back to him as soon as he can and take better care of him than ever before and lavish him with basketfuls of cat-love.

All of a Kitten's deepest love to his dear unique, irreplaceable Steed.

[Autograph letter with glued-on addition]

Wednesday. [2 June 1965, New York]

Dearest Stallion:

Little news of any interest to report. Old Cat is just dragging around in the cruel metropolis (when he isn't sitting sad and alone on a sooty cushion in his barren cage, which is most of the time) missing his Sweet Pony (all of the time) and pining for the acrid summer smell of the stable.

On Sunday I had lunch at Kaye Ballard's with Brian Bedford and Stanley Papich and several New York musical comedy spirits (singers, lyricists, composers) who are a world apart, at least most of the time, thank god. Not that they aren't easy to be with, cheerful and even quite amusing. It is just the endless sunny-side-up brightness, the insistence on ignoring The Chasm, that makes me feel the hopelessness of being *with* them. After three hours I was as nervous as a Cat.

7. Ballard (b. 1925) appeared on Broadway, in T.V. sitcoms and game shows, and in movies.

I went to see Kaye Ballard in a revue of little-known Cole Porter songs and was very impressed by her. She is a singing funnywoman and is really very good at both, and completely professional. She is one of those who is at their best on stage—her intense concentration and desire to please manage to hold her personality together, at least for a couple of hours. To try to draw her as she sits alone in a room is to try to draw an unfocused, unpredictable, moody mass of nervous ticks. Even the face, which on stage is a good, Martha Raye type, seems totally dispersed. Also, she is [. . .] sentimental [. . .] and quite fond of confessing it.

Saw Joan Elan and her (still undivorced, I think) friend on Sunday evening. She looks slightly better than when last seen in California and he, Bud Something, is a good man, unthrilling certainly, but good. My repetition of good makes me realize I have the smallest suspicion that, finally, he's not going to marry Joan.[1] He is forty-fiveish, fair, short, stocky and faceless. With all that, it might still not be disgusting to find oneself in bed with him. He writes copy for an advertising agency, but, as though that weren't bad enough, writes "seriously" on the side and reads current best sellers to "see how it's done."

Monday night I had dinner at Joe LeSueur's with Frank O'Hara and Joe's ex, J.J. Mitchell.[2] They were friendly and amusing and even quite cosy to be with, and yet I felt remote from them. The whole evening I was aware of making an effort to like and be liked and feeling vaguely frustrated in both efforts by the end of the evening. Frank was teasing Joe a lot, mostly about his affairs but also about his lack of judgement in his publishing job, and Joe's silliness was quite cruelly revealed by his own guileless swallowing of even the tiniest bit of bait. Both Joe and J.J. submit unquestioningly to Frank's superiority. Indeed, he is superior—in intelligence, wit and strength of character—and he accepts their submission quite naturally, which is partly responsible for my failure to love him.

Dinner with Lincoln tonight, and *Don Quixote* again, which I am both dreading and curious to see a second time. I am hoping to get some kind of coherent statement about Lincoln's plans for me, or lack

1. British actress Joan Elan (1929–1981), who worked in Hollywood in the 1950s and appeared on Broadway, did later marry advertising executive Harry Nye, known as Bud, and settle with him in New York. She sat for Bachardy in the 1950s and 1960s.
2. Mitchell was LeSueur's lover and then O'Hara's.

of them. I really want to leave here as soon as possible, which is the only thing that is keeping me from doing so. I don't want to leave feeling defeated, dejected and depressed, which is pretty much my state right now, though I feel somewhat better for having done some painting today.

Thursday. [3 June]

Drub's dear parcel arrived this morning to cheer and feed a needy Kitten in one of his darker hours.³ How that dear Old Pony is missed and loved and needed by his adoring xxxxxxx Fur

[*Typed letter, signed*]

Tuesday 8th [June, 1965]   [Santa Monica]

Dearest darling Puss,

Here are your photos. God, that one of Betty leaning back! There one sees the Master's paw.¹

Lincoln woke me at six with a special delivery letter. Quite unnecessary, as they always are. His Selma march and Washington poems are good in their way, but Lincoln's Jewish patriotism embarrasses me to death. Every time he says I'm an American, I'm a Harvard boy, I'm a Bostonian, I think[,] No you aren't, you're a Jew.² And Wystan's two poems embarrass me too. These seem to epitomize all the damage that Chester's influence has done to his work. I do wish he wouldn't use words like "diffy."³

---

3. Isherwood baked and sent brownies.

1. Isherwood enclosed photos (now lost) of Bachardy's recent drawings of Betty Harford.
2. Kirstein sent at least three drafts titled "March" and "Arlington" about the march and about Washington, D.C. and some of the national leaders buried at Arlington Cemetery. These evidently became the two-part poem "Star, Bar & Stripe" published in *Rhymes and More Rhymes of a PFC*. He also sent a draft called "Temples" about the architectural structures that members of various religions erect and worship in, opening with the Jews. "Temples" was later published as "Domes."
3. In a letter of April 16, Auden sent Isherwood "To H.K." about his paid sex-friend known as Hugerl; he later published this poem as "Glad," the first of his "Three Posthumous Poems." Auden describes marriage as "A diffy undertaking" in "Epithalamium," completed in April for the marriage on May 15, 1965 of his niece Rita Auden to Peter Mudford.

From these remarks you may gather that old Drabdub is in his mad-bad-and-dangerous-to-know mood. Only Sweetcat could approach him this morning. He is in a rage with the world, bored with being old and alone, and just waiting for some woman to offer him a novel to read, so he can kick her ass in.

A dull evening at Henry and Michael's.[4] But they are nice. Lee Heflin's novel really has something; he's the bearded beat.[5] Bill Jones came by and sang a sad klong about being lonely, but the minute some little boy appears ready to love him, he presents the boy with a list of ground rules a yard long, and the little boy runs off back to the Red Raven in disgust.[6] This evening I sup with a bore named Cortes. Because he's a friend of Paul Fox.[7] Haven't seen *Bay of the Angels* yet but mean to.

Grey weather. The sun will never shine till Kitty comes.

At the weekend I'll make my darling some more sweet brownies. Would he like that?

Klaus von Wahl's address is: Berlin 33. Humboldtstrasse [. . .]. Joachim's name is Kuester (in case you'd forgotten and can't read his writing on the drawing, it's rather ambiguous).[8]

The Ted Gibson framing work will be ready in a day or two.[9]

All Dobbin asked for was his Kitten, and they took him away.

I find that I only really want to see Swami, Jack-Jim, Gavin. And maybe, oddly enough, Chris Wood. Bill Brown is said to be in New York. Haven't seen Paul at the gym.

---

4. Henry Guerriero and his lover, Michael Leopold, an aspiring Texan writer with whom Isherwood had had an affair in 1949–1950.

5. Heflin attended Isherwood's writing class at UCLA, where he worked at the University Research Library (later called the Charles E.Young Research Library); he was also an abstract painter.

6. Jones was an aspiring writer; Isherwood had been encouraging him with his work for about five years (and they were sometimes sex partners). The Red Raven was a gay bar in West Hollywood.

7. Enrique Cortes and his friend Steve Jackstand took Isherwood out to supper that night and then stayed at Adelaide Drive. Paul Fox was a set decorator at Twentieth Century-Fox; he won Academy Awards for Best Art Direction for *The Robe* (1953), *The King and I* (1956), and *Cleopatra* (1963).

8. Von Wahl was a writer and dialogue director for Berliner-Synchron, dubbing English-language movies into German. He had also worked as an actor and was the German voice of Danny Kaye. Bachardy had done individual portraits of him and his friend during the visit home from New York.

9. The framer, Ted Gibson, did not frame the portraits of the two Germans, but something else.

The tears roll down Dub's nose, thinking of his faraway furry love. He forced himself to eat a little breakfast, very sad.

Saw a bit of *Star is Born* on T.V. [James] Mason marvellous. [Judy] Garland looked old enough to be his mother.

Don't forget old Nag, and don't stay away too long. Perhaps Kitty will return to find Rubbin lying dead on the stable floor; those workhorse blues are killing him.

poordub

[*Typed letter, signed*]

Monday morning. [June 14, 1965, Santa Monica]

Dearest Love,

[A] little sweetness, a mere drop to be added to that ocean of sweet love. Dubbin made them with tears, because every grain of flour reminded him of the whiteness of his kitten.[1]

I think the novel will be finished before his Love returns.

Last night I dreamed about a railroad station that had four names: Fee, Landis, Goldwater, and another name I have forgotten. Fee means fairy in French. Landis defeats me. As for Goldwater, it was explained to me that they had changed the name of the station for him during his campaign. To which I answered, well now this is probably the only way he'll ever be remembered. The people to whom I said this were not pleased . . . It occurs to me that Fee, in the English sense, may be a joke about our business dealings with Lee Garlington. Not an ill-natured joke, because I really feel quite warmly towards him, and his name, which seems to have invaded my life lately—Lee Prosser, Bob Lee (not that horror but Richard Montague's Negro boyfriend),[2] Lee Heflin, Lee Galloway, a very pretty friend of Bill Jones who has just written a novel and brought it to me the other day, and a charming man named Lee who is repairing the tape recorder!

But why Landis? AND WHAT WAS THE FOURTH NAME OF THE STATION? (*SCREAM!!!!!*)

1. The letter accompanied a box of home-made brownies.
2. That is, not the partner of Jerry Lawrence, but the partner of American mathematician and philosopher Richard Montague (1930–1971), with whom Isherwood had become friendly at UCLA, where Montague was a professor.

And what was the station? BANG!!!

Dub wishes he could send fresh cream for his pretty dear, but it would spoil.

With squashing horsehugs and great sloppity kisses, his everfaithful Good Steed,

D.

[*Typed letter, initialled*]

[Friday, 11 June 1965, New York]

My Darling Onlydrub:

At last a letter from that artful Steed. Kitty had begun to feel quite forgotten without the smallest note from that busy old faithless Nag, and then this afternoon when Kitty, bedraggled and exhausted from the heat and his painful struggle, got back to his wretched quarters, he found a large envelope outside his door. His poor weighted little heart gave nearly its last jump at the thought of a message, however small, from his beloved Horse.

And Kitty read and wept, in spite of his own dreadful ordeal, to know of that Dub's hardship. Those Old complaints racked that already feverish, limp little body and Kitty cried out for his Dear, and the pain of missing him was almost too much for a kitten to bear. But he recovered himself, somewhat, after several prolonged sobs.

Old dub must be as brave as his kitten, whom he taught, and not weaken with the Animals' reunion in sight. Whenever Kitty's strength seems about to give out, he thinks of the Animals sitting up, hoof in paw, hearts together, being shown *Senso*[1]—and then he knows he can go on.

I can hardly believe it, but after Tuesday I will have only five more dancers to draw. I have been drawing two people a day all this week and one or two of the drawings are my very best. I am determined now to lay the completed job in Lincoln's lap and let him sink or swim with it. I did object tactfully to his putting up the drawings of the actors outside the theater and he was enormously relieved, saying it would have cost $1,000, probably more, to have had them framed and shipped and

1. Visconti's 1954 film.

installed (outstalled, actually). I said, *sotto voce*, that that money could go towards the printing costs of the book of ballet drawings.[2]

Virgil has had me to dinner twice this week, both times at short notice. I realize I fulfill two functions. The first is the satisfaction of Virgil's maternal instincts by bringing me together with important New York figures—a composer named Ben Weber, fat, scaley, little known but very much admired by those who do know,[3] and then with Kirk Askew, who runs the Durlacher Brothers gallery, wears a glass eye in place of a cancerous one which has been removed and has the distinguished, gaga opaqueness of Monroe Wheeler, and that same self-pleased, rich-false friendliness, and discomfiture, of the queen who passes.[4] My other function at Virgil's dinners is to satisfy his hostess's desire for youthful decoration. (Imagine Old Tabby still being considered decorative! If they but knew, Kitty would be cruelly exposed and chased away with a stick.) Virgil explains my presence in the palace by saying, in front of me: "His manners are very good." That's only because K.'s been raised in the Stables by that master of social graces, M. Cheval. But what Virgil really means is that Kitty knows how to be nice and pay attention to old things, and where that know-how comes from nobody will ever guess.

Saw the LeSueur-O'Hara gang last night, including Larry Rivers (our first encounter since his cat-snubbing—Kitty was extremely gracious and composed, without the slightest discernable ruffle of his fur[5]), and all of us sat up in the El Quijote till after two in the morning. Rivers has a young and quite pretty wife who is Welsh[6] and sounds very like Sybil Burton. They were most of them quite drunk and Kitty was able to observe with his piercing, sleepless eyes. Frank was querulous and bitching Joe again.

2. Kirstein had proposed an exhibition at the Shakespeare Festival Theater in Connecticut of Bachardy's drawings of the festival actors, as well as a book to be sold in the lobby at Lincoln Center of Bachardy's drawings of the New York City Ballet.

3. Ned Rorem, Aaron Copland, John Cage, and Elliot Carter, as well as Virgil Thomson, were among the admirers of William Jennings Bryan Weber, called Ben (1916–1979).

4. R. Kirk Askew (1903–1974) opened the New York branch of the London gallery for the Durlacher Brothers in the 1920s, and he acquired both galleries in 1937. He dealt in Old Master drawings and paintings and then increasingly in contemporary painters. He was married to Connecticut heiress Constance Atwood McComb, former wife of his Harvard art history professor, Arthur McComb.

5. When Bachardy rang Rivers to arrange the sitting proposed by LeSueur and O'Hara, Rivers refused.

6. Clarice Price, a schoolteacher; she arrived in the U.S. in 1960 as an au pair for Rivers's sons and became his second wife and the mother of his two daughters.

Kitty must stop because Patricia Wilde, the prima ballerina,[7] is coming to be drawn and some effort must be made to make his poor dingy box slightly presentable.

With all of his love and his infinite devotion to his Only Darling, the wors
^x ^xx _xhi_{x x x x x}ping Fur

[*Typed letter, signed*]

Thursday. [17 June 1965, New York]

Dear Precious Pony:

As you will see from the enclosed, another Darling has been saved. Kitty is so glad to know that his Old Dubbin is so many miles away from that dreadful New Jersey slaughterhouse. Kitty likes the look of that old white nag with his muzzle in the feedbag—perhaps the Cat will pay him a visit and tell him a nice story about the Dear Drub in Santa Monica that Kitty misses so, and stroke him and give him a sweet carrot.[1]

Drubbin's brownies arrived to strengthen frail Kitty, who has already gobbled down several—they're even more delicious than the first ones and not quite so crushed by the mailing.

Not much news of any interest to report to my Darling. Lincoln came to see my latest drawings on Sunday night and gave them a very lukewarm reception. I wouldn't allow myself to indulge in the fury I felt, realizing he was in a low state of mind and anyway doesn't have the faintest idea of what's any good, and if he did, wouldn't have the courage of his conviction. He will never be able to stop thinking of me as a dear little boy from the West. I don't fit into any of his

7. Wilde (b. 1928), a Canadian, danced for Balanchine at the New York City Ballet from 1950 to 1965.

1. Turnout, a nineteen-year-old roan horse rescued from a New Jersey slaughterhouse, had served as a training aide and mascot at the ASPCA in Manhattan, and was now being retired to a dairy farm in upstate New York. Bachardy sent Isherwood a clipping that includes photographs of Turnout's farewell party, with a white horse pulling a hansom cab on Fifth Avenue and Turnout's first steps in his new pasture. "ASPCA Horse, 19, Put to Pasture," *The New York Times*, Wed., June 16, 1965.

preconceived ideas about The Artist. He can't explain to himself how I could possibly be any good *really*. His only way of coping with me is to treat me like a student in need of guidance and so I have to listen to talk about "form" and "vision." Lincoln suffers more than anybody else I know from knowing too much for his own good. He even discourages himself because there is always some form of opposition, some basis for criticism, if you look for it, for any stand one might take—and Lincoln, as you know, is the most awful coward, and will back down at the slightest bark from any ass, including Madam Balanchine, who may be a genius as a choreographer but is just a vain, silly know-nothing about other things, most particularly "the visual arts."

Nevertheless, Lincoln is pushing forward with plans for publishing the ballet drawings. The idea now is to have a portfolio of reproductions, each on single sheets without binding and with perhaps a biography of each dancer on the back, to be sold at the theater but quite independent from the souvenir program. The best arrangement I think, though I can't imagine any kind of notable sales.

Kitty is still struggling valiantly and in spite of all doubts in him has done some first-rate drawings, but I think a phase of his career is coming to an end. I don't think he will ever work in this way again, once the ballet drawings are done. The period of the Bachardy Drawing, as we know it, is over, and if he draws again, which is not absolutely certain, his work will be totally different from what has gone before. Anyway, Kitty is anxious to get into his painting smock again. He is strong enough now to be an artist, and he doesn't feel any longer that he has to keep proving himself by getting a likeness of any old fool. He really is stronger—all of this feverish, intensive drawing of the last two weeks has been done without even the aid of Dexamyl, except for one day when Kitty wasn't feeling quite well. It is possible though that this sense of strength is just a delusion resulting from too much time spent in New York, where everyone else is so weak, stupid and silly that, by comparison, a simple little furred thing from Los Angeles feels like Lao Tse!

Virgil had me to dinner again and was very sweet as usual, but an elegant pair of refined New York queens who came along for the ride produced more boredom than they were worth. Otherwise, when Kitty isn't working (though he usually is, thank goodness), he feels very sad and lonely for his old leathery Dub and longs for the warmth of his old flanks and the moist smell of hay in his long mane. Kitty loves that old Horse so much, more than ever, and can't wait to be beside him again.

His adoring Tabby XXXXX

[Typed letter, signed, with enclosure]

Monday [June 21, 1965, Santa Monica]

Own Cat,

Here's the American Express bill.

This morning I finished the rough draft of A Meeting by the River. Exactly three months to a day. I don't dare read it yet. It is awful, certainly. And even if it weren't awful, I don't know if I could ever publish it without mortally offending the Ramakrishna Order. There isn't one word about them in it, but they are so touchy and they will identify, in one way or another.

Glorious sunshine today. Dobbin got a moment to warm his poor old hide.

Tonight, I'm watching Jim Bridges's Hitchcock story about the demon drag-queen nurse, which is being rerun.[1] Jim will come and watch it, too. Jack is rehearsing every evening for Androcles.[2]

Tomorrow, I'm going to see Dutchman and The Toilet, because one of the dinge actors came by with Jerry Lawrence and suggested it.[3]

Wednesday is Selznicks. Jennifer called, as I told you.

Thursday is blank, because Swami called and said he couldn't make

1. "An Unlocked Window" (1965), based on a story by Ethel Lina White and starring Alfred Hitchcock, first aired February 15 on "The Alfred Hitchcock Hour." Bridges wrote sixteen episodes for the series.
2. Larson had the lead in a revival of George Bernard Shaw's Androcles and the Lion directed by John Kerr for the American National Theater and Academy at Beverly Hills High School on June 25 and 26.
3. Gene Boland, an African-American actor and T.V. writer, came to Adelaide Drive with Lawrence and others for drinks on June 20; he was playing in The Toilet. Both plays were by African-American writer, actor, and activist LeRoi Jones (later known as Amiri Baraka) (b. 1934); they were first produced in New York in 1964, where Dutchman won an Obie Award. Dinge is slang for black.

it, this week. Incidentally, there has been quite a good notice of *Rama-krishna* in the *L.A. Times*, which pleased him.[4]

Friday is Stravinskys.

Thus does Dub try to "bundle Time away Till the Cat come." (Yeats, nearly).[5]

Gavin is rejoicing that he is free of Budd Cherry. I still don't know just exactly what their involvement was, but evidently not much. We had supper with an Australian film journalist named Charles Higham[6] yesterday. He made Australia sound glamorous. Had interviewed various stars here. Liked Bette Davis best, [Josef von] Sternberg least.

Drub is longing so to be with his dear again, so he can whisper in Animalese into Kitty's ear while he holds that snowy paw. And then he will make little breakfasts for his treasure and pet him and surround him with all the attentions of home, so Kitty will be glad to be back and not sigh for far-off rooftops for a little while.

Give Dob one final call on Sunday morning.

Till then, all love,

Rubdub

[Typed letter, signed, enclosure lost]

• • •

4. "Mysticism of a Hindu," review by Stanton Coblentz of Isherwood's *Ramakrishna and His Disciples*, the *Los Angeles Times*, June 20, 1965, B 27.
5. Cf. "To bundle time away / That the Night come." From "That the Night Come," *Responsibilities and Other Poems* (1916).
6. Higham (b. 1931) is English and moved to Australia in 1954 and then, later, to California. He published poetry, worked as a journalist and editor, and became known in the 1970s for his numerous best-selling biographies of movie stars and royalty.

February 21 [1966]   [Santa Monica]

Dearest Love, I feel so sad thinking of Kitty freezing in that New York weather.[1] We get reports of how cold and awful it is, and the only consolation is that that tiny love isn't exposed to the flu, which is sweeping us. Even tough old Gladys Cooper has it, she called to tell me, sent you her love, has the part of the murderess-mother in Maugham's *The Sacred Flame* which they're reviving in England—she played the wife of the cripple who has an affair with his brother in the original production in the thirties.

Gavin also has flu. Before he came down with it, I went over and with the help of Gavin and Michael Sean moved your car into his port, at the back, where it isn't in the way. Now I have the key but Gavin says to wait till Thursday, when I am going to dinner with him, to move it back up here.

Your telephone has been put on vacation rates. They suggested having the special operator give a message to anyone who calls to call my number. This costs nothing extra, so I said yes, because it is possible some business might arise and I could tell those concerned to call your number in New York. Okay?

Dorothy is cleaning here today. She is in bliss, because she had a dream in which her niece appeared to her and said she was sorry because she and Dorothy had had words and she wanted to make everything all right, because she was about to pass on. So Dorothy called Ohio (or wherever it was, long distance) and was told that the niece was indeed in hospital and at death's door. They had gone out to her house in the deep snow and found her on the floor with her tongue hanging out, in a diabetes coma. They don't know yet if they can revive her.

1. Bachardy returned to New York on February 15 to supervise engravings of his New York City Ballet drawings for the portfolio publication proposed by Kirstein. He stayed at 26 Second Avenue in a one-room apartment Jim Bridges had rented.

I saw *La Notte* again. It still seemed awfully good but perhaps not quite so shattering. The fight between the two boys was almost the best thing, and of course Moreau's marvellous bitchery at the party, especially when she kisses Monica Vitti. And the Negress in the nightclub. The last bit of *The Red Desert* seemed pretty terrific, the color is so marvellous.[2]

Gavin said that both Mulligan and Pakula were terribly upset because of the bad N.Y. notices of *Clover* (I didn't tell him I'd seen them, of course) but consoled by the good business it is doing—people standing in long lines, despite the cold.

Jack and Jim keep on about the apartment. They say they told Joe Le-Sueur to get a cleaning woman in, and he didn't, but that they will gladly pay for one.[3] Last night they gave a roaring party for the cast of *The Candied House*,[4] in a queer bar in the Valley. I didn't go, remembering Kitty's lectures on dub-drunkenness. Meanwhile, they have a project that Jack, Betty Harford and I shall do, an evening of readings from Victorian humorists, Edward Lear, [C.S.]Calverley, [W.S.]Gilbert, Lewis Carroll, to be presented at the County Museum Theater. I said yes, because I think it might be a thing we could repeat on various campuses and earn a bit of money.[5]

Here is the Ginsberg interview. I think is makes an awful lot of sense, even though one questions if G. himself really has all that love to spread around. But it *is* a corrective to the Animals' paranoia about the Police! Am very anxious to hear what you'll think of it.[6] The other chores are being taken care of. Don Murray's pictures aren't ready yet, I checked this morning, but I'll deliver them very soon.[7]

Dubbin misses his Darling so, and, every day, is reminded how truly unique he is and how half-dead nearly everybody else seems by comparison.

2. Michelangelo Antonioni's *La Notte* (*The Night*), also starring Marcello Mastroianni, came out in 1961. *Il deserto rosso* (1964), again with Monica Vitti, was Antonioni's first color film.
3. LeSueur had a one-room apartment in a second building at the same address. Both buildings had one-room apartments only.
4. A mystery play by Larson based on the story of Hansel and Gretel and written in rhymed verse; Bridges directed it at the Leo S. Bing Theater at the Los Angeles County Museum of Art.
5. Nothing came of this.
6. Ginsberg told Thomas Clark that drugs and anal sex should be included in literature since they were part of the real lives of himself and other writers he was close to, in particular Kerouac and Burroughs. "Allen Ginsberg: An Interview, The Art of Poetry," *The Paris Review* 37, Spring 1966. Ginsberg had visited Isherwood and Bachardy on January 6, 1966, with Peter Orlovsky and Stephen Bornstein.
7. Two pencil and ink-wash drawings by Bachardy, one of Don Murray and the other of his second wife, Bettie; they were being framed.

Don't forget weird old Drub, so bad and only to be excused, if at all, because of his love for Mr. K.

xxxx Rubbin

[*Typed letter, signed, enclosure now lost*]

March 5, 1966 [New York]

Dearest Only Pony:

I've only just gotten this typewriter back from the repair shop. Freddy Maddox had managed to jam the carriage and hadn't bothered to do anything about getting it fixed. But even though I have the typewriter I don't have a table to set it on, so I have to have it on my lap. Oh this place is so uncomfortable and sad-making.[1] I try to get out of it as much as possible, which is why I haven't been writing. I haven't even written to Jack and Jim. If you thought the other apartment on West 20th was uncharming, you really should see this. On one side of me there's a mother who screams frantically at her moppet. The moppet has some kind of rocking chair or cradle which she keeps going a good part of the day and the floor of my apartment echoes and trembles with the action, though I can still manage to hear their television over the rumble—it's on throughout the day.

Maurice Grosser (Virgil's painter friend) very kindly offered me his apartment on West 14th but he won't be out of it until sometime around the 15th, when he leaves on his annual six-month trip to exotic places, so it wouldn't be much good to me.[2] But it is a quite pleasant place (comparatively speaking) and convenient.

I missed you so terribly today, and worried about you and wondered if you are taking proper care of yourself. Kitty couldn't bear it if something happened to his Old Dear. He fears so that he might fall down in the street and Kitty wouldn't be there to drag him home.

I don't know what I'm doing here. It seems pure madness. I'm having an awful time. Nothing and nobody amuses me. I'm not working and minding that, and yet I hesitate to get started for fear of getting involved

1. Bachardy had moved from Jim Bridges's, but the new apartment is unidentified.
2. Grosser (1903–1986) painted, wrote about art for *The Nation*, and published several books about painting. He lived partly in Tangier. Bachardy was then planning to return to Santa Monica on March 21.

and wanting to stay on. Every minute away from my Nag seems foolish and wasted. The Animals have so little time to be together—really there is so little time anywhere. Kitty gets so sad here thinking about time slipping away and the meaninglessness of every moment spent so far away from his Dear Love, whom Kitty loves more than anything in the world. Dub is the only thing in Kitty's life that he cares about, the only One who makes Kitty's life worth saving. Kitty really only takes care of himself for his Horse because he knows that it would hurt him so if anything happened to Kitty. And Kitty needs to know that Dub feels the same way and guards that sweet, irreplaceable hide with the greatest care. Kitty will come back to the stable as soon as he can.

More later. All of a cat's love. Fur

[*Autograph letter with autograph addition*]

March 11, 1966 [New York]

Dear Treasured LoveDub:

No news of any real interest. I've done more work this last week than I've done since I've been here and I'm surprised that it has done little to lift my general mood. Two afternoon painting sessions with Anita produced only mediocre results, though Anita was pleased with a couple of them. The best thing I've done in the last weeks is a drawing of Miss Moore which I've given to Gladys.[1] To my amazement Miss Moore sat like an angel, better than any other child of seven I've ever drawn and the drawing itself was correspondingly better. I wish you could see it— but then you will when you come here again, though when you do you may have to come alone. Old Cat is in a very anti-N.Y. state of mind and wouldn't mind at all if he never saw this place again. I will certainly never return here without a definite job to do. Even that might not get me here. The simple fact that I've discovered this trip is that I don't much like N.Y. people, with a few, too few, exceptions.

I saw Wystan again. I took him to lunch. He was very much friendlier but there was still the underlying sense of duty between us. He is very cross about the appearance of his pornographic poem in *Fuck You.*

1. Miss Moore was Anita Loos's adopted daughter; Gladys, a middle-aged black woman, was her factotum.

Apparently it says "ascribed" to W.H. Auden so that he can't sue even if he were willing to face the publicity.² Besides, as he says, he *did* write the thing, and in fact he's got others but is keeping them under lock and key until posthumous activities begin.

I had dinner with Frank Moore who is really very nice and appealing in an unthrilling, weak-natured way. He spoke frankly about Tony and is much offended by Tony's treatment of him.³ He has an attractive, for N.Y., apartment, though unmistakably decorator-queen in its modest tastefulness. He drinks a great deal, though how N.Y. life is bearable without drink is becoming more and more of a mystery to me. Even poor Kitty has had his head forcibly held down in the liquor bucket. I think that's part of the reason for his uncontrollable depression—he's only used to his healthy stable diet. Already his coat has noticeably lost its usual gloss.

I have seen strangely little of Lincoln, though he has been out of town this week. I'm having dinner with Virgil tonight, but a sad weekend of dreary engagements promises to wrench more lonely sobs from that already weakened furred body.

The only sparks in the dim near future are Lauren Bacall's play on Monday (I don't even seem to have enough drive to get after her again about sitting for me)⁴ and an evening with Elaine de Kooning.⁵

The only thing that makes Kitty's survival possible is his constant devotion to that all-important Horse and his determination to be alongside that dear Old Hide once more.

With a kitten's purrpetual love,

F.

[*Typed letter, initialled, with enclosure⁶*]

---

2. "It was a Spring day, a day for a lay," printed without a title in *Fuck You: A Magazine of the Arts*, Vol. 5, No. 8, March 1965; described as "A gobble poem snatched from the notebooks of W.H. Auden." The publisher, Ed Sanders, also produced a pamphlet edition titled *The Platonic Blow*, with drawings by Joe Brainard.
3. Moore had been a friend of Tony Richardson since at least 1960.
4. Bacall had been starring in the Manhattan comedy *Cactus Flower* since early December 1965.
5. American painter, teacher, writer, lecturer (1920–1989), married to Dutch-born artist Willem de Kooning.
6. "Police Horses Move to New Home, Not Always Happily; Police Mounted Unit Ends 50 Years at Armory," *The New York Times*, March 10, 1966. The clipping is illustrated with two photos showing the horses of Police Department Troop C being led from the Eighth Regiment Armory at Madison Avenue and 94th Street to new quarters on West 55th. In one photo, a riderless horse has bolted and nearly unseated the policeman leading it. Bachardy underlined and annotated the article with flirtatious allusions to his and Isherwood's animal personae.

March 14, 1966 [New York]

Dear Longed-for Colt:

When a certain cat saw the enclosed full-color picture of a Dub in holiday decoration, he shed tears of sadness and longing.[1] He misses and worries about his Old Dear so terribly.

I was told this morning the final prints of the ballet drawings will not be ready until almost the deadline, which is the opening of the spring season on the 29th. I'm not at all sure that Kitty's strength will last that long. His energy seems to be diminishing daily, especially without the reviving effects of the stable warmth and smells to keep him going.

No news of any interest. Kitty sometimes doesn't even put his head out of doors till late afternoon. He was so desperate for company last night that he went for drinks to neurotic, unpleasant John Kennedy[2] who was as neurotically hypochondriacal as usual (a mysterious upset stomach which prevented him from drinking anything but a little weak tea) and maybe even more unpleasant than I'd remembered (he very cruelly, in front of me and his other guests, reprimanded his silly defenseless roommate for being drunk and "slurring," and finally forced him out of the apartment).

Kitty has been reading and quite enjoying Agee's film reviews,[3] though they are often very self-consciously "serious," with involved sentences of such clumsiness that I must sometimes read them three and four times and even then I don't always know what I've read. Also reading Vivekananda's *Raja Yoga* and being amazed by its readability and lack of depressing effect. It is a wonderful antidote for the symptoms of acute anxiety and gloom which the reading of the morning newspapers produces.

Kitty only lives to be with his Darling Drub again. He has set April 1 as

---

1. Bachardy enclosed the cover page of *New York, The Sunday Herald Tribune Magazine*, March 13, 1966, a photograph of the head of a grey carriage horse with a green carnation in his harness to celebrate St. Patrick's Day, March 17.
2. John F. Kennedy, coincidentally named like the president; he later came to Santa Monica where Isherwood met him and Bachardy did several portraits of him. The acquaintanceship ended when Bachardy backed into Kennedy's car parked awkwardly on Adelaide Drive and Kennedy insisted on contacting Bachardy's insurance company rather than allowing Bachardy to pay for repairs.
3. From *Time Magazine* and *The Nation*, collected in the first volume of *Agee on Film* (1958).

the deadline for their reunion, if that fragile feline stamina permits, and if it does, upon arrival in the stable Kitty will need immediate massive intravenous doses of Horse Essence.

All of a kitten's unswerving love and devotion, F.

[*Typed letter, initialled, with enclosure*]

· · ·

as from c/o American Express
Salzburg Austria
Sat. Sept. 24 [1966]

My darling only Love,

Sorry Dub's cable was worded so coldly, but he wrote it knowing that it was about to be read aloud by a dyke operator at the desk in the presence of Danny Mann![1] Dub misses Kitty so, and is only glad Kitty was spared a few of the travel-griefs. To start off with, our flight to N.Y. was a bugger, ending with nearly two hours circling around before we finally landed in thick rain fog and air-traffic jams. The bumps greatly demoralized Danny, Dub was high on Librium and liquor and acted calm and nonattached. Then we were told (by a dreamy but dreadfully square Kraut chick in uniform) that we'd missed our Luft Hansa plane to Munich. So we had to crowd into another later one, going to Frankfurt. Again Dub got drunk with a Kraut rubber manufacturer and spouted Deutsch until he passed out and woke fresh as a daisy due to applications of eau de cologne which they give you in tiny impregnated towels. Danny, who hadn't slept, was so demoralized that he decided we should take the train, not the plane, to Munich. So we didn't arrive till late Thursday and had to squeeze into this third-rate hotel. But Munich is lively and enjoying a beer festival, and we have rented a car and are going to see lots of local lakes today and drive to Salzburg tomorrow and settle in the *best* hotel—so now I do wish Kitty were here to help Dub enjoy the scene—because Danny, though

1. American film and T.V. director Daniel Mann (1912–1991) asked Isherwood to write a script for an ABC Christmas special about the song "Silent Night," so they travelled together to Oberndorf, near Salzburg, Austria, where the words and music were written and first performed. The cable, probably announcing Isherwood's safe arrival in Europe, is lost.

truly well meaning and friendly and even unstingy is definitely not up to This Sporting Life![2] Gottfried and Silvia Reinhardt[3] are at Salzburg and apparently raring to make with the hospitality. Dub is fighting for his waistline against the most delicious wicked cream cakes, and the local wine is out of this world. But he keeps pretty sober because there's no one to drink with.

My typewriter got psychosomatically damaged in transit and so I hope I can get a secretary in Salzburg and rattle off this script, then dash to Vienna to see Wystan if there, then England and I hope home soon to my darling who is all the Dub wants to be near, ever.

Still I hope Angel is having a fun vacation and also working to his satisfaction. Give Swami my love when you see him. And I'm of course curious to know if Gerald likes the idea of having the novel dedicated to him.[4] As for Dub, *he* is dedicated to Kitty *forever*.

Am writing this real early in the morning, after getting home late from a visit to Herbert List,[5] who looks like an old lady, lives alone collecting 17th-century drawings and is sad, sad—though bravely setting off to Greece on a trip. He sends you his love and has admired your drawings of Max,[6] and of me, he says. He gave me a very nice book of pictures of boys in Haiti.

Am wearing Kitty's robe, to feel nearer to him.

Eternally,

Pluggin

[Autograph letter on letterhead of Eden-Hotel-Wolff, Munich]

2. The 1960 novel by David Storey, and Lindsay Anderson's 1963 film, expose the glamorous life of a professional rugby league star as a nasty, rough slog. Isherwood is suggesting that Mann is not a seasoned pro like himself in the harsh reality of show business.
3. Austrian producer (1911–1994) and his wife; from 1940 to 1954 Reinhardt worked at MGM, where he was Isherwood's favorite Hollywood boss.
4. *A Meeting by the River* (1967); Isherwood had completed a third draft in May.
5. German photographer. Isherwood met him in the early 1930s when List was working as a coffee merchant in Hamburg in his family's firm.
6. Max Scheler, German photographer, friend and pupil of List; Isherwood and Bachardy first met him during the filming of *War and Peace* in Italy in 1955. Afterwards Scheler visited Los Angeles where Bachardy drew his portrait.

September 28, 1966 [Santa Monica]

Dearest RubbleDub:

His dear letter arrived yesterday and made Kitty so happy, though he winced for that aching hoof to which the pen was strapped.[1]

No mail of any interest, as you can see from what I've enclosed— mostly bills, fan letters and the usual unurgent stuff.[2]

I've had no communication from Josué Corcos.[3] I begin to think I won't be going east now, which is all right with me. Instead, I am planning a trip to San Francisco next weekend. John Goodwin and Anthony [Russo] are going to be there and maybe I can even arrange finally to do that commission I got when I had my show at the museum.[4] John and Anthony have suggested I drive with them to Los Angeles with a stopover in Big Sur but I doubt if I will because that would mean waiting until they were ready to leave San Francisco, which would not be before the tenth of October. Six days is a long time in San Francisco—not that very much is happening here.

The big concern is whether or not Jack (Larson) is going to flip. His yakking long since passed the flood mark. Nellie[5] tells me he's not been able to sleep and is suffering from paranoiac suspicions as well as delusions of grandeur beyond even his usual susceptibility. I got an early morning call from him—he was full of deep appreciation for the simple things in life. You can imagine how well that all went over with Kitty who had dragged himself from his warm (but lonely) basket in order to answer the phone. I am supposed to spend tomorrow evening with Jack and Jim, and maybe Gavin. I'll know more then.

I did see Gerald but intuition told me that the offer of the dedication should come from you, not me, so I didn't mention it. He looked well and was very affectionate and talked nonstop. Occasionally his talk

1. Isherwood had arthritis in his right thumb and usually typed, but his letter from Austria was written longhand.
2. Enclosures lost.
3. New York doctor known for his research into rheumatoid arthritis and for his use of acupuncture in the 1970s to treat smoking and overeating. He was from Marrakesh and studied acupuncture in France. Jack Larson and Jim Bridges introduced him to Bachardy, who later drew his portrait when Corcos visited Santa Monica.
4. The commission to draw William Silva was outstanding from Bachardy's show at the M.H. de Young Memorial Museum in Golden Gate Park, April 10–May 10, 1964. See below p. 223.
5. Nellie Carroll (d. 2005), American artist, born Jean Dobrin. She designed and drew greeting cards.

seemed quite independent of him, like an automatic mechanism he couldn't control—rather like our toaster. It made me feel somehow closer to him. There was a kind of union resulting from neither of us paying strict attention to what he was saying. As with your visit, Michael [Barrie] was out of the room the whole time.

I had an uncomfortable evening with Michael [Leopold] and Henry [Guerriero] due to the presence of Gavin and Clint.[6] Michael and Gavin were exchanging minor bitcheries and Clint was in his sulky silent aspect, an aspect I've noticed that he saves largely for his evenings spent with the unfamous queer.

Michael Sean is in his house and has returned to the gym. Lyle [Fox] has been cast in the role of physical therapist—at last he has something to do.[7] Kitty, due no doubt to despondency, weighs little more than 140.

Two more sittings with Ian Whitcomb,[8] both of which went quite well, another sitting with Fords (I may at last have sold one of Glenn to him),[9] a painting sitting with Maggie which bored the hell out of Michael, who had come to be tutored (but at least they want to buy two drawings of the children)[10] and a nude session with part of the Horne brood.[11] I'm supposed to draw Rachel Roberts[12] tomorrow but I more than expect a cancellation.

I've seen Swami once, on Sunday, and he seemed well. He was alone and I think pleased to see me. He sent you his love. I will try to see him or call him tomorrow and will give him your love.

Poor Kitty waits patiently for further word from his roaming stallion.

6. Clint Kimbrough (1933–1996), American actor and director, sometimes credited as Kimbro; he was then having an affair with Lambert.
7. Sean was in a bad car accident in May and spent a long time recovering in the hospital and in a clinic in Downey before being allowed home.
8. British pianist, singer, and later record producer, author, and radio host (b. 1941); he moved to Los Angeles when he had a hit song in 1965.
9. Glenn Ford married actress Kathryn Hays that year.
10. Margaret Leighton married British actor Michael Wilding (1912–1979) in 1964, her second marriage, his fourth. He was an aspiring painter and sketched all his life. The children were his two sons with his second wife, Elizabeth Taylor: Michael Wilding Jr. (b. 1953) and Christopher Wilding (b. 1955).
11. Geoffrey Horne (b. 1933), American actor and acting coach, was then married to Collin Wilcox with whom he was raising three children, Kimberley Horne, Christopher Mann Horne, and William Wilcox Horne. The three sat for Bachardy clothed on August 24, and they sat again unclothed on September 15 along with the son and daughter of Betsy von Furstenberg, Glyn and Gay Vincent, who were staying at their house. The children ranged in age from about nine to eleven years old. These are the only nudes of children Bachardy has ever done.
12. Welsh-born stage and film actress (1927–1980); she was nominated for an Academy Award for her role opposite Richard Harris in *This Sporting Life*.

He feels very alone and unprotected and spends most of his evenings by himself, eating half-heartedly from a jagged tin of old fish. There seems little point to his life without the Old Nag.

Hoping Dub will take time out from his merry rounds to think of his loving, loyal and devoted

Kitty

P.S. Alan Searle called. He is staying at [George] Cukor's. I am having lunch with him on Monday.

[*Typed letter, signed, with autograph insertion*]

October 3 Hotel Mirabell Salzburg

Angel Sweetcat,

His dear letter only arrived today—in fact, they'd already told me at the American Express that there was nothing, and old Dub was getting very upset, imagining disasters. But then Danny Mann, off to Vienna until tomorrow night, to inspect the studios there, happened to go by the Express office to get his own mail, and asked for mine too, and yours had just come in and he very considerately phoned me. Dub was just about to send off a cable, appealing for a message that his Kitty was all right. He is sending one anyway, so Kitty will know that Dub will probably be in London by the weekend and to write next to c/o American Express[.] I will tell the American Express here to forward anything that may arrive in the interval to their London office.

Work has gone very quickly and quite well, I think. Danny is very pleased. Also, he has found all his locations for the picture. Oberndorf itself wasn't right but a nearby village was perfect.[1] I find these lowland villages suicidally depressing—peasants, cowshit, a church and sometimes the sun. (The weather has been heavenly so far but they say it rained the entire summer.) And then, just as you get to Salzburg, within less than twenty miles, everything changes, a landscape of stunningly picturesque hills, marvellous lakes, rich woods with autumn flaming colors—sort of

1. "Silent Night" was first performed in the church of St. Nicholas in Oberndorf in 1818, but the show was made in Eugendorf.

Disney heaven, but still absolutely beautiful. And Salzburg, the old part, is as thrilling as the behind-the-canal-front Venice, marvellous warrens and alleys and tunnels and beer cellars right out of the Middle Ages. And what a dobbintown! Dobbins everywhere, shaggy old live ones pulling carriages, and mad marble ones in fountains squirting water out of their nostrils (perhaps Dub will have learnt this trick by the time he gets home) and painted dobbins on walls, very noble and gracious[2] and of course The White Horse Inn, which is near here on a huge lake. (The lake out of *The World in the Evening* is also in the neighborhood.) *Neigh*borhood—I never realized what that word meant before!

Yesterday we drove to the house Hitler had on a huge crag above Berchtesgaden. It is now a restaurant, but you still get a real chill from the architecture, the grim utterly humorless, meant-to-be-impressive use of bare stone. To think of that grim little bore, detaining us all with his corny old-fashioned paranoia. The drive up to the top of the crag was very sheer, with vast views and vertical precipices. Danny was frankly terrified—which I not only felt for, due to my own vertigo, but liked because it made me completely calm; Dub fairly craned his neck over the abyss. However, I must admit that some of these cable-car lines which are all over the hills here simply are *not true*. Dub would have to be blinkered and shot full of morphia first. They are said to be absolutely safe, not more than three or four cars fall in twenty years.

By the time I get to London, the first draft of the screenplay will be done. I suppose I'll rewrite it in California. Danny is longing to get back to his Gigi (emphatically *not* a gee-gee![3]) and will probably only stay a short while. As for me, well, we'll see what offers. But Dub can't bear to be separated from Kitty much longer. One of them must come to the other. I am taking Bob Regester and Neil up on their invitation. If they back out, I might try Stephen. I talked to Wystan by phone at his house and he's leaving for London almost at once, to preach not at St. Paul's but at Westminster Abbey! He will be staying with Stephen but I think there are two spare rooms.

Am going to lunch with Gottfried Reinhardt today. He and Silvia are

2. Isherwood enclosed black-and-white illustrations, evidently cut from a tourist pamphlet, of the paintings and statues of horses that decorate the *Pferdeschwemme* (horse pond), where the royal horses were once watered and washed, and of the *Residenzplatz* fountain, which has marble horses squirting water from their mouths.
3. That is, not a horse (British slang).

the only fun people I see. Danny is well-meaning, stingy, rude to servants, terribly sentimental about his love life, eager for friendship, conscientiously liberal, quite bright on film ideas, saddeningly homely. His two vices are buying expensive sweaters and eating rich Austrian cakes; the sweaters have difficulty covering the effects of the cake! With this warning, Dub guzzles less than he otherwise might—sadness at Kitty's absence gives him a pathological appetite—but still, I fear he's curving a bit, too.

My love to everybody, as they say. And all of my true love where it is already unalterably bestowed between those paws the very thought of whose whiteness and purity brings tears to the eyes of

Old Plugdub

[Typed letter, signed, with enclosures]

October 4, 1966 [Santa Monica]

My Darling Horse:

His dear telegram[1] arrived this morning to cheer old Sadcat and make him know his Sweet Dubbin hadn't forgotten him. How joyless and empty the old stable is without that Drub and how cold and comfortless the basket without that resting Rump.

This will be a short letter since it may not reach you before you leave Salzburg. I will send my next letter to London. There is very little news and no mail worth sending on.

I had dinner with Gavin and Michael Sean last night at the Bellevue and we went to see *The Wild Angels* (about the Hell's Angels). The film is really very good and beautifully photographed. You will love it. Kitty will take His Dear to see it when he is home again. There's a pale horse in it who is set free by the cyclists—Dubbin will like that scene especially. Michael was his usual overwhelmingly complimentary self. He is very slow still on the crutches but made a great struggle to keep up. We had to go in my car and getting in and out of it (an ordeal for anybody) *three times* was almost too much for him. And we would go to probably the only restaurant in Santa Monica with an upstairs men's room and, of course, Michael had to go to it.

I did two nice drawings of Maggie yesterday and she gave me a check for $400 for two of the drawings of the children. Rachel *did* stand me up but she's being given another chance today. Alan Searle took me to lunch yesterday and was very sweet. He misses Willie very much he says. He told some horrendous stories about the last days, or rather years, during which Willie was apparently quite crazy, not even knowing who Alan was. Alan said he was sometimes awakened in the middle of the night by Willie's beating on him. A ghastly story too about what the daughter did near the end[2] which I shall save for a cozier telling.

---

1. Not preserved.
2. Liza Paravicini Hope (1915–1998), Maugham's daughter with Syrie Wellcome, whom Maugham married in 1917. She had been Maugham's heir until 1962 when Maugham tried to disinherit her and adopt Searle. Maugham argued that she was the daughter of Henry Wellcome, Syrie's husband at the time of Liza's birth. A French court ruled Maugham was the father, and Liza eventually inherited the Villa Mauresque, as well as receiving in Maugham's lifetime, in an out-of-court settlement in England, half the proceeds from the sale of paintings Maugham had bought in her name. Everything else was inherited by Searle, who had nothing good to say about his rival.

I am going to San Francisco on Friday and will probably drive back with John and Anthony after all. I am staying with Ben Underhill whom I called and rather brutally put on the carpet. He was taken aback, to say the least, but submissive, about my self-imposition. I hope neither of us will be sorry. John and Anthony are planning to leave S.F. on Monday the tenth and be here on the twelfth, spending one night in Big Sur. In Kitty's brave battle against depression and oblivion, he also bought two dear little suits from the Ohrbach's boys' department for his trip.

Jack Larson seems out of danger at present—the babbling is back to a modest (for him) level.

Kitty will fly off to the post office now. His most important message is: he wants his Pony back, as soon as possible, double-quick, pronto, and if he doesn't get him back soon he'll come to London, harness-in-paw.

With all of a kitten's undying love, always,

K.

[*Autograph letter*]

[Los Angeles, Oct. 7, 1966]

"Among horses, you may know me as Uchchaishrava, who was brought forth from the sea of nectar."
Sri Krishna to Arjuna, Bhagavad Gita[1]

[*Autograph postcard; verso shows full-color nursery illustration of well-dressed mother and father cat with seven kittens causing domestic mayhem*]

1. 10.27, when Krishna makes known some of his divine manifestations, including the snow-white seven-headed horse, king of horses. Bachardy quotes the Prabhavananda-Isherwood translation, p. 115. He sent this postcard c/o American Express, London, where Isherwood had gone on to from Austria.

Tuesday. October 11 [1966, San Francisco]

I'm going down to Ernie's[1] to make a hit, and to hell with all the rest. Frisco Fur.

[*Autograph postcard; verso shows color photo of blue-eyed tiger-and-white kitten*]

October 12, 1966 [Santa Monica]

Dearest Raggledub:

They just dragged Old Cat's exhausted body into the Casa tonight after more than five days on the road. His desperate attempt to forget his loneliness and drown his Dubless despair would be ridiculous if it weren't so poignant. I think maybe Kitty and San Francisco are chemically incompatible. Anyway, the trip was more effort than entertainment, as I guess most trips are—at least the ones I make. One good thing: I more than paid for the trip by doing a commission—a dressmaker who runs a shop there named William Silva. He is tacky and has a garish house with friends to match, and the most awful collection of "artworks" anyone would dread to see. I shudder to think of a Bachardy being added to those walls. But, he is easy to get along with and has a hairdresser friend who is ready to be drawn on my next trip to S.F., whenever that is going to be.

I stayed two nights with Anthony and John in their apartment and two nights at Ben Underhill's place. I had hoped I would get to know Ben by staying with him but he almost never allowed us to be alone together for more than a few minutes at a time. He was forever asking somebody, anybody, up to his place or taking me over to see them or just running into someone on the street and suggesting they have lunch with us. Even on Sunday morning he had *two* people in for breakfast! And you know what Kitty is like when he hasn't had either his morning toilette or his coffee-flavored cream. *Oh* the socializing and the San Francisco brand of elegant politeness. And, since Ben never permitted us a chance to have any but the most superficial conversation, I feel I hardly know him any better than when I arrived there. One hunch I have got: I think

---

1. The San Francisco restaurant at 847 Montgomery Street; used by Hitchcock in *Vertigo* (1958).

he is determined to be a disappointed queer and force himself into a sad corner from which the only escape will be marriage. Also, I feel he was a little frightened of me, or suspicious, or disapproving, and maybe a little of all three.

Anthony and John were, on the other hand, very sweet and genuinely glad to see me and quite fun to be with. Their apartment is small but their Mercedes-Benz made the trip home very comfortable. We had lunch at Nepenthe, stayed last night at a motel in San Simeon and saw Hearst's folly this morning. I am really very fond of them both now.

Mason [Wells] and Frank [Hamilton] were away. Thom Gunn[1] is in New York but I did have lunch with Mike Kitay,[2] who looks older but is on the whole unchanged, except he seems less sulky, less rigidly success-minded, and decidedly less stuck on Thom. He works as a kind of writer-associate producer on a daily T.V. interview program.

Poor old Cat is so tired his unclipped claws are catching on the typewriter keys. He must put himself into that cold basket.

There is still no urgent mail, other than what is enclosed,[3] unless you take seriously a threat from the Writers' Guild of America, West, to place you in bad standing unless you report your employment and sales record and pay your dues for July–September. I will send you the forms if you want them, and I will pay your annual membership dues to the Authors' Guild ($30) if you want me to.

Old Greywhiskers, tired and bent as he was, jumped from the car this evening as they brought him back, hoping he'd find a letter from his dear Horse waiting for him. He had to hang onto the mail box to hold himself up when he didn't find what he was looking for, but he didn't let the others see the pain-filled tears in his great eyes.

Hoping that prancing cosmopolitan Stallion won't forget his loyal and devoted Fur who loves him with all of his heart.

K.

[Typed letter, initialled]

1. English poet (1929–2004) living in San Francisco and teaching at Berkeley from 1958 onward.
2. American companion of Gunn and, later, housemate; he studied at Stanford and at Cambridge, where he met Gunn in 1952.
3. Not preserved.

Oct. 14 [1966]

Angel Lovecat,

[H]ave just been by the American Express and found Kitty's dear letter, forwarded from Salzburg. There is still Kitty's account of his visit to San Francisco to look forward to.¹ Am starting to write this on a bench in St. James's Park, before going to lunch with Eric Falk at the Reform Club. The sun is shining but it is sort of chilly and damp and yellow-leaf-littered, with old sodden deck chairs standing out under the trees. If you dared sit in one you wd not only get pneumonia but be charged 2/6.²

It was such a joy hearing Kitty's voice yesterday. Dub thinks about him at least once every few minutes and it sometimes scares him to realize how utterly Kitty has become what he lives for and does things for. At the other end of this seat sits a man of Dub's age, in despair, with a grey London face. He is simply Dub without a Kitty. Even to have a Kitty 6,000 miles away makes Dub the most fortunate of nags. (The man has just gotten up and walked away, as if he knew he was being written about!)

As I told you on the phone, I was really quite horrified by *Sailor from Gibraltar*. Moreau so fat and old, Bannen sheerly repulsive, the continuity fucked up, horrible narrated thoughts (Bannen's) on the sound track. "Was this happiness? Had I found what I wanted at last?" (That's not exact, but a perfectly fair specimen of what they're like.)³ I was frank about all this to Bob Regester, less frank to Neil. Haven't talked to Tony yet, as he has been away on vacation location (a Freudian slip—"your play, dear boy, your play"!⁴) I shall merely try to get them to take out some of the narration, as they easily can.

As for Vanessa, she is radiantly beautiful in the film, which makes nonsense of it—no one would leave her for Moreau. And no one would *not* leave Bannen for absolutely anyone . . . Incidentally, Tony made me a strangely frank speech shortly after I arrived—almost as if he were giving evidence at a divorce trial—about how he'd had this affair with Moreau and how she had then started an affair with a Greek boy who plays one of

1. Isherwood had received Bachardy's letter of October 4, but not the letter of October 12.
2. That is, two shillings and sixpence in British currency before the decimal system was put into use in 1971.
3. Isherwood saw the film at Twickenham Studios on October 13. Scottish actor Ian Bannen (1928–1999) played opposite Moreau and Redgrave. The film came out in 1967.
4. Oscar Wilde's reported reply to an amateur writer who asked Wilde's opinion of his "work."

the sailors on the yacht, and how this had made Tony so insanely jealous that he had "lost control" of the picture. This confession was somehow too pat, but I suppose it must be mostly true. (What I cannot believe in is the jealousy.) As for Vanessa (who is coming to California early in November and taking Gladys Cooper's house) she is apparently in the process of divorcing Tony on the grounds of adultery with Moreau. But this is ghastly *hush* until it actually happens, for fear the papers play it up—Vanessa now being a very famous actress here and a maybe movie star!

I am still awaiting word from Richard about when I must go up there.[5] I figure I shall do this sometime later next week, and stay a week—and then finish off here in 3–4 days. I picked Nov. 2 to return because that would be exactly six weeks since I left. If I come that day it will be by Pan-American, arriving between 4 and 5 in the afternoon.

As I told you on the phone, the *Torrents of Spring* deal looks promising.[6] But there wd be no question anyhow of doing that for quite a long while. And Danny Mann will certainly want alterations on "Silent Night," if ABC okays it. He has told me that in advance. So staying on here wd be impossible, even if you came.

London is as full of traffic as every other place, but at least you can get around on the tube. Haven't yet seen the vaunted high tower over Tottenham Court Rd—but it's not nearly as tall as the Empire State— only 600. Am sending you a picture of it, along with a bunch of Dubbin cards for various moods.[7] From now on, I'll try to write very often, so Kitty will know how he is loved and missed.

Lunch with Eric was nice though in no way thrilling or surprising. He sent you his love. The Reform Club looks stunningly beautiful now it has been cleaned—like an Italian palace.[8]

All Dubbin's devoted love.

D. xxx

[Autograph letter]

5. That is, to visit his brother at home in Cheshire.
6. The BBC had proposed that Isherwood write a T.V. adaptation of Turgenev's novel, but in the end he did not.
7. The Post Office Tower, the tallest building in London and in England when it was completed in 1964, is 581 feet high, not including the telecommunication aerials on top, which make it 620 feet high. It was later called the B.T. Tower. Isherwood sent a postcard on which it is visible (see p. 231 below), but the Dubbin cards are evidently lost.
8. It is not clear where Isherwood broke off and restarted the letter. The Pall Mall premises of the Reform Club, founded as a base for the Liberal Party after the passage of the Reform Bill in 1832, were designed by Charles Barry and are celebrated as one of England's finest Victorian buildings.

October 18, 1966 [Santa Monica]

Darling Pluggin:

His long awaited letter arrived this morning to relieve and comfort Kitty. Also the postcards of cavorting Dubs, exhibiting more than enough rump, the saucy, flagrant things.[1]

These last days have been quite eventless for Kitty. Little or no work, disproving the theory that Dubbin's presence keeps Kitty from working as much as he might. On Saturday Kitty entertained alone, for the first time in the Casa, and cooked for seven (Jack, Jim, Gavin, Ronnie,[2] Clyde[3] and a cute little friend of his named Mike Van Horn[4] who would make Dubbin dance) but though the evening went well and the food (tried and true as ever jambalaya with fried parnsips and hot pears for dessert) was good, Kitty's heart wasn't in it. He missed his old faithful helper, in spite of his clumsiness.

Sunday I was supposed to eat at Jo and Ben's on the condition that Paul Wonner would come, too. Otherwise no din for Kitty. But though Paul agreed, Jo got sick at the last minute (stomach again, but with a headache this time and fever chills for variety's sake) so Paul and I ate alone at Casa Mia. A small, fond, would-be intimate evening which we were both unreluctant to end early.

Last night to Jack and Jim's to watch Clyde on Stanwyck's "Big Valley."[5] Jack and Jim have a color set now so all T.V. rendezvousing is done there. Clyde was good in a too small part. He is not nearly as handsome on film as he seems in the flesh, but he is a good actor. The show was unmercifully dull and hideous. Clyde was very upset about it

---

1. Isherwood's October 3 letter from Salzburg enclosed the cut-out horse pictures above, p. 220, but Bachardy probably means the lost postcards sent from London.
2. Ronnie Knox (1935–1992), American football player. He was a star quarterback for USC, UCLA, and Montreal during the 1950s, then turned to writing fiction. His real name was Raoul Landry.
3. Clyde Ventura (1936–1990), American actor, director, acting coach.
4. American artist and fashion illustrator.
5. The T.V. Western in which film star Barbara Stanwyck (1907–1990) appeared from 1965 to 1969.
6. Miss Wiesenthal, known as Wiesen, had fled Augsburg, Germany during World War II, and ended up in Hollywood where she was a companion to the aged mother of Polish actress and writer Sara Salomea (Salka) Steuermann Viertel (1889–1978) and later an assistant and housekeeper to Salka. Salka, first wife of Isherwood's London and Hollywood boss, Berthold Viertel, was Greta Garbo's screenwriter, co-star, and confidante and the center of a close-knit émigré circle during the war. She had befriended Isherwood as soon as he arrived in Hollywood in 1939 and, later, was briefly his landlady. Salka was blacklisted during the McCarthy era, and in 1954 she moved back to Europe.

all in spite of our valiant praise. Wiesen (Salka's legacy)[6] was on hand to thicken the mixture, which also included Nellie and Miguel.[7]

Today I am going to David Hockney's studio for the first time to see what he has been doing,[8] then to my parents' for dinner and then to that awful drawing class that Margot Smith got me involved in.[9] Poorcat has nothing better to do.

Yesterday at the beach (the weather for the fifth day in a row is that most glorious clear warm magic fall weather—just in case Old Drub might be getting used to that London dreariness) I pointed out to Clyde my Bluesuit[10] and got Clyde really turned on to him. Clyde, who is wonderfully shameless, began vamping and finally langored down the beach and got Bluesuit to follow him. Unfortunately, Bluesuit had a skinny black-hair-on-white-skin friend with him who also followed along. Anyway, Clyde did manage to get them into conversation and found out that they live together, Bluesuit goes to school and works part-time at a Broadway store somewhere, the skinny friend is a "landscape artist," and they are canvassing for threesomes, which turned Clyde off. He also objected to Bluesuit's rolling his eyes and licking his chops, queen fashion, at the mention of Richard Chamberlain.[11] Apparently Bluesuit and friend are queer-actor devotees (they also know and revere Tom Tryon[12]) and so another dear illusion of Kitty's is shattered forever.

Which brings Old Fur back again to the familiar thought of his dearly loved Plug who is adored and missed more than ever and who means much more to Kitty than anyone else in his life. He is Kitty's "raisin" d'etre. Please come home to Kitty soon.

With all of a kitten's dear love,

F.

7. Not his real name. Mexican artist; he worked in wood, made light fixtures, and also earned money as a carpenter and builder. He had a wife and child, but for many years he was Nellie Carroll's lover.
8. Hockney, the British artist (b. 1937), was teaching drawing at UCLA and using the front room of his apartment on Pico Boulevard in Los Angeles as a studio.
9. Smith studied art at Chouinard, where she and Bachardy became friends in 1956; the class was conducted by Chouinard instructor Edward Reep (b. 1918), a watercolorist, at his house.
10. A beach regular who always wore the same trim, blue bathing suit; he had a good body and great legs, but was perhaps nearly forty and too old to be Isherwood's type. Bachardy never spoke to him, though he and Isherwood often discussed him and his imagined life.
11. American actor (b. 1935), famous for his starring role in the T.V. series "Dr. Kildare," 1961–1966.
12. American actor (1926–1991), mostly in T.V. Westerns and "Walt Disney Presents"; he had an acclaimed film role in The Cardinal (1963).

P.S. Kitty has finished the Gita and is onto Drub's journals and is loving them, and Drub, more than ever.[13] They make Kitty sob a lot with an exquisite mixture of recognition, pain and joy.

Also, while in San Francisco Kitty bought from Gump's two wicker chairs for the Casa, but they won't arrive for many weeks.

[*Typed letter, initialled*]

October 16 [1966]   [London[1]]

Darling own Snowpaws,

Am starting to write this in the bar of Le Petit Club Français, on St. James's Place, where I'm waiting to have lunch with Joe Ackerley. I'd asked him to come down with me to Cambridge—to visit Morgan. But Morgan can only see me for supper, so I'm going alone, because Joe has a supper date.

Yesterday I had lunch with Marguerite [Lamkin and her companion]. She sends you much love, and wished you could come over, and she said, of her [relationship], "I've been *so lucky.*" I had the feeling that [her companion] pretty much agrees to anything she wants. He was very meek and quiet, and endured all Marguerite's in-talk with me about people he'd never met. I couldn't judge how Marguerite looked, because she sat with her back to the light, in dark glasses. She wore an elegant tweed suit with pants and didn't seem at all fat. We sent you a postcard. "Ivin" *does* seem fatter to me, and older. Wystan can never possibly look older—Stephen was bitchy about this, saying that someone had remarked to Wystan's doctor that W. wd live to be eighty—and the doctor had replied, "But he is eighty." I don't believe this.

After the lunch with [Marguerite and her companion] I visited Amiya in her new flat. It was very depressing. I had to listen to a long drunken monologue about George's death[2] and Amiya's selfless dedication to the welfare of everybody. She said, "Why is Swami worried about me—he

13. Bachardy was reading the Prabhavananda-Isherwood translation, *The Song of God, Bhagavad-Gita* (1944), and Isherwood's wartime diaries, 1939–1944, which are the only ones he read during Isherwood's lifetime, at Isherwood's request.

1. Isherwood was staying with Neil Hartley and Bob Regester at 38 Princes Gate Mews.
2. That is, her husband, George Montagu.

always thinks I must be in some sort of trouble." I said, "He thinks you drink too much and give all your money away to anybody." This sort of pleased her, but also made her think a bit.

Last night I saw Patrick Procktor[3] (who sends you much love) and I went with him and Bob Regester and the director named Anthony Page[4] (not sure you'll remember him—quite youngish, bold, rather nice) to that Chinese restaurant in Limehouse—"New Friends"—and then on a tour of pubs. The Dockland has been radically cleaned up—you could take the kiddies there at any hour of the night—but it still has glamor and there was a quite acceptable queer pub. (I know I ought to be writing about impressions of London—but that's something to be hatched out later in talk.)

Joe Ackerley (with whom I've in the meantime had lunch—am writing this waiting for the Cambridge train to start) sends much love, is very deaf and old, and says his life is over, he will write nothing more. He says he is only interested in animals, whereas Morgan at 88 still thinks of cocks. Indignation against Stephen, who bought a Henry Moore drawing from him for £10, now says, "Joe, I hear you're very poor and you should have had £1000 for that drawing—will it be all right if I give you a check for £500 and the rest next year?"

All love to my darling—Rubb'n

[Autograph letter]

[October 17]   [London]

Hope I shall see you soon in N.Y. love Wystan[1]
We're eating at Chez Victor. Saw Morgan yesterday—he sends you his love. Dodie and Alec on Wednesday[2]—all love, H.

[Autograph postcard in two hands; verso shows detail of a Christopher Wren monument in the City of London commemorating the Fire of London]

3. Dublin-born painter (1936–2003), trained at the Slade, a close friend of Hockney and a subject in some of Hockney's early work.
4. Page (b. 1935), British actor and director, was then Artistic Director at the Royal Court.

1. In Auden's hand, evidently written during supper.
2. Isherwood planned to visit British novelist and playwright Dodie Smith (1896–1990) and her husband Alec Beesley (1903–1987) at their cottage in Essex. The Beesleys had been intimate friends of Isherwood when they lived in California during World War II.

Oct. 18.   [London]

Just got your letter about San Francisco. Please phone the Writers' Guild (Crest 48601) and tell them I never got their form, and that I'll contact them after my return Nov. 2. Heard Wystan preach in the Abbey this morning,[1] shall see Beatrix in a play tonight. Am writing tomorrow. Walter Baxter acts hurt because you didn't write him 58 Addison Rd. W. 14. All my love, more tomorrow—N.A.G.

[Autograph postcard with autograph addition on verso, which shows Queen Mary's Gardens with roses in bloom, Regent's Park, London and Post Office Tower in the distance.[2]]

Oct. 19 [1966]   [London]

Dearest Snowtail,

Just setting forth for the Beesleys'. After torrents of rain last night it is a beautiful morning. Old Rubbin is feeling liverish—all this rich restaurant food is starting to nauseate him—you can't get anything that isn't drowned in goo. Yesterday Bob Regester and I went to hear Wystan preach—except that we actually didn't, because he had a mike hanging round his neck and every time he raised his head and looked out over the congregation his voice became nearly inaudible. However, as a show, it all worked wonderfully. They played trumpets before singing "God Save the Queen," and the boy soloist in the choir really chilled the spine with those spooky high notes. (I remember your commenting on the choir at King's Chapel, saying they really were like angels, uncanny.[1]) Then I had lunch with Robert Medley and a very saucy blond named Gregory Brown who he seems to be going with, and who's also a painter. And then I saw Alan White at Methuen's, who was quite clear that you were having your drawing on the back of the jacket but had apparently forgotten all about the idea of the river photograph—so now they are having a drawing of a river instead. I know this will look awful but

1. Auden gave the sermon in "A Service for Those Engaged in Science, Medicine, and Technology" in Westminster Abbey.
2. Attached to the Post Office Tower inside a bubble, Isherwood wrote, "Terribly disappointed in this—it's tiny."

1. February 13, 1956, when Isherwood took Bachardy to Cambridge for the first time, to visit Forster and sightsee.

there's nothing to be done. The art director wanted it and I could see that Alan wasn't going to resist him.

Yesterday evening I went to see *The Storm*, a classical Russian play by Ostrovsky, at the Old Vic. The Russians can keep it. Reason for going was Beatrix Lehmann, who played an old lady in her usual blue-jay voice. Also in it is a girl named Jill Bennett, who is John Osborne's latest love. She was as good as the play wd allow.[2]

Relations with Neil Hartley and Bob Regester remain good. I'm only embarrassed because they are constantly paying for meals etc. Finally I tried to restore the balance by getting them a rather expensive, rather hideous ice-cube container from Dunhill's. But I'm feeling guiltily obligated, still. However I do think they like having me here and they keep talking about how wonderful it wd be if I could get a job here later and come back with you. Actually I don't see them much. They are out a lot. Neil spends long days at the office, Bob goes out dancing at night. Bob is at a loose end and unhappy about it. He was hoping to work on a film of John Osborne's *Inadmissible Evidence*—but it has fallen through. He says he will never work for Tony again—Tony bitches and bullies him so. He also complains that Neil is so cold and undemonstrative. I feel I still don't know Neil. Bob I know rather well. He isn't a very bright boy, snobbish, a dresser-up, apt to flirt around with girls in a way which looks surprisingly like trying to pass—and his legs are catastrophic—and he plays bridge. But still and all he is genuinely kind and thoughtful—he is always taking little precautions for my comfort—and he isn't about to express his opinions, which are mostly the opposite of Neil's—Neil being quite reactionary. (Which reminds me, Wystan says we have to go on fighting in North Vietnam until the North surrenders.)

Well, Dodie and Alex are pretty much as last seen, except Alec looks fatter. Dodie is very little and her skirt is short though not a miniskirt. She says she loves the new clothes and wishes she was young enough to wear them. The cottage is as beautiful as ever and now almost covered with pigeons. There used to be 2 and now there are 50 or 60, Alec says. There is also the new Dalmatian named Disney (ugh!) who is a very good-natured dog and doesn't bark.[3] Also 2 donkeys who are furry eared

2. British actress Jill Bennett (1931–1990) starred as Katerina in Aleksandr Ostrovsky's 1860 play adapted by Doris Lessing for the National Theatre. Bennett also starred in several of Osborne's plays and was his fourth wife from 1968 to 1977.
3. The Beesleys had kept Dalmatians since before Isherwood first met them in 1942; earlier

and quite adorable. They live in a sort of national park at one end of the property and never have to do anything but eat. (Dodie just came by in rubber boots from feeding the pigeons and said to give you her love.)

Angel, I do miss you so and now I long to return, wish I could leave tomorrow. But first there is the visit to Richard, beginning the day after tomorrow and ending the middle of next week. I have now definitely booked a seat on the Pan-Am plane which arrives on Nov. 2 in Los Angeles around 4:30 p.m., nonstop from London—BOAC and Trans-World don't have flights that day, so you can easily identify it.

Old Dub loves his dear Kitty so very much and longs to be with him again. Will send little messages of love as often as possible, so Kitty's sweet mailbox won't be empty.

Old Faithful Plug. xxxx

[*Autograph letter*]

October 23, 1966 [Santa Monica]

Dearest Pony:

Two letters and three postcards from that roaming Roan.[1] Kitty's glad that Dub's trip seems to be turning out so well. Everybody seems to be in London. I thought Stephen was supposed to be in California this fall. I hope I am safe in assuming his stay has been cancelled. Please give my love to Patrick Procktor and tell him David's studio here is very comfortable and certainly big enough for two and so he should come. Love too to Joe Ackerley and Morgan, Marguerite, and Patrick Woodcock if you've seen him—I don't remember your mentioning him. You might also call Richard Buckle if you feel like it and say hello for me. I am curious to know why he never answered my letter. His number is COVent garden 2111, his address 34 Henrietta Street, W.C. 2. You also mention nothing of Cecil so I presume he is still in N.Y.

Before I went to N.Y. Anita sent a copy of her book[2] to me with an

---

ones had been nervous and barked at the slightest provocation. The Disney film of Dodie Smith's 1956 novel *The Hundred and One Dalmatians* came out in 1961.

1. The third postcard had been written by Marguerite Lamkin and her companion over lunch on October 16. Isherwood added only, "Having lovely lunch—D."
2. Her memoir *A Girl Like I* (1966).

inscription, so I wrote to her last week to tell her I had read and liked the book and took the opportunity of getting you off the hook about not having written a blurb by telling her that you were in Austria working on a script, making it sound as though you might have been there for months, and referring to the "treat" you have in store for you when you get back.

The good news here is that Clint has gone, to Boston for two months anyway, to play Marat in that awful play by Peter Weiss about him and de Sade and the loonies, which I had to see again here last week because Anthony [Russo] wanted to go.[3] Gavin seems in good spirits though he says he misses having Clint in the house. We had an evening alone together last Thursday. We went to see *The Women* in Anaheim (a good title) with Pamela Mason, Dagmar, Margaret O'Brien and Joan Caulfield, all in the round, in more ways than one.[4] We only stayed for the first act which was more than enough and then Gavin took me to dinner at Mateo's which was nice but expensive. He told me he is on the verge of leaving the Frenches[5] for a variety of reasons, the most important being the fact that they've not come up with a job for him in more than a year. Also they turned down a T.V. offer without even telling him and then sent him on a wild goose chase to see a producer about doing a script of Lawrence's *The Fox* and Gavin didn't discover that another writer had already been signed to do the job (which the Frenches knew) until he'd given the producer a very good solution for the ending. I think Gavin is considering Famous Artists.

Kitty entertained again this week with a pot of his famous chili. David Hockney brought Peter Schlesinger who had flown down from Santa Cruz in hushed secrecy just to be with David.[6] Apparently the affair really is an affair now. David, in his indiscreet show-off way let me

3. Kimbrough was appearing in the Theater Company of Boston's production of *Marat/Sade: The Persecution and Assassination of Marat as Performed by the Inmates of the Asylum at Charenton under the Direction of the Marquis de Sade* (1963) by Swedish playwright Peter Weiss. It had been performed by the Royal Shakespeare Company in 1964, and the Broadway production won four Tony Awards in 1965.

4. Clare Boothe Luce's 1936 play was staged in the round, exposing the cast from all angles: British actress Pamela Mason (1916–1996); comedienne and T.V. personality "Dagmar" (1921–2001), born Virginia Ruth Egnor and known for her full, curvaceous figure; American actress Joan Caulfield (1922–1991), a voluptuous pin-up; and American former child star Margaret O'Brien (b. 1937), a more delicate beauty. All were past their primes.

5. That is, former actor Hugh French (1910–1976) and his son Robin (mentioned above, p. 144) who were film agents for Lambert as well as Isherwood.

6. Schlesinger (b. 1948), later a painter, photographer and sculptor, was then an undergraduate at the University of California at Santa Cruz. He had met Hockney when he took Hockney's summer drawing class at UCLA.

read a letter from Peter with statements to the effect of: "I want to see you, be with you, hug you and kiss you." At least they seem to be making headway. Peter was also more talkative at dinner and told Jim [Bridges] (who was there with Jack [Larson] and a dreary pick-up from the beach) that he had deplored Clyde's performance in *Mame* the last time he'd been to the house⁷ and was also shocked by Jim's drunken behavior. [. . .]

John Goodwin I know would love to read *A Meeting by the River*. If you would like me to send it to him, enclose a small note to him in your next letter so that I can put it with the manuscript when I send it. He would also love to read Morgan's *Morris* (*Maurice?*) but you have probably got that in the bank vault. I am reading, or rather wading through, *The Idols and the Prey*. It is very, very tedious work. What a vast improvement the second book is. Kitty saves The Journal of a Dub, B.C., for dessert and what delicious dessert it is.⁸

Saw Gerald again on Friday. He looked and talked well in spite of a slight slurring every once in a while and a just noticeable difficulty in completing some thoughts and sentences. He was gloating over having found out that Aldous used to have quite bad trips with LSD which he never told Gerald about.

Swami is in Laguna now and is taking walks around the garden three times a day.

Jack Allen and Hal Buckley⁹ invited me up to dinner one night last week with Gavin and two semi-attractive guys named Ray and Rod, one of whom was taken by Hal into the bedroom at the end of the evening and joined soon after by Jack, leaving Gavin and me to let ourselves out without any send-off. It was a tacky, debauched, extremely low-class evening which was nevertheless amusing. The amyl nitrite was passed around as though it were potpourri.¹⁰

7. Clyde Ventura did a spontaneous performance in the living room at 145 Adelaide Drive, impersonating one or several actresses he'd seen in the role. Bachardy recalls that Ventura was a gifted and funny mimic and that Bachardy himself, Isherwood, and their guests were mostly laughing hysterically and urging on the wild and inspired display of camp, the likes of which, Bachardy now reflects, Schlesinger had probably never before encountered.

8. Forster's then unpublished gay novel, *Maurice*, was written 1913–1914 and revised 1959–1960. *The Idols and the Prey* is Goodwin's 1952 novel about Haiti; his second was *A View from Fuji*. The Journal of a Dub, B.C.—i.e., Before Cat.

9. Buckley (1937–1986) was an American actor, mostly on T.V. Allen had a New York stage career; later Allen bought the Four Oaks Café, which they ran together, in Beverly Glen Canyon.

10. Amyl nitrite, inhaled as a recreational drug, induces a brief euphoric effect and relaxes involuntary muscles, especially blood-vessel walls and the anal sphincter.

Jo and Ben finally gave me a dinner last night, having well insulated themselves with Peter and Alice, Ann Gowland and daughter Tracy[11] and Sandy Grigg with daughter Raina. Sandy and Ricky are living separately now.[12] Sandy served her celebrated marinated meat-sticks and marinated butter fish—delicious if you like marinade, lots of it, thick and sweet. Echh!

Bill Brown is back from his trip, having seen and liked Albee's *A Delicate Balance* and *The Killing of Sister George*.[13]

Do try to see Jocelyn Rickards (Mrs. Leonard Rosoman) if you can and please give her my love. Her address is 7 Pembroke Studios, Pembroke Gardens, W. 8. and her number WES 3638.

If Kitty doesn't go with Nellie to see an Andy Warhol film called *My Hustler* tonight, he will stay home alone, thinking of and missing his Old Hide, as usual, and looking forward to his return to Kitty's humble basket.

With a kitten's dearest love and devotion,

as always,

Tabby

[*Typed letter, signed*]

[October 20]   [London]

We are about to have supper here at Pelham Place after seeing a long and not very successful play—am hoping to see Christopher again on his return from the north. Maybe we all meet in L.A. later this winter. Wish you were here—Love Cecil.[1]

11. Ann Gowland, daughter of Peter and Alice Gowland, divorced Tracy's father and used her maiden name until she later married David MacMillan and took his surname.

12. Sandy Grigg was the wife of surfer and, later, oceanographer Ricky Grigg, who left Santa Monica to pioneer big-wave surfing on the north shore of Oahu. Their daughter, Raina, became an artist and schoolteacher in Hawaii.

13. Both were running on Broadway that autumn. Albee's *A Delicate Balance* was nominated for a Tony Award for best play and won the Pulitzer Prize for Drama in 1967. *The Killing of Sister George*, by Frank Marcus, won the Tony for Best Play and also for Best Actress (Beryl Reid).

1. In Beaton's hand. The play was *Days in the Trees*, adapted from Marguerite Duras' early novella, *Des journées entières dans les arbres* (*Whole Days in the Trees*); Peggy Ashcroft starred in the RSC production at the Aldwych Theatre.

Saw Harry Miller, Julian Jebb and Dicky Buckle this afternoon. All send love. Tomorrow I'm off to see Richard. Roll on next Wednesday week! Always,

P.L.U.G.

[Autograph postcard in two hands; verso shows a London policeman]

Oct. 21.   [London]

Angel Whiskers,

This is just before starting for Stockport. I know the train will probably joggle too much for me to write while we're moving. Got his dear Puss's letter just before leaving Neil & Bob's house—the first one addressed directly there. It's wonderful not to have to wait at the American Express counter, suspecting that Dobbin's precious beloved puss-mail has been filed incorrectly under Horse, Plug, Nag, or what not. Dubbin can't bear to think of Kitty lonely. Couldn't he at least enjoy a frisk à trois with Bluesuit to while away the hours?

Well, yesterday I saw Henry Miller, Julian Jebb, Dicky Buckle and Cecil Beaton. Harry sent love—Loudon Sainthill is busy producing a musical about Houdini called *Magic Man*.[1] (This reminds me that Neil Hartley read a rather unfavorable notice of *Cabaret* in *Variety*—that is, about its out-of-town opening, of course. Cecil maintains that our director (his name has left me for the moment) is marvellous, nevertheless.[2]) Harry asked a lot about your work and said he hoped you'd have another show at the Redfern before long and he wished he could see some of your painting. He sent his love and so did Dicky Buckle, who really was very friendly and said he had loved your portfolio but that he hadn't been able to do anything for you with Lincoln because Lincoln had suddenly stopped speaking to him.[3] The underlying impression I got was that

1. Harold Fielding's *Houdini: Man of Magic*, book and lyrics by John Morley and Aubrey Cash, music by Wilfred Josephs, opened at the Piccadilly Theatre in November but was not a success.
2. *Cabaret* had a three-week trial at the Schubert Theater in Boston starting Monday, October 10. Harold Prince directed (and produced in association with Ruth Mitchell); choreography and musical staging were by Ronald Field. The early review praised the dancing and also the music and lyrics by John Kander and Fred Ebb, but criticized Joe Masteroff's book, Prince's direction, the singing and some of the acting. *Variety*, Oct. 12, 1966, p. 70.
3. Kirstein had printed Bachardy's drawings of the New York City Ballet dancers as a loose-leaved portfolio publication, but then abandoned plans to sell them at performances.

probably Dicky and Harry would only be set in motion by your actual appearance, plus paintings. Julian Jebb, also sending greetings, came on very strong about a T.V. interview with me and paying my way to come over. And Anthony Page continues to make big noises about possible stage and film work. And so does Willie Fox's father, Robin.[4] But I'm sceptical. I'm afraid England is on the verge of a terrific economic collapse, for one thing, and no one will have the money for any projects.

Cecil (who wrote on a card I sent you last night) is still seeing Kin [Hoitsma] from time to time. He will go to San Francisco before very long—then possibly on to China. He says Kin is more wonderful than ever. But he is off Truman—says he has been changed by success and only associates with rich women and is giving gigantic parties costing thousands. Cecil himself has just put on a new production of *Lady Windermere's Fan*, which people say isn't nearly as good as the old one. . . .[5]

In the midst of this letter, the train started, and I am actually finishing this in the house where Richard is living, and where I shall stay. We have eaten a vast tea, and supper looms. *Thank god*, there is television!! But all this must be described in my next letter. At present Dubbin is feeling wrapped in Midlands gloom, and dreadfully far from the Home Basket.

God bless his own darling beloved kitten, for whom he longs so, and roll on the hour of reunion! This too will pass. Don't write to this address—13 Bentside Road, Disley, via Stockport, Cheshire—unless it's something to be urgently cabled. I leave here Oct. 26.

Xxxxxx GULP spelt backwards.

Richard sends his love

[*Autograph letter*]

4. British actor James Fox (b. 1939) had been proposed for the BBC adaptation of Turgenev's "The Torrents of Spring"; his real name was William. His father, Robin Fox (1913–1971), was an actor and theatrical agent.
5. Beaton designed John Gielgud's 1945 production of Oscar Wilde's 1892 play; its lavish splendor was said to embody the return of British elegance after World War II. The 1966 production was directed by Anthony Quayle.

Oct 22 [1966]   [Disley, Cheshire]

A Kitten is a brumby's world. Yesterday evening was television of the great landslide disaster in Wales, today 2 walks to the village, letters, and study of my mother's book about Marple,[1] tomorrow a Quaker meeting and a visit to Wyberslegh—during which we're going to phone Amiya! R's hosts here are *really* nice and easy to get along with, and the food as abundant as on an ocean liner. Pray for old Dub, who is so homesick for his basket.

[*Autograph postcard; verso shows a grey kitten balancing on a globe*]

Oct. 23 [1966]   [Disley, Cheshire]

No time to write a proper letter today. What with R., my hosts and my homework—copying out a lot of stuff about Marple—these days do go by fast. Which is a blessing, of course. Will write properly tomorrow. I don't think I'll ever be able to face a visit like this again—and yet everybody is being so kind. It is all a sort of funeral, and in the end one has to stay and be buried, or leave and live—which Dub hopes to do.

[*Autograph postcard; verso shows Lyme Hall, Disley*]

October 24 [1966] Disley

Adored Pinktongue,

What a rat race this is! I'm just through copying some truly wonderful passages from my mother's diary about my father's death, because Richard doesn't want to part with the diary even temporarily. However, I am bringing back a couple of volumes of copies she made of all my father's letters from the front. And I have the official account of the Marple ghost story, and other goodies ... Meanwhile the food here is suffocating, and Dobbin has to rush out for trots up and down

1. A family history—about Marple Hall, the Bradshaw Isherwood family seat, and Wyberslegh Hall, also on the family estate, with a family tree and accounts of Isherwood's ancestors— which Kathleen wrote out longhand or cut from the newspapers and which she illustrated herself with watercolors and drawings.

the hill to keep his liver working. Richard now practically refuses to go out. He says that since he had bronchitis four year[s] ago he gets breathless if he walks uphill and since that's unavoidable he won't walk. Yesterday he drank beer all day and today he started at breakfast time. He remains quite lucid and maybe it is a way of life. At least he doesn't smoke anymore. As for me, I am refusing to drink at all as long as I am up here because somehow that would be more than I could bear, to have hangovers in this place. Yesterday the family was home all day. Mr. Dan Bradley is 55, very sweet really, big like a house but short. Works in a dye works not far away. Left-wing views. We get along fine, and on Wednesday we are all driving down to London together because he wants to see the motor show. Then I shall be free. What is very good is that Richard ha[d] only expected me to stay the weekend so I have proved to be more generous than he'd hoped, whereas I felt guilty!

He is really very sweet and we live entirely in the past, he remembers everything about everybody and is a mine of information about the family. But what will become of him? Mrs. Dan is a plump smiling and I think truly good-natured and undesigning woman and she cooks enough for ten people; all the meals are profuse. She and Dan look after him and he is much cleaner though his fly is still usually open. He drinks until he vomits and then goes on drinking. He helps them a lot with money, I think, but they don't need or demand much, and the place is clean. What my mother used to call sniffily "a council house"—i.e. built by the town council. You hear the neighbors' television, but then so you do everywhere. The weather is perfect—sometimes on the verge of rain with a great tragic sky and the low hills sodden as if by Dubbin's tears. But that's how it should be—this landscape isn't meant to make you laugh. I long to walk miles, but, as I say, Richard can't or won't. I went to Quaker Meeting yesterday, discovered one right by the church, in a three-hundred-year-old house which used to be a pub called The Ring O'Bells, a hundred years ago. The British Quakers are bleaker and less effusive than the Philadelphia ones, but I was welcomed as our American Friend, and it was heaven to sit perfectly quiet. Whenever I try to meditate in my room, Mrs. Dan comes in with a cup of coffee. (Tea, this trip, suddenly disagrees with me, I go into spasms as if I had taken poison—but the coffee, well, you know all about that!)

We also went to Wyberslegh, which is now quite frankly a tomb. My father's pictures are rotting, but what am I to do? R. says take one, but it's like being told to save one refugee child from Vietnam, and then he doesn't want to wait while I go right through the portfolios. I hope, however, if you and I return fairly soon we may find a few of them still alive! Am also trying hard to read Wedekind's *Pandora's Box* (the Lulu plays, in fact) for a stage adaptation; but I just do not have the time. Richard longs to talk, I must get the copying done, and then in comes the family and there is supper and telly.

God, my mother's and father's letters are fascinating! In one of them, my father makes a strange apology to her for "lack of reciprocity" and he seems to mean some sort of coldness, sexual or emotional. As for my mother, she says, bitter against Uncle Jack, "None of the Isherwoods feel things much"!

Oh Catkin, how Dub needs him! That old horse is restless and uneasy in this graveyard among the mildewy ghosts. He is afraid a mean old skeleton will jump on his back and ride him away to the glue factory! Meanwhile, terrible on the horizon, stands that curious little tower, Lyme Cage.[1] It is like something you see in a dream which means something else, thoroughly Freudian and unpleasant. No more for now, Love, because Richard, who is just sitting and drinking beer and doing nothing, is beginning to show impatience and slam his hand on the arm of the chair to indicate that I must talk to him. And I have got to get out in the air and take at least a few deep breaths, before sunset! One more whole day, then we're off!

Kitty is to take the most precious care of himself and make a list of things Dub can do to please him, when he returns.

As always, his adoring old plug,

D.

Richard just asked who I was writing to and I told him and he said, "Give him my love."

[*Typed letter, initialled*]

---

1. Built in the sixteenth century as a hunting lodge for Lyme Hall.

Oct. 26. [1966] London

Just got back from Disley, and found that nice letter. Will try to see
Jocelyn Rickards—anyhow they are coming to the States very soon, I
hear. John Goodwin shall see *Meeting* as soon as I've used it to correct
the proofs. Tomorrow William Plomer, Francis Bacon; Friday, Edward
Upward. Will write once more before I take off. Meanwhile all my love
as always—

    Mr. Hide (Senior)

[*Autograph postcard; verso shows Lyme Cage, Disley*]

October 27, 1966 [Santa Monica]

Dearest Silkmuzzle:

Many sweet communications from that Old Dear to keep Kitty's great but fragile heart from breaking. But that racey Drub had better come soon—there's no telling how much longer that small body can hold out. Less than 140 lbs. and disappearing fast! Little more than eyes and fur left. Only massive transfusions of Dublove can save him now, but it had better be quick.

No mail of any interest, and little news of any kind. The drabness of the life of a kitten alone is indescribable. No wonder he's wasting away.

He did go to see Andy Warhol's *My Hustler* (with David Hockney and Nick Wilder[1] instead of Nellie and Miguel) which was shown with two other films, *Vapors* (about an encounter in a steam bath house) and *Gay Life*, all purporting to be about homosexuality and all missing the subject by a mile. You can't make a movie about "a subject" anyway, but these were either inept or silly or dirty, and all of them misleading. Warhol's was the most professional and finally the most irritating and boring because of its unfulfilled promise. The movie theater was small, hot and crowded, which did nothing to strengthen Kitty's patience.[2]

On Monday night I went with Jack Jones to see *The Bible*, obviously not knowing when I'd had enough. Oh! the paralyzing boredom. Huston has managed to make a movie about the creation of the world in which nothing happens, for three hours! True, Michael Parks looks pretty and poses prettily, but his scenes are short.[3] Richard Harris, as Cain, manages to overact with only one line of dialogue. And then Huston as Noah—a case of the cutes that would make Disney turn away and retch. Kitty's attention was held, but only for an instant, when two fat white ponies were lured into the ark, followed by some very restless striped and spotted kitties, clearly very critical of the whole proceedings.

Tuesday to Gavin's with Jack, Jim, Bill, Paul, Michael [Leopold], Henry [Guerriero] and Clyde, in fact an anti-Clint celebration, though Gavin still promises Clint's return. The evening was enjoyable in spite of Michael's

1. Nicholas Wilder (1937–1989), American art dealer; he later represented both Hockney and Bachardy, and was also a subject for both.
2. *Vapors* (1965) was made by Andrew Milligan, and *Gay Life* (1965) was made by Clifford Solloway; all three films were screened at Cinematheque 16 on Sunset Boulevard. Isherwood had met Warhol (1928–1987) in 1962, when Warhol drew his feet.
3. The American actor and singer (b. 1940) appeared nude as Adam.

barbs which were bigger and sharper than ever. Michael, referring at the dinner table to Gavin's loss of weight: "You look like a death's head stuck onto a skeleton." To Clyde, whom he'd never met before: "I love your hair. I don't think you're attractive but I love your hair. I mean, you're not attractive to me. If we went to bed together I wouldn't know what to *do!*" He had an unpleasant compliment to pay to practically everybody, but he was so extreme that no one took him seriously.

Last night I took Carlos[4] to dinner at Bellevue. We got along all right but in spite of his friendliness and humor, there is still something about him that puts me off, an underlying, constant, put-upon attitude to himself. He forgives Carlos for everything but none of the monsters, whom he claims to love, for their long history of crimes against him. Poor little Carlos has been badly used indeed but still he goes on, bruised and beaten but still there. However, he praised Kitty's nudes. He gets points for that. There was a small motive behind Kitty's dinner treat. Kitty visited Carlos's shop the other day and saw some pretty things that might look very nice in the Casa. Perhaps, if they pass Dubbin's inspection, some little bits of furniture might find their way into the Animals' warren at a very good price.

Still Kitty hasn't worked, but strangely enough he isn't fussed. Betty Harford is coming to be drawn today so that she can use a drawing in the program for a new Houseman production she is doing next month out Pasadena way.

Coincidentally, referring to your last letter written from Richard's place with your statement of the horrors of tea, Kitty has given up coffee, believe it or not, and now drinks only tea and feels so much better.

Tiresome Department: Jack Allen at the gym yesterday begged me to ask you to please try to get him a 90-day supply of a French sleeping mixture in suppository form unavailable in this country. He says it is called SUPERONERIL, but is unsure of the spelling, irritatingly enough. He thinks you can get it at a chemist's in London. If not, maybe Patrick Woodcock could get some.

Less than a week now until Dubbin's promised return. Kitty has his stall all swept and scrubbed clean, and fresh hay will be ordered next week. Kitty can hardly wait to hug that old Rump again and purr

---

4. Carlos McClendon, American designer (b. 1923). He ran Chequer in Manhattan, selling clothes and furniture of his own design as well as ethnic textiles and folk art sourced on his travels around the world and, later, a second shop, Chequer West, in West Hollywood.

into those pointed ears. Kitty won't send any more letters and will wait anxiously for the dear telegram announcing his Plug's flight.

With all of a kitten's loving thoughts and stored-up kisses,

His waiting Fur.

[Typed letter, signed]

Friday [October 28, 1966, London]

My darling,

Just a wildly hurried line to tell you how much I love you and long for our meeting next Wednesday. I have seen or shall see nearly all of the people I most want to. A man (I'll find out his name before I leave[1]) at the Mercury Gallery on Cork St. recognized me yesterday and said, without any prompting of any kind from me, that he used to work at the Redfern and remembered your show, and that, if the Redfern couldn't give you a show, *he* would be delighted to give you one at the Mercury. So we'll see! Pan-Am Flight 121 (?) arriving L.A. 4:15 p.m.

Dub does love his Kitty so.

H.

[Autograph letter]

·   ·   ·

1. Stan Hardy. See below, pp. 246–247 and 251.

c/o Regester, 38 Princes Gate Mews, Exhibition Road, London S.W. 7.[1]

Monday 8th May [1967]

Dearest Angel,

Dob arrived quite safe but so drunk that he wandered right past the customs without showing his baggage—and wasn't even called back! Saw Patrick Procktor yesterday. He sends love. Has a show on at the Redfern which I'll report on tomorrow, when I've seen it. Tomorrow I shall deliver the photographs to the Mercury. Didn't do so today as I want to put them personally into Stan Hardy's hands. Bob Regester's legs are even thinner and he is really quite fat, but is making lots of woo while Neil's away. Tonight we are supposed to meet Moreau, then I dine with Hugh French to discuss job. Write here for the present— but I'll keep checking the American Express, in case. Love my furry darling and wake weeping for the touch of a vanished paw and a rough little pink tongue. Couldn't sleep last night so got up at 4.30 a.m. and went downtown, roamed around Covent Garden, walked on Waterloo Bridge and all that jazz. No Kittens anywhere, only very dirty rude pigeons.

Thinking of my darling nonstop—
Old Hoof.

[Autograph letter]

1. Isherwood flew back to London on May 6 to do newspaper and T.V. interviews for the late-May publication of A Meeting by the River. He intended, while he was there, to collect family papers for his next book, which he was then calling Hero-Father, Demon-Mother, and to pursue several other work proposals. He also hoped to pin down a show for Bachardy at the Mercury Gallery. For the first twelve days, he again stayed at Neil Hartley and Bob Regester's.

May 9. [1967]   [London]

My Darling,

[I]t's really heaven this morning as I am all alone in the house after a long blissful sleep and the wear and tear of the trip recovered from. Bob went to supper with Jeanne Moreau last night. He wanted me to come but I couldn't because of going with Hugh French to see this elder brother of Jimmy Woolfe about "Anastasia." I doubt if it will come to anything but Dub scratched his old mane and came up with a couple of ideas.¹ For his outing with La Moreau Bob selected a heavy white silk Russian-type blouse which has to be buttoned from behind, and a powder blue velvet jacket. He must have returned, changed and gone off to some lover. Tonight I have supper with Patrick Woodcock and a batch of elderly literary dummies, Rosamond Lehmann, L.P. Hartley,² Lionel Trilling.³ John Lehmann will hear of this and so thereby learn that Dub is displeased with him. I am avoiding the bores, duties, nuisances and bloodsuckers for the present. Funny—I find I only really want to see Marguerite! Patrick Procktor's show was showy, eye-hitting, billboardish, indiscreet but some of the smaller portraits had quite a lot of charm. Am sending you a catalogue, which shows you almost none of the charm; also a catalogue of the Bacon show.⁴ If he were a writer I'd say he was getting bogged down in his mannerisms, but who is an old plug to speak of a painter? Today I shall deliver your books to Mr. Hardy at the Mercury. Bob asked to see them and raved and raved—nothing so good being done anywhere, etc. I hope Kitty is working? Dobbin has resolved to be very useful and get things accomplished so he can come home to his dear. He thinks about Kitty all day long, as well as about God, and tries so hard to be good. The weather is sort of so so, one keeps expecting rain; but it's not cold at all. Am waiting to hear from Richard, about going up there, which I dread. There is to be a big party for me on Friday—that's to say, a catchall with me as an excuse. Bob has to leave this house before long

---

1. John Woolfe (1913–1999) was also a British film producer and the founder of Anglia Television; the brothers often worked in partnership through their independent production company Romulus Films Ltd. Isherwood decided not to get involved in this project about the youngest daughter (1901–1918) of Tsar Nicholas II.
2. British novelist (1895–1972).
3. American literary critic and professor of literature at Columbia University (1905–1975).
4. Procktor's May 1967 show was his third at the Redfern. "Francis Bacon: Recent Paintings" had been on at the Marlborough New London Gallery during March and April 1967.

and we are supposed to move to some mod slum, a really crowded Pad. But at the last moment, Dobbin will canter away. Kitty has accustomed him to his sweet comforts and he needs them. Oh, I ran into Alan Searle at the Dorchester; he was dining with Cukor and dreadful old Whitney Warren,[5] who licked Dub's ass. Alan is very fat, sort of a theatrical widow, *not* married. He sent love, says he's coming in August. Love to Kitty from his faithful old four-footed foolish fond Nag XXXXX

[*Autograph letter*]

May 12, 1967 [Santa Monica]

Dear Silver Steed:

Your second letter arrived this morning to cheer momentarily an old forsaken fur. It also managed to irritate him slightly. Couldn't you at least have gone to shake hands with Moreau so that a pent-up cat, starved for news of the world outside, might know how his favorite actress looked and behaved? Cruel Horse. I think Hugh French might have waited a few minutes.

Enclosed is all mail of any interest, including a thank you note from Romulus Linney which I found of especial interest, so much so that I answered it. A copy of my note to him is attached.[1] Also enclosed is a list I

5. New York art collector and philanthropist (1898–1986), son of the architect of Grand Central Station and a cousin of the Vanderbilts; he was a longtime friend of Cukor.

1. Of the enclosures Bachardy mentions, only three survive: a note from him about Gerald Heard (printed below, pp. 250–251); a letter to Isherwood from Romulus Linney IV (1930–2011), American playwright, novelist, and professor of writing, about a dinner Bachardy gave for Virgil Thomson on May 3; and Bachardy's reply to Linney:

> Montecito Hotel, Los Angeles, Calif. [May 1967]
> Dear Mr. Isherwood,
> Many thanks for the food, drink and fine company. It was a great pleasure.
> When things progress a bit more at the theater, I hope you will come to see the play.
> Best wishes
> Romulus Linney
> [*Handwritten letter*]

> May 12, 1967
> Dear Mr. Linney:
> Mr. Isherwood is in England now. I am answering his mail at his request. I will convey your thanks to him, though I expect he will be somewhat mystified by them,

MAY 1967 · 249

found on your desk which I thought you might have forgotten to take with you, and an article from the current *Free Press* about Kent Chapman.[2] I know that St. Dub is always curious to know of the whereabouts of His little ones who strayed. (Note enclosure of letter from Caskey, unopened, and note from a Mr. David Dowdy (mispell?). I took the enjoyable liberty of writing a short note to Mr. Dowdy informing him of your condition and pointing out to him delicately that he did not allow you ample time to respond.)

A letter from Rex, who did receive my last letter, to say that he and Jim will not get to London until May 21 and will be staying at the Cavendish (I thought it must have been torn down), not Brown's.[3]

A *Cabaret* check came this week and has been deposited.[4] Also a check from Rio Hondo Junior College[5] for $350.00, to be deposited today. A money transfer by order of Jonathan Cape Ltd. has put $463.88 into the bank here and $1125.00 has been deposited into the Chase Manhattan account by Curtis Brown (advances from Random House

---

since it was I who gave the dinner for Virgil.
When Virgil called me to ask if you might come, I agreed as a favor to Virgil. I assumed then that you would know who was your host.
Had it been Mr. Isherwood's dinner, he would have done the cooking. He is an able cook and enjoys cooking much more than I do.
Sincerely,
Don Bachardy
[*Typed letter, signed*]

The Mark Taper Forum was staging Linney's *The Sorrows of Frederick* as part of its first season in 1967. The play opened in July.
2. Chapman (b. 1935), a student when Isherwood met him in the 1950s, was a Vedanta devotee and an aspiring writer; during the 1960s he developed a drug problem, then around 1967 or 1968 got clean, married, and converted to Roman Catholicism. Years later, he became a Benedictine monk. *The Los Angeles Free Press* was a weekly underground paper distributed free.
3. Rex Evans (1903–1969), British music-hall comedian, Broadway actor, and Hollywood character actor, ran an art gallery on La Cienega Boulevard and had been showing Bachardy's work there since 1962. His companion, Jim Weatherford, was also his silent partner in the gallery. In London, they planned to pursue the show for Bachardy at the Mercury.
4. *Cabaret* opened November 20, 1966, at the Broadhurst Theater on Broadway, played for fifteen weeks to sold-out houses, then moved to the larger-capacity Imperial, where it was continuing to sell out. In March, 1967, it won eight Tony Awards: Best Musical, Best Director Musical, Best Featured Actor and Actress Musical, Best Composer and Lyrics, Best Scenic Design, Best Costumes, Best Choreography. In June, it won the New York Drama Critics Circle Award for Best Musical. Later, it moved to the Broadway Theater, eventually playing 1,165 performances altogether. Isherwood received only a small percentage of the proceeds, but with tours and, later, the film and revivals, *Cabaret* gave intermittent boosts to his income for years to come and a feeling of longterm financial security.
5. Where Isherwood gave a lecture on the evening of April 20.

for Ballantine editions of *World in the Evening* and *Prater Violet* at $625.00 each).

Regarding the letter from Gore, you might combine a visit with him in Rome and a stay with Rex and Rachel in Portofino.[6] I saw them on Sunday at Jennifer's (a dull occasion with only (besides Gavin) Frank McCarthy,[7] Rupert Allan,[8] & Marti Stevens[9]—all of my most favorite people) and they both implored me to beg you to visit them. They will be there at least a month from May 20. Why not? It's only catmoney. Kitty will probably be dead of neglect anyway in another week or so. His coat has already lost its sheen and his poor ribs can be seen through the limp fur—he can't bring himself to eat stale crumbles from an unwashed dish. If he's not dead of starvation, he'll probably be found hanging by his untied ribbon from the clothes rod in Dubbin's closet. Kittens aren't good at understanding desertion. They can live for a while without food, but not for very long without affection.

Still, Kitty remembers his Old Horse with that same unswerving love and devotion which only kittens are capable of. He blindly hopes to see that old Muzzle again, before it's too late.

Tragicat

[*Typed letter, signed, with enclosures*]

[May 12, 1967]

Dearest Wanderplug:

I forgot to tell you that Gerald has had another stroke apparently, though a milder one this time. I did write a long letter to him in which I gave him your love. I think he must have gotten it before the stroke. Jack [Jones] says he is more or less the same now as he was before. I got a birthday greeting from Michael yesterday, signed by both of them, so at least Gerald can still sign his name.

6. Rex Harrison was then married to Rachel Roberts, his fourth of six wives. He had built a villa in Portofino after World War II.

7. American film producer (1912–1986), a brigadier general in World War II and a head of public relations at Twentieth Century-Fox.

8. American journalist, magazine editor, publicist (1913–1991); from 1955 he handled public relations for Marilyn Monroe and other major stars.

9. American singer and actress (b. 1931), on Broadway, T.V., and in a few films.

A word of advice: I think it is unwise of Old Dubbin to roam around Covent Garden unattended in the early hours of the morning—he might suddenly find a fruit cart attached to that old rump.

With all of a lonely kitten's loving thoughts,

True Mew

[Typed letter, signed, enclosed in previous letter]

May 10 [1967]   [London]

Dearest Angel—

[I]t's so warm! Real summer with bright green leaves out in all the gardens. Yesterday I had a brief telephone chat with John Gielgud, who was leaving within an hour or two for Venice. It seems just as well neither of us took the house as now they have found something wrong with one of the floors![1] John says that Martin [Hensler] made a great speech to Harry Miller of the Redfern about the marvellousness of your work. However, when I saw Harry, *not one word* about you! He is a sleek slimy crook, and dumb with it. He doesn't really admire Patrick Procktor or anyone else; but he was working hard on a millionaire to buy a de Stael for £25,000, though he admitted that its front legs were weak—it was of a dobbin. At the Mercury I gave your two books of drawings to Mrs. Raffles (who behaved quite interestedly) and to Stan Hardy who came on very intimate with me.[2] So they will study the drawings before Rex [Evans] arrives. Then I started getting all this publicity set up for the novel—interviews, T.V. etc. Poor Dobbin is wearying of his silly plumes already and longs for the simplicity of the dear stable.

To a dinner party at Patrick Woodcock's (he sends you much love and is off shortly to join the outfit in Turkey. He says two horses have been killed already).[3] Rosamond Lehmann looked like a very fat white goose, still pretty, rather drunk. She bitched [her brother] John and Stephen— whose name has been further muddied because it has been proved that *Encounter* was supported by American CIA money. Stephen has resigned.

1. Possibly Isherwood or Regester was considering borrowing Gielgud's house when they had to move out of 38 Prince's Gate Mews.
2. The Mercury was opened by Gillian Raffles in 1964; Hardy was her assistant.
3. On the set of *The Charge of the Light Brigade* (1968), which Tony Richardson was directing.

Rosamond says of course he must have known about it all the time, but now he acts horrified and indignant. "He's always double," R. said, "he knows things and doesn't know them."[4]

Bob Regester is out *again*—this time spending the night in the country with John Osborne. The night before last, he brought Jeanne Moreau back to the house, and danced with her to the record player for hours without waking me. Then he rushed out and spent the rest of the night with some friend. Very relaxing and quiet for old Dub.

He thinks of his Kitty all the time and wonders what he is doing. Hopes dearly for a letter soon!

All Dub's eternal love—XXXXXXX

Sent off the Bacon and Procktor catalogues yesterday.

[*Autograph letter*]

May 16, 1967 [Santa Monica]

Dearest Muzzle:

I would like to be with my Old Darling but there wouldn't be anything for me to do really. I am working some here, painting as well as drawing, and I have hopes of getting down to it more effectively—the Bacon catalogue is great inspiration. (The Procktor catalogue is no inspiration at all, though the stuff is at least better than the little else I've seen. He is still suffering from a severe case of the cutes.) And, if you are going to have to move into a hotel, my being there would only double the expense. So Kitty has decided to be brave and stay on at the Casa. He appears every morning now in full state costume on the deck (we are having a terrific heat wave— 95° today), very much in residence, defiantly in residence, prouder than ever, though in his small secret heart he longs only for his Dubbin, and his quick little heart beats DubDubDubDubDubDubDub ...

Another *Cabaret* check today. I thought the money would have stopped by now. Also an announcement that Phil Anderson is a

4. Leftist friends had warned Spender that *Encounter* was funded by the CIA through the Congress for Cultural Freedom, and many presumed he knew. He made formal enquiries as early as 1963 and even found new funding for the magazine, but this funding may also have come from the CIA. He resigned as co-editor on May 7, 1967, after finally confirming the allegations about a month before.

candidate for the degree of Doctor of Medicine, ceremonies to be held June 9 in spite of the conspicuous absence of a furry Grey Eminence. Colin Wilson has sent a copy of his new book *The Glass Cage*, signed to both of us.

Saw *Accident* on Saturday with Jack and Jim and very much enjoyed it, though it gets very contrived and unconvincing at the end. But it is very well directed and acted and nicely photographed. It took the three of us about an hour of discussion afterwards to figure out what had happened in the film. Under analysis all of the contrivances begin to stick out.[1] But it's fun to see and I could easily see it again with Dear Hide. There's a cute boy in it, too, complete with legs, who will appeal to equine tastes I think, a boy named Michael York.[2] He is also Lucentio in *Taming of the Shrew*, which I saw last night with Paul Wonner. As I thought, it is handsome to look at, costumes and sets and period atmosphere all very good (with the exception of a few "studio" country roads and streams). Richard, too, is excellent. He plays the role with great comic charm and looks good, too. Just about the best thing he's done. She is not good—back to her tinny voice and fake lustiness and passion. Still, the first half of the film is very successful, second half much less so.[3] Paul was friendly in his usual remote way and Jack and Jim were indulging themselves in their usual brand of nervous, tense togetherness.

I saw Gerald on Sunday. He seemed exactly the same to me in spite of this last stroke. I was still unable to keep him from talking and still able to understand almost all of what he said if I listened very intently. He and Michael both send you their love. Great warmth from both of them. They seemed sincerely pleased that I came, and on short notice, too. My long letter had gone over big.

I'm enclosing two *Cabaret* ticket order forms, one for Klaus Peter Adam[4] who has been torturing poor Kitty mercilessly and another one in case anyone else comes along. Just sign and send back when you write again. No mail of any interest aside from enclosed.

1. Harold Pinter wrote the screenplay, based on Nicholas Mosley's 1965 novel. It was directed by Joseph Losey.
2. British actor (b. 1942), born Michael York-Johnson; he later played the Isherwood character in the film version of *Cabaret*.
3. Richard Burton played opposite Elizabeth Taylor in Franco Zeffirelli's film.
4. A German friend of Patrick Woodcock; he lived in London, where Bachardy met him at a dinner party at Woodcock's. He sat for Bachardy on a visit to Los Angeles. (Because he was noted for his large penis, Bachardy portrayed him nude.)

Love to Marguerite if and when you see her & regards to Buckle if you run into him and all unadulterated catlove to that dear treasured Plug whose hide is worshipped from afar by a brave Tabby.

[*Typed letter with autograph corrections and additions*]

[May 19, 1967, London]

Dearest Fur,

[A]m scribbling this under the eye of John Cullen[1]—how surprised he'd be to read it! Am just about to go to a book lunch where Dub will prance for the press—then straight off to Coventry to see Morgan and the Buckinghams. Will write from there. Got his Angel's letter this morning; it was so beautiful that Dub cried. And Marguerite has a photograph of Kitty when very tiny which I kiss. What great trustful eyes!

XXXXX

and a lick of that rough old tongue

[*Autograph letter on printed letterhead of Methuen & Co. Ltd. Publishers, 11 New Fetter Lane, London E.C. 4*]

May 21, 1967 [Santa Monica]

Beloved Hide:

Kitty has patiently waited to write until he'd heard from his Old Dear, but also no sweet note to cheer him on, so "That moving paw, having writ, writes on."[1]

A call on your phone this morning from Laura [Huxley], wanting something as usual. She has finished her book about Aldous, which she of course wants you to read, though it seems that her publishers, Strauss & Co., already have the manuscript. She is in a big tizzy (I don't know why the big rush since she still expects you to give her advice on the manuscript before it's published) about the title. She wants to

1. Isherwood's editor at Methuen following the retirement of Alan White in 1966.

1. Cf. "The moving finger writes, and having writ, moves on," in Edward Fitzgerald's 1859 rendering from Persian of *The Rubáiyát of Omar Khayyám*.

call the book *This Timeless Moment*. The publishers, who she likes, want a subtitle which explains what kind of book it is and Laura has come up with *This Timeless Moment—with Aldous Huxley*. The publishers say this is "ambiguous" and "not English" and suggest instead *This Timeless Moment, an Evocation* (period). Laura doesn't like this, nor do I for that matter, and she likes less the other suggestions of the publishers, *A Portrait* or *A Memory* of A.H. She wants you to telegraph her *collect* your opinion of the matter. She at first wanted you to call her collect but then she called back to say a telegram would be better because she could then send it on to the publishers. In any case, here are both her telephone numbers and her addresses: 6233 Mulholland Highway, L.A. 28, HOllywood 48024, or 6110 Graciosa, Apt. 11, L. A. 28, HOllywood 64981. She expects the telegram to be sent collect. By way of inducement she said she is intending to use my drawing of Aldous in the book.

Diane had its L.A. Television Premiere last night and it was sad to see, far worse than my memory of it. The acting and the direction were unbelievably bad, so awful that it wasn't even funny. If Miller and the "actors" had set out to sabotage the script they could not have done a better job of it. Every detail was so ludicrously wrong. Only Daniell and Hardwicke conveyed the smallest hint of style—at least they could speak. And yet, deep under the dreadful soggy mass could still be seen the makings of a marvellous film, the work of a clever Old Horse. It is one of the rare times when that Great Rump was almost completely covered up, but it took all of MGM to do it.[2]

David Hockney and Peter "dropped by" yesterday, quite unannounced as is their custom, hoping for some words of wisdom from The Great Sire himself. David is disenchanted with California. He has managed to foul himself up with income tax problems and is now delinquent and at best will have to pay a 6% penalty if he can ever figure out how much he owes. I offered to put him on to Arnold Maltin if he couldn't work it out himself. Also, he has had a notice to appear in court this week with regard to suspension of his driver's license. If it is only a warning that he has had too many traffic tickets and will lose his license if he gets one more,

2. Isherwood wrote the script for this 1956 film about Diane de Poitiers starring Lana Turner, Roger Moore, Pedro Armendáriz, and Marisa Pavan. It was directed by David Miller. Henry Daniell and Cedric Hardwicke had supporting roles.

he at least can go to court well prepared, having received the required ticket on his way down from S.F. this week. Of course he has decided that it is all California's fault and is in a mood to flee the country with his common-law wife. Peter has now become a complete, full-fledged woman and doesn't even flinch when David speaks of their "eloping" to England. Elopement is considered necessary because Peter's parents are still being obstructive [. . .]. Though Peter is not living at home, he has not gotten a place of his own. He is just "staying" in Nick Wilder's pen above the Strip. Peter's story might well turn into The Fall of a Woman.

Kate is here, and Jennifer [Selznick] and Diana Lynn[3] gave a trash bash for her and Ivan at Diana's exclusive Tower Road establishment on Friday, complete with Frank McCarthy and all that heaven doesn't allow, including a clear plastic bag with zippers and a false grass floor which served as mess hall for nearly eighty messes. To my surprise I was placed on Kate's right (perhaps guilty conscience since she only called to invite me the day before). I do like Kate. In the middle of the evening she came up to Gavin and me and said, "I wish we could go home but we can't . . . we're staying here," though this weekend they move into Richard Harris's huge Bel Air villa.

Speaking of Richard Harris, a sitting with him this week was totally unsuccessful because he would not or could not sit still, though after four irritating hours with him I don't hate him—he just bores me deeply. A drawing was supposed to be used for an advertisement for this reading he's giving at the Coronet early next month, but I don't like anything I did and don't know if I can face another sitting.[4]

Gavin and I went to The War Game yesterday. It is very effective and chilling, but it is not art, and its purpose is being defeated by merely showing it in a movie theater with a $2 admission price. It should be shown on television three times a week for several weeks until everyone has been made to see it. Last night was the first Saturday night of its run and the theater was practically deserted.[5]

---

3. American film and T.V. actress (1926–1971), born Dolores Marie Loehr; she started her career as a concert pianist.

4. Irish actor, singer, writer, director Richard Harris (1930–2002) appeared in *Il deserto rosso*, *This Sporting Life*, and *The Bible*, mentioned above, and was now starring as King Arthur in the film of *Camelot* (1967). He later played Dumbledore in the first two *Harry Potter* films. The reading at the Hollywood Coronet was part of an anti-war program, with Edward G. Robinson, Mia Farrow, and others (see below, p. 276).

I'm going to a showing of Alan Pakula's *Up the Down Staircase* tonight at the Screen Directors' Building (you were also invited, by separate telegram). Ned Rorem arrives this afternoon to stay with Gavin for two days. Gavin is giving a party for him tomorrow night. The Mouse of Rothschild[6] called today and I said I would see him today on my way into town. Also, Glenn Porter[7] called today from San Francisco for the second time, telling me about his LSD-type experiences after a week without sleep. He may well be on the verge of madness or spiritual experience or both. He talked calmly and sweetly and with innocent affection about his doings and sayings and writings, all of which made little sense to me but I didn't mind listening.

Kitty will go now to the P.O. and then to his studio to make some kind of effort to work. The ache in his little heart for His Old Grey Dear gets worse every day, so that Plug had better come soon.

With all of a Kitten's sacred love, Snow Paws.

[*Typed letter, signed, with autograph addition*]

May 21. [1967] Coventry

Most loved Fur,

[W]ell, I'm leaving here in a couple more hours and going back to London and the Mansion of Marguerite. I shall get in touch with Rex Evans early tomorrow morning.

Morgan and May Buckingham send their love. Bob went to London for the day this morning, and Joe Ackerley left this afternoon. I think on the whole that this has been a very successful visit. Morgan is in surprisingly good shape, not paralysed, able to speak perfectly, very bright and sweetly affectionate. I had to sleep in his room, and this was sort of a great success with him—it appealed to his baby persona.

---

5. *The War Game* is a fictional, documentary-style film in which nuclear war breaks out between Russia and the U.S. and warheads are dropped on Britain. It was made for BBC T.V. by Peter Watkins in 1965, deemed too horrifying to broadcast, and released in U.S. theaters in 1967. It won the 1966 Academy Award for Best Documentary.

6. David Roth, a young friend of Bachardy, for whom Roth often posed.

7. A student of Isherwood at Los Angeles State College during the spring of 1962; he was an aspiring writer, served in the navy, and later became a Vedanta devotee called Chandala.

He liked to have me sleeping across from him in the opposite bed—
and when we chatted in the morning after May had brought in the tea,
there was a kind of nursery atmosphere. He sleeps a great deal, and not
noisily—although of course every time he did make any noise in his
sleep I was apt to wake and wonder if he was starting another stroke!
May is ruthlessly bossy with all of us, which is probably necessary but
sometimes one feels a bit embarrassed for her because it's so square
and unstylish. Joe is awfully like Chris Wood, sulking because of
life's unkindness, saying he wishes he could die, he loved nobody but
his dead dog, nobody likes his books etc. etc. Bob is very solid and
outspoken and quite intelligent.

Henry Heckford, the young man who is writing about me,[1] turned
out to be old-maid-young, prim, awkward, with a white mournful
fattish face, little lady-hands and a tiny rosebud mouth. Also he's a
Catholic. I found him adequately bright and talkative when alone with
me but he was a frost when the Buckinghams asked him to supper.
He just sat.

More about all this in my next. Must now close, as I have to talk to
Morgan.

Do so dearly love my Fur—
Drub. XXXXXXX

[Autograph letter]

May 22 [1967]   back at 79 Chester Square [London]

Darling Snow-whiskers,

[P]romptly at 9:00 this morning I called the Cavendish, but neither
Rex nor Jim could be reached, and they had left no message for me
although I had left one for them before I went off to Coventry. So
now I've left another message and I'll keep after them. The worst of
it is, every time I make a call from the phone in my bedroom, I find
Marguerite on the line so I feel I'm being a nuisance. I'm not to have
supper with her tonight, as they have a date, and old Pat Trevor-Roper
whom I thought I'd work off, is unexpectedly leaving for America,

1. The book was never published.

Olive[1] is in France, Amiya can't be reached (thank God), Pat Woodcock has left for *The Charge of the Light Brigade*, [Erik] Falk is never home— even Jonathan Preston, whom I called at his office, didn't return the call.[2] No one wants dull old Drub, who noses shabbily around hideous byways, trying to snitch or cadge a few gulps of hay. Alas, where is his darling, his only love and tiny furry protector? Will he ever see Kitty again? Sometimes he panics, and has visions of ending in some foreign trashcan, far from that longed-for basket.

Now I'm off to buy a wooden salad bowl as a thank-you present for May Buckingham. She happened to remark that theirs had broken and they were making do with a ceramic one she didn't like. May is definitely the one who has to be handled. Her tongue is rash and probably sometimes dangerous. For instance, Joe Ackerley had confided in her that he didn't like staying at Cambridge because it meant sharing a bedroom with Morgan, and he hated sharing bedrooms. So she promptly tells this to Morgan (in my presence) and I could see it hurt his feelings because he took it as a rejection. Furthermore, May thereby made an indirectly bitchy comparison between Joe and me, who *hadn't* minded sharing a room with Morgan. Women, women! Oh yes, and Joe also tells me that May recently told him in all seriousness that Bob had never known Morgan was queer until about six years ago!! Joe was dumbfounded, naturally. What kind of lies can Bob have been telling her? Or was it a mad female attempt at a cover-up?

I wish you could have been with us on a drive we took 2 days ago—it really was a little pocket of rural England amid all the factories. A disused 13th-century church. A great house with parklands, where a young man made glider experiments and got killed, in the nineties.[3] An old steam traction engine called Flaming Elias, brought down for a show of traction engines in the park. The River Avon, at that point no bigger than [a] brook. Swans. A road that crossed a ford, and had cattle gates you had to open and shut. I was reminded of those villages we visited outside Stratford-on-Avon . . . Hugh French just invited me to lunch, darling

1. Olive Mangeot (1885–1969), English wife of Belgian violinist André Mangeot, for whose string quartet Isherwood worked as secretary for about a year, beginning August 1925. She appears as Madame Cheuret in *Lions and Shadows*.
2. Preston was a publicist; he had lived for a time in Los Angeles, where Isherwood met him in 1958, and they had a sex friendship.
3. The church is at Stanford, Leicestershire, and the house is Stanford Hall, where Percy Pilcher crashed his glider in 1899.

boy. Do I smell a job? Anyhow, Drub will hang up the horse-phone for now. More very soon. Neck-rubbings and tongue-licks for his Angel. XX

[Autograph letter]

May 27, 1967 [Santa Monica]

Dearest Show Pony:

Two sweet letters to tell Kitty of the Dubbin Adventures, though Kitty suspects here and there a little editing has been done. There is a suspicious lack of any of that spontaneous applause that Old Horse loves so. He is so clever at getting it, too. I'll bet Jonathan Preston didn't return his call because there were too many people in the office who might have overheard all the cooing noises. The catguess is that Bad Steed has by now much more than heard from Nora Preston, whose mouth, as we all know, was meant for kissing, not for tell(ephon)ing.[1]

Enclosed is an ad sent by Curtis Brown. I think you might put in a well chosen word or two at Methuen. If they are going to use that awful Ayrton drawing, they should at least give him credit for it—otherwise people will think the drawing is *mine*, Heaven forbid![2]

A bill from Heywood Hill for 5-3-7[3] which you might want to pay while you're there.

Michael Leopold has had a letter from Gerald Hamilton asking to give you his telephone number (FLA 9578) since it is not listed. I told Michael that I doubted you would be desperately needing it.

Went with Gavin last night to see *Two for the Road* with Audrey Hepburn and Finney. It will make him a big star.[4] She is as false and calculated as

---

1. *Nora Prentiss* was a 1947 film noir about a nightclub singer who, at his own request, allowed her lover to be unjustly executed rather than reveal the story that proved his innocence. Posters for the film showed the sultry, scantily clad singer, played by Ann Sheridan, with the slogan "Would you keep your mouth shut if you were Nora Prentiss?" Patrick Woodcock told Bachardy that one poster in the Tube had a large penis drawn on it beside Sheridan's face.
2. Methuen's advertisement for *A Meeting by the River*, featuring a drawing of Isherwood made in February 1956 by British artist and writer Michael Ayrton (1921–1975), appeared in *The Bookseller*, April 29, 1967, p. 2069.
3. That is, 5 pounds, 3 shillings, 7 pence.
4. Finney had already taken his role in *Luther* to Broadway in 1963, and he had also starred in Tony Richardson's *Tom Jones* (1963). Isherwood first met British-Dutch star Audrey Hepburn (1929–1993) in 1951, but neither he nor Bachardy knew her well.

usual and looking more and more like the toughest, scrawniest bird that even the hungriest of primitive debased cats would reject as unappetizing. The film is deeply slick, like a *Time Magazine* version of *An Anatomy of a Marriage*. It is proof that lies can be told about imaginary people.

Gavin's party for Ned Rorem was an embarrassed flop, due largely to an ill-assorted cast consisting of Jack and Jim, Antoinette and Jim,[5] Clyde, Nellie and Miguel (God must know why), Marti [Stevens] (even God may not know why), most of whom barely knew Ned; and Ned made little effort to pretend he wanted to alter that situation. The evening got so desperately tense that even Clyde performed (his umpteenth farewell appearance—I have decided that I have made *my* farewell appearance in his audience) and dismally failed to amuse. I hated the whole evening and thought of nothing but fleeing throughout. Ned and I made hollow efforts to be friendly but our voices echoed and finally died away.

The catmood, especially since that evening, is one of not wanting to see people. It is difficult though, to avoid a slight feeling of resentment since they obviously don't want to see Kitty. But the Old Fur struggles on valiantly, even painting some. He must rush off soon to draw the Christopher Plummer-sired moppette of Tammy Grimes[6]—probably another of life's cruel jokes on an old cat. But he still has his faith in Mr. Hide to keep him going, and when Dread Dub tires of terrorizing London, perhaps he'll remember his old loyal Stablecat who sits patiently by the stall waiting for his large friend to return.

With all of a tiny kitten's pink and white love, Fur Angelico

[*Typed letter, signed, with enclosure*]

May 24 [1967]   Chez [Lamkin, London]

Sacred Pinknose,

Got his dear letter (May 21) this morning. Actually I dislike all the alternatives proposed for Laura's book, so must wire her to tell her so. I loathe this publishing hysteria. There is no hurry really, and we can

5. Antoinette Bower, Canadian actress, and Jim Gill, an American painter. They lived together for a time but never married.
6. Amanda Plummer (b. 1957), later an actress. Christopher Plummer and Tammy Grimes were married from 1956 to 1960.

discuss it when I return. *This Timeless Moment* sounds like Adela Rogers St. John or some such swooning supercunt.[1] Well, after talking to my Darling yesterday I phoned Rex Evans and he agreed that it wasn't really necessary for you to send the paintings—he quite understood your feeling that it would be better if the Mercury people saw them in frames. Anyhow, he will let you know direct what happens when he sees the Mercury again next week for their decision. I shall still be with Richard, but Rex will leave me a message. I really feel he is quite reliable and as good a representative with the Mercury as you could find.

Have been worrying about this war situation,[2] because I hate to be separated from my Fur when any danger threatens. Dobbin's *dharma* is to die shielding that tiny Snowball from harm. The Jews here are hysterical of course. George Weidenfeld[3] was at supper here last night, advocating that the U.S. should threaten to use atomic weapons to protect Israel! Dobbin bit his lip, but later, when G.W. had gone, he SPOKE. As for [Marguerite's companion] he is far more sensible. I really like him—but what a pale shattered man, with his skinny twisted body. Marguerite drives him up the wall, I think, when he comes home exhausted to find the house full of women and decorator-boys with drinks. She teases him with threats of extravagance; she'll buy a [Graham] Sutherland, or a 17th-century commode, or repaper the top bathroom with mink. *She* looks exhausted, too. Oh, and Nicky Haslam (Lady Jim)[4] was there last night, wearing a black silk Russian blouse, green cowboy boots and a tiny jewelled cross which had belonged to Mary Queen of Scots or Svetlana Stalin or someone.

Dub committed an extravagance the other day. While in Liberty's he saw an alarm-clock with painted insides, different colors, very pop art, and he bought it (only 8–9 dollars) and sent it to Kitty. If Kitty doesn't like it, we can give it to someone. Dub thought it was so pretty.

What to give Dorothy? An awful man who runs *The New York Review*

1. Girl reporter for the Hearst papers and silent-screen writer (1894–1988), known for her purple style. Laura Huxley did use this title.
2. Tension was rapidly building between Israel, Syria, and Egypt toward the Six Day War. On May 19, the U.N. Emergency Force began withdrawing from the Gaza Strip and Sinai. On May 23, Egypt blockaded the Gulf of Aqaba, cutting off Israeli shipping and raising the crisis to a new level. See below, p. 277.
3. Viennese-born British columnist and publisher (b. 1919), trained as a lawyer and diplomat; founder, with Nigel Nicolson, of Weidenfeld & Nicolson. In 1949, he served as political adviser and Chief of Cabinet to the President of Israel, Chaim Weizmann.
4. British interior designer Nicholas Haslam (b. 1939) was then the lover of James (Jimmy) Davison, an American banking heir; they bred Arabian horses on a ranch in Arizona.

of Books came by last night with a miniskirted mistress, and murmured to Marguerite, "Don't judge her by appearances, she runs the biggest Negro paper in the country"!!![5]

After raising Dub's hopes, all that Hugh French wanted to do when he asked me to lunch was to introduce me to his representative or partner here, a corrupt toothy grinner named Nicholas Thompson.[6] He is trying to pry me loose from Curtis Brown. But Dub's famous loyalty frustrated them.

Have just read Diane Cilento's novel *The Manipulator*, which is most obviously about Tony Richardson and John Osborne. It wd be quite good if she could write better, but the loathing it expresses is basically a bore, and the plot is stupid.

I hope Kitty can read Dobbin's crabbed hoof-marks? His old hoof aches so when he tries to write. He only loves his darling and longs to be back with him. Dreads the Cheshire visit, and all the *effort!* Longs to lick that paw. Gave Marguerite your letter to her, which pleased her very much. She is writing you.

XXXXXX

Aye, there's the Rub.

[*Autograph letter*]

May 26. [1967] at 13 Bentside Rd. Disley—till May 31 or June 1st, then back to [Marguerite's]

Sweet longed-for Flufftail,

Old Drub's hooves have trudged northward and now here he is, feeling farther than ever from his love. However, the atmosphere here is pleasant. Richard seems far more in one piece, his cough has nearly disappeared and he hasn't sipped a sip so far—which gives Dub an extra excuse to stay on the wagon, after all that London slurping. Mr. & Mrs. Bradley are really sweet—but thank God, if you and I came up here, we would *have* to sleep elsewhere; things would be too crowded even for

5. Jason Epstein (b. 1928), a founder of *The New York Review of Books* in 1963, was at dinner at Marguerite Lamkin's that night with Weidenfeld, Haslam, and socialites Judy Gendel and Spider Quennell. The woman newspaper editor is unidentified.
6. Thompson was an American theatrical agent, but based then in London.

northern hospitality. Every time life at the Casa seems drear or dim say to yourself, "*At least* I have my own bathroom!" Dub is certainly longing for his—though, I have to admit, I get one at Marguerite's.

Saw Penelope Gilliatt (spelling?) before leaving town. She came on like gangbusters. What does she *want*? Well, she was just about to leave for a week in Los Angeles before taking up her job on *The New Yorker*, so I surmised it was some kind of contact there. She's staying with Mike Nichols. She spoke of Kitty and his art in handsome terms and said she wanted him to draw her daughter (who, however, is only joining her when she gets to New York) so I gave her your number.[1] You can always wriggle out of it if you want to. Incidentally, we were talking of who'd be the next poet laureate—dear old Masefield just died—and names were named, and some said Bjetcheman (why can I *never* spell him?)[2] and someone else Plomer, Robert Graves and finally Stephen. And Dub's dear old loving tongue suddenly became forked and darted out and hissed, "I was a poet laureate for the CIA"—and Penelope laughed so much that I feel uneasily sure she'll repeat it all over hell. Well, shit—I've endured quite enough of Stephen's cracks. Also saw Amiya—very sippy and soggy and such a bore, poor dear. And Jocelyn Rickards—cordial, but it didn't *quite* work. Maybe because Bob Regester was with us, striking the wrong note.

Oh love, it has begun to rain and today is only Friday! I love my darling so very very much always.

Old Faithful XXXXXX

[*Autograph letter*]

1. English critic, novelist, and screenwriter Penelope Gilliatt (1932–1993) had been a staff writer for *Vogue* and *Queen* and film critic for *The Observer* and was about to become film critic for *The New Yorker*. Her second husband, from 1963, was John Osborne, with whom she had a daughter. The marriage broke down in 1966, and she began a two-year relationship with stage and film director and producer Mike Nichols (b. 1931), settling with him in New York.
2. John Masefield (1878–1967) had been poet laureate since 1930. He was succeeded by Cecil Day-Lewis (1904–1972); John Betjeman (1906–1984) became poet laureate in 1972.

May 27 [1967]   13 Bentside Road Disley

Far-distant Angel,

Sad rain is falling, so no one shall enjoy the holiday weekend. Patrick Monkhouse[1] whom I phoned, was to leave for the Lake District today! Well at least I'm under cover and occupied, and Mrs. Bradley makes marvellous fishcakes, but oh the sadness. Yesterday we went over to Wyberslegh and I collected bunches of letters and all my mother's diaries from 1897 to 1915. These I shall be allowed to take, but not the Marple book—that's sacred. Now I'm going through my manuscript[2] with Richard page by page and it is just marvellous what he remembers. I'll be busy with that until Wednesday, when I return to London. Then I'll fix a day for my return to Purradise.

Did I tell you how I remarked to Mrs. Bradley that I had been moving around London (this to explain why I had dirty laundry I wanted her to wash) and she said wistfully, "That's how I'd like to live"? It was sort of heartbreaking. Oh God, Wyberslegh is sad! Everything speaks of death and dead Dobbins, separated from all they loved best. And the cracks in the walls are bigger and the papers in the drawers are wetter, and my father's pictures are probably in a state of hopeless mold. I wish we could go to the movies but Richard won't, and the telly is pretty grim.

Loves his dear Kitty so
and will try to survive long enough to lick
that sweet paw once again—
Blub.

Richard particularly asks me to send his love.

[Autograph letter]

1. Childhood friend, raised in Disley. He was at Oxford a year or two ahead of Auden and became a journalist at the *Manchester Guardian*.
2. For *Hero-Father, Demon-Mother*, later called *Kathleen and Frank*.

May 29, 1967 [Santa Monica]

Dear Plumed Pleasuring-Plug:

A happy day for a lonely kitten with three letters from his Old Hoofer to give him courage. And poor Furred Thing was feeling very grey and bedraggled this morning as he dragged that listless little body from the basket. I'm afraid He's getting very run down with no one to care for him. His fur hasn't been combed out in days, his claws need clipping and his pads are dry and rough for want of oiling. I think Old Dub had better come soon. Otherwise there's no telling what kind of state he'll find that small creature in. He's already wasted away to little more than a few ounces, minus fur weight, due to his diet of scraps and bits of bitter grass. He has neither the heart nor energy to run after mice even, and now the cruel birds, seeing his reduced condition, have started swooping down on him and taking away bits of tangled fur. Another week and he'll be little more than a grey blur haunting the once happy Casa. Only the desperate hope of smelling once again that warm hide keeps him going.

I wonder if it didn't work with Jocelyn because of cool reports from Leonard Rosoman of the general lack of warmth and response he got from the Animals when he was in California.

Also in the mail this morning a thank you note from Rachel Redgrave[1] for the photographs of the drawings I sent her, sending you her "very best wishes." She refers to the pleasure of her visit to the Casa "with it's (her apostrophe not mine) delightful calm atmosphere." She also hopes to see us when we come to London. If you feel like giving her a call the number is KEN 9572. She says they go to Venice June 10.

I don't think it's really necessary to bring something for Dorothy. I gave her an extra ten dollars for her birthday. She retaliated by sending me a chocolate cake by special delivery which arrived at 6 a.m. I took the cake to my mother who wouldn't touch it, I'm sure because it had been made by black hands. I got into a big argument last week with my mother and father over their deep prejudice against Negroes. In the heat of battle my mother declared that a Negro is "five steps above a gorilla." My closing statement was that I, with all of what they call my

1. English actress Rachel Kempson (1910–2003), wife of Michael Redgrave and mother of Vanessa, Corin, and Lynn Redgrave.

"communist" ideas, was a much better American than either of them since they were undermining the very principles of the Constitution and the Bill of Rights.

On the subject of Dorothy, she, while thinking of you in England, suddenly announced that the Duke and Duchess of Windsor were also in England "for the unveiling of Queen Mary." My only thought was that it's about time she was unveiled.[2]

Went to dinner at Gavin's last night with Kate and Ivan. A difficult evening, though I am fond of them both. Gavin must be going through a period in which his instinct for entertaining is quite off. After having too many of the wrong people for Ned Rorem, last night he had only me and the ever-present never-pleasant Clint. The four of us could have made it alone, though only just, due to a slight but always underlying tenseness between Gavin and Ivan—something to do with Gavin's basic resistance to many of the British. But Clint was the fifth wheel who as usual refused to turn. Gavin had also invited Betty Harford who begged off because of a terrible hangover. Betty loathes Ivan anyway. It would have been worse if she'd come.

According to Gavin, one night at a recent party Ivan got him into a corner and asked him about the boys in North Africa, where he was going soon because of *Justine*. He wanted to know if they were really as good as they were said to be because he was planning to try them. *Quien sabe?* is all I can think, except that anyone who has sex with Speed under the delusion that he's a boy, doesn't really know what a boy is.[3]

Saw *Persona* by myself the other night and had a big reaction to it. I was very involved in it and very much moved by it, though a lot of the time I had little idea what was going on. It is a truly extraordinary movie and I think very frightening and powerful. I haven't had such a

2. The Duke and Duchess of Windsor attended the unveiling of a plaque at Marlborough House commemorating his mother, Queen Mary (1867–1953), who had lived there. The visit attracted media attention because it was the first public meeting with his sister-in-law, Queen Elizabeth the Queen Mother, since the Duke, then Edward VIII, had abdicated in 1936, forcing his brother to take the throne as George VI.
3. Moffat was working with Lawrence Durrell on the screenplay for George Cukor's 1969 film of the first novel in Durrell's *Alexandria Quartet*. Bachardy had the impression that the sexual encounter between Moffat and Speed Lamkin had taken place before 1952 when he met them, and perhaps as early as 1949. He believes it was Moffat's only sexual encounter with a man, undertaken in a spirit of scientific discovery. Moffat told Isherwood about it, in Bachardy's presence, saying that there had been laughter on both sides and various attempts at experimentation. *Quien sabe?* is Spanish for "Who knows?"

reaction to a movie since *Paths of Glory*.[4] A lot of it might just have been my mood (the little Creature was feeling particularly lost and friendless) but it is undeniably good strong stuff, much his best picture. Don't see it because I certainly want to see it again.

The Mouse of Rothschild has turned into a long-haired rodent with beard and turquoise choker, very much the in-habitant of the San Francisco [. . .] scene, full of musings about the quality and meaning of life. He is still basically an irritating kind of innocent and as self-dramatizing and self-obsessed as ever, but something around the edges worried me. I think he might be steering toward [trouble] of some kind. He is very split now between the beatific, cool, uninvolved, inactive attitude to life, which is not natural to him [. . .] and his very natural [. . .] ambition for acclaim and power. He [. . .] can't make up his mind and instead strikes one pose after another. I had dinner with him and his actor friend Neil Elliot[5] who is a very simple, good-natured believer in the Establishment, if only it will acknowledge his membership. He is rather alarmed by David's dabblings in the far out. Significantly, David's relationship with Mike Nichols has come to little and he only works very occasionally on the film when they are on location in the S.F. area, due to union restrictions. I'm inclined to think David didn't put out sufficiently for Nichols, but I couldn't ask him because Neil was always there.[6]

Enclosed is a psychodelicat which arrived in the mail this morning.[7]

Kitty only lives for the return of his Dear Rump. He has polished the old harness and painted the sadly disused catcart pretty gay colors and tied it with new velvet ribbons as offerings to the Horse gods to appease them and coax them into returning his dearly loved Nag who is a kitten's only reason for being.

With all of a Tabby's constant love and adoration. Baskit

[*Typed letter, signed, with enclosure*]

---

4. *Persona* is Ingmar Bergman's 1966 minimalist film, often considered to be his masterpiece. *Paths of Glory* is Stanley Kubrick's 1957 film set during World War I.
5. Elliot had bit parts in films and T.V. and worked as crew.
6. Mike Nichols (not the well-known film director) also aspired to work in the film world.
7. A concert flyer printed in green, hot pink, and electric blue with a pair of cat's eyes. The Miller Blues Band and The Doors were playing at the Avalon Ballroom in San Francisco, June 1–4.

May 29. [1967]   13 Bentside Road Disley

My darling Love,

This morning suddenly there was sun, and I went for quite a long walk up the road to the moors above Lyme. It was warm, and everything was green and with blossoms, and there were lambs, and the hills were so beautiful and springlike that Dobbin felt almost like a colt again, and if Kitty had been there he would have taken that dear paw between his hooves and whispered vows of love. He did long for his Kitty beside him. Oh, it was poignant, like the sad-happy parts of *Wuthering Heights*.

Today is the bank holiday, so even up in the lanes among the hills there were tiny cars tearing about, and fat girl hikers. But still it was beautiful and peaceful and miniature; and you would have adored it, just for that moment. But of course back at home there was Richard, who won't walk uphill anymore, and hence I had guilt feelings for staying out so long.

It seems that he *does* still drink, lots, but he is evidently determined not to as long as I'm around—which suits me because I was really getting the drink-blues in London. Now I am very well again except for that sore old tongue, which Patrick Woodcock looked at and said, "Grin and bear it, I'm afraid." The Bradleys are quite concerned what to do with Richard but they most certainly won't turn him out. He must be an awful nuisance though, because he is really quite despotic; he won't let them leave him alone, and he won't come with them to visit their relatives.

However, I can't complain: Richard will let me have all my father's letters and all the volumes of my mother's diaries that I need. Only the Marple Hall book he won't part with, and I have nearly all the information I needed from that. Also I have been through my manuscript with him and he has corrected me on all sorts of points—his memory is astounding.

Am leaving here the day after tomorrow, May 31. Am hoping for a letter from my Darling tomorrow—no mail today.

Dobbin says to Kitty, just as though this was the first time he was saying it: "I love you." Then he takes Kitty in his forelegs.

Interminably,

Dob.

[Autograph letter]

79 Chester Square London S.W. 1   June 1st [1967]

Dearest Snow-gaiters,

This is in great haste, as I'm about to fly off shopping with Marguerite. Kitty's darling letter (May 29) arrived here this morning. Kitty's mews nearly burst Dobbin's already full heart, he wished he could fly instantly to his dear, but there are still things to do. I hated breaking the irritating news to you on the phone yesterday about the paintings, but I suppose it's better than nothing. I'll go round to the Mercury next week and try to find out what they really do intend.[1]

Have spoken to Methuen about that awful Ayrton drawing being reproduced, and Alan White agreed it wasn't to be compared with yours and said it wouldn't happen again.

Three notices of the book this morning—*Times* poor, *Daily Express* fair, *Daily Telegraph* very good.[2]

I like being with Marguerite because I feel she really loves Kitty and thinks of him as one of her best friends, quite independently of Dobbin. You would be very welcome here, they both say. Even now, if you were suddenly to decide to come over—!!?

There has just been a domestic crisis, the Spanish couple, lazy and unwilling, refused to serve us a last-minute supper last night, and this morning Marguerite fired them.

Bob Regester leaves for Turkey on Saturday (day after tomorrow) unless those selfish Israelis are so little interested in *The Charge of the Light Brigade* being filmed that they declare war!

Kitty's letters are so clever and interesting and Dub's are so dull—chiefly because he's being constantly interrupted by the phone, Marguerite with decorators, rude pansified heters with matching ties and handkerchiefs, who drop cigarette ash on the floor. How *amazing* about Ivan! Is *A Meeting by the River* coming true,[3] or is it his way of being faithful to Kate?!

All a Dubbin's devotion to his Treasure XXXXXXX

[*Autograph letter*]

1. The gallery wanted to see actual paintings and drawings rather than the photographs Isherwood had shown them, before they would decide whether to exhibit Bachardy's work.
2. Paul Barker wrote the notice in *The Times*, p. 7. The *Daily Express* review, possibly by Robert Grosvenor, called the book "skilful and humorous," p. 9; and Robert Baldick in *The Daily Telegraph* said it was "a remarkable *tour de force* . . . convincing and satisfying," p. 21.
3. The Patrick character was based partly on Moffat.

June 2. [1967]   [79 Chester Square, London]

Darling beloved Fur,

[T]he rain is coming down in clumping torrents and well it may, this being John Lehmann's birthday, which I am about to attend, after being interviewed by an Italian newspaper editor—Dr. Zampa of *La Stampa*, believe it or not! Then to see *Three* (count 'em) *Sisters* at the Court with Anthony [Page] because he believes a girl in it, Marianne Faithfull,[1] might do for Lulu. Tomorrow [Marguerite and her companion] propose to take me on a picnic, *if* the weather improves. Last night I took them out to a restaurant on the Fulham Rd. which serves fish cakes, shepherds pie, steak and kidney pudding *and* treacle tart. And guess what it's called— The Hungry Horse! I long to take Kitty there. Indeed I have found a couple of good new places.

Just got my ticket definitely made out for Friday June 9—flight 771 due to arrive Los Angeles at 7:00 p.m. or 7:05; they told me both. Oh, may the Animals be safely reunited!

Am hoping so much that your paintings will reach the Mercury Gallery before I leave, so I'll be able to bring you some stop-press news of their reactions. Incidentally I now find that the Redfern is also holding a summer show with a great variety of artists represented, so there was no earthly reason why *they* shouldn't have shown a couple of yours, too. However, the few times I have seen Harry Miller (twice, actually) I have been careful to hide my feelings and be friendly—business before pleasure (of fury). He may still be useful.

The city is very lively, green and crowded. But it is catless and therefore a desert for Dobbins.

Bob Regester sends his love to you. He leaves for Turkey early Sunday, and I shall be spending the day with the Beesleys.

I imagine Richard is floating high on beer, now I've gone.

Geraldine Fitzgerald[2] wrote to ask me to read a school novel called *Lord Dismiss Us* by a writer named Michael Campbell, who wanted a blurb. I had the pleasure of telling her I already read it, I think it's awfully good and I am seeing the author on Monday.

1. Faithfull (b. 1946) was then reaching the height of her fame as a singer and as Mick Jagger's girlfriend. The Chekhov play directed by William Gaskill was her stage debut, running since April 18 and about to close.
2. Irish-American actress (1913–2005), on Broadway and in Hollywood from the late 1930s.

All love to my darlingest Pinkpaws—
Drudgin. XXXXXXXX

[*Autograph letter*]

June 2, 1967 [Santa Monica]

Loved Velvet Muzzle:

Rex's letter arrived today. I have decided not to send any paintings. The tone of Rex's letter is very unimperative: "If you would like to have two of your acrylics in the summer group show, Stan said he would be glad to include them." Thanks a million department. They still can't make up their minds about a show, but I'm supposed to be glad to hussle big framed and glassed paintings over to England by air freight (which certainly wouldn't be cheap) just on the off chance that they will deign to honor me with an exhibition. Once they take a look at the paintings they might very well tell me I can't have a show, and if the paintings don't sell in the summer show, I'm sure I'll be expected to pay the return shipping as well. Therefore, circumstances force me to decline their generous offer. And if it costs me the show, what does it really matter? Thinking it over, I'm not all that mad for a show in England. I can perfectly well concentrate on my show at Rex's in November, and if that's a success I can perfectly easily go to London, taking some work with me, and do what I can to arrange a show in person, wherever I can. All this negotiating by proxy is no real good and usually ends badly. I will send them a telegram saying there is insufficient time for me to have the paintings framed and sent to them before the opening of the show. I am also enclosing a letter to Stan which you might take by the gallery if you approve of the tone of it. If not, don't take it. It doesn't really matter.[1] But I would like you to go by the gallery sometime before you leave London so that you can get the book of photographs of the drawings and bring it back with you.

Kitty's Dubless life continues drably. An evening at Jack and Jim's (at last they got around to feeding the nearly forgotten old cat) with David [Hockney] and Peter [Schlesinger] and Bob Gordon.[2] David's

1. Bachardy did not write the letter, as he explains in a different enclosure, printed below.
2. American writer, settled in San Francisco; Jack Larson and Jim Bridges introduced him to Isherwood and Bachardy.

license hasn't been taken away and Peter has become a redhead via ye olde peroxide bottle. Among other noticeable changes in Peter is a new and more than slight tendency to contradict his lord and master. Still they are planning to go to England together (around the 15th of June I think) and are hopeful of glimpsing Old Father Drub before departing, and getting his blessing.

Significantly, both of us were invited to a showing of Curtis Harrington's movie with Signoret, called *Games*, on Wednesday evening at Universal.[3] I went with Gavin, and Clint, who reached a new low in childish sulky behavior. I couldn't tell whether or not the decidedly chilly air between him and Gavin was the cold calm before or after the storm. Anyway, I have taken a turn in my tactics with Clint. The sulkier and more childish he gets the more I treat him like an intelligent, responsible, contributing grown-up, forcing him against his will to feel himself included in the conversation. And I kiss him religiously both arriving and leaving. And the remarkable effect all this has had on Saint Tabby is to completely rid Him of His aversion to Clint. Kitty fairly glows with sweet acceptance.

The audience for the showing of the film was a cross section of the Hollywood intelligentsia with many fringe benefits and drawbacks. Notably present were Fritz Lang,[4] Ray Bradbury,[5] John Saxon,[6] Anne Baxter, Bernadine Fritz,[7] Jack and Jim, the Hoppers,[8] Eadie Breckenridge[9]

---

3. Harrington (1926–2007) was an American director of underground and studio films. In 1954, Isherwood punched him in the face at a party at Iris Tree's because Harrington brought a friend who made advances toward Bachardy. Harrington sued, and they settled out of court. Afterwards, Isherwood avoided Harrington, although he was forced to work with him in 1956 at Twentieth Century-Fox where Harrington was Jerry Wald's assistant.
4. Revered Austrian director and screenwriter of German and Hollywood films (1890–1976).
5. American novelist, poet, playwright, and screenwriter (1920–2012); best known for his science-fiction classics *The Martian Chronicles* (1950) and *Fahrenheit 451* (1953).
6. American actor (b. 1936), he starred in Harrington's 1966 science-fiction horror film, *Queen of Blood*.
7. American journalist (d. 1982); she worked as a reporter in Chicago and New York then lived in London and Paris and travelled in India and China where she met her fourth husband, Chester Fritz, a metals trader, financier, and horseman from North Dakota. They married in Manchuria in 1929 and divorced in Hollywood in 1946, though he continued to support her socialite lifestyle and salon.
8. Dennis Hopper also starred in *Queen of Blood* and in Harrington's earlier supernatural thriller, *Night Tide* (1961). His then-wife, Brooke, briefly an actress in her teens, is the socialite daughter of film star Margaret Sullavan and agent-producer Leland Hayward.
9. A well-dressed art-crowd dilettante in her seventies, slim, elegant, and party-going; Bachardy knew her by sight from drawing classes they both attended early in his career.

and Renate,[10] who cut me twice before the film and embraced me afterwards.

The film is a horror thriller, very Diaboleaky,[11] not badly directed but just so unconvincing, predictable and badly constructed in its story that all is lost finally, or rather long before finally. Signoret again demonstrates with great expertise the fact that she is not a very good actress. It is quite nicely and prettily photographed in pale, subtle color.

Bill Brown is back and I went there for dinner last night. Jo and Ben were the usual fixtures. It was pleasant though, largely because Bill and especially Paul were in obvious good spirits. In spite of protestations and pleadings for mercy from Whitefur, I'm afraid notation has been made in the Black Catbook of the fact that Jo and Ben, with the negligible exception of a couple of offhand last-minute invitations to join in on preorganized evenings, have failed to feed or even pay attention to Lonelypaws. I tremble at the thought of the impending Catcourt trial.

To console himself and in an effort to camouflage the stark boniness of his dreadfully thin little body, Kitty has been shopping recently. He managed to find two pretty ice-cream-colored suits which will do happily for his summer wardrobe, and some dear little boots with buckles on them.

A dreaded sitting tomorrow morning with an awful ass who calls himself, and probably is, the Consul of Brazil.[12] I encountered him at a not-to-be-believed German Fiesta at Margot Factor's[13] for Horst Buchholz and wife (a dainty French contriver)[14] about which I will tell you all when I see you, after we have exhausted every other possible topic of conversation.

Michael Leopold, very manic, calls me almost every morning shortly before nine full of schemes to get me commissions and sales and an exhibition at the New Orleans Art Museum. Who needs London? Bang!

10. Druks (1921–2007), Austrian-American painter, actress, film director, scenic designer, settled in Malibu from 1950. She had a role in Kenneth Anger's experimental film *Inauguration of the Pleasure Dome* (1954), in which Harrington also appeared. She was a girlfriend of Ronnie Knox, and she often sat for Bachardy.
11. That is, like the 1955 French horror-thriller *Diabolique*, also starring Simone Signoret.
12. Raul de Smendek, of Dutch background.
13. Middle-aged German socialite.
14. German stage and screen star (1933–2003), known in Hollywood for his role in *The Magnificent Seven* (1960); his wife, Myriam Bru (b. 1932), was an actress, and, later, a talent agent in Paris.

John Rechy[15] is in town. On Sunday Kitty is giving for him the first dinner party of his period of ordeal-without-Dub. Jack and Jim are invited and Gavin and Clint, though I haven't yet dared to let John know that Clint is still obligatory. John was disappointed that you were away but will still be here, as will Ivan and Kate and David and Peter, all of whom clamor for Horse droppings, if Dub still comes on the 9th. Also a tax bill from the Internal Revenue Service for an installment of $2,500 which is due June 15, awaits. And last but not least, a tiny heart waits and pines for that Treasured Rump who is all a kitten knows of love in his small life, and all he needs to know. Please come soon.

Your adoring

Furtail

[*Typed letter, signed, with two further notes enclosed (printed below)*]

Drubble:

I've decided not to write a letter to Stan. There is no need of it—my telegram said all that needed saying.

If and when you see him, if they still want to give me a show, tell him I will bring with me when I come enough drawings for a show and also enough paintings for a combined show, if they like that idea better. I will plan to arrive in London in plenty of time to have everything framed there before the show opens. However, don't push the issue if they are reticent. As I say, the whole idea of a London show is not now of any burning importance to me. If it's going to happen, it will happen.

What is of burning importance to Kitty is the return to him of the Real Hide. XXXXXX K.

[*Autograph note*]

15. American writer (b. 1934); known already for *City of Night* (1963) and about to publish *Numbers* (1967) with thinly disguised portraits of Isherwood, Bachardy, and Gavin Lambert.

Dearest Rump:

It is very late. I have just gotten home from the reading Gavin organized for Richard Harris at the Coronet. Most of the evening was a chaotic mess with only a few of the old performers managing to come across with something—among those Dorothy McGuire,[16] Walter Pidgeon,[17] Elsa. The real criminal of the evening was Harris himself, who even dared to read his *own* poetry and *not* know it. He is revealed forever as a sloppy, self-indulgent, undisciplined egomaniac. He is proof that charm most decidedly is not enough.

Kitty's dinner for John Rechy last night was all right—John is stranger than ever. Tomorrow afternoon Ray Henderson is playing and singing for me the last of the music he's written for *Dog Beneath the Skin*—it will be our second session. What I've already heard is really quite impressive.[18]

This will be Kitty's last communiqué and is only meant to tell Old Drubbin how very much Kitty longs for that Horse Flesh—oh to get his claws into that tough Hide again. His stall is already cleaned out (Dorothy comes tomorrow for a final scrubbing), his blanket steamed and scented and the feed bag filled to capacity with deluxe-quality oats. Kitty can hardly wait for Friday to come.

With a heart full of love for his Nag,

Whiskers.

[*Autograph note*]

16. American stage and movie actress (1916–2001). She appeared on Broadway from 1938 and was first brought to Hollywood by David Selznick to reprise a stage role in *Claudia* (1943).
17. Canadian star of Broadway musicals, Hollywood films including silent movies, and T.V. (1897–1984).
18. Henderson, an American composer and pianist, was Elsa Lanchester's musical director and piano accompanist, performing in her nightclub act in Los Angeles and on tour and on her T.V. show. He was also her lover. His lyrics and score for a musical version of *The Dog Beneath the Skin* developed into a project to be directed by Burgess Meredith; it was never produced.

June 5, [1967]   [London]

Darling Purr,

[N]ot a proper letter—just a signal to let Kitty know that Dub is thinking about him more constantly than ever, and worrying because of this horrible war.[1] It is too dreadful to be separated from Kitty when the least danger threatens. Dub wishes he could whizz off to the Basket tonight. At least it's good he has a reservation, in case people start hurrying home.

Kitty's dear letter just arrived, and of course I'll see the Mercury people and tell them. (If only it had arrived by the first post I could have done it today.) The Beesleys sent their love. They seemed much older. Am seeing Edward and the Mangeots tomorrow.[2] Tonight I have been trapped into seeing Beatrix Lehmann in *Hecuba*[3]—just the right entertainment for a crisis!

Marguerite has finally written you today.

Must stop now—doubt if I'll write again or it may not arrive before I do. Roll on Friday!

TWA. 7:05 Flight 771.

Pegasus.

XXXXXXXXXXX

[*Autograph letter*]

•   •   •

1. The Six Day War broke out that day, June 5, when Israel made a surprise preemptive strike against the Egyptian air force, destroying much of it on the ground. Later the same day, Israel launched air strikes against Jordan and Syria, and Jordan, Syria, and Iraq struck back.
2. Edward Upward, Olive Mangeot, and her younger son Sylvain Mangeot (1913–1978), a journalist. He worked at the Foreign Office and then became a diplomatic correspondent, an editor, and an overseas radio commentator for the BBC. As a child, Sylvain made the animal paintings that inspired the Isherwood poems published with them much later as *People One Ought to Know* (1983).
3. A Euripides double bill, with *Iphigenia at Aulis*, at the Mermaid Theatre.

Sept. 13 [1967, Santa Monica]

Dearest love,

I feel a need to tell Kitty today how dearly Dobbin loves him and how faithfully he waits and guards the stable until Kitty's return.¹ Dub has been quite off his feed since Kitty hasn't been there to tempt him with morsels held by those pure paws, but whether that great bulk has diminished so that Kitty would notice—there's the question.

A letter arrived from your ex-landlady—pages of self-justification but very careful not to enrage you further. All the blame is thrown on Fred, and a check for $100 is returned (which I deposited) with promises to send the balance when she has found out how much the repair of the furniture etc. comes to.² Do you want this letter sent to you?

Mrs. Dinsmore called, to ask if they had liked your drawings at the New York office.³ She says they never tell her anything. I said they *had* liked them, oh yes indeed.

Jim Bridges showed me a mad card Lincoln Kirstein sent Jack—from the looney bin, presumably—"don't come (here)."⁴

I hesitated about sending the money to Glenn Porter, awaiting a

1. Bachardy flew to New York on August 28; he stayed in Maurice Grosser's apartment at 219 West 14th Street and returned September 27.
2. Fred Maddox had moved into Bachardy's vacated apartment at 418 West 20th Street. The landlady, a nit-picker and suspicious of all youth, was unfairly trying to retain part of the security deposit when in fact no damage had been done.
3. Nancy Dinsmore, Los Angeles representative for *Harper's Bazaar*; Bachardy had done portraits for the magazine of prominent Los Angeles personalities—Fred Astaire, Billy Al Bengston, Betsy Bloomingdale, Diana Lynn and her daughter, Nancy Reagan, and James Stewart's daughters.
4. Kirstein had had a severe breakdown while directing his play *White House Happening* for Harvard's Loeb Theater. A week before the play opened on August 7, he was committed to Baldpate Sanitarium in Georgetown, Massachusetts, near Boston, and remained there for seven weeks.

"signal from life." Then, a few hours after I talked to you, Robin French called to tell me that a check had come in for my share of the record-album sales on *Cabaret*—$3,139.47! The surprise was nice because I hadn't known I would receive *any* share of these earnings. So Glenn got his $100.[5]

It also looks as if "Black Girl" may get started.[6] And Long Beach State have offered me $1,500 to spend the day there and give two talks.

Lyle loved the Greek ashtray so much that I have loaned it to him—I think he identified with it; but Rez, when this was suggested, smiled scornfully.[7]

Am returning *The Ring* today separately.[8]

Jo and Ben get more and more boring. It's really criminal, this public fuss. Now Ben is going through a sort of breakdown, a psychofiesta, in which neither Jo nor Dee really matter.[9] Jo thinks that when he gets through this he will be a truly *great* writer.

But Dubbins don't understand such things. They only wait for their kittens till death. Wet-tongued kisses and shaggy mane-rubbings for his darling. Horse. XXXXXXXXXXXXX

[Autograph letter]

. . .

5. Probably a loan.
6. George Bernard Shaw's story, "The Adventures of the Black Girl in Her Search for God," which Isherwood had been asked to adapt for the stage by Lamont Johnson, who proposed to direct it at the Mark Taper Forum.
7. Lyle Fox, who ran Isherwood and Bachardy's gym, was blond and muscular; the ashtray evidently bore a figure with a similar physique. He married Rez that year.
8. Richard Chopping's 1967 novel, which Bachardy had given Isherwood for his birthday. Isherwood may have been returning it so that Bachardy could read it.
9. Masselink was in the process of leaving Jo for Dionyse (Dee) Humphrey, the wife of their friend, Bill Hawes. He married Dee in August 1968.

Tuesday. April 23. [1968, London]

Dearest Only Angelhorse—

Kitty's longing for his Hide is especially bad this morning. I so regret not getting on that plane yesterday. At the last minute I decided it was so silly to rush off just in order to keep from paying another $90 when I'd already spent nearly $500 to get here[1] and accomplished only one thing: the realization that his dear old Nag is the one thing in the world that really matters to him. As if he hadn't realized that countless times before. Why do I have to keep doing these awful things just in order to remind myself of something I already know, and have known for a long time now? Anyway, I did the only bit of good work since I've been here yesterday morning (the drawing of Jill Bennett—now Mrs. Osborne[2]) with my bags already packed and a cab waiting for me and I knew if I left then I would never see the drawing again and they would probably make an awful muck-up of the poster for which it was done. Now I realize I don't give a fuck what happens to the drawing (Anthony Page has said he will buy it and give it to the Osbornes for a wedding present) or the poster. As it turns out, the man in charge of designing the poster who I met yesterday afternoon is I think probably quite bright and will know what to do with the drawing. Anyway I will see his roughs on Thursday and will at least be able to bring back a reproduction of the drawing to show Oldpony.

Bob Regester's place is quite nice[3]—at least there is lots of light—but madly uncomfortable and inconvenient due to there being only one bathroom, and due to the fact that he keeps all of his clothes in the closet

1. Bachardy flew to London April 1, 1968. He planned to return April 18, then April 22; now he had again postponed his return because Anthony Page had hired him to draw portraits for the posters and program for John Osborne's new play Time Present, which Page was directing at the Royal Court. It cost Bachardy $90 to change his ticket and extend his stay.
2. In fact, she and Osborne married a month later, May 23, at the Chelsea registry office, the day she opened in Time Present.
3. 81 Cadogan Square, S.W. 7.

of the bedroom in which I am sleeping so that I feel like I'm sleeping in a train station. Neil is away—I think with Tony in the South of France—but maybe coming back tomorrow. And Mrs. Potter (the cleaning lady whom you met who, after exchanging half a dozen words with me, asked Bob if I were a friend of Mr. Isherwood's) is a finely wrought torture instrument for the nerves. I have had enough of servants here to last a lifetime.

I have forgotten to mention to you both of the last times we talked on the telephone that Iris is dead—since a week ago Saturday.[4] A relatively painless but difficult death apparently. She hung on determinedly up to the very last in spite of doctors doing nothing to keep her alive. Boon[5] told me that on the Friday night before, it was obvious that she hadn't anything left to go on but, seeing that it was night, she asked him, "Help me to wait till it's light—noon light." She died at eleven the next morning. Neither Kate nor Ivan have made any ado about it. Both Friedrich[6] and Boon were with her. I had a drink with Boon who is exactly the same only older, and much more vulnerable and alone in his dullness. He wanted to see me in order to communicate to you that he hoped you'd forgiven him for something or other he thought you were cross with him about. I was so amazed by this that I almost said it was ridiculous for him to imagine you cared enough about him to be mad at him. Anyway, I assured him I knew nothing about any such matter. Apparently Ivan had been telling him you were cross about something—God knows what?

There is much more to tell of minor interest but I will wait till I see you. Your telegram was telephoned in this morning. I haven't telephoned Angela Baddeley because I couldn't think of a good enough reason for seeing her, unless she wants to buy one of the drawings which is unlikely since your telegram didn't mention that.[7] I would anyway not be able to get a drawing to her until I got back to Stableland. The effort of "just seeing people" seems far greater since I've been here than ever before. I

4. Iris Tree (1896–1968), English actress, poet, playwright. She was introduced to Isherwood by the Huxleys during World War II and remained one of his closest English friends in California until she moved to Italy in 1954. Ivan Moffat was her son by her first husband, Curtis Moffat. She died of cancer Saturday, April 13.
5. Christian Ledebur, known as Boon (b. 1928), a doctor. He was Iris's son by her second husband. Boon was raised partly in California and lived in Santa Monica intermittently.
6. Count Friedrich von Ledebur-Wicheln (1900–1986), Iris's second husband until they divorced in 1955. He was a cavalry officer during World War I, trained horses, and had some small movie roles in Hollywood.
7. English actress (1904–1976), best known for her role as Mrs. Bridges in *Upstairs Downstairs*; she was the elder sister of actress Hermione Baddeley. She sat for Bachardy December 1, 1967 in Santa Monica, and he did two drawings of her.

haven't called half the people I know. I don't even want to call Marguerite & [her companion], who get back today from Morocco, to tell them I still am in London, though I'm afraid she might find out anyway.

I will send a telegram to let you know my flight number as soon as I make a reservation. I will not do that before Thursday in case some unforseen emergency arises concerning the posters. Both Bob and Anthony Page require a lot of resisting. They've suddenly developed a great concern about my welfare in London, born of a desire to please you on Bob's part and I think guilt towards you about the Lulu plays on Anthony's part.[8] Kitty dreams of his basket and longs to hook his claws into that dear tough old Hide. With all of a kitten's love.

Fur XXXX

[Autograph letter]

Tuesday [April 30, 1968, London]

Dearest Love Plug—

A few hurried words to my only Darling before taking Marguerite to lunch at a chic Italian restaurant on the King's Road (Don Luigi's). I finally called her yesterday to declare my lingering presence here. I was so afraid of running into her or [her companion] on the street, or, even worse, Speed. Though Speed and I have officially buried the hatchet, if we are to establish any semblance of genuine friendship it cannot possibly begin with trust.[1]

The only other person I've called to say I'm still here is Patrick Woodcock. All the others I can't be bothered to take leave of again. Anyway I am so busy doing the drawings for the theater I barely have

8. During his trip to England in May and June 1967, Isherwood agreed to go ahead with the adaptation that Page had proposed during Isherwood's October 1966 visit to London, and Page gave him some books and some notes. On his return to Santa Monica, Isherwood mentioned in his diary, June 16, that he ought to begin roughing out a translation. Page was so immersed in his Osborne productions that he had done no work on the Lulu plays but he recalls that he did not feel guilty because Isherwood had not communicated with him about the project. It never gained momentum, and later, on Christmas Eve 1969, Page finally asked Isherwood to return all the materials.

1. Speed Lamkin was a gossip. Tom Wright, or possibly Marguerite, had once repeated to Bachardy some comments Speed had made about Bachardy, causing a rupture. Although the friendship had been renewed, Bachardy assumed Lamkin would gossip about him again.

time for anything else. I showed the cast drawings to Anthony yesterday. He was enthusiastic about all but three so I am going to try to set up second sittings with each of the three actors which shouldn't be difficult to do. Alas, the only drawing I've done of John Osborne is not right and that really will be hard to redo. John is so elusive and grand, though still kind of lovable and funny in his feminine way. And looking better than I've ever seen him look—very slim with long flowing hair and a handlebar moustache which isn't half as ludicrous as it may sound, especially since it camouflages his cruel little stung mouth.

My drawings of Anthony Page are some of the best I've done here though he is alarmed by the best one and much more in favor of a weaker, more romantic looking first drawing. He has been really kind and helpful to me, and now he has begun to talk about your working on a movie script of some idea he and a woman friend of his have for a thriller. I have to keep reassuring him that you like thrillers and don't feel they are beneath you, but I fear there is little chance of any real backing for the project, even if he does ask you to do it. He is *very* unreliable about money matters, his own as well as everybody else's.

Later

Marguerite was well and undemanding. Hers and [her companion]'s trip to Morocco had been quite a success though it rained most of the time. We ran into Kate Moffat at the restaurant. Deeply embarrassing because I had not told her I was still in town and Iris's memorial service was last Friday. I have not even seen Ivan since I've been here.

I must fly off to the theater to see a run-through of the play and set up sittings for tomorrow. I am planning to get a reservation on the Monday flight. Should anything interfere I will call you at the weekend—Sunday morning in fact—but only if I can't come on Monday. Don't call me here except in an emergency. I feel very uncomfortable around Bob & Neil and so spend most of my time away. I miss my Old Hide terribly and think of him always and long to stroke that dear muzzle. With all of a kitten's loving heart. F.

[*Autograph letter with enclosure*2]

2. Bacardy enclosed part of a newspaper story about American abstract expressionist painter Mark Tobey (1890–1976). On the clipping, he underlined Tobey's recollection of Dartington in the 1930s, "You could hear a horse breathing three fields away at night," and added with an asterisk, "So? Kitty can hear a horse breathing more than 7,000 miles away."

Jill Bennett

[*Pencil and ink wash drawing by Don Bachardy; printed as program cover for* Time Present]

John Osborne

[*Pencil and ink wash drawing by Don Bachardy; printed in program for* Time Present]

Anthony Page

[Pencil and ink wash drawing by Don Bachardy; printed in program for Time Present]

Thursday. [May 2, 1968, London]

Dearest Sugardub—

Old Cat misses his Angel Horse so very much and thinks of him so much and pines pitifully for his warm basket with the huge Hide cushion which comforts him so. But Kitty is being terribly fussed and rattled and dazed by all these Show Biz people who keep plucking at his fur and spinning him around. What still has not been settled is whether or not I'm going to get another sitting with John Osborne. I am pushing for Sunday, in which case I can keep my Monday reservation. But he is so capricious and grand that nobody dares find out definitely. If it's a question of staying on a little while longer to draw him, I think I will. Also, then I can get back the originals of the drawings I've done of the cast which I know I will never see again if I don't take them with me. Not that I mind so much about them, except for the one of Jill Bennett, but I don't even have any reproductions of them because I don't know of any place here to get them done. Oh it is so uncomfortable and inconvenient and inefficient here! I can't tell you what I went through doing those first drawings. A nightmare. And here I am doing the same old portrait drawings I've been doing for years. I've already gotten bored by that very familiar Bachardy drawing—but at least I am better off doing that than I am doing nothing. I was so miserable those first weeks here. At least now I have somewhere to go and something to do each day.

I am staying with Anthony Page (68 Ladbroke Grove, W.11). I was so ill at ease at Bob and Neil's that I asked him if he would put me up for a few days. The place is *very* primitive (but still preferable to Bob's) and though much more inconvenient than Cadogan Square, I at least can get a ride into town in the morning when Anthony goes to rehearsals. He has been having [. . . an] affair of many months with a guy named Norman who lives in the flat above with a lover [. . .]. I've still not clapped eyes on him yet—all I know is that he's an actor turned real-estate agent, which is more than enough to sink him as far as I'm concerned.[1] But Anthony still suffers [. . .]. I am very fond of Anthony and he is fun to be with, except that much of the time he is so wrapped up in the play and rehearsals that

1. In fact, Norman Swallow was a painter turned real-estate agent. Page recalls that the affair, a serious one, took place while Swallow's partner was away and that it was now over.

he can't really concentrate on anything else. He still talks of the possibility of your writing this thriller for him though I hear nothing that makes me think it might really happen. It could very easily happen if you were here. He is a terribly out-of-sight-out-of-mind person.

Kitty is sorry for all of these changes of plans. He feels so silly and scatterbrained and guilty because he remembers so many other times when he's behaved like this. But he trusts his Dear Rump will be patient with him and never forget that Kitty loves him more than anything or anyone in the world. I miss you so much and long to be near you and hold you and talk to you like I can talk to no one else.

I will either call you or send a telegram on Sunday. With all my love, Furheart.

The telephone here if you don't have it: PAR 0560.

[Autograph letter]

Wednesday. [May 8, 1968, London]

Beloved Hoof:

It is cold and rainy today and poor old Cat has to drag himself out to draw Anna Massey, daughter of Lincoln and ex-wife of half-man Jeremy Brett.[1] Yesterday I had to do over again one of the drawings for the program—a good but endlessly tiresome old actress named Valerie Taylor.[2] She made an awful stink because Anthony wanted to use one of the drawings of her of which she didn't approve. She was so hysterical she swore she would leave the play if he insisted on using the drawing she'd vetoed. So little Kitty was sent into battle again, and battle it was. After doing another drawing it took nearly an hour to persuade the old bird that it was all that heaven allowed. I must say it was a small miracle of flattery and likeness, but she was so mad with vanity and

1. British actress Anna Massey (1937–2011) was the daughter of Canadian-born actor Raymond Massey (1896–1983), who played Abraham Lincoln so many times on Broadway, in Hollywood, and on T.V. that a fellow actor said Massey wouldn't be satisfied with his impersonation until someone assassinated him. Anna Massey's first husband from 1958 to 1962, Old Etonian actor Jeremy Brett (1933–1995), left her for a man, although he later married another woman.
2. (1902–1988).

silliness she couldn't see it. All she could think of was the envelope full of photographs of her, taken literally thirty-five years ago, which she'd brought to the sitting with her. Given a free hand she would have put one of *those* in the program.

The company leaves for Brighton on Saturday for the Monday night opening. I think I will go down on Sunday evening or Monday morning because I have a sitting with Keith Vaughan on Sunday afternoon. Patrick Procktor I've not seen since the second day I was here when he said, "Let's have breakfast, lunch and dinner every day." I called him the next afternoon and got told he was busy and never heard from him again. He is in for a little sobering talk before I leave this place.

I have not seen Tony again (he's been in the South of France most of the time) but did have a nice note from him in answer to a letter of praise I wrote him about *The Charge of the Light Brigade* which I really did like a lot and am anxious to see again, though I'm told it won't open in the U.S. until October. There may be a showing of Anthony's *Inadmissible Evidence* on Friday. I'm very curious to know if he knows anything about making movies. He's been offered by Paramount here a movie based on a French thriller called *Praying Mantis*.[3] He is allowed his choice of a screenwriter with whom he would work on the script. There is no script as of now. He mentioned you without any prompting. He hasn't even read the book yet but from what he's been told and what he's told to me it sounds like a highly contrived melodrama, involving two women and a man, with strong dykey undertones. But he is so caught up with the Osborne play that he can barely think of anything else for more than a few seconds at a time. Jill Bennett has started getting panicky and hysterical (hers really is a terribly long & difficult part and the whole weight of the play is on her) and she's beginning to crack a little. She's now blaming Osborne for the difficulty of the part, saying it's unplayable and calling him a shit pig—this from Anthony who spent last night with them. I had lunch with them on Sunday and there were no signs of stress then, but the screws on her are getting tighter every day. I do like her though, but I fear she may be no match for John.

3. Hubert Monteilhet's *Les Mantes religieuses* (1960), published in English as *The Praying Mantises* (1962).

The enclosed is a picture of a poor lost Tabby wandering the cold London streets (on tiptoe to avoid the cruel puddles), all glassy-eyed with loneliness.[4] If he were home in the Stables I hope his protecting Dubbin would never let him go around in such a dreadfully baggy suit. Oh he longs for his dear old Pony—I'm sure if he can only get back to him he'll never go wandering again. He thinks of his Dear Drub always and loves him so dearly. XXXXXXXX
Smallpaws

I will send a telegram next week about flight home.

P.S. Anthony has not yet read *The Praying Mantises* but still talks of asking you to do it. I think it's a lot of fairly boring nonsense about "really evil" people with lots of French-cynical psychology and endless ass-backwards contrivances thrown in for bad measure. But it still might make an amusing movie thriller. Simon & Schuster published it.[5] If Anthony does ask you to do it, a kitten might lend a paw if asked. That way the Animals could put their heads together out of the basket as well as in. But you might hate it and think it unworkable. Anyway, we'll see.

Furry.

4. Enclosure lost, but Bachardy wrote his P.S. on a separate half sheet to which he glued another picture of a pure-white kitten, printed opposite.
5. In the U.S.; in the U.K. it was Hamish Hamilton.

Only a desperately lonely kitten would be over at the foot of a woman!

[Autograph letter with glued-on addition]

Wednesday [May 15, 1968, London]

Dearest Plug—

It looks as though poor Cat is going to spend his birthday all alone. He'd *rather* be alone really if he can't be with his Dearnag. It's not only the theater drawings that are keeping me here, but they *are* being incredibly slow getting the program and poster done. They only just today showed me a sample of the reproduction process for the program they'd planned to use and thank goodness I stayed on to keep them from doing their worst. If I hadn't been here they would have gone ahead and used what they showed me today and honestly you could barely tell it was a drawing by me. It would have been disaster for the program—they wanted to use a straight black & white line reproduction instead of a grey half tone but I screamed and hollered sufficiently I think to discourage them. Their main reason quite naturally turns out to be a money one—the line reproduction is less than half the cost of the half tone. My argument was that they got the drawings for almost nothing (£25 for the lot!) so they can afford to spend a little something on making them look halfway decent in the program. I've almost definitely decided not to do drawings for the second play.[1] I'd hoped I might at least get started on them this week but then I found out that several of the cast are on holiday and won't be back in London till rehearsals start a week from Monday and that is too long to wait to get started, and too much work to do for only another £25. There are ten people in the cast.

1. *The Hotel in Amsterdam*, again by John Osborne, and again directed by Anthony Page, opening at the Royal Court on July 3.

I went to Brighton for the opening of the first play (*Time Present*) on Monday night. Everyone was moaning and groaning with dread and despair beforehand but the performance was actually a very good one. Everyone even knew their lines. And the audience too was a respectful one. Nobody left in the middle as they did when *Inadmissible Evidence* opened in Brighton. Which brings me to Anthony's film of same which, though good in many ways, is certainly not the work of a master.[2] It is at its worst terribly hit or miss, often confused and disorganized, weighted by much theatrical actory overacting and finally not building to any real climax. For me what I thought was the point of the play was, if not missed entirely, certainly somewhat bypassed. So much of the emphasis of the film seems in the wrong place. Anthony even makes in the last quarter of the film a fundamental error in style—he completely changes the point of view of the film. He shifts from the dilemma of the main character (Maitland) to the dilemma of a very subsidiary and inessential character (the queer who comes to Maitland for help) in such a way that, though the shift takes only a few minutes, when we get back to Maitland his life-mess seems insignificant compared to that of the queer. So much sympathy is lost for Maitland just as the film is ending, and it's all accidental and unnecessary and Anthony can't even see it, though I told him as tactfully as I could. All the queer stuff should go anyway— it's sentimental and heavy-handed. I'm afraid that though Anthony is as queer as you know whose hatband, he has the psychology of a bisexual and they (Tony R. comes to mind) are never a queer's best friend. Lots of crocodile tears but no real jism (spelling?), not on that score anyway.

Back to Brighton, the pavilion there is maybe one of the most depressing buildings I've ever been in in my life.[3] I finally took a look through while I was there. And finally took a look through the baths on Jermyn Street for the first time and what a waste of fifteen shillings. Lots of darting hot eyes but no *action*. After an hour and a half in there Kitty came out as pure as when he went in (and that's very pure indeed), only a lot damper.

Kitty also quite lost his head early this afternoon (it may be delirium

2. Page directed the 1964 Royal Court production of Osborne's earlier play *Inadmissible Evidence* and also the 1968 film adaptation.
3. That is, the Royal Pavilion, built 1787–1823 for the Prince Regent, later King George IV.

induced by oncoming birthdays) and bought a Helleu etching for £55 (already quite nicely framed) partly because it was so cheap and mostly because it is so beautiful—one of his glorious ladies in a big hat. The Casa is going to be brimming, what with that and the Keith Vaughan I am going to select on Sunday, which is my other reason for staying on past Saturday (Catday),[4] because he won't be back from Essex till then and it would look like I was skipping out of the country after just *saying* I wanted to buy one if I went before. I'm told he will probably sell me an oil painting for £90 or £100 which would be a real bargain. He said too I could pay on a time plan. I hope I can pick one that will please an Old Muzzle and make him not begrudge the loss of oats. Kitty loves his Old Dear and thinks of Him so much and pines for Him and is coming home to the Stables as soon as he can because there's no life for a kitten without his Horse.

XXXXX His loving and devoted Tabby.

[*Autograph letter with cuttings glued to each of three folios*]

Catday [May 18, 1968, London]

Dearest Hide—

Kitty was so glad to hear his dear Voice this morning. It cheered an old Cat very much and made it easier for him to bear the burden of the mounting years (no pun intended).

I am assured that I will have copies of the poster on Monday and the program on Tuesday. I don't know yet if I will stay on for the opening on Thursday. There seems no reason in the world why I should, having seen it several times already. But if I see that my leaving is going to be considered desertion, I will stay on for it and come back on Friday or Saturday. Kitty thinks now of nothing but the stable and his dear basket and his dearly loved companion.

Kitty treated himself to a delightful double bill on his birthday afternoon—Bergman in *Gaslight* and Stanwyck in *All I Desire* at the Waterloo Station Cinema—just a little furred thing sitting up alone in the dark with his bright eyes fastened on the screen. (Perhaps a wee bit of

4. That is, his birthday, May 18.

the brightness of his eyes was due to tears at the absence of his Hoofed Friend—how he would have loved to share the delights of Bergman and Stanwyck with Him.)

But Kitty will be home soon to stroke his Old Dear and soothe that bad old aching back. I will send a telegram with flight time, etc.

With basketfuls of catlove,

K.

P.S. Had a very nice evening with John G. and Martin on Thursday. Martin cooked. They were both very sweet. XXXXXXXX

♪ I'm dreaming of a White Stallion
He is the Only One I love
With those eyes that glisten
And ears that listen
To hear mewing from above ♪

[Autograph letter with autograph verse and glued-on cutting enclosed]

Wednesday [May 29, 1968, London]

Dearest Muzzle—

I have started in on the drawings for the second Osborne play (*The Hotel in Amsterdam*). Yesterday was the first day of rehearsals and I drew two of the actors. I'm going to see if I can't do them all in one go—one drawing each that is. Both drawings yesterday were first drawings and both quite adequate I think. John O. sits for me tomorrow morning at 11:30, at least two actors today and maybe three tomorrow which, if I'm lucky, will leave only two drawings for Friday. Doing Paul Scofield over without his beard may be a bit difficult (he still has the beard and must be persuaded to shave it for me) but I think it can be managed.[1] He is extremely charming and kind, so much so that it is worrying. But anyway we are on the best of terms, if only superficially, and I think that will be sufficient. Kitty's fierce determination to be with his Old Dear has turned him into a Supercat for whom no task is too difficult. No obstacle is insurmountable now. Anything that brings him closer to his Hide will be done with *alacrity*. Sunday I have set as the deadline for the doing of the drawings. And, they will be done.

Last night Kitty (alone as usual) slipped into the National Film Theatre to see D.W. Griffith's *Lady of the Pavements* with William Boyd (awful), Lupe Vélez and Jetta Goudal (sublime). The whole film is irresistible but Jetta Goudal especially was extraordinary. You would have loved it. Kitty kept thinking of his Dub and wished he were there with his great eyes watching and his muzzle moving rhythmically as he chomped on some delicious sweet.

Last week I saw the great Carl Dreyer's *Gertrud*, having seen only his Joan of Arc film and having heard for years of the greatness of the later films.[2] Well! It is so awful and amateur and silly that it would be perfect as an example of "what not to do if you are going to make a film." It contains practically every crime in the book. It is so appalling that it has its own fascination and I stayed right to the end.

Anthony's cleaning woman has just arrived which means I won't have a moment's peace for a good hour.

1. The British actor (1922–1986)—an international star after his Academy Award performance as Thomas More in *A Man for All Seasons* (1966)—was playing Laurie, the screenwriter character modelled on Osborne himself. Bachardy thought that Scofield delayed shaving his beard because he craved the excitement of changing his look at the moment when he transformed himself into his new character.
2. *The Passion of Joan of Arc* (1928), shot in France, is a silent film, like Griffiths's *Lady of the Pavements* (1929); *Gertrud* (1964) was the last film by Danish director Carl Theodor Dreyer (1889–1968).

I will cable or call at the weekend to let you know when I am coming. I plan to have the drawings photographed on Monday, get prints to the theater on Tuesday and leave on Wednesday. Will let you know definitely. Kitty's heart is already beating faster at the thought of seeing his Darling again. With endless furred love, Gatito

[*Autograph letter*]

John Osborne

[*Pencil and ink wash drawing by Don Bachardy; printed in program for* The Hotel in Amsterdam]

Paul Scofield

[Pencil and ink wash drawing by Don Bachardy; printed as program cover for The Hotel in Amsterdam]

Anthony Page

[*Pencil and ink wash drawing by Don Bachardy; printed in program for* The Hotel in Amsterdam]

•   •   •

Wednesday. [October 9, 1968] The Casa.

My darling Love,

I know I can't expect a letter for two or three more days at the earliest, but I will write this off—just a quick note—so Kitty will have at least a love-signal from Drub.[1]

Am going to see Robin this afternoon and give him Jim's copy of the play to read. Jim was talking about making a Xerox of it which I discouraged because it can only mean that it starts wandering from hand to hand. I don't think he will do it now—in fact I'm sure he won't without asking me again. Is there *anybody* here you think should see it?[2]

Then I'll go on to Vedanta Place and read, and see Swami, who's still a bit sick however. Then dash back to get some of *Strangelove*. And, if I stay up late, there's that absurd (I imagine) first picture with Tab Hunter I'd like to see a bit of, *Island of Desire*.[3]

Went to have supper with Gavin last night at La Grange. We got a table all right and bouillabaisse (?) which Gavin raved over but I just thought too rich. Gavin was quite confidential and told me that he would rather not live alone but has had such bad experiences with his mates that he is very very cagey about trying again. He really is a good friend to us both and loves us both, I feel. He maintains that his meditation makes all the difference to his life and also makes him much more energetic for work.

Leonard Barclay (?) called on your phone and wanted us/me to come and see *The Golden Fleece*.[4] Doubt if I shall. Am going to see *Niagara*

1. Bachardy flew to London on October 8 to stay with Anthony Page and to draw portraits for a new production of Osborne's *Look Back in Anger*, which Page was directing at the Royal Court.
2. The play was a stage adaptation of *A Meeting by the River* that Isherwood and Bachardy had drafted during July and August. Isherwood had earlier begun collaborating on the project with Jim Bridges, and Bridges, who read their script in September, was now interested in directing it.
3. *Dr. Strangelove* (1964) and Tab Hunter's 1952 debut film were playing on T.V.
4. Jered Barclay (b. 1930), American T.V. actor, was directing the world premiere of A.R. Gurney Jr.'s play, at the Mark Taper Forum.

Falls[5] on Monday afternoon, then have supper with Chris Wood. Shall go to the end of Jim's rehearsal tomorrow night and have late supper with him after.

I almost think I am getting properly started with the book![6] And I plug along at the Vedanta article for the encyclopaedia.[7] Yesterday I went on the beach and met old Jo, so I'll have to see her soon. Apparently Alice Gowland is making almost as much fuss as Jo does, and Peter is going to an analyst. I said, "Is he getting shots for adultery?" Jo thought this remark not in perfect taste, though she had to laugh.[8]

Am picking up the *Filmgoer's Companion* today if I have time, from Larry Edmunds. They are holding it for me. As for *The Pure and Impure*, Gavin lent it to me and I thought I'd read it first because it may not be worth buying for ourselves. So I won't buy it yet unless you want me to.[9]

No mail for you except a card from your folks in Hawaii. It shows the interior of a motel bedroom on Kauai!

Angel, I miss you so much I mustn't think about it. But I aim to keep very busy and indeed I have been on the go since breakfast. I ran on the beach yesterday, if you can call Dob's broken-down trot a run, and had meant to do it today, but it's getting late and it's so grey and sad. Almost as if it might start crying for Kitty.

Sweet wet kisses from its wet old mouth,

Naggin

XXXXXX

[Typed letter, signed]

---

5. Leonard Melfi's play, which Jim Bridges was directing.
6. *Kathleen and Frank.*
7. "Vedanta" in *Man, Magic and Myth: An Illustrated Encyclopaedia of the Supernatural* (1972), twenty-four volumes, edited by Richard Cavendish, issue 105, pp. 2930–2935.
8. Peter Gowland was also having an affair.
9. Larry Edmunds is a bookshop on Hollywood Boulevard. Farrar Straus published Herma Briffault's new English translation of Colette's *Le Pur et impur* (1932) with an introduction by Janet Flanner in 1967; the earlier translation was 1933.

Wednesday p.m. [October 9, 1968, London]

Dearest Rubble—

Old Kitty has arrived safely. The flight was uneventful and quite painless except for a 73-year-old Russianess from San Francisco in the window seat who was so bored and incapable of amusing herself by herself that she kept ruthlessly dragging Poor Kitty away from Joe's book. Nevertheless I've managed nearly to finish it and think it is amazing, very moving, sad but strangely not depressing, sometimes shocking and occasionally even irritating—but a wonderful, relentless, fiendish book. It makes me love Joe terribly in spite of longing to kick him quite often. He is such a surprising writer.[1]

Anthony is [. . .] in mid-rehearsal and terribly upset because Tony has not only stolen away Nicol Williamson (whom Anthony "discovered, created and made a star") by putting him into his Nabokov film in the Burton part, but also taken away the project dearest to Anthony's heart—a *Hamlet* production starring Williamson.[2] [. . .] Tony must be humming with delight. As soon as Anthony went off to rehearsal I left a message with Tony's secretary saying I was in town and hoping to see him—just to go on record right away as not being part of this stew. The fact that I left Anthony's number is bound to intrigue Tony and ensure our meeting.

Anthony now says he does not want drawings of the cast of *Look Back*, only a drawing of the actor playing Jimmy Porter (someone called Victor Henry[3]) for the poster and cover of the program. I am expected at rehearsal this afternoon to look him over. Then dinner with Jill Bennett after her performance in *Time Present*,[4] by which time I shall be pie-eyed. I tried to nap a bit just now but couldn't manage even a doze.

1. *My Father and Myself* by J.R. Ackerley, published in 1968, the year after Ackerley died.
2. Two weeks into filming his 1969 adaptation of Nabokov's novel, *Laughter in the Dark*, Tony Richardson fired Richard Burton for failing to keep to the shooting schedule and hired British actor Nicol Williamson (1936–2011) to replace him. Williamson had played the lawyer, Bill Maitland, in Page's *Inadmissible Evidence* at the Royal Court and in Page's film, and he had taken the role to New York where he was nominated for a Tony Award. Richardson went on to direct Williamson in *Hamlet* at the Roundhouse, where Williamson won a Drama Desk Award before transferring to New York. Williamson also starred in Richardson's 1969 film of *Hamlet* based on the Roundhouse production. See below, pp. 321 and 389.
3. British actor (1943–1985) who had a number of stage, T.V., and film roles, and died at only forty-two.
4. It transferred to the Duke of York's Theatre July 11.

Anthony says Jill and John are warring so I shall probably get that saga tonight.

I've called Marguerite who was still asleep and said to be not feeling well. She has not returned my call. David Hockney was very sweet and has invited me for Sunday. Peter was away at the Slade.[5]

Must leave for the rehearsal now.

I think Anthony rather dreaded my visit. I called him this morning, admittedly earlier than I said in my telegram (I got to the bus terminal at ten to eight, rang 15 times at 8 A.M. and got no answer, called back at 8:30 to get a very groggy Anthony on the line [. . .] not about to rush over to pick me up and even asked *me* to pick up a bottle of milk on my way over in a taxi.) Still, I managed to reassure him at breakfast that I'm only staying three weeks, was cheerful and gave him very good advice on how to cope with Tony. Kitty loves his Dear Hide so very very much. F.

[*Autograph letter*]

Saturday 12th [October, 1968], mourning   [Santa Monica]

Angel Paws,

Drub just hobbled up to the mailbox in red[1] and got his sweet letter. Now Drub has something new to worry about—on the radio yesterday they said there's a mail strike in England, so I wonder if his letter (written last Wednesday) has arrived or if this one will! If not we must phone.

To begin with a bit of tiresomeness, Michael Barrie wants to know if you would get a record for Gerald (he phoned about this this morning) MagnifiCAT by Pergolesi and Gloria by Vivaldi. London-Argo Z 505.[2] I realize now that he didn't say if it was monaural or stereo, so I guess better get mono. Chris Wood tried to get me to bother Kitty too—to buy a copy of Ackerley's book, but I bypassed that by writing direct to Heywood Hill and telling them to send Chris a copy airmail direct. It should arrive much quicker that way anyhow.

5. Where he had begun studying painting in September.

1. That is, in his much-worn red terry cloth robe.
2. Elizabeth Vaughan (soprano), Janet Baker (contralto), Ian Partridge (tenor), Christopher Keyte (bass); the Choir of King's College, Cambridge; Academy of St. Martin-in-the-Fields; Leader, Neville Marriner; directed by David Willcocks.

Your Polanski drawings got back, but only after Dobbin had called and issued an ultimatum.[3] He threatened to rear! I have also sent a recommendation for Ken Anderson for the Fulbright.[4]

The weather is sad. Dob forces himself to trot on the beach and is now quite stiff. The gym is nearly uninhabitable. That great floppity cunt is there almost always, and she *again* plunged into the men's room when it was full, sending John Tomassi[5] in first to get us to stay in the steam room! I am going to speak to John Wilkinson[6] as soon as he appears, but he doesn't. I shall ask him if she has bladder disease!

Both Nicholas Thompson *and* Bob Regester are here! Thompson asked about the play, so I told him we had done a draft but we didn't want to show it around until we had worked on it more. Of course he will find out that Robin is reading it; I can't help that. Anyhow he seems to be switching to being a literary agent. Bob was very friendly and full of gossip. He thinks Tony will remarry[7] (don't tell anyone he said this). Of course he feels Tony acted badly toward Anthony but he also feels very warm toward Tony at present. He seems to regard *Inadmissible Evidence* as a disaster. He talked a lot about *Meeting* (the novel) so I told him we had done a play, because even if you don't show it in England they are certain to know about it soon.

I also saw Steve Cooley, who seemed much more mature as a hairdresser and learning French. He really is very nice, quiet and good-natured and not trashy. I think he was slightly shocked by Dobbin's ruined appearance, after six years the last time we met.[8]

Still toiling at the first chapter of *Kathleen & Frank*. I would like to have that done to show you. Also this motherfucking Vedanta article.

---

3. Bachardy made three drawings of Roman Polanski in August, commissioned by Sharon Tate, who bought the second one. He loaned the drawings or reproductions of them to Polanski's agent or directly to *Variety* and *The Hollywood Reporter* because the same one Tate had chosen was also being used as a full-page ad. See below, p. 328.
4. Anderson studied art at UCLA and had studio space in Venice. Bachardy bought a drawing of his from a UCLA student show, later met him, and bought two more drawings and a painting. He was applying for postgraduate funding.
5. Aspiring writer friend; Isherwood was reading a manuscript for him.
6. A manager at Lyle Fox's gym, where Fox split each day into separate men's and women's sessions.
7. Richardson and Redgrave divorced in 1967. Afterwards Richardson had a long relationship with Grizelda Grimond, who is the mother of his third daughter, Katharine, born in 1973, but by his own account he met Grimond only in 1970 while working on *The Edible Woman*.
8. Steve Cooley (not his real name) was previously an aspiring actor. They had an affair in 1945 when Isherwood was working at Warner Brothers, where Cooley was then a messenger boy.

Also I have to read Trabuco Cliff's book on Vedanta,[9] and a chapter of Elsa's opus.[10] And then there is [Marguerite's companion] coming. So Drub feels rattled. He is being *very* good about drink.

A few drear hours ahead—Oldjo Hasntben, Sean & Sethfink,[11] Camillinda.[12]

How he loves his darling. Oh the sweetness of the thick ruff of fur where poor old Nag used to bury his muzzle in deepest lovesnooze! They have had to bring out blankets to stop his shivers. And now the moppets down below have another puppy which really squeals like a slate pencil.

Kitty now has three postcards from his parents in Hawaii. They return this evening. Am going to entertain Ted and Ted soon.[13]

Greetings to Anthony. And of course all the others according to taste and discretion. Oh yes and Swami sent his love. I had a long session with him Wednesday. Sarada had been to see him. It was a failure, she seemed mad and smelled bad.[14] Swami was very distressed because he felt she was terribly hungry so he sent for food—you can imagine Ananda's expression as she brought it![15]

Eternal Naglove—

XXXXXXXX

A card from David Burns in San Francisco, thank God.[16] No word from Paul Bowles, Tennessee, Michael & Henry.

[*Typed letter, signed*]

9. Clifford Johnson, also known as Bhuma, an English professor who was living as a brahmachari at Trabuco. He was managing editor of *Vedanta and the West* for some years. The book may have been *Vedanta, An Anthology of Hindu Scripture, Commentary and Poetry* (1971).
10. Elsa Lanchester had begun to work with a teacher and children's T.V. presenter, Ned Hoopes (1932–1984), on a biography of Charles Laughton; it was never published.
11. Michael Sean and Isherwood and Bachardy's neighbor in the house just below them, Seth Finkelstein.
12. Camilla Clay (d. 2000), American stage director, and her companion, American novelist, Linda Crawford (b. 1938); they were friends of Gavin Lambert, who introduced them to Isherwood and Bachardy.
13. Ted Bachardy and his boyfriend, Ted Cordes, who worked in publicity.
14. She had left the society in 1965, causing Swami great pain, married a few years later, and became a painter.
15. Pravrajika Anandaprana, Ramakrishna nun; she was a German-Jewish refugee, educated in England before she came to the U.S. during World War II. Her previous names were Ursula Bond and then Usha.
16. A persistent, crazy fan who came to the house uninvited and without telephoning ahead, sometimes left his luggage, and had his mail delivered to Isherwood and Bachardy's address because he was sleeping on the streets. He was jailed later that autumn, and confined to the Camarillo State Mental Hospital, but managed to get out by the end of the year. David Burns is not his real name.

[October 10, 1968, London]

Dearest Angelhorse—

Have just had lunch with Marguerite in Chester Square with John Craxton[1] and a couple of others (Joan Axelrod[2] was there for a drink). Marguerite is well and was very sweet. Sends you her love. Now she is talking of going, with or without [her companion], to Arizona to stay with Jimmy Davison. [Her companion] is travelling with 3 or 4 others which is why she doesn't want to go with him. He says he'd be afraid to drive my car. I don't think he will accept an offer of staying with you either, though I haven't mentioned it.

Dinner with Anthony & Jill last night (at Rule's) was nice. Kitty had steak and kidney pie. *Time Present* is closing in a week or two. Jill is wondering what she'll do. No offers have been made since she opened in the play.

Saw a rehearsal of *Look Back* yesterday. The actor playing Jimmy Porter is very homely and will be difficult to draw. Our sitting is supposed to be tomorrow morning. He and the actor playing Cliff are very good I think, but the women are poor.[3] The play itself seemed surprisingly good, very theatrical and sound and really about something. Am supposed to see a run-through now at which Osborne will be present.

Have spoken to Patrick Woodcock and he's invited me for Saturday. Don't know if I can go because Anthony has suggested an overnight trip to Dublin to see a play by a friend of his called Tom Murphy.[4] The play sounds awful and I'm not keen anyway to see Dublin. Still haven't been able to speak to Tony. Have told no one so far of the play and begin to feel that maybe I won't show it to anyone. I'm sure it's not worth showing it to Anthony—I doubt if he'd understand it.

His flat is [. . .] as usual and in my delayed-reaction, semi-depressed state of mind I fear sometimes I can't even cope with the effort of taking a bath. But I'm sure it's just part of not being accustomed to being here yet. Of course trying to meditate is a major feat—like a scene in a

1. British painter and stage designer (1922–2009).
2. American actress and interior designer (1922–2001), second wife of playwright George Axelrod (1922–2003), who wrote *The Seven Year Itch* (1952) and the screenplays for *Breakfast at Tiffany's* (1961) and *The Manchurian Candidate* (1962).
3. Martin Shaw (b. 1945) played Cliff. Jane Asher (b. 1946) played Jimmy Porter's wife, Alison Porter, and Caroline Mortimer (b. 1942) played his mistress, Helena. All three are British.
4. *The Orphans*, by Irish playwright Thomas Murphy (b. 1935), opened October 7 at the Gate Theatre in Dublin as part of the Dublin Theatre Festival.

farce[,] with Mrs. Potter, that tiresome woman from Bob Regester's flat (who sends you her greetings—she's substituting for Anthony's regular woman who has just had her gall bladder out) coming in in the middle. Bob Regester left on Monday for N.Y. and will be away almost until I leave. Supposed to have tea with David & Peter today.

Miss my old darling and think of him so much. All of a cat's love. XXXXX

Tabby.

[*Autograph letter inside a birthday card bearing a color photograph of a kitten*]

October 14. [1968] 145 Animal Avenue

Beloved Fluffpuss,

Monday morning and here is a second letter from Fur with such a *darling* portrait.[1] (By the same mail a card from David Burns in San Francisco with a white puss on it rather grandly but wistfully ignoring a pink carnation.) And Dorothy announced she'd had a dream Marguerite was coming here, not knowing what you'd said in your letter or that [her companion] was coming!

I do rather hope you *will* show the play to Tony (and Anthony too for that matter) because I am so curious for an opinion, even an unfavorable one. But this is entirely up to you of course, and I won't show the play to anyone else. (Have heard nothing from Robin yet.) If you aren't showing the play, I'm sorry I told Bob Regester about it—not that it matters in the least, nobody is *that* interested and unless they actually see the play they'll forget all about it very soon. In bed this morning I had a thought: should we have at least one speech in which Patrick says *sincerely* how he is feeling, his doubts, fears etc.? Or is that wrong? Think this over, please. Gavin and I went yesterday to Varda's show (where Gavin bought a Varda for $800!)[2] and to the gruesome rally for the Chicago police victims at Burt Lancaster's house.[3] The house is of an incredible vulgar

1. Enclosure lost.
2. Jean Varda (1893–1971), Turkish-born Greek painter and collage artist living and working in California.
3. Nearly 600 protestors were arrested and 100 injured, some beaten severely, in violence between antiwar demonstrators and Mayor Richard Daley's police outside the Democratic convention in Chicago, August 26 to 29. Film star Burt Lancaster (1913–1994) outspokenly

spacious deadpan emptiness with buckets of artificial flowers hanging from chains like in a torture chamber, and the worst obtainable (genuine) Impressionists hanging beside local Jewish daubs (very *strong*). Neither Burt nor Paul Newman showed but Hope did and Don Murray. The one speech by an actual boy who'd been there was truly shocking, however; the police seem to have been let loose deliberately, like Attila telling his men they could loot the town—*exactly* like storm troopers but less disciplined. Most of the crowd only wanted to see the stars however, and a couple of fucking politicians who spoke were just using the Chicago scandal to get votes for themselves . . . I felt like the "Ah, love, let us be true . . ." part of Matthew Arnold's "Dover Beach"—the world is so disgusting sometimes. But courage! Today *Niagara Falls* & Chris Wood. Tomorrow Elsa and Hoopes & their book to be discussed. Wednesday Larry Holt[4] & Swami. Am keeping on with my book & the Vedanta article. Yesterday I actually went in the ocean but the weather is so half-assed. Maybe this rain will clear it. Maybe it's waiting to welcome Kitty home. Love him so.

Hope he doesn't forget his old Trot XXXXX

This is my third letter. Is it true that there's a mail strike?

[*Autograph letter*]

October 11, [1968, London]

Adored Hide—

Kitty had tea with David and Peter yesterday in the sumptuous, newly and completely redecorated Hockney studio. My breath was almost literally taken away by the transformation. I had consciously to check my praise, realizing I was making the place as it was when I stayed in it sound like the sty that it most certainly was. And it is now so *neat*. Peter is really making his presence known and quite visibly too. They could not have been more adorable, real almost Animal-like sweetness. I felt great affection and happiness between them and from them. In his

---

opposed the Vietnam War and had campaigned for peace candidate Eugene McCarthy during the Democratic primaries.

4. Dr. Hillary Holt, a Hollywood devotee of German or Austrian background.

studio David had the painting of us on which he is still working. After the preparation provided by you and Anthony, I was not at all horrified by the likeness of me, which really does seem quite a likeness now. I think he's been working on it since either of you saw it. In fact, the figure of me is in grave danger of being *over*worked. Otherwise I very much like the painting. Peter has started at the Slade, likes it but is not overwhelmed by enthusiasm. He says he just goes and draws. I am seeing them again on Sat. Robert Medley is giving a party. Anthony is very possibly going to Dublin to see a production of a play by a friend of his (Tom Murphy) at the festival there on Sat. I don't think I will go, not wanting to get onto a plane again so soon and preferring the Medley party to Dublin. Anthony, if he goes, will be back on Sun. for dinner with David & Peter who are cooking.

I am up early this morning to say my prayers and call Tony and go off to the theater for an early sitting with Victor Henry (Jimmy Porter). Anthony is still in bed. Tony, who can only be reached at this hour apparently, was very friendly and invited me for a drink on Sun. but I must call first. I asked if I could see any of his new film[1] and he said "maybe later." He is post-syncing now. I still have not mentioned the play to anyone. Kate Moffat had asked Marguerite for my number here so maybe they are not cross with me. Anyway I have called them and left a message. Must fly out now. I think so much of my Old Dear in his stall. Please keep him well. XXXXXX His devoted Tabby.

[*Autograph letter*]

Tuesday Oct. 15 [1968]   [Santa Monica]

Treasured Flufftail,

[A]nother dear pussogram arrived this morning. Drub could hardly believe such good fortune. And to think that Puss finds time in the midst of his quick dartings to remember that loving anxious old plug away there in his western stable, that makes plug very happy.

Am so glad that David and Peter are so happy and nice. I take it that our portrait hasn't been sold to the Tate? Do they have any idea where it

1. That is, *Laughter in the Dark.*

will land up? Hope it'll be in London, at any rate I don't want to have to make a pilgrimage to some obscure provincial gallery.

Yesterday it rained and today it is beautiful but windy and cold. Yesterday afternoon I went to the Mark Taper for the dress rehearsal of *Niagara Falls*. It really went very well, and Jim says the opening last night was definitely good. The actress you liked,[1] and Billy[2] were the best. I still think, and indeed so does Jim, that the boy who played the Marine in his play has something, when he walks on stage you know it.[3] Kathy[4] was quite good though awful loud. Of course that slow dying presents an almost insoluble problem, so hard to make it keep going and at the same time jump from person to person and group to group without letting the others interrupt and get the audience's attention away. Jim certainly did a very good job, he is really gifted as a director I feel. But he is terribly lacking in confidence and scared. After the opening it seems there was a real fight with the critics ([they] all showed up although they won't write anything about any of these Monday night shows, by arrangement). Melfi the author got practically ready for fists, and Jim just went away and lay down somewhere and pretended to be asleep. In fact, it seems Jack actually got in the act, though it was certainly none of his business, and made one of his declarations of art.

Nothing from Robin French. I called him and he didn't call back so I suspect he hasn't read the play and is guilty. Fuck him. But really, love, I now am *certain* that it is good, not only intrinsically but even as it stands, and I don't care, I feel just as I usually do about my books, *somebody* will like it and it will be performed somehow. So let us risk a little disapproval. All this is *not* to say you should show it in England if instinct tells you not to. Do exactly what *you* think. But don't ever have doubts about the play in itself.

This afternoon I am going to see Elsa and Hoopes about their book. They have produced a specimen chapter, in which the material from the taped interviews is "presented" mostly in a quite unnecessary journalistic way. "'Charles taught me everything,' says Shelley Winters,

1. Barbara Minkus (b. 1942).
2. William Gray (b. 1938), famous as teenage son "Bud" on the T.V. series "Father Knows Best" (1954–1963).
3. Paul Gleason (1939–2006), American T.V. actor who appeared in a few films, had been the Marine in Bridges's one-act play *Rehearsal of Sterling Underhill*, staged with two other one-act plays at UCLA, and he now had a role in *Niagara Falls*.
4. Kathleen Nolan (b. 1933), American actress, mostly on T.V.

drawing her Chinese robe about her and dipping greedily into the candy box . . ." That's not a real quote, but it's how it is, exactly. He has such a vulgar little mind. Shall point this out, but tactfully.

Last night I had supper with Chris Wood who seems pretty sad. He says Paul[5] insists on staying in New York all winter and until next June, and he misses him terribly but can't go there or go away except for weekends anywhere as long as Gerald is alive. And Gerald is certainly brightening up again. He really talked more than ever yesterday and you could understand him. I don't feel Michael quite likes me to see this, it spoils the deathbed atmosphere.

Now I am going to the gym, resolved to be a good little Vedantist and see if I can't relax toward that cunt, because it isn't her fault that she makes me sick. The funny thing is that Bob Regester (whom I may or may not see again, if I do it will be only a quick stop-by at Mel Carney's where he's staying[6]) told me an identical story of how he had been enraged because they brought some women into his gym in London, something to do with television, and how he came out stark naked and refused to put on his clothes until he was good and ready and the ladies had screamed but the gym manager could do nothing because he was in the wrong. Bob is really even more aggressive than I am. And where does it get one really?

Angel Love, I had such a terrifically vivid dream of you this morning, at exactly seven. You were absolutely *there*, but at the same time I knew you weren't, you were sort of sliding away from me. It was terribly painful and you didn't really want to go, but then I woke up . . . Don't ever slide away from old Brumby, because his Kitty is his all.

D. XXXXXXXX

[*Typed letter, initialled*]

5. Paul Sorel (b. 1918), American painter, born Karl Dibble. He and Wood lived together in the early 1940s, and Wood supported him thereafter.
6. Mel Carney (d. 2001), Chicago-born, Princeton-educated banker and aspiring writer, settled in Beverly Hills.

Saturday. [October 12, 1968, London]

Dearest Nag—

The enclosed item about Sybille Bedford is from yesterday's *Times*.[1] The Wilson review of Joe's book I had taken off by mistake[2]—I think it's a nasty, petty put-down by someone who knows who his betters are and hates them for it. Dreadful little man. I love Joe's book. I finished it today. Overwhelmingly bleak and sad finally—Joe's obstinate self-indulgence and fanatical self-criticism. And then to be made happy at last by his dog. It's heart-rending. It makes me cry horribly just to think of it. Such genuine and yet senseless suffering by someone who had so much and apparently nothing at the same time.

Am now reading one of Jean Rhys's books, *Good Morning, Midnight*, the writer Gavin was telling us about, who's also written a book about Rochester's wife (*Wide Sargasso Sea*). Coincidentally Anthony is very impressed by her, even I think would like to make one day a film based on the book I'm reading now, though he says he would have to be a very much better established movie director than he is now. I don't yet see an interesting film in it. She writes quite well (with affectation though—largely in her resonating repetitions) but so far little of real interest and lots of self-pity and self-indulgence of a much lower order than Joe's. I doubt if I will get much beyond the first seventy pages I've read. I think I will try the *Sargasso Sea* which is a much later book. *Good Morning, Midnight* was written in 1939. I see so clearly why Gavin likes her. She's an intensely feminine writer, natch.

1. *The Times* "Diary," Oct. 11, p. 10, announced that German-born English writer Sybille Bedford (1911–2006) had become Aldous Huxley's official biographer: "'I myself suggested Christopher Isherwood but he didn't want to undertake it,' she says."
2. Angus Wilson's review of *My Father and Myself* appeared in *The Observer*, September 22, 1968, p. 30, and it also mentioned Isherwood: "Indeed, it seems to me that the line of ironic mockery runs from Samuel Butler through E.M. Forster, a close friend of Ackerley's, to Ackerley himself and Christopher Isherwood. It is a powerful, important stream of English literary thought, rejecting first Victorian institutions and Victorian Christianity, then questioning all family life because of its hidden economic foundations, finally in Ackerley and Isherwood standing back in self-accusation from the mockery itself. Central to it is the idea—essential to all 'Bloomsbury' thought—of rescuing personal relationships, above all sexual love, from all falsities and hypocrisies, especially from hidden bourgeois entanglements of money, and establishing them in some hoped-for pristine honesty that would irradiate life." Bachardy probably received the review in the post from London, stuck it inside his copy of Ackerley's book, and took it back to London by mistake without showing it to Isherwood.

Anthony has gone to Dublin to see this play by his friend which is reviewed in today's *Times*. Very bad review. I've been invited to a party at Robert Medley's tonight starting at nine. David & Peter are going. I have spent the whole day in bed reading and feel disinclined to make the effort to get myself out but probably will.

I drew the Jimmy Porter actor yesterday. He looks, at 25, like a slightly more male Judith Anderson[3] and you will know what that means. He moved a lot and talked endless, total shit, complete with his opinions of the unfortunate lot of the homosexual. I don't even think it was for my benefit because on the tube last night I found an *Evening Standard* with an interview of him which contained most of the same stuff he'd given me, including the homosexual line. Because I was in a turned-on drawing mood I did one very good drawing of him, far too accurate for the purpose I'm afraid, but it's good and fiendishly like him. Anthony hasn't seen it yet. [. . .] We've spent little time by ourselves. My Sun. meeting with Tony is put off till Tues. David & Peter tomorrow night & Buckle on Mon. As I half-expected, I've lost confidence in showing *MbyR*[4] to anyone with my name on it. More later.

Kitty misses his Old Warm Rump. With pink kisses,

Whiskers.

[*Autograph letter*]

October 16 [1968]   [Santa Monica]

Darling Whitewhiskers,

[A]nother dear pawscript arrived this morning, so I hope the strike never happened and that you are getting my letters too. I have answered every one of yours.

Yes, Angus's review is full of his peculiar awfulness, such a dainty little governess presiding over the class and rapping the pupils' fingers. I'm sure Joe would have been overwhelmed to know that he had made Miss Wilson "sad"! Incidentally, the copy which I ordered for Chris Wood from Heywood Hill has already reached him, so he is happy and

3. Australian-born dramatic star on Broadway (1898–1992), known for her role as the housekeeper, Mrs. Danvers, in Hitchcock's *Rebecca* (1940); a longtime friend of Isherwood.
4. That is, the play script of *A Meeting by the River*.

no doubt it will also be read aloud to Gerald, rather wincingly, by Jack Jones! I'd love to be there when he gets to the sex confessions at the end!

Am a bit worried to hear that Kitty spent the day in bed. Not that a real rest isn't good for those frisking creatures from time to time, and Dr. Dobbin would certainly approve, but it sounds so unlike Kitty with his demonic energy that I fear he may be sick and not telling Dub about it?

Robin French called this morning and really carried on wildly about the play, said it was "perfect" and was particularly impressed by the idea of using the Cubes.[1] He said he had imagined that we should somehow do a straightforward conventional stage version of the novel but that now he realized that would have been impossible and that he thought this stylization exactly right. He asked me to be sure and congratulate you. All of which is fine, but the question still remains, how is the play going to get performed? Robin says he'll think about this. I do wish we had someone who had real initiative plus know-how in these matters.

Love, you say you will tell me more about your feelings with regard to showing the play with your name on it. I suppose you mean, just in England? Well, I can't argue with you until I hear what you say. But I do think we are going to have to take some sort of plunge, at least as soon as you get back here. As I said yesterday, this time I have real confidence, not just fuck-them confidence but confidence that the play will actually be liked, at any rate by some of the people some of the time. But, I repeat, if you decide not to show it or admit to anyone that you have a copy with you, that's entirely up to you. It certainly can't do any harm. And I do believe in Kitty's hunches.

Saw Elsa and Ned Hoopes last night and took them through a sort of interview on tape, asking them how they got the idea for writing the book etc. They want to use some of this by way of preface. It was interesting because Elsa began a long confession (which she said she had never made before) about how she had hated Charles, chiefly for marrying her without telling her he was queer, and then she claimed that he had told Paul Gregory[2] she'd refused to have children, because

---

1. Each character was to work inside an individual cube, either a minimalist abstract prop or a lighting effect, to enhance the suggestion of psychological isolation. (Bachardy recalls that he and Isherwood were vaguely relieved when they were eventually persuaded to abandon the cubes.)
2. American film, T.V., and theater producer (b. 1920); he began managing Laughton in 1950 after a small acting career of his own, and arranged tours, T.V., stage, and film productions for which Laughton acted, directed, and sometimes wrote material.

she was afraid to. Which is ridiculous, says Elsa, she would gladly have had children but not with Charles because he wouldn't have been possible as a father. Why wouldn't he? Because he ate shit. But then Elsa admitted that she didn't really know this, it was only hearsay. I said, it's the sort of accusation that rather *sticks* to one, doesn't it? (Privately I really begin to think that Elsa herself must have a thing about shit, she harps on it so!) Anyhow, all this confession was delivered in a rather marvellous gentle all-passion-spent voice, like Madame X. testifying in court.[3] I wish you could hear the tape. Later we had excellent roast beef, and Elsa once again went into her thing about how much she admired your painting (at your last show). Today the weather really is warm and not much wind so am going on beach to trot old Brumble. Have now risen above the cunt at the gym and decided she is really a very stupid moo-cow who might even be trained to give Kitty cream. She wallows on the floor like a cow resting. And then she did facial isometrics which was almost endearing because she looked exactly like Bill Van Petten![4] Her mouth got right over one ear!

Loves his darling Pinkmouth so and loves to hear from him. I guess [Marguerite's companion] will be calling me on Friday? Well, roll on the week after next! XXXXXXXX Hoof

[*Typed letter, signed*]

Sunday [October 13, 1968, London]

Treasure Pony—

To my surprise I have finished *Good Morning, Midnight.* Don't like it much, I guess because I really don't get it. Seems to me intensely feminine in a derogatory sense, trivial and both intentionally and unintentionally meaningless—so that I feel I just may have missed the whole point, though I doubt it. Anyway, neither she nor it are my bag! She writes well though and is even funny sometimes in quite a genuine, unexpected way. Her tone of voice is very good and convincing. I'm

3. At her murder trial, when she is defended by a young lawyer who doesn't know she is his mother. The role in Alexandre Bisson's play *Madame X* was first played by Sarah Bernhardt in 1910, often revived, and filmed more than half a dozen times with as many stars.
4. William Van Petten (d. mid-1980s), a reporter for the *Los Angeles Times* and other smaller local papers. His face and eyes had been damaged by radiation treatment for cancer.

curious to know what you'll make of her. I doubt very much that you would like this one anyway. Where Anthony sees a movie in it I can't imagine. It makes me wonder seriously about his "nose," which also *doesn't* smell a movie in *The World in the Evening.* He has read it all, he says, and though praising it, has shown no indications of interest in a movie of it. Oddly enough the part about the Quakers and the character of Aunt Sarah seemed to have made the strongest impression on him.

He is back from Dublin and taking a nap in the next room.

Monday.

Anthony woke up in the middle of this letter. [. . .] I often find myself just standing around, waiting for sometimes I don't even know what. But he has gone off to the theater now and peace and calm have descended. Except this morning is Mrs. Moss's day (she's the cleaning woman) and though she is out now shopping, her little boy is in the next room. She brought him along because he's sick today—some kind of pain around his ribs. He's about 12 and quite sweet and quiet. But still he's there and complete peace is postponed.

Robert Medley's party on Sat. was big, mixed and tedious, largely I think because I wasn't in much of a party mood. My mood was not improved by being introduced around by Robert as "Christopher Isherwood's friend." David & Peter were there, and Arthur Lambert & Larry Stanton (both of whom I dread—they also came in after dinner at David & Peter's last night).[1] Also at D. & P.'s were Jim Dine & his wife,[2] also Henry Geldzahler[3] and various fringers of the art world. Too many people but still D. & P. create a cozy relaxed atmosphere. It turned out to be a kind of inauguration party of the pleasure dome—all the decorating

1. In fact, they were staying at Hockney's. Lambert, once a Washington banker, managed a Los Angeles company that ran telephone answering services. In Los Angeles, Hockney was often at his house near La Cienega Boulevard. Stanton, an American painter (1947–1984) noted for his beauty, was still a student and had been studying painting and drawing in New York and then in Los Angeles, where he lived with Lambert.

2. American painter, graphic artist, sculptor (b. 1913), identified with the pop art movement from its inception. He lived and worked in London from 1967 to 1971 with his wife Nancy Minto and three young sons.

3. American art historian and curator (1934–1994). He zealously promoted contemporary artists, supervising the creation of the Department of Twentieth Century Art at the Metropolitan Museum of Art and serving as the first director of the Visual Arts Program at the National Endowment for the Humanities, where he was responsible for grants to young artists. He was also a frequent Hockney subject, and he was staying with Hockney.

is only just finished, in fact still in progress. Richard Buckle tonight. Old Fur thinks so much of his dear Basket Mate and misses him. Please take good care of that Sweet Hide that Kitty loves so. XXXXX K.

[*Autograph letter*]

Thursday Oct. 17 [1968]   [Santa Monica]

Basket Jewel,

I fear my letter of yesterday went off late, so maybe you will get none and then two together. It is suddenly very hot and still, with a murderous smog in town, I imagine. The bug destroyers have just fixed an enormous tent, striped white and green, over the house where the woman lives below us who once told us to "live with our neighbors" or whatever, because of that poodle. As a matter of fact, touch wood, the squealing puppy hasn't been heard from, yesterday and this morning, or maybe it has lost its squeal and now only barks occasionally.

I saw Swami last night and he sent you his love. He said (during the reading) that he has been thinking a lot lately of Shankara's saying that we must *not* say we are in bondage, we must say we are free.[1] Ananda was being terribly bossy about the new heating system which is required for the temple, they are so afraid they will be cold during Kali puja on Monday. When Swami refuses to make a snap decision she rolls her eyes in heavenward patience and sweetly says well, we must all wait until you tell us what to do, but meanwhile Yogini[2] has been up late three nights getting the books ready for the general meeting which would have been unnecessary if we'd known that the meeting would be postponed etc. etc. etc. No wonder Vidya fled the country![3]

1. See *Shankara's Crest-Jewel of Discrimination*, translated with an introduction to Shankara's philosophy by Swami Prabhavananda and Christopher Isherwood (1947), p. 127. But perhaps Swami meant Ramakrishna, who said: ". . . by repeating with grit and determination, 'I am not bound, I am free,' one really becomes so—one really becomes free," in the *Gospel of Sri Ramakrishna*, p. 138.
2. American Ramakrishna nun, a disciple of Prabhavananda since World War II. She was later called Yogaprana.
3. In 1966, Swami Vidyatmananda transferred to the Centre Védantique Ramakrichna in Gretz, France, partly because he objected to the fact that Prabhavananda had initiated so many women and allowed them to live alongside the men in the Hollywood center. In India, only men could join the Ramakrishna Order; women joined the separate Sarada Order.

From there I went on to Mel Carney's because I hadn't seen him the time before, when I saw Bob Regester, and it seemed rude not to. Bob was still there and several other aging cronies who I am supposed to know, and don't. Bob was carrying on like crazy about the beauties of *Good Morning, Midnight* and how everybody but everybody in England thinks it is the greatest. He also said that Tony and Neil are leaving at the weekend for Italy and then Australia (Italy because Tony is going to redo the two Graves Claudius books, and Australia because of *Ned Kelly*, but you doubtless know all this).[4] So I hope you'll see Tony before he leaves, though I understand now more than ever that this probably wouldn't be at all the moment to show him the play.

Meanwhile George Schaefer has popped up again and Ray Henderson is apparently to write the song for "Christmas Carol" at once, because Rex *still* hasn't signed and won't till he gets the song.[5] I really begin to feel that Rex doesn't mean to do it, but George swears Rex really wants to. What with the arrival of [Marguerite's companion] and having to discuss the contents of the song with Ray and George, and interviewing my would-be BBC television interviewer, Derek Hart, to see if I finally decide to do the interview or not,[6] this weekend promises to be busy. I am pushing on with the Vedanta article and my book by sheer brute force but I do long for some uninterrupted days. I even grudge having to go on the beach, but I feel I must as long as the weather is like this.

Kitty doesn't sound to me as if he is having much fun, I'm afraid. I hope I'm wrong about this? Of course I know the doubleness of Kitty's attitude toward parties because it is much like Dobbin's. Imagine Medley saying that about your being C.I.'s friend. That's the side of the world I hate most, I think, more than its so-called cruelty—this brutal thick-skinned don't-care tactless stupidity. I could thrash it—and of course I do exactly the same thing myself.

---

4. Richardson was considering how to recreate ancient Rome for a proposed film of Robert Graves's *I, Claudius* and *Claudius, the God*. Isherwood and Bachardy were among those who later worked on scripts, but the film was never made. Richardson's trip to Australia, reconnoitring for a film about the Australian outlaw Ned Kelly, did result in a 1970 film, starring Mick Jagger.

5. Schaefer, an American director and producer (1920–1997), was proposed to direct a T.V. film of Charles Dickens's *A Christmas Carol*. Isherwood wrote the script during the first half of 1968. Rex Harrison was considering the lead.

6. "Christopher Isherwood—Born Foreigner" (1969), a fifty-minute documentary about his life and work. It was first broadcast as an "Omnibus" program on November 2, 1969.

Gavin is going with Camilla and Linda tonight to see *The Golden Fleece* and *Muzeeka*.[7] They asked me and I accepted and then backed out, I just plain old didn't want to. Now I'm seeing them separately. Thinks of his Darling all the time, the constant dialogue with him goes on, what would he say to this or that, how would he react. Breakfast seems not worth fixing and even the few steps to the deck are a drag, but Dobbin has great style and appears because, after all, we belong to Our People and seeing that life goes on in the Casa helps them so much in the miserable existences they lead in their squalid huts.

Be very very careful, Angel, and don't get some dull London marsh-fever or loathsome dirt-rash. Are you going to see Rosamond Lehmann? I know you will be wonderful about me and her book. But, who knows, silence is so often best.[8]

the love of an old old old draggin naggin

XXXXXXXXXXX

[*Typed letter with autograph additions*]

Tuesday [October 15, 1968, London]

Darling Drubble—

Two very dear letters from his Old Hide to gladden Londoncat, who will see about the records for Gerald and could easily have seen about the Ackerley book for Chris, too.

A very pleasant evening with Richard Buckle last night who took me in a cab all the way to Croydon to see a ballet company called Western Theatre Ballet. They were premiering a new work called *The Throne* about a jester who takes the place of his dying king, very sentimental and muggy. The company itself though is very good I think and Richard is in the difficult position of wanting to encourage them and yet hating this particular work.[1]

7. *Muzeeka* by John Guare, directed by Ed Parone, was on at the Mark Taper Forum with the Gurney play Jered Barclay was directing.
8. *The Swan in the Evening: Fragments of an Inner Life* (1967), her account of her continuing spiritual relationship with her daughter, Sally, who died of polio aged twenty-four in 1958. Bachardy brought a copy from London, so Isherwood had read it, but he didn't like it.

1. The company was founded in 1957 by Elizabeth West and Peter Darrell; they moved to Glasgow and became, in 1969, the Scottish Theatre Ballet and then, in 1974, the Scottish Ballet.

Richard was extremely sweet and affectionate, more so than I've ever known him. Ever since Drub's kindness to him in California he's been so much nicer to Old Stray. His hair is very long now, so are his sideburns—down to the jawline in fact. Oddly enough he manages to carry it off quite well—the only person of his age I know of who can. He is full of invitations to the country but, embarrassing for me, he lives very near Cecil in Wiltshire and sees Cecil constantly because he is designing a huge exhibition of Cecil's photographs at the National Portrait Gallery. The NPG has asked Cecil to donate a selection of his photographs of famous people and in return is paying for this exhibition which is going to be huge and very elaborate and include a picture of a certain Ponyfriend of Kitty's, though which picture I don't know—Richard's description was too vague.[2] I don't want to tell Richard I don't want to see Cecil because that would make too big a thing out of it. I'm not cross with Cecil even, I just want to avoid seeing him. To tell Richard my reasons would make such a situation of minor drama. And I am rather ashamed of my reasons for not wanting to see Cecil. I feel I could only tell them to Cecil himself.[3] Luckily the exhibition opens a few days after I leave, though I can't help regretting not being able to see the show itself.

Lunch tomorrow with Joan Axelrod who I saw the other day at Marguerite's. The woman who owns the house they are living in has seen my drawings of them and wants to be drawn herself, so Joan is bringing us together.[4] Then, if Anthony can get tickets for *Hair* we are going with David and Peter.

Snowpaws misses his Dear Muzzle and thinks of him so much and loves him more than anything. He worries about him and hopes his supply of oats and straw and carrots lasts till a Kitten's return. With baskets of pure Catlove. Fur Angelico XXXXXX

[*Autograph letter*]

2. "Beaton Portraits: 1928–68" ran from October 30 to the end of February 1969, attracting huge press attention and attended by 80,000. It included a small portrait of Isherwood, see below, p. 355.
3. Beaton had been a close and supportive friend of Bachardy and assisted him in his career as a portrait painter, but in his 1964 book, *Cecil Beaton's Fair Lady*, about making the film, he wrote in effusive detail about intimate evenings spent "once a week" at home with Isherwood, as if Isherwood lived alone (pp. 111–112). Bachardy, who was always there and usually did the cooking, refused to see Beaton again and never allowed him back into their house, although he made no objection to Isherwood seeing Beaton elsewhere. Beaton never once at later meetings asked Isherwood, "Where's Don?"
4. A Mrs. James, see below pp. 323, 327, 341.

Wednesday. [October 16, 1968, London]

Dearest Treasured Trot—

His third adorable missile arrived this morning, hoofwritten with that aching hoof, the thought of which makes Kitty wince for his Old Darling. Such a demonstration of devotion brings tears into those great eyes of Kitty's.

My first reaction to the idea of a sincere speech from Patrick is that it would be out of character, and anyway tell the audience in an underlining way something they ought already [to] know or at least have guessed. I fear it might be too on the nose. Does Patrick really know or allow himself to know what he sincerely thinks? It seems to me to be a contradiction of his carefully established personality, but maybe for that very reason it's good. I will think more about it.

I saw Tony last night and told him about the play. Though he was interested and thought it a good idea and was impressed by all the work you've been doing lately, he did *not* ask to read the play. Should I ask him to read it? Let me know what you think. He was very friendly and amazingly relaxed and communicative. He said he would maybe let me see a showing of his Nabokov film on Tuesday. He is pleased with it though he says it *can't* make money or be popular because it is so black and uncompromising. Nicol Williamson he says is wonderful in it. Tony is now planning a film of *I, Claudius* with Williamson and is going to do at last a Ned Kelly film based largely on a script by John Arden written years ago for Karel Reisz, and rejected by him in favor of a script by David (*Radcliffe, Sporting Life*) Storey which Tony says is dreadful.[1] But before either film is the stage production of *Hamlet* which Tony says he has "always wanted to do." He still thinks movies are much more fun and wouldn't be returning to the theater except to do something he's dreamed of doing *always*. And Nicol he says is "ideal" casting.

I suspect that part of the reason for Tony's warm and private reception

---

1. Karel Reisz was inspired, like Tony Richardson, by Melbourne artist Sidney Nolan's paintings of Ned Kelly, which were exhibited in London in the early 1960s, and he planned to make a film about Ned Kelly starring Albert Finney. British playwright and novelist John Arden (1930–2012) first drafted a script in 1962. British novelist David Storey (b. 1933) may have written his Ned Kelly script for director Lindsay Anderson with whom Storey adapted his first novel *This Sporting Life* (1960) as a film, mentioned above. *Radcliffe* (1963) was Storey's third novel. Richardson later wrote his own Ned Kelly script with Ian Jones (b. 1931), an Australian writer specializing in Ned Kelly.

for me might have been his expectation that I was bringing some kind of message from Anthony or some inside gossip about Anthony's agonies. I said nothing and the only reference Tony made to the affair was right at the end of our interview when I said I was going to *Hair* with David & Peter (*both* of whom Tony is very fond [of]). Knowing full well that Anthony would probably be with us, Tony said why didn't we all come round after—as long as we didn't bring Anthony. I told him Anthony was indeed coming. "Well," said Tony, and even he himself was unable to resist laughing slightly, "I won't have him in the house." Very typically Tony has, I can see, decided that it is *he* who has been misused and betrayed by Anthony.

Tony says, though *The Charge of the L.B.* is doing quite well, it *can't* make back its cost. Notices in N.Y. have been mixed—raves, pans and in-betweens. Vanessa (see enclosure) is demonstrating again after a long series of films one right after the other. She liked doing *The Sea Gull* and predictably has made a great friend of Signoret who's also in it. Before that she did an Italian film with Franco Nero [. . .]. Tony says it's a disaster—she even plays an Italian in it, is very miscast to say the least and was very unhappy while doing it. Before that was *Isadora* which Tony hasn't seen yet, he says. He "hears" Vanessa is wonderful in it but that Karel Reisz has characteristically turned Isadora into a troubled introvert, as he had wanted to do to Ned Kelly.[2]

No word from Tony of his forthcoming marriage, but then I didn't expect there would be. There is maybe going to be a male evening tomorrow night to which I'll be invited if it happens. I think I am considerably a more desirable guest in Tony's house now that Tony knows I am staying at Anthony's—Tony can underline the fact that Anthony is unwelcome. Tony has not dared to ask me anything about my relations with Anthony, but that too I'm sure makes me a more eligible guest—Tony hopes that Anthony will get jealous. Anthony, in fact (and

2. Vanessa Redgrave led a "pushchair protest" outside the U.S. Embassy in London on October 15; 400 women with children and babies demonstrated against the Vietnam War and the prison sentence imposed on Dr. Spock, the American pediatrician, author, and antiwar activist. Bachardy enclosed photographs clipped from the front page of *The Times*, October 16. Redgrave starred with James Mason and Simone Signoret in Sidney Lumet's 1968 film of Anton Chekhov's *The Seagull*. Her film with Italian actor Franco Nero—her lover and the father of her son born in 1969—was *Un tranquillo posto di campagna* (1969, *A Quiet Place in the Country*) directed by Elio Petri. (Redgrave married Nero in 2006.) She was nominated for an Academy Award for her role as Isadora Duncan in Reisz's 1968 film (re-edited and released in a much shorter version, *The Loves of Isadora*, in 1969).

it is to be said in his favor), makes no objection whatsoever to my seeing Tony. Quite the contrary, he too is eager for news of the other side.

David & Peter are spending the weekend at Tony's place in the South of France, all expenses paid including plane fare. They are both excited by the occasion. We saw them at dinner last night (Anthony at the last minute couldn't get tickets for *Hair*) along with Patrick Procktor who is just back from Morocco with his love, Gervase (not at dinner),[3] Nick Wilder, Ron Kitaj and girl.[4] I was glad to meet Kitaj. There is something defensive, evasive and self-protectingly square about him. He is going to be in L.A. in Jan. & Feb. so maybe we will see him.

I got to speak very little to Patrick but he seemed his usual self. In the street after dinner he put his arm around me in his usual fulsome[5] way, a kind of mock gesture of pseudo friendship.

A call from Joan Axelrod's secretary to tell me she and her commissionairess waited lunch for me yesterday. I'm *certain* she told me Wednesday. I had a sitting with John Craxton planned for Tuesday before she even asked me. I will write a note of apology but I fear it may mean that commission will not happen.

John Craxton was very difficult to draw, a subtle mover. He is quite nice I think and even somewhat complimentary about my work. He suffers from a very usual kind of English smallness of mind and a self-protective sneer. Also, he took it upon himself to tell me where I had gone wrong in my drawings of him, though he liked one enough to want a photograph of it.

I am having drinks with Kate and Ivan tonight so I will know at last the temperature there.

After being very difficult for several days, Anthony has suddenly become much nicer and more relaxed and easier to be with. A relief since I was regretting having come, due in part to his behavior and in part to my usual reaction against arriving anywhere except the Casa.

But Kitty still loves his Dear Muzzle best and always will and misses him and worries about his falling into disrepair without Kitty's daily tune-ups. Kitty is helped by knowing the Dear is getting his run on the

---

3. Gervase Griffiths, Oxford-educated English model and aspiring pop singer; Procktor painted him many times.
4. R.B. Kitaj (1932–2007), American painter and graphic artist. The girl was not his first wife, Elsi Roessler, who died of a drug overdose in 1969.
5. Bachardy wrote "foulsome," then, typing out the letter himself three decades later, typed "fulsome."

beach and even a dunking. Kitty will return soon and get him back into tip-top working order. With eternal love & devotion. Pussboots.

[Autograph letter with enclosure]

Friday [October] 18th. [1968]   [Santa Monica]

Darling Fur,

[T]wo dear letters arrived today, Tuesday and Wednesday. This doubtless means no letter tomorrow, but Dub will reread them with kisses then and on Sunday.

I'm glad you told Tony about the play but if he didn't ask to read it I wouldn't offer it to him; that just might be his loss later. Anyhow let's see what we can do with it here first. I talked about it some more to Jim last night, had supper with the two of them, cooked by Jack. They are feeling *very* poor. They say they have spent nearly $20,000 on fixing up the house! It is nearly finished now. Jim doesn't want to have to do any more movie work, he longs to direct. He talks about arranging for a reading of our play, but the awful question remains, who in hell is there to play Patrick and Oliver? Jack and Jim also are convinced that Maltin is not only inefficient but headed for the penitentiary as he has been gambling wildly with and on behalf of Rooney.[1] I don't quite see how he can play any dirty tricks on us, but the Animals must keep on the alert.

Am very happy to detect a happier note in Kitty's letters, had begun to fear the whole visit was being a flop.

Up to now, noon, have heard nothing from [Marguerite's companion] and a check of the B.H.[2] and other hotels showed no booking by anyone of that name, but of course it may be a block booking by his gang for so and so many rooms. Anyhow, I'll cope. Paul Bowles also called and he is settled with his friend[3] at the Shangri-La in Sta. Monica! But the friend has said he daren't drive in our traffic and is anyhow homesick and may leave soon, and return to Morocco. So I told Paul I will see him very soon and maybe come sometimes to drive him to market, as he does all cooking at home and hasn't the transportation. It is a drag, that one has to talk French or Spanish to the friend. A student from the college comes

1. Film star Mickey Rooney (b. 1920), who had a gambling addiction.
2. The Beverly Hills Hotel, where the friend checked in on October 20.
3. Mohammad Mrabet (b. 1936), Moroccan storyteller and painter.

to drive him to his classes.[4] Paul tells me that he has seen Tennessee and that Mike Steen is very much in command there; this must mean that Mike doesn't want Tenn to see us! I shall call however. I heard through Jack that Paul told them how he and Oliver Evans[5] had gone up to see Tenn and how Mike Steen had made them drunk (he pours drinks relentlessly, according to Paul, and doesn't drink himself) and on the way home, Oliver Evans was driving madly and was signalled by cops and made a run for it and was caught and protested violently and was finally taken away in handcuffs! I think I should call Oliver and sympathise? I guess he has himself a drunk-driving sentence, maybe with jail.

Last night I saw *Inadmissible Evidence*. I went because I fear it can't run long. It was at the Plaza in the Village.[6] As a film I thought it was truly brilliant and that Anthony had made everything out of it that could possibly be made, and I guess I admire Williamson too, though I don't warm to him much, and cannot imagine that he will be particularly interesting as Hamlet. All that was wrong I blame on Osborne.[7] I don't think the queer thing works, although one saw why it is there, Williamson is being confronted by a reverse image of his own life, so to speak. Jill Bennett is really extraordinary looking; that nose! I thought a lot of the acting was brilliant, and that supper party was about the best thing of its kind I have ever seen on the screen—with the wooden bowls! That's *real* comedy and shows you how crude such scenes are as a rule. Please tell Anthony how much I liked it.

The weather is less good today, but Drub will be taken down to the beach and trotted, and made to go to the gym later.

It's a long time since I had as much trouble with a piece of writing as I'm having with this book. This morning I saw that I must scrap it all and start over.

What you say about Patrick is very true and maybe I am wrong, but we'll talk it over; I just got a feeling that the play might seem kind of lopsided if P. *doesn't* speak.

I do wish you could somehow have it out with Cecià (you see, I was trying to write Cecilia!) Beaton, because it would be so awfully good

4. Bowles was a visiting professor at San Fernando Valley State College, where he was teaching courses in the modern European novel and advanced narrative writing.
5. Poet, biographer, literary critic, and English professor (b. 1915), from New Orleans. A longtime friend of Williams.
6. That is, the Plaza movie theater in Westwood Village.
7. Who was the author of the screenplay as well as the stage play.

for him and would clear the air, *if* he could take it, which I doubt. He *just* might. But all that is your affair. Perhaps the photo exhibit will come over here later. It would probably be popular.[8] As for the Axelrods' frump, you are probably well out of that.

All Dobbin's love to his Darling who is Dub's sole reason for doing everything, from trotting to page blotting. Always remember that Dub is thinking of his Dear with so much love and lavishing kisses on his sacred basket-spot. XXXXXXXX H.

Had just sealed this up when Ed Ruscha called. The girl who was with him and works for Guernreich[?] named Leon Bing was so impressed by your drawing of Ed that she wants to be drawn.[9] I said you'd call when you got back.

[*Typed letter, initialled, with autograph additions*]

Thursday [17 October 1968, London]

Darling Drubchen—

Greyfur has been thinking so much about his dear Brumbie today and missing him and wishing he could stroke that Old Muzzle and chew on his sweet ear. Cat has just come from an interminable run-through of *Look Back*, nearly four hours of it. It was so *slow*, largely due to the actors and the awful long breaks between acts. I begin to wonder now if it can have any kind of success. Not that it's not good but just that it's still very familiar, and, though no longer up-to-the-minute modern, is not yet aged enough to be "period." The cast is good, but I am *not* drawing them finally. There has been a great deal of indecision and disorganization of a boring kind and the end result is that nobody really wants the drawings enough, nor do I want to do them badly enough to make a big fuss. There is now no longer time either. As I expected, Anthony was quite taken aback by my drawing of the leading actor, felt it too downbeat for the poster. Anyway, Victor Henry is not really a recognizable nor a commanding star here, so his face on the poster would be no real draw.

8. It reopened in New York in May 1969 as "600 Faces by Beaton: 1928–1969" and toured the U.S.
9. Bachardy drew American pop artist Ed Ruscha (b. 1937) on September 27, 1968. Leon Bing worked for Rudi *Gernreich*; Bachardy never drew her.

However, I had lunch with Tony Gibbs (the editor of *Petulia*) and his wife today and the commission to draw her is very much on—Saturday in fact.[1] They are both very nice and she is drawable, too (if you can imagine Frank Merlo as a not bad-looking woman?), so I am looking forward to it. Also, the misunderstanding about the Joan Axelrod lunch has been cleared up and I am to meet her landlady on Monday at 5 p.m. to arrange a sitting. Otherwise, no drawing plans, unless I try to arrange through David Hockney to draw Ron Kitaj, and I don't know if I will. Ran into Alexis Rassine on Bond Street yesterday so got John Lehmann's telephone number from him (it's not in the book) and called John this morning. He was very friendly and invited me to lunch next Thursday. Rosamond I've not gotten a hold of yet.

I'm on my way to drinks at Tony's. He and David and Peter leave tomorrow morning for the weekend at Tony's place in the South of France. Tomorrow night is a late party for the casts of the three Osborne productions. *Time Present* comes off Sat. night so the three won't quite manage to be all on at the same time.[2] Lunch with Marguerite tomorrow. Poor Nag will be saddled with her companion this weekend. Kitty's brave old Darling! I hope he's still staying off the sauce like his true kitten.

Had drinks with Kate and Ivan yesterday evening and to my amazement and delight there is no ill-feeling there whatsoever—they were both charming and sweet and looking well and sending love to you. Kate says she wrote a two-page letter to me last July to thank for the drawing I sent. She didn't seem to be lying so I guess it got lost. They neither of them mentioned wanting one of the originals of Iris so I didn't either. Ivan is on some new pill for perking up the middle-aged, called KH3—expensive he says but it seems to work—at least he can concentrate in the mornings. Should Catkin bring some back to the stable to mix in with Rump's oats? Mountains of densely packed furred love for a Tabby's only companion.

[*Autograph letter*]

1. Influential New Wave British film editor Antony Gibbs (b. 1925) became famous when he introduced the flash forward into Richard Lester's 1968 film starring Julie Christie. His first wife was called Jocelyn, see below pp. 332–333.
2. *The Hotel in Amsterdam* had transferred from the Royal Court on September 5 and was still playing at the New Theatre in the West End. *Look Back in Anger* was to open at the Royal Court on October 29.

Roman Polanski

[*Pencil and ink wash drawing by Don Bachardy; printed in* Variety]

Oct. 19, Saturday. [1968]   [Santa Monica]

Dobbin's Furry Saint will be pleased, I hope, with the reproduction of his Polanski drawing in *Variety*.[1] I sent a copy off to him airmail today in case he needs it for any reason in London. Have ordered half a dozen other copies. I wouldn't have known about it if Gavin hadn't told me. I think it looks good?

Today a bound proof copy of Salka's book *The Kindness of Strangers* arrived. Kitty gets what I believe is his first mention in a book of memoirs, "Christopher Isherwood and a young painter, Don Bachardy, joined us for dinner." Otherwise there doesn't seem much about Dobbin, considering all he did for the family, but then he wasn't a Jewhorse. It only says that (in 1939) he was "boyishly handsome"![2]

A volume of poems also arrived from Ralph Pomeroy.[3] No comment needed. Bill Otis called just now. I told him you were in London till the end of the month. He said he'd ring again.[4] And the Ruscha picture is framed, so I'll pick it up and pay for it.

Today is a day which demands all of Drub's courage. Very thick sad fog. The vague threat of [the arrival of Marguerite's companion] has efficiently fucked up the weekend and I can get no clue as to where he'll be staying and he hasn't phoned or wired, I suppose he is being considerate. Well, it doesn't matter really. I waited in till late yesterday and then fixed up a last-minute date with Basil Gordon, that skinny Maths professor. We went to the Fuji Gardens. He really is quite bright and he has a nice little house all to himself on 15th St., and a little money apparently, which is a drag because he wants to "return my hospitality." He is very closet, or rather, not even that; just restrained and somehow reserved for something, like a folded napkin. He played the piano to me afterwards, Brahms, quite fairly nicely but not well. I imagine he would be good to draw; his face is rather endearing when playing, like a fish

1. The full-page drawing appeared in *Daily Variety*, Friday, October 18, p. 5.
2. *The Kindness of Strangers: A Theatrical Life, Vienna, Berlin, Hollywood*; see p. 241, where Viertel records the friends they had in common and her view that, during the war, Isherwood "was going through great emotional strain," and see also p. 319.
3. Probably *In the Financial District: Poems* (1968) by American poet, painter, art critic, curator (1926–1999). He lived in New York and in San Francisco and had occasionally been an Isherwood sex partner before Isherwood met Bachardy. Isherwood did not admire his poetry.
4. An acquaintance who had visited Bachardy's studio September 25 at 5 p.m., evidently a sex date, as it was too late in the afternoon for a sitting and no portrait is known.

rising to the surface. The enormous advantage of mathematics is that they *can't* be explained so one is excused from all that.[5]

I did a terrific drive yesterday and found another opening for my book so feel better about that.

No letter from my Darling this morning but then, as I said yesterday, I didn't expect one, having received two.

Will probably spend the evening discussing the lyrics for the two "Christmas Carol" songs with Ray. And tomorrow, as I think I told you, I have to make up my mind about having this BBC interview, so shall see what the interviewer is like.

Inadmissible Evidence is posted as coming off in 3 days.

Some woman just called up to ask me to help get the vote out for Nixon. I told her what I think of him. She said, "Well you're entitled to your opinion." The minute she hung up I wished I'd answered, "I shan't be, if he gets elected."[6]

Angel Love, Old Drubplug is thinking of him so and loving that dear pink tiny nose and whiskers.

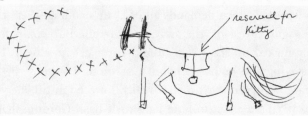

[*Typed letter with autograph additions*]

Friday [October 18, 1968, London]

Adored Loverump—

Furry is sitting up at table, dressed to his tiny teeth in his new blue-grey Swedish suit, waiting for Marguerite to arrive. We are having lunch (it seems as though Kitty has only just finished breakfast but somehow or other, due to perserverance mostly, he usually manages to swallow a small bite or two) at an Italian restaurant in the Fulham Road called San Frediano. Tony Gibbs brought me here yesterday and it's really quite

5. Gordon (1931–2012), a mathematician and physicist, was a professor at UCLA. While in the U.S. Army, he had worked with Wernher von Braun, the ex-Nazi rocket scientist.
6. In the upcoming presidential election, against Hubert Humphrey, November 5.

good—much better anyway than those dreadful crowded noisy but "fashionable" places Marguerite likes to go to. Since I am entertaining her I suggested this place—there was an appreciable drop in the tone of her voice on the telephone this morning. I also spoke to Rosamond today who was dashing to (Rosamond dashing? Let's say gradually moving towards) the Isle of Wight for the weekend. I said I would call her on Monday to know if she could have lunch with me one day next week. Also spoke to Leslie Caron[1] who was nice and invited me to dinner next Wednesday. She recognized the telephone number I left yesterday as Anthony's and invited him to dinner, too. I suspect he may be a large reason for her cordiality to me. Her dear little calculating French mind could hardly fail to take into account a smart young director about town. Anyway they already know each other slightly. I doubt if Anthony can come because *Look Back* starts previewing on Tuesday and Anthony says he will have to see it every night till it opens.

Later.

Marguerite was very sweet and talkative and even wound up liking the restaurant I think. One thing helped: John Schlesinger[2] turned up there and came over very friendly and I introduced them. Marguerite said later in very respectful tones, "He's so talented," so I gather she was impressed. John looked very well and tanned, said he was leaving tomorrow so we wouldn't be able to meet. Marguerite was full of Jackie's marriage which was announced this morning. What she had heard was that Onassis was Lee's friend and supposedly Jackie and Lee always want what the other has.[3] Marguerite said I was the only one she'd talked to this morning (and that's a distinction of some kind I guess, if only of numbers) who'd been in favor of the marriage. (Kitty can't help being prejudiced in favor of May–September matches! In fact, Kitty would surmise a 30 year age difference is just about right—the papers here say she's 39 and he's 69.)

Had drinks at Tony's last night. Neil was there and an assortment of males, mostly mixed bags with one or two sweet meats, one of whom looked exactly like Liza Minnelli without a nose job. Tony made rather a point of lolling over his end of the sofa—especially after I told him I

1. French dancer and actress (b. 1931); Isherwood and Bachardy had known her since the 1950s.
2. British film and stage director (1926–2003).
3. The widowed Jacqueline Kennedy married Aristotle Onassis on October 20. Lee Bouvier (b. 1933), her sister, was then married to her second husband, Prince Stanislaus Radziwill.

thought the boy much the best of the bunch. Tony also did this naughty thing of whispering invitations to dinner to the selected few in front of the definitely unselected majority. Even I got an invitation, all the more pressing once I'd refused, most certainly because Tony guessed I was having dinner with Anthony. He would so love to have been able to spirit me away as well as Nicol Williamson, if only for the evening. Even Neil started in to persuade me in his famous, high-powered, unctuous, Mephistophelian manner. Kitty was firm, not because he especially wanted to have dinner with Anthony but only because he knew *why* he was wanted. And anyway, they were only going to play bridge after dinner. Tomorrow Kitty goes to Cobham to draw Mrs. Gibbs in their 16th-century house. He is looking forward to working again, and so looking forward to hooking his claws into that Old Hide again.

With heartfelt Catkisses, Furchen XXXX

[*Autograph letter*]

Saturday [October 19, 1968, London]

Sacred Brump—

Furpaws is riding on a train back to London after having spent the day drawing Jocelyn Gibbs, so forgive if the paw errs. The Gibbses are both likable. I gather she is rich, and he is kind of subterranean arrogant, the king of mad arrogance born of years of "servitude" to apparent incompetents like Tony Richardson. I'm sure he feels that anybody could do Tony's job as well or better than Tony, quite overlooking the fact that a certain amount of beastliness and lack of talent actually makes one more qualified for such a job as Tony's. As far as being a movie director goes, Gibbs is possibly too competent and serious and knowledgeable for his own good. Nevertheless he is determined (and frightened too I think) to do it. He has a script based on an Isak Dinesen story which he's offered to Ingrid Bergman and she is interested. They are meeting on Thursday in Paris to discuss it.

Jocelyn is a rich girl, I learned today, but nice in spite of it, though she is unmistakably tainted. She could not have sat more patiently or stiller than she did, which made me like her, but it was still a struggle—maybe because I've drawn so little since I've been here. I did four drawings (we worked steadily about five hours—no, six!) and they are talking big about buying 3 out of the 4. He anyway pressed £75 into my hand (the price I gave for one) and said they would most certainly want more. I didn't make my usual concession of half price for a second since £75 anyway is less than my "usual." And once I'd heard about her rich daddy, Kitty's great eyes narrowed to such an extent he might have been mistaken for a furry Anna May Wong.[4]

Tonight is the last night of *Time Present*. I feel quite determined not to sit through it though Anthony feels obligated and pressured by Jill to do so. *Bluebeard's Eighth Wife* is at the Natl. Film Theatre where there might just be an extra seat for a somewhat tattered Pussy.

There was a party last night for the casts and crews of the three Osborne plays [. . .]. Oscar Lewenstein paid but it was really all Anthony's idea [. . .]. Champagne & shepherd's pie [. . .].

Later.

No *Bluebeard's 8th Wife* but the first half of *Jekyll & Hyde* with Bergman[5] which Kitty can never resist. Must fly off to meet Anthony for the last few minutes of *Time Present*.

Kitty is tired but never too tired to think of His Dear and miss him with his small but true Animal heart. With ribboned love for his Only Naggin. XXXXXXXX Pinkears.

[Autograph letter]

Monday 21st [October 1968]   [Santa Monica]

Sweetest Silkwhiskers,

[T]wo dear letters from his Darling today and so they saw an old Plug smile. He opened them very carefully with his tongue.

Couldn't write yesterday, there was a continuous interruption. First talking to the BBC people. This miserable interviewer was exhausted after her trip and so couldn't get her ass out of bed and come over.[1] What

4. Chinese-American movie star (1905–1961).
5. That is, *Dr. Jekyll and Mr. Hyde* (1941), starring Ingrid Bergman and Spencer Tracy.

1. Leslie Megahey (b. 1944).

a contrast to Kitty when he lands in London and bravely rushes out to conquer the city at once! A contrast to [Marguerite's companion] for that matter, too—*he* went straight off to supper with Tennessee Williams and Rita Hayworth![2] (Rupert Allan took him along; it seems that Tennessee is entertaining these days. [Marguerite's companion] had never met him before and Tenn didn't strike him as particularly drunk or gaga. But no call to the Casa!)

Well, after that George Schaefer came down and we had a talk with Ray Henderson about the songs for "Christmas Carol," and then I had to go over to the Beverly Hills Hotel and meet [Marguerite's companion].

He is very busy with official lunches and dinners and meetings of the International Steel Board or whatever it's called. Apparently the American steel industry is in a mess, old-fashioned and incompetent, and the Japs are selling steel cheap and the Americans are scared and want to clap on tariffs to prevent it from coming into the country and competing with them.

I invited him to stay (when I was quite certain he'd refuse) and he refused, but was much pleased by all these hospitable noises.

So then we went out and visited Nick Dunne ([Marguerite's companion's] idea). I must say Nick wasn't so bad at all when seen in the intimacy of his huge apartment. He was very friendly, and only embarrassed me by showing a wild desire to meet Paul Bowles! He carried on in a most unconvincing way about how broken up he was by the separation with his beloved Lenny.[3] I suppose this was for [the benefit of Marguerite's companion].

He has a Japanese houseboy, however, who is a jewel (we didn't see him). He also carried on about the pleasures of pot and how much nicer it was than drinking. And of course he talked about *The Boys in the Band*, but quite guardedly and I don't think [Marguerite's companion] even knew what it is about.[4]

Then I took [Marguerite's companion] to Por Favor, because he said he liked Mexican food. The food was cold, so I was humiliated. Marguerite

2. American dancer and Hollywood star (1918–1987).
3. Dominick Dunne (1925–2009), film and T.V. producer, later a novelist and special correspondent for *Vanity Fair*, was divorced from Arizona ranching heiress Ellen Griffin Dunne (1932–1997).
4. The play, by Mart Crowley (b. 1935), is about a Manhattan birthday party attended by nine men, eight of them gay. It opened off-Broadway on April 14, 1968, and was still running to sold-out houses. Dunne, a close friend of Crowley, was an executive producer of the 1970 film for which Crowley wrote the screenplay. Dunne himself was bisexual and in the closet until near the end of his life.

had given him a list of places to eat at, all stuffy as well as expensive, Perino's, Chasen's, Au Petit Jean. Also the Bistro. With a groan inwardly I said the Bistro was the only lively one, so I called it but thank God it was closed Sundays! And now Nick Dunne is taking him there today.

I don't think I shall see [Marguerite's companion] at all till tomorrow and probably not much then as he is very busy, but I have offered to drive him up to Santa Barbara, where he has a nephew teaching on campus; which also kept up the hospitality impression. Finally, after Por Favor, [he] wanted to see the Strip, so we went into a couple of places and did get a sort of whiff of hippies, though there weren't many around and Whisky a Gogo seemed more given over to tourists now, from what I could judge. There is a strange kind of mission place, with a huge cross, but hardly anyone in there, and how I do hate slumming! I felt embarrassed, especially as the kids obviously just want to be left to do their thing. But [Marguerite's companion] seemed interested. He seems much turned on by very young girls and he confessed to me he liked them boyish! (This was a sort of concession to prove that we all have a bit of queer in us, I think!)

His chief preoccupation is Marguerite and he is worried because he feels he is square and always the one who has to say No. I pointed out that Marguerite absolutely needs someone like that. I do like him, but he is so awfully hung up and inhibited and stooped and tied into a knot.

Now I have to go see Gerald and Michael. Then the BBC people are coming, and I'm almost certain I shall call the whole thing off but must give them a fair hearing. And then there is Kali puja, which I am going in for an hour of (give or take half) at ten this evening! Swami wants me to talk to some Indian journalist first! Well, I pray that life will get back to normal again after tomorrow, and then Drub can sit down and wait quietly for his Darling and get on with his work. I still have to see Oldjo, Michael Sean and Seth Finkelstein, Paul Bowles, and have sessions with Ray about the songs. If this letter is incoherent it's because Dobbin is feeling so pressured, which he hates.

Only loves his Darling and longs to have him near, and bury his muzzle in that divine furball.

Eternally, Dragnag.

XXXXXXXXXXXXX H.

[Typed letter, initialled, with autograph additions]

Sunday [October 20, 1968, London]

Best Pluggin—

A quiet day today, almost the first that Anthony has not had to dash off to the theater in the morning. He did go though, around three, so I went into town with him and went to see *Belle de Jour* while he checked out the set for *Look Back* which is being put up today. Kitty very much enjoyed his movie, having been fed a big late breakfast. He was feeling quite full and satisfied but did manage a little ice cream bar covered in orange ice to see him through the movie. It is not the best Buñuel—it's a little too clever for its own good and oddly slick in an unBuñuel way, but very enjoyable and well done and full of Buñuel details. An actress named Geneviève Page gives the best performance, as the madam.[1] Kitty will take his Old Pony to it when it comes to L.A. because he will enjoy it.

Kitty then took the underground back to Ladbroke Grove and watched Minnelli's *The Clock* which I hadn't seen since it was new and always wanted to. Imagine the joy of T.V. here—I saw the whole film without a single interruption! But, in spite of the bliss of being without commercials, the film is shockingly sentimental and obvious and phony—full of horribly self-conscious cute "naturalism." I almost had to turn it off, and would have at the sight of the first commercial, but finally after the first 45 minutes I became numbed to the overplaying and watched it till the end in a kind of grimly mesmerized state. Both Garland and Walker suffered terribly from the calculated cutes but, even so, demonstrated shrewd professionalism, like two Shirley Temples, both of them older than Time in their know-how but playing young & innocent.[2]

Later.

Anthony came back from the theater and we went out for a late supper at a Chinese restaurant called Fu Tong's, distinguished mainly

---

1. French actress Geneviève Page (b. 1927) starred with Catherine Deneuve as the housewife who works as a prostitute in the 1967 film directed by Spanish-born writer and director Luis Buñuel (1900–1986).
2. Vincente Minnelli directed Judy Garland opposite Robert Walker in the romantic comedy about a soldier and a girl who agree to find one another under the clock in Pennsylvania Station in New York. Minnelli married Garland the same year, 1945.

for being expensive, being open on Sunday and serving late. Anthony is in a very nervous state due largely to this production of *Look Back* which is not doing well. Little things keep going wrong, the actors are all quite young, inexperienced and unreliable[3] and on top of all this, the Court without letting Anthony know in advance has committed them to play in front of an audience on Tuesday (two days earlier than Anthony was first told) though the official opening with press is not till the following Tuesday (the day of a certain Kitten's departure from London en route for the Basket). How glad I am not to have to endure the opening!

Anthony's high-strung state is due also, according to him, to doing too many Osbornes in a row & too many productions in a row without sufficient breaks in between. [. . .] His danger is that he is really too bright. He is capable of doing so many things quite well but none of them really well enough unless he concentrates. Did I tell you he can draw surprisingly well and also plays the piano and once considered a concert pianist's career? And in spite of his success in the theater I don't think he's quite given up thoughts of these other careers which take on added attraction when things go wrong in the theater. [. . .] But I'm not really very worried about him because I think he really does enjoy directing while he's actually doing it, and what is so impressive in watching him do it *is* his ability to concentrate. Every ounce of his nervous energy is poured into attending to what's going on onstage and the actors feel it and respond to it and therefore often enjoy working for him more than anybody else.

Anthony is also upset about his film of *Inadmissible Evidence*. Paramount is refusing to release it here and Anthony fears they maybe never will. In spite of several good notices in N.Y. it has not made money there and so Paramount executives are down on it. There is also a purge going on in the executive offices here and so the question of release will be suspended until it's over. So for the time being Anthony's career as film director is at a standstill. [. . .]

I think my being here is some help to him but also an added (though, I keep telling him, imaginary) responsibility. He continually half-worries about my being "entertained." I finally had to make a scene about not wanting to be treated as a guest which made some impression

---

3. Four were only in their twenties, but they had already had a number of professional roles. Edward Jewesbury (1917–2002), though, playing Colonel Redfern, was experienced and highly skilled.

on him. But still he is aware of being totally wrapped up in the play and not being able to attend to much else for more than a few minutes. Actually his absorption in the play gives me much needed breaks—if I were around him all day while he's in this state of mind I would soon crack. It's largely this consideration that makes me glad I'm not doing drawings for the play.

You might not guess from this letter that I am so glad I made this trip, but even gladder that I am returning to my Only Rump next week.

His adoring
Snowpaws
XXXX

[*Autograph letter*]

Tuesday 22 [October 1968]   [Santa Monica]

Treasured Tabbycat,

[A]nother fogged-in morning which makes olddub restive in his stall, he scatters the straw with his hoof and whinnies uneasily. Had hopes for a short canter on the beach but now it looks like he'll have to settle for Miss MooCow's gym.

Have at length, after much hesitation, agreed to do the BBC interview film on Thursday. They aren't pressing their silly idea of acting bits out of my books. They will just have an interview and maybe show some old photographs and background material from newsreels like Berlin in 1930 and China in 1938. They also said they would like to get a picture of Wyberslegh. Richard will probably tell them to fuck themselves but that is his business.

Am not seeing [Marguerite's companion] any more. He has a lot of stuff to do today, anyhow, and obviously didn't want it. He *was* interested in going to discotheques, however; he digs young girls as I think I told you. When I told him you'd had lunch with Marguerite he asked, "Has she been behaving?" and immediately added, "Better than I have, I hope." What this may have meant I didn't ask.

Yesterday evening there was an unusually crammed Kali puja, you could hardly get into the Temple with instruments. Swami very cheerful. He actually went in there for the first hour and was planning on getting up at 2 a.m. to do another stint. There was a terrible Peter Sellars-type Indian journalist there, someone I'd met in Calcutta, more religious than the entire Ramakrishna Order and false in exactly the same way as Rudi Anders—it was astonishing to see how little difference race makes, the same state of mind produced the identical grimaces, particularly that monkey grimace when Rudi shows his teeth.[1]

Mark had made the Kali statue, very well done and as embarrassing as they always are, but I guess it is wonderful karma yoga, taking all that trouble over an artwork which is then thrown into the ocean next day.[2] Franklin came up with the other boys—you remember, the grey-haired nice-looking one who got into trouble with some kind of voyeurism in a movie theater? Well, as I was getting into my car around 11 p.m. in the dead of puja with no one else around, I saw Franklin hurriedly come down the lot from the direction of the steep hill which leads down to Vine St.! If he *was* up to anything I only pray he doesn't get caught.[3]

Am going with Gavin tonight to see a French film called *Judex*, which comes off tomorrow. Am wondering about a film I see advertised in the Oct. 13 London *Sunday Times*—*Forty Years On* with Gielgud and Alan Bennett.[4] Also there's the play with Gladys Cooper in it, *Out of the Question*.[5] Both opening next week. I do hope *Forty Years On* comes here.

Am quite concerned about Larry Holt, who seems to be having a nervous breakdown. He won't see me but calls.

Am of course still guilty about the people I haven't seen yet, but I'll do something about some of them.

1. The journalist was possibly D.P. Tarafdar, who wrote for *Amrita Bazaar Patrika*; Isherwood met him December 27, 1963. Rudolph Anders (1902–1987), a German actor who often played Nazi villains, was also a regular at the temple.
2. Mark was John Markovich (193[2]–2008), American painter and Ramakrishna monk. When he took his first vows, he was called Nirmal and then, at sannyas, Swami Tadatmananda; he later became abbot of Trabuco. Each year, for Kali puja, a statue of Kali, about three-and-a-half feet high, is made for worship. About a week after the puja, the statue is taken out to sea in a boat and immersed, with devotees singing and celebrating on the way. The immersion symbolizes Kali's return to her celestial abode where her husband Shiva resides.
3. Franklin Knight (*circa* 1924–2005), American Ramakrishna monk. He became Asima Chaitanya, known as Asim, when he took his brahmacharya vows. He was never allowed to take his final vows because of the episode to which Isherwood refers, which took place in 1963 and involved the police.
4. It was a play, not a film; Alan Bennett (b. 1934) wrote and acted in it. It was his first West End play. The London paper would have been given to Isherwood, possibly by the BBC crew or by Marguerite's companion.
5. By Ira Wallach. Cooper turned eighty while she was appearing in it.

Oh Love, I long to see you and talk and hear all your impressions. Your letters are certainly far more amusing than mine but then you are getting around more. However Dobbin has his tasks and that is a great blessing; even when he is lazy he can feel that he has something to neglect. I suppose there are a lot of people who simply don't have anything to do or refuse to do. And then there is always the thought of his Darling to give him courage, and make him remember how lucky he is and how he must never cease to give thanks that that Saint descended out of the Catnipananda heaven to cheer an old plug.

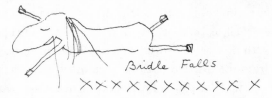

Bridle Falls
X X X X X X X X X X X

[*Typed letter with autograph additions*]

Monday [October 21, 1968, London]

Darling Colt—

Two dear letters for a lucky Pussy this morning, and the copy of *Variety* which I have been meaning to ask you to look out for. I'm relieved to see they have reproduced my drawing properly. The typeface and the placement of his name is wrong but not disastrously so. There is something vaguely ridiculous about the page as a page. I can't quite put my finger on it. I wonder what kind of good it can possibly do *anybody*, but maybe the very silliness of the idea of it gives it a certain strength.[1]

Anthony will be so delighted to know you like his film. He asked me just last night at dinner if you'd seen it. I told him I'd made you promise not to see it until I got back (Capricious Pony) but he will be very encouraged to hear what you say.

1. Polanski received enormous acclaim for *Rosemary's Baby*, beginning in June 1968 when the film was released. His next project, *Donner Pass*, with a screenplay by Ivan Moffat, was not announced until the end of November, and in the meantime the Bachardy drawing of him in *Variety* promoted him as the hot director of the moment.

Later

I've just come from the Axelrods' where I at last met their landlady, my commissionairess. The Axelrods I am genuinely fond of, they are really funny and nice and sympathetic, *but* I will have my work cut out for me with Mrs. [. . .] James, a chatterbox of such energy and determination I tremble to think of the sitting. Her husband, said by the Axelrods to be dishy and only 32, is a self-made real-estate baron and [Mrs. James] is his Lady Macbeth—I can hear her saying quite unemotionally, "Give *me* the eviction notices." She could even pass for being pretty in a totally meaningless way, which will only make it infinitely more difficult to draw her. I'm glad I asked for £100. I'll believe it when I see it (the cash). I've got, too, on Wednesday, a woman who calls herself C.M. Allen coming up to Ladbroke Grove from Sussex to be drawn, also for her husband at Christmas. She wrote a letter to me c/o The Court asking did I do commissions?—the letter only arrived a few days after I did—and I answered, "Yes indeed!" So who knows that I won't manage to pay for my trip after all? One of the actresses from *Time Present* also thinks she wants her drawing. Off now to Patrick Woodcock for dinner.

With many lickings from Kitty's rough tongue. XXXX Saint Kit

P.S. Have you heard whether or not Kathy Nolan has used her drawings for an ad? I don't suppose any money has come in from her.

[*Autograph letter with enclosure²*]

October 23 Wednesday [1968]   [Santa Monica]

Darling Velvetpaws,

Dobbin got a letter from his Angel this morning which had been written on Monday which is a record for speed. Am not sure how long I should go on writing (always assuming that Kitty isn't detained at the last moment for some reason) but I suppose if I send a letter off on Friday it will be all right. How Dobbin longs to see his Darling again.

2. Bachardy folded in half a photograph cut from a newspaper magazine of a long-haired white cat lying on a brown carpet. On the outside, he wrote, "Inside: a picture of Kitty on a stretch of imitation Hide! Says Kitty: You can't fool me with this fake stuff! I want the real thing!!"

No, there has been nothing from Kathy Nolan. Her two performances in *Niagara Falls* were well thought of, it seems, so she should be in an upbeat mood.

Dobbin didn't mean to see *Inadmissible Evidence* without his Dear, but it was so obvious that it wouldn't last at that theater and it may very well not appear again, so I didn't want to risk it. For the same reason I went last night with Gavin to see *Judex* which is directed by Georges Franju, who made *Eyes Without a Face* (?).[1] Last night was the last night. It is a film based on an old silent serial about a sort of noble avenger who warns and then punishes the wicked banker and his assistants. I think it is the best thing of this kind I have ever seen, because they don't get too cute about it. It is in the manner of a silent thriller, but with dialogue and not made too much fun of, and the period atmosphere is preserved and the thrills are really thrilling. I do wish you could see it. If they bring it on anywhere else I would certainly like to go again. But otherwise I'm not about to go to anything which we might want to see together. And in fact I don't anticipate any more movie going, unless I invite Ted and Ted to come out with me Saturday and we see something; if we do, it shall be some bore or other which they want.

Tomorrow I have this BBC recording most of the day, and then I am going to take [O]ldjo out and drink her tears. Friday I am going to see Paul Bowles because his friend Mrabet is leaving Saturday for Morocco. Nothing will cure those Arabian sulks. Mrabet refuses to leave the house and complains of psychosomatic pains; Paul says that's what Arabs are like, take them away from their social environment and they wither. I think it's rather a fucking bore. But Paul seems very calm and good-natured about the whole thing.

On Sunday I'm to have dinner with Bill [Brown] and Paul [Wonner]. Paul's show is on the following Sunday, the 3rd. Tonight I am going to Vedanta Place again and to bed early; as I'll have to rise early to receive the BBC.

Heard from Gavin that Rupert Allan has actually been hired by Tennessee (of course in reality Mike Steen) to be his press agent! It seems absolutely incredible but Rupert told Gavin so himself. Maybe that is why the Animals are excluded, but I don't really think so.

---

1. Franju's *Judex* (1963) was the second remake of the original 1916 silent. *Eyes Without a Face* (1960) was adapted from Jean Redon's 1957 novel *Les Yeux sans visage*.

Have just been down to the beach. The sunshine is only hazy but I promised Kitty to take care of Brumb, so I trotted him up the beach a bit and then made him go in the water. How he neighed and shook his mane and squirted water out of his nose! It was cold for him.

Ray Henderson is making my life tiresome, calling up all the time to consult me about his lyrics, but I must say, he has already whacked out t[w]o passable tunes, which is something.

Thinking so much about his Angel and dreaming of white fur and a pink tongue in Drub's old hairy ear.

XXXXX D. XXXXXXXXX

[*Typed letter, initialled*]

Tuesday [October 22 , 1968, London]

Treasured Trot—

Kitty is sitting up again in San Frediano, waiting to have lunch with Mont Blanc Lehmann. She's not late yet, it's just that I am early. I took Patrick Woodcock to a meal last night. He suggested a new restaurant in the King's Road called The Melita, an Italian place run by the same people who run Alexander's. Patrick was much as usual, looking well in spite of long stories of his sufferings at the hands of this friend of his (David[1]) with whom he is painfully in love. I met David when I was here in the spring. I don't think he gives a fig about Patrick except as a provider of entertainment, friends and money (Patrick's invested quite heavily in David's business—manufacturing objects made out of caning). But Patrick obviously enjoys being unhappily in love, I suspect the more unhappy David makes him the better he likes it. They had some unpleasant weeks together in Greece this summer. David [. . .] had just found a steady [boy] before he came to Greece and of course told Patrick all about it the moment he arrived. Their sex together sounds peculiar and infrequent. From what Patrick says [. . .] that seems to be that. Patrick had never been interested in that particular form of sex but says he now sees the point of it (no pun intended).

1. David Mann.

Later

Rosamond looked bigger & pudgier than ever, due in part to being noticeably fatter. I saw her avoid the liver she'd ordered in favor of some delicious fried potatoes. I told her you hadn't much liked her book, "disappointed" is the word I used, and you'd been sorry not to be able to write something really enthusiastic about it and therefore, according to your rule, you didn't write at all. She more than understood, she said, and didn't want you to think she'd minded or held it against you, though she had hoped and expected that you would be able (open-minded enough was the idea she was getting across) to appreciate it. Then she went on to say that as a matter of fact she hadn't liked A Meeting by the River (she really is such an ego maniac!) because she couldn't accept the device of the letters and thought Patrick too unsympathetic. (More self-protective tit for tat would hardly be possible.)

Patrick says Rosamond's the most hostile of his women friends. I don't find her especially hostile. She's so squidgy I can't quite take her hostility seriously. We yakked quite easily and pleasantly for an hour and a half and then I dropped her at her flat.

Later in the afternoon I went to a showing of Tony's new film with Nicol Williamson and Anna Karina ([Jean-Luc] Godard's leading lady & ex-wife) and very much enjoyed it. It's a big change of pace for Tony. You'd hardly believe the story. Williamson plays an English lord, a very rich art expert with elegant houses and an elegant wife and child, who falls crazily in love with a sleezy, troublemaking, calculating slut and gives everything up for her. The wife leaves him, the child dies suddenly and he goes off to Majorca with the girl and her lover, who's been hired by him as a kind of art-buying assistant—the girl tells him the lover is queer. In spite of Williamson's insane jealousy, she and the lover fuck quite recklessly right under his nose. Then he finds out, drives off wildly with the girl and gets into a wreck and (believe it or not) loses his sight as a result of the accident. The girl then takes him off to a private villa, reads him a letter of goodbye from the lover (who claims he left because the girl was jealous of his love for Williamson) and then she and the lover share the villa with him without letting him know the lover is actually there. This situation (a little far fetched wouldn't you say?) is what attracted Tony in the first place, I'm sure. He mercilessly drains it dry and, I think, goes more than a bit too far. But there are very good things in it and it's great fun to watch. Williamson is really wonderful and Karina is revealed as one of the super sow cunts of the cinema. And Tony is relentless in exposing the indifference and, finally, total contempt of the pair for Williamson. Tony is delighted at the thought that the movie is so black that no one will like it. I raved to him though, and to Neil & Williamson who were also present. It will be fun to show the movie to Kitty's Old Drump. He may snort but it'll amuse him.

With noisy purrs to his Darling, True Tabby.
                                              x x x

[*Autograph letter*]

Thursday 24th [1968]   [Santa Monica]

Dearest & best Pinkpads,

[A]m writing this in the midst of being telefilmed by the BBC. Ah, how usual it all is—the tired questions and the bright answers; bright only because they have been given a hundred times before or are quotes from my books. I really do not know why one does this kind of thing. If only it were somehow in aid of something! The interviewer (Derek Hart—Gavin who used to know him says rightly that he isn't very bright) shows not the faintest interest in any of our pictures or other mementoes & possessions. He seems to want to talk about the smog & how horrible America is.

A letter arrived for you from Mart Crowley excusing himself and saying that he was on Fire Island and the mail there is unreliable etc. etc., but that he indeed loves and wants "the full-front figure for my very own." More apologies, and then he says will you contact Paul Wolfowitz at the Charles Renthal Company 641 Lexington Avenue New York "and he will take care of what I owe you for your marvellous drawing" and then he says he'd appreciate it if you'd send him the drawing to the Algonquin Hotel, where he will be staying for approximately another 2½ weeks. The letter is dated October 21st so I guess you will have time to take care of this after you return. I'm just telling you the details in case you want to send him a line explaining where you are. The Algonquin is 59 West 44 N.Y. 10036.

Reason I'm writing this hoofwise is because my typewriter had hysterics yesterday and would print nothing but 00000000 (sheer negativism) so I had to take it to be fixed.

Swami was wonderful last night, talking about Brahamananda. I mean, the *way* he talked about him was wonderful. He said, "I *saw* him, Chris," as if he couldn't believe it. I said, "And we see you," and he said, "You see the dust of his feet."

Now, after messing around since 9 a.m., they have gone out to lunch, which I know will take forever; but I excused myself as I want to mail this to my Darling. How Dobbin longs for the moment when the stewardess opens the hamper and Kitty walks majestically down the red carpet from the plane with all the peasants cheering.

His adoring Drub XXXXXXXXXXXXXX

[*Autograph letter*]

Friday 25 [October 1968]   [Santa Monica]

Spotless Ruffneck,

[H]is dear letter today, so looked forward to and eagerly read, as usual. This will be Drub's last to his Darling, unless he hears of a change of plans, because a letter written tomorrow might not arrive in time.

That plump old Rosamond (she really *is* Hedda Gobbler) won't ever really forgive Drubb, I fear. How tiresome. The awful thing with these creatures is, they have been flattered too long. Not so much praised as taken seriously—until the poor silly old turkey believes every word of it.

I long to see Tony's film. I'm sure it will fascinate me, though I hate that sort of "cruel" story.

The BBC filming continued all day, from 9:00 a.m. to 6:30! They insisted on going out with me. I sat in the back car, an open convertible, with the interviewer driving and we followed a station wagon with the T.V. camera in the back. Our conversation was relayed to the front car by a pocket radio. We drove all around Sycamore and Rustic Roads and then out to Venice. God alone knows what the pictures looked like. I was exhausted and made very little sense, I'm sure, but they shot 2¾ hours worth and only need 50 minutes, so I suppose something can be extracted.

Then last night I took Oldjo to supper. She has been suffering from exhaustion and doesn't want to go to New York, as she must, for Cole's,[1]

1. Cole of California, a company for which she designed bathing suits.

and doesn't want to go to Florida, as she promised, to see Ben's father. I think she may just possibly start drinking a lot—no, I don't really. She says meditation (the Maharishi's kind—or was it maybe what Swami told her to do) is no good. Perhaps what she should do is to marry absolutely anyone she can get. She is on a great kick of saying the men have it so much easier than women—they can always get some young girl!

This morning I picked up Paul Bowles and drove him to the San Vicente market to do his shopping. Mrabet and he and Gavin and I are to eat together tonight. Mrabet leaves tomorrow. Paul told me he has seen Tennessee again. He asked him, "Have you seen Chris?" and T. said, "Yes"—nothing more. This was probably vagueness, not a deliberate lie, do you think? When T. and Paul were alone, T. complained bitterly that Mike Steen had engaged a psychiatrist to come and see him. T. said he had thrown the psychiatrist out. It's getting to sound a bit Hitchcock, isn't it?

Tomorrow night I'm having supper with Ted & Ted Cordes—my return for the supper they gave me last time you were away. Sunday I'm going to Bill & Paul as I told you.

A letter from Robin Maugham, who arrives back here in another week. He entirely agrees with my suggestion of queering up the character of Gerald Haxton & wants to show my letter to George Schaefer.[2] G.S. has heard Ray Henderson's "Christmas Carol" music and likes it very much.

Am ¾ through Salka's book. The part about Salka & Berthold is very interesting but far too many outsiders are dragged in and then dismissed with a couple of adjectives.

Thick fog this morning, then it cleared a little and I took Dob down & trotted him and ran him into the water. It's over 90 in town; cool here but you can feel the smog. Plug is so longing to see his adored Puss again. XXXXXXXXXXXXXXX

[Autograph letter]

2. Probably for a T.V. script about Maugham and his American lover Gerald Haxton (1892–1944), eighteen years younger than him. They met in 1914 when they were both working for a Red Cross ambulance unit in Flanders during World War I.

Wednesday [October 23, 1968, London]

Longed-for Stallion—

C.M. Allen turned up at Ladbroke Grove this morning to be drawn and turned out to be a round-faced, 44-year-old (she told me because today is her birthday) member of the titled classes—Lady Allen. She was so coy and cagey about being "Lady" Allen in her letter that I didn't even know what sex she was and simply wrote back to her "Dear C.M. Allen." However, once into the flat, she couldn't keep herself from hinting this way and that about her "wonderful secret" and, when I didn't pick up on it, she finally had to produce her card (printed "Lady Allen") under the guise of recommending me to some friends of hers in Delaware. I didn't turn the card over in her presence (only in the bathroom) and was still feeling perverse enough not to mention it because I could see she was dying that I should know. (I'd introduced her to Anthony and Mrs. Moss, the cleaning lady, simply as "Mrs. Allen"). After the sitting (one drawing turned out well and she liked it too) she had to go to the bank to cash a check for me because I told her I couldn't cash a pound check myself. I accompanied her to the bank and while we waited in line she was so desperate to fill me in that she showed me a card with "Lady Allen" typed on it (the card enabled her to cash checks up to £30) pretending to wanting only to enlighten me as to banking procedures in England. I still would not acknowledge that she was a "Lady"—I was punishing her for not letting me know in her letter. Had I known from the start I would have charged her a lot more than £25, the sly old bird.[1]

Tony Gibbs showed up today, too, with another £75 for a second drawing which makes a total so far of £225, and Kitty ain't through yet! He hasn't even cashed any of his traveller's checks.

Last night David Hockney took me, Patrick Procktor, a dress-designing friend of theirs named Ozzie Davis,[2] and Peter, of course, to a very good Indian restaurant in the Fulham Rd. called Tandoori. Anthony was invited too but because of it's being the night of the first

---

1. Consuelo Maria Linares Rivas Allen (1924–1991) was the second wife of British chemist and industrialist Sir Peter Allen (1905–1993), who helped develop plastic fibers, including polythene and a polyester called Terylene. He was then chairman of the chemical company ICI. He also wrote books on railways and on golf. He had been knighted only the year before, in 1967.
2. In fact, it was Ossie Clark (1942–1996), who studied at the Manchester School of Art and the Royal College of Art with Hockney and was a close friend and, later, a subject of the large painting Mr. and Mrs. Clark and Percy.

performance of *Look Back* in front of an audience, he was an hour and a half late, by which time the cook had gone home. So he only got a plate of cold Indian sweet meats (ugh!) but was in a good mood anyway because the performance had gone well. We went to Patrick's after the restaurant for tea and a look at the Olympics gymnasts on his color telly. [Ossie Clark], a great pothead I gather, prepared a big pipeful of hash for the guests[. . . .] A certain Saint Kit [. . .] graciously abstained.

Patrick is working on several new canvases, all of them single figures based on photographs he's taken of Gervase. All but one of the paintings were quite poor I thought but maybe that's because they're "works in progress."

Dinner tonight with La Caron. I dread her sulky French-heel boy-friend.[3] Anthony is supposed to come in after dinner by which time Leslie & friend will most certainly be in bed. His lateness is being carried to the extremes of human expectations. I am getting very good at coping with it, by which I mean I just go ahead and make my own plans quite independently of him. This morning was a classic situation. He was supposed to be *at* the theater at 10:30 a.m. as I knew in advance, so I asked "Lady" Allen to come at 11 a.m. Anthony was so curious to see my mysterious sitter that, though she arrived fifteen minutes late, he was *still* there. As though he and Mrs. Moss weren't enough to drive me round the bend, Anthony asked the girl who lives downstairs up for a Bloody Mary, and *she* brings a girlfriend with her! The joint was jumping, but not as high as those taut cat nerves. Anthony cannot resist a childish, mischievous desire to rile me if he can. I think my patience irks him a lot—he smells the smoke of rage beneath it and that both intrigues him and frightens him a little bit, an irresistible combination when he's in a certain devilish mood. So far, Cat patience has triumphed. Kitty is only impatient for his Sweet Old Steed and so looks forward to the 29th.

With a kitten's heart, Furkin

[*Autograph letter*]

3. Caron divorced her second husband, Peter Hall, in 1965 and married her third, Michael Laughlin, in 1969. The French boyfriend is unidentified.

Thursday. [October 24, 1968, London]

Darling Velvet Muzzle—

Had lunch today with John Lehmann who was very friendly and I think pleased that I'd called him and taken the trouble to come. For the first time since I've known him I got a feeling of loneliness from him. He looks much older now than when I saw him last (several years ago admittedly) and I think he is feeling his age, too, feeling it is much more of an effort to keep up and yet not wanting to be out of it or thought out of it. He'd just been to stay with Gore and Howard in Rome, said he thought Gore had become slightly pompous (that's the kettle criticizing the pot!) and also said he thought Gore's health not good, though he couldn't say exactly what was wrong. He complained that Gore & Howard didn't get up in the morning till after 11 and said he never saw Gore doing any work while he was there. First thing after breakfast Howard got onto the phone to get the day's stream of boys flowing. John said they arrived at 2:30 and 6 p.m. daily.

John had a novelist-playwright-painter named Colin Spencer to lunch also. He has a play opening tonight in the West End called *Spitting Image*, about two queers, one of whom gets pregnant and gives birth. Spencer is about 38–40, quite attractive (a sort of blunt-faced Ivan Moffat) but not altogether "nice." He shares a house with Richard Simon[1] but they are no longer lovers. He's being divorced by his wife who is trying to keep him from seeing his 7 yr. old son on the grounds that he is a practising homosexual. He quoted his current friend as saying indignantly: "You're not practising, you're full-fledged!" His sex talk, a combination of bragging and salivating, was somehow distasteful and made him unlikable in spite of his charm. He is definitely not a first-rate writer. There is an unmistakable cheapness in him. Maybe you know his novels. The latest (the third of four related books) is called *Tyranny*. They are long books which John complained about. John liked the play though—he'd seen it the night before.

John sends you love but complains, natch, that you've not written in more than six months. He fixed lunch for us himself which quite surprised me—shrimp cocktail, cold Fortnum & Mason meat pie & hot

1. Simon (b. 1932) was a literary agent at Curtis Brown and represented Isherwood in London. Later, in 1971-1972, he set up his own firm, Richard Scott Simon Ltd.

veg. He seemed too large for his kitchen and moved clumsily in and out of it, carrying dishes and bottles. In the middle of lunch he suddenly called me "Caskey, I mean Bill, I mean *Don!*" I honestly don't think he meant to do it but he does show so clearly how his mind works. With Martin Hensler tonight to see *Hotel in Amsterdam.*

Kitty loves his old Dear so much and longs to chew his soft ears. XXXXXXX T.

[*Autograph letter*]

Friday [October 25, 1968, London]

Worshipped Glossyhoof—

To my surprise and enormous relief I *very much* enjoyed *Hotel in Amsterdam* last night, in spite of a few of the performances which seemed quite wrong, including Scofield's. He gives an eccentric, mannered and obviously virtuoso performance which is never dull and never right. I'm sure, like Olivier, he knows so much about acting that he can never again give a good, straight, simple performance. But the play itself is fascinating on stage, full of atmosphere and sadness, very like Chekhov sometimes. I had to go backstage afterwards because I was sitting in house seats and I noticed at the curtain calls Scofield was straining to see who occupied them and I thought, if he recognized me it might cause a situation if I didn't go back, since he probably knows I am staying with Anthony (and they are about to do this T.V. show together[1]). He was very friendly and pleased that I came back so I guess it was good.

Martin Hensler (John G.'s friend) came to the theater with me though he'd already seen it. I've never before spent very much time with Martin, except when I drew him and then we hardly talked, so it was a pleasant surprise for me last night to realize I really like him; underneath the bad English and vain exterior is somebody quite friendly and aware, even quite intelligent. We went to the Melita and Anthony & Eleanor Fazan (she played Nicol Williamson's wife in the film of *Inadmissible*) joined us later for dinner. She is a very nice woman, you'd like her I'm sure—she is

---

1. "Emlyn" (1969), the third play in Alun Owen's trilogy "The Male of the Species," for "Saturday Night Theatre." Scofield won an Emmy.

also a choreographer and Nigel Davenport's mistress. I hope you liked her in the film as much as I did. I think she looks a lot like Jeanne Moreau.

Later.

I went to John Craxton's house today and got shown a lot of bad paintings which were horribly difficult to say anything positive about. He lives in Hampstead in a weird crazy-built Edwardian house with his old father and endless relative-type people. He did a drawing of me, quite like me only making me look a good 10 years younger. It's not much good as a drawing. He said he would send a photograph of it to me. I then got the record for Gerald & tonight, dread dread, I see Look Back and have a champagne supper at an Indian restaurant with Anthony and the cast afterwards.

So characteristic of my adventures in London, especially those having anything to do with Anthony, this morning only, knowing full well I'm going on Tuesday, he had the idea that I should do a drawing of Kenneth Haigh for the poster of Hotel in A. when Scofield leaves.[2] I'm supposed to be paid properly this time because it's a successful West End production now. Anyway, a sitting has been set up for Monday afternoon. Wouldn't you know it wouldn't be set up over the weekend? So more of Kitty's frantic last-minute pencil waving. Nevertheless, regardless of the outcome of the sitting, Kitty is determined to get onto his Tuesday plane.

This letter will barely arrive home before Kitty so the next news old Dub will have of him will be delivered in pusson. He is so looking forward to his dear basket and that warm giant rumpcushion.

With tender loving cat thoughts, Purrpaws.

[Autograph letter]

2. British actor Kenneth Haigh (b. 1931) played Jimmy Porter in the original stage production of Look Back in Anger in 1956 and took the role to Broadway in 1958; he replaced Scofield as Laurie in The Hotel in Amsterdam in January 1969.

Tuesday (deep) Mourning [October 29, 1968]   [Santa Monica]

Darling Faithless Fur,

As soon as the bad old phone rang, Dubbin KNEW,[1] and later when Kitty's letter from last Friday came, speaking of Kitty's certain arrival, a few tears fell. At least, one would have sworn they were tears but doubtless it was only rheum, since the University of Cats at Los Angeles absolutely assures us that Dobbins have no feelings or hearts and we needn't worry how we treat them. (Soviet scientists have, it is rumored, declared that Dobs not only have hearts but that they are so *enormous* that the kittens never noticed them; they were actually *inside* one and thought it was the Red Room at El Caballo.[2]) Anyhow Rubble promises to be brave and not feel sorry for himself like Oldjo, the public nuisance, because after all what could be stupider than a thing that can't feel being sorry for a thing with no feelings?

Tonight I'm going with Gavin to see the *Nazarin*. Tomorrow we are both having dinner with Jim and Jack—this was arranged yesterday and you were invited. Jim wants to have a reading of the play but I told him to wait and not set it up until you are back and we can discuss it—I mean, discuss who we get to read it and all the diplomacy and care needed not to raise false hopes.

Since Anthony has now read the play, what about Nicholas Thompson and Bob Regester, who both begged to see it? There are the most serious objections to both—and neither one of them knows that it is finished, even. But I *was* impressed by Nicholas as a true eager beaver. As for Bob, he is simply significant as a flea in Tony's, Neil's and I guess Anthony's ear. This isn't really a suggestion even. Just turn it around in your head, as long as you are there.

Seth has moved in with Michael Sean. I mean, he is in the downstair part of the same house, with a roommate named Richard. Not that kind of a roommate I feel sure. I went around to see them and they were very sweet and then two more boys and a girl came in. They wanted me to stay for supper (this was on Sunday) but I couldn't, as I was having

---

1. That Bachardy had delayed his return. See below, p. 355.
2. That is, the bedroom at 145 Adelaide Drive. During their first year there, 1959–1960, Bachardy painted the whole house himself, choosing scarlet for the master bedroom and a bedcover and curtains of off-white denim with a thin, charcoal grey stripe, "*very* jazzy for 1960," he recalls.

supper with Paul and Bill (maybe you should send Paul best wishes for his show next Sunday Nov. 23rd). John Zeigel was there, bearded and very healthy from all this butch bike-riding. He went off a bit looped and I wondered if he'd make it home. He went on all through dinner about his German boyfriend Manfred, who is also a bikeboy and very beautiful. They went to Greece together. Zeigelita is also going up to San Francisco for a whirl with Thom [Gunn]. I guess Mike [Kitay] doesn't mind this any more. I thought Paul looked terribly tired and much older and sadder. Now they talk of going to live for a while in Taos. Bill dreads it but it's what Paul wants. I guess this is one of their really serious problems, a place they both like.

I finished Salka's book which is awfully good as a portrait of her and her feelings toward Berthold and her sons (not of Berthold himself, though some of his letters are marvellous). Everybody else in the book is shadowy. I think this is partly because of drastic cutting. But the book does have a shape and is certainly a successful piece of work. I'll say something about it for the publishers.

Never did hear a word from that horrid old Academy.[3]

It is now thought that [Hubert] Humphrey might just squeeze through, but it would be very very close, and so many people have vowed not to vote that I doubt it.

Darling precious treasure of my old life, don't please think of Drub as a drag. Do everything in London that you feel you should, or want to do. Naggin will be waiting and chewing quietly.

　　　　　　　XXXXXXXXXXXXXXXXXX Dusty Prancer XX

[*Typed letter, signed, with autograph additions*]

---

3. Isherwood was joining the Academy of Motion Pictures so that he could take Bachardy to screenings there. Films were often shown before public release, and the quality of the projection, on a big screen, was good. They first attended on March 2, 1969, to see *The Girl with a Pistol*, a 1968 Italian comedy starring Monica Vitti.

Wednesday [October 30, 1968, London]

Dearest Silkmane—

His disappointed neigh on the telephone yesterday when Kitty said he wasn't coming home yet nearly broke Sillycat's heart. He does long to see his Old Dear and his reasons for staying on do seem to be frivolous ones today. But still it is good that Kitty doesn't leave London feeling he's leaving behind unfinished work and unfulfilled duties. His drawing of Kenneth Haigh has turned out well—I got the photographs of it last night. If I'd left yesterday I could not have taken the original drawing with me or seen how the photographs turned out. My still being in London will also make it easier to get proper money out of Oscar Lewenstein for the drawing. And these people the Davisons (he's Jimmy Davison's cousin) Marguerite put me onto not only bought both drawings I did of their seven-year-old son but want me to draw their twelve-year-old son, too, so I will try to set that up before I go.[1] Also I'm drawing Ron Kitaj tomorrow morning and Robert Medley in the afternoon.

I'm having tea today with Wystan who's leaving tomorrow and is understandably booked up all other times. He let out a cry of surprise and delight when I called him which warmed a kitten's heart. I will see the Gielgud-Alan Bennett play on Saturday and also be able to see a big Balthus show at the Tate. Richard Buckle gave me a preview of the Beaton show at the Natl. Portrait Gallery Monday evening. The gala party is tonight but I don't think I will go though Richard wants me to. The show is wonderful and Richard has done a very good job of mounting it. Kitty's one major criticism of the show is the postage-stamp size of Dubbin's photograph and it is not even one of the good ones of him. Cecil has taken beautiful pictures of the Old Nag but the one in the show has Him giving his Granny-Dub grin, which doesn't fool anybody, at least not any Cat.

John G. & Martin took me to *Hair* on Monday night which Kitty very much enjoyed. It even made him laugh and clap his paws. Both John

1. Daniel Pomeroy Davison (1925– 2010), American banker, then running the London branch of J.P. Morgan. He was the fifth generation of Davisons to work for J.P. Morgan and was later known for reviving the United States Trust Company. His wife, Katusha, née Cheremeteff, was the daughter of a Russian count. Bachardy drew their youngest son Henry (Harry) and, later, on November 2, their middle son, George, at the Davisons' house in Chester Square. The following spring, May 2, he drew Davison (see below). The eldest son, Daniel P. Davison III, was away at boarding school in the U.S.

and Martin were very sweet and took me afterwards to dinner at the Escargot in Greek St. which was very old-world snug and delicious. I think it was Kitty's reward for taking Martin to dinner when John was away in Brighton. Sunday night was dinner with Alfred Lynch and his friend Jimmy,[2] both of whom I like, and Anthony—we all went to a movie called House of Cards, entertaining but totally undistinguished. Orson Welles has a small part in it.

I think Anthony is quite impressed by the play and rather intrigued by it, too. I can hear wheels going around in his head even. [... He] dared, without saying a word to me about it, to take the play off to the Court on Monday—I'd left early to draw Colin Spencer and left the play in the flat because Anthony had only read half of it on Sunday—and let an assistant there [...] read it.[3] When Anthony told me this on Monday night, I was furious and lost my temper in a way I have never done with him before. As you can imagine, he was very surprised. We had quite an argument. This is another reason why I didn't want to leave yesterday, in a cloud of ill feeling.

Apparently the assistant adored it though, even called after midnight on Monday to enthuse about it, but I was still so cross I wouldn't speak to him. I'm sure a production at the Court could and would be arranged if we wanted it. But as far as I'm concerned we don't—anyway not without the very best cast and director. Anthony has not yet said anything about wanting to direct it himself but I'll bet he is seriously considering it. He suggested Peter O'Toole for Patrick, or Dirk Bogarde, though I said I thought him too old.[4] The only criticisms he's come up with so far are: 1) he thinks it is occasionally too underlined, too on the nose; he would prefer a slightly less straightforward approach in a few of the speeches (I will try to get him to specify); 2) the convulsive laughter with which the play ends is, practically speaking, impossible for most actors, at least impossible to produce night after night. Jack Larson also said the same

---

2. British actor (1931–2003) and his longterm companion James Culliford. Lynch had many small roles in the new working-class drama staged at the Royal Court in the 1950s and 1960s, and he was in the 1959 film Look Back in Anger and worked in T.V.

3. Nicholas Wright (b. 1940), British playwright and director, who directed his own play, Changing Lines, at the Royal Court that summer and who, from 1969, was the first Artistic Director of the Royal Court Theatre Upstairs.

4. Irish actor Peter O'Toole (b. 1932) became a huge star as Lawrence of Arabia in 1962. British actor Dirk Bogarde (1921–1999) was in his late forties. Page recalls that he finished reading the play soon after Nicholas Wright, and that he told Bachardy he did not feel the play could work.

thing to me on the phone before I left. He said it's an actor's nightmare, far worse than having to cry. I do see why, too, but don't feel it will be difficult to change if you agree.

Last night *Look Back* opened officially. I dreaded going but do think the performance was the best I've seen. The notices this morning are very good indeed. I've only read the *Times* and *Mail*, both good, especially the *Mail*—Osborne is likened to Ibsen, of all people—and I hear the others are all favorable, too. Anthony is excited and pleased. He has gotten a lot of personal praise for the production. David and Peter were also there and the four of us had a wonderful meal at the Hungry Horse (Kitty's favorite restaurant, natch)—Kitty had kedgeree and steak and kidney pudding. David and Peter were very sweet as usual.

Kitty must fly to his tub and wash his fur for Wystan.

Don't give up on Old Kitty. He really will be on the plane Monday. Besides longing for his Loved Hide, he has to cast his small catvote.[5]

Kitty loves his Dear Horse so very much and wants desperately to avoid another tragic Bridle Falls incident.[6]

With basketfuls of furred love and musical purrs,

Pink Pads XXXXXXXX

[*Autograph letter*]

Wednesday 30th [October, 1968]   [Santa Monica]

Bestloved Snowgaiters,

[H]ow Dobbin thinks of him and longs to feel the brush of his great tail! We are having such weird weather here, rain last night and now it can't make up its mind, shall it be nice or cloud up again. Am just off to see Gerald. At Michael's suggestion they switched it to Wednesday, hoping you'd be back. I think Gerald gets some healing vibrations from holding that paw, and who shall blame him?

---

5. In the presidential election on Tuesday, November 5.
6. At the close of his October 22 letter, above, Isherwood sketched a horse collapsed on the ground, weeping, and he labelled it Bridle Falls, a punning reference to the spectacular and dangerous Bridal Veil Falls on the Yosemite Valley floor. Isherwood and Bachardy visited Yosemite many times.

A card for you from Terence McNally[1] thanking you for the photos and apologizing for his long delay in writing.

Last night I went with Gavin to see *Nazarin*, *The Andalusian Dog* and *The Criminal Life of Archibaldo de la Cruz*. I do think the actor in the *Nazarin* is awfully good but somehow it didn't impress me nearly as much as it impresses Gavin. Buñuel had told Gavin that he made it to show "what's wrong with the Christian idea"—that is, the humble love-everybody approach. But, if so, Buñuel is too subtle for Drub's schoolmasterish tastes, he doesn't lay it on the line. The climax, when the old woman gives the Nazarin a pineapple, is supposed to be a tremendous wow, but I couldn't see it, because actually quite a lot of other people have been nice to him already. I really more enjoyed *The Criminal Life*, which Gavin scorns. It seemed very vivid and realistic and then quite shocking and mad, like a dream. And *The Andalusian Dog* is fun but you can have only so much of surrealism.[2] It did seem far better than Cocteau's *Blood of a Poet* though. I enjoyed our evening but didn't feel any more than a half-and-half Buñuel fan. We ended up eating at Matteo's, too, which was a drag. It was rather a masked evening. Gavin didn't make any interesting confessions or comments. Incidentally the audience at the Buñuel was one of the wayoutest I have ever seen, as though Tiny Tim's whole family had assembled.[3]

At last I really have got the book started and am quite turned on about it. It's fun jumping about in time like this, and I think it works. Am still toiling on the Vedanta article for the encyclopaedia. I must have been mad to accept it.

Richard Simon couldn't get the Ethel Mayne books from the publishers, *Inner Circle* and *Nine of Hearts*. So he is advertising for them. Heywood Hill is hopeless. I must have that line about my grandmother described as "the old serpent"![4]

---

1. American playwright (b. 1939), author of *And Things That Go Bump in the Night* (1965) and, later, *Love! Valor! Compassion!* (1994), *Master Class* (1995), *Corpus Christi* (1998), and the books for the musicals of *Kiss of the Spider Woman* (1992) and *Ragtime* (1997).
2. *Un Chien Andalou* (1929) is a surrealist silent short, Buñuel's first film, made in France with Salvador Dalí. Spanish actor Francisco Rabal (1926–2001) played the beleaguered priest in *Nazarin* (1959), which was made in Mexico, as was *Ensayo de un crimen* or *The Criminal Life of Archibaldo de la Cruz* (1955) about a would-be serial killer.
3. That is, the ringletted American singer and ukulele player (1932–1996).
4. Ethel Colburn Mayne (1870–1941), Irish journalist, critic, biographer, translator, novelist, short-story writer. She had an unconsummated romantic relationship with Isherwood's father,

Have just returned from Gerald. His voice is amazingly much stronger although it is very difficult for him to talk and he only gets a word or two out now and then. I took him the Gita record, having got an extra one from Vedanta Place to give him. I'm really awful on it, so dead and dull.[5] They have read the Ackerley book (Chris's copy) right through already and of course that must have been meat and drink for Gerald, I wouldn't wonder if it isn't the reason why he's got temporarily stronger. Michael seems to get a little bit smaller and skinnier every time I see him.

Am starting to read Mailer's articles on the two conventions, which are supposed to contain his notorious confession that he is getting tired "of Negroes and their rights, bored with Negroes triumphantly late for appointments, depressed with black inhumanity to black in Biafra" and that he's becoming a "closet Republican." So much for him! It seems he has been praised for these remarks in *Time Magazine*.[6]

There's also a book of Paul Bowles stories I didn't know about. It includes the ones in that little paperback we have and several more. Have got this too.[7] Haven't seen Paul the last few days. I should take him to the market again.

A hoofclasp across the sea from his loving old
XXXXXXXXXXXXXX Drub the Waiter XX

[*Typed letter, signed, with autograph additions*]

---

conducted mostly by letter, and afterwards became a family friend. Frank Isherwood referred to her as Venus. Her short story "Still Life," published in *Inner Circle* (1925), evokes a visit to Kathleen Isherwood and her mother, Emily Machell Smith, who is presented as a serpent.

5. *Selections from the Bhagavad-Gita (The Song of God), A New Translation in Prose and Poetry* by Swami Prabhavananda and Christopher Isherwood, recorded on Caedmon TC 1249 (1968). Isherwood read from the Gita translation he made with Prabhavananda in 1944.

6. Norman Mailer's "Miami Beach and Chicago" was the eighty-nine-page cover story in *Harper's Magazine* for November (pp. 41–130); Isherwood paraphrases from pp. 58–59. *Time Magazine* called Mailer's piece in *Harper's* "some of his best writing," see "Comment: Mailer's America," Friday, October 11, 1968.

7. The four stories in *A Hundred Camels in the Courtyard* (1967) were included in *The Time of Friendship* (1967), both of which Isherwood read in 1968. The same year, he also read *Up Above the World* (1966), a novel by Bowles, and *Love with a Few Hairs* (1967), a novel by Mohammad Mrabet translated by Paul Bowles. Isherwood and Bachardy also owned *Delicate Prey and Other Stories* (1950) and *Cold Point and Other Stories* (1968).

Thursday [October 31, 1968, London]

Cherished Pluggin—

Oldcat had a very nice hour and a half with Wystan yesterday. He is very well I think—much thinner than when I saw him last. I don't know whether he lost weight intentionally or whether it was the result of several weeks in his cast. He showed me snapshots of him in the cast. I was amazed to see how elaborate it was—going right around his middle, over one shoulder and propping up one arm (his right arm) in midair. It must have been hellishly inconvenient for him. He said he could manage to unbutton his fly to pee but could not rebutton himself[1].

He showed and read me bits of what he calls his "autobiography," by which he means it's the closest he will come to one. It is compilation of extracts, bits and pieces, quotations, etc., which have interested him over the years. A kind of abstract autobiography compounded of what he is interested in—quite like Horse's book of quotations & excerpts from other people's work, except that Wystan had things like a list of various odd terms for a cock and a corresponding list of terms for a cunt. I also think some of Wystan's own poems are incorporated too. At any rate the book looks and is very long, and he is determined not to cut it.[2]

He is staying in a nice flat in Bryanston Square belonging to a music critic called Peter Heyworth who is away now. He leaves for N.Y. today. I suddenly decided without any premeditation to tell him the story of the split with Lincoln. He had never heard anything about it from Lincoln, nor ever anything unpleasant about me from Lincoln. He said he would speak to him and fix things up. He seemed very confident that he could do so and said he would write to me about it. Lincoln is supposed to meet him at the airport today. I wonder what will happen.[3]

Wystan sends you his love. He was very curious to hear what you

1. Auden had had a car accident in Austria the preceding winter and broke his right shoulder. He was driving back to his house in Kirchstetten with his groceries, reached across to stop the eggs falling off the seat, and drove into a telegraph pole.
2. *A Certain World: A Commonplace Book* (1971). Isherwood's commonplace book remains unpublished.
3. The split occurred because Kirstein could never bring himself to ask George Balanchine's permission to sell as ballet souvenirs the folio of drawings commissioned from Bachardy, even though he had them printed. Kirstein was irrationally afraid that Bachardy would be perceived as a boyfriend he was trying to promote. Auden was not able to bring about a reconciliation.

are doing and how the book about your parents is going. He grunted with a mixture of satisfaction and envy to know that the *Cabaret* money keeps coming in each week. Chester has been sick from some kind of Russian fever which brought on a gradual numbness in the limbs which frightened them both. Apparently it was quite serious and Chester had to be in hospital, and be given cortisone for four weeks. Chester still maintains his Athens life and has gone back there now.

A brief drink with Lady St. Just (Maria Britneva to those who know better, and worse)[4] whom I met at Leslie Caron's. She called up and was determined (why I don't know) we should meet before I go. She is as determinedly and indefatigably pushy, fanatical and possessive as ever, but still somewhat likeable in small, infrequent doses. Much talk about Tennessee. She is definitely pro-Mike Steen and anti-Bill Glavin[5] and thinks Paul Bowles chilly and cynical and unloving.

I'm drawing Ron Kitaj in the morning, having lunch with Marguerite and Kate and drawing Robert Medley in the afternoon. Am seeing John G.'s play on Sat. And whizzing home to Dearolddrub on Monday. Kitty is missing his basket so and pining for his warm companion and dreaming of sinking his tiny teeth into those soft pointed ears.

Kitty will save all further news for Monday.

With tender sweet kitten kisses, Claws XXXXX

[*Autograph letter with enclosure[6]*]

Thursday 31st [October, 1968]   [Santa Monica]

Don't know when this will arrive but will send a word of love to my Darling, though there isn't much news.

It's sort of dull today. Yesterday Drub was trotted on the beach and then dipped in the ocean, and then taken to the gym so today he is

4. Russian-born, English-educated actress (1921–1994). In 1956, she had married Peter Grenfell, 2nd Baron St. Just (1922–1984), the heir and putative son of English banker and politician Edward Grenfell. She was a close friend of Tennessee Williams and became his literary executor.
5. Paid companion to Williams from 1965 to 1970.
6. Newspaper clipping titled, "The Cat-Snatchers," about cat dealers, thieves, and breeders supplying cats for laboratory research. At the bottom Bachardy wrote, "I hope they don't get Kitty before he boards his Monday flycart. K."

resting on orders from Dr. Dobbin who reminds him sternly that old racers must proceed with caution.

Had supper with Jack & Jim last night and took Paul Bowles. Gavin was there too. Paul says that Mike Steen phoned him to say that Tennessee has disappeared! By which he only meant that T. has gone off with Bill Glavin without leaving an address. Since T. had remarked to Paul—referring to life with Mike—"Isn't fascism wonderful?" this is hardly surprising.

After all that work done on the house, water from the recent rain poured into Jim's bedroom the night before last! Jack was hysterical and the builder was sent for at six in the morning. The truth is[,] that old dump is incurable.

Loves his treasured angel Halopuss so *very very* much and longs to fondle that paw that never knew the touch of sin.

Kitty's Plumed Servant. XXXXXXXXXX

[*Autograph letter*]

Friday [November 1, 1968, London]

Darling Patient Pony—

A sweet picture for him and floods of catkisses.[1]

Kitty dreams of the Red Room at El Caballo and longs for nothing else. The Animals will have a champagne supper there on Monday night.

With a kitten's as always devoted heart and soul,

Constantcat

P.S. Have had supper with Nancy West, drawn Robert Medley and Ron Kitaj and tomorrow draw another of the Davison children (for $). Cashcat

[*Autograph letter*]

· · ·

1. Enclosure lost.

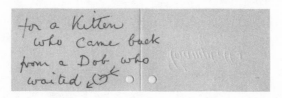

[Autograph note on gift tag from Campbell's Books for All Ages, Westwood Village]

[Autograph note on greeting card]

•   •   •

April 18 [1969]   [Santa Monica]

Angel, in an old Drabbin's darkness,

[J]ust want to get a few lines off to my darling today to tell him of Rub's ceaseless love. Yesterday he was so sad he ate up all the peanut brittle without stopping, so the night was gassy.[1]

Had supper with Jim. He said how you got more and more handsome and marvellous, and then how Jack was a great poet, and he said to Dub, "We're both *so* lucky!" Jim wanted to go to a hippie bookshop called Papa Bach's, and there we ran into Jim Gill, who looks thinner and very distinguished. We went up to his place for a few minutes. He doesn't paint, just studies mysticism in great big books. Meanwhile there was some kind of flap at the liquor store below, and no less than five cop cars arrived with cops who entered with drawn guns. But all seemed calm. Jim Gill says it is getting to be a very alarming neighborhood and all the maximum security cases from the Sawtelle funny farm keep escaping and attacking people.[2]

Yesterday Rub trotted. The beach is quite wrecked, all rocks and dirt for about half a mile.[3] Met the skinny maths prof., Basil Gordon, so am going with him tonight to see (Ugh!) *The Illustrated Man*. Also met Mike Van Horn, who is all alone, Jim Crabe[4] being in New York, so am having dinner with him tomorrow, no Sunday—tomorrow is Chris. And Jo is Monday, we are going to the Miramar together to vote first.[5] (So you see

1. Bachardy returned to London on April 17, 1969, and stayed with Anthony Page. He had been hired to draw the Earl and Countess of Harewood, a commission arranged by Richard Buckle.
2. That is, the Sawtelle Veterans' Hospital; the surrounding neighborhood, close to Sawtelle Boulevard, was known as Sawtelle (south of Santa Monica Boulevard, north of West Pico, east of South Centinela, and west of the 405 freeway).
3. Following heavy rainstorms.
4. American cinematographer (1931–1998), for T.V. and feature films.
5. There was a meeting at the Miramar Hotel about the Santa Monica Freeway.

I am having a real mercy-killing time, should have been a St. Bernard instead of a plug). Tuesday is Gavin, Wed. Vedanta, Friday Sta. Barbara for the Writers Conference.[6]

Jim says that Tony Harvey is so hysterical and more and more I begin to feel he will throw up this *Cabaret* project.[7] He told Jim on the phone yesterday that he and Dan, after a year's love, have come to an understanding. That is, Dan has agreed to live with him on the following terms—Tony must guarantee to earn *at least* as much money as he does![8] Shades of Krishnamurti! I opened his book at random and read an attack on marriage which is based entirely on the belief that it is a relationship like that.[9]

Talking of money reminds me of business ... I went to Western Union, they couldn't have been sweeter, and the bill is to be revised and practically halved; they admitted they had billed you for a direct wire, not a night letter. I called Amellican Expless and they are going to query the $5.50 listed for Sinclair, but they said I should pay the rest of the bill—which would be $32.91 instead of $38.41. What shall I do? Pay nothing and wait? Or just pay the $20.16 which is the only clear item: the bill at the Bellevue Rest[aurant], on March 14 when we took John Lehmann there? Be sure to let me know about this. I agree with you, the rest of the bill seems utterly obscure and I think it is probably a mistake.

A letter came from Tom Wright but you will be seeing him in England anyhow. He just flaps on and mourns over his bounced check and the vagueness of the publishers about printing your drawing on his jacket.[10]

Have got the two hippie boys coming this afternoon. They are being driven to see me by the father of one of them, who is a psychologist at Cal. State. We talked on the phone because apparently the boys are too helpless to get the directions themselves! He said he wouldn't come in himself as the boys wanted it to be "their scene." What a late nineteen-sixties scene!

---

6. At the Adult Education Center, where Isherwood was to speak.
7. British child-actor-turned-director Anthony Harvey (b. 1931) was planning a film version of *Cabaret*. Isherwood and Bachardy had been asked to collaborate on a treatment for a screenplay.
8. Dan Tondevold. Harvey had just had a big success with *The Lion in Winter* (1968), for which he received an Academy Award nomination.
9. Krishnamurti often attacked marriage for institutionalizing possessiveness and sexual gratification without real communication, mutual self-understanding, or love. Isherwood had a number of his books, including *Freedom from the Known*, published that year.
10. Bachardy's drawing of Wright appeared on the jacket of Wright's travel memoir, *Into the Maya World* (1969); Wright's check for the drawing had bounced.

I felt like the madam of a whorehouse to which a father is bringing his sons to get laid! I'm sure he serves them breakfast in bed and attends symposiums on the question: should you smoke pot with your boy? There is a very Henry James comedy lurking within this situation.

Old Horse is rattling on so as not to be sad, but great tears keep slithering down in his coffee. Don't forget old loyal Hoof.

To London →

Something went wrong with this drawing!

[*Typed letter with autograph additions*]

April 19 [1969]   [Santa Monica]

Darling Treasurepaws,

[N]o mail this morning and anyhow it's impossible I should hear from you, but will just keep the channel open with a few items. It's a glorious day but chilly and windy. Olddub was wakened out of some merciful sleep by Oldjo who wants to give a birthday party for Paul Wonner on Thursday—BUT we have to start at 6:30 because Jo is going to work next day so must not be kept up late for this banquet. (Doubtless there will be *double* portions of enchilada etc. ordered up from Cas Mia!) Now I have got to get him a present!

Just had a talk with Jim Bridges. He says Gavin is in bliss. Christopher is "just a child" and so happy and Gavin bought him a secondhand V.W. in return for his painting the upstairs (so I fear we can't afford him!).[1] Not only this but Gavin is going to Ensenada this weekend with SOMEBODY ELSE!! The prime of Miss Jean Brodie![2] Jim had just seen *The Immortal Story* and raved over it.[3] At the end of the month, Warhol

---

1. Christopher Wedow, an aspiring critic.
2. Isherwood, Bachardy, and Lambert went together on April 6 to see Maggie Smith in the 1968 film about the schoolmistress pursued by her special pupils, by her music-teacher lover who wants to marry her, and by her art-teacher ex-lover who is married to someone else.
3. Orson Welles's 1968 film based on Isak Dinesen's story.

arrives with a cargo of superstars and they are going to take 2 houses with 2 swimming pools.

Nellie on the other hand is cross. She told Jim he had betrayed her by not coming back from N.Y. to [be] at Miguel's deathbed (he's fine now). Nellie is going to tell Miguel to leave his wife, she says.

Last night I saw *The Illustrated Man* and believe me it was *worse* than you thought it was going to be. Strictly a family affair, really only Rod and Bloom and Bobby Drivas, they kept cropping up in the future, and Steiger took off all of his clothes, and even eyes accustomed to seeing Dobbin in the boudoir might well have been stricken blind with horror. Bobby did his best, but it was a screamer part, and when he screams he suddenly looks like a middle-aged Italian countess having hysterics.[4]

The two little boys who came to see me, Peter and Jim, were quite adorable, even for little boys. The little curly-headed Jewish (?) one is a magician; I am to see him perform at a hippie theater in Venice next weekend, and the tall thin one, blond with a weak moustache, is a pacifist and a Vedantist. It was impossible to guess if they were making it together or even if they were "lovers", they were just sort of magically involved with each other and I saw a great deal of the relationship I had with Edward Upward at Cambridge in it. Their conversation with me was kind of dubbed in with a mimic dialogue they kept getting into in which they talked to each other and gave imitations of me. When I showed them the D.H. Lawrence candlestick they got down on the floor and prostrated, banging their heads, sort of ironically but adoringly. It was very amusing and I wished so much you had been there, but probably they won't seem quite as stunning next time, and a great deal less later. Perhaps one should only meet people like that once.[5]

---

4. *The Illustrated Man* was Jack Smight's science-fiction movie based on Ray Bradbury's 1951 story collection. Steiger, who had a lifelong problem controlling his weight, plays the illustrated man who is covered in tattoos. The tattoos unfold as stories that terrify a drifter, played by handsome, gay actor Robert Drivas (1938–1986).
5. Peter Schneider (1950–2007), a student at Santa Monica College and afterwards of English, at UCLA. He worked as a magician. Later he was a writer, editor, teacher, and Vedanta devotee. Jim Gates (1950–*circa* 1990), also briefly a student at Santa Monica College, was a violinist, and later, for a short time, a monk of the Ramakrishna Order. Schneider was straight; Gates was gay and somewhat in love with him. The D.H. Lawrence candlestick was made by Lawrence from a twisted tree branch and given to Isherwood by Frieda Lawrence, Dorothy Brett, or Mabel Dodge Luhan when Isherwood visited Taos in 1950.

Did I tell you Mr. Walsh[6] put the new lock on the studio? It works so much better than the other.

The man who cuts your hair called today. (I mean Rudy—he says be sure & call him when you get back. He'd expected you to call before leaving. I told him you left in such a hurry.) Ted [called] yesterday. No one else.

No news of our play or of Tony Harvey. I think he's in San Fran.

An old plug's love and hopes that his Darling is well and frisking and that London isn't too cold or rainy or anything.

XXX D. XXXXXX

When you go to Heywood Hill, about the Klimt, will you order the Caravaggio too? It's by Robert Payne. Published by W.H. Allen.[7]

[Autograph letter with autograph additions]

Sunday, April 20. [1969]   [Santa Monica]

Dearest love,

[N]ot much to report today. I saw Swami yesterday afternoon. He asked after you but of course I haven't heard from you yet. He says he has heard, from India, that Vandananda has been writing to them and wants to return and work there, which seems extraordinary to me; of all the swamis I'd have thought he was the one who likes being here the most. He seems to adore all things western. But actually Swami talked most about devotion and how Krishna (*Sri*, not George!)[1] had said that he gave liberation freely to all but that he was niggardly about giving devotion. And then Swami said that of course if you had devotion it wouldn't matter to you if you had liberation or not, because this world was just as good a place to feel devotion in as anywhere else.

6. A builder and handyman; not his real name.
7. Probably *Gustav Klimt with a Catalogue Raisonné of His Paintings*, by Fritz Novotny and Johannes Dobai, translated from German by Karen Olga Philippson (1968); the Payne book was *Caravaggio: A Novel* (1968).

1. That is, Lord Krishna, not George Fitts, the American Ramakrishna monk who joined the Vedanta Society in 1940 and, in 1958, took his final vows and was renamed Swami Krishnananda.

So then I had supper with Chris Wood at the Swiss Café. He told me that Paul Sorel (who'll be coming back for the summer after eight months in New York) has found a new interest in life, he is teaching a retarded boy of fourteen to read! So maybe he'll end up just another (yawn, yawn) saint.

Chris told me quite seriously that he now thinks of nothing but the past—that this comes over you as you get older! But since when did he ever think of anything else? He keeps talking, as if it was stop-press news, about how someone seduced him at Charterhouse;[2] but it isn't really a bore, because Chris is so interested. Chris says Peggy is now rather at a loss with no one to look after—though she does have Ben's children. She is going visiting around with relatives in the East, so they'd better watch out![3]

Last night I watched the whole of *Advise and Consent*—which shows how far a lonely old Dob will go, to win sleep. Charles was terribly unconvincing, and the faces he pulled [were] truly revolting at moments. The queer part was either much cut or it never had any impact anyhow, and nowadays Don Murray's inability to tell his wife seems merely sadistic refusal, not any kind of weakness. Never for an instant do you believe he killed himself.[4]

Yesterday a catalogue arrived for you called *The Faces of Authorship*. It is of an exhibition they had at the University of Texas at Austin, from November of last year to January of this. Busts, drawings and paintings of authors; Beerbohm, [Augustus] John, Coldstream, Tchelitchew, Topolski, Wyndham Lewis, Epstein, Roger Fry, Rothenstein were among the artists. (There's the Coldstream painting of Wystan and a Topolski of Forster and Edith Sitwell and a Dorothy Brett and an Alfred Wolmark (?) of Huxley. I'll put it in your room, of course.) On the cover, Anaïs Nin (who sent it to you) has written: "Dear Don, they should be interested

---

2. His English public school.
3. Peggy Kiskadden (*circa* 1900–1990s) thrice-married East Coast socialite living in California; Isherwood had ended their close friendship when she failed to accept his relationship with Bachardy. Her third husband, plastic surgeon Bill Kiskadden, died in February 1969 after a long illness, and her four children were grown-up. She was closely involved with the children of her eldest son, Benjamin Bok, who married in 1950, got a degree in music from USC in 1955, and then raised wolves near Llano, California.
4. Murray plays the senator and family man who is blackmailed about a past homosexual affair with an army buddy.

in your portraits! Did the Professors buy your drawing of me? Love, Anaïs."[5]

Should I call her for you? I stupidly forget—was it the "Professors" at Cal. State who wanted to buy your drawing, or where? There doesn't seem to have been any picture of Anaïs in the exhibition and I'm not sure how or why she got the catalogue. Let me know if I should call her and thank her and say you're away.

No other letters for you so far.

Talked to Bill Brown this morning, to find out what Paul wants for his birthday. Mercifully, Bill had heard him say he wanted a copy of the book of Swami's lectures with the introduction I wrote.[6] Bill says the Strawinskys just left for N.Y. Vera told him to excuse them for not calling us!

This as you see is a new sort of air letter & it took me by surprise when I reached the end of it. So Drub's boundless love has to be squeezed in tight!![7] Does love his adored Paws so much. XXXXX XXXXXXXX

[Typed letter with autograph additions]

Friday 4:15 p.m. [April 18, 1969, London]

Sacred Stallion—

A red-eyed and very Old Cat arrived this morning after a longer than usual flight (11 hrs.) and found himself strangely unexcited by the sight of London—almost as though he hadn't been away for very long. The flight was devoted to reading *Nicholas and Alexandra*,[1] bought at the L.A. airport. Ideal plane fare. Kitty transported to St. Petersburg of the 1890s, feeling quite regal in a high stiff choker of pink pearls. Very good and enjoyable history lesson—Kitty even wept a discreet diamond or two.

My arrival at 68 Ladbroke Grove was a typical tableau: Anthony deep

---

5. Huxley sat for Polish-born British artist Alfred Wolmark (1877–1961) in 1928. Paris-born American writer and psychoanalyst Anaïs Nin (1903–1977) sat for Bachardy three times in 1962 (July 12, October 18, and December 7).
6. *Religion in Practice* (1968).
7. Written by hand, sideways, in top right corner.

1. (1967), by Robert K. Massie.

in a telephone conversation in the bedroom, a strange mute secretary woman staring into a wall in the other room. I was met at the door by a boy named Stephen, on my last trip referred to by Anthony (in French) as "one of the beautiful young men," implying that he was fundamentally idle as well. Not only is he no longer idle, he is now Anthony's personal assistant, fully equipped with an efficient telephone tone.[2] He didn't introduce me to the staring secretary and the three of us sat dumb and motionless until Anthony finished his telephone conversation in the next room. After Anthony and I engaged in a limp handshake as the other two stood by, Anthony picked up his dictation to the secretary where he'd left off and Stephen offered me the dregs of an electric coffee pot which could not be believed for horror, even in England. The plot soon thickened with the arrival of Anthony's cleaning woman, the female set designer of *Women Beware Women*[3] and a third woman, never identified. I took to the morning *Times* in refuge for more than an hour until I could get a minute with the telephone in the next room (Stephen was in possession of it while Anthony dictated). When at last I got to it I called Buckle but was cut off twice by Anthony's faulty wall plug which kept tilting to one side everytime the telephone cord was moved, thereby cutting off the connection. Finally on the third try managed to arrange to have lunch with Richard who, while I was in his flat, very efficiently put through a call to the Harewoods. I am supposed to leave with them for their country house tomorrow morning at 9:30 a.m. for an unspecified number of days (maybe until Tuesday), driving with them for three hours. What will we talk about? They are both experts on music and musicians and live in a grand house with precious antiques.[4] Kitty already feels a bit choked by his collar of pink pearls. Anyway, the show is on the road in jig time and Kitty braves the unknown again! Mrs. Harewood is however under the impression that she is not the

2. Stephen Frears (b. 1941), who became well known as a film director. His work includes *My Beautiful Laundrette* (1985), *Dangerous Liaisons* (1988), and *The Queen* (2006). Years later, he sat for Bachardy.
3. Possibly Sally Jacobs (b. 1932), who designed the sets for the production of Middleton's play, which Page directed in 1962 for the Royal Shakespeare Company. Page was starting to plan a new production in Watford, starring Jill Bennett and Marianne Faithfull.
4. George Lascelles, 7th Earl of Harewood (1923–2011), was a grandson of George V, first cousin of Queen Elizabeth II and in line to the throne. He was then Director of the Royal Opera House; his publications include Kobbé's *Complete Opera Book*. His second wife was Patricia Tuckwell (b. 1926), an Australian violinist.

unknown, insisting we met with the Tynans God knows when. I clumsily faked remembering the occasion.

During the precious few minutes I had with Anthony's telephone I called the Natl. Port. Gallery and was told by Dr. Strong's secretary (he's away until Monday) that alas I missed the meeting of the board of trustees which was yesterday, as though it were by no means definite that they want my drawing. I expressed cold surprise but will save my ammunition for my meeting with Dr. Strong.[5] Tune in next week for the further Purrills of Pawline.

Kitty already pines heartbreakingly for his one and only Beloved Hide. F.

[Autograph letter]

Monday April 21 [1969]   [Santa Monica]

Sweet treasured and above all others preferred Fur,

[O]lddub shuffled up to the mailbox this morning and there was that unmistakable pawscript, so the old thing began his week happily. But what a grim arrival in London! If the Nt. Port. Gallery *dares* to reject the drawing one will have to send them a picture of Dorian Gray but an improved model which turns into a horror monster and comes out of the frame and shits everywhere and has to be fed on etchings. And how will Angel make out amidst the titled country set? No doubt with great style and sparkling repartees. Oh I can just see him in his best ribbon being coaxed with cream by a duchess! Buckle has earned honorable mention for his conduct and you can tell him that Dubbin said, "We are *amused.*" Dub might even decorate him with the order of the horseshoe if he keeps this up.

Robin just called to say that I'm to come in and sign the papers for the film-rights sale of *Cabaret*, so that much is to the good & the poor Animals will have a little mad money for the next few years, it seems. Meanwhile Tony Harvey had gone up to San Francisco for the weekend and nothing more has been said by Ed Parone about

5. Roy Strong (b. 1935), Director of the National Portrait Gallery, was acquiring for the NPG Bachardy's 1967 portrait of Auden.

Meeting.[1] Tomorrow I am to appear on T.V. with Susan Batson as you know.[2] In this week's Calendar that snooty fart Dan Sullivan has another article on *Black Girl*: "*Black Girl* May Be Preachy but It's Shaw." He is trying to make amends but determined not to take back one word he said against the production.[3] He'll be dealt with later.

Just talked to Jim Bridges who says that Virgil has a cold and has become (temporarily, one hopes) absolutely deaf! He was told this by Jack on the phone. Jack is planning to stay at least till the end of the month in N.Y. Jim wants to dash hysterically over there this weekend, although he has to start rehearsing his one-act play on Monday.[4] He would like me to come with him but I'm not about to—will have quite enough with the Sta. Barbara thing, not to mention Esmereldo the Magician's performance![5]

Last night I went out with Mike Van Horn which was very nice but hardly thrilling. (He hadn't seen either *Bullitt* or *Point Blank* and they were playing together in Sta. Monica, so we went. I enjoyed *Bullitt* very much but *Point Blank* seemed awfully thin and fakey and you felt the director having a ball at your expense. Oddly enough, what seemed most powerful in *Bullitt* were the genuine hospital shots; the sense of crowding and old-fashioned accommodation and emergency and somehow making do.)[6] It's so amazing, to hear Mike talk you'd think

1. Ed Parone, once an assistant director with the Professional Theater Group at UCLA, was developing new plays at the Mark Taper Forum. He was interested in staging *A Meeting by the River*.

2. American actress Susan Batson (b. 1944) won the 1969 Los Angeles Drama Critics Circle Best Performance Award for her Black Girl in Isherwood's adaptation of George Bernard Shaw's *The Adventures of the Black Girl in Her Search for God*.

3. Sullivan, the *Los Angeles Times* drama critic, gave *Black Girl* a long, tepid review when it opened March 19, calling it "an illustrated lecture . . . pleasant . . . but not involving," even though he called Susan Batson "a find" and twice mentioned how little she wore (*Los Angeles Times*, March 21, 1969, pp. 1 and 20.) In his "Calendar" piece, April 20, 1969, he said the acting had improved but that the play was still fundamentally flawed, a sermon of ideas. But he spent many words discussing the ideas.

4. Jim Bridges's one-act play was probably *A3*, which Isherwood and Bachardy saw as part of a double bill with *Slivovitz* by Joel Schwartz at the Mark Taper Forum on May 15. Jack Larson and Virgil Thomson's opera *Lord Byron* had auditioned successfully at the Met.>

5. That is, the Writers' Conference and Peter Schneider's magic show—Schneider's professional persona was Esmereldo the Magician.

6. The box-office hit *Bullitt* (1968) starred Steve McQueen as the San Francisco cop guarding an underworld witness who is shot and hospitalized before dying of his wounds. *Point Blank* (1967), directed by John Boorman, starred Lee Marvin as a loner tracking down criminals who had robbed him and left him for dead.

that he is the difficult one, he makes scenes, he says, just for the sake of creating a situation, and Jim [Crabe] is supposed to be the soul of kindness and consideration and loyalty!

Saw Gerald and Michael this morning. They sent love. Gerald better than ever, though a little confused sometimes in the midst of one of his long sentences. He has now started to talk about the absolute utter importance of meditation. But he was also very lively and laughed until he nearly fell out of bed at some quip of Dobbin's, forget what it was.

I may miss a day tomorrow or else miss the mail, as I have to fool around in town so much, but will try to get a word off to my beloved treasure. Mid pleasures and palaces, don't forget that lowly stable where a melancholy mare whinnies sadly.

Always, a kitten's adoring slave,
Drub XXXXXXXXXXXXXXXXX

Just got a brochure from an outfit in San Diego called ALCOHOL INTELLIGENSIA, urging Dob to sign an appeal and say that he has found that abstaining from alcohol has brought him health, happiness and success. As they put it, they need cultural leaders in the community to say why they don't drink. Am wondering if this is another put-on by Eddie James[7] or even Clyde Ventura!?

[*Typed letter, signed, with autograph additions*]

Wednesday April 23 [1969]   [Santa Monica]

Absent Angel,

I didn't get to write to you yesterday, chiefly because I knocked the phone off my desk and broke it and had to stay home while the repair man came and that meant that I had to have Michael Sean and Seth Finkelstein to tea up here instead of going down to their place and *that* meant that they stayed two hours and Seth was almost silent

7. Edward James (1907–1984), American railroad heir. He was an early patron of the surrealists (especially Dalí), and was married briefly in the 1930s to Tilly Losch, the Austrian ballerina. Isherwood knew him by the start of the 1950s, probably through the Stravinskys. James spent much of his time in Mexico where he had a coffee finca in Xilitla, near Tampico.

while Michael bored me silly with stories about "Uncle Filthy" who is my least favorite non-fiction character.[1] The rest of the day was really quite busy. I had lunch with Kimmis Hendrick, that *Christian Science Monitor* journalist[2] whom we met at King Vidor's. When he invited me I imagined he wanted to talk about *Black Girl* but no, he wanted to admit to me that, though married, he had always been a queer at heart— news which surprised rather than thrilled me. Then I went to KHJ and appeared with Susan Batson on "Tempo." Michael Hall was hovering rather ineffectually around. Like in all those studios there are lots of young persons pretending to be producing something. Susan looked marvellous and was very articulate and altogether I rather adored her. The show is now quite a hit and every performance ends with a discussion with the audience, something which has arisen more or less spontaneously. Also all the later notices in local papers, even including the *Free Press*, were excellent. And we will even have a replacement for Douglas Campbell who is said to be first-rate and much thinner and younger.[3] It is a shame it can't run for another month. Instead they are pushing in some tired Frog farce after May 4th.[4] From the broadcasting I went on to Robin's office and signed the *Cabaret* film sale papers. It seems we shall really get very little, about 6 or 7 thousand a year for six years; still and all, *I Am a Camera* only netted ten thousand altogether. And we *may* get more from the Cinerama lawsuit or if it is found that Macy has no claim on the movie money.[5]

Julie Harris won a Tony for her Broadway play, did you hear?[6] I sent her a wire from both of us. Another letter for you from Tom Wright, enclosing a check for $50 (which I'll deposit) and yakking away about his publishers, who haven't *yet* decided about using your

1. An eccentric acquaintance of Sean's; Isherwood and Bachardy never met him.
2. (1910–1979).
3. Scottish actor and director Douglas Campbell (1922–2009) played Bernard Shaw and God in *The Adventures of the Black Girl in Her Search for God*. He was replaced by Michael Allison, a British actor who came to Broadway in 1960 to play Henry Higgins in *My Fair Lady*, the third replacement after Rex Harrison.
4. *Chemin de Fer* by Georges Feydeau.
5. Evidently, Cinerama had undertaken to make a film version of *Cabaret*, then backed out because so many people had rights in the material; they were perhaps being sued for breach of contract. New York stage manager and producer Gertrude Macy co-produced the 1951 stage version of *I Am a Camera* with Walter Starcke and thereby had a substantial financial stake in *Cabaret*, reducing Isherwood's earnings.
6. *Forty Carats*, Jay Allen's adaptation from *Quarante Carats* (1966) by French playwrights Pierre Barillet (b. 1923) and Jean-Pierre Grédy (b. 1920, Egypt).

drawing! I guess you know his address—it's 8 Nevern Place, Flat C, London S.W. 5.

Just got a small bill from Heywood Hill. If you order those books will you ask them to tell you how much they'll cost; then I'll add that to my check and mail it to them at once. They always write surface, so it'll be much quicker that way. I took OldJo to the Fuji Gardens on Monday night, which she liked enormously. But she dropped a tear or two into the tempura. She says if she can't have Ben she doesn't want anyone. This is a THREAT!

Oh God, I get so impatient with her and then I remember how desolate I am without my darling. Miss him so when I'm in the kitchen early and there's no one to pop out and scare old Plug. And when that sacred dear Fluff scratches on Dub's door to be let in, and when . . . but Dub mustn't continue, the tears are flowing fast.

This morning he was very good and went jogging on the beach with Jim, to get rid of the big dinner up at Four Oaks which Gavin bought him last night. It is so much better now that they have an upstairs room, quite snug. Christopher was with us and the atmosphere was very happy but *not* I felt loverlike. I asked G. what he had been doing and he didn't say one word about Mexico, so maybe that trip was cancelled! Jim is very busy conferring with Tony Harvey about Tony's love life. Dan sounds the most businesslike bitch in the world but he claims he only wants security and loves Tony nevertheless! Jim thinks that Tony *is* going to take on *Cabaret*, but he is awfully cagey; I'm sure he knows something he mustn't say. Well, patience! I dread the boredom of Santa Barbara on Friday–Saturday, and then there's that horrid surgeon for Drub's hoof next Wednesday.[7] But Drub will get Kitty's permission first, he promises. Am picturing Kitty on some royal cushion. No letter today or yesterday, let's hope for tomorrow. The weather is by no means great; sunshine but windy and chilly. Going to Vedanta Place tonight.

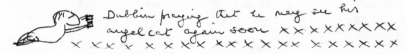

Dubbin praying that he may see his angel cat again soon ×× ×××××××
× ×× × × × ××× ×× × × ×× × ×××××

[*Typed letter, signed, with autograph additions*]

---

7. Isherwood's doctor, Alan Allen, had referred him to a specialist hand surgeon because Isherwood had lumps developing in the palm of his left hand; see p. 403 below.

Saturday [April 19, 1969, London]

Hallowed Hide:

An exhausted fur slept till 12:30 today and feels now somewhat revived. Toward the end of yesterday he was feeling very peculiar indeed, so he took a nap while Anthony went off to the Court to see a new play by David Storey (*Radcliffe* & *This Sporting Life*) called *In Celebration*, directed by Lindsay Anderson & starring Alan Bates. He liked it and wants to go again later in the week and will take me along. After the play we met at the Hungry Horse (Kitty's wish) and a sleepy Pelt supped on kedgeree & steak and kidney pudding and thought of his Old Muzzled Companion and swallowed hard.

This afternoon Anthony picked up the color prints of pictures he took in Peru, many of them very good.[1] We went to an early showing of Welles's *The Immortal Story* and Buñuel's *Simon of the Desert*, both very short (only about an hour each) and neither very good. The Welles is nicely photographed and colored but very arty with self-consciously poetic dialogue and awful narration which tells you what you're seeing. Jeanne Moreau is enjoyably ridiculous in it. The Buñuel is a very obvious and very minor effort, a heavy-handed kind of parable. Afterwards we had a fish supper at a place called Manzi's in Soho, very near Chez Victor. I'd never been before. Kitty had some nice fish, whitebait for beginners and a lovely big grilled Dover sole. Anthony is still not drinking due to his malady so we had just Pellegrino both evenings.

When I got back late yesterday afternoon, after lunch with Buckle and a workout at the gym which I thought might finish an already shattered Tabby but actually helped revive him, for a few minutes anyway, there was a call from Dr. Strong's secretary. She had obviously spoken to Dr. Strong since I'd called earlier in the day and she was calling to apologize for giving me misinformation. The NPG has indeed definitely decided to buy my drawing of Wystan. What they are undecided about is David's painting of us which they are considering buying as well.[2] I am supposed to see Dr. Strong on Monday at 3 p.m. to deliver my drawing but will have to call and postpone since I decided not to drive to Yorkshire with

1. Page's sister was married to a diplomat then stationed in Lima, where Page had been visiting her. They travelled to Machu Picchu and other sites together.
2. The NPG did not buy Hockney's portrait of Isherwood and Bachardy, but did later acquire a 1976 Hockney lithograph of them.

the Harewoods this morning but to take a train in the morning and come back sometime on Tuesday. Good thing too. I needed the sleep this morning. All furred devotion and whiskered kisses. K.

[*Autograph letter*]

Sunday [April 20, 1969, Leeds]

Dearest Drubchen—

It is 12:45 a.m. A distant lonely furkin is sitting up at a dear little night desk (accidentally enough in front of a tilting mirror) in *Harewood!* The train journey took four hours (an hour and a half more because it's Sunday) so only arrived shortly before 5:30. Lady Harewood and four-year-old child met me at the station, apparently recognizing me (a big black portfolio I carried was a hint) from a meeting in 1961 with the Tynans and Joan Littlewood, an evening we all spent together, having dinner in some King's Rd. restaurant.[1] What she in fact remembered was having met a *dear* old Horse who had made quite an impression on her. She had not at that time married Harewood. In fact, she only married him two years ago though they have a four-year-old son, a fact they both referred to this evening though Buckle had already filled me in beforehand. I gather quite a scandal even for nowadays. Buckle told me that Benjamin Britten, a longtime friend of Harewood, told him to his face he'd never see him again because of his actions. B.B. has I'm told remained a good friend of the first Lady Harewood.[2] The current one is an Australian, very lively and talkative, an easy averter of awkward silences, a great appetite for life's challenges, a grabber of bulls' horns, short haired and well seated. Will be difficult to draw.

1. The Ox on the Roof, July 16, 1961. Isherwood tells about the evening with Ken and Elaine Tynan and leftist theater director Joan Littlewood (1914–2002) in his diary entry for July 17, 1961. He does not mention the future Lady Harewood, but in his day-to-day diary he records the presence of "a girl from Australia called Patricia."
2. Harewood's first wife and the mother of his three older sons was Austrian-born concert pianist Marion Stein, later Mrs. Jeremy Thorpe (b. 1926). Her father Erwin Stein was Britten's music editor at Boosey & Hawkes, and Britten and Peter Pears had shared a house with the Steins in the 1940s. When Harewood's son with Patricia Tuckwell was born out of wedlock in July 1964, Britten ended his friendship with Harewood, and the following January, 1965, he fired Harewood as president of the Aldeburgh Festival and banned him from attending. The son was called Mark Lascelles.

He is a perfect cross between Milton Berle and Chester Kallman, if you can imagine an English aristocrat being *exactly* that! Never has the psycho-physical analysis been more certain or more revealing. He too is likeable, and talkative thank God—even so it has not been easy. The real fun begins tomorrow morning, God help a very tiny Kitten who is also expected to draw the four-year-old. To bed now, an especially small trundle bed in a cozy little room with a ticking antique clock. Kitty is prepared for the morrow, if prayers and facial isometrics are sufficent preparation.

XXXXXXXXXX Furkin

[*Autograph letter*]

Monday night [April 21, 1969, Leeds]

Adored Velvet Muzzle—

Kitty is sitting up here in bed, unable to sleep. I don't know if it's still the time difference or the residue of an awful day of nervous tension. I drew them all (the Earl, his Lady and their four-year-old boy) and none of the drawings is any good. I started this morning with the Earl who hadn't the faintest idea he wasn't sitting properly, then went on to the child who could win a prize for the most unpleasant, spoiled little beast I've come across in a long, long while. By lunchtime I was a nervous wreck.

After lunch in the sitting room where I'd worked all morning I saw the same awful distracting situation was going to repeat itself—me trying to draw one of them while the other two fussed around in the same small room doing everything under the sun to distract whoever it was I was trying to draw and succeeding brilliantly, with the help of two poodles, a cuckoo clock man-servant and a blasting loud speaker. I could have screamed with nervous agony but instead went to my room to lie down on the floor for half an hour. After lunch I insisted on taking Her Ladyship into the dining room, to everyone's disappointment and dismay, but by that time my nerves were so shot I couldn't do anything anyway.

An awful day altogether. I was an ass to let myself in for it. What *could* I have been thinking about? I've *never* enjoyed staying in anybody's house, let alone total strangers', and to do so in order to try to draw them seems to me nothing but madness. Of course I would feel more than ever the anxiety to please and the torture of not being able to. I got myself into such a state of self-consciousness and frustration I nearly lost (but didn't) my cool. And then to have to make with the conversation and sit down to meals with the same three people I am by this time loathing—well I'm sure you can imagine.

And of course the Harewoods expected to come out looking like their Beautiful Highnesses and to see their offspring looking like an Angel. I couldn't even let a couple of the drawings be seen! This really may be the end of my career as portraitist. I doubt if I could go through something like this again. I feel really awful—like a failed imposter, and guilty, partly for being exposed but mostly for exposing myself, with eager, careful, diabolical cunning. It makes me wonder if the whole purpose of this trip might not have been to make me give up, once and for all, this pointless charade, this seemingly endless ability of mine to get myself into situations in which I feel I have to please people.

Writing this has helped to make me feel better. It certainly can't be news to you though—I've been getting myself into these situations for what seems an eternity. And the Harewoods really aren't bad. They make an effort anyway. She has that unmistakable energetic brightness and self-satisfaction of the newly titled (funnily like Amiya and a Lady Allen I drew last year, all of them fatly pleased with themselves and so graciously ready to show they haven't gone high hat). He is eager to be friendly and prove he's a regular fellow who hasn't forgotten the importance of the common touch. He is dutifully humble, especially in the presence of culture, but always ready to cheer the footballer on. But underneath one feels a certain complacent self-indulgence and arrogance, and all of it simply gushes forth from the boy heir who has become like a familiar of his father, parodying in burlesque style all the unpleasant qualities his father thinks he's risen above in himself. And he seems to think they look cute in the little boy. Ugh! A more spoiled brat is impossible to imagine. And [I suppose] she lets the boy get away with murder because she likes his being the apple of his father's eye, [which might justify] her adultery and claim to be called Her Ladyship. And to think I started this passage by saying they weren't so bad! It seems especially ungrateful to be putting these things down on their own stationery.

It's now 6 a.m. and hardly worth trying to sleep any more. I think I'll read some more of *Nicholas and Alexandra* which is really so enjoyable. Rasputin is such fun.

Breakfast is at 9:15, then I get taken on a tour of the house and then, mercifully, a 12:30 train back to London. I'm supposed to do more drawings of them next week when they are in London again but we shall see.

This may be all part of a Foolish Fur's readjustment blues but he's feeling now he never wants to see another Bachardy portrait drawing. He longs only for the comfort of his dear basket and the security of his Hide blanket and the warm smell of old hay and the soothing susurrus of the Old Drub chomping away in the feed bag.

With all of a Kitten's loving devotion and quickly beating little heart. T. XXXX

[*Autograph letter on letterhead of Harewood House, Leeds*]

Tuesday [April 22, 1969]

Darling Drumpkin—

Am on train heading back to London. After all Kitty's harsh words old Harewood was very nice this morning and gave Kitty a personally conducted tour of the house instead of answering a large pile of mail which arrived this morning and I know was weighing on him. Then he drove me into Leeds to catch my train. He seemed altogether more sympathetic, an harassed old pooch faithfully guarding the family house. The Chester Kallman-Milton Berle likeness still seems profound and, alas, appeared even stronger in yesterday's drawings. In contrast to Harewood's semi-transformation, the little Master would barely speak to me at breakfast this morning and formally gave me a goodbye handshake only when bidden to by his mother. Until then we only regarded each other sulkily from across the table. Oh, I am so relieved to be away from there, though this morning's tour was of interest, especially since I'd read through a guide book Buckle had edited and given to me before I left London, so at least I had a vague idea of what I was being shown most of the time.[1] The paintings are the most distinguished and dullest kind of masterworks but the Adam ceilings

1. *Harewood* (1962), by Richard Buckle, illustrated by Bertram Unne, revised and reissued several times since.

are pretty and the Chippendale, if not nearly as ravishing for me as it seems to be for others, is at least impressive in its workmanship and variety of design. But oh the weight and gloom of the place with all of its objects and furnishings, the slow grim Hell of possessions and the heavy yoke of position and responsibility they impose. And as though he hadn't suffered enough, Harewood started a collection of Leeds pottery only two years ago. He already has a whole great case full.

What *is* attractive is the country itself. It's a very big estate with brown or pale green grassy slopes and hills, dotted with black sheep and edged by woods. A pretty artificial lake, too. Old Dubbin could have grazed quite placidly or cantered gracefully in and out or up and down, tossing his mane in the misty air. Frazzle-Fur misses him so.

[Autograph letter]

145 Adelaide Drive Santa Monica Calif 90402
Thursday April 24 [1969]

Dearest Pinktongue,

Naggin got his sweet three letters today, Saturday[,] Sunday and Monday–Tuesday, all in a clump. The Harewood visit must have been too ghastly, and Kitty is quite right to decide not to go on torturing himself like this. That paw of genius should never be lowered to the mud of monarchy, or he will descend to the level of a Mrs. Beaton.[1] How interesting that Harewood looked like Chester; it's that tainted Jewish blood his mother got from Edward VII who got it from Prince Albert.[2]

Very little news after that long bulletin I wrote yesterday. I went up to Vedanta Place as usual and read. Jim Gates, one of the two boys I told you about, came up there for the reading and I drove him back to Venice after. I think you would like him, if he doesn't turn out too terribly earnest. He gave me a letter he'd written to me, telling all about his past,

---

1. That is, Cecil Beaton.
2. Harewood's mother was Princess Mary, the only daughter of George V and Queen Mary; Edward VII, eldest son of Queen Victoria and Prince Albert, was his great-grandfather. Prince Albert's mother, Princess Louise of Saxe-Gotha-Altenberg, was dismissed from the court of her husband, Ernst I, Duke of Saxe-Coburg and Gotha, for having an affair with Baron von Mayern, a Jewish court chamberlain rumored to be Albert's real father.

including pot, LSD and a boyfriend. It seems that he and Peter aren't lovers. I am very curious to see Peter's magic act on Saturday, when I get back from Sta. Barbara, at this hippie theater, called The Walrus.

Meanwhile this morning I heard from Tony Harvey and he is coming to see me tomorrow. It seems that *Cabaret* is suddenly very much on, but who knows? Tony is very hysterical, wants everything to start now or never. But Robin has to make a deal first. He is asking for $25,000 for a treatment and then, if that is accepted, $60,000 for the screenplay. If Beckerman[3] accepts we presumably will be expected to start at once. However, let us not get in a flap about it. If things get really definite I will phone you and see what we decide. This is just a distant early warning, so don't change any plans. Even if the deal actually goes through we can probably stall them for a week at least.

Am glad that the Nat. Port. Gal. isn't making any difficulties. It *would* be rather marvellous if they buy the Hockney portrait. Kitty would be the first Amellicat to be admitted![4]

Dobbin was to have gone for a quiet trot with Jim Bridges this morning but now he is busy with Ed Parone. I told him to get some news of *Meeting* at all costs, but fear that fart Gordon Davidson is still away.[5] It's a beautiful day but windy and so cruelly cold. Paul Wonner's birthday supper with Oldjo this evening. Alice is coming. I fear a gloom-ridden feast.

Drub misses his darling so with his purring and tiny ways and his paw hooked deep in that horrid hide. Fear the humble old stinky stable will soon be forgotten amidst the delights of London and the rich fish-puddings. But his Mare loves him so.

FAITHFUL TIL DEATH

[*Typed letter with autograph addition*]

3. Producer Sidney Beckerman (1920–2008), president of Allied Artists, was putting together the deal for *Cabaret*.
4. The policy of the NPG is to acquire portraits of "the most eminent persons in British history from earliest times to the present day," and these have always included non-British citizens and Americans. For example, there are four portraits of George Washington, the last acquired in 1936.
5. Parone's boss, American stage director Gordon Davidson (b. 1933), who had worked with John Houseman's UCLA Professional Theater Group, was artistic director at the Mark Taper Forum and would make the final decision about putting on Isherwood and Bachardy's play.

Friday April 25 [1969]   [Santa Monica]

My darling Love,

[T]his is sort of a provisional letter because I may quite possibly be talking to you on the phone tonight or tomorrow. This whole Tony Harvey thing *appears* to be going through and, according to Tony, Beckerman has given him the impression that he is about to accept Robin's terms for us (which are still, I presume, $25,000 for the treatment and then, if they still want to go on and do the screenplay, $60,000 for that). As soon as this is definite (and Robin *may* telephone to tell me it is tonight when I am up at the Warshaws'),[1] I shall call you and we can discuss what to do next. At present Tony is wild to get started ... well, anyhow, it is ridiculous to write all this because, as I say, it's all provisional ....

A brilliant day but with this terrific hot wind which will be hell to drive through. I leave for Santa Barbara in about two hours.

Today I finished page 100 of my book.

Yesterday evening we had supper with Jo. Paul really did more about the birthday than she did. He brought a dessert *and* little presents for each of us. I got a can of marrons glacés (which I hope bad Glutdrub will have the strength of mind not to eat!). Alice Gowland rather amusingly arrived in a twenties dress which used to belong to Aileen Pringle;[2] it looked marvellous. Jo sang quite a lot of blues, but it was all right; just ungay.

Jennifer has invited me to supper on Sunday. We are supposed to be alone. Ha! Wonder if I'll get to sit at her table.

Angel I feel so irritated about all this sudden jostling by Harvey and Beckerman after this long long pause. But perhaps it will come to nothing, or drag on long enough until you're ready to get back here. Do love my Kitty and miss him so, but most certainly do not want him dragged back here early unless there really really is good reason for it.

Oh, that agent of David Hockney's (Casman?) called and asked if I would consider writing an introduction to a book of David's drawings.

1. Where he would be staying for the Writers' Conference.
2. Silent film star (1895–1989).

So I said Yes, because I really didn't feel I could refuse, especially as I'd refused to do the Grimms' Fairy Tale book.[3]

Still nothing definite about our play, which is what I'm most interested in. Last night, Jim tells me, he and Ed Parone and Tony Harvey were together, and Ed asked Jim what was happening about our play, was Jim going to direct it? So Jim said, it's not up to me, Ed has the power. And Ed said, "Right!" Nothing else. God, I would love to have that little cunt flogged. Even better I would love it if we could set up an entirely other deal, including Jim, and then just blandly tell Parone and Davidson, "Well, you never even spoke to us, we have no obligation to you."

Always Kitty's adoring devoted lonely old

Plug XXXXXXXXXXXX

[*Autograph letter with autograph additions*]

Wednesday [April 23, 1969, London]

Treasured Only Pony—

Two dear letters filled with hoof prints waiting for an old Veteran Cat returning from the latest war yesterday, cheered him so and gave him strength to go on. And go on he did, to the opening of Patrick Procktor's exhibition at the Redfern—a big show, maybe a little too big, of watercolors and prints, lots of them very nice and some of them among the best work he's done.[1] Richard Buckle bought one which I picked out (a small watercolor for £60). Patrick was his usual effusive superficial self, except for a short blond moustache which is not a success. Harry Miller and Loudon were both there and I had the pleasure of informing Harry that the NPG had bought a drawing of mine. He was quite taken aback I'm happy to say. Patrick said he hoped he'd see a lot of me while I'm here and referred to one time I'd been here and he'd been depressed

3. Hockney's London dealer, John *Kasmin* (b. 1934), known by his surname, Kasmin, asked for an introduction to Hockney's *72 Drawings: Chosen by the Artist* (1971), but Isherwood's piece was not used. The book Isherwood had refused was Hockney's *Illustrations for Six Fairy Tales from the Brothers Grimm* (1970), for which both he and Auden were invited to make new translations. Auden also turned it down.

1. Procktor's 1969 Redfern show ran from April 22 to May 16.

and not seen enough of me. This was delivered in a smiling casual way in front of several people and strangely failed to melt a rather frosted Fur.

Richard and I afterwards went to Pasolini's *Oedipus Rex* which in spite of a lot of quite beautiful photography is absolutely *no good* at all. I will even go so far as to say that Pasolini is maybe no good at all. It's not just a bad movie by a good director but much worse. He has a dull mind and is overwhelmingly humorless, and arty and false. And having had about two hours sleep the night before didn't help much. Ate afterwards at the Escargot. Lunch today with Marguerite at a Japanese restaurant called Hiroko. She is very well and was very sweet. We went afterwards to Henry Guerriero's show, which opened yesterday,[2] and ran into Tom Wright. Then to the NPG to deliver the Auden to Dr. Strong who I think really was impressed by the original. He'd forgotten I'd written about the size of the drawing and was surprised to see how big it is. He remarked what a good postcard it will make. Only drawback is that it won't be exhibited till Wystan's dead (NPG policy) and I could not get cash for it, so an international money order is being sent to Santa Monica.

Please pay Am. Ex. bill minus Sinclair charges. And take exquisite care of that antique Horse Hide which Kitty prizes above all else. That snake's head drawing didn't fool old Kitty.[3]

With "all of a kitten's" love. F.

[*Autograph letter*]

Thursday [24 April 1969, London]

Dearest Worshipped Rump:

Two sweet Stablegrams for Kitty's soul breakfast this morning. How Kitty misses that Hoof and thinks of him so much and longs for those steamy, smothering nights alongside that Dear Bulk in the dear dilapidated basket. But Kitty must be brave for the time being and try to cover his Horsesickness with bright London chatter.

Saw a farce last night (Kitty did try to laugh) written by Joe Orton who

2. At a small London gallery, unidentified.
3. That is, at the end of Isherwood's letter of April 24, 1969.

was murdered by his lover (hammered to death) in 1967. Ralph Richardson (who was so good) and Coral Browne were the stars and it was really very enjoyable and maybe even good. I do love farces if they are anywhere near well done and though I have a few doubts about this one it is still very clever.[1] Had dinner at Chez Victor afterwards. It was more crowded than I've ever known it but still good.

Finally got Tony [Richardson] on the phone yesterday. He is going to N.Y. with *Hamlet* on Sat. for a week. He was very busy replacing three of the actors in the cast so I won't see him till he gets back. He's invited me to his place in the So. of France for the weekend of the 4th but of course he may be delayed in N.Y. and Kitty will miss going again. I'm going to see *Hamlet* tomorrow night and having dinner with Anthony & Nicol Williamson tonight after the performance. Before dinner Anthony and Jill Bennett (Osborne) are coming with me to see *Ziegfeld Follies* and *The Great Lie* (Mary Astor & [Bette] Davis) at a film club I always check up on. Richard Buckle has invited me to his place in the country for the weekend and I think I'll go—he may even be able to scare up some commissions there, he thinks, so has suggested I bring my drawing board along. Anthony's production of *Women Beware Women* has almost for sure collapsed, to his mixed reactions of relief, disappointment & rage, but his sister arrives from Peru on Sunday so he will have to devote at least the whole of that day to her. I will come back from the country on Monday morning and am then supposed to have lunch with and later draw the Harewoods, who according to Richard "adore" me—imagine that! Anyway Old Tabby glutton-for-punishment feels he should try again if only for Buckle's benefit. I don't want to discourage his attentions. Ran into Stan from the Redfern days who is running another gallery across from the Mercury and asked me please to bring in my work to show his boss lady who was also there.[2] I said I would call on Monday.

Eternal rough tongue lickings and limitless catkisses from His Paws.

[*Autograph letter*]

1. This was the first production of *What the Butler Saw*, the last play Orton (1933–1967) wrote before he died; it opened March 5. Orton's lover since 1951, Kenneth Halliwell, swallowed twenty-two Nembutals and died with Orton after delivering the nine hammer blows.
2. Stan Hardy was now working at the Hamet Gallery in Cork Street; the gallery was established by Rose Adeane (1944–2006) in 1967.

Friday [25 April 1969, London]

Treasured Steed—

A day of upheaval. I quite suddenly decided this morning to leave Ladbroke Grove. I've felt very uncomfortable with Anthony for several days and I knew there would be a row if I stayed on. Wanting to avoid that, I asked Richard Buckle if he could put me up for a while. So I am now set up at Henrietta Street, which is very pleasant (if staying with other people can *ever* be pleasant). At least there are attractive views of Covent Garden etc. from the windows. And Richard is very sweet. I've not told him why I left Anthony's, nor has he asked.

Anthony has been in a terribly tense state due to the collapse of the *Women Beware Women* production. [. . . U]nder the strain of these last few days (really since I got here) being with him has been very difficult. He has very little idea I think of what he's like and so it's almost impossible to talk to him and I knew that even to attempt to tell him how I felt would only have meant a quarrel. So I packed up and left while he was out to lunch today, leaving a brief note to say where I'd gone to. I hope he won't be angry or upset but even if he is, I can't help it. It seemed the best, if not the only, thing I could do. We've been finding it increasingly difficult to get along together. In fact the only way we could manage it was for me to keep my mouth shut. The fact is, I think we are chemically an unsafe mixture and, being as we were in very confined quarters, there was bound to be an explosion if I didn't get out. I'm very sorry in a way, but glad at least to have found this out without too much unpleasantness. I can't help feeling a sense of relief. I asked him in my note to leave any letters for me downstairs in the hall (so Kitty will collect all Horse messages), but write to me c/o Buckle, 34 Henrietta St. W.C. 2 from now on. Kitty needs so his Old Naggin's encouragement.

With all of a Kitten's loving heart as always. T.

[*Autograph letter with enclosure*¹]

1. A black and white photograph cut from a newspaper of a Siamese cat wearing around its neck a collar with a leash attached and a handmade sign saying, "Well done, Chris."

Saturday [April 26, 1969]

My Own Plumed Pony—

Old Cat is very cross with himself for having left behind in Richard Buckle's flat his Friday letter to his Dear, so now He won't be hearing from his Catkin for several days and will probably get this before the Friday letter. So I will have to repeat some of Friday's news and maybe decide to throw away the unmailed letter when I get back to London on Monday morning. I am writing this on the train going down to Wiltshire with Buckle to stay in his country house there.[1] Of course I am already wondering why I am going to stay with someone again, having sworn only last week that I would *never* do it again. You will have got (I hope) my telegram telling you to write to me c/o Buckle. I moved into his flat yesterday afternoon. I decided quite suddenly I could not take much more of the nonstop tension and confusion [. . .] without there being some kind of explosion. We were beginning to get on each other's nerves due to the closeness of the quarters, his anxiety over the collapse of his production of *Women Beware Women* and my increasing impatience with an all-too-familiar situation.

Miraculously, though, we've managed not to quarrel and are still on good terms and I think will be able to take each other much better in small doses. Richard is being very kind and agreeable and has made me very comfortable (that is, as comfortable as I can ever be in someone else's place) in the end room of his flat, with a nice big window overlooking the market.[2] Saw *Hamlet* last night. Though I do dislike the play and find it endlessly tedious, it is clear that Nicol Williamson gives a very intelligent and interesting performance, but *Oh!* he is so unpleasant.

With a kitten's undying love & eternal devotion to his Naggin. XXXXXXX Furpaws.

[*Autograph letter, labelled "Letter #1"*]

1. In fact Buckle's country house was in Dorset—Roman Road, Gutch Common, Semley near Shaftesbury.
2. That is, Covent Garden Market.

Sunday [April 27, 1969, Dorset, England]

Worshipped Shiny Rump.

As well as having left in London Friday's Dubnote, Kitty also forgot his tiny pen and so hates this one he has borrowed from Richard, as though Kitty's paw marks weren't clumsy enough already.

Alone in the country in Richard's small, snug and surprisingly remote house. Not quite alone since Richard is here too. And he is not the easiest person to be alone with, partly because I think he himself fears he is boring to be alone with. Anyway, he is desperate to organize some kind, any kind, of distraction to prevent our spending another evening alone together. Last night was a bit forced. I had little to do but stand around and dutifully admire the surrounding countryside (which really is pretty, even for one who is not keen on the country). I longed to help Richard prepare the evening meal but he's a do-it-yourself kid, in spite of not knowing very well how to do it, and so Chat le Chef had to stand by mutely & witness unspeakable crimes of the kitchen. Really it didn't turn out all that badly, but then Tabby, not fed at lunchtime, was so hungry he would gladly have eaten tinned catfood.

Today, a colleague of Richard's named John Whitley brought his girl Sue Richardson to lunch. He writes criticism for *The Sunday Times* and she works on the paper, too. They'd driven down from London to look at a house to rent in the neighborhood, behaving like young-marrieds though not married. He is very much like Tom Courtenay[1] in all ways & she is a plump-faced girl with masses of real red hair and one bad tooth (the others are all right). Richard gave them a lamb joint (tough & fatty), leeks, potatoes & cold salmon, finished off by a rhubarb fool which was like a thin, sour milk shake. Kitty this time was allowed to make the gravy—not his specialty & he had little to work with, but it wasn't bad. To see Julian Bream this evening. He's England's greatest guitarist & Richard's closest neighbor, the latter being his prime recommendation.[2] XXXXXXX Tail

[*Autograph letter, labelled "Letter #2"*]

1. British actor (b. 1937) who became famous in Tony Richardson's film of *The Loneliness of the Long Distance Runner* (1962).
2. Bream (b. 1933) is a classical guitarist and lutenist.

Saturday April 26 [1969]   [Santa Monica]

Own dearest Pinknose,

[G]ot back from Santa Barbara to find his sweet letter of Wednesday plus a cable saying that he'd moved to Dicky's, which provokes that Nosey Nag's curiosity but he will wait till he's told the reason!

Meanwhile, nothing from Beckerman or Harvey, so I shan't phone you as I thought I might. I still think the deal is most probably on, but it is truly irritating because there you are, getting disturbing letters from me and not knowing what the score is. All I can say as of now is this: Tony is away for the weekend. When he returns he'll stay here till a week from Monday, May 5th, when he'll go to New York for one week to shoot a commercial for T.V. *If* the deal goes through and we are signed, then he hopes to work on the picture during this coming week, from the 27th to May 4th. So then the question will arise, does it matter if you aren't here then and come and join me later in the work, while he's still away in New York. This is what I shall phone you and discuss, but only when the deal is absolutely definite and set because *I don't rely on Harvey*, I mean emotionally. He is all excited now and so mad to start and asking how long I think the treatment will take to write; but he may just as easily get deflected onto something else. I fear we have a true film-faggot on our hands. I wouldn't bet money on any plan he makes. He *says* that after the treatment is finished (and presumably passed by Beckerman and his associates) he will want to go with us to Berlin and look for locations. But who knows? The one thing definite is that the film-rights sale has been made and Beckerman has an arrangement with ABC to distribute the film. So that much looks like business.

Please forgive all this crap. Nothing is more boring than Brumby the Businessman. But I have visions of you getting all these letters with scraps of news and poor Puss's head so confused and nervous and losing all pleasure in his little fish suppers and other frolics.

At Santa Barbara, I found Howard [Warshaw] just as usual and really very nice. [Douwe] Stuurman remarried, hated it, went mad, tried (not very hard) to kill himself with some World War Two cyanide which must have gone stale, he wasn't much damaged. Now he seems exactly the same closet queen as of old.[1] Fran [Warshaw] (who hates

1. Stuurman's first marriage was to a blind poet, his second, very brief one, to Phyllis Plous, director of the UCSB art museum. He had served in U.S. military intelligence during World War II.

my guts I feel—but *why?*) had a cancer operation (I mean they thought it was cancer but no, only a benign tumor). She looks very fat and heavily powdered dead-white like Madam Goddam or the Chinese wife in *The Letter*.[2]

The Writers were sort of Sunday writers, mostly middle-aged, so Drub gave them the number two charm number complete with modesty, eyelashes, British jokes and wry grins. I think it was a little much even for my staunch fans, Howard and Geo Dangerfield,[3] though they were polite. The most terrific Santana I have ever experienced very nearly wrecked Stuurman's car, with Naggin in the horsebox, on the way home from the lecture. It blew hard on the way back here today.[4] Tonight I am having a bite of supper with Elsa, then going (not with her) to the magic show. Tonight our clocks are put forward for summer, so we'll be only eight hours' difference from London again.

Will call my furred Soul of my Soul only in case of definite news, which is now of course most unlikely before Monday.

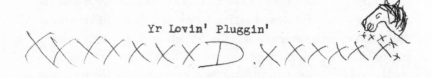

Yr Lovin' Pluggin'

[*Typed letter, initialled, with autograph additions*]

2. Madam Goddam is proprietress of the brothel in John Colton's 1918 play *The Shanghai Gesture*; she is called Madame Gin Sling in Josef von Sternberg's 1941 film adaptation. Somerset Maugham's story "The Letter" was staged in 1927 and then filmed in 1929 and again in 1940. Isherwood had probably seen both of the original stage productions as well as all three films.

3. British historian George Dangerfield (1904–1986) was a lecturer in the history department at the University of California at Santa Barbara. Among his books, *The Era of Good Feelings* (1952)—about the shift in America from Jeffersonian to Jacksonian democracy, 1812–1829—won the Pulitzer and Bancroft Prizes in 1953.

4. The dry wind, also called Santa Ana, possibly after the mountain range, blows out of the northeast from the desert, down across southern California, and out to sea.

Sunday, April 27, 1969   [Santa Monica]

Dub's Own Adorable Snowfur,

[B]eautiful today but still a bit windy. Have put all the clocks forward and have been running after them all day long. Now it's getting time to dash up to Jennifer's and wait 2–3 hours for her to come to sup with me—and how many others?

No more news yet. The opinion seems to be that Beckerman will settle the deal with Robin tomorrow for our services, but I still am not sure. Meanwhile, I am going to MGM on Tuesday to see a screening of the *I Am a Camera* film. I wish you could be here but after all I suppose it can easily be run again if necessary. Miss Tony Harvey flaps ever more wildly, says if Beckerman doesn't close the deal he'll walk off the picture. Oh fuck them all with their jitters. Anyhow I shall not phone until the deal is set and *then* we can discuss if and when you should come back. What is so boring is that, being unable to trust Harvey, I can't even be sure if he will go to New York next week or not, and of course that makes all the difference in the world to our plans, because if we are to work while he's away we must both discuss the whole thing with him together before he leaves (May 5th, I think).

The magic show never took place. I went down with these two boys to a really, fascinating place on Washington Blvd. in Venice, the Walrus Theater; dancing, hippies, hair, children, blacks, a light show, a toilet bowl to collect money, the music blasting, the whole house quaking— and then little Peter who is cute but an awful little curly-haired prima donna didn't feel that the audience was "right for it." However I laughed a lot and it was preferable to the alternative, an evening at Elsa's with Gavin, Rita [Hayworth], Jim Bridges, Tony Harvey, a man who worked puppets (brilliantly, I must say),[1] Antoinette [Gill], Ray Henderson, and his landlady, a jazzy girl who has flown the Atlantic solo. I saw them all, said I was coming back and then didn't. Ray and Rita clicked which didn't please Elsa, I'll bet.

This morning Bill Jones appeared and talked very lengthily about his novel. He is fatter but very jolly and I only dread his disappointment if

---

1. Welsh screenwriter Elwyn Ambrose (b. 1912); he had appeared on British and American T.V. with his puppets, including on "The Ed Sullivan Show" in 1966.

they don't accept it, but then why shouldn't they accept it? If they do he plans to leave all and become a real writer.[2]

Oh Angel I do miss you and yet it makes me so mad to think that you should be dragged back here prematurely after waiting all that long and postponing leaving on account of these fuckers.

Just had a call from Collin Wilcox, who is at the Chateau Marmont because they are going to film the rest of the picture here! She instantly reminded me of her breakdown, denounced Christopher, who is only to be allowed back into the family if he will consent to go to a head shrinker every day for six months, reminded me of my "godson" William's birthday and asked if she could be considered for Sally Bowles in our film. Her psychiatrist has convinced her that she is to go all out to be a film star.[3]

Darling Treasure, do be so careful of that stainless fur and think of old Drub and have a good time. Drubbin will guard the stable till that Saint comes scratching on the door.

[*Typed letter, initialled, with autograph additions*]

Monday A.M. [April 28, 1969]

Revered Shag Mane—

On the train with Richard heading back to London. Richard is sitting across from me with a table between us yawning and yawning (Richard, not the table) and there is a small boy (across from us sitting with his mother) making incessant hooting sounds like an owl. Kitty's nerves are not at their best. He wasn't fed his breakfast and so has had 2 cups of vile coffee (as only the English know how to make it) on an empty stomach. Richard left a telephone call for 7 a.m. last night & it didn't

2. The novel was never published.
3. She had roles in *The Babymaker*, *The Revolutionary*, and *Catch-22*, all released in 1970. She was probably then working on *Catch-22*.

come through. It was Kitty who saved the day by waking up miraculously at 8 a.m., just in time to wake Richard & get us to the station to catch the 9:10. I suspect the inner Fur foresaw disaster & set a private alarm—today is Harewood day and Kitty is expected for lunch in Maida Vale at 1 p.m. and it wouldn't do to arrive late. How I dread the day but am eager to have it behind me.

The Julian Breams last night turned out to be not the Julian Breams at all but another (synchronicity) unmarried couple. She is a very Jewish-looking-&-behaving woman, a sacred mother type who, in between caring for her brood, makes daily deep bows before the shrine of art & culture, of which Julian Bream is an embodiment. For some unfathomable reason her husband refuses to divorce her. Bream is a short, stocky, working-class peasant type who [I imagine] has pulled himself up with the energy born of pure ambition [. . .]. He apparently has earned a great deal of money and has from the way he talks invested it shrewdly. He seems to own all kinds of property, and his house near Richard is somewhat grand.[1]

Later

Back in London at last, and in good time to get to the Harewoods since, as we came in the front door, there was a call to put me off till 1:30, which means I will probably not have enough daylight to draw by. Richard told me in the taxi coming here that the little boy across from us was mentally deficient and couldn't speak properly, which explains his hooting. Kitty just dumbly accepted him as another instrument especially designed for the torture of cats. Dinner with Patrick Woodcock tonight and lunch with Marguerite tomorrow. She's invited the partner of David Hockney's gallery manager, Kasmin, to please me? Dread Dread. Oh for a kitten's dear Basket and Old Silky Ears standing over it. How he misses His Darling and wants never to be parted from him again. XXXXX Pink Nose

[Autograph letter, labelled "Letter #3"]

1. A few years earlier, Bream had sold his house in Chiswick and his country cottage in order to purchase Broad Oak House, a Georgian farmhouse near Semley, Wiltshire, that was his main residence for the next forty years. "Synchronicity" is Jung's term, first adopted by Gerald Heard and then by Isherwood, for pairs of events that happen close together in time—like meeting John Whitley and Sue Richardson, immediately followed by meeting Bream and his unidentified girlfriend.

Tuesday [April 29, 1969, London]

Old Satin Ears—

His first dear missile c/o Buckle arrived this morning and Lank Pelt only got from Ladbroke Grove his Thursday and Friday messages late yesterday, so an Old Fur is quite overwhelmed by the developments and lack of them. I was quite worried last night that you might have tried calling me on Sunday and I wouldn't have known because I was at Richard's place in the country. I'm glad to know that, as of this morning's letter, nothing definite has happened. I know you may call any day now. Though I am likely to be at Richard's in the mornings up to noon anyway, it is chancey your calling station-to-station in case I might be out (uncharacteristically) the day you call. So I guess it's safer to call person-to-person but do it during the cheap hours, between 5 p.m. & 5 a.m. Calif. time isn't it? Check to be sure. 5:30 p.m. Calif. time would be 9:30 a.m. in London, which would be fine for me. By the time you get this we may already have spoken, so little use in going on. Of course I will come as soon as I can, if necessary, but I hope it won't be before Friday as I must stay here till then or else pay the regular fare.

I drew both the Harewoods again yesterday and to my surprise the drawings were a great success, as far as they were concerned anyway. They called Richard last night to say they are delighted & want to buy both and the drawing of the little boy as well. Harewood suggested £400 for the three to Richard which is £100 more than I would have asked myself, so I wrote a note today to say that would do.

Saw Patrick Woodcock last night. He is still in love with David (who has both T.B. and a lover) but doesn't see him and is suffering. He was very sweet and we had a nice evening. He roasted a chicken. Today went to Marguerite's for lunch. She had Lady Caroline Blackwood Freud Citkowitz,[1] Kasmin's (Hockney gallery) partner Sheridan Dufferin

---

1. Caroline Hamilton-Temple-Blackwood (1931–1996), Irish-born novelist who came to be known under her own name, Blackwood. As the daughter of the 4th Marquess of Dufferin and Ava and of Maureen Guinness, she was both an aristocrat and an heiress; in addition, she was a great beauty. She was married to English painter Lucian Freud from 1953 to 1958 and to Polish-born American composer Israel Citkowicz from 1959; later, from 1972 until his death in 1977, she was married to American poet Robert Lowell. Among her other lovers was Ivan Moffat, who fathered one of her three daughters born during her marriage to Citkowitz.

& wife,[2] and Patrick Procktor who Marguerite had never met. The party was a great success, particularly for Marguerite & Patrick who got along marvellously, rather to my surprise & certainly to my relief. Caroline looks much older but quite wonderful in a way. She's turned into quite an original sort of English eccentric with a quirky walk and unbalanced stance and very black teeth. Even the Dufferins were quite pleasant.

I forgot to tell you I think that Marguerite has, believe it or not, got John Foster to buy the Hockney painting of us for her birthday Sunday.[3] I don't know whether I'm pleased or not. I'd rather begun to see it in my mind's eye in some terribly distinguished museum. But she swears the deal has been made. I stupidly forgot to send David Hockney an opening telegram (yesterday was it?).[4] Did you think of it?

Am going off now to a Wheeler's restaurant in the Brompton Rd. to have an early dinner with Anthony, who has to give a lecture on *Godot* at some school. He's going off to Devon tomorrow to stay with Alfred Lynch & friend[5] without a certain cat's company. So Kitty is ready for his return to the Casa, though, as usual as He begins to ready himself to go, drawing commissions begin to come in. Saw with Marguerite this afternoon Mrs. Davison, who now wants me to draw her husband (I drew her two boys last fall), but I can do that tomorrow or Thursday I think. I hope so. Think of the commissions I'll get when I give up portrait drawing altogether!

XXXXXXXXXX Your Furred Equestrian temporarily unseated

[*Autograph letter*]

2. Sheridan Hamilton-Temple-Blackwood, 5th Marquess of Dufferin and Ava (1938–1988), and Belinda (Lindy) Guinness (b. *circa* 1941), his cousin, a painter. They married in 1964 although he was essentially gay. Caroline Blackwood was his older sister.
3. Brigadier Sir John Foster (1904–1982), Australian-born lawyer, Q.C., Conservative M.P., human-rights activist, and socialite, was a close friend of Marguerite.
4. "David Hockney" at the André Emmerich Gallery in New York, April 26–May 5. The big double portrait *Christopher Isherwood and Don Bachardy* was in the show.
5. That is, Jimmy Culliford.

Wednesday [April 30, 1969, London]

Golden Love Pluggin—

A kitten's drooping whiskers suddenly stiffened this morning at the sound of that Old Naggin neighing, and his tired little heart started beating so quickly. Kitty is delighted by the news.[1] It probably would never have happened if Kitty hadn't come to England. How Kitty looks forward to working side by side with his Dear, that warm rough hide rubbing against the soon-to-be-revived fur. Already the Old Pelt is bristling with expectation. I sent a telegram this afternoon after confirming a reservation on Pan Am Fl. 121 arriving Tuesday May 6 at 5:35 p.m. That will be Kitty's May Day this year.

I had dinner last night with Anthony, the first time we've talked since I left Ladbroke Grove. It was a good meeting, by which I mean I managed to make several of my points without getting upset or angry, and Anthony was quite surprised and often at a loss for replies. At one point he even complained that everything I said was so "articulate." He meant it as a sneer but I laughed out loud and he had to admit it was funny. Anyway, I said I wouldn't go to Devon with him but said I would see him in London if he wanted to. I begin to feel the big mistake was in staying at Ladbroke Grove. I certainly don't ever want to do that again. Anthony has free passes to see *Oh! What a Lovely War* tonight so I'm going with him and Jill.

After dinner last night he went off to speak to a class who were studying about *Waiting for Godot*—which he'd directed at the Court some years ago with Alfred Lynch in one of the parts. I went by myself to see Pasolini's *Theorem* which exonerates him as far as I'm concerned considerably. I still think he's got no humor but in this case it doesn't matter. Only a humorless filmmaker could have made it. Anyone else would have seen how corny and laughable and simpleminded it is and would have given it up. But not Pasolini. He just goes straight for the mark as though he'd never heard a wrong laugh, and by being so direct manages something extraordinary every once in a while. He does have a marvellous eye and it is often thrilling to watch. I think it's Pasolini's *Mademoiselle* and I think it's his best so far, as *Mademoiselle* is Tony [Richardson]'s best. A great mistake of *Theorem* is the casting of Terence Stamp in the role of irresistible saint-tempter who changes the lives of everyone he comes into contact with.

1. An agreement was reached that day to go ahead with the *Cabaret* film, and Isherwood telephoned Bachardy to let him know.

Imagine. This very usual, actory pseudostud Stamp in that part. There must be some financial reason why. The producers must have insisted on some kind of name because Pasolini usually has such an eye for faces.[2] Anyway, I look forward to seeing it again with my old Stablemate. Oh! What a Lovely War must be awful, though it has had an ecstatic reception.

Am longing to sharpen some very dulled claws on that rough hide and then curl up between those dear knobbly forelegs. The enclosed is intended as a warning to the Old Drub to keep that Muzzle out of the honey pots. Kitty doesn't fancy having to dive into a water tank.[3] XXXXXX P.

[Autograph letter with enclosure]

1969 MAY 1

FROM SANTA MONICA CALIF

BACHARDY CARE BUCKLE, 34 HENRIETTA STREET, LONDON WC 2 (ENGLAND)

HARVEY NOW SAYS NO NEED WE THREE WORK BEFORE HE LEAVES SO OKAY YOU STAY TILL MAY 8 IF NECESSARY HAND SURGERY NOT REQUIRED YET LOVE CHRIS

[Western Union International Telegram]

Thursday [May 1, 1969, London]

Beloved Brumby—

Spent last night with Anthony and so missed His dear call this morning. I was waiting for the cheap calling hours (when Dubbin would have had his restoring snooze) to return the call when His telegram arrived. At least Kitty is relieved to know he won't be coming home to a three-legged Nag, but is anxious to know the details of the diagnosis.

2. British actor Terence Stamp (b. 1938) had been nominated for an Academy Award and a BAFTA for his film debut in the title role of Billy Budd (1962) and became widely known as Sergeant Troy in John Schlesinger's Far from the Madding Crowd (1967) with Julie Christie, Peter Finch, and Alan Bates, even though the film was poorly received.
3. Bachardy enclosed the following item, clipped from an unknown paper: "Bees kill donkey: An angry swarm of bees stung a donkey to death at San Marcos de Leon, Mexico. Its peasant rider, badly stung, escaped by diving into a water tank nearby, and was taken to hospital. He said he would sue the bees' owner, who replied that either the donkey or its rider must have tried to nibble at the bees' honey."

I guess Kitty will have to go to the vet himself. It might turn out to be quite a nice little scene to play—Kitty pleading for Dubbin's hoof, even placing his own soft white paw under the scalpel in lieu of the Old Hoof (after first removing with great care a delicate lace glove).

As for Harvey's vacillations, as soon as I changed my May 6 flight to May 8, he'd decide something different, so I will stick to May 6 unless there's a last-minute reason for staying on a day or two, in which case I will cable you. But there doesn't now seem to be any point in staying beyond Tuesday. I will have done all the business I have. I'm doing the Davison commission tomorrow afternoon and soon I will call Stan at the Hamet Gallery to know what he thinks of the book of photographs of my drawings which I took into the gallery yesterday. I went into Heywood Hill yesterday, too. He was eager to do whatever he could for you but doubtful about both the Klimt and Caravaggio books, neither of which he knew about. I will check with him at the first of the week to know if he's been able to get hold of them.

Finally got to see Tom and Flavio and delivered the Horse drawing.[1] Flavio, after disappointing weeks with no job offers, had decided he must go back to Mexico. Suddenly within two days he got signed by both the Portugal & Sweden ballet companies. He leaves for Portugal on Sunday for three months and then to Sweden in July for I don't know how long. He and Tom will be seeing very little of each other but I don't think that will bother either of them. The flat they've got in Earls Court is depressing but I suppose bearable when you've gotten used to it. Saw *Oh! What a Lovely War* with John [Osborne] & Jill & Anthony last night and nearly died of it. A more boring, unimaginative and totally untalented movie has never been made. The 4 of us, after 2 hrs. 24 min. without an intermission, were overcome by pent-up fury and raged against it for at least an hour. No film has gotten such universally ecstatic reviews in years.[2]

Kitty so looks forward to seeing that Dear Rump tethered to the waiting post at the airport on Tuesday.

XXXXXX His eternally loving Snowpaws.

[Autograph letter, labelled "Letter #1"]

1. A portrait of Isherwood.
2. Adapted from Gerry Raffles and Joan Littlewood's 1963 stage musical and directed by Richard Attenborough; many British stars appeared, including Dirk Bogarde, Edward Fox, John Gielgud, Laurence Olivier, Corin Redgrave, Michael Redgrave, Vanessa Redgrave, Ralph Richardson, Maggie Smith, Ian Holme, and Susannah York.

This is Kitty's Last written London report. The next to be delivered "in Pusson."

Friday [May 2, 1969, London]

Sainted Rubble—

I hope I'm not making another foolish mistake by letting Anthony persuade me to accompany him to the country to stay with Alfred & Jimmy. I really hadn't anything else to do in town over the weekend and Anthony is anxious to make up for his behavior during my first week at Ladbroke Grove. It seemed obstinate and petulant of me not to give in. He promises not to be difficult. We shall see. Oddly enough, it seems we've spent so little time with each other, and almost no time alone. [. . . I]f there have to be other people around, Alfie and Jimmy are the nicest I can think of. And I suspect that maybe Anthony is right and I shouldn't insist on our being alone together. We're going to Devon on a sleeper tonight, arriving early tomorrow morning and coming back Monday afternoon—that is, if I can stick it for that long.

Last night I went to dinner at the Harewoods' with Richard Buckle and Vanessa [Redgrave] and Franco Nero. Vanessa has become a great buddy of Richard's as a result of Isadora. She had never met the Harewoods and wanted to in order to enlist his support for some cause of hers, a Birmingham playground in fact. Strangely enough, though she brought up the subject at dinner, she never got around to popping the question to Harewood. She said in the car on the way home that she suddenly felt awkward and shy after coming on so openly about the project. I was surprised to hear she ever felt shy. She seems to me so untuned-in to other people's wavelengths. I think she really does live in a world completely of her own in which she moves like her idea of a free soul. It's all make-believe, even her relationship with Franco—a tacit understanding between two Egos. A colder pair is difficult to imagine. I think they're both pod-born replacements for real humans. Even Richard, who is devoted to fame in general and to Vanessa in particular, said of her when we got home that she had been "coy" he thought that evening, which was putting it mildly. The evening had not been a success really. The Harewoods came on rather jolly, talky Establishment, as though this is what they feared Vanessa would think of them, and she behaved as though it was in fact what she did think of them. Franco was playing it rude Wop male peasant, though I saw him scratch his scalp and then carefully pat his head where he'd scratched in case he'd mussed it. After dinner, in the street, Vanessa did a few high kicks and free form movements, the obligatory behavior of a natural free soul. I asked her if she received our letter rather too pointedly. She had.[1]

Am longing for my Sweet Muzzle as always. Silverclaws.

[Autograph letter, labelled "Letter #2"]

May 1. Thursday [1969]   [Santa Monica]

My dearest darling Love,

I will take a chance and send this one message to the Puss of my Heart. Came back last night meaning to send you a night letter, then found it was after midnight so it wouldn't be delivered until May 2nd. So tried to phone but you'd gone out, so I waited up till 3 a.m. and kept calling, and then the phone was busy and I gave up and sent a straight wire to let you know about Tony [Harvey]'s change of mind and plans. And then this morning your cable arrives saying you are coming back on Tuesday! Well, maybe this mess will untangle. Anyhow Dobbin will be waiting for his love, no matter when.

Incidentally, when I finally got to sleep I was woken at 7 by Collin Wilcox, saying oh dear is it that early but I wanted Geoffrey to say goodbye to you—he's leaving for Washington. So she screamed to Geoffrey to come to the phone and he thought he was about to talk to Jane Fonda! I think she must have flipped again. Could I see her tonight? No I said, I'm going down to say goodbye to the cast of *Black Girl*. Can't I come with you, she said. No, I said, because I'm going with the director. That stopped her.

I talked to Tony Harvey yesterday and it was then he suddenly said he will leave early Tuesday for New York and then to England, quickly quickly to pack up his apartment and come back here in about three weeks. So, he graciously said, why need we three get together until his return? Meanwhile you and I would draft an outline. To which I agreed, because it really is much better that way. But Miss Harvey has once again (as she will many many times in the years ahead) fucked up your

---

1. Isherwood and Bachardy saw the uncut version of *Isadora* soon after it opened; they both liked it and wrote to Redgrave to tell her so.

plans. I hope my cable will arrive soon enough to unfuck them again if you have any reasons of any kind for wanting to stay on till Thursday. Not that Dub doesn't long for Kitty's return, and not that he doesn't urgently need him for discussion, because there are grave problems to be solved in our story, including some things which Harvey wants and I don't and I'm pretty sure you won't want either. I've taken notes on our conversation, so you and I can discuss it.

The hand doctor said yes indeed, Dob's hoof had this thing Dr. Allen said, a Dupuytren's contracture. It is a racial hereditary thing, much to be found among the northern races, British and Scandinavian, never in Asia. Sometimes it arrests itself for years or the rest of a lifetime, sometimes it races ahead. It is never malignant. If Dub's hoof looks the same in four months, the Dr. says it will be arrested, but anyhow it can be corrected at this early stage by a slight operation which would mean having the hand in a splint for a couple of weeks and produce a complete cure. Most patients he said only come in when their hands have almost turned into clenched fists! Then there's not so much he can do. He doesn't believe in the X-ray treatment, it may cause deep burns. It was funny being in the clinic because you saw all these patients in little rooms having their hands held and examined by doctors, like people consulting palmists.

All Saddleplug's devotion to his darling Rider, and how he longs to feel the dig of those spurs and the delicious thrill of that velvet whip!

Your letters just arrived!

[Typed letter with autograph additions]

· · ·

[May 18, 1969, Santa Monica]

A story about a Dobbin's (ugh!) devotion.

There was an old Dobbin who wanted to give Kitty something of a certain shape and color which he had lost part of, so he went to a place in Sta. Monica and they said better go to a place where they sell men's clothes, and they said have you tried the hotel but the hotel didn't know. So old Dob went to Pacific Palisades where the lady said no unfortunately but I hear there's a place on Ventura Boulevard at Coldwater Canyon where they have *nothing else*. So Dub trotted over the hill and how hot it was and the flies got under his hat and stung him but he found where it was and they said sorry but our Mr. So-and-So has taken them all to the Pan Pacific where there's a Home Show—so Drabbledug trotted back over the hill dragging his tail through Laurel Canyon through all the dust and he got into the Pan Pacific and they laughed at him and tried to run him out but he neighed and reared and at last he found Mr. So-and-So who was kind but said I've sold them all. But Mr. So-and-So told him to go to Gorham, just off San Vicente, and there, in a pet shop of all places, he found some—and this isn't really what he was thinking of but he hopes Kitty will like it—anyhow it's truly a token of Love on Kitty's birthday.[1]
XXXXXXXXXX

[*Autograph note on the recto of a plain white envelope containing two color gift tags and a color picture postcard that squeaks, all with autograph additions, printed opposite*]

1. Isherwood and Bachardy were together in Santa Monica for the birthday. The gift is unidentified.

Even a sow dubbin
    can wish a heppy
birthday
    to
a

saint puss

A Gift for You

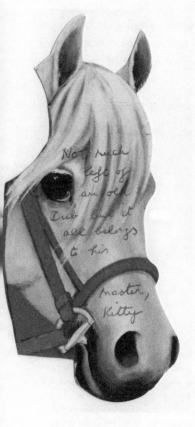

•   •   •

August 18 [1969]   [Santa Monica]

Dearest Angel,

[J]ust to let you know that Dennis sent back your address book. You don't want it, do you?[1] In the same mail a bill from American Express, $21.82, which I paid.

Swami was saddened to hear that he wouldn't see you and sent his love. (I'm having lunch with him on Wednesday.) Saw Gerald, just the same as ever. Very affectionate but really wanted Kitty. Said he'd thought about us every single day since we left and had had some very strange dreams about us. I couldn't ask him to elaborate for fear of bringing on a verbal traffic jam.

Also a letter from Bob Regester telling me to call, look after and show the sights to Jeanne Moreau, who is here doing a film. This is not Drub's idea of amusement but I'll do the minimum so Kitty can maybe draw her.

Just wanted to get this word off to my Darling and hope he won't forget his old

[Typed letter with autograph additions]

---

1. The address book had been left behind in Australia, where Isherwood and Bachardy visited the set of *Ned Kelly* during August 1969 after travelling to Tahiti. They left the film set August 7 and flew from Canberra to Sidney, where they spent time with Australian academic and gay activist Dennis Altman (b. 1934). Bachardy evidently left the address book in the hotel after consulting it on August 10 to phone Anthony Page in London and arrange to visit him there. He returned to Los Angeles August 11, and then flew to London August 18. He again stayed with Page.

Thursday [August 21, 1969, London]

Adorable One—

I have been waiting to write to you until I had some definite news to tell you. Still none, and nothing to tell that you won't already have heard from Robin before you get this. I saw him and Jessie¹ for a drink the evening of the day I arrived. They were leaving for Ireland the next day and should be on their way back to L.A. by now. She is about five weeks pregnant and only discovered it once they were here. She's felt sick most of the time they've been in London and so has not gone out much.

Robin says Jim only that morning (Tuesday) had had a telegram from the Robert Wise people to say they are ready to go and want him back as soon as possible. According to Robin, Jim thinks he should not direct our play and Robin agrees with him. Says Robin, Jim will be involved in his film till February and he, Robin, thinks it would be wrong to wait that long to do the play.²

Jim is in Edinburgh (Jack, too) and was due back yesterday. I sent a telegram asking if we could have dinner last night and to call me as soon as he got in. I waited all day and all evening for him to call. He didn't and it's already after 10:30 this morning and still no word. Until I've spoken to him there's no way of knowing how he really feels about doing the play. I told Robin we did not want to get into production with the play if we could avoid it before November because of *Claudius* (apparently Neil has offered only $15,000 for the screenplay).³ Also, the longer we put off the production the better the chances that Christopher Gable will be available.⁴ However, for whatever reasons, Robin is pushing for the play to be done this fall without Jim.

Robin also knew without my telling him that I was staying with Anthony. He said too that Jim knew Anthony wanted to direct our

---

1. Jessie Homer French (b. 1940), his wife, a painter.
2. American director Robert Wise (1914–2005) was producing *The Babymaker* (1970), for which Bridges had written the screenplay and which he was going to direct, thus threatening to interfere with his plans to direct *A Meeting by the River*.
3. Tony Richardson had asked Isherwood in May 1969 to do rewrites on a script he already had for *I, Claudius*, and Isherwood introduced Bachardy as his collaborator. They had discussed the script with Richardson and made an outline during their visit to Australia.
4. Royal ballet star Christopher Gable (1940–1998) had recently turned to acting, and Isherwood and Bachardy hoped to cast him as Oliver in *A Meeting by the River*.

play. I told Robin that as far as I knew Anthony still had not even read the revised version and had never said anything to either of us about wanting to direct it. I begin to wonder if maybe some mischief has been done and Jim is feeling betrayed. Impossible to know without talking to him. I played it grave disappointment with Robin, and not all that insincerely either. I think Robin has been encouraging Jim to back out. Also I think Robin is against a Royal Court production and would rather a straightforward West End production—which I'm sure has been Nicholas Thompson's line from the beginning and he has, I'm also sure, influenced Robin. I'm having lunch today with Nicholas so will maybe know more later. But still, Jim is the person to talk to. He should be back today and I will just keep calling until I get him.

Anthony went to Nottingham yesterday to see some Scottish repertory company—he's on the lookout for actors for the *Macbeth* production. He comes back today. He has not even mentioned the play, so neither have I. I am waiting at least till I've spoken to Jim. But then, I have nothing to talk to Anthony about as far as the play goes. Surely he is the one to speak. If Robin knew I was coming to stay with Anthony, I suspect that Jim probably knew, too, and it would be very easy for him to imagine some kind of plot against him. And the truth—that I have never really even discussed the play with Anthony—is so unlikely. Nevertheless, I will go out of my way to reassure Jim when I see him—if I ever do. He's supposed to be leaving for L.A. on Saturday.

I had a nice a lunch with David and Peter and Wayne Sleep,[5] who's staying with them, on Tuesday, the day I arrived. They were very sweet and their relationship seems to be working. We ran into them at the Hungry Horse that same night. They were there with Ron Kitaj to whom I was very cool. Peter's hair is much longer and reddish from bleaching. David looks a bit fatter. A drink with Patrick Woodcock this evening and lunch with Jill Bennett tomorrow.

Later

A dear note and such a sweet drawing from his Old Muzzle just arrived. Kitty feels so cheered. He has been undergoing those familiar London

---

5. British ballet dancer (b. 1948), educated at the Royal Ballet School and, from 1966, a member of the Royal Ballet, where he was to become an international star.

blues and wondering, as usual, whatever is he doing here. Delighted to know Jeanne Moreau is there. I hope you'll be able to endure her long enough to allow Kitty at least to get a look at her. I must call Bob Regester today. Glad to know my address book arrived. Let me know if I should write to Altman to thank him. I could send a letter to him to you, or you could send me his address. Also let me know if I should get after a copy of *Heart in Exile* here.[6] I'm going into Heywood Hill today to see about the Klimt and Caravaggio.

Must hurry to get out to lunch. Kitty thinks of His Only Dear constantly and misses him and loves him more than ever. XXXXXXXX Snowpaws.

P.S. *I, Claudius* is such a bore. An awful book I think and Graves is so odious. What drudgery it is to get through it.

[*Autograph letter*]

Friday August 29. [1969, London]

Dearest Love Cob—

I have not written before now because the situation here changes from day to day, if not from minute to minute. After our telephone conversations on Sunday and Tuesday in which we decided to back Jim, what does Jack do but call me up on Wednesday to propose a highly confidential heart-to-heart in which he more or less advised us, "unless we really really want Jim," to drop him. His reasons were mostly practical and quite convincing: no N.Y. producer was likely to accept a package deal including Jim; chances of a proper legit production in L.A. had been exhausted with the possible but by no means sure exception of the Huntington Hartford;[1] Jim by his own admission felt very intimidated by the London scene and Jack thinks he will have trouble getting any first-rate English actors to work with him; also, Jack feels that American

6. A 1953 gay novel by "Rodney Garland," possibly a pseudonym for Adam de Hegedus (b. 1906), a Hungarian-born writer settled in London.

1. The theater at 1615 North Vine Street, in Hollywood; A&P grocery store heir Huntington Hartford bought it in 1954 and ran it for ten years before selling it to James Doolittle, who renamed it the Doolittle Theater. It now operates as the Ricardo Montalban Theater.

and English styles of acting are so different that English critics, and maybe English actors and producers as well, will be unable to accept Jim's ideas.

Of course I am interpreting (and of course editing drastically) Jack's remarks, but that seems to me the gist of what he was trying to say. It is possible, too, that Jack's intention might be to save Jim from what he thinks will certainly be another London disaster for him,[2] as much as to save us from disaster. I guess that the agreement between us and Jim which Robin is drawing up will not be valid until I have signed it too, so we will have an opportunity to discuss it when I get home. In the meantime the situation concerning Anthony and the play could not be more ambiguous. He has still only read part, if any, of it and I can't pressure him any further because he is immersed in troubles with Nicol Williamson who is behaving quite madly. As of this morning the *Macbeth* production is off because Anthony feels he can no longer cope with Nicol. I have told Clement Scott Gilbert[3] that we are seriously considering waiting till March or even April for Jim and he is very dismayed. He has in the meantime given the play to Alec McCowen[4] (who might be free for a Jan. 1970 production) & is still hoping to ditch Jim. Continued in next letter. K.

[Autograph letter, labelled "Letter #1"]

II   Friday, August 29 [1969, London]

Old Darling—

What hell all this "negotiating" is and how I hate it. I wish I'd not come here now. There's so little point in my getting involved in all this mess

2. Bridges directed Larson's play, *Cherry, Larry, Sandy, Doris, Jean, Paul,* for a one-week run in a student theater in London (the Jeanetta Cochrane Theatre, attached to the Central School of Art and Design) before taking it to the Edinburgh Festival, August 18 to September 4. Opening night in London was a disaster because two actors missed their entrance cue and the actors on stage had to ad-lib extensively; the play was in rhymed couplets of iambic pentameter, and their ad libs were not. Nevertheless there were some good reviews, and Bridges began filming London exteriors for an independent film version. He dropped the project, though, and hurried back to Los Angeles when he was offered the chance to direct his own script, *The Baby Maker.*
3. British theater producer trying to put together a London production of *A Meeting by the River.*
4. British actor (b. 1925) proposed to play Oliver.

without your being here too. And Anthony and I have been more at odds than ever before. Even if he loved the play and was dying to do it (which I think unlikely now) I wonder if it would be really possible for us to work with him. Anyway, no point in considering that until he's read the play (if he ever does) and says what he thinks of it. I am determined to get at least some kind of reaction out of him. Whatever else may be wrong with him, he does certainly know the ins and outs of the theater here, and what kind of chance the play would have of success here.

I am having a drink with Nicholas Thompson tonight—a vague attempt on my part to pacify him. I feel he's been misled by Jim and us to a certain extent and I feel a bit guilty. He has after all only been doing his best and now he's in the middle, between Jim who wants to direct his film and the producers who want to get on with the show and don't want Jim anyway. Clement (we're on first-name basis now) also told me on the phone yesterday that April would really be too late to begin production—it would take at least a month to cast and if rehearsals began in May the play could not possibly open in London till sometime in June which is already the summer & off-season. He thinks that would mean a fall 1970 production and he doubted his money men would wait that long. And who knows if Jim might not have another film to do?

An end to all of this tiresome business stuff. I will call you if anything important develops. I can't tell you how much Kitty longs for the happiness of his basket and the warm snug smell of his Only Hide. What joy to be with him again. At least I am not going to Morocco[1] but don't know if I can get away now by early next week as I'd planned. I won't leave here until I've settled with Anthony and gotten some kind of word from him about the play. But Old Catkin will cable as soon as he knows what plane he's getting on and will call if anything of interest comes up to do with the play. He thinks of his Dearest Pony so much and never wavers in his love for him. And longs so to be with him again. XXXXX Fur.

[*Autograph letter, labelled "Letter #2"*]

·   ·   ·

1. A conjectured trip with Anthony Page.

Sunday 25 [January] 1970 5:20 p.m.[1]   [Santa Monica]

Just off to see Bill & Paul at Gerald Davis show.[2] So far unable to contact Nick Wilder but will let you know at once if I do.[3] Jack Larson made such a fuss about your seeing Warhol & how he'd written him a huge letter praising you that I've just sent you a telegram to call Warhol direct.[4]

Loved talking to his darling just now. Adores his precious angel treasure.

[Autograph note with autograph additions]

. . .

1. Bachardy flew to New York on January 22, and Isherwood spoke to him on the telephone on January 25, just before writing this note, which he sent to the Hotel Chelsea, 222 West 23rd St.
2. An exhibition of paintings at the Jacqueline Anhalt Gallery. Davis was a friend of Wonner and Brown.
3. Bachardy was arranging to do Wilder's portrait for an upcoming show of artists, art dealers, and art-world figures. The sitting, on January 17, 1970, proved to be the start of their important friendship.
4. Warhol sat for Bachardy on January 29 at The Factory, and Bachardy did three portraits, starting at 3 p.m. The same day, in the morning, he did two drawings of Jasper Johns.

[March 2, 1970]

Adored One-Horse—

Old Fur is starting this on the plane, which is about to start its descent. It's later than I thought—the landing gear sounds as though it's just being lowered.

I stupidly came away with the keys to Moore St. but will hang onto them rather than send them through the mail. You probably won't be needing them (unless that roaming stallion takes on a "live-in" to take care of Kitty's chores), so I will bring them back with me unless I hear from you that they are needed.[1]

I also came away without anything to read so had to make do with *Newsweek, Harper's Bazaar* & the London *Times*. I meant to take *Nest of Ninnies*.[2] Please don't throw it out before I finish it.

The flight has been fairly smooth. This plane seems less beat-up than the other BOAC one we came on, but still it's shabbier than the Pan Am planes, and the lunch almost totally inedible, which is saying a lot of a meal on a plane. I can usually eat anything (but horse meat of course). In fact, the tiny, gristled lamb chops tasted rather like I imagine horse meat. The broccoli offered the worst of both worlds—as tough as it would be if it were raw, and tasteless as though it'd been boiled for several hours. The canned mixed-veg. salad was covered over with a damp blanket of salmon as though it had died and was, with reason, being concealed from sensitive eyes.

1. Bachardy was arriving in New York en route to Los Angeles from London. He had spent a month there with Isherwood working on rewrites for their play, A Meeting by the River, and was now returning home for the March 8 opening of his exhibition at a new gallery, the Irving Blum Gallery (see below, pp. 416–418). Isherwood remained in London continuing to work towards a production and staying in a flat belonging to an old friend, Bill Harris (see below, p. 420) at 3 Moore Street, S.W. 3.
2. The 1969 comic novel written by John Ashbery and James Schuyler.

6:30 p.m.

Have got a very cheap, very basic room at the Chelsea. I'm having dinner with Virgil tonight in order to collect my gear. I think I will stay through tomorrow and leave on the noon plane Wed. Henry Geldzahler has invited me to have dinner with him and David Hockney & Celia[3] tomorrow night—they're supposed to arrive sometime tomorrow afternoon. Elaine de Kooning is in town and has even asked to see my drawings, so I will see her late tomorrow afternoon, though even if she offered to set up a sitting with the old man[4] I doubt if I'd have time to do it. Also supposed to see Joe LeSueur for lunch and maybe drop by Joe Brainard's in the early afternoon. So all is fairly well organized and I'm trying hard to stay awake through this evening—have taken a tiny D. for support.[5]

I hated leaving my Darling Dubbin this morning and miss him so much already. Please guard well that beloved, *only* Hide which is Kitty's all.

With Catkisses thousandfold. Fur.

[*Autograph letter*]

3 Moore St. [London] S.W. 3   March 3 [1970]

Dearest Sweetruff,

Oh the longing for his angel since that sad snowy departure and oh the cold since, both in heart & thermometer! Drub couldn't sleep last night until he was wrapped in his chemise & robe, with socks on his icy hoofs. And yet that tiny kitten could warm his old hide through & through.

St. Rubble has been engaged as usual on tasks of charity—supper with Sylvain Mangeot last night, lunch at the Vedanta Society today, supper with Robert Medley tonight, visit to Peter Schlesinger's studio tomorrow & to theater with Norman Prouting.[1]

3. Celia Birtwell (b. 1941), British fabric designer, wife since 1969 of fashion designer Ossie Clark.
4. That is, her husband, Willem de Kooning whom Bachardy held "second only to Bacon."
5. A Dexamyl.

1. (1924–1983), Isherwood's landlord; Prouting owned 3 Moore Street, where he lived upstairs from the flat that he let to Bill Harris. He was a train buff and had worked on commercial film shorts about English transport.

Now Clement is getting very mad at Clifford because of the *Oh Calcutta* commitment. At present it wd mean that Clifford wd be off our project from the 1st of April to the 2nd of June! And in addition to this he is going to New York to talk about it, until the end of the week![2] We are to discuss all this as soon as John Roberts & Richard Schulman (?) have read the play—maybe tomorrow afternoon.[3] Of course I shall express no definite opinion until I've talked to you on the phone— in a way, your not being here is a tactical advantage, it gives time to consider!

But never mind all that shit. The point is, we have got the play revised and now we'll get it cast, with or without Clifford. If we have to get another director, we will. Meanwhile we hear that the Germans (who read an earlier version of the play which Nicholas Thompson sent them) are definitely interested in doing it![4]

Angel, remember I shall be up north with Richard from Friday 6th to Monday 9th. You'll call me late Monday so I'll be early Tuesday morning.

Will be thinking of beautiful genius Kitty with so much pride, during his show. Do hope his treasured Love is all right.

Always his adoring
Rump XXXXXXXXX

[*Autograph letter*]

March 6. [1970, Santa Monica]

Dearest Hide—

I've been thinking over the situation with the play since your call last night. First of all, I'm amazed that Williams & Roberts have behaved so badly—not communicating with you directly about something as basic as their proposals seem to be. I agree with you totally that not only would the rewrites they require mean virtually writing a whole other

2. Clifford Williams (1926–2005), British actor and director, then an associate director at the Royal Shakespeare Company. Kenneth Tynan's sex revue *Oh! Calcutta!* had opened in New York in 1969 and Williams was to direct it in London in 1970.
3. Roberts, a British theater producer who had produced two plays on Broadway in the 1950s and later worked in South Africa, was proposing to work with Clifford Williams. Schulman was Scott Gilbert's producing partner.
4. At a theater in Düsseldorf (see below, p. 431), but nothing came of it.

play but also a play which would be much more usual, mechanical and "West End" in the worst sense of the word. Knowing that, how could we conceivably sit down and rethink the whole thing (it might take months, even if we could do it)? I'm against it. But alas, Williams and Roberts are the only ones I had any confidence in. The prospect of pushing on with Clement and Schulman is a sad one. I don't think Clement has any taste or professional instinct. I think he will saddle us with incompetents in every department, and how would we be able to defend ourselves from them, not knowing anything of the London theater? I am inclined to wanting to back out, but certainly will come back and pull with my Old Naggin if he feels we must or should go on with the project. I am vague about exactly how binding is the contract we've signed with Clement. Can he in fact go ahead without us if we both leave England?

Jim and I are getting along well.[1] It takes a bit of adjusting to, having anyone but the Dear Rump in the sacred Casa, but he is very sweet and responds to any show of affection, however forced it may be at heart. (Only Dubbin knows where that tiny heart is hidden, in the deepest part of the fur.)

There is surprisingly little for me to do about my show. Irving[2] says the interest in it is "fantastic," everyone is "talking about it and wanting to be in on it." He says there are already several orders for commissions, all of which must wait if Capt. Dub decides the Animals can't desert the ship. (It occurs to me that Jim's film is finished shooting now—I don't know how long the editing will go on or what his plans are—should we suggest all over again that he do the play in London? Jack I know is against it, but still I can't see what any of us would have to lose if Jim doesn't have anything better to do at the moment.)

I had dinner last night with Henry Geldzahler & Larry Stanton who've just arrived here. They are coming to my show on Sunday—Henry's presence will have good prestige value.

1. Jim Gates had moved into 145 Adelaide Drive to housesit. He didn't have much money, so Bachardy let him stay until near Isherwood's return at the end of April.
2. Irving Blum (b. 1930) was Bachardy's new Los Angeles dealer. Blum joined the Ferus Gallery in 1957, then in 1967 opened his own gallery, where he showed contemporary Californian artists including Ed Moses and Ed Ruscha, as well as Bachardy and more widely known talents like Diebenkorn, Lichtenstein, Warhol, and Johns. Portraits of them all, by Bachardy, were to be exhibited in the show.

Miss my Sweet Angel Hooves so terribly. I'll call him Tuesday a.m. London time, around 10 a.m. if I can, to give as much chance for this to arrive beforehand.

With every beat of a kitten's secret heart. Whiskers

[*Autograph letter*]

Friday, March 13, 1970 [Santa Monica]

Beloved Velvet Rump:

The enclosed is mostly junk mail. I thought you would rather cope with the English stuff while you are there instead of having to face it when you come back to the Casa. The letter from Danny Selznick I find false and oily in its lack of commitment on any point. I think he must be a very weak character and definitely hiding under Mama Hawk's dry old wing.[1]

Also enclosed is a review of my show from this morning's *Times* which I found out about soon after I spoke to you this morning. I'm amazed to see it featured as it is, with even a picture, and ahead of such distinguished figures as Hanson, Weeks and even Billy, who won't like it at all. Happily he and Penny are out of town for a few weeks. I think the review is on the whole favorable, though grudgingly so—"mannerist line," "muzzily modelled," "glamorous" technique, "*Vogue* magazine illustrations" are all phrases of scented derision, as is the "vaguely disturbing" with which the review ends, but nevertheless the space it occupies is impressive. Irving is very pleased, and surprised too—says he has almost never been given such coverage.[2] He called this morning

1. Daniel Selznick (b. 1936), writer and producer, was the younger son of David Selznick and his first wife Irene Mayer (1907–1990), who became a theatrical producer after the marriage. Isherwood and Bachardy had given Daniel Selznick a copy of *A Meeting by the River* in December 1969 at his request so that he could show it to his mother.

2. Isherwood preserved the review, although the other enclosures are lost. Henry J. Seldis and William Wilson, "Art Walk: A Critical Guide to the Galleries," *Los Angeles Times*, Fri. Mar. 13, 1970, Part IV, p. 8:

> La Cienega
>
> Pencil portraits of art people by Don Bachardy are a divertissement after vanguard art watching. Bachardy's supple, mannerist line focuses on muzzily modelled faces, describing features with a deftness both accurate and decorative. His technique is, itself, glamorous, existing in a tradition stretching from Ingres to *Vogue* magazine illustrations. But he gives us more than the superficial gloss of faces from a public demi-monde. They are finally psychological studies.

with a commission from Mrs. Weisman. She and her husband were the subjects of Hockney's first big double portrait. I haven't spoken to her yet but Irving seems to think it's definite.[3]

Jim [Gates] is going away to Santa Barbara for the weekend to see Swami before coping with his draft board summons. He is calm about the event and trying to see it as a meaningful, even possibly beneficial, change in his life. I have very little of his philosophical optimism on the subject. I have got very fond of him and feel I understand him better than I used to. I can't imagine sitting up to breakfast in the Casa every morning with anybody else. Don't imagine though that he has

---

Robert Irwin looks like a Western guru: Billy Bengston, shrewd; Larry Bell, aloof: Betty Asher, grandmotherly; Henry Geldzahler seems to be hiding behind his glasses. There is tragedy in the ravaged heads of Dalí and Francis Bacon. Brooke Hopper looks so soft that any man who doesn't develop a crush has no soul.

Seeing such work in a far-out establishment contradicts the notion that vanguardists hate traditional art. It's also vaguely disturbing, like finding John Jones's house full of portraits of John Jones. (Irving Blum Gallery, 811 N. La Cienega; through April 10.).—W.W.

Prints and paintings by Southlander Hardy Hanson have grown as delicate as watered silk, Hanson is frankly influenced by the civilized satanising of Paul Klee and the color theories of Joseph Albers. He finds a niche between them through tight compositional sensitivity and a brand o˙ light eccentricity that reminds one of Satie's music. Current work falls into two broad categories; ordered mosaic strokes that organize in optical color-blushes and computer-blips; and emblematic works, mostly small, woven in lines of metallic color. (Rex Evans Gallery, 748¼ N. La Cienega: through March 28.)—W.W.

James Weeks paints pleasant terraces, studio corners and other relaxed subjects in the brushy, blocky style of 50s San Francisco art. (Felix Landau Gallery, 702 N. La Cienega; through March 28.)

Billy Al Bengston shows new bravura-style abstractions, on shiny, rumpled metal. Here his chevron trademark appears between beautifully orchestrated splashes of color in an installation illuminated by candlelight. (Mizuno Gallery, 669 N. La Cienega; to March 31.)

Art dealer Nicholas Wilder

American artist Billy Al Bengston (b. 1934 in Kansas), who had his first one-man show at the Ferus Gallery in 1958, had been a friend of Bachardy since 1967. He was an admirer of Bachardy's work, as was Bengston's girlfriend, Penny Little, who worked in interior design.

3. Hockney's *American Collectors* (1968), now in the Art Institute of Chicago, depicts Marcia and Fred Weisman in their Los Angeles sculpture garden.

by any means taken a certain Pony's place—in fact, Kitty has assumed Dubbin's place at the head of the table and Jim sits in the lowly Cat's chair.

Doug Walsh has hitched up both the washer and dryer. The dryer is by the wall next to the stove. I didn't think it would fit or look as good as it does there. But now Doug himself has suggested putting them both downstairs in the basement and I think it's a good idea. I wish I'd thought of it sooner.

I'm having dinner with Paul Wonner tonight. Hopefully I will get to talk to Jim [Bridges] about the play first. I am very doubtful though that he will commit himself to doing it even if we're prepared to wait till after May 29. I think Peter Gill is a much better prospect if the Court furies don't fuss him.[4]

I saw Gerald and Michael on Monday. Gerald has had another stroke Michael says but still seemed much as usual, though maybe a bit dimmer and vaguer. The record *was* the right one.[5]

I'm going with Ted to see a showing of *Inspiration* (with Garbo) tomorrow night somewhere in the wilds of Highland Park. I haven't seen him since I've been back. He had a brief crazy spell a few weeks ago and according to my parents it is over now, though I think he still sounds high over the telephone. In the past the short bouts have usually been merely curtain raisers but I will know better tomorrow.

Have just spoken to Mrs. Weisman who says she does *not* want a "Hockney likeness" of herself. For the first time ever I told her she ought to want a drawing by me more than she wants a flattering likeness. She took my point very well. I tackle her on Monday.

Leonard Stanley's boyfriend tomorrow morning.[6] Leonard wants to take pictures while I'm working. And Dale[7] is going to take photographs of the drawings in the gallery on Wednesday so that Old Sweethide can at least get an impression of the way it looks.

Chris Wood called today to say he'd seen the show. He invited me to

---

4. Welsh-born actor, playwright, and director Peter Gill (b. 1939) had been an assistant director at the Royal Court since 1964 and became an associate director in 1970.
5. That is, the Vivaldi and Pergolesi recordings mentioned above p. 303.
6. Stanley was an interior designer and photographer introduced by Tony Duquette. His boyfriend was Lars Stensland, young, blond, and pretty.
7. Dale Laster, photography assistant and lab man for Peter Gowland.

dinner with him and Sorel on Monday, alas.[8] Bill Harris[9] also called. I said I might drive down to Laguna on Tuesday to spend the day with him and Jack and Ray, who he says are about to move into a new house they've built on the site of the old one.[10] Bill wanted to know how much longer you would be wanting the house and referred to the "three weeks" I originally quoted him in my letter. I got the impression he was a bit anxious to make plans for returning to London. I told him about our director trouble and said I didn't know how long it would take to find a new one. He was not especially pressing and didn't say anything about coming to "share" the place with you or us. I will know more if I see him on Tuesday.

Jim Weatherford came to my opening on Sunday and brought the Vietnam soldier, just returned, who had bought two of my nudes. You read I think a couple of his letters. The soldier is quite bright and even quite attractive but Jim was making very proprietary noises. Jim took us to dinner at Raphael's on Tuesday. I'm eager to encourage Jim's demonstrations of no hard feelings (very stylish of him I think) and so don't dare do any poaching, in spite of vague signs of encouragement from the guy, Dan Luckenbill. He's twenty-five, now bearded, and working in a library.[11]

Kitty must get now to the gym. He misses his leathery Darling so much and thinks of him all the time. The Casa just doesn't seem like home

8. Bachardy was disappointed that he had already arranged to have dinner with Jim Gates on Monday, to hear about Gates's weekend in Santa Barbara with Swami.

9. American artist (d. 1992), a beautiful blond with a magnificent physique. Isherwood had an affair with him in 1944 while living as a celibate at the Hollywood Vedanta Society, and this weakened his determination to become a monk. Harris is referred to as "X." in Isherwood's 1939–1945 diaries and appears as "Alfred" in My Guru and His Disciple.

10. Jack Fontan, American actor, artist, astrologer, known to queers as "The Naked Sailor" because he appeared in South Pacific in nothing but cut-off blue jean shorts, which put his genitals on view to anyone seated in the front rows. He was photographed in youth by George Platt Lynes. Once a lover of Bill Harris, he spent fifty-three years with his companion, Ray Unger (d. 2006), American artist and astrologer, also known for his beauty. For some years, they managed a gym together in Laguna Beach, the Laguna Health Club. Their house burned to the ground in a forest fire, and even though the canyon in which they lived had a long history of such fires, they rebuilt in the same place.

11. Luckenbill (b. 1945) worked at the UCLA library in the manuscripts division, and he began to publish short stories around this time. Later, he curated exhibitions and wrote catalogues on gay and lesbian studies. Rex Evans, Jim Weatherford's companion and his partner in the Rex Evans Gallery, had died in 1969; Weatherford made no fuss when Bachardy left the Rex Evans Gallery for Irving Blum.

without his Dear. Basketsful of catkisses, and love from Jim [Gates] who's just come back from school. XXXXXXXXX Pinkpads.

[*Typed letter, signed, with autograph additions and one surviving enclosure*]

March 25, 1970 [Santa Monica]

Darling SugarHoof:

The enclosed booklet arrived this morning to worry Kitty.[1] At first Kitty thought he ought to shield his Old Dear from the knowledge of such ugly facts of life (as the fate of those poor Greek ponies), but then he reconsidered and decided it might help that Curried and Pampered Colt to value a bit more his snug stable and his faithful old furred Stablecat, who waits so patiently by the stable door, currybrush in paw, for the return of his Wandering Stallion.

The rest is near-junk mail (including that foulsome missile from Bury Taxman[2]) and various odds and ends, such as the Academy list of nominations with checks beside those whom Kitty, assuming Purrer of Attorney, voted for. I trust Drub will agree with his choices. Those categories without checks obviously deserved no recognition by the Animals.[3]

The "Estimated Tax Declaration" should be signed by you and returned to Arnold. The envelope has his address on it. It's not serious

1. The booklet is lost.
2. Bachardy's derisive pun on Barry Taxman, a composer and music teacher with whom Isherwood had an affair in 1950; the letter is lost.
3. The only enclosure still with this letter, a list of the Academy of Motion Picture Arts and Sciences' "Nominations by Category" for 1969, torn from a larger list of nominations and screening times for Academy members. Isherwood had been admitted sometime after October 29, 1968 and voted every year in consultation with Bachardy. Bachardy cast their 1969 votes as follows: Best Actor, Jon Voight, *Midnight Cowboy*; Best Supporting Actor, Jack Nicholson, *Easy Rider*; Best Actress, Liza Minnelli, *The Sterile Cuckoo*; Best Supporting Actress, Dyan Cannon, *Bob & Carol & Ted & Alice*; Best Cinematography, *Bob & Carol & Ted & Alice*; Best Director, John Schlesinger, *Midnight Cowboy* (Bachardy wrote beside this entry, "At least he's queer"); Best Film Editing, *Midnight Cowboy*; Best Foreign Language Film, *My Night with Maud*; Best Picture, *Midnight Cowboy*; Best Visual Effects, *Marooned* (Bachardy added, "to keep the other from winning." The other was *Krakatoa, East of Java*); Best Screenplay, based on another medium, *Midnight Cowboy*; Best Story and Screenplay, original material, *Bob & Carol & Ted & Alice*. Bachardy added "not *The Damned* which certainly doesn't have a chance and why let any of the other three win?"

if it should arrive late—Arnold will just sign another voucher himself and put in brackets "Tax Accountant" for you, or something of the kind. The two check stubs are from checks I got from the bank which have the number of the joint account on them. (Slydub carefully took away all the joint account checkbooks so that Drabcat couldn't buy any pretty new ribbons to cheer him through his lonely vigil.)

Jim [Gates] has managed to get a job with the Goodwill.[4] It is one of the few available jobs in L.A. which satisfies his draft board requirements. He has to drive all the way downtown, work from 8:30 (which means getting up at dawn) till 5:30, and all for $1.60 an hour (a sub-scab wage I would think). It sounds pretty grim, too, and Jim is as close to depression, defeatism and self-pity as I've seen him, though certainly not without cause. I try to cheer him by telling him that this job may only be a breather to satisfy the draft board for the moment. Later on he can start looking for other jobs on his day off. He found out yesterday that certain jobs with KPFK meet draft board requirements—I told him I thought you might have some pull there as a result of your efforts on their behalf.[5] I hope I was not exaggerating. He became quite encouraged by the thought. He has had to quit his Black Whale job[6] and school of course, which he was beginning to enjoy perversely enough, particularly his English class for which he was doing a lot of writing. I told him he ought to write about his experiences at the Goodwill, also the Inside Story of Vedanta Place which quite turned him on. At least he will now be able to stay on in the house for as long as we might be away. Then, when he won't have a car anymore, he intends to find a place by himself in Hollywood near the temple and get to the Goodwill by bus.

Kitty's days have been uniformly uneventful. No more commissions. Irving is in New York, presumably arranging a show for me there, among a great many other things I'm sure. He's due back this weekend, with some news I hope. Chris Wood took me to dinner with Paul Sorel who, after some perfunctory praise of my show, proceeded to tell me "candidly" just what it is that my work "needs."

4. Nonprofit provider of education and training for the poor, homeless, ill-educated and physically and mentally disadvantaged, organized around mending and reselling used household goods and clothing.
5. Isherwood occasionally appeared at KPFK Radio fundraisers and spoke or read on KPFK broadcasts.
6. A restaurant in Marina del Rey; Gates washed dishes there and maybe even bussed tables and served.

Saw Gerald and Michael on Sunday. Gerald was a bit brighter and talked quite a lot though he was almost totally unintelligible. I took Evelyn Hooker out to lunch on a three-hour pass she got from the Mt. Sinai looney bin.[7] She insisted, too, on being taken to my show, but once there was hardly able to cope with it. I've seldom seen anyone so at a loss to know how to react to my drawings, and so unable to cover her bewilderment. But still she was determined to make a "meaningful experience" out of our time together. She's eager to be reassured and loved, but in that way that seems only to require demonstrations. Such demonstrations the Animals are well-equipped to supply, and do so while thinking of nothing more immediate than their next meal.

Just about the only weight left for old Drudgecat to pull is Jo, though I did call to suggest taking her out to dinner one night and she was mercifully busy. Jack Jones, in recognition of his buying the drawing of Dalí,[8] is being given the rare experience of feeding the old Pelt (quite spiritless and numb I should think after a can of fish-flavored Kat Krumbles—is $650 nearly enough?). On the credit (?) side is the opening tonight of the film version of *The Boys in the Band* with Gavin.

One more noble Catdeed which also cleared the Muzzle of any obligation: I was able to supply Bill Harris with $40 worth of amyl nitrite, at far greater cost in Cattime and effort. Bill was very grateful indeed and said it was far better than anything we might have bought for the flat. (That Proud Pusson reduced to the role of common pusher in order to spare his Horse a tiresome responsibility.)

The weather has turned grey and cold and Fogfur can almost smell the vapors steaming off that sun-drenched Carcas in Carcassonne.[9] But Old Tabby still dares to hope that under that drowsing mane there's still an occasional vague memory of a distant but ever-devoted

Whiteruff XXXXXX

[*Typed letter, signed, with autograph additions and one surviving enclosure*]

7. She had a breakdown while trying to write a major academic book on homosexuality and was being treated for depression.

8. That is, Bachardy's portrait of Dalí, done in New York February 1, 1970 and exhibited in his show at the Irving Blum Gallery.

9. From March 23 to 31, Isherwood, Hockney, and Schlesinger joined a house party at Tony Richardson's farm in the South of France, and on March 24 Hockney took the three of them off by car on a three-day sightseeing tour which included Carcassonne and Les Baux, several fine restaurants, and visits to Douglas Cooper and Natasha Spender.

April 1. [1970] 3 Moore St. [London] S.W. 3

Wishes he was still young like those frisky dobbins,[1] for then he'd have rushed to answer that sweet catcall this morning & quickly swum the few ponds between him and the Casa stables. But, alas, old Vieux Cheval is kept locked in his icy northern stall (snowed this morning!). David's lunchtime opening went over very big, with "everybody" there.[2] David sent his love and regrets that Kitty wasn't. Will have to see *Tiny Alice* (uncut version) tonight—then supper with Albee,[3] Neil & Peter. Never forget how Rub yearns for his dear home & longs for reunion. Proper letter tomorrow. X

[*Autograph postcard with black-and-white photo on verso; labelled "CAMARGUE. Chevaux sauvages dans les étangs" on recto*]

April 2 [1970] 3 Moore St. [London] S.W. 3

Dearest Snowruff,

Poor old shivering Drub is writing this under the wall heater in the kitchen, the only spot in the house which is *at least* subarctic. Charming weak sunshine outside, with light snow! Fuck this island. Now I remember why I never liked to live here. Rub's old back, just where Kitty used to snuggle, is permanently cold. What joy if Velvetpaws were pattering in the chow cupboard to prepare a hot soup! Wrubbin longs to lick that pink nose and try to express his love with fond muzzlings in that warm ruff.

Well, the trip to France—aside from terror on the roads, discomfort at Tony's and chills in bed everywhere—was at least not ghastly; I came away not hating anyone. David & Peter got most marks—they were both lovable, though David got on Peter's nerves a lot, by public fondling, burping, nagging about the right road, etc. He got on my nerves by driving, literally, at 100 mph. But he *is* careful about passing other cars, I will admit.

1. Isherwood was writing on a postcard showing wild horses running through the marshes of the Camargue in the South of France.
2. Hockney's retrospective, "Paintings, Prints, Drawings 1960–1970," opened April 1 at the Whitechapel.
3. American playwright Edward Albee (b. 1928). Isherwood and Bachardy had seen his play *Tiny Alice* in New York on January 30, 1965, during its first Broadway run.

Tony seemed withdrawn, suspicious, ruthless, very much the mad Czar—but he never *quite* got around to ordering anybody's execution. He doesn't much like Albee, who certainly is square, pompous and a layer-down-of-the-law on all matters from politics to bridge. "The Men" (Tony, Albee, Bob Regester, Neil or Jan the chauffeur[1]) played bridge every night and just let the rest of us get on with amusing ourselves. Tony had had a fight with Bob but then relented—Neil had said he wouldn't come without Bob. While they were together at Le Nid de Duc they got along uneasily well. Tony also disapproved of Albee's boyfriend, Roger Stock, who is a clothes buyer for some firm, with a Cockney accent, an ungracious fag air of grandeur and good legs. (He has now decided to be friendly to Dob, however.) And there were Tony's attendants, Anna O'Reilly[2] (who went out alone to dance at the St. Tropez bars nearly every night, explaining that she had "two personalities, one for England and one for France [. . .]," Giancarlo Cesaro, a really magnificent man-woman, with a body like a Michelangelo, who plays Carmen really *well*, and Tony's "friend," Will Chandlee, the American[3] (Bob says they do mild S. & M. things together), and a boy named Jean-Pierre, who looks after the place when it's unoccupied. It is quite beautiful—a deserted village of 8 houses away up in the wooded hills in back of St. Tropez.[4] Tony must have spent thousands, putting in baths and lights and closets. It's still madly uncomfortable, nevertheless. And it is definitely not Dob's scene to sit down 20 to the table, as we often did—especially with Tony's 2 little daughters,[5] their nurse, five miniature greyhounds, a parrot, and peacocks tapping on the windows!

David is supposed to fix up one of the buildings for a studio; it will cost him at least seven thousand pounds—and for what? A pad on someone else's property! I can't help remembering the Hookers and "my" garden house, but I daren't say anything to David lest I'm branded

1. Jan Niem (d. 1973), born in Poland, imprisoned in Siberia during World War II, and afterwards a British citizen, was Richardson's driver for twenty years.
2. Personal assistant to Richardson from 1964 to 1971; she sometimes helped as his hostess and eventually worked as an associate producer on several of his films. Later, as Anna Cottle, she became a T.V. producer in Los Angeles and worked in literary and film management on book-to-film projects.
3. William H. Chandlee III; he had worked at the Philadelphia Museum of Art planning lecture series and writing seasonal publications before joining Woodfall Productions. Later he returned home and ran an antique store.
4. Near La Garde Freinet, Var.
5. Natasha (1963–2009) and Joely, (mentioned above).

as a mischief-maker.[6] I only hope his Yorkshire caution and his Yorkshire brother (who manages his affairs) will dissuade him.

No more news about the play, except that Richard Chamberlain has now, of his own accord, asked to read it. Nothing heard yet from Ian McKellen, or from Terry Hands, the possible director.[7] A nice note from Dirk Bogarde claiming that he likes it enormously but is doing no more stage acting. He also implies that, if he were doing any, he'd be afraid of another queer part. Says he's "done his bit" in that direction! He's now at Venice, filming *Death in Venice*.[8]

On Saturday I'm going down for the day to see Dodie & Alec. Dodie has sent me her dreadful-looking new novel *A Tale of Two Families*. I'll try to skim through it before seeing them so I'll be spared the horror of writing any more lies.

Did I tell you that Mr. Cullen of Methuen's tells me that he has read Henry Heckford's book about me and it's no good? So now it seems I have to break the news to Heckford. What a drag. Cullen wanted *me* to read it, but I refuse to take the responsibility. I should end up rewriting it.

I called Nicholas Thompson and gave him a severe wigging about his tactlessness to Robin. He should *never* have sent a cable. He promised to call Robin personally this evening and explain the whole situation. Anyhow, he isn't asking for any share in any royalties, *so he says*.[9]

There is said to be a partial reprint in *The Listener* of that notorious T.V. interview with me.[10] If it's anything I'll send you a copy.

All an old shivering Nag's love and frozen tongue kisses—

XXX D. XXXX

[*Autograph letter*]

---

6. Isherwood spent a sizeable sum fixing up the garden house at Evelyn and Edward Hooker's property on Saltair Avenue in Santa Monica, hiring Jim Charlton to design it. But he lived there for only a year, August 1952 to September 1953, because the Hookers became anxious there would be a scandal when Bachardy, thirty years younger, began to stay with him there.
7. British actor Ian McKellen (b. 1939) was to say no, as was British stage director Terry Hands (b. 1941).
8. Bogarde also starred in *Victim* (1961), pursuing blackmailers responsible for the death of a boy with whom his character was chastely in love.
9. Thompson, already assisting with negotiations on *A Meeting by the River*, had been presumptuous in taking forward independently a new idea, a film of Isherwood's adaptation of *The Adventures of the Black Girl in Her Search for God*. See below.
10. "A Fortunate, Happy Life—Christopher Isherwood Talks to Derek Hart," from Hart's 1969 BBC1 documentary, appeared in *The Listener*, April 2, 1970, p. 449.

April 3. [1970] 3 Moore St. London S.W. 3

Beautiful Sacred Fursaint,

Dreardub draws nearer every day in loving thought to his dear. If only his prayers to that Purrity could produce a mystic experience of the True Fur! It's so clammy in Dob's dungeon stall that actually it makes no difference if he sleeps in his red blanket or not; only the tiny heart of a kitten could warm him.

Talked to Nicholas Thompson again today who assures me he has talked to Robin and that all is perfectly understood and Robin has already mailed him a copy of the *Black Girl* contract so he'll be able to study it before talking about the film to the Shaw Estate. Furthermore, Nicholas agrees that we should not overexpose the script of our play. If we can't find some response by the end of next week he thinks we should confer and decide what to do—which might include waiting for Jim Bridges to be free (his suggestion, not mine). Anyhow, I am more & more thinking of leaving here this month unless there are some very positive results before long.

Have just finished Dodie's novel, which I really find quite empty, smug, valueless—a perfect example of middle-class domestic female Christian Science art. *The Eustace Diamonds*, which I have also just finished, seems as stinging as Zola by contrast—and yet I suppose she thinks of Trollope as one of the masters of her School. How can she write such stuff? And what can I tell her about it? Am going down there tomorrow, which will mean no time to send a letter to my Love. Will send a report on Sunday, however.

Don't forget that poor old nag lost in the snowdrifts but plodding on in the faith that somehow he will find his kitten again.

XXXX D. XXXXX

[*Autograph letter*]

April 3, 1970 [Santa Monica]

Adored Velvet Muzzle:

I went to the reading on Wednesday night and saw Swami before and after, which explains the enclosure of the Dubtask.[1] He was uncharacteristically hesitant to burden the Old Plug but then decided it would be better to load him up well in advance (June 1 is the deadline) rather than at the last minute. Kitty of course would be the last to want to curtail the Filly Follies—London's biggest hip (I mean hit), I'm sure.

Also enclosed, for morbid curiosity only and to be destroyed by burning after examination, is a particularly gagging bit of drool from David Smith. The return address on the envelope read: "David Smith and Bob Christian (in absentium)." "People who love people" are not only *not* the most wonderful people in the world, they don't even love people.[2]

Also included in this shipment is a graphic reminder for Wayward Roans of what can happen to defenseless furred creatures when left alone and unprotected, forgotten by those they love and depend upon.[3]

The rest is largely stuffing. Now that almost everyone knows The Rump is no longer in residence, the Casa mail is decidedly unscintillating.

Kitty's sad grey days follow each other with regularity and sameness. Saw Beverly yesterday. There was an awkward ordeal last Saturday when she was brought to the gallery to see my show. She refused to let her air machine be plugged in because of the noise, but then soon after being wheeled around in her bed to each of the drawings (having to look at them at such an angle and from such a distance she must have been able to make nothing at all of them) she suddenly had to be rushed back to

1. Swami had made a six-page translation of Shankara's "A Garland of Questions and Answers," and he wanted Isherwood to polish it for him. This became Part IV in their translation of Shankara's *Crest-Jewel of Discrimination* (1947) when it was published in a second edition in 1975.
2. David Smith had been a student of Isherwood at Los Angeles State College in 1962 and remained a fan. Bachardy drew both men, including a nude session with Bob Christian, with whom he once had a sexual liaison in New York. Christian is African-American. Barbra Streisand sang "People," with its lyric, "People who need people are the luckiest people in the world," in *Funny Girl* on Broadway in 1964 and made it a hit all over again with the movie in 1968.
3. Bachardy enclosed a black-and-white photo, clipped from a magazine, of two cats in a small, dirty wire cage, captioned "Cats used for experiments, kept in this cage for many months."

the car and plugged into the portable battery. It was her neck muscles, not her lungs, which gave out.[4]

Miguel's show opened on Tuesday at a very tacky gallery on La Cienega which was so hot Jack referred to the evening as Suddenly Last Sauna— we were all sweating like pigs. Miguel's things were poorly hung and he shared the room with a very slick fourth-rate painter, but he managed to sell two, one of them a quite nice piece at $500.

I'm still seeing Cukor films two or three afternoons a week with Gavin. This week we saw two Judy Hollidays, both of them well directed but both written by Garson Kanin, with and without Babe Ruth, and the scripts are extremely clever (even desperately clever) and deeply horrible when it gets around to message time. I had a genuine experience of actually seeing the devil's work being done. Quite chilling and shocking. It became suddenly clear that no one of any quality can possibly have anything to do with the Kanins, especially him. His production of *Idiot's Delight* with Jack Lemmon and Rosemary Harris is now playing downtown and said by all to be a dreary bore.[5]

I took Jo to the Fuji Gardens and *Downhill Racer*. It was downhill all the way. Jo was her usual grateful, humble, self-pitying self. "Oh it's so *good* to go to the movies!" then wistfully, "I never go anymore—I can't face going alone . . ." The film is a disappointment, largely because the sport of skiing is so monotonous unless maybe you're actually doing it. And judging from this film, there is no way to photograph it interestingly. It's a thrill movie with no thrills, like *Grand Prix* with only one car.

April 4.

Last night was Nellie's birthday so with enormous effort I cooked some chicken fricassee. Jack and Jim came too and Jim Gates helped a bit with the chores. Unfortunately at dinner we got into a semi philosophical-religious discussion, triggered off by an adamant declaration from Jack saying that there was *nothing* in astrology. I realized right away that

4. Beverly Baerresen, a friend introduced by Jack Larson and Jim Bridges, had had polio and depended on artificial respiration.
5. Gavin Lambert was preparing to write his book, *On Cukor* (1972). Ruth Gordon (1896–1985), American actress, playwright, screenwriter, whom Bachardy calls "Babe Ruth," was married to actor, writer, and director Garson Kanin (1912–1999), and she collaborated with him on many films. Kanin was directing Robert Sherwood's *Idiot's Delight* (1936) at the Ahmanson Theater, March 17–April 25, 1970.

Jack was in one of his unhinged, hysterically argumentative moods, and kept out of it. Jim Gates, however, sailed into the wind and made several surprisingly good sound points, far too good for Jack's liking, and I think I saw the healthy young buds of new love withering. Up until last night Jack and Jim both liked Jim enormously and he liked them too, though Jim, naturally, better than Jack. But I'm almost sure that Jack was offended last night by "the young whippersnapper" and love was lost. I, too, though Jim was surprisingly articulate and sensible, thought him the tiniest bit glib and impertinent. I am still (or again) undecided about him. Every once in a while I hear the sound of goody two shoes being punctuated by a cheeky kind of arrogance, a faint smug intellectual pride that permits him the subtlest sneer at his "inferiors." Can you imagine Jack cast in the role of "The Deluded"?

I finally spoke to Irving and there is no question of a N.Y. show this spring. I suspect he met with more opposition there than he expected but he claims to be working on the idea still. He is going to S.F. next week and is "sure" he can set up something there, alas. Kitty again made to draw pretty pictures of the rich. Anyway, since the N.Y. show is off, at least for the present, Kitty could join his Old Hide if and when required, that is, if he's still wanted.

In London or en Casa, Kitty wants his Dear Drumpkin as soon as possible. He misses him painfully and has been deprived of him too long now. If they don't ship that Glossy Rump back fast, Kitty will climb into his tiny travelling hamper, have it placed in the belly of a great iron bird and FLY to his Only Darling, TWA (Trans Whiskers Airlines).

Baskets of Catkisses and showers of Pusspurrs,
Furkin XXXXX

[*Typed letter, signed, with enclosure*]

April 5 [1970] 3 Moore St. [London] S.W. 3

Darling Flufftail,

I saw Dodie & Alec yesterday. It was a wretched day of cold rain with some snow. Alec met me at Audley End in his Teddybear coat, much fatter in the face and all around but with his usual brick-red tan. Now they have *two* Dalmatians—one of them a problem dog who belonged to a U.S. sergeant at the airbase who chained him up and thrashed him (so the sob story runs) and who then was rejected by three other owners because he smashes things. So of course the Beesleys *had* to have him! On meeting Dobbin he jumped right up in his face. Dobbin kissed him (ugh!) but then he put his muddy paws on Swami's scarf and Dub was *displeased.* I've spent ½ an hour brushing those [illegible] bristles out of my jacket. The Beesleys thought this was perfectly okay. But when I drooled over the angel donkeys, who are really little *ponies* and so dear, they thought me a bit *bent,* I could see.

Dodie looks much older and quite weird, almost a *Thing,* with its white weaving arms and its head sunk deep into its hump. But they were both very sweet and said repeatedly to give you their love & tell you how they wished you were here. Dodie has written *two* more plays, and she says her new novel is getting far better notices than the last, which was marvellous because it excused me from raving about it. She has given me a play to read, however.

Saw David & Peter today and D. said he has sent you a catalogue. His show is a smash hit. I'll send you some notices tomorrow, also an interview with Jill Bennett.

Now the German theater at Dusseldorf has allegedly offered us a world premiere of our play! That wd be in German, of course. I talked to Edward Albee about this and he didn't pooh-pooh it at all. *The Zoo Story* was done that way, also a Beckett play (don't know which). He says it creates great prestige and is covered by the British press too. But he says it should only be a European premiere, so we can reserve the right to do it here first in English, if we want to. What do you think? I'm going to find out more and ask around. There's no hurry deciding.

But I do feel more & more that I'll be coming home before long. That dear Pussn's mews are reaching me through the airwaves and calling back Kitty's loyal old shambling inflated Dub. (Some of David's photos of him on the trip are *sobering.*)

An adoring tongue lick for Kitty under his ruff.

XXXXXXXX

[Autograph letter]

April 6. [1970, London]

Beloved Pinkpaws,

[H]ere are a couple of Hockney notices & an absurd interview with Jill Bennett.[1] Haven't see the Osbornes again. Haven't seen Rosamond, Beatrix Lehmann, Connolly,[2] William Plomer, Jean Ross,[3] Robin Maugham, Gerald Hamilton etc. etc. And now I begin to think I shan't. It is pouring down rain and icy and I just loathe being here—except when I'm "amusing" myself, which is all very well but I must get back to work. So—*either* something so dramatically encouraging must happen to the prospects of the play that it's worthwhile for Kitty to return (which wd transform this Siberia into a tropical paradise) *or* I plan to leave on the 19th and return to my Darling. I shall see Richard in the middle of next week. Amiya must come up to town or I won't see her. Won't see Philip Toynbee[4] either, unless *he* comes.

I have wasted an awful lot of time and quite a lot of money sticking around here. If we return for the play eventually, we'll get stringent guarantees first that it will be performed instantly—*and* they'll have to pay us.

The things I *don't* regret about this trip are that we did all that truly valuable work on the script, that I got a lot more material for my book from Richard and that I made the trip in France with David & Peter (but that wd have been far more fun with you along).

Peter & I are going to *The Damned* this afternoon.[5] He is now wearing silver paint on his eyelids. So suitable!

Larry Madigan, the New Zealand seaman, is a great big man, queer, Catholic, very intelligent, tried being a monk, drinks a lot & gets into fights. He is definitely not my dreamboat but he is probably someone

1. Enclosures lost.
2. Cyril Connolly (1903–1974), British journalist, critic, editor, autobiographer, a prolific contributor to English newspapers and magazines, including the *New Statesman*, *The Observer*, and *The Sunday Times*.
3. (1911–1973), the original of Isherwood's character Sally Bowles in *Goodbye to Berlin*. After Berlin, she returned to England where she lodged for a time with Olive Mangeot and joined the Communist Party. She had a daughter with the communist journalist and author Claud Cockburn (1904–1981), though she never married.
4. English communist novelist and critic (1916–1981).
5. Visconti's 1969 film *La Caduta degli dei*.

else's. I like him quite.[6] We had supper last night. David & Peter came into the restaurant. Their appearance shocked him a bit, but he is off to see David's show today.

An actor named Basil Hoskins actually *wants* to play Patrick! Must find out about him. He's about 38, tall, good-looking (says Clement). No word from the prospective director, Terry Hands. (Dub's hoofwriting keeps getting indistinct because his arthritis is paining him so.)

Dob loves his Darling so much
and will come to him *soon.*
XXXXXXXXXX

[*Autograph letter*]

April 7 [1970]   [London]

Longedfor Fur,

[A]m writing this at a table in a post office just off Regent's Street amidst a whole bunch of rather sympathetically giggling Dutch girls, sympathetic chiefly because one can't understand what they are saying. They are all writing telegrams. Am in Regent's Street because I have just been to the BOAC and got a reservation for Sunday, April 19—flight 591, arriving L.A. 5:50 p.m. So that's that, unless circumstances change the plans, which doesn't seem likely at the moment. The man who directed *Three Months Gone*[1] has just turned the play down, saying that it's too literary and doesn't have any conflict. But, you know, I am now more than ever convinced that the play is *good* and so I feel strangely exhilarated, as I often do when I'm convinced that The Others are wrong. Also I feel that all these minus votes are preparing for some big plus in the near future.

This morning the copy of the Unity magazine arrived. How typical of those sloppy creatures, spelling your name wrong! I like the drawing

---

6. Leo Madigan shipped out as a merchant seaman while still a teenager. His early writing appeared in a magazine called *The Seafarer*, published by the Marine Society in London, and which he edited for a time; he also contributed to *Blackwood's Magazine*. His first novel, *Jackarandy* (1973), is about the professional gay sex scene in London. Later, he settled in Fatima, Portugal, and published religious books and Catholic novels for children.

1. Ronald Eyre (1929–1992) directed Donald Howarth's hit play; it opened at the Royal Court in January 1970 and transferred to the West End.

very much indeed. It makes me want to meet him. I wonder what he thought of it?[2]

At lunchtime today I went with Clement Scott Gilbert to see a performance of Sam Shepard's *Red Cross* by three Americans in a cellar which appeared to be a Chinese night club. We went because the male actor (James Gary) had written to us applying for the part of Tom—he hadn't read the play, only heard of it. He was not only mediocre but a very oriental-looking Jew. One of the girls was very good. The play is all about behavior and should be called *As We Like It*.

All a Dub's love—XXXXXXXXXXX

[Autograph letter]

April 8 [1970]   [London]

Darling Snowtail,

[W]as hoping for perhaps a word from my Angel to cheer old Drub's path through life until the Blessed Nineteenth. I think the mails are being delayed. Have kept writing to Kitty nearly every day since the 2nd or 3rd and will continue to do so.

Am now definitely going up to see Richard again on Monday next, the 13th, staying till the 16th, then back here for the last 3 days.

What do you want done with your drawing paper which was left down in the workroom? I presume you'll say, "Leave it there, with a note to Bill [Harris] asking him to keep it till I'm in London again"? Otherwise I wd have to buy a portfolio to carry it home in.

OH JOY! A lovely letter just arrived from Furkin. (As I wrote this word, Mrs. Gee, who is cleaning, scratched the door *exactly* the way Kitty does when he wants to be let in to Dobbin's workroom! It made Old Horse's heart jump.)

Dodie & Alec seem *really* to like our play, though D. admits to being somewhat put off by the distasteful subject of God. She thinks it is very well made and has lots of conflict and the two parts excellent for actors

2. Bachardy had forwarded the first issue of *In Unity*, the magazine of the homosexual Metropolitan Community Church of Los Angeles. On the cover was his portrait of the Reverend Troy D. Perry (b. 1940), a gay activist and former Baptist minister who founded the church in 1968. The portrait was attributed to "Don Bachady."

and the dialogue *not* "literary" and she doesn't see why it shouldn't have a West End success! Her only criticism is that Oliver should sell the reasons for living a monastic life a bit more energetically and lucidly. I think that's true.

All my love and kisses for that Only Treasure.

XXXXXXXXXXX

[*Autograph letter*]

April 9 [1970]   [London]

Dearest Whiskers,

I begin this while waiting for a visit from the disc jockey named Christopher Isherwood[1] who wrote me from Bristol. He is already nearly 50 minutes late and Dub is getting restive and pawing the straw.

This morning a somewhat dubious breakthrough has occurred, the director named Robert Chetwyn (spelling may not be quite right) has read the script and is enthusiastic, though he claims that he doesn't understand the lighting, which sounds as if he must be stupid. Anyhow I am to meet him with Clement the day after tomorrow. He is said to be fortyish and much liked by actors and a specialist in light comedy—including *There's a Girl in My Soup* and some Restoration plays. Sounds more like farce, which usually means a heavy hand.[2] However, if he's at all possible, I'll probably phone you on Sunday and we'll consider what to do. In the meanwhile we should have also conferred with Nicholas Thompson and heard from Richard Chamberlain.

Dodie, who phoned me yesterday, sent you her love and said she was going to "do something" so I wouldn't leave England and you'd come over. One of her horrid Christian Science spells, no doubt. I begged her to be careful, pointing out that the result she wanted could easily be

---

1. Known professionally as Chris Connery.
2. Chetwyn (b. 1933), British director and former repertory actor, took Terence Frisby's *There's a Girl in My Soup* from the West End to Broadway in 1967. His stage work also included Shakespeare, Shaw, and Wilde, and he directed and produced for BBC television and ITV. In 1979, he directed Martin Sherman's *Bent* at the Royal Court.

achieved by killing me in some sort of accident. Now I begin to wonder if Chetwyn may be a sign that the spell is working!

This bastard hasn't shown up yet and it's 2! Fuck all fans.

All of a Rump's devotion

XXXXXXXXXXXX

[*Autograph letter*]

April 9, 1970 [Santa Monica]

Worshipped Plumed Steed:

The mail deliveries have been very weird. Nothing at all last week from dear Plumprump and then two letters and a wild-pony card on Monday and two letters yesterday, one just after seeing Dodie and Alec and the other with the paeans to Hockney. (The deification ceremonies have already begun. Such demonstrations of love and admiration must be almost unprecedented. Well, at least it couldn't happen to a nicer person.) It helps poor Kitty in his Soledad to have word from his Adored Mane. He puts the treasured letters into his little vest and wears them next to his beating heart which then begins to beat even faster. How he clings to the hope of seeing his Naggin on the 19th!

Kitty's days have been filled with duties as usual. Gerald and Michael again on Monday. Gerald was very energetic this time and talked more than he has for many weeks. I could even understand some of it. He referred twice to death and was quickly silenced each time by Michael. He thanked me for bothering to come to see someone "so inept in every way."

On Saturday I went with Antoinette (now forgiven) to see Betty Harford in a one act O'Casey (*Bedtime Story*) at the New Hope Inn, now renamed the No Hope Inn. We had a lousy table with a two-foot-thick pillar between us and the acting area, were served with total indifference a plate of nearly cold, indistinct "grub" and a bottle of Gallo-quality wine at $7.50 a head, and then told at the end of the meal that Mr. Ford Rainey, Betty's co-star, was delayed due to television filming but that, lucky us, the distinguished actor Richard Hale would entertain us with recitations from Stephen Vincent Benet. (The old ham was down to the place in a tuxedo five minutes after being rung up he was so eager to bore an audience.)[1] Light years later, after Mr. Hale and an indefatigable couple who sang Irish songs forever, ending with a reprise of "Danny Boy," Mr. Rainey arrived and the O'Casey, scheduled to end shortly before ten, began a wee bit after eleven. And if I never hear another Irish brogue, including Betty's, it will be a little too soon. Incidentally, O'Casey is all cuteness and Irish "charm" and nothing else—a totally imaginary playwright I think. Betty gave her usual eccentric, tense performance which always makes me want to take a deep breath (in the No Hope Inn?) the moment she leaves the stage. Her stage presence is extraordinary and bizarre, but in some basic way her performance is always a disappointment—*at* you rather than for you.

Bravefur even invited Elsa over for a drink with Antoinette before we went to see Betty. She came equipped (such a coward) with Jack G.,[2] David Graham (the fat agent)[3] and a silent young actor friend of his. Elsa was not drinking that weekend, somehow managing to imply that this was a slap at me ("You don't have to worry, I won't drink up any of your liquor"). She arrived late, knowing full well that Antoinette and I had to go off, so that we had less than half an hour together. The subject of conversation inevitably turned to Elsa's favorite, hypocrisy and her loathing of it (the hypocrite!), I suppose expecting me to wince because I'd kissed her when she arrived. Her loathing of me is really quite phenomenal and on such a deep, primitive level that I can't take it personally. It's too much of a spectacle. It goes so far beyond me or anything I've done that it would be sheer vanity to assume any responsibility for it. Her hate is a thing of such purity that I can only feel awe in its presence. I think I would be quite worried if she practised witchcraft, though such a demonstration of deep negative emotion *is* a kind of witchcraft, isn't it?

Jim Gates and I have twice gone to see The Company Theater on Robertson at Jack and Jim's urging. We actually went with Jack and

---

1. Hale (1892–1981) played character bits in Hollywood movies and T.V., often as a Native American or a "foreigner" (Russian, Chinese, Arab, French) and once as the soothsayer with the line "Beware the Ides of March" in the 1953 film of Shakespeare's *Julius Caesar*. Rainey (1908–2005), also American, was much better known, both in T.V. and movies, especially Westerns and action pictures. He had been appearing on stage with Betty Harford since the 1940s, when they were members of Iris Tree and Alan Harkness's High Valley Theater Company in the Upper Ojai Valley.

2. Jack Grinnich, an actor who occasionally spent weekends with her.

3. He was Elsa's own agent, as well as representing other actors, writers, and directors. Later, he became a casting director for movies and T.V.

Jim on Sunday, Jack having decided to overlook, if not forgive, Jim's impertinence a few evenings before. I had a rousing experience the first time—an entertainment called *The Emergence* which is very impressively staged. I look forward to guiding the Old Plug there to sniff at it. Sunday's performance was an audience participation evening which, though quite fun and worth doing once (Kitty danced *onstage!*), is at heart a kind of basically square group therapy demonstration. Like a Rorschach test, you couldn't, and wouldn't want to, do it twice. But as a company of actors, I think they create the best atmosphere around themselves of any I've seen.[4]

Watched the Academy Awards at Gavin's with Camilla and Linda (boring and the usual stupid awards) on Tuesday, had lunch with Lee Garlington yesterday (Greg[5] has left him to be on his own and try his charms on others, so Kitty could play his understanding and sympathetic Sweetfur role which is one of his best loved), and last night I saw Richard Hopper who is fatter and more settled than six months ago but still yacking away a mile a minute. He's pleasant to be with, every once in a while.

I see *Bhowani Junction* with Gavin this afternoon, then drive to Santa Barbara to have dinner with Bill and Paul. *Two-Faced Woman* tomorrow afternoon, which I'm looking forward to.[6] I even draw occasionally. Did some quick and not uninteresting drawings of Peter [Schneider] the other day, a good drawing of Peter and Jim's fat girlfriend Allyn on Sunday.[7] But no painting yet for no good reason.

Kitty pants at the thought of the return of his Only Muzzlelove and lives only to lick that salty old Hide with his rough little pinktongue and make it tingle again.

Furballs and pink catkisses,

Purrpuss

XXXXXXXXX

[*Typed letter, signed*]

•   •   •

4. The Company Theater was an actors' commune on Robertson Boulevard founded by Gar Campbell in 1967. It lasted until 1981, when some of its members became part of the Powerhouse Theater.
5. Greg Pavlich. Bachardy did his portrait November 22, 1969.
6. Lambert and Bachardy were still working their way through all George Cukor's films for Lambert's book.
7. Allyn L. Nelson. She lived in Oxnard and attended Claremont College, where she met Gates and Schneider.

[May 18, 1970, Santa Monica]

Happy Birthday!

This seems a silly way of saying how much Dub loves Kitty and wishes him all the things that *can't* be given—but Dub liked the color and perhaps it'll do to keep mice in or plump little birds.[1]

XXXXXXXX

[Autograph note attached to a gift]

---

1. Isherwood flew home from London to Santa Monica on April 29, 1970; the gift is unidentified.

Frequently Used First Names

Alice – *see* Gowland, Alice
Amiya – *see* Sandwich, Amiya
Anita – *see* Loos, Anita
Anthony – *see* Page, Anthony
Arnold – *see* Maltin, Arnold
Ben – *see* Masselink, Ben
Betty – *see* Arizu, Betty Lathwood
Bill – *see* Brown, Bill *and* Caskey, Bill
Bob – *see* Craft, Robert *and* Regester, Bob
Budd – *see* Cherry, Budd
Camilla – *see* Clay, Camilla
Carter – *see* Lodge, Carter
Cecil – *see* Beaton, Cecil
Charles – *see* Laughton, Charles
Chester – *see* Kallman, Chester
Chris – *see* Wood, Chris
Clint – *see* Kimbrough, Clint
Clyde – *see* Ventura, Clyde
David – *see* Hockney, David
Dick – *see* Foote, Dick
Dig – *see* Yorke, Dig
Doris – *see* Dowling, Doris
Dorothy – *see* Miller, Dorothy
Edward – *see* Upward, Edward
Elaine – *see* Tynan, Elaine
Elsa – *see* Lanchester, Elsa
Emlyn – *see* Williams, Emlyn
Eric – *see* Falk, Eric
Frank – *see* Merlo, Frank
Gavin – *see* Lambert, Gavin
George – *see* Goetschius, George

Gerald – *see* Heard, Henry FitzGerald
Glade – *see* Bachardy, Glade
Glenn – *see* Ford, Glenn
Gore – *see* Vidal, Gore
Harry – *see* Miller, Harry Tatlock
Henry – *see* Guerriero, Henry
Hester – *see* Chapman, Hester
Hope – *see* Lange, Hope
Howard – *see* Austen, Howard *and* Warshaw, Howard
Igor – *see* Stravinsky, Igor
Irving – *see* Blum, Irving
Ivan – *see* Moffatt, Ivan
Jack – *see* Larson, Jack
Jen – *see* Yow, Jenson
Jennifer – *see* Selznick, Jennifer
Jerry – *see* Lawrence, Jerry
Jill – *see* Bennett, Jill *and* Osborne, Jill
Jim – *see* Bridges, Jim *and* Charlton, Jim, *and* Gates, Jim
Jo – *see* Masselink, Jo
Jocelyn – *see* Rickards, Jocelyn
John – *see* Gielgud, John *and* Goodwin, John
Julian – *see* Jebb, Julian
Julie – *see* Harris, Julie
Kate – *see* Moffatt, Katherine Smith
Keith – *see* Vaughan, Keith
Ken – *see* Tynan, Ken
Lincoln – *see* Kirstein, Lincoln
Linda – *see* Crawford, Linda
Loudon – *see* Sainthill, Loudon
Manning – *see* Gurian, Manning
Marguerite – *see* Lamkin, Marguerite
Martin – *see* Hensler, Martin
Michael – *see* Barrie, Michael *and* Leopold, Michael
Molly – *see* Williams, Molly
Morgan – *see* Forster, E.M.
Neil – *see* Hartley, Neil
Nellie – *see* Caroll, Nellie
OldJo – *see* Masselink, Jo

Patrick – *see* Procktor, Patrick, *and* Woodcock, Patrick
Paul – *see* Wonner, Paul
Peter – *see* Gowland, Peter *and* Schlesinger, Peter
Prema – *see* Prema Chaitanya *and* Vidyatmananda
Richard – *see* Isherwood, Richard
Robin – *see* French, Robin
Rosamond – *see* Lehmann, Rosamond
Rouben – *see* Ter-Arutunian, Rouben
Russell – *see* McKinnon, Russell
Speed – *see* Lamkin, Hillyer Speed
Stephen – *see* Spender, Stephen
Swami – *see* Prabhavananda
Ted – *see* Bachardy, Ted
Tennessee – *see* Williams, Tennessee
Terry – *see* Jenkins, Terry
Tony – *see* Richardson, Tony
Truman – *see* Capote, Truman
Vanessa – *see* Redgrave, Vanessa
Vera – *see* Stravinsky, Vera
Vince – *see* Davis, Vince
Virgil – *see* Thomson, Virgil
Willie – *see* Maugham, William Somerset
Wystan – *see* Auden, W.H.

Index

Works by Isherwood appear directly under title; works by others appear under authors' names.

Prema Chaitanya (*earlier* John Yale)
xv, 34, 51, 82, 138–9, 145
presidential election 1964 157, 200
presidential election 1968 xxviii, 357
Preston, Jonathan 259, 260
Price, Clarice 202
Price, Vincent 179
Prime of Miss Jean Brodie, The (film) 366
Prince, Harold 237n2
Pringle, Aileen 384
Procktor, Patrick xvii, xviii, 230, 246,
247, 251, 252, 289, 323, 348, 349,
385–6, 397
Prosser, Lee 177–8, 200
Prosser, Mary 177–8
Prouting, Norman 414
Pure and Impure, The (Briffault's
English translation of *Le Pur et
impur*, 1967) (Colette) 301

Quakers 239, 240
Queen (magazine) 91
Quennell, Spider 263n5
Quintero, José 167, 168, 183

Raffles, Gillian 251
Rainey, Ford 436, 437
Ramakrishna, birthday puja 50, 51;
sayings 317
Ramakrishna and His Disciples (C.I.):
writing 79, 84, 86, 102, 131; reviews
206
Random House (publishers) 249–50
Rasponi, Lanfranco 90, 96, 105, 108–9
Rassine, Alexis 57, 327
Rattigan, Terence 92, 118–19, 120
Ray, Joan (Doya) 87, 92
Raye, Martha 196, 197
Reagan, Nancy 278n3
Rechy, John 275, 276; "A Quarter
Ahead" 88

Red Desert (*Il deserto rosso*; film) 208,
256n4
Red Raven (West Hollywood gay bar)
199
Redfern Gallery, London xiv, 68, 79,
80n11, 85n4, 88–9, 92, 100, 102, 105,
109, 112, 150, 237, 245, 246, 271, 385,
387
Redgrave, Vanessa 144, 157, 180, 225–6,
304n7, 322, 401, 402
Reep, Edward 228n9
Reform Club, London 68, 225, 226
Regester, James Robert (Bob) xvii,
xviii, 128, 211, 225, 229n1, 230, 231,
232, 246, 247–8, 252, 264, 270, 271,
280–1, 282, 283, 287, 304, 307, 311,
318, 353, 406, 409, 425
Reid, Nick 97, 98
Reid, William Wallace Jr. 7
Reinhardt, Gottfried and Silvia 215,
219–20
Reisz, Karel 45n5, 321, 322
Renaldo, Tito 82
Reno, University of Nevada at 132
Republican Party 359
Rex Evans Gallery, Los Angeles 157n5,
272, 418n2, 420n11
Rhys, Jean: *Good Morning, Midnight*
312, 315–16, 318; *Wide Sargasso Sea*
312
Richardson, Joely 180n7, 425
Richardson, Maurice 92
Richardson, Natasha 425
Richardson, Ralph 387
Richardson, Sue 390, 395n1
Richardson, Tony: commissions D.B.
to draw cast of *A Taste of Honey*
xii, 19n1; feud with Anthony Page
xxii, xxv, 302, 303, 304, 322–3, 332;
and stage adaptation of *A Meeting
by the River* xxiv–xxv, 306, 307,